"FOR THE SOVEREIGNTY
OF THE PEOPLE"

For the Sovereignty of the People

A Conversation with
Niccolò's Ghost and
a Defence of the
Crown in the
Westminster
System

Nigel Greenwood

First published in 1999 on behalf of Nigel Greenwood from a completed manuscript presented to Australian Academic Press Pty. Ltd., Brisbane. All responsibility for editorial matter rests with the author. Any views or opinions expressed are therefore not necessarily those of Australian Academic Press.

Distributed by
IBIS EDITIONS AUSTRALIEN
PO Box 1004, Indooroopilly QLD 4068, Australia.
www.sovereignpeople.com

National Library of Australia
Cataloguing-in-Publication data:

Greenwood, Nigel, 1967–.
For the sovereignty of the people: a conversation with Niccolò's ghost, and a defence of the Crown in the Westminster system.

ISBN 1 875378 28 6

1. Democracy — Australia.
2. Legislative power — Australia.
3. Monarchy — Australia.
4. Republicanism — Australia.
5. Australia — Politics and government — 20th century.
I. Title.

321.870994

Cover photographs: Richard Nixon, Paul Keating, Russian tank crew, courtesy of Associated Press, London; Winston Churchill, Adolf Hitler, courtesy of Mary Evans Picture Library, London.
Back cover photographer: Alastair Bett
Cover and text design by Andrea Cox of Australian Academic Press, Brisbane.
Typeset in Goudy by Australian Academic Press, Brisbane.

Foreword

———————————————— ▪■▪ ————————————————

I am delighted to pen a brief Foreword to this book which, as the title page indicates, is a "Defence of the Crown in the Westminster System". It is rather daunting to be asked to say something relevant about such a well-researched and thoughtful work, but at the outset, may I say that I am most impressed not only with its structure and contents, but also with the industry and sagacity which the author has displayed.

Dr Greenwood admits in his introduction that he is a confirmed constitutional monarchist, and one finds it difficult to accept, in the light of the persuasive arguments, that any diligent and thoughtful reader of this text would not be led to adopt a similar point of view. This book is the product of a great deal of solid research into the problems of government, but it is far from being merely a dull legal tome, or a textbook on political science.

Later in this year, Australians will face up to a referendum as to whether they consider this nation should become a republic rather than remain a constitutional monarchy. I am convinced that all who advocate changes to the Australian Constitution in favour of a Republican system of government should read long and hard each chapter in this publication. Dr Greenwood sets out exhaustively the considerations which militate both for and against any constitutional change for this purpose. His analysis of the systems of parliamentary government is erudite, and he does not avoid giving adequate explanations of the several reasons motivating those who wish to do away with our present Monarchial system.

It would be unfortunate if some persons, upon perusing the title, take the view that this volume is based on a particular conservative foundation or political philosophy, and that it shows prejudice or bias. This is simply not so, because all types of view are frankly and openly discussed. Although his approach is primarily an historical one, the whole work is methodical, and he writes in plain language which is easy to understand. Those who fancy calling themselves "Republicans" should read this book. It constitutes a real challenge to them, and may I say that they should be persuaded to show great caution in their seeking answers to many salutary points raised by the author. In short, what is said in these chapters demands answers.

Much has been written on this topic of Republicanism over the last decade, but these chapters do not constitute just a repetition of views expressed by the several protagonists of one form of government or another; they are based on sound historical research and are a keen analysis of the many governmental structures in society, both at the present time and in the past.

The reader is made to reflect on such concepts or principles as ministerial responsibility, the independence of the public service, the necessity of the retention of reserve powers of the Crown by the Head of State, be he or she Monarch or President, and so on. He or she is taken through much of the writings of great thinkers on governmental structure, such as Voltaire, Plato, John Stuart Mill and others, not omitting that eminent statesman, diplomat and writer Niccolò Machiavelli. Indeed, so vast and thoughtful is this publication, that it would be idle for me to endeavour to highlight any particular issues, or to analyse and dissect any of the points which are made. Suffice it for me to say it is a most persuasive work.

The book is well footnoted, and has a good bibliography.

I commend this book wholeheartedly to all concerned Australians.

The Hon. Sir Walter Campbell, AC QC
1st July, 1999.

Contents

powers, duty of servants of Crown to disobey manifestly unlawful orders. Implications for armed forces and police, "Her Majesty's Prisons" and *habeus corpus*. The Crown as emblem and the Oath of Allegiance.

Imperial Presidency and the Lawless State 64

Contrast: the United States of America. Teapot Dome and Watergate. Findings of Watergate Congressional Committees: profound executive lawlessness entrenched in system. The Schlesinger Report. Presidential knowledge and superior orders: the Justice Department's stance. Executive-ordered illegal espionage, kidnapping, and possible murder. *Congressional Quarterly* suggests "awful new flaw" in US Constitution. Contrast with Crown and modern interpretation of Bill of Rights (1689): New Zealand High Court and *Fitzgerald v. Muldoon (1976)*.

Illegality and the Crown 75

Viceregal witnesses of executive illegality: what should they do? Evatt and criticisms of his stance. The sacking of Premier Jack Lang by Sir Philip Game, New South Wales 1932. Lack of practical justiciability in many executive actions.

3 Beyond Our Shores 91

The republican form and the republican ideal: Switzerland and England, de Tocqueville's views. Collapse of the Weimar Republic and the rise of Hitler. Influence of Westminster upon French Republics. Collapse of France's Fourth Republic in 1958 military *coup d'etat*. De Gaulle, the Fifth Republic and virtual dictatorship. Democracy and Asia: Aung San Suu Kyi's view.

4 Bagehot Revisited 109

Bagehot's authority questioned. His perceptions of the Crown and his own 19th Century prejudices: hatred of the "lower classes", disdain for the "upper". The Crown as "disguise". Heredity and personal ability. Morality. Efficacy of reserve power or its lack: Bagehot v. Machiavelli, illustrated by the Irish Presidency. A different, modern paradigm: the monarch as "potent witness" of executive government.

BOOK TWO — CIVIL POLITICS AND THE CROWN 131

1 The Necessity of Reserve Powers 133

Existence (and Need for Existence) 133

Conflict of interest inherent in representative democracy: constituency and elective oligarchy. Need for safeguards. Justiciability and non-justiciability. Difference between Charter of Rights and reserve powers; Machiavelli and *lo stato*. Hitler and the last days of the Weimar Republic: judicial impotence. An attempt to subvert democracy in Australia: *Australian Capital Television Pty Ltd v. The Commonwealth of Australia (1992)*. The High Court's ruling.

Canada: D.P.O'Connell QC, Dr Geoffrey Marshall, 1978 Regina Protest of the Canadian Premiers. A solution to current dangers: 1930 framework of viceregal appointment and nomination by community leaders via a "Convocation of State".

3 Military Considerations, or Uncivil Politics and the Crown 229

The Issue of Military Command 230

Necessity of a commander-in-chief in all political systems. Current role of our Governor-General as commander-in-chief. Inherent safeguards.

Military Aid to the Civil Power 236

Necessity of Military Aid to the Civil Power. Used in Australia: 1978 Sydney Hilton bombing and the Bowral call-out. Used in Canada: 1976 Olympic Games, 1970 kidnapping by Quebec Liberation Front. Used in UK: Northern Ireland. Dangers in partisanship: 1970 Kent state Massacre in United States. Rules of engagement. Sombre contrast: 1919 Amritsar Massacre.

The Army and the President 241

1787 Philadelphia Convention recognises armed oppression an obvious threat in republican form of government. Historical experience in military dictatorship during 17th Century English republic, arbitrary reign of James II, failure of English safeguards in colonial context during American Revolution. American solution: institutionalise Congressional ability to wage civil war upon President and US Army, through Second Amendment, the so-called "Right to Bear Arms". Alternative in Switzerland: conscription for all male citizens at all levels of military expertise, in a national conscript army. Third path attempted by Commonwealth republic of the Gambia: total disbandment of army. The Gambia becomes longest-lived democratic republic in Africa, but is obliged to restore army. Collapses in military *coup* in 1994. No solution proposed by Turnbull Committee; problem conveniently ignored. Alternative danger: army rises against resented government. Conventions surrounding Crown that act to discourage this.

BOOK THREE — THE FLIES OF A SUMMER 251

1 Of Nations 253

Historical Inevitability? 253

An African confrère: postcolonial attitudes driving Australian debate obsolete, a retro-'70s ideological fashion in the 1990s. Of monarchists and royalists. Socialist monarchists: irrelevance of "left-wing v. right-wing" taint to debate. Role of Crown and ignorance of "experts". Becoming "a republic for Asia", a contradiction to multiculturalism. Imperial China and the British Civil Service.

FOR THE SOVEREIGNTY OF THE PEOPLE

Whosoever considers the past and the present
will readily observe that all cities and all peoples
are and ever have been animated by the same
desires and the same passions; so that it is easy,
by diligent study of the past, to foresee what is
likely to happen in the future in any republic,
and to apply those remedies used by the
ancients, or, not finding any that were employed
by them, to devise new ones from the similarity
of the events. But as such considerations are
neglected or not understood by most of those
who read, or if understood by these, are
unknown by those who govern, it follows
that the same troubles generally recur in
all republics.

Niccolò Machiavelli, *The Discourses.*

Niccolò's Ghost
(An Author's Introduction)

———■■■———

This book has its genesis in the speeches of two debates, the first of which was held in September 1992 in the Legislative Council Chamber of Queensland's Old Parliament House, Brisbane. In that chamber, itself a dignified casualty of misguided constitutional "reform", the author appeared on behalf of the Queensland branch of the Royal Commonwealth Society against members of what was then known as the Australian Republican Party, to argue in favour of retention of the Crown.

The second debate occurred four months later in the bleak English January of 1993, in the rooms of Wadham College, Oxford, during the World Universities Debating Championships. There the author was required to devise a passionate defence of republicanism, and denounce constitutional monarchy in the United Kingdom and Australia. The unusual experience of having argued both sides of the debate, having endeavoured to construct the strongest possible case for each side, left the author a confirmed constitutional monarchist. This manuscript was embarked upon to explain the reasons why.

It swiftly grew to be a more impassioned and polemical work than a mere "explanation". The more research undertaken, the more the implications of a republic were contemplated, the more the manuscript acquired the nature of a vehement exposition of argument and belief, a political manifesto advocating retention of the constitutional monarchy. In *Leviathan*, the political philosopher Thomas Hobbes once described the state of "nature", the plight of humans without ordered society, as being a condition "where every man is enemy to every man… continual fear, and danger of violent death; and the life of man, solitary, poor, nasty, brutish and short".[1] Yet many ordered societies create circumstances which fulfil this description: not only the totalitarian regimes which have disgraced the face of this earth throughout the 20th Century, and in places like Chinese-occupied Tibet continue to do so, but also societies under democratic constitutions. A long walk through the streets of West South-Central Los Angeles (it can be done, if you're as foolish as the author of this book in attempting it) irresistibly summons Hobbes' description to mind. Although the misery of South-Central and inner cities like it throughout the United States are in large part due to the profound inequities which exist in that society, they also owe a great deal to explicit measures adopted in the US Constitution — measures like the Second Amendment which, as shall be discussed, were not taken by accident but were instead a calculated risk by its authors, a cool-headed acknowledgment of the dangers posed by a republican form of government. The leaders of the republican movement in Australia are unwilling even to acknowledge such dangers, let alone present the Australian people with attempted solutions.

To write a proper work of political philosophy is to endanger public perception of the author's character. History remembers Machiavelli as an Italian cad not because of anything he actually did, but because he was astute enough to realise Italy lay in a lamentable state of disorder and oppression and attempted to devise a theory of politics to remedy this condition, realizing that virtues like compassion and conscience weren't conducive to survival in the Renaissance. For the offence of intellectual honesty, writing down his analysis without sugaring the medicine, this scholar and diplomat has been condemned as being as dark as the tyrants he studied. Monologue, particularly polemical monologue, becomes rapidly a bore. Invoking whatever occult powers of literature a writer can invoke, I have summoned the ghost of Machiavelli to sit opposite me while I write this manuscript: to interject from time to time, and to keep me company while I write. His presence reminds me whenever I stray, that lucidity of thought is a more potent weapon against oppression than a fistful of warm fuzzy sentiment.

At the moment it isn't intellectually fashionable — particularly among the sort of people who find nothing incongruous in the phrase "intellectually fashionable" — to oppose republicanism. But ambiguity dwells in the very word "republicanism", thrown about so casually in the popular press. One must distinguish between a republican *form* of government, and what might be described as the republican *ideal*. The republican form of government, so eagerly championed by the Australian Republican Movement, is to extinguish the hereditary component of the Crown and invest (in the minimalist model) all the powers of the Crown in a figure elected either by Parliament or the nation. In the more radical republican models these powers of the Crown are themselves to be dismantled, so that the Prime Minister acquires more power. The republican ideal (*res publica*, government for the public good) on the other hand is perhaps best summed up in Abraham Lincoln's words in his Gettysburg address as being government "...of the people, by the people, for the people".

It is this ideal which is the valuable part of the constitutional debate, for the republican form of government is only valuable if it enhances this democratic ideal in our society. The central proposition to this book is that a republican *form* of government imposed upon Australia will not only fail to enhance this ideal, but may very well destroy democratic government in this country as it has been destroyed in so many other countries throughout the world.

Until the appearance of the ghost, the provisional title of this manuscript was "A Commonwealth of the Crown". The reader might have assumed the title referred to the (British) Commonwealth of Nations, but that wasn't the principal connotation intended. In the 17th Century Thomas Hobbes defined a *commonwealth* as being a body established when a multitude of people make a mutual covenant among themselves,

> made by covenant of every man with every man, in such a
> manner, as if every man should say to every man, I authorize
> and give up my right of governing myself, to this man, or to
> this assembly of men, on this condition, that thou give up thy
> right to him, and authorize all his actions in like manner.[2]

This is done so that this person or assembly of people to whom the right of government is given "*may use the strength and means of them all* [the multitude], *as he* [that person or assembly] *shall think expedient, for their peace and common defence*", and that person or assembly is "... called SOVEREIGN, and said to have *sovereign* power; and everyone besides, his SUBJECT".[3]

Perceptions of sovereignty have evolved in sophistication since Hobbes' day, but the intrinsic idea of a government created by the populace for the common good remains strong. Quick and Garran, two Australian constitutional authorities who in 1901 published a large and learned commentary, directly upon the Australian Constitution and indirectly upon that of Britain,[4] traced the usage of this word through the centuries, originating from the phrase "common weal", the common wellbeing, spoken by Shakespeare and Bacon, written in the King James Bible, employed by the political writers Hobbes, Harrington and Locke, and invoked by the republican poet Milton.

The most famous polity of former centuries to be graced with the name of commonwealth was the 17th Century English republic praised by Milton, the Commonwealth of England. The name survived the regime, and was carried by English colonists on their ships into the New World, where it may be found to this day: the Commonwealths of Massachusetts, of Pennsylvania and of Vermont.

Unlike the word "republic", debased from connoting government for the public benefit merely to denoting a system in which all principal authorities are directly or indirectly elected, "commonwealth" retains its ancient meaning. It pertains to the democratic ideal without confusion with any specific form of government. In particular it is invoked in the 20th Century by a number of parliamentary democracies endowed with constitutional monarchies: the Commonwealth of Australia[5] and the Commonwealth of the Bahamas.

Underneath the essays of this manifesto rests the proposition that the Crown of the Westminster system, represented in various form throughout the world, is no mere relic imposed by history but can and should be defended in contemporary times and terms as an intrinsically valuable component of the parliamentary government of sovereign countries, government established to express the will and preserve the liberties of its citizens. This proposition becomes clearer to be seen when we look away from the class obsessions of Britain, to other countries that possess Elizabeth II as their Queen; countries that in their constitutions have consciously reconciled the historical legacy of the Westminster system with the objectives of modern government, to compose variations upon the theme of parliamentary democracy.

This book was written by an Australian for his fellow citizens of the Commonwealth of Australia, yet it is hoped other citizens, other readers from other countries will also find something of value in this work. In this century the word Commonwealth has acquired a new meaning, of a free association of sovereign States who, without sacrificing any of their sovereignty, gather in a congregation inspired not merely by financial gain and trade but by a shared history and a sense of community created by a common legacy. Parliamentary democracy of the Westminster system is a potent part of that legacy for the Commonwealth of Nations, and it is to be hoped the debates and tensions which currently disturb Australian society may shed some light upon the future of political institutions in other Commonwealth countries — and indeed, communities within those countries, such as Northern Ireland, Scotland and Wales, themselves immersed in political debate about their constitutional future.

References are made in this manifesto to a written Constitution and a High Court, a federal system, an elected Senate as an Upper House. All these institutions may seem alien to British readers, being things existent in their own country merely as insubstantial ideas sketched in the air, theories without tangible foundation. Yet in Australia these institutions are real, interwoven with the historical traditions of Westminster to provide our own form of parliamentary democracy under the Crown. The United Kingdom is itself in a period of constitutional turbulence, confronted with fundamental political challenges and threats, externally from the European Union, internally from alienated communities advocating devolution and a discontented awareness seeping through all strata of society that Britain's constitutional structures are in serious need of reform. It must be hoped that in the years ahead the United Kingdom may benefit from understanding the successes and failures Australia has experienced with its institutions, even as my country's Constitution owes much of its success to the knowledge and understanding its authors possessed of the historical experiences of Britain.

Much attention is given in this work to Canada and the opinions of Canadian monarchists. It isn't startling that Canadian threads are woven so conspicuously in this fabric of argument, when an Australian travelling beyond his own shores witnesses another New World monarchy protecting a parliamentary democracy, in a country holding a shared history with his own; with a federal and provincial governments, a written Constitution with a powerful judiciary; a country which committed itself to multiculturalism before his own, and has apparently undergone a more profound metamorphosis from the experience than his own; a country also under Queen Elizabeth II, but as Queen of Canada wearing the Maple Crown. Despite their apparent similarities the Crowns of Canada and Australia hold different implications, for the constitutions (and hence the power structures that bind citizens) of the two countries are different. In comparing political experiences upon the soil of these sister countries both accordance and dissonance yield enlightenment to observers, irrespective of the accents with which they speak.

A point of difference between the three countries of the United Kingdom, Canada and Australia lies in the power invested in their judiciaries. In the republican debate in Australia there's a subconscious awareness that in dismantling the powers of the Crown, some power residing in the Crown must nonetheless be placed beyond the reach of politicians. As a consequence, what we are actually witnessing in debate isn't the establishment of a republican parliamentary democracy, but a judicial aristocracy in a republic.

In saying this, something very different is meant to the figure of Lord Denning in his wig and gown. By a judicial aristocracy I mean a council tenured for life, endowed with power beyond that based on their authority in law and able to wield unaccountable political power in an executive or legislative manner. The actions of our judges are not hedged about with the safeguards we have placed about our executive government, such as the responsibility of cabinet ministers to Parliament, nor are they subject to the punishments we impose upon our legislature, the threat of members being dragged from their seats by an angry constituency enraged at the passage of bad law. Nor would it be appropriate to surround judges in their usual capacity with such constraints. Citizens' liberties rely in large part upon the presence of competent and independent judges, so these are appointed on the basis of legal expertise, not popularity, and once appointed are difficult to remove; the most important kind of judicial independence is independence from political pressure exerted by the dominant faction in Parliament. Those qualities required for an effective judiciary acting in its ordinary capacity, upholding the integrity of law, render judges totally unacceptable for extraordinary duties which would poison ordinary judicial integrity, and hence poison the integrity of law.

To retain coherency of argument one must adhere to a consistent world view, but such audacity immediately carries the stigma of being an "ist" or an "ite". I'll therefore nail my colours to the mast right now as (for want of a better description) a "Forseyite monarchist" — what this means shall become clear — and shall argue as such throughout this book. The first (and I hope, the only) casualty of this clarity shall be the opinions of a small clique of constitutional lawyers whose opinions have of late been remarkably fashionable in the popular Press. They shall doubtless feel their opinions to be dreadfully neglected by this book. I confess this was deliberate: their so-called "modern" views are divided from those of the Forseyite monarchists by an enormous conceptual gulf, upon the far side of which are perched their legal opinions. In reality their doctrines are vintage 19th Century, whereby the struggle is between an hereditary Crown (represented by an aristocratic viceregal figure) and elected politicians representing democratic government, so the more progressive Constitution has the Crown more marginalised — or deleted altogether.

In contrast, the Forseyite view is that this struggle is dead. It has been dead for almost an entire century. The real struggle in our representative democracy is between elected politicians and the people, and it's a struggle in which the remaining residual powers of the Crown are of enormous value in protecting the people and their interests, when properly invoked. How and when these powers should be invoked is the crucial question confronting our modern democracy.

Drawing breath, I must acknowledge my debts. If one knew nothing of parliamentary history — or had only the report of the Republican Advisory Committee as a source of knowledge — one could be excused for believing that at some time in centuries past, at a particular phase of the moon, antecedent creatures of this form of democracy crawled on stumpy fins out of shallow primaeval seas onto all the shores of Earth, whereupon they waddled into the forums of the nations of the world, squatted down, and promptly started evolving. In reality, for much of its history parliamentary democracy is a creature having evolved in a particular environment, from particular circumstances, from which it spread out throughout the rest of the world, adapting then to local environments. Names like "cabinet minister", concepts like a Prime Minister, institutions like a vote of no confidence; all these come, like parliamentary democracy itself, from the "Mother of Parliaments", Westminster.

In these days of politically correct and expedient historical whitewash it's deeply unfashionable to acknowledge one culture may owe debts to another. Even as the Western world owes a great deal to Ancient Greece for its contribution of formal ideas of participatory democracy, formal logic, philosophy, geometry, music and the dramatic arts; as it owes much in the understanding of large scale practical government to Ancient Rome, the preservation and extension of this learning through the Dark Ages to the Arabs, of much culture since then to the French; the contributions of Imperial China, the Renaissance Italian states, the

Austro-Hungarian Empire, and so on; so too does our society owe a great deal in its political institutions to English and British history.

This doesn't imply owing any debt to contemporary Britain. In a rare moment of lucidity Malcolm Turnbull's Republic Advisory Committee declared,

> In acknowledging the importance of British models of parliamentary democracy and law, Australians often speak of having "inherited" these institutions from Britain or even of Britain having "given" these institutions to Australia. Whatever may be the correct characterisation in other countries, the British subjects who settled Australia brought with them British concepts of law and parliamentary government just as they brought with them the English language, the Christian religion (in its various forms) and other elements of British culture. The settlers did not *inherit* British institutions; they were as much entitled to those institutions, and understood them as well, as any British subject living in the British Isles.[6]

The Committee is only a little wide of the mark: the settlers did inherit British institutions, in the same sense as their contemporaries in the British Isles inherited them. Both British history up to the 20th Century and the institutions thereof, by being incorporated in our constitutions as the birthright of our settlers, have become the birthright of all Australians, all New Zealanders, all Canadians, irrespective of ethnicity; even as the political experiences of the American Revolution, incorporated into the Constitution of the United States, have become the birthright of all Americans irrespective of ethnicity. This shall remain true irrespective of modern or future Britain; thus are our debts to history, not to a contemporary country.

What are the important aspects of the Westminster system?

> Its major characteristics are: a sovereign bicameral legislature in which the lower house has final authority; government by a cabinet which is drawn from the parliament and is responsible to it; an "above politics" constitutional monarch as the ceremonial head of state, distinct from the effective head of government, the Prime Minister; the rule of law and judicial independence; a career public service impartially serving the government of the day; and armed forces which are outside politics.[7]

Each country or territory to have inherited this system has made amendments in whatever way the constitutional drafters of that country thought would provide improvements appropriate to local conditions. For example,

> This system provides the basis of governmental processes in Australia, but has been amended in important respects. The sovereignty of the parliament is limited by the Australian Constitution, in particular, the federal system. Also the

powers of the Senate, especially as asserted in the 1975 constitutional crisis, weaken the relative position of the House of Representatives.[8]

Australia has an elected Senate representing its States; Canada, an appointed Senate modelled on aspects of the House of Lords, and New Zealand, most radically, has dispensed with an Upper House altogether. Britain emasculated its House of Lords in 1911, depriving it of potency, whereas within the Australian Senate is preserved an ancient right formerly held by the Lords to block Supply. Australia and Canada hold written constitutions, although Britain and New Zealand do not. The constitutions of these four countries, as well as those of the other twelve countries throughout the world also under Queen Elizabeth II, and the States of Australia, and the Provinces of Canada, may be regarded as different subspecies of the same tree; a tree which, for want of a more precise title, is known throughout the world as the Westminster system.

Comprehending the role of the Crown in this system requires looking further abroad than the United Kingdom. During the 20th Century the purpose of the Crown in upholding parliamentary democracy has gained far clearer definition from the experiences of other Parliaments throughout the Commonwealth than from that Parliament physically residing in the Palace of Westminster. This has happened to such an extent that it can be said the role of the Crown can no longer be understood simply by looking at British experiences. An illustration of this occurred in 1950, when an argument was waged among constitutional authorities as to whether the King held the right to refuse a dissolution of the British House of Commons to his incumbent prime minister. The battlefield was the letters page of *The Times*; the protagonists concentrated on British events: what Asquith said early this century; what Queen Victoria was advised to do or not to do by Lord Aberdeen last century. There appears to have been no awareness among the majority of them that the most systematic and authoritative study on this question had been performed by a Canadian at Oxford in 1943, a study that required assessment of events throughout the Commonwealth realms. The exception was the most authoritative letter written; by Sir Alan Lascelles, Private Secretary to King George VI. Although not mentioning the Canadian by name, Lascelles' summary of the King's discretionary power was consonant with this study, and explicitly cited events in Canada and South Africa as illustrations.

Understanding modern institutions of Parliament and the Crown requires understanding political history, and this in turn requires access to voices of the living and voices of the dead. For the latter, to be heard in books, I am deeply grateful to my father in Brisbane for his encouragement, patience and support (particularly after I ransacked his law library); to Don Markwell in Oxford, through whose hospitality I gained access to the priceless repository of documents in the Bodleian Library during my stay at Merton College; and to the Australia-Britain Society who, after deciding the manuscript was of mutual importance to the two countries, granted me a Menzies Scholarship to pursue research in the United Kingdom. Of the voices of the living: this manuscript has passed through the hands of a number of constitutional and political authorities who have been kind enough to read drafts of it and offer constructive criticism. In particular I would like to thank the following people:

> His Excellency the Hon. Sir Walter Campbell AC QC, *Governor of Queensland (1985–92), Chief Justice of the Supreme Court of Queensland (1982–85), Judge of the Supreme Court (1967–85).*

> The Hon. Sir James Killen KCMG, *Barrister-at-Law; Minister for the Navy (1967–71), Minister for Defence (1975–82), Vice-President of Executive Council and Leader, House of Representatives, Commonwealth of Australia (1982–1983).*

> Peter McDermott, *Queensland Law Reform Commissioner; Senior Lecturer in Law, University of Queensland Law School; Barrister-at-Law.*

> Professor D.J. Markwell, *Warden of Trinity College, University of Melbourne; former Fellow and Tutor in Politics, Merton College, Oxford; Queensland Rhodes Scholar.*

> Colonel the Hon. John Greenwood RFD QC, *Member of the Queensland Legislative Assembly (1974–1983), Cabinet Minister (1976–1980); Delegate to Australian Constitutional Conventions (Hobart 1976, Adelaide 1983); former Army Judge Advocate and member, Reviewing Judge Advocates Panel, Australian Defence Forces; counsel in constitutional cases before the High Court of Australia and the Privy Council in London.*

Thanks also to Dr Geoffrey Marshall, Provost of Queen's College, Oxford, and J.R. Lucas, Fellow and Tutor in Philosophy at Merton, for their encouragement and discussions. To all these people, my editors Elizabeth Slade (caught between a venomous spider and a difficult author) and JWG, my long-suffering mother and sisters, as well as the ever-patient and friendly people at Australian Academic Press — Stephen, Andrea and Lucy — and my friends who have endured my opinions argued over in coffee-shops and bars in Brisbane, Melbourne, Oxford and London… my warmest gratitude and thanks.

The opinions (and any errors) residing in this work are my own, but the inspiration, encouragement and support required to write this manuscript came from them.

Whispers of History

The danger of royal absolutism is past; but the danger of Cabinet absolutism, even of Prime Ministerial absolutism, is present and growing. Against that danger the reserve power of the Crown, and especially the power to force or refuse dissolution, is in some instances the only constitutional safeguard. The Crown is more than a quaint survival, a social ornament, a symbol, 'an automaton, with no public will of its own'. It is an absolutely essential part of the parliamentary system. In certain circumstances, the Crown alone can preserve the Constitution, or ensure that if it is to be changed it shall be only by the deliberate will of the people.

The Hon. Dr Eugene Forsey, *The Royal Power of Dissolution of Parliament in the British Commonwealth.*

Prelude

—▪■▪—

[*Scene: The interior of a library, late at night. A solitary man is writing at a long wooden desk, its surface covered with faded green leather. Around him are untidy piles of books. He's writing by the light of an old-fashioned electric table-lamp, which illuminates a stack of loose-leaf manuscript pages at his elbow. Pausing for a moment, the Author re-reads what he has just written.*]

Author   In the study of politics, Niccolò Machiavelli once warned...

[*Enter Niccolò's ghost, an old white-haired man, shuffling in a dressing-gown covering what appear to be threadbare Renaissance clothes. He is carrying a cup of tea.*]

Niccolò's ghost   Whosoever considers the past and the present will readily observe that all cities and all peoples are and ever have been animated by the same desires and the same passions; so that it is easy, by diligent study of the past, to foresee what is likely to happen in the future in any republic, and to apply those remedies used by the ancients, or, not finding any that were employed by them, to devise new ones from the similarity of the events. But as such considerations are neglected or not understood by most of those who read, or if understood by these, are unknown by those who govern, it follows that the same troubles generally recur in all republics.[1]

[*He seats himself in the chair across the table from the Author, and observes him with a quizzical eye.*]

Author   [*open-mouthed*] Oh my...Lord...

Niccolò's ghost   No, a good political analyst instead, alas. Still, it will have to do. [*Takes a sip from his teacup. Long pause.*]

Author   Er...are you offering to lend a hand with this?

Niccolò's ghost   Well, I don't know about a *hand*. A willing ear and a critical mind, certainly. Much more to the point.

Author   [*dazed, and clearly at an utter loss what to do or say at this bizarre bit of supernatural intervention*] Ah...[*drops his pen.*]

Niccolò's ghost   Oh, don't mind me. Please, continue writing. I think you were about to discuss troubles in your own country.

[*At a loss to do anything else, the Author picks up his pen and resumes writing.*]

◙ ◈ ◙

Prospero: ...What see'st thou else
In the dark backward and abysm
of time?

The Tempest, Act I Scene 2

Beyond the Painted Chamber

———————■■■———————

Adebate, that is no debate, has imposed a crisis on us all. The most profound constitutional question posed since Federation, of whether to become a republic, is being asked of us in a nonchalant, even careless, manner. The task may not appear difficult, but only because it has been presented to us in a vacuum. Curiously for such a matter, its public controversy remains innocent of philosophy, almost unheeding of history and careless of political principle. A nationalist box of time and place has been drawn around the Australian continent, and all broader historical and political influences on the Westminster system discarded by the Fourth Estate. The apprehensions of many members of the populace — republican and monarchist alike — remain formless and unuttered, through lack of awareness of the historical precedents that would reveal them to be well-founded. As a substitute for individual thought, orthodox conformity is being urged upon us, an acceptance of the Oz Republic. Clichés have been pressed, to persuade the recalcitrant they are out of step with history. The most obvious starting-point is the claim by members of the republican movement that we should look to the American Revolution for our political inspiration and attitudes to Britain.

The fact we attained full independence peacefully, and with the free will of British and Australian parliaments, would seem to suggest an analogy with the 18th Century American colonies' tensions is inappropriate. Yet leaving the argument there would allow chardonnay revolutionaries to escape unscathed a field of contention, on which they have fired the opening shots and upon which they could not hope to win. Allowing the constitutional struggle of the North American colonies to fade into a cheap republican slogan insults the memory of its American and British protagonists, and buries the truth. Before anything else, we must accept the challenge and look to the American Revolution, in its proper historical context. This is not only for its own sake, but because the context of the Australian republican debate cannot be entirely grasped without a thorough exposure to four centuries of history and the philosophies that have emerged. Once these are understood, the current republican question will be seen to produce a very different answer. Our gaze turns first to England in the late 17th Century, and the legacy of two earlier revolutions.

> The fall of the English republic and the Restoration of Charles
> II in 1660 had been essentially a return to government by law.
> It implied primarily a repudiation of the arbitrary rule by
> civilian or military juntos, parliamentary or republican, which
> eighteen years of armed force had imposed on the nation.
> Equally if less obviously, it implied a repudiation of the [earlier,
> royal] arbitrary rule…which had been overturned by the Long
> Parliament between 1640 and 1642.[2]

Since the collapse of the republic there had been an uneasy compromise between two conflicting views of government: one held that effective political authority should rest with Parliament, and the other, that political authority should flow entirely from the Crown. This conflict had been reflected in the emergence of two political parties by 1680, the "Country" party upholding the former view, and the "Court" party upholding the latter. Despite Charles' efforts, grievances from the recent civil wars found fresh expression, as republicans adhered to the country party and cavaliers defended the Court. Mutual hatred between the two parties led to an exchange of unflattering nicknames: courtiers dubbed members of the Country party "Whigs", in reference to Scottish Presbyterians, while they in turn retaliated by describing the courtiers as "Tories", a name describing Catholic Irish outlaws.[†]

Charles himself was the undoubted head of the government, and freely wielded the Crown's prerogative powers to prorogue or dissolve Parliament. On occasion this proved necessary: the behaviour of the House of Commons during his reign at times resembled that of a lynch mob. Yet the House of Commons frequently forced him to acquiesce to measures and assent to laws which he personally disliked and of which he disapproved. Shortly before his unexpected death from a fit at the age of fifty-five, he acidly warned his younger brother, "I am too old to go again on my travels: you may, if you choose it."[3] This was a wry reference to their exile abroad during the republic, and the power of Parliament. The younger brother failed to take his advice and, as James II, precipitated the Revolution three years later which cost him his throne and reinforced the authority of Parliament.[4]

---

† This is the origin of Britain's two famous parties. (The Labour Party is much more recent, dating from the beginning of the 20th Century.)

THE LEGACY OF REVOLUTIONS

In Duke Humfrey's mediaeval library at Oxford may be found an ancient folio-sized book bound in worn brown leather: volume II of Sir Anthony Woods' *Athenae Oxonienses*, published in 1692. A 17th Century *Who's Who* of all the writers and bishops who had been educated in Oxford from 1500AD to 1690AD, it would have been a fascinating work to read even if it had never passed through human hands since leaving the printer's press three centuries ago. Sir Anthony was a stout Cavalier who repeated not only biographical details if he knew them to be true, but also salacious gossip he heard about prominent Roundheads involved in the recent Civil Wars. Of this he seems to have heard a great deal.

Yet this particular copy of the work has passed through the hands of various owners, one of whom has transformed the value of the book. A "Jo. Gadbury", possessed of the irritating habit of scribbling notes in the margins, performed an invaluable service to historians. Transcribed in the broad margins of *Athenae Oxonienses* in archaic handwriting browned with age, by a hand long since dust, are written extracts of the debates of the Convention Parliament of 1688, when assembled in a free conference of the Commons and Lords to discuss the implications of the Revolution for the monarchy and its succession.

That this assembly in the Painted Chamber, debating on the constitutional future of England, was a "free conference" is important, for a free conference was, in the words of one delegate, a "way of intercourse between both Houses…where there is full liberty of objecting, answering and replying".[†] Yet as significant as the form of debate were the participants, among whom were some of the finest English legal minds of the period. Of this number perhaps the most influential was an elderly Oxford-educated republican prosecutor, Serjeant Maynard, whose life thus fell within the scope of Wood's busy pen even as his speeches lay within that of Gadbury's.

John Maynard, the man who was "a great promoter of the Revolution, he being the person according to common fame that first started using the word Abdication for King James 2[d] leaving the Kingdom instead of Desertion",[5] was born about 1602. Educated at Oxford's Exeter College and in the Middle Temple, he became a famous prosecutor, legal authority and parliamentarian. Elected MP for Totness for the parliament of 1640, he drew up the evidence for the prosecution of Thomas, Earl of Strafford on a charge of High Treason. Strafford, Charles I's right hand man, was tried, found guilty and executed. Maynard gave an eloquent speech to both Houses of Parliament in reply to Strafford's unsuccessful defence, a speech immortalised in hostile Cavalier verse:

---

† Marginal note, Sir Anthony Wood's *Athenae Oxonienses*, vol II, cols. 769–772. (Spelling and punctuation have for the most part been rendered into 20th Century form). This quote is taken from the speech of Mr Hampden, a member of the House of Commons and member of the family of the republican parliamentarian John Hampden. John Hampden was one of the early enemies of Charles I and "a Colonel for the Parliament in the beginning of the rebellion": text *ibid.* col.770. He was killed in June 1643 fighting against the King's army.

The Robe was summon'd, *Maynard* in the head,
In legal murder none so deeply read:
I brought him to the Bar, where once he stood,
Stain'd with the (yet un-expiated blood)
Of the brave *Strafford*, when three kingdoms rung
With his accumulative active tongue...[6]

His deep knowledge of "legal murder" was again employed to draw up the prosecution case against Dr Laud, Archbishop of Canterbury, who met the same unpleasant fate as Strafford. During Cromwell's Protectorate Maynard, a Serjeant at Law, was by letters patent made the Protector's Serjeant, and held a notable career as prosecutor in the republican High Court of Justice, being responsible for the execution of several Cavaliers. He recanted at the Restoration of the monarchy, swore oaths of allegiance to Charles II and "by the corrupt dealing of a great man of the Law"[7] was made the King's Serjeant. By the end of November 1660 he had been knighted and made a judge, but "by several excuses he got clear off from that employment".[8] His legal expertise proved profitable:

This Sir *Joh. Maynard* was a person, who, by his great reading
and knowledge in the more profound and perplexed parts of
the law, did long since procure the known repute of being
one of the chief Dictators of the Long Robe, and by his great
practice for many years together did purchase to himself no
small Estate.[9]

Elected MP for Beralston in 1661, he continued a lengthy career as a parliamentarian until 1689, when he retired having "grown very infirm by his great age".[10] Now at the age of about eighty-seven, he was about to engage in the last great political and legal action of his life.

In the 20th Century two things are sometimes said about the Bill of Rights which emerged out of the debates of this Convention Parliament. The first is that it made the Crown elective as well as hereditary, the second that it merely limited the powers of the King *vis-à-vis* Parliament, unlike a modern Bill of Rights which limits the powers of the government over the citizen. Neither assertion appears sustainable.

Rather than making the Crown *elective* (each individual monarch in effect having to meet with the approval of the parliament at the Coronation) as well as hereditary, it would be more accurate to say it made the Crown *contractual* as well as hereditary (so each individual monarch must comply with conditions set out in the statutes relating to the monarchy, both at the time of her Coronation and throughout the rest of her reign). Yet as we shall see, the concept of the contract goes much deeper.

Maynard himself, the great urger of the concept of James's abdication, a "Great Stickler in the free Conference between the Lords and Commons about that weighty and Criticall affaire",[11] explicitly rejected the notion that the events of the Revolution and actions of the Convention Parliament would render the Crown elective: "My Lords, when there is a present defect of one to Exercise the Administration of the Government I conceive the declaring a vacancy and provision of a Supply, for it can never make the Crown Elective".[12]

He wove two themes in his speeches, and repeated them so often as almost to become monotonous in discourse. The first is the existence of a defect — the absence of government, the neglected sceptre left by James' hasty departure — and the consequent need of a replacement, explicitly devoid of any implication of an elective King. This emphatic rejection appears to have been a necessary condition in persuading the Lords to the course of action urged by the Commons. Memories of republican experiments in England were still fresh and bitter in many minds. The second is the existence of a contract between subject and sovereign, violation of which was a breach of trust and consequently an abdication, hence his claim that James' earlier violation of the Constitution represented an abdication:

> If the attempting the utter destruction of the subject and
> subversion of the Constitution be not as much an Abdication
> as the Attempting of a father to cutt his Sons throat I know
> not what is, my Lords. The Constitution, notwithstanding the
> vacancy, is the same, the Laws that are the foundations and
> Rules of that Constitution are the same: But if there be in
> any particular instance a Breach of that Constitution that will
> be an Abdication. And that Abdication will infer a vacancy.
> It is not that the Commons do say the Crown of England is
> always and perpetually Elective, but it is more necessary that
> there be a supply when there is a defect and the doing of that
> will be no alteration from a Successive one to an Elective…
> sure we must not be perpetually under Anarchy, the Word
> Elective is none of the Commons' word, neither is the
> making the Kingdom Elective the thing they have in their
> thoughts and intentions.[13]

This second argument of a contract or trust was expanded further by Mr Serjeant Holt, commanded by the Commons to assist in the management of the conference. He spoke upon the definition of abdication, and argued that actions which violate a trust are a renunciation of that trust, and hence an abdication, without requiring a formal abdication in writing.[14] Another member of the Commons, Mr Somers, rose to his feet and argued in support of Holt's case, quoting legal authorities and defiantly declaring

> King James the 2[d] by going about to subvert the constitution
> and breaking the original contract between King and
> people, and by violating the fundamental Laws and with-
> drawing himself out of the Kingdom, hath thereby
> renounced to be a King according to the constitution, and
> avowing to govern by a Despotic power unknown to the

Constitution and inconsistent with it he hath renounced to
be a King as he swore to be at the Coronation, such a King
to whome the allegiance of an English subject is due, and
hath sett up another kind of Dominion which is to all
intents an Abdication...[15]

This belief in a contract between Sovereign and subject appears to have been one dear to the hearts of many members of the Commons, and so they believed of James II that "by these Acts, his subversion of the Constitution, his breaking the Original Contract and Violation of the fundamental Lawes he hath Abdicated".[16] Whether any Stuart King before the Revolution would have agreed to the existence of this contract is extremely unlikely. James I and Charles I had made their own views on the Divine Right of Kings well felt, and Thomas Hobbes, tutor to the younger Stuarts, held political theories which explicitly rejected the kind of contract conceived by Maynard and his fellows.[17] Yet irrespective of whether the contract conceived by Maynard and his fellow orators existed before the Revolution, there can be no doubt that it existed for all time after the Revolution.

Reading the speeches of the debates and the circumstances of the Revolution, it is difficult to derive any other conclusion but that the Bill of Rights *was* intended as a partial expression of this contract, and does limit the authority of the government over the people by defining conditions under which the allegiance and obedience of the subject is not longer owed to that King and his servants. When Maynard says:

If two of us make a mutual agreement to help and defend
each other from anyone that should assault us in a Journey
and that he that is with me turns upon me and breaks my
head he hath undoubtedly abdicated my Assistance and
Revoked [the agreement][18]

the two travellers alluded to were not the King and his Parliament but the King and his subject. This fundamental concept of the basis of the Crown's authority over the country being a trust between the Crown and the people which, if violated by a King, caused his authority to be revoked, was utterly radical throughout Western Europe at the time. It remains the basis of the authority of the Crown in every realm of Elizabeth II throughout the world today, and the events which gave birth to it are rightly regarded as the first of the revolutions of modern Europe.

The Convention Parliament bestowed the Crown upon Mary (Stuart), Princess of Orange, the Protestant elder daughter of James, and her husband William, Prince of Orange, to reign jointly as William III and Mary II, with the understanding that "the sole and full exercise of the regal power be only in and executed by the said Prince of Orange "in the names of them both, with the succession passing to:

the heirs of the body of the said princess; and for default of
such issue to the princess Ann of Denmark [James II's
younger daughter, Mary's sister] and the heirs of her body;
and for default of such issue to the heirs of the body of the
said Prince of Orange.[19]

At the same time the Parliament presented them both with the text of a declaration outlining the origins of the Revolution, the offences of James II which it
desired to be declared illegal in perpetuity, the desire to establish circumstances
such that "their [the subjects'] religion, laws and liberties might not again be in
danger of being subverted",[20] its confidence that the Prince of Orange would
"perfect the deliverance so far advanced by him, and will still preserve them
from the violation of their rights, which they have here asserted, and from all
other attempts upon their religion, rights and liberties"[21] and consequently, its
willingness to bestow the Crown upon them. In turn William and Mary gave
their assent to this declaration, which passed into law and was entered upon the
statute books with a now famous title, the Bill of Rights.

Although the Revolution was effectively bloodless in England, the same
cannot be said of its implications for James' former kingdoms of Ireland and
Scotland. In Ireland the Catholic Irish regiments of James II fought against the
Protestant Irish and allied regiments of William III, and were defeated at the
Battle of the Boyne, devastating any hopes James had of regaining any of his
Crowns. In Scotland, the homeland of the Stuarts, fears of an uprising led to
the tragic massacre at Glencoe and the seeds were sown for the Jacobite rebel-
lions of the next century.

These political arrangements were also endangered from another direction.
William and Mary had no children in their marriage, and when Mary died
of smallpox in 1694 he never re-married, dying childless in 1702. The
Crown passed to Anne, whose private life was also marred with tragedy.
Despite her many pregnancies, she frequently either miscarried or the child
did not live long. Her longest lived child, the only one to even approach
adulthood, was her son William, Duke of Gloucester, who died in 1700. He
was eleven years old.

At the year of the death of Queen Anne in 1714, the parliament of the newly-
created country of Great Britain remained divided into the Whigs and the
Tories, but the positions of these parties had shifted and evolved over the
decades. The Whigs now regarded themselves as the defenders of the Revolution
twenty-six years earlier, the moderates among them monarchist, regarding the
institution of monarchy as a political instrument which existed not because it
was ordained by God but because it was useful as a safeguard against arbitrary
power. Again in the language of 1689, they believed that the "constitution of the
government is actually upon pact and covenant with the people",[22] and a duty of
the Crown was to defend the Constitution. The Tories, on the other hand,
believed a monarch held her position because she was anointed by God rather

than by any pact, and they sympathised with the overthrown James II and his exiled heirs, endowed with the divinity of kings but not much else.

The Tories had come to enjoy the favour of Anne, dominating her court during much of her reign. Many of them (the "Jacobites") even expected that at her death they would be able to restore the deposed line of James to the throne, undoing the Revolution and its principles. Unfortunately for them Anne, who had for a long time suffered from poor health, suddenly fell very ill on the 29th of July, and it rapidly became clear she was dying. The Whigs were swift to act. The Act of Settlement had been passed in 1701 to prevent reversal of the Revolution and restoration of James II's line. This Act instead gave the throne in "Protestant succession" to Princess Sophia of Hanover (a granddaughter of James I) and her heirs, in the absence of Anne's children surviving. Sophia had since died at the grand old age of eighty-four, but she had left an heir, George, Elector of Hanover. The Whigs were determined to see the Settlement fulfilled. They had maintained correspondence with George, and he was ready.

In Kensington Palace, a gracious building resting among the beauty of Kensington Gardens in London, there remain only a few echoes of Queen Anne's presence, and none of a dying Queen and a bloodless palace *coup* which would transform constitutional history, not only within the realm but beyond the shores of Britain. In those few days as she lay sometimes sleeping, sometimes conscious, slowly dying in the quiet elegance of Kensington, her most trusted adviser and leader of the Tory party, Henry St. John, Viscount Bolingbroke, was proceeding to select Jacobites for positions of power in preparation for the crisis precipitated by her death. Meanwhile her deathbed at the Palace was attended, not only by Bolingbroke and the Tory members of her Privy Council,† but by the uninvited Dukes of Argyle and Somerset. These two men were Whigs, members of the Council but excluded from the Cabinet, who were secretly intriguing with Charles Talbot, Duke of Shrewsbury, one of Anne's most senior ministers.

Bolingbroke had been deceived by Shrewsbury into thinking him compliant with Tory ambitions, and had bestowed on him the powerful offices of Lord Chamberlain and Lord Lieutenant of Ireland. When Argyle and Somerset now unexpectedly appeared at the doors of the Council chamber it was Shrewsbury who rose from where he had been sitting and thanked them for their offers of assistance, bidding them take their seats, while the rest of Cabinet watched in dismay. Argyle and Somerset imme-

---

† The Privy Council was (and in the UK, symbolically still is) the formal body to which the Crown's advisors belonged. In the 17th Century the monarch would choose members of the Privy Council to form committees to advise her on government policy. These advisors were known as "ministers of the Crown". The most important ministers were those belonging to the clique most trusted by the monarch. They became known as "Cabinet" ministers in reference to an inner room, or "Cabinet", of the Council apartments in the royal palace (hence the modern title). Politicians out of favour with the monarch might belong to the Council yet not to the committees formally advising her. See A. Todd, *On Parliamentary Government in England*, vol. II pp. 60–144, for the history of the Privy and Cabinet councils.

diately seated themselves and suggested that the Queen's physicians be consulted to see if she was still coherent. When told that she was, they proposed that the vacant post of Lord Treasurer be promptly filled, and that Shrewsbury be recommended to the Queen as the best candidate. The Jacobite ministers, taken off guard and not yet realising Shrewsbury's duplicity, did not object, and so he visited her bed to tender what appeared to be the unanimous verdict of her ministers. Anne, roused to consciousness, acquiesced in a faint voice and gave him the treasurer's staff, bidding him use it "for the good of her people". When he offered to surrender the staff of Lord Chamberlain she refused to accept it, telling him to keep them both. He thus became for a crucial period the most powerful man in Britain; simultaneously Lord Treasurer, Lord Chamberlain and Lord Lieutenant of Ireland. Back in the Council chamber Argyle and Somerset had argued that in this time of crisis all privy counsellors in or near London should be allowed to meet in council irrespective of their party. This had met with agreement, and a special summons was sent out. A large number of Whig counsellors promptly appeared at Kensington the same afternoon, including their leader Lord Somers. By the fifth of August 1714, Anne was dead. On that day, with the Tories outmanoeuvred in Council and demoralised at her death, George, Elector of Hanover was declared in the assembled Parliament of Great Britain to be King George I.[23] Many Tories subsequently fled the country for Europe.

Few, if any, members of Parliament sitting that day in their powdered wigs and frock-coats could have realised precisely the vast wheels of change being set in motion. Until the accession of George I, conflicts over government policy between the Crown and Parliament had been resolved (where possible) by ministers of the Crown. The power of Parliament by this time was becoming concentrated in the House of Commons: the House of Lords had been abolished in 1649 during the English republic, but the excesses of a single-chamber Parliament during the republic had proved the need for a second chamber, and so Cromwell had set up an Upper House also termed the "House of Lords", the members of which were nominated by him. The traditional House of Lords had been re-established at the Restoration but with diminished authority. Its power continued to wane for the rest of the 17th Century, until by the mid-18th Century politicians were known to avoid the Lords until their careers in the Commons seemed truly over.

By the end of Anne's reign these ministers all were parliamentarians. Although they advised the monarch on policy, she was neither obliged to ask their advice nor to accept it, nor to limit herself to them when seeking advice. It was their often unpleasant task to act as mediators between the monarch and Parliament: a task rendered more dangerous by the fact they were held personally responsible by Parliament for the Crown's actions, and that they held their authority as advisers, not because they held the confidence or respect of Parliament, but because the monarch liked them or found their abilities or political beliefs useful. Within the constraints imposed by Parliament she had remained the author of the government's policies, the arbiter of its goals, the definer of its conduct.†

The parliamentarians in their powdered wigs therefore knew they were witnessing an historic turning point. It was the final fall of the House of Stuart, the Scottish dynasty of monarchs who had ruled England, Scotland and Ireland since the time James VI of Scotland had come south to fill the vacuum left by the death of Elizabeth I of England, to reign there as King James I. It was the final burial of the doctrine of the Divine Right of Kings, that despotic monarchical belief, foreign to the English Constitution, advocated by James VI of Scotland in his book *True Law of Free Monarchies* and by Louis XIV of France, *le Roi Soleil* of Versailles whose splendour the later Stuarts had admired. By choosing the Elector of Hanover to be King, Parliament had set aside the lineage "ordained by divine grace" for one defined by Act of Parliament, representing the consent of the nation.[24] Internationally it was the forging of a religious, political and military alliance with the German state of Hanover, just as the recent coronation of William of Orange had represented the forging of a similar alliance with the Dutch Netherlands. Yet perhaps the most important point, and the one least appreciated, was the simple fact that George was a middle-aged German prince who spoke no English.

The deliberations and debates of the committees of the Privy Council were doubtless often tedious to a British-born monarch who understood both the language and the constitution. But George was fifty-five years old, and set in his ways. Apart from the increase in wealth, prestige and military strength which the British throne provided, he was neither interested in British affairs nor in the intricacies of its constitution, preferring instead to concentrate upon the intrigues of the German states. Scarcely any of his British ministers could speak German, and he was bored to distraction by debates he could not understand. Conversations with his ministers were conducted in Latin, not particularly fluently on either side. Consequently, his cabinet ministers began to meet and decide policy in his willing absence. They no longer had to struggle with the monarch's will, but were themselves the entire authors of much government policy, the arbiters of goals, the definers of conduct.[25]

No sooner had they found themselves freed of the King's will than they found themselves shackled by that of the Commons. With the view that political authority flowed entirely from the Crown rendered so obviously untenable, the alternate view, that effective political authority should rest with Parliament — in particular, the House of Commons — asserted itself with vigour. Cabinet ministers could only keep up their old role as mediators, negotiating with the Commons without submitting to it, while they were actively backed up by the Crown's authority and support. In the absence of that support they now found it

---

† Although this was the position of the Crown during the reigns of William and Mary, and Anne, it was not a vantage exploited by Anne, whose chronic illness and limited abilities led her to rely heavily upon her Cabinet. William III on the other hand made full and energetic use of his position; an example admired fifty-eight years later by George III in his struggles.

---

necessary to acquire the assent of the Commons to transact the business of government. The country's effective Executive found itself reliant upon the good will of the Commons, without which it could not govern.[26]

This made it a matter of urgency for Cabinet to acquire debaters whose eloquence could persuade the Commons, and leaders whose insight and qualities inspired enough fellow ministers and parliamentary factions to support unpopular measures. What was needed was a new kind of minister, whose authority could persuade or compel others and fill the vacuum left by the abstinence of the King from heading the government of Great Britain. In short, a person whom later generations would describe as a prime minister or premier.

Enter stage left one Robert Walpole, Whig politician. Aged thirty-eight in the year of Anne's death, he had already distinguished himself in the House of Commons as one of its ablest members.[27] He had been made Secretary at War in February 1708, and as such was the Duke of Marlborough's political and administrative arm in England while Marlborough was fighting in his campaigns abroad. Within a month of his appointment Walpole had to deal with an attempted Jacobite invasion of Scotland — an invasion supported by strong French naval and military forces. To his relief the invasion was successfully repelled at sea, and forced to return to Dunkirk empty-handed.[28] In London he made his presence felt among the Cabinet ministers, for although not himself a member of Cabinet he attended its councils when military affairs were being discussed.

When the Tories rose to power during the reign of Anne he was dismissed from office. They retaliated to his stinging attacks upon Tory ministers in the House by formally accusing him of graft in handling military contracts during his time in office. The accusation was probably true: bribery and corruption, profiteering and graft were in this era regarded as necessary elements of the business of government. The disgrace lay in being caught with one's fingers in the till. On the 17th of January 1712,

> he was committed to the Tower by order of the Commons and
> expelled from the House...Walpole remained in the Tower for
> six months, until Parliament rose for the summer recess. His
> physical well-being was ensured by a reasonably comfortable
> apartment, but the effect of imprisonment upon his mind was
> bitter...Released on 8 July 1712, [he] was not allowed to take
> up his place in Parliament again until after a general election.[29]

Such was the man now waiting with the other parliamentarians assembled at Greenwich on the 19th September 1714, to greet their new king upon his arrival from the Continent, and manoeuvre for office or favour.

At the beginning of George I's reign Walpole had to be content with the post of Paymaster-General. Although not a Cabinet position, it was nonetheless lucrative, involving as it did the handling of the country's military budget. In the elections of 1715 the Whigs won a resounding victory over the Tories, with 341 Whig seats won as against 217 Tory. This victory was pushed even further when the Whig Richard Hampden was appointed Chairman of the Committee of Elections in the Commons, to adjudicate disputes over electoral results. Under his management of his position, thirty Tories successful at the elections "were unseated in favour of their petitioning rivals, while all petitions from unsuccessful Tories were defeated".[30] George I had already purged Tories from political offices in his government; what the Whigs now purposed was the utter extinction of the Tory party.

When the Commons established a committee to find evidence for the impeachment of the former Tory ministers Bolingbroke, Oxford and Ormonde, it was Walpole who was chosen to chair it. Bolingbroke had already fled the country, soon to be followed by Ormonde. Elderly Oxford "bravely disdained to follow his colleagues into exile and was duly committed to the Tower of London",[31] still protesting he'd done nothing not ordered by Queen Anne.

That same year Scotland was convulsed by the first of the two great Jacobite Rebellions. Amid this crisis the coincidental deaths of two senior Whigs led to Walpole being appointed by the King to both the posts of First Lord of the Treasury and Chancellor of the Exchequer — the highest ministerial position possible. Meanwhile,

> in the absence of an assurance from the [Old] Pretender
> that he was willing to adopt the Protestant religion very few
> Tories stirred on his behalf in England. The Duke of Argyll
> was dispatched north to deal with the rebellion, and by the
> early months of 1716 it was defeated both in Scotland and
> in Lancashire.[32]

During this period of Walpole's power Parliament repealed the Triennial Act of 1694 (requiring the Commons to go to general elections every three years) in favour of the Septennial Act of 1716 (requiring general elections only once every seven years).† Humiliated by fellow Whig ministers over North European foreign policy, Walpole resigned from the government in March 1717. From the backbenches of the Commons he organised a dissident Whig group in Parliament, headed by himself in the Commons and by his kinsman Lord Townshend in the House of Lords.

Such a breakaway dissident group would have been unthinkable in August 1714. It had become possible through the annihilation of the Tories: with no external threats, the Whig movement was now free to splinter from within. Walpole seized the opportunity, and gained notoriety as the destroyer of party unity.

Events favoured the dissident during his three-year exile on the backbenches. The Prince of Wales, who disliked his father the King intensely, established a

---

† The excuse given was fear of a Tory electoral victory, with its implications for the legacy of the Revolution; Adams, *Parliamentary History of England* p.398.

THE LEGACY OF REVOLUTIONS

rival court based in Leicester House. Opposition to the senior Court of George I could now be conducted by Walpole under the shelter of the Prince's favour and the Prince's court. The Prince went further, and supported the new Opposition in the Commons by commanding his Household followers in Parliament to vote with them. At the same time Walpole negotiated an alliance with the remnants of the Tories, many of whom had now abandoned loyalty to the Old Pretender but were still not trusted; the so-called Hanoverian Tories.

In 1720 the investment scheme infamous to history as the South Seas Bubble finally burst, bankrupting and beggaring a multitude of English investors. Walpole became man of the moment, for he had been a critic of this financial scheme in Parliament and was regarded by an enraged public as an unheeded prophet. He was restored by the King to the posts of First Lord of the Treasury and Chancellor of the Exchequer in April; earlier in the year he had already regained his position as Paymaster-General in a move calculated to reunite the divided Whig movement. Walpole mounted an unsuccessful salvage operation after the Bubble's collapse, losing him much of his public popularity but enhancing his standing within the government. His prestige increased still further when his counter-espionage network and information leaked by the French minister Dubois combined to reveal a conspiracy for an Irish-officered Jacobite invasion from France. The revelation of the plot impressed George I and the other Whigs of the senior court greatly, and left the remnant Tories isolated. By 1724, for the first time ever Walpole and his followers

> were without a serious rival in the Cabinet, the House of Commons was quiescent and the King well disposed. Twenty-three years after Walpole's entry to Parliament, ten years after elevation of the Whigs to a position of supremacy under King George I, Walpole-Townshend influence was firmly in control.[33]

This immense personal power was in large part due to his influence over the House of Commons:

> [His] greatest strength lay in the House of Commons. It is an historical truism to remark that he preferred to remain in this House, setting aside the practice of predecessors who had usually chosen at some point to commemorate success by moving to the House of Lords. Even Harley, whose pioneering methods in the post-Revolution Commons showed Walpole the way to mastery of that same body, had been misguided enough to take an earldom at the height of his career; the result was that [his] last years in office had been marked by a serious loss of control in the Lower House. Walpole was determined to make no such mistake.[34]

So the King's personal character and his difficulties with English language and customs had contributed in creating a power vacuum, which Robert Walpole filled through his control of the Commons. But how did this control come to lie in his hands?

In part it was through his ability to manage both Houses of Parliament, an ability that had become legendary even within his own lifetime. He was aware of the diplomatic necessity of acceding to backbench opinion from time to time, and was astute in his use of patronage to bribe impecunious peers and bishops.[35] Most importantly, his grasp on both the Lords and the Crown — a grasp peculiar to him alone of the Commons — was through the supply of money vital for government.

> [S]ince 1689 the growing power of Parliament *vis-à-vis* the Crown was partly due to the Commons' control of taxation. In the increasingly expensive modern world, the political role of the House of Lords was diminished. Financial initiatives were almost entirely in [Walpole's] own hands as First Lord of the Treasury and Chancellor of the Exchequer.[36]

His personal grip on power was illustrated following the death of George I in 1727. The Prince of Wales became King George II, a man embittered by Walpole's defection to the senior Court seven years earlier. Upon his accession to the Throne he sought an alternative.

> George II well understood that he needed the Commons' support and thought to obtain it by securing its Speaker, Compton, as his intermediary; but the chair of the House was not the important government post it had been in the seventeenth century or even in Anne's reign, when Harley had once held it in conjunction with a Secretaryship of State. The chair was slowly moving towards the modern position of impartiality and independence…To direct the Commons in Walpole's time a 'manager' needed to be not only a respected parliamentarian like Compton but a minister with the patronage resources of the Treasury behind him. Walpole had the combination of skills needed, being an administrator of proven ability as well as a leading Parliament man. Compton, however, lacked talent for office.[37]

Thus the new King, a man who *could* speak English and was concerned with British affairs, came to realise he was dependent upon Sir Robert Walpole's abilities and retained him, with reconciliation between the two men being negotiated by George's wife Caroline. Sir Robert remained in power for another fifteen years;† he resigned from office in February 1742 and died three years later, in his sixty-eighth year.

---

† It was George II who gave Walpole a convenient building in Whitehall for the use of the Treasury and its First Lord. Sir Robert moved in, using the house as his London residence. Its address? 10, Downing Street.

THE LEGACY OF REVOLUTIONS

The nature of his twenty-two years in government was described in a hostile motion proposed in both Houses of Parliament in January 1741, censuring him for having acted as a "prime" minister — an insulting turn of phrase. A distinguished statesman towards the end of the previous century had declared that nothing was so hateful to the English as a "prime" minister; they would rather be subject to a usurper (like Oliver Cromwell) who was first magistrate in fact as well as in title, rather than a legitimate King who referred them to a Grand Vizier.[38]

To parliamentarians accustomed to the idea of a system of government in which the business of government was conducted by a loose association of ministers loyal to the King but not to one another, there was something sinister about Walpole's methods. It was he who devised the now-familiar concept of collective responsibility for Cabinet decisions: ministers could privately criticise policy proposals before Cabinet reached a decision on the matter, but once that decision was made all ministers had to accept equal responsibility for it.[†] Behind Cabinet stood Walpole himself, not merely "first among equals" but the controller of all aspects of government, either personally or by immediate direction.[39] This accusation was levelled against him by a hostile Whig in the Commons that day, that Sir Robert had become "sole minister, a name and thing unknown to England".[40] Walpole rose to his feet and vehemently denied having been a "prime" — much less a "sole" — minister. His denials were hollow, and all sides of the House knew it, but he was saved that day by the action of the Tories, who either abstained or voted in his favour, for they were sickened to their stomachs of parliamentary persecution.[41] This clemency of his ancient enemies allowed his novel style of government to survive formal censure, to be remembered favourably in later years.

Time now passes some nineteen years beyond, to 1760. Sir Robert Walpole has been long since dead and buried, his audacious political experiments not repeated by his successors; the Crown's ministers have once again fallen from a cohesive and disciplined body into a loose coalition of individuals, nominally led by the Duke of Newcastle, the most eminent among them William Pitt the Elder, nicknamed by some "the Great Commoner".[42] George II has just died at the age of seventy-seven, his corpse interred with the solemn pomp and mourning of a State funeral. His twenty-three year old grandson has succeeded him to the thrones of Britain and Hanover, reigning from London as George III. Britain is immersed in the Seven Years' War with France, a war that encompasses the continent of North America, upon which soil the rival armies of Britain and France engage in bloody conflict. In that British Army is serving a young colonial officer by the name of George Washington.

---

† This practice was originally imposed by Walpole for entirely practical reasons: provided ministers were willing to backstab one another publicly over an unpopular policy, it had been easy for an angry Commons or an irritated King to hold the actual author individually responsible for the measure, and punish him by impeachment or dismissal. Once ministers closed ranks over responsibility for policy the government became a more formidable body, less vulnerable to external criticism. If the entire ministry was to be replaced over an unpopular measure, an alternative ministry had to be found capable of transacting government — not an easy proposition in the days before party discipline.

The new king is of a very different temperament to his predecessors, reigning under very different conditions. George I had been willing to delegate (although not completely surrender) the administration of his British realm to British ministers. George II, English-speaking, had been keen to play an active part in government but his hand had been constrained. The early unpopularity of German-born monarchs couldn't be ignored. Other constraints lay within his own personality: he had been scrupulous not to violate the apparent constitution of his island realm, and so refrained from actions once persuaded they were unconstitutional.[43] He was a man of limited abilities upon whom circumstance had compelled talented ministers, first Walpole, then — much later — Pitt, who forced upon him their policies. But this third George has been born and educated in Britain, and lives in a time when the Hanoverian dynasty has firmly taken root in his adopted country.

The Jacobite threat is practically extinct after the failed Rebellion of '45. Even the Highland Scots, previously loyal to the Stuart cause, provide regiments for the House of Hanover. The Tories, never quite eradicated from Parliament despite being denied power for most of the century, have become socially and politically palatable again. They have abandoned attempts to reverse the Revolution of 1688, so their superstitious theories on royal sanctity have ceased to be a threat to the new dynasty. Instead those same theories are now bent to serve the incumbent family, and the Tories now perceive themselves as the especial supporters and servants of the Crown.

Now is the era in which parliamentary corruption has been elevated to an art form. Electoral boundaries for English seats in the House of Commons have remained unaltered since before the middle of the 15th Century. Since then there have been considerable changes in population, as rural communities wither and mercantile cities like Manchester swell, so although all electorates are represented by politicians in the Commons, this House can no longer be regarded as being particularly representative of the general public. Some of these electorates (the "pocket" boroughs) are such that their voters lie under the influence of a powerful landowner. Other electorates are populated only by a handful of voters, openly corrupt, their votes sold to the highest bidder. The qualifications for the right to vote differ markedly from one electorate to the next: in some the right is broadly held, so it may be that every male resident who hasn't been in receipt of poor relief holds the right to vote, or else the "potwallopers" have the vote, every financially independent man who owns a dwelling of his own with a hearth at which he can cook his food. Elsewhere the vote is more confined; for instance, in some possession of the vote is tied up with the holding of land, a condition that allows wealthy men to buy up the votes of an underpopulated borough, the infamous "rotten" boroughs like Old Sarum (which is altogether uninhabited). The populations in the cities are grossly under-represented: Portsmouth, with twenty thousand inhabitants, has only eighty voters.[44]

The Whigs have exploited this state of affairs over the decades, establishing an oligarchy of aristocratic families who dominate both Houses of Parliament even as they dominate Society and the countryside. The heads of these families sit in the House of Lords, while lesser members of each sit in the Commons. Not all of these ruling families are of particularly ancient vintage, for a number of them have recently come from what might be described as the upper middle class, being the families of Whig politicians who have celebrated their political fortunes by taking hereditary peerages in the House of Lords. Old blood or *nouveau riche*, they hold Parliament in their grasp. In the middle of the 18th Century fifty-one peers and fifty-five commoners "made or effectively influenced the return of over 190 members of the Commons".[45] Twenty years later, in 1780, a majority in the Commons will be elected by only about 6000 voters. Out of 658 members of the House, 487 will have been virtually appointed, not elected.[46]

Niccolò's ghost Such control of Parliament is in many ways useful. Most obviously it reduces (although, inconveniently, it doesn't eliminate) the whole ghastly problem of public opinion. One only needs to bother about a sprinkling of voters out of the entire population. The business of creating and destroying governments can then be left largely to the feuds and alliances of families and factions. Second, it gives the heads of these factions the power to hire and fire parliamentary supporters, to enlist new talent into the House or remove incompetent or disloyal followers. Third, it provides a line of retreat for controversial politicians unfortunate enough to possess actual, independent-minded constituents. If the voters are ungrateful enough not to appreciate all the hard work expended on their behalf by their local member at Westminster, they may actually have the cheek to vote him out. It's a comfort to know that should this appalling ingratitude occur one can remain in Parliament by retreating to a nice quiet rotten borough, where the only constituents are a large flock of sheep tended by a halfwit called Reuben.

Australian interpretations of 18th Century British history place a strong accent upon the harsh legal code and heavy penalties inflicted, which weighed down upon the lower classes and filled prisons and squalid rotting hulks with miserable humanity, impelling the First Fleet to sail across the globe to establish a penal colony upon the shores of New South Wales. Yet it must be remembered that Britain at that time had one of the most liberal societies in Europe. "In no European country save Holland were freedom of discussion and intellectual liberty more complete or individual rights so adequately protected."[47] While deploring the corruption of the Whig aristocracy one must remember the real vindication of their style of government lay in their creation of this society. "A cultivated and liberal upper class, highly cosmopolitan in its culture, created a world in which literary, artistic, philosophical and scientific pursuits could flourish. Its political as well as its social hegemony was readily accepted."[48]

That this society existed in Britain of all places was astounding to Continental eyes. In the previous century the English had held the reputation for being a turbulent and rebellious race immersed in internecine strife, who not only killed their anointed king (and forced the abdication of another) but also the archbishops of their own national church. The reputation of the Scottish had been little better. That the two should combine into one of the most stable and tolerant countries of the period made it the subject of study for political observers. Voltaire was a conspicuous admirer, and for Montesquieu the British Constitution of the time was the inspiration for his now-famous doctrine of the separation of powers.

Life for the Whig parliamentarians is not, however, all snuff and rosewater. At the accession of George III a rather unpleasant reality presents itself: the foundations of their power are being eroded.

> [They] could no longer justify their monopoly on power by posing as the defenders of a dynasty now unchallenged, or of Revolution principles now generally accepted by Tories as well as Whigs. No longer united by the need for defending these principles, they had become resolved into a multitude of mutually hostile factions each mainly held together by personal loyalties.[49]

Their former noble ideals have decayed into lust for power and wealth, a decay now increasingly conspicuous.

On the other extreme of the ideological spectrum from the Tories, a few adherents remain in the wider community who adhere to the previous century's legacy of Puritan democratic radicalism. Discontented with the rule of the Whig families and the betrayal of their ideals, these adherents advocate popular sovereignty and radical reform. They provide the genesis of a Radical party. Within a decade large political meetings and public rallies will make a regular appearance on the landscape. The Society of Supporters of the Bill of Rights and the Constitutional Society will be formed, providing a party structure to this movement.[50]

In mainstream society people are also becoming more aware of political matters, illustrated by a steep increase in political pamphlets and journals in circulation. Two rival London journals, the *Gentleman's Magazine* and the *London Magazine*, had taken to reporting parliamentary debates some decades earlier, although both Houses had condemned the practice as a breach of parliamentary privilege. Despite the imprisonment of a bookseller and the forcing of the editors of both magazines before the bar of the Lords to make an apology in 1747, the reporting of debates had proved sufficiently popular for journalists to continue to risk it. When Pitt the Elder had been dismissed from government in 1757 by George II, public opinion had been expressed by gifts sent to the ex-minister: it "rained gold boxes".[51] Public opinion during the Seven Years' War had forced his return to Cabinet upon the King; as Dr Samuel Johnson subsequently remarked, whereas Walpole had been a minister given by the King to the people, Pitt was a minister given by the people to the King. During the war George II had himself conceded to Pitt "You have taught me to look for the sense of my subjects in another place than the House of Commons".[52]

At this time other people sit in the Commons than elected Whigs or Tories. "Placemen", members of the royal Household or Crown pensioners who take their orders directly from the King also possess a certain number of seats in the House, although he usually places their votes at the disposal of the government of the day. The Commons have repeatedly attempted to purge these people from Parliament, but each time a Bill for their exclusion passes the Commons it has been rejected in the Lords.[53]

An unresolved conflict festers within political circles over the constitutional position of the Crown, between its apparent state as exercised during the reign of the late King and a traditional, legalistic interpretation of its role. In strict legal terms the position occupied by George II was very much like that of William III after the Revolution; the head of his own government and the architect of his own policies. This perception of the King's powers and duties was an important component of the broader "classical" view of the 18th Century British Constitution, which assumed that:

> ministers were primarily the King's servants, conducting his government and policy and dispensing his patronage, in which task his authority underlay theirs; that Parliament ought not to impose upon him ministers he found distasteful; that the creation of a "formed opposition" was disloyal and factious; that it was the duty of members who could with good conscience do so, to support the King's government, even if they had to be stimulated by material or social rewards to vote according to their consciences; that no impropriety attached to the use of "influence" towards this end; and that the judiciary and the Church ought to be regarded, as far as they could be enlisted for the purpose, as instruments available for the support of the government.[54]

This "influence",

> consisted in the distribution of the royal patronage, offices, employments, and contracts, of various rewards, titles and pensions which the king had to bestow, sometimes perhaps in the direct use of secret service money, all to influence elections or more directly to influence members of parliament themselves. Not infrequently punishments were used as well as rewards and men dismissed from office, in some instances

even obscure and old men who had nothing to do with opposition but were dependents or appointees of those who had.[55]

In reality, during the reign of both Georges,

the practice was being fixed, though more by unnoticed
precedents than by conspicuous cases, that the king must not
act without the advice of responsible ministers, and that he
must take his policy from the cabinet; that is, that he was
bound to follow the advice given him [on policy].[56]

Underlining this practice, the "influence" necessary for persuading parliamentarians to approve government policies is now negotiated, not by the King, but
by his responsible ministers. Their advice to him gains weight from the fact
they are the people who arrange the bribery required for government. During
the reign of the late King influence has been organised into a coherent system
by the Duke of Newcastle as head of the ministry.

The idea that the King must follow the policies dictated by his Cabinet is not
one which has been consciously devised, but one which has simply grown out
of the fertile soil of circumstance. Its implications shall only be realised by
parliamentarians once they are confronted by systematic royal opposition, by
a King determined to reassert his classical role.

George III's entire upbringing and education has been a reactionary one, with
a single theme, expressed in the words of his mother: to "be a king". By that
she meant a king such as was comprehensible to a continental European; a
king along the lines of the classical interpretation of the Constitution. "His
text books in political science had been Bolingbroke's high tory argument, *The
Idea of a Patriot King*, and Blackstone's account, in his *Commentaries on the
Laws of England*, then still in manuscript, of the place of the king in the constitution".[57] Blackstone's description of the royal role was "the account of a
lawyer who naturally stated the law as it stood and disregarded the interpretation now conventional".[58] George took these accounts of his constitutional
role quite literally. A man with a strong sense of duty but of limited intellect,
stubborn disposition and vindictive nature, he took upon himself with fanat-
ical zeal the duty of defending the Constitution — as he understood it. This,
then, is the year 1760.

His first task, as he saw it, was to sweep aside the outrageous conceits of his
Whig ministers as to who was the proper source of government policy; to
knock down the frail and tentative structure of Cabinet government as a
broom brings down a cobweb.

It is necessary at the beginning to make clear just how far the
plans of the king went, as we know them historically, and what
they did not include. He never attacked the sovereignty and
supremacy of parliament. That is, his plans, so far at least as he
had time to develop them, never contemplated the sort of royal

power which was aimed at by Charles I and James II, an absolute and arbitrary royal power, limited only by the responsibility of the king to God. The primary results of the revolution of 1688, he did not attempt to change. Rather what he strove to reestablish was the royal control of government policy which William III had enjoyed...

We must remember also in forming our judgement upon George III's plan, that no one at that time could think of it as an unconstitutional attempt. It would be unconstitutional in a king of today. It has been called unconstitutional in George by a modern scholar, but that is carrying a judgement from present day conditions back into a time when they did not exist. No one of that day could deny that the king had a perfectly legal and constitutional right to do all that he did in regard to his ministers between 1760 and 1782. We can see clearly that the attack which he made upon the cabinet system of government was deadly, and that it would have destroyed it, if it had succeeded. But the cabinet system was certainly not legally recognised at that time, nor was it so firmly established, so habitual in practice, or so understood in common thought, as to be fixed in the conventional constitution. George III was undoubtedly struggling against the whole current of English history, which had steadily led on to ministerial responsibility of the modern form...but he cannot be accused of violating the constitution as it then existed.[59]

George lost no time declaring his intentions. On the day his grandfather died the new king offered to make his own favourite courtier, the Earl of Bute, a Secretary of State. Bute was a mediocrity, but a loyal mediocrity. He refused the offer of such rapid promotion, but George put him in Cabinet anyway. The King then relieved Newcastle of the reigns of influence and took control of them himself, to the minister's consternation. Pitt resigned in October 1761 because other ministers refused to follow his advice over the conduct of the war, followed by Newcastle May the next year. The Seven Year's War ended with the Treaty of Paris in February 1763, sealing ultimate British victory with the acquisition of — among other things — all Canada, including Nova Scotia and the French territory of Quebec. Bute was now the principal minister, and it was his administration which negotiated the peace treaty. After this his position rapidly became untenable, forcing his resignation in April 1763. His was followed by a number of other short-lived governments of various political flavours, until January 1770, when George appointed a man by the name of Lord North the head of his ministry.

North's twelve-year era in office marked the height of George's bid to be the head of his own government, with the principal minister reduced to nothing more than his chief responsible agent in parliament. During this time George was indeed the author of his own policies, North merely his amanuensis, performing his royal master's instructions even when he disapproved of them.

For this behaviour North has attracted the odium of historians on both sides of the Atlantic, yet he was motivated not by ambition but a sincere belief that it was the King's right to be served this way. As for his own abilities,

> [I]t is necessary to insist on Lord North's skill as a parliamentary leader, his deft handling of the Commons, his aptitude for finance, his conciliatory disposition, and his ability in debate as essential factors in his long tenure of office, which lasted until 1782.[60]

Yet George's government didn't rely merely on North's ability. The number of placemen and Crown officers in parliament increased, forming an influential body of supporters known as the "King's Friends". Tories were enlisted to support the King against Whig critics. Influence was put to work in both Commons and Lords on such a scale that this period represents the summit of organised corruption in British history. In modern terminology, the King had stacked the numbers. Every aspect of government had fallen under his control: policy, Cabinet, Parliament.

The Whigs were appalled. Forced into opposition, they could only sit and watch as their own techniques were turned against them. Powerless, their only hope of ever returning to office was for George's government to meet with some terrible disaster.

Niccolò's ghost   For all his faults, George III is a conscientious man, dedicated to hard work and scrupulous to details. If there is to be a disaster it must be of a kind whereby a fatal defect in his character cannot be remedied by diligence.

We have not raised armies with
designs of separating from Britain
and establishing independent states.
Necessity has not yet driven us into
that desperate measure.

Thomas Jefferson, 1775.

"...Stained with the Blood of Her Children."

The American Revolution flowed from manifold sources. Colonial resentment at Imperial policies of taxation and trade grated against Imperial frustration with the colonies' petty jealousies, disorganisation and fondness for smuggling. Many of the American colonies had retained a Puritanical element that did not sit well with the cynical and decadent brilliance of 18th Century England. Nor was religious Puritanism the only 17th Century English export to cross the Atlantic to the colonies. Radical theories on democratic government that had emerged in England during the Civil War were carried by the colonists to the New World, there to remain in currency in the New England colonies like Massachusetts long after they had fallen into disuse on English soil.

Other aspects of the colonists baffled the members of the Imperial Parliament at Westminster. The members of the various American colonies viewed one another with suspicion and distrust; to the Boston merchants, the plantation-owners of Virginia were almost foreigners, although both merchant and plantation-owner were swift to claim links with Britain. Contemporary commentators feared that if direct Imperial control was ever removed, the result would be chronic civil war from Maine to Georgia. In 1756 armed conflict actually broke out between Georgia and South Carolina over the navigation of the Savannah river.[61]

These were people who were intensely proud of their British ancestry, whose rhetoric on liberty was frequently expressed, not as Americans, but as colonial Britons who had inherited English political institutions and possessed as their birthright English rights and liberties. Yet whenever the Imperial

Parliament attempted to assert its sovereignty over them, they replied with defiance and disdain.

Ridiculous humiliations were imposed upon them by an Imperial policy which, in attempting to create an entirely self-sufficient empire not reliant on foreign commodities for survival, had ordained that the colonies should produce raw materials and Britain the manufactured goods created from those materials. Colonial attempts to manufacture goods in competition with British exports were suppressed: wool and bar iron (1719), felt hats (1732), molasses (1733) and steel furnaces (1750). The knife didn't just cut one way; tobacco growing in the west of England in competition with American plantations was ruthlessly extinguished. However, the colonists on the other side of the Atlantic weren't likely to be aware of this, and justifiably felt that the trade laws were rigged against them.[62]

For their own part many British intellectuals despised the institution of slavery deemed so essential by colonial plantation-owners. Dr Johnson, an opponent to American independence, was "sarcastic on the subject of the freedom-loving slave-owners".[63] This contempt obscured their understanding of the motives of their colonial counterparts. Even of Edmund Burke, one of the greatest British parliamentary advocates of American independence during the Revolution, it can be said,

> [F]eeling as he did about American slavery, Burke must have felt uncomfortable with the copious American revolutionary rhetoric about freedom. Especially so, when the rhetoric came from the slave-owners, as in the case of the momentous 'Virginia resolves' (i.e. resolutions) of 29 May 1765, which opened America's campaign of defiance against the Stamp Act. He favoured repeal of the Act on rational grounds, but he is unlikely to have been impressed by an assertion of the importance of 'American freedom', coming from Virginia's House of Burgesses.[64]

Nonetheless, from the constitutional perspective the Revolution was not a colonial revolution so much as a British civil war fought on colonial territory. It was not inspired by hatred of Britain but of her government's policies; even less was it inspired by a desire for a republic. Even in July 1775, when after the battle of Bunker Hill George Washington came to Cambridge, Massachusetts to take command of the army, he had not yet decided whether the objective of the war was to be the independence of the colonies.[65] That same month Thomas Jefferson stated the situation explicitly: "We have not raised armies with designs of separating from Britain and establishing independent states. Necessity has not yet driven us into that desperate measure."[66]

When, a year later, he drafted the Declaration of Independence, he wrote in it the melancholy words "We might have been a free and great people together".[67] These words were later deleted by the Continental Congress before the manifesto was approved on the 4th of July 1776, but they are as eloquent a reminder that the Revolution was a civil war as the fourteen loyalist American regiments which fought for George III.[68]

If any single event can be said to have triggered the Revolution, it was the ending of the Seven Years' War. England had held colonies on North American soil since 1583, with the founding of the colony of Newfoundland during the reign of Elizabeth I. Throughout the 17th Century the Stuarts had encouraged the settlement of colonies along the Atlantic seaboard and in the West Indies. Farmers, convicts, traders and adventurers all settled there — as did exiles. Refugees from every war and struggle of that turbulent century fled across the Atlantic: Puritans, Cavaliers and Jacobites all escaping from persecution crossed to the colonies when the tide turned against them in the British Isles. Occasionally colonies would become actively involved in the turmoil of the day; in 1649 the coalition of Virginia, Barbados, Bermuda and Antigua rebelled against the regicide English republic, only to be suppressed by the Parliamentary navy. A diverse congregation of colonies grew, with a bewildering variety of political systems, some democratic, some mercantile or military, but all at least nominally under the English Crown.[69]

After the Restoration an elaborate network of Imperial regulations on commerce and trade had been imposed upon the colonies by the English Parliament, demanding tariffs on various goods, but further Stuart attempts to impose stronger ties between home and colonial governments fell in the Revolution of 1688. Pragmatism flavoured subsequent dealings between the Imperial government and the colonials. When Sir Robert Walpole was asked why he did not approve of a scheme for taxing the colonies he laughed, retorting "I have half of Old England set against me already, and do you think I will have all New England likewise?"[70] The dominant question was not whether or not Britain had the right to tax her colonies, but what the colonists were willing to stomach.

The absence of any coherent political order underlying the First British Empire could be ignored so long as external threats existed. Britain wanted trade and territory, while the colonists wanted the protection of British armies and the Royal Navy. Until the end of the Seven Year's War an obvious threat to the colonists was France's imperial presence in French Canada. But at the Treaty of Paris France ceded all of its Canadian territory to Britain, an event which doubtless filled most Britons with elation and most French with a sense of humiliation. A few astute observers, however, saw the deeper possible implications of the treaty. The French ambassador at Constantinople at the time, the Comte de Vergennes, reportedly told an English traveller that:

> the consequences of the entire cession of Canada are obvious.
> I am persuaded England will ere long repent of having
> removed the only check that could keep her Colonies in awe.
> They stand no longer in need of her protection; she will call
> on them to contribute towards supporting the burdens they

have helped to bring on her; and they will answer by striking off all dependence.[71]

Events of the next twenty years were to prove the brilliance of this assessment. France's chief minister at the time of the treaty, the Duc de Choiseul, appears to have based his foreign policy upon it. Uninterested in the recovery of Quebec (it was expendable; indeed, he appears to have been relieved at its loss), no sooner had the treaty been signed than he immediately began naval rearmament, trebling his country's naval strength within seven years and engaging in an alliance with Spain in preparation for eventual intervention and war against Britain in the West Indies.[72]

As Vergennes had predicted, the immediate problem confronting the British parliament following the Treaty of Paris was the expense of the war just concluded, a war George III had wanted to describe in the first address of his reign as "bloody and expensive"[73] and one many felt had been waged for the benefit of the colonists. Who should pay for it? There was, furthermore, the problem of ongoing costs. What the colonies now needed to uphold the peace was a permanent standing army of about ten thousand soldiers. The threat from hostile European powers had declined, but the perpetual threat from the Indians remained,[†] and the colonists were too feud-ridden and suspicious of one another to raise and maintain coordinated forces of their own. In the year of the treaty an Indian revolt under Pontiac "captured many forts, slew, tortured or drove off thousands of settlers, and devastated their lands".[74] The Assembly of Pennsylvania refused to organise self-defence. Colonial frontier-dwellers, confronted by the terror of Indian raiding-parties, appealed to the British for protection and marched upon Philadelphia in protest. After heavy fighting British regular troops suppressed Pontiac's uprising.[75]

Who should pay for this standing army? The Bute administration had been replaced by that of George Grenville. He at least was in no doubt of the answer: the colonists required the services of British regular troops, therefore let them contribute to the upkeep of those troops. An Imperial stamp tax imposed upon all colonial legal documents should raise a nice bit of revenue to that end. He therefore introduced Declaratory Resolves in the House of Commons in 1764 announcing the government's intentions, and passed the Stamp Act in 1765.

The way this tax was supposed to work was that it required all legal documents to bear stamps, varying in price from threepence to ten pounds. The idea had been suggested by a number of royal governors in the colonies during the war: Shirley of Massachusetts (commander-in-chief of the troops in America), Dinwiddie of Virginia, Sharpe of Maryland, Hardy of New York and others.[76] Over two centuries after the event opinion is still divided among historians as

---

† This threat was largely the colonist's own fault. "In dealing with the natives, they had showed a violence, ruthlessness and lack of scruple to which the constant danger of an Indian rising must largely be attributed" (Keir, *The Constitutional History of Modern Britain since 1485*, p.359).

to the justice of this notion. American historians point to Benjamin Franklin, who stated the colonies had

> raised, paid and clothed nearly twenty-five thousand men
> during the last war — a number equal to those sent from Great
> Britain, and far beyond their proportion. They went deeply
> into debt in doing this; and all their estates and taxes are mort-
> gaged for many years to come for discharging that debt.[77]

One such scholar has observed,

> That the colonies had contributed more than an equitable share
> toward the expenses of the war, that their contributions had
> even been in excess of their ability, had been freely acknowl-
> edged by Parliament, which, on several occasions between 1756
> and 1763, had voted large sums to be paid over to the colonies,
> in partial compensation for their excessive outlay[78]

therefore Parliament clearly could not make defrayal of the war debt the grounds for imposing a new tax upon the colonies. Other historians (mostly British) have swiftly riposted that there was still the matter of paying for the peacetime army. Colonial defence was calculated to be costing the government £3 million a year "to which the colonies contributed not a penny".[79] The stamp tax was calculated by Grenville to raise £100,000 from the colonies, which he regarded as a reasonable contribution to defence costs.[80] All the more so since the Pontiac uprising had revealed many of the colonists unwilling to take alternative arrangements for their own defence. These histo-rians also invoke Franklin, who wrote in 1764 that he thought it very possible,

> that the Crown may think it necessary to keep troops in
> America thenceforward, to maintain its conquests and defend
> its Colonies, and that the Parliament may establish some
> revenue arising out of the American trade to be applied
> towards supporting those troops. *It is possible, too, that we
> may, after a few year's experience, be generally very well satisfied
> with that measure.*[81]

Justified or not, Grenville's Stamp Act made a lot of people in America very angry. Patrick Henry, in Virginia's House of Burgesses (their colonial assembly) drew up a series of resolutions in which he declared that colonists were enti-tled to all the liberties and privileges of natural-born British subjects, that "the taxation of the people by themselves, or by persons chosen by themselves to represent them,…is the distinguishing characteristic of British freedom, without which the ancient constitution cannot exist";[82] that attempts to vest the power of taxation in any body other than the colonial assemblies was thus a menace to British freedom even as it was to American freedom, and that the people of Virginia weren't obliged to obey any law enacted in disregard of these essential principles, with any who asserted to the contrary being properly regarded as public enemies.[83] Opposition to the Stamp Act had begun.

A lawyer by training, Grenville at this time also acquired the odd and dangerous notion that customs and excise laws existed to be enforced. A lot of very astonished customs officers theoretically employed to administer these laws in the colonies, which they did by proxy whilst remaining within the coasts of the British Isles, found themselves packed off to the colonies. Their shock was nothing compared with that of the colonists. An estimated nine-tenths of their usual supplies of wine, fruit, tea, sugar and molasses was contra-band. In the past British officials inspired by a mixture of tact and comfortable inefficiency had winked at this practice, but now all of that was to be changed. The laws of trade were to be rigorously enforced, much to the indignation of the colonists, one of whom later exclaimed "it is this new invention of collecting taxes which makes them burdensome".[84] An ominous example was the Molasses Act of 1733, the tariffs of which would have been prohibitive had they ever been enforced. They *had* been enforced during the Seven Years' War as a means of cutting off trade in sugar with the French West Indies, but the colonists had assumed this was merely a ghastly exigency of war which would cease at the outbreak of peace. Imagine their horror at this Act being resur-rected now as the Sugar Act, with reduced duties aimed not at crippling an enemy but at increasing public revenue. Merchants hitherto uninterested in political principles found their attentions wondrously focussed by this turn of events. George Grenville and his entire government found themselves really very unpopular indeed.[85]

Throughout the colonies lawyers agreed to ignore the absence of stamps on legal documents. Both stamps and effigies of stamp officers were burnt by mobs. Boxes of stamps arriving by ship were burnt or thrown into the sea. Passions were running very high; yet rebellion against Britain was as yet not a certain threat. Benjamin Franklin, sent to London to represent Pennsylvania's opposition to the Stamp Act, wrote that if the colonists couldn't agree,

> [T]o unite against the French and Indians, who were perpetually harassing their settlements, burning their villages, and murdering their people, can it reasonably be supposed that there is any danger of their uniting against their own nation [of Great Britain]…with which they have so many connexions, and ties of blood, intercourse and affections, and which it is well known they all love much more than they love one another.[86]

Two arguments of protest were developed by the colonists and their supporters in Parliament. The first, more moderate argument acknowledged the right of Parliament to impose external taxes through imposing seaport duties on ship-ping (i.e. imposing duties on merchandise imported into the colonies) but rejected the imposition of internal taxes intended to raise revenue from within the colonies. The other, more extreme argument was a direct appeal to the ancient English adage of "no taxation without representation", and denied the right of Parliament to impose any taxes at all upon the colonies.

Niccolò's ghost   Underlying all this talk of taxation rested the essential quarrel, which was the disagreement between colonists and parliamentarians over the status of colonial legislatures. To most of the parliamentarians and their supporters there was only one true Parliament which held the right to legislate over all British subjects. Colonial legislatures were tin-pot municipal governments afflicted with delusions of grandeur. To the colonists, however, colonial legislatures were Westminsters in replica, with King, Lords and Commons substituted by Governor, appointed Council and elected Assembly. When colonists spoke of their rights under the Common Law and the inheritance due to them as Britons (as they did), they were interpreting these rights and this inheritance in terms of their own legislatures being "Parliament". For many members of the Imperial Parliament this was an absurd pretension.

The Grenville government fell in July 1766, replaced by that of the Marquis of Rockingham, a Whig whose faction was to prove influential in the Revolution. A fiery debate broke out in the Commons over the proposed repeal of the Stamp Act, with Grenville and his friends now in opposition asserting the justice of their actions and the base motives of the colonists in resisting them. To refute their arguments Pitt the Elder, leader of a pro-American faction, left his sick-bed and stood in the Commons, delivering speeches in which he declared he rejoiced in the resistance of the Americans, and that had they submitted tamely to Grenville's measures they would have shown themselves fit only to be slaves. He argued the colonists were upholding essential principles of British constitutional government, and that victory over them would be of ill omen to liberty on both sides of the Atlantic, warning "In such a cause your success would be hazardous. America, if she fell, would fall like the strong man with his arms around the pillars of the [British] Constitution".[87] He therefore urged the Stamp Act to be repealed immediately, the reason for this repeal to be stated explicitly to be because the Act "was founded on an erroneous principle".[88] In conjunction with this statement he proposed a Declaratory Act to be passed in which the Parliament's sovereign authority to legislate for the colonies in all matters apart from taxation be boldly asserted. His advice, and that of his learned ally Lord Camden, was only partly heeded by their fellow parliamentarians. The Houses repealed unconditionally the Stamp Act, but passed also two other measures destined eventually to be the forerunners of war. One was a Declaratory Act, which asserted the right of Parliament to legislate in every respect, including taxation upon the colonies. The other was a modification of the Sugar Act, reducing the duty for foreign molasses of threepence a gallon to a penny on British and foreign alike.

At the time these other measures were disregarded by the colonists, who saw them merely as face-saving gestures. News of the repeal spread swiftly throughout the colonies, with bonfires of thanksgiving lit in every town and addresses of thanks to the King voted in all the legislatures. Demonstrations of loyalty were made, including a lead statute of George III erected in New York. No interest or desire for rebellion was now apparent, nor would be for some months to come. That this same statute of George would some years later be melted down to make shot to kill his soldiers was not dreamt of by those who erected it. In London also, crowds greeted news of the repeal with delight, cheering Pitt when he appeared upon the streets and hissing at Grenville when he did the same.[89]

In July 1766 the Rockingham government fell, to be replaced by that of Pitt, now elevated to the House of Lords as the Earl of Chatham. His ministry, possessing such a diversity of people that it was compared to a tessellated pavement by Edmund Burke, was composed almost entirely of pro-American parliamentarians, nominally led by a man who, even before his opposition to the Stamp Act, had become a legendary figure throughout America as well as in Britain. Among the colonists he was as venerated as George Washington was later to be, and retained this respect even through the violent years to come.[90] It seems a strange twist that his was the administration which inspired the outbreak of war. But then, Chatham was gravely ill.

Niccolò's ghost 18th Century medicine was an imperfect science. Although accurate diagnosis of his illness eludes us, it is known the disease caused excruciating pain and induced bouts of profound melancholia, verging on madness.

Because of his illness Pitt was unable to lead an administration in the Commons, so he accepted the position of the Lord Privy Seal and the earldom of Chatham in the Lords. The Duke of Grafton was the actual head of the ministry, under Chatham's guidance. Three staunchly pro-American politicians who took the extreme colonial view on constitutional matters were awarded senior portfolios: Conway, Secretary of State; Lord Shelburne, Secretary of State; Lord Camden, Lord Chancellor. Added to this number was a man then regarded as one of the most knowledgeable experts on American affairs in England — the Chancellor of the Exchequer, Charles Townshend.[91]

[*The Ghost reaches across the table, plucks the page from under the Author's pen, and re-reads it.*]

THE LEGACY OF REVOLUTIONS

Niccolò's ghost On paper this appears an admirable arrangement. In reality the personalities and predicaments of the men involved made it disastrous. Chatham's ailment overwhelmed him, so he was unable to participate in government at all. All of these other ministers were in the Lords except Conway and Townshend, who alone were in the Commons, where the real direction of government was negotiated. Grafton held insignificant authority without Chatham, which meant Townshend became the most powerful member of Cabinet. Undoubtedly talented, he was a man devoid of conscience or any sense of responsibility. Possessed of a capricious nature, he was a most dangerous man to be left in power.

[*He drops the sheet dismissively on the table. The Author retrieves it, and continues.*]

Described by one historian as "the evil spirit of the administration",[92] unbound by any modern convention of Cabinet solidarity, Townshend relied upon the favour of George III to protect him from the anger of his fellow ministers, whom he now defied. In 1767 he placed a series of proposed measures before Parliament which revealed in an incredible display of misapplied ingenuity that he'd devised a way of levying revenue from the colonists which was constitutional, yet could be used to destroy colonial self-government. His scheme was funded using the "external" taxation of port duties, a means of raising money which American moderates had already conceded was legitimate for Parliament to employ. What objection could there be to the raising of revenue? Had the colonists complained at the Rockingham amendment to the Act? No, even 'though the penny per gallon of molasses was used for revenue. So how could they complain at *his* proposals to aquire revenue? His measures imposed duties on wine, oil and fruits if carried directly from Spain or Portugal to America, and upon glass, paper, lead, painter's colours and tea. Smuggling, which would undermine this income, was to be stamped out. To ensure this, revenue commissioners for all of British America were to be headquartered in Boston and armed with extraordinary powers. The money raised was to provide the Crown with the means of creating a civil list in every colony: paying salaries to the royal governors, judges, and anyone else in the colonies the Imperial government thought fit, irrespective of the opinions of the colonial legislatures. Having arranged alternative sources of income for Crown servants, recalcitrant legislatures could then be punished. The colony of New York, previously given the task of providing supplies for the garrison of British regular troops stationed there — a task it insisted on doing its own way, ignoring instructions from London — suffered the suspension of the legislative powers of its assembly as punishment for non-compliance with Imperial orders. Townshend had devised a grand scheme for centralising power and destroying self-rule.[93]

Introducing his proposals in the House of Commons, he light-heartedly declared "I expect to be dismissed for my pains".[94] His Cabinet colleagues were livid with rage. Chatham, who was in a stable period when Townshend's extraordinary scheme was announced, took advantage of his temporary good health to journey to London and request the dismissal of the Chancellor of the Exchequer by the King. But George III hated Chatham and admired Townshend, and the only adequate replacement for Townshend would have been a certain Lord North, a man who refused to do anything which would displease the King, and so declined the offer of the Exchequer. Before Chatham could resolve the problem he suffered a relapse of his illness. The one minister who could have stopped Townshend was thus forced to return home, where he remained.

Niccolò's ghost   Hour after silent hour he sat, remote and inaccessible at North End. His higher mental faculties stolen by disease and melancholia, he remained unresponsive to the entreaties of his bewildered colleagues.

Townshend himself remained in control only a little while longer. Within three months of his Bill passing the House of Commons he fell sick with a fever and died, at only forty-one years of age. After his death his scheme found a new champion in the person of George III, who had been delighted at his minister's ingenuity and resolved to stake his own political career as monarch upon the implementation of his servants' plan: a plan which would enable George to "be a king" over his American colonies even as he intended to be over Great Britain.

The vacancy at the Exchequer caused by Townshend's untimely death was filled by the King with a young and affable Tory lord, who despite his good nature held no sympathy with democratic government. The eldest son of the Earl of Guildford, this young man was Lord North. Colonial affairs were stripped from Lord Shelburne and given to the Tory Lord Hillsborough. Conway was dismissed by the King, who replaced him with Lord Weymouth, a supporter of the Stamp Act. The Earl of Sandwich, who despised American colonists, was made Postmaster-General. The following year, Chatham resigned the privy seal. Two years after that George's personal government began.

[*The Ghost rises, agitated at the discussion, and begins to pace the floor of the library.*]

Following Townshend's Revenue Acts the only colonial stance of opposition to Imperial taxation left was the extreme one: an appeal to the fundamental principle of "no taxation without representation". The uses to which Imperial revenues were put made opposition urgent for those who cared about self-government. The suppression of smuggling which went hand-in-hand with the levying of duties was also enough to provoke anti-Imperial sentiments among pragmatists.

But "no taxation without representation" held huge implications on both sides of the Atlantic. It posed an immediate threat to the contemporary political theory of "virtual" representation, a theory which had been devised to reconcile a centuries-old tradition of elected representation in the Commons with the reality of a suffrage that had always been limited and an electoral system now conspicuously corrupt. Under virtual representation,

> The argument was that Members of Parliament represented
> the entire nation, indeed the entire empire, not merely the
> districts or electors who had actually sent them to the House
> of Commons. It was not necessary, the British asserted, that
> an individual or a group participate in an election in order for
> him or them to be authentically represented in Parliament.
> The majority of men resident in the home country either
> were not qualified to vote or lived in areas not yet granted a
> seat in the Commons, yet they were truly represented in
> Parliament. So likewise with the Americans; it did not matter
> that they did not vote in parliamentary elections. They were
> a part of the British nation and empire, and therefore they
> were "virtually" represented in the House of Commons.[95]

Determined colonial opposition to virtual representation would clearly undermine the two tenets upon which it was based. One was the belief that the British people, nation and empire held a single cohesive interest common to all its members, which could be represented by a few privileged residents of the British Isles. The other was the attempt, underlying the theory, to dissociate representation from the active processes of election, accountability and removal. On this second point the Scottish-born colonial lawyer James Wilson (later to assist drafting the US Constitution) wrote:

> Can [parliamentary] members, whom the Americans do not
> elect; with whom the Americans are not connected in
> interest; whom the Americans cannot remove: over whom
> the Americans have no influence — can such members be
> styled, with any propriety, the magistrates of the Americans?[96]

The obvious answer to these rhetorical questions was "no". But if it was accepted that these members were not representative of the colonists, and various subjects of the British Empire on either side of the Atlantic possessed diverse and sometimes conflicting interests, then it required no great leap of intellect to see that virtual representation was also discredited within the

British Isles. It failed to accommodate residents of regions as yet denied seats in the House, or members of disenfranchised social or economic classes. What of the vast urban populations of the new mercantile cities like Manchester or Birmingham, whose interests were sometimes in conflict with those of rural Britons? What of the lower classes? "No taxation without representation", if pushed to a successful conclusion in the colonies, wouldn't just imply reform in Boston and New York but reform in Portsmouth and London.

Niccolò's ghost This forced the Whig parliamentarians in Opposition to do some serious thinking. If reform of this sort took place at all it would have an effect on British political institutions little short of revolutionary. It would inevitably destroy the elaborate system of tenure, influence and patronage upon which the Whig ruling families had relied for the best part of a century for their power. But the foundations of their power had eroded, and this system had been hijacked by the King who was using it to great effect to destroy whatever power they had remaining. And destruction of the system, although a frightening threat to their future, would also certainly be fatal to the future of George's personal government.

The King could only remain the architect of government policy so long as the Commons listened to him instead of to public opinion, for he would always need the Commons to supply him with the money required for government. If the American cause were to be victorious, the Commons would be eventually reformed and public opinion would become impossible to ignore. In making this bid to restore royal power His Majesty had already discarded the traditional shield that protects a monarch from the anger of his subjects, the institution of ministerial responsibility. It couldn't be pretended that "the King could do no wrong"; his entire attack on Cabinet government had involved taking personal responsibility for government. He would never now be able to defy a hostile Commons. If a transformation to that House made it hostile to him he would have to acquiesce, or be forced to abdicate. Whoever dominated that House would return to controlling government. If the colonists won their struggle.

On a cruder level, even if no reform took place in Britain but the American colonists won the humiliation for George would be enormous. Again, there was now no longer a shield between the King and the consequences of his actions. Provided the humiliation was big enough, and the indignation inside and outside the House therefore strong enough, he and his attempts to destroy Cabinet government would be permanently discredited. Parliamentarians again would return to controlling government. Provided the colonists won. Otherwise the King would remain in power indefinitely, with a subjugated Parliament.

THE LEGACY OF REVOLUTIONS

Niccolò's ghost Is it any wonder Chatham, in one of his times of lucidity, said of the struggle between Britain and her American colonies "be the victory to whichever host it pleases the Almighty to give it, poor England will have fallen upon its own sword"?[97]

Many of the Whigs decided to throw their weight behind the colonists. Chatham's followers, who had always been dedicated to parliamentary reform, wanted the American demands accommodated, to be followed by Imperial reconciliation. The Rockingham Whigs, traditionally associated with the system of ruling families, proved willing to push an even harder line: victory to the Americans even to the extent of total American independence.[98] As far as these parliamentarians were concerned, truly it could be said that,

> what was at stake in it for England, beyond colonies and empire, was the continuance of this personal royal dictation, under the forms of the constitution established in 1688, or a return to the system of cabinet government taking its direction from the [H]ouse of [C]ommons and responsible to it and to public opinion…It was no doubt the perception by the king that this question was involved that made him so reluctant to bring the war to an end. The fact was recognised clearly enough by the opposition party, and is the explanation of their vigorous support of the American cause. The colonies were fighting the battle of Englishmen at home.[99]

The Tories, on the other hand, approved of the system of royal dictation, approved of the war, and refused to countenance the loss of the colonies. As hostilities escalated, British merchants became frightened of the permanent loss of trade independence seemed to imply, and threw their weight behind the government.

Many American colonists themselves desired reconciliation once the Imperial Parliament recognised the justice of their position. Two plans were devised to accommodate colonial representation within an Imperial framework. The first, supported by Adam Smith in Britain and by Benjamin Franklin and James Otis in America, was for a certain number of seats in the Commons to be allocated to the colonists. This suggestion was also mooted by loyalists during the first Continental Congress in 1774.[100] The second was the acknowledgment that all powers of taxation should remain in the colonial legislatures; that a system be established whereby British and colonial governments would exist equally under the Crown. As late as 1779 Joseph Galloway, a colonial politician and former Speaker of the Pennsylvanian Assembly, advocated federal union with two co-equal Parliaments in Britain and America, asserting before a parliamentary committee at Westminster that "many more than four-fifths of the [American] people would prefer a union with Great Britain upon constitutional principles to…independence".[101] By that time this was doubtless an exaggeration, but ten years earlier it would have been true.

The 1774 Continental Congress of the colonists certainly subscribed to the view that the conflict with the Imperial Government was of the nature of a civil war.

> ...Congress believed that the ministry had conceived "a deliberate plan to destroy, in every part of the empire, the free constitution, for which Britain has been so long and so justly famed". Not even the people of England were safe, the delegates believed, for if the ministry subjugated America, it would doubtless turn its instruments of oppression against the mother country. "Soldiers who have sheathed their Swords in the Bowels of their *American* Brethren, will not draw them with more reluctance against you", Congress warned the British people.[102]

Evidence of colonial desire for reconciliation is also to be found in the actions of this Congress, which at the insistence of Virginian delegates refused to complain of any grievances against the Imperial Parliament dating from before 1763; for earlier grievances would doubtless include the British Navigation Acts. An attack upon the Navigation Acts would render reconciliation impossible, for, as Richard Henry Lee warned, "the Kingdom could not exist without them".[103] This self-imposed restraint remains in the Congressional papers of 1774 and 1775, and was incorporated even in the Declaration of Independence of 1776. Even that document was drafted with an eye to reconciliation: a passage of Jefferson's draft that implied censure of the people of England was deleted before publication.[104] But all this was in the future in 1774, when the Assembly of Pennsylvania and the Continental Congress dined at a banquet in the City Tavern, and all rose to the toast "May the sword of the parent never be stained with the blood of her children".[105] War was formally declared the next year.

A detailed discussion of the further events of the Revolution lies beyond the scope of this book. Suffice to say, reminders of the way it divided British society continued throughout the duration of the war.

When the democratic government of the Commonwealth of Massachusetts was dissolved by Imperial statute in 1774, the enraged Duke of Richmond in the House of Lords declared "I wish from the bottom of my heart that the Americans may resist, and get the better of the forces sent against them".[106] General Sir William Howe, commander-in-chief of these forces in the early years of hostilities, was opposed to fighting the colonists and once even declared he would refuse to do so.[107] He accepted his military post in the hope he could help achieve conciliation; when this proved impossible he proceeded to prosecute the war. The Scottish philosopher and historian David Hume objected to "mauling the poor unfortunate Americans"[108] and Edmund Burke's fiery eloquence in the Commons provided a continual reproach. When a British army surrendered at Saratoga in 1777, the announcement in the House was answered by a group of Opposition Whigs with whoops of delight.[109] That same event brought France into the war.

Niccolò's ghost   De Choiseul had believed in 1770 that Britain and the Americans were sufficiently estranged to intervene. He attempted to push Spain into confrontation with Britain, giving France an opportunity to engage in war. But Spain refused, and the elderly Louis XV of France was irritated and disturbed at these events. He dismissed de Choiseul and replaced him with a more patient man…de Vergennes. When news of Saratoga came to Paris on 2nd December 1777 the former ambassador decided the time had come. Within a fortnight France recognised the United States as an independent power. In February the next year treaties were signed between the two countries, and France declared war on Britain.[110]

By this time hopes of reconciliation had been soured by war. Loyalists fled persecution in the United States for refuge in the Canadian colonies or Britain; British government forces, aware the American colonies were probably lost, fought more savagely. Yet even if the United States was lost to Britain as territory the war continued to serve its purpose in the Imperial Parliament. The parliamentarian John Dunning achieved a majority in the Commons in 1780 for the famous resolution "that the influence of the Crown has increased, is increasing, and ought to be diminished".[111] The following year came the final defeat at Yorktown. When news of the British defeat reached Lord North in Downing Street his usual good humour deserted him. He "walked up and down the room, throwing his arms about and crying 'O God! It is all over! It is all over! It is all over!' ".[112] In the battle had fought not only American troops but French regular forces. Spain by now had also entered the war against Britain, as had Holland. Hostile fleets were sailing the Channel and engaging in manoeuvres in the West Indies. Naval battles took place in the North Sea and the Caribbean, and invasion of Britain was threatened.[113] Lord North persuaded George III to accept his resignation on the 20th of March 1782. The only ministry capable of possessing the confidence of the Commons was that of Lord Rockingham, who dictated terms to the King. His principal demand was that no further obstruction to recognition of the independence of the United States of America be attempted. The preliminary articles of peace were signed on the 30th of November 1782.[114]

At sea the Royal Navy defeated the French fleet in a devastating battle near the West Indian island of Sainte-Marie Galante, relieved the three and a half year siege of Gibraltar by Spanish forces, and defeated a Dutch squadron of warships in the North Sea. Peace treaties were signed.

The Rockingham government, composed of a coalition of pro-colonial Whig factions, lasted only for a matter of months before the marquis died. It was succeeded by one headed by a former Rockingham minister, Shelburne. These two administrations passed Acts abolishing a number of government and court offices, excluding government contractors from the House, and preventing the votes of Crown revenue officers from being used to manipulate elections. Secret pensions were ended. Parliamentary reform had begun.[115]

Niccolò's ghost	In the modern United States the American Revolution is reduced into the nationalist myth of the "War of Independence", a hollow parody—
Author	Of heroic all-American patriots with nice broad accents fighting the nasty horrid British. No remembrance of the painful dilemmas of civil war, of kindred fighting kindred. No recollection that many of the revolutionaries were fiercely proud of their constitutional inheritance, and attempted to retain their allegiance to the King whilst holding enmity against the ministers of the British government, a juxtaposition impossible to maintain during the reign of a king who insisted upon taking personal responsibility for the policies of his government. Just a version of history with the easy simplicity of a cartoon.

The chief fascination of the Revolution to a non-American lies in the fact it was *not* a war of independence in the 20th Century postcolonial sense of the phrase. Rather, it was a civil war which aimed at reform, not separation. But the bitterness of war made reconciliation impossible. The momentum of hostilities forced total independence to be the only feasible ambition for the revolutionaries and their supporters on both sides of the Atlantic, and hence the republican experiment became necessary.

In the two centuries since its drafting, the US Constitution has attracted a vast quantity of rhetoric and praise. Much of this is deserved: for perhaps the first time in history, political thinkers and lawyers were forced by circumstances to sit down and draft a constitution from first principles, the results being remarkably successful. Some of the institutions they devised have travelled beyond the shores of North America, to be adopted in the constitutions of more recent countries, including Australia. But this praise has engendered a belief that America benefited from the Revolution whereas Britain lost by it, and the US Constitution is more "modern" than the British. In fact Britain also benefited from the Revolution. Two centuries later, in constitutional terms we can argue Britain actually benefited more than the United States did. It lost a huge chunk of its Empire—

Niccolò's ghost But what did it gain?

— but won parliamentary government as an institution. Now direct royal government had been disgraced for all time, some form of Cabinet government had to be restored. But if Cabinet was to determine government policy there was an implication the King should follow the advice of his responsible ministers, the authors of the policy. Furthermore, it no longer made sense for Cabinet to be a loose aggregate of minsters serving the King but unbound by a collective mutual loyalty. If they were to impose their policies upon a reluctant king mutual loyalty among ministers was essential, as was consistency in their policy across portfolios. For this cohesion and consistency the imposition of a coordinating will was necessary. A chief minister with only nominal authority over his fellow ministers now made no sense, but Sir Robert Walpole's historical example of a "prime" minister or "premier" did.

Not all of this was immediately apparent at the time. It would be an anachronism to believe the logic obvious with hindsight was understood equally by British reformers picking up the pieces immediately after the America *débâcle*. George III never completely understood the transformed nature of his position. Yet seen or unseen, this logic dictated the shapes of things to come. In the year 1783 he sought a parliamentarian to form a government that he could stomach, and which could salvage Britain from the mess it was now in. He found it in the person of William Pitt the Younger, Chatham's son, who at the tender age of twenty-four had distinguished himself as a minister in the Shelburne cabinet. Unlike his father, Pitt the Younger was a Tory, but a Tory of a fresh breed who acknowledged and supported the validity of cabinet government. From December that year, when he was asked by the King to form a new government, Pitt remained in power for seventeen years. During that period, although the King continued to intervene in questions of policy, the modern position of prime minister crystallised. The title "prime minister" ceased to have its old insulting undertones, and became merely a description of a necessary political office. In 1803 Pitt's views on the subject were made clear via Lord Melville, who wrote in a letter that Pitt had:

> stated not less pointedly and decidedly his sentiments with regard to the absolute necessity there is in the conduct of the affairs of this country, that there should be an avowed and real minister, possessing the chief weight in the council, and the principle place in the council of the king. In that respect there can be no rivalry or division of power. That power must rest in the person generally called the First Minister, and that minister ought, he thinks, be the person at the head of the finances.[116]

From this point issued the evolution of modern parliamentary democracy.

But the Pitt administration by its existence also tied together the legacy of previous revolutions.

> In other words, we may date from the formation of Pitt's ministry, at the end of 1783, the full establishment of the

compromise of 1660: a king in the nominal possession of almost all power, a cabinet in the real exercise of the king's powers, and a parliament with the power of final decision in every question, because it was the voice of the people in whom the ultimate sovereignty resided. The cabinet as the instrument by means of which parliament was to make real in practical government the sovereignty of the people was at last in existence.[117]

On the other side of the Atlantic political revolution went down a different path. The late G.B. Adams, emeritus professor of history at Yale, lamented:

> Three years after Pitt's triumph the Constitution of the United States was framed by an assembly of the most experienced public men and students of politics in America, who considered with care the question of setting up a government to operate in the best way. One great problem before them, set by the situation of the time, was to secure a really efficient executive while leaving ultimate authority in the legislature as representing the people, exactly the problem which ministerial responsibility solves. In their constitution, however, not merely did they entirely separate the executive and legislative departments, then becoming closely united in England, but they gave little attention to the cabinet, and they seem to have had no idea whatever of ministerial responsibility.[118]

Under these conditions parliamentary democracy, the control of the executive by and through a parliamentary majority, was impossible. An alternative form had to be devised.

The United States is a republic because its Head of State is (usually) elected.[†] But the office of President was based very heavily upon the contemporary British monarchy — as the drafters understood it to function. As colonists, what they understood wasn't the actual prosaic way it operated during the early Hanoverian period but its theoretical role in the classical Constitution. Consequently they immortalised in the Presidency a late-17th Century English monarchy, albeit bestowed upon an elected figure instead of an hereditary prince. Nor was this the only archaism incorporated into their system of government. The classical British Constitution of course employed a large measure of separation between the Executive (the King and his ministers) and the Legislature (the Houses of Parliament), an arrangement that inspired Montesquieu's theory on the Separation of Powers.[‡] The drafters embraced

---

† In 1974 Gerald Ford became the first unelected President of the United States of America. In August that year President Nixon was forced to resign to avoid impeachment over his illegal actions in the Watergate scandal. Vice-President Spiro Agnew had already been forced to resign the previous year, under threat of indictment, and so was replaced by Ford, appointed at Nixon's recommendation under the 25th Amendment. When Nixon resigned, Ford became President. Later he gave Nixon a full pardon. (V. Wilson, *The Book of the Presidents*, pp. 80–81.)

‡ The third branch, the Judiciary, is not discussed here as it isn't directly relevant to the matter at hand.

THE LEGACY OF REVOLUTIONS

Montesquieu's theories in the design of their new polity (although with some important modifications by James Madison), so the Executive was represented by the President and his officials, and the Legislature by the chambers of Congress. It's an irony the same war exploited by British reformers to destroy the classical separation between Executive and Legislature was used by American reformers to enshrine it forever. The difference between the resulting modern systems has been argued in Oxford by Dr Geoffrey Marshall, who recently wrote:

> In the first and basic sense ministerial responsibility stands for the system of government that contrasts with the separation of powers as exemplified by its American model. In that system the executive and legislative branches are separately elected for fixed terms as autonomous bodies each deriving its power independently, neither subordinate to the other and each irremovable by the other. A 'responsible' executive is legally and constitutionally non-autonomous, removable and answerable to the legislative branch and in theory thereby to the electorate.[†]

The US Constitution is a living fossil, an offshoot of 17th and 18th Century political ideas and institutions which, unlike their Westminster counterparts, haven't been forced to evolve much further. As an elected late-17th Century "monarchy" with a dissociated Executive and Legislature, it's a constitutional coelacanth, a primitive fish spawned in a primitive ocean.

Contemplating the power associated with the executive and legislative branches of the American polity reveals the strange nature of the creature. The President is supposed to be in charge of executive government, and the chambers of Congress, the writing and passage of laws. Being separated bodies they're elected at different times (to provide a balance) and neither can force dissolution and elections for the other. If the President needs any laws enacted or revoked he needs Congress to do the job for him, although he mightn't have any control at all over Congress, so they can flatly refuse to comply with his requests. Congress can pass Bills, but before they become law they must gain the assent of the President — which he can refuse to give, vetoing their measures and destroying their efforts.

The United States claims it's a democracy because President, senators and congressmen are all elected by the people. But the electoral process obtains whatever validity it possesses through the power of choice it offers the public, so the voters may choose the nature of the government which will rule over them. Essential to this choice is knowledge of the various sets of policies corresponding with each candidate government, so the "right" set of policies is put

---

† Quoted from the introduction to Marshall, *Ministerial Responsibility*, p.1. Of the latter system Marshall warns "In practice the degree to which the constitutionally superior legislative branch can enforce its authority has depended in different parliamentary systems — and in the same parliamentary system at different times — on the structure and organisation of political parties".

in power. But if (as is the case at the time of writing) the President is of one party and Congress is dominated by the other, where is the popular will? Why elect Mr Clinton President on a platform of reform when the legislation he needs to fulfil these promises is gutted by a hostile Congress? Why elect a conservative Congress when its measures are struck down by a hostile President? Does this predicament yield the actual government Democrats wanted? That Republicans wanted? That anybody really wanted? Of course voters who want to stalemate an unpopular President will elect hostile congressmen, but as neither branch of government can force the election of the other, this stalemate shall last until the next fixed-term election, perhaps years away. This stalemate is an inherent risk of the US system — otherwise described by less critical admirers as a "check and balance" of the system — and shall remain a risk year-in, year-out, for the centuries to come. Is this government "of the people, by the people, for the people"?

The Westminster system holds the solution in its link between the Legislature (Parliament) and the Prime Minister of the day. As the latter is simply the leader of the party which possesses the confidence of the Lower House, if the Lower House attempts to gut his or her legislation the government can decide whether to back down over the issue, or resign, or advise an election. In the latter two cases either a change of government or an election results. The Lower House asserts its dominance as the expression of the popular will, or else fresh elections are held to re-establish the popular will; a far more democratic arrangement than the US counterpart.

Niccolò's ghost [*irritated*] Enough of this fireside musing; a conclusion is called for. Who benefited the most from the Revolution?

The United States won independence and an important constitutional experiment, perpetuating 18th Century structures, whereas the United Kingdom gained the necessary environment to begin parliamentary reform, Cabinet government, the office of prime minister and parliamentary democracy. In the long run it's arguable the United Kingdom got the much better deal. However, the countries which benefited most from the Revolution were neither the United States nor the United Kingdom but the more recent Commonwealth realms. It's not just that the Revolution forced the British to understand the apparent paradox of a devolved empire: that there comes a time when, to retain former colonies as friends and allies, they must be given complete self-determination and independence, dismantling that empire. (One American historian remarked that the idea of Dominion status first being employed in its rudimentary form towards the end of the 19th Century actually originated in the Revolution.[119]) More than this, the Commonwealth realms have been placed in the historically rare position of being able to benefit from both sides of a civil war, without suffering strife within their own communities. From the

British side they acquired common law and Cabinet government, the prerogatives of the Crown and parliamentary democracy. On colonial soil they developed their own distinctive two-tiered (or as we shall loftily call it, "bipartite") monarchies, where the Crown is composed of the Queen and her appointed viceregal representatives. From the American side they received understanding of the possible workings of a written constitution and a constitutional court, a federal structure and an elected Senate as an Upper House representing the States of the federal union, the opportunities and defects of a constitutional Declaration of Rights. Were I to be asked to name the North Atlantic country or territory which benefited most from the Revolution, using it to acquire the most sophisticated form of democratic government, my reply would have to be…Canada.

As a consequence of these revolutions, every Queen's Realm of the Commonwealth has its constitution constructed upon the reconciliation of two apparently contradictory notions, the ancient Whig and ancient Tory conceptions of sovereignty. The validity of the Whig view, of effective sovereignty residing in Parliament as the representatives of the true sovereign, the people, is fairly evident. The usefulness of the Tory view, of all sovereign authority welling from the Crown, as a superficial form to clothe the Whig substance of our constitution will soon be revealed.

What remains now for the chardonnay revolutionaries, those who defy armies, compel nations, shift history and erect novel forms of government to last a thousand years somewhere between *entrée* and coffee? The Australian Constitution has already extracted the maximum benefit from both sides of that tragic but necessary war two centuries ago, without throwing tea into Sydney Harbour. Let the true revolutionaries rest in peace.

> [*He returns to working among his papers. The Ghost watches him for a while, then wanders off among the bookshelves, browsing among the titles, and disappears from view. Silence, but for a clock's muted ticking.*]

The laws of England have taught us that kings
cannot command ill or unlawful things. And
whatever ill events succeed, the executioners
of such designs must answer for them.

> Sir Dudley Digges, impeachment speech before the
> House of Lords, 1626.

Every civil servant should remember that, while it
is the duty of the servants of the government to
carry out all lawful orders, it is equally their duty
to disobey unlawful orders.

> Brigadier-General (Sir) Victor Windeyer KC,
> later Justice of the High Court of Australia, 1949.

Ancient Responsibility

On the eleventh of November 1975 in the Australian House of
Representatives, Mr Frank Crean, a former Treasurer of the Whitlam
Government, rose to his feet and delivered a speech attempting to expound
upon the role of the Crown.

> "What needs to be spelt out is that the Queen's representative in
> Australia, the Governor-General, does not act on his own initia-
> tive but acts on the advice of his Ministers", Crean told the
> House. "Who the Ministers are is conditioned by who has the
> majority in the House of Representatives. I would hope that
> everybody, in this House at least, would assert that as a funda-
> mental ground rule of the Australian Parliamentary system".[120]

Although honestly intended, Crean's version of the relationship between the
Crown and its responsible ministers was a gross over-simplification, omitting
details essential to the way the Westminster system operates. To understand
these details we must return to history.

A number of authors this century have written remarkable rubbish upon the origins of the doctrine underlying ministerial responsibility, namely "the King can do no wrong", and over the years this detritus has drifted more and more into mainstream acceptance. Lord Esher, for example, claimed early this century:

> If the Sovereign believes advice to him to be wrong, he may refuse to take it, and if his minister yields the Sovereign is justified. If the minister persists, feeling he has behind him a majority of the people's representatives, a constitutional Sovereign must give way.
>
> It is precisely at this point that the dual personality of the Monarch becomes clear. Hitherto he has exercised free volition, he has used his prerogatives of criticism and delay, of personal advice and remonstrance. At a given moment, however, when he is forced to choose between acquiescence and the loss of his minister, the Sovereign automatically, under the Constitution which by the Constitution Oath he has sworn to maintain, ceases to have any opinion.
>
> The King can do no wrong. This cannot be said of anyone who is a free agent. Within certain limits, and under certain circumstances, the King ceases, constitutionally, to be a free agent. Hence the meaning of the pregnant phrase, the King can do no wrong. With due regard to the security of the Throne, the Sovereign cannot retain the final right of private judgement.

Asking rhetorically "Has the King then no prerogatives?", he replies,

> Yes, he has many, but when translated into action they must be exercised on the advice of a minister responsible to Parliament. In no case can the Sovereign take political action unless he is screened by a minister responsible to Parliament.
>
> This proposition is fundamental, and differentiates a constitutional monarchy based upon the principles of 1688 from all other forms of government.[121]

In a similar vein one or two other writers have recently claimed "the King can do no wrong" originated in the 18th Century, when the Hanoverian kings were no longer the authors of government policy and "therefore" couldn't be held responsible for it. But enough history has already been discussed in these pages to realize most of Esher's view is a version of convention and history with its head screwed on backwards. The Revolution of 1688 is almost irrelevant to the matter: contrary to Esher's theory, William III freely hired and fired his ministers and actively imposed his will on government. In reality the principle "the King can do no wrong" originates from an earlier period of history, before either the Hanoverians or 1688, when the King was very much the author of policy. And contrary to Esher's assertion, it emerged precisely *because* the King was chief author of policy. These origins must be understood if we're to comprehend how the modern reserve powers exist and operate.

Probably the best way of dating the origins of ministerial responsibility is by the revival of ministerial impeachment by the 17th Century English Parliament. Confronted by the reign of the House of Stuart, a Scottish dynasty with little patience for the workings of the English Constitution, Parliament had to devise a way of criticising and opposing the King's more controversial policies without appearing to enter into conflict with the King himself. A solution to this problem was of mutual importance to both monarch and Parliament: parliamentarians needed a way of criticising the government without being accused of disloyalty or treason, while the King couldn't afford dissatisfaction against his policies to explode into outright rebellion against his person.

A rather elegant solution was found by resorting to a legal fiction, "the King can do no wrong". Any policy pursued by the King was taken to have been advised to him by one of his servants, his ministers. They were to be deemed the authors of all royal policies, and so could be criticised and punished by Parliament without directly implicating the King, who was taken to have acted in good faith. Better yet, they could be executed. The mediaeval procedure of impeachment, of trial by Parliament, had been revived during the reign of James I/VI to punish corruption in a number of powerful public figures, including the Lord Chancellor Sir Francis Bacon, and the Lord Treasurer, the Earl of Middlesex. In this method of trial the House of Commons drew up charges against the accused, and sent managers of the impeachment to the House of Lords, before which they acted as counsel for the prosecution. The House of Lords itself was traditionally competent to act as a court of law, sitting in judgement not only upon its own members when charged with offences, but upon any English subject whose case was brought before them, including upon criminal charges. As well as deciding innocence or guilt it was empowered to pass sentence upon the guilty, including the death sentence. This weapon of ministerial impeachment was now to be used against the King's servants to curb the King's policies.

An early illustration was the trial of the Duke of Buckingham, Charles I's favourite minister, in 1626. Brought up to believe in the Divine Right of Kings, Charles found it difficult to comprehend the blunt pragmatism underlying the impeachment of his favourite. In reply to the Common's complaint against Buckingham, the King protested "Certain it is, that I did command him to do what he hath done. I would not have the House to question my servants, much less one that is so near to me".[122] Two of the managers of the Commons, Sir Dudley Digges and Sir John Eliot, both of whom had been briefly imprisoned for their role in this trial, gave formal answer in their speeches before the Lords. In the words of Digges, "The laws of England have taught us that kings cannot command ill or unlawful things. And whatever ill events succeed, the executioners of such designs must answer for them".[123] In his closing speech for the prosecution Eliot provided an even more definite outline of the ancient doctrine of ministerial responsibility, declaring:

My Lords, I will say that if his Majesty himself were pleased to have consented, or to have commanded, which I cannot believe, yet this could in no way satisfy for the Duke, or make any extenuation for the charge, for it was the duty of his place to have opposed it by his prayers, and to have interceded with his Majesty to make known the dangers, the ill consequences that might follow.[124]

Because Buckingham had failed to do so, he was to be held responsible for those ill consequences. As G.B. Adams remarked,

The modern doctrine of ministerial responsibility can hardly be more fully stated in the same number of words, though of course all that was implied in it was not yet seen. Here is, however, the principle that was the minister's duty to resist the orders of the king if he knew that they were wrong, and to protest against the attempt of the king to carry out his will contrary to the law; and because he did not do that the minister is responsible and must be held accountable.[125]

It was Charles I's tragedy that he didn't understand these measures protected himself as well as his parliamentary critics. His insistence upon taking personal responsibility for government policy led to the outbreak of civil war and his own death.

His son, Charles II, made no such mistake. A satirical poem composed by a member of his Court, Lord Rochester, suggested an epitaph for the King's tomb when the time eventually came: by one account the lines went

Here lies our sovereign lord the King
Whose promise none relies on;
He never said a foolish thing,
Nor ever did a wise one.

When this came to Charles' ears he replied acidly "This is very true: for my words are my own, and my actions are my ministers'."

During his reign the process of impeachment was perfected with the trial of the Earl of Danby, begun in 1679 but never completed. In its final form it obeyed the following principles:

[T]he minister could be put on trial on charges known to be unfounded against him but well founded against the king; that a pardon from the king could not avail to stop the trial— embodied in law in the Act of Settlement of 1701; and that prorogation or even a dissolution of parliament was not to interrupt the proceedings and require them to begin anew. This last was an application of the principle already adopted in the ordinary judicial business of the House of Lords.[126]

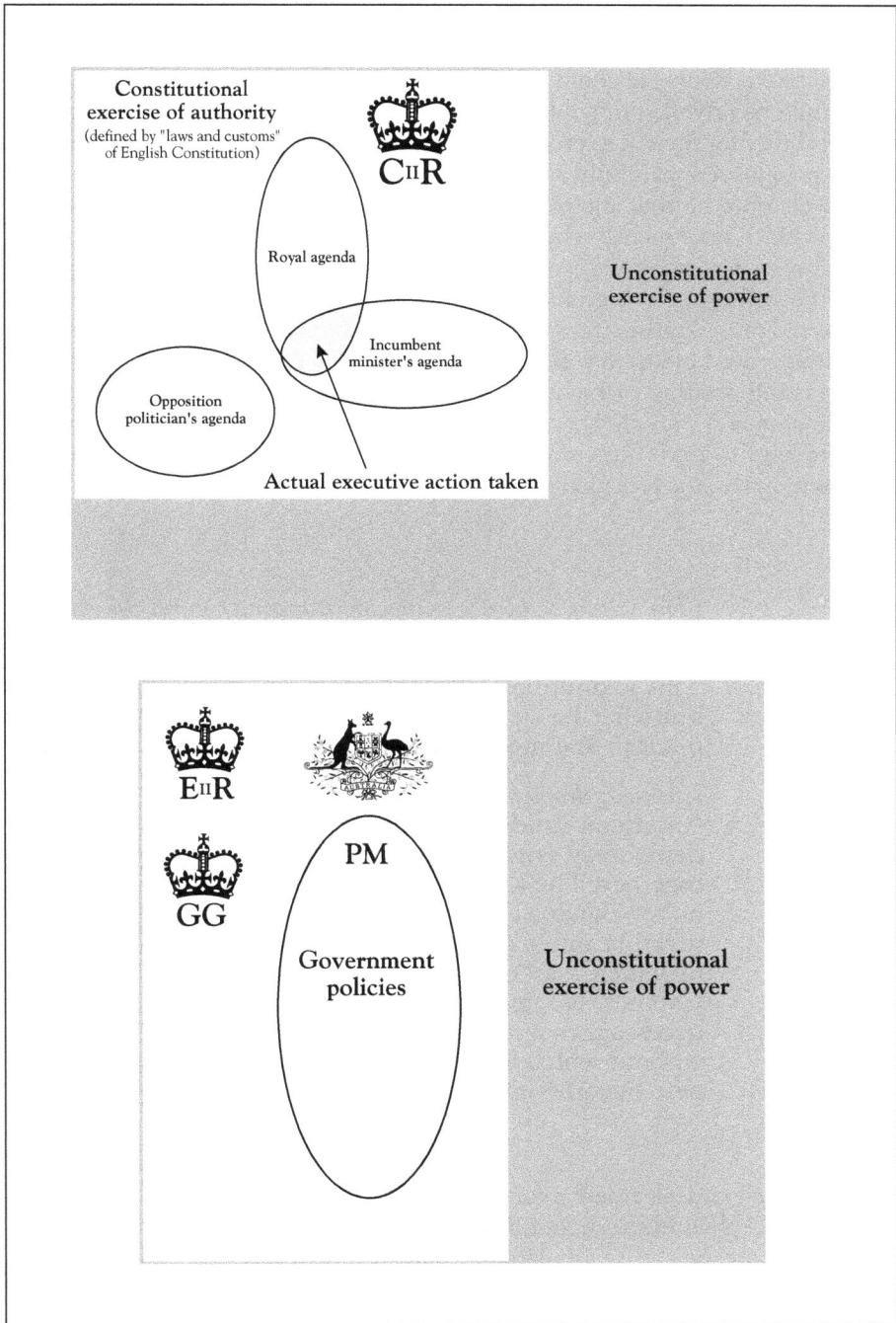

Diagrams of the two forms of ministerial responsibility, the 17th Century form (*top*) as perfected during the reign of Charles II, and the modern form (*bottom*) as exercised in Australia. Authorship of policy has moved from the King (modified by his responsible ministers) to being the domain of the Prime Minister and Cabinet. Instead of being authors, the Queen and Governor-General have become observers...except for the reserve powers.

In a nutshell, what the ancient form of ministerial responsibility achieved was a parliamentary constraint over executive policies or other actions actively devised by the King. He could conceive whatever schemes he liked, but before they could be unveiled in public view he had to persuade his ministers to take responsibility for them, i.e. pretend it was they who suggested the ideas to him. These people were painfully aware that they were the ones risking parliamentary displeasure — that their heads could quite literally end up on the chopping block. Consequently they would modify the royal plans to a mutual compromise, to something with which the King would be satisfied and they would be willing to risk endorsing in public. If no compromise was possible they would resign, rather than face execution or imprisonment over something they disapproved of anyway. If this happened the King would be placed in the embarrassing position of having to find alternative ministers to carry on his government and provide the screen between himself and Parliament. Good staff are hard to find. But contrary to Esher's assertion, the King was entitled to remain obstinant provided he could find other ministers.

> [*The Ghost suddenly reappears standing behind the Author, reading over his shoulder.*]

Niccolò's ghost   This is doubtless all very interesting to an antiquarian, but what has it to do with modern democratic government or the modern reserve powers?

Author   [*startled, drops his pen.*] As we saw in the account of the American and previous revolutions, parliamentary democracy emerged from a number of factors braided together. The King was forced to surrender control over policy-making to his ministers, who became bound together into a cohesive unit, the Cabinet, the solidarity of which was enforced by the Prime Minister. For a Cabinet to remain capable of governing it became necessary that it retain the confidence of the Commons, without which the business of government would otherwise become impossible to transact legally.

Parliamentary and electoral reform forced members of the Commons to be answerable to their electors, and in a more general sense to the British public. Policy was now therefore formulated by ministers with an eye to public opinion rather than to the royal pleasure, a consequence of the 19th Century Reform Acts rather than the Revolution of 1688. Throughout the reign of Queen Victoria the monarch fought a final rearguard action over issues of policy, but by the beginning of this century complete control over these matters was held by the government ministers under the Prime Minister, with the proviso that the monarch retained private rights of consultation.

These ministers remained responsible to Parliament, but in the modern world this responsibility found expression in a different form. Impeachment had long since fallen into disuse, the disapproval of Parliament being usually expressed by a vote of no confidence passed by the Commons. The Lords retained until early this century their own way of expressing extreme parliamentary disapproval of a ministry, through their control over Supply, but this died when the Lords' power withered in 1911.

An illustration of the emerging difference between modern ministerial responsibility and its ancestral form — one which shows the way the ancient version remained for the reserve powers after it had fallen obsolete for government policy — was provided by the effective dismissal of the Melbourne ministry by William IV in December 1834, triggering a general election. At the next sitting of Parliament, in February 1835, the new Prime Minister Sir Robert Peel assumed full responsibility for having tendered the "advice" to the King for these events, despite the fact he'd been travelling in Italy at the time and hence out of all contact with London. As he put it,

> although I have not taken any part in procuring the dismissal
> of the late Government, although I could not, from circum-
> stances which are notorious to the world, hold communica-
> tion with any of those with whom I have now the honour to
> act, much less with the [King]…still I do conceive that by the
> assumption of office, the responsibility of the change which
> has taken place is transferred from the Crown to its advisers;
> and I am ready — be the majority against me what it may —
> to take all the responsibility which constitutionally belongs to
> me, and to submit to any consequences to which the assump-
> tion of that responsibility may expose me.[127]

Although the 20th Century Westminster system is now profoundly democratic in conception, with the government's policies devised by the elected representatives of the people, and although the modern form of ministerial responsibility obscures its ancestry, relics of its ancestral form remain and retain their validity for the particular narrow purpose they possess in the modern world.

The most obvious modern remnant of the ancient form, one provoked to mind by Mr Crean's speech, rests in the modern exercise of the Crown's reserve powers. The purpose of these powers, their usefulness in defending constitutional government and Parliament's democratic privileges against arrogant trespassers, will be argued in later chapters. It suffices at this point merely to remark that although the prorogation (i.e. closing) and dissolution of Parliament are actions usually (and wisely) performed by the Crown on the advice of its incumbent ministers, they are Crown powers which, unlike power over policy, were historically never surrendered to complete control by the incumbent government.[128] In extreme and reprehensible circumstances the ancient form of responsibility remains available to the Crown, if needed — as existence of a discretion requires, for Esher was accurate at least when he said

"In no case can the Sovereign [the Queen, represented here by her Governor-General or Governors] take political action unless [she or he] is screened by a minister responsible to Parliament". The necessity for these powers to remain discretionary and with the Crown has been argued by a number of distinguished figures, whose voices will be heard soon.

Deferring for the moment further discussion on this matter, we instead come face to face with another modern discretionary power of the Crown that *couldn't* be exercised under some kind of obedience to the incumbent Prime Minister, or any other way than under the ancient form of responsibility: namely, the task of actually appointing the Prime Minister.

If the previous one's resigned there *is* no incumbent. If the previous one's headed a minority government in the House, and has now suffered a no-confidence vote, then it would be clearly outrageous for the Queen or her representative to be compelled to obey this person's advice on who should now be commissioned from the former Opposition. As Dr David Butler has recently remarked in Britain,

> while there may be problems about the Queen trying to act as a
> neutral umpire, there could be even greater problems if she
> were obliged, in default of anyone else, to act on the advice of
> a lame-duck Prime Minister. It would be widely seen as outra-
> geous if, in an essentially adversarial situation, the umpire had
> to act on the advice of one of the protagonists.[129]

Furthermore, choosing a Prime Minister in a House dominated by two parties is relatively easy, being determined by who holds the leadership of the majority, but what of a House shattered into, say, five jealous parties? Here a discretion is essential, an ability for a Head of State to act on her own initiative in deciding who's most likely to cobble together a viable coalition (ask Italy's President Scalfaro how easy this job is). This process, irreconcilable with the usual form of modern ministerial responsibility, is readily explicable under the ancient form. Whoever is commissioned by the Head of State to form a government *ipso facto* takes responsibility for the act of commissioning, for providing the "advice" to be made Prime Minister, just as Peel did.

Niccolò's ghost   So even if we wanted to pretend all other reserve powers didn't exist, we would have to concede the ancient form of responsibility must still be available to the Crown, for a Prime Minister or Premier ever to be commissioned. Consequently the chap you quoted earlier was wrong — under certain circumstances your Governor-General *must* be able to "act on his own initiative".

Author   And consider the converse side of the coin...

With the power of appointing ministers must come the reserve power of dismissing them, also to be exercised under the ancient form of responsibility. Otherwise an absurdity takes place: a Prime Minister loses a vote of no confidence, so the Governor-General attempts to commission the Leader of the Opposition, who *does* hold the House's confidence, to be the new one. But before person B can be PM, person A has to cease to be PM. What if person A doesn't want to go? If ministers could only be dismissed on the advice of the incumbent Prime Minister, person A wouldn't have to go, because the required advice would simply never be tendered. Elementary logic concurs with history, in saying that the Crown's power to appoint ministers under its own discretion must be accompanied by a discretionary reserve power to dismiss them for appointments to be properly enforceable.

Yet this raises other questions. These two powers (really the converse sides of the same power) are exercised as a response to particular circumstances on the floor of the House, a vote expressing no confidence. And the fact the House has expressed this resolution justifies what would otherwise be an unnatural act by the Crown in sacking its ministers, for here it's simply throwing what power it does possess behind the House, to force the old ministry to submit to Parliament. Had the Crown failed to do so it would have been the target of justified public outrage.

Accepting this implies that the Crown has a valid role to play in upholding the privileges of Parliament, when these privileges are being flouted by a recalcitrant ministry. But votes of no confidence don't happen in a vacuum. For them to occur the House must be given the opportunity to sit and debate, deliberating over the heavy question before it. If it were true Prime Ministers wielded entirely the power of proroguing Parliament (in other words closing it for months, causing the dispersal of its members throughout the country) rather than this power being entrusted to the Crown, then they could compel the House's silence, rescuing their own administrations from accountability. It's surely a ridiculous proposition to say the Crown should fight to uphold the House's decision, but stick its hand in its pockets and whistle while ministers gag the House's mouth and bind its hands, preventing that vote from taking place.

Niccolò's ghost	[*irritated again*] But this brings us right back to worrying about entrusting discretionary powers to the Crown over the closing or dissolving of Parliament. I thought you said we'd defer that until later.
Author	I did.
Niccolò's ghost	Then do. You said the reserve powers were the "most obvious" of the surviving relics of the ancient form of responsibility. What, pray, is a less obvious example?

During his 1930s Sydney University law lectures a subsequent Justice of the High Court, (Sir) Victor Windeyer KC, drew attention to another ancient remnant when, commenting upon the speeches of Digges and Eliot, he remarked that a modern consequence was that all servants of the Crown are personally liable for unlawful actions.

> They cannot justify any wrongdoing by alleging that they were acting in the execution of the orders of a superior. The constable, who makes an unlawful arrest, is personally liable at the suit of the injured party, although he may have been acting upon instructions. The King's minister of state, who acts in contravention to the law, can be brought before the King's courts. It will not avail him that he was acting in the King's service, even though it were at the King's actual command, for the law will not impute wrongdoing to the King…Every civil servant should remember that, while it is the duty of the servants of the government to carry out all lawful orders, it is equally their duty to disobey unlawful orders.[130]

In both Australia and Britain this principle remains true as an inheritance of common history, an aspect of what is known in both countries as "Responsible Government". For the latter society the case has been argued by Sir Ivor Jennings LL.D., who, after pointing out that in Britain all civil servants are equally servants of the Crown, the Postmaster-General in common status with a maintenance worker,[131] remarked:

> since the King can do no wrong, he can authorise no wrong. Therefore any servant of the Crown who commits a wrong must commit it without authority. He thus renders himself personally liable, even though he was acting as a servant of the King and on behalf of the King.[132]

This attribute of ministerial responsibility under the Crown has been reiterated in a number of other writings, like those of the late Lord Hewart, Lord Chief Justice of England earlier this century.† It transforms, among other things, the significance of the Oath of Allegiance to the Queen (rather than to some vaguer object, like a flag, or the nation, or "democracy"), and the symbolic importance of the Crown upon badges of office. It restores to stark significance the faded emblems of the Crown still displayed on older Post

---

† Lord Hewart, *The New Despotism*, p. 27. Notice that Windeyer, Jennings and Hewart, all three of whom drew attention to implications of ancient aspects of the Westminster system for modern executive government, were lecturing and writing in the same period, the late 1920s and the 1930s, when governments throughout Europe were collapsing and even some of the surviving democracies throughout the Western world were forced to institute versions of "constitutional dictatorship" to cope with the Great Depression. One of the virtues of having a political system which stretches back centuries is that someone somewhere in the past may have encountered an analogous crisis to that of the present — like a dangerously powerful Executive — and devised an effective solution which remains latent in the system to the present day.

Offices and post boxes, telephone exchanges and other buildings pertaining to the free passage of information in a democratic society.

We're so used to seeing the emblem of the Crown upon insignia and buttons that many of us never give it a second thought. Yet when Paul Keating altered the Oath of Allegiance, did none of his ministers pause to think that the old Oath to the Queen of Australia was worded that way for a reason? That the fact all government ministers, all the judges, barristers and other servants of our courts of law, all State and federal police, all members of our armed services have been required to swear an oath to Her Majesty maybe was done for a particular purpose rather than through a fit of historical absent-mindedness? That the symbol of the Crown is placed upon the badges and buttons of all the police, the armed services and indeed (in at least some States) upon the insignia of all emergency services (fire brigade, State Emergency Service etc.) that might need to wield extraordinary authority in a crisis or natural disaster, is perhaps for a reason other than it looks pretty? Might it not be that, upon acquiring particular positions of power, officials are required to swear allegiance to the Queen because they're given that authority formally *as servants of the Queen*,[†] thus constrained in the manner set out by Windeyer?[‡] That the conspicuous display of the Crown upon uniforms, as well as displaying the source of authority wielded by officials, also offers promise and warning — a promise to all other citizens and a warning to that official — that if he or she abuses that power by acting unlawfully, he or she is personally liable for the consequences?[§] No special executive order, no excuse of "national security" or secret agenda of high state can alter that.

[†] An interesting slant on this was provided by the senior officers of the Rhodesian Army at the time of Prime Minister Ian Smith's illegal Unilateral Declaration of Independence from Britain. Southern Rhodesia was strictly speaking a colony under the British Crown, not an independent Dominion under its own. Smith was attempting to enforce permanent white minority rule in Southern Rhodesia, South-African style, while the British Government was insisting on black majority rule as a necessary reform. Smith retaliated by declaring UDI in 1965, effectively creating a white republic. Prior to his declaration his own military commanders warned him that they would not oppose a British landing: if faced with conflicting instructions they would obey the Queen, from whom they held their commissions, rather than the unlawful orders of an illegal regime. Smith dismissed the GOC Rhodesian Armed Forces, Major-General John Anderson, who had indiscreetly declared his own loyalty to the Crown and hostility to UDI too soon, and then tricked the Governor, Sir Humphrey Gibbs, into signing an undated declaration of a state of emergency. The declaration was used to gag Gibbs and any further utterances by the Crown. With Anderson removed and no clear lead of defiance by Gibbs, Rhodesian troops then acquiesced to Smith's regime. Their offer to cooperate to restore constitutional government was not taken up; British Prime Minister Harold Wilson lacked the courage to attempt a military intervention, despite urging by black Commonwealth leaders. (See Lapping, *End of Empire*, pp. 489-496.)

[‡] By this argument, such an oath would be distinct from swearing allegiance at a citizenship ceremony, which has been done traditionally as part of becoming a subject of the Queen of Australia. Jennings (who doesn't explicitly contemplate the Oath) quotes N.E. Mustoe, *The Law and Organisation of the British Civil Service* (1932), p. 15: "The term 'Crown servant' has not been authoritatively defined. But there are cases in which the courts have had to consider whether or not the holder of a particular office was a Crown servant. In each case the decision was based upon the facts of the case before the court, and no comprehensive definition of 'Crown servant' appears to have been attempted." (Jennings, *The Law and the Constitution* p. 178.)

[§] Of course this isn't the only implication of the emblem of the Crown, nor is it under all circumstances necessarily the relevant one. Many organisations with a royal appellation also display the Crown on the uniforms of their staff. When the author was travelling in Canada in 1991 the province of Ontario even displayed the Crown on all its car registration plates, presumably to remind American tourists that they were now north of the Border.

Niccolò's ghost   Aren't *all* citizens in your society expected to obey the law? If that's the case, where's the difference between a servant of the Crown and anyone else?

Author   A difference may be found in the way authority flows through the hierarchy.

Imagine a hypothetical private company controlling telecommunications, the senior partner of which decides to tap particular telephones for private or political advantage. Consider then the plight of the technicians actually ordered to install the illegal intercepts. They don't approve of it, but the boss is still the boss regardless of what he orders, even if he's a bad 'un. They've got families to provide for and mortgages to pay off, and good jobs are hard to find. We can't help but understand their motives if they choose not to rock the boat.

But now consider a similar scenario when it's the government controlling the telephone lines, and a senior public servant ordering technicians who are junior public servants to install the phone taps. All sympathy for technicians who obey now flies out the window, for they are servants of the Crown being directed to engage in an illegal act by another servant of the Crown. If they know it's illegal they know the order has no authority; that despite their subordinate position they are under no obligation to obey, for the hierarchy which compels their obedience has for the moment been set aside; that indeed this hierarchy requires their disobedience of such an order, the Crown they serve being also guarantor of the laws of the land now being flouted.

Of course there are regions of uncertainty over what is or is not a lawful order, an issue which is particularly painful for members of the armed services, who are conspicuously servants of the Crown bound by strict discipline. When they should obey and when disobey is an uncomfortable question summed up neatly last century by Sir Charles Napier, who protested that it:

> reduces the Soldier to a choice between the hanging —
> awarded to him by the Local Law — for obeying his Officer,
> and the shooting — awarded him by the Military Law — for
> disobeying his Officer. In such law there is neither sense nor
> justice, and (being one of those unlucky red-coated gents thus
> agreeably placed between shooting and hanging) I beg to
> enter my protest against this choice of deaths. If such is Law,
> the Army must become a deliberative body, and ought to be
> composed of attorneys, and the Lord Chancellor should be
> made Commander-in-chief.[133]

This question is a complex one, existing for armed forces throughout Her Majesty's realms of the Commonwealth. Windeyer himself was no stranger to it, having served in World War II as a Brigadier commanding in the 2nd AIF, fighting in North Africa. The difficulties arise with orders that are in fact unlawful, but not manifestly so. In the Hope Report on Terrorism, commissioned by the Fraser Government following the 1978 Hilton bombing in Sydney, both he and Mr Justice Hope of the NSW Supreme Court gave detailed consideration to the issue in Australian, British, New Zealand and Canadian contexts.[134]

As both Dicey and Hewart took pains to point out, this aspect of ministerial responsibility is particularly relevant to the liberty of citizens in the matter of imprisonment. Traditionally prisons are titled "Her Majesty's prisons", with conspicuous display of the Crown upon buildings and the uniforms of warders. There's an implicit allusion in this to the ancient writ of *habeas corpus*, whereby citizens in custody are entitled to prompt trial, enforced by the courts of law. Such a writ can be made by the Court, through application by either the prisoner or any other person who satisfies the Court or judge that the prisoner appears to be detained unlawfully. Upon receiving this writ from the Court, failure by warders to produce their prisoners promptly before it, showing the day and cause of detention, carries heavy penalties — penalties to be inflicted upon the individual warders, who as servants of the Crown have no excuse for engaging in unlawful detention.[135]

Niccolò's ghost   **From your tone of voice I gather you think all this a remarkable thing, that in hierarchies under the Crown servants of the Executive are expected to disobey illegal orders, and if they fail to do so they are punishable in a court of law. But isn't this true in all Western democracies?**

In his 1929 treatise *The New Despotism* Lord Hewart defined the behaviour of servants of the Executive in three categories:
* the Rule of Law,
* the *droit administratif*, and
* executive lawlessness.

The Rule of Law, exemplified by the English common law traditions central to the modern legal systems of Her Majesty's realms throughout the Commonwealth, he defined as obeying certain criteria, the most obvious being that all citizens either within or outside the government are held accountable to the same body of law. In contrast with this, the *droit administratif*, a system of law employed during the 1920s in most continental European countries,[136] exempts servants of the Executive from the ordinary laws that bind ordinary citizens.

> Under this system, the ordinary Courts of Justice are regarded
> as having no jurisdiction to deal with any dispute affecting the
> Government or its servants, all such disputes being within the

exclusive cognizance of the administrative Courts, the chief of which, in France, is the *Conseil d'Etat*. This Council was originally a purely administrative body…and it has gradually become more judicial in character, the members have always held office at the pleasure of the Government of the day.[137]

Although the *droit administratif* is a system "fundamentally opposed to the English conception of the 'Rule of Law'"[138] and hence contradicting the most basic principles of the Westminster system, it nonetheless is still a form of law.[139] The third category, however, is not: executive lawlessness.

The distinction between illegality and lawlessness is important. Leafing through the dictionary at my elbow, an "illegal" act is defined as being one "contrary to law". A "lawless" act, however, is one "regardless of, disobedient to, uncontrolled by" law; "unbridled, licentious". A "lawless" country or government is one "where law is non-existent or inoperative". So a thief who picks a pocket is guilty of an illegal act, that of theft, but isn't necessarily committing this act within a lawless society. Provided crime is repaid with just punishment and police constables are adequately efficient, thieves must live in fear of retribution for their offences. The law still rules, despite the existence of offenders. Acts of lawlessness, however, are something more profound, setting aside or destroying the instruments by which the rule of law is enforced so that illegality can flourish unconstrained. A petty thief can't achieve this; he has insufficient power to disable these instruments.

From time to time throughout the world, including Australia, governments have instructed their servants to engage in illegal activities to provide a solution to political problems. From time to time the servants have obeyed. Like our hypothetical thief the authors of these actions have lived in fear of arrest and punishment, but unlike our pickpocket they've held resources through office by which justice might be averted. In many countries these resources have been exploited to sabotage the operation of law.

Although never experienced in Australia, lawlessness at the highest echelons of government is something which can afflict all countries; Hewart for example was afraid of its emergence in Britain through regressive constitutional practices appearing in that country earlier this century, fears later reiterated by a number of other eminent British commentators throughout the 20th Century. France suffered executive lawlessness in the 1950s and '60s. Yet the victor's laurels for most spectacular example in any modern industrialised democracy must surely be awarded to the United States of America, a lawlessness entrenched through its constitutional arrangements.

Author   [*looking up*] In discussing this behaviour in the United States we're not motivated by some holier-than-thou anti-American cant, but merely studying a particularly chronic case of a general disease —

Niccolò's ghost   [*shrugs*] Of course. If politics is the art of the possible, then surely an option's illegality is an inconvenience rather than a disqualification.

Author   Accepting this, look closer at modern American history.

This memorandum addresses the matter of how we can maximize the fact of our incumbency in dealing with persons known to be active in their opposition to our Administration. Stated a bit more bluntly – how we can use the available federal machinery to screw our political enemies. [Hit list of two congressmen and eighteen private US citizens follows, to be destroyed through selective IRS audits, denial of federal grants and contracts, prosecution and government litigation.][140]

> 1971 White House internal memo written by John W. Dean III, a member of Nixon's staff. Hit list subsequently given to Dean by special White House counsel Charles Colsen, for priority. Tendered as evidence to Senate Watergate Committee, 1973.

"[T]he President's ability to govern is at stake. Another Tea Pot Dome scandal is possible and the government may fall. Everybody else is on track but you. You are not following the game plan. Get closer to your attorney."

"You know that if the administration gets its back to the wall, it will have to take steps to defend itself."[141]

> Testimony by Watergate conspirator James W. McCord Jr before the Senate Watergate Committee, allegedly quoting an ex-Nixon presidential aide attempting to bribe and threaten him into committing perjury.

Imperial Presidency and the Lawless State

At 2:30 am on the 17th of June 1972 five men were arrested after having broken into rooms of the Democratic Party's national headquarters, located in the Watergate hotel and office complex in Washington DC.

Wearing surgical gloves to avoid fingerprints, the men were discovered carrying electronic surveillance equipment. Once they and two accomplices had been arrested, it became disturbingly clear that here were no common burglars. Out of the seven, five were US citizens while the other two were anti-Castro Cuban *émigrés*. Five were either former employees of or had associations with the Central Intelligence Agency, three had connections with the White House, one worked in narcotics intelligence and another was an ex-FBI agent. All either pleaded guilty or were convicted of felonies within eight months.[142] Yet as the intricate events surrounding their burglary slowly began to unravel, they revealed profound and longstanding executive illegality reaching through the White House, to Presidents themselves.

The idea of executive illegality in the United States wasn't born at Watergate. To public knowledge there'd been at least two earlier administrations tainted with corruption, those of President Warren Harding and President Harry S. Truman. The scandal of Harding's reign broke after his death on the 2nd of August 1923 and is notorious to history as the Tea Pot Dome affair. In 1920 Congress had passed the *General Leasing Act*, permitting (under some conditions) the Secretary of the Navy, a government minister appointed by the President, to lease naval oil reserves on public land to private oil operators. At the urging of his Secretary of the Interior, Albert Fall, and his Secretary of the Navy, Edwin Denby, President Harding signed an executive order in May 1921 transferring jurisdiction over naval oil reserves to the Department of the Interior. The next year Fall granted oil leases over the Elk Hills reserve in California and the Tea Pot Dome reserve in Wyoming to private oil companies, without public notice or competitive bidding. After Harding's death it transpired that Fall had accepted bribes of at least US$400,000 from these companies, a vast sum of money at the time. The next occupant of the Oval Office, President Coolidge, sacked Harding's Attorney-General, Harry M. Daugherty, for failing to prosecute any of the guilty participants. Daugherty's replacement, Attorney-General Harlan Fiske Stone, promptly purged the Bureau of Investigation (now the FBI), later writing "When I became attorney-general, the Bureau of Investigation was…in exceedingly bad odour…The head of the Bureau…had himself participated in serious infractions of the law and obstructions of justice".[143] Fall was imprisoned and Denby resigned, and Tea Pot Dome became the posthumous hallmark of Harding's era.

During the Truman administration a number of his White House aides and personal assistants were publicly confronted with allegations of corruption, including his military aide, General Vaughan; the assistant Attorney-General in charge of the Tax Division, T. Lamar Caudle; the general counsel to the Bureau of Internal Revenue, Charles Oliphant; the Internal Revenue Commissioner himself, George Schoenman; former Internal Revenue Commissioner Josef Nunan; chief of the General Services Administration, Jess Larson, and Truman's appointments secretary Matthew Connolly. Sixty-six officials in the Justice Department and the Bureau of Internal Revenue were forced from office. Nine, including Caudle and Connolly, were imprisoned.[144]

But the revelations of Watergate went far beyond simple monetary corruption. Described as "a mediaeval morality play, acted out in 20th Century terms"[145] it forced the Senate's most distinguished constitutional scholar, chairing the Senate Watergate Committee,[146] to query the continued viability of the United States as a representative democracy.[147] Discussing the gross executive illegality it revealed without sounding as paranoid as Fox Mulder is difficult. Enough crackpot conspiracy theories exist without further contributions from this or any other book. Fortunately the vast — although incomplete — quantity of evidence and testimony collected by presidential and congressional committees of inquiry since Nixon's fall, annotated by commentaries and memoirs written by disillusioned ex-government agents, are more than enough to counter claims of paranoia. The Ervin Senate Select Committee investigating Watergate, the Rockefeller Commission headed by the US Vice-President to investigate the CIA's illegal domestic activities, the Senate Committee chaired by Senator Frank Church and the House Committee chaired by Congressman Otis Pike, both investigating general illegal activities by the US intelligence community, heard testimony from serving and former Directors, Deputy Directors and agents of the CIA, FBI and other government agencies, subpoenaed documents and White House officials, and offered limited immunity from prosecution for informers in return for evidence delivered under Oath.

One of the most damning documents was the secret internal report ordered by newly-appointed CIA Director James Schlesinger in May 1973, ordering all Agency employees to inform him of inappropriate or illegal Agency activities past or present. To his horror the data he received as a result, nicknamed by the Agency the "family jewels", consisted of 693 pages of illegal actions: domestic espionage including warrantless wiretaps and illegal mail interception on a vast scale, in gross violation of the Agency's 1947 congressional charter forbidding the Agency from wielding "police, subpoena, law enforcement powers or internal security functions"; the training of foreign insurgency groups; assassination plots and assassination squads and the possible murder of foreign officials.[148] Schlesinger remained Director for only five months;[149] his successor, the late William E. Colby, used the report to brief President Ford. Although the Schlesinger Report was never publicly released, parts of it were leaked to the *New York Times* and CBS News. Taken together with other evidence gathered by the committees of inquiry, a diorama is revealed of executive-approved espionage, blackmail, burglary, political persecution, manufacture of false and incriminating documents against political enemies, kidnapping, illegal possession of lethal or incapacitating drugs, monetary corruption, the running of secret armies abroad and links with organised crime at home.[150]

The sense of betrayal felt by many decent Americans was expressed by Senator Philip Hart of Michigan, a gentle and honourable man who, appalled when confronted with the truth about the FBI, objected:

> I have been told for years by, among others, some of my own family, that this is exactly what the Bureau was doing all the time, and in my great wisdom and high office, I assured them

that they were wrong – it just wasn't true, it couldn't happen. They wouldn't do it.[151]

But they could, would and did.

What spares this litany of illegality from the banality of ordinary brutality, endowing it instead with a bleak epic quality, was the nature of middle- to late-20th Century history and the role of the United States in it, as the supposed guardian of Western civilisation's democratic ideals.

In wartime, executive government takes on a very different aspect from that of times of peace. Even as a civilised society puts aside self-fulfilment and individuality for sacrifice and discipline, its government becomes more secretive in deliberation and authoritarian in rule, a state of affairs acceptable to a democratic society simply because now the entire society is struggling for survival. These measures assist the coherency of the war effort, and while the security of the country is in doubt there's a basic community consensus that the war must be won. Having acquired emergency powers to cope with World War II the White House failed to relinquish them in 1945, choosing instead to retain them in the struggle for survival that was the Cold War. The President claimed the right of wielding them in defence of national security, the nature and interests of which he would define himself.[152] But over a protracted cold war the national consensus breaks down as to the identity of the enemies and how they are to be fought. Obviously the Soviet Union under Stalin and the People's Republic of China under Chairman Mao posed an immediate and lethal threat, but could the same be said of, say, Chile under President Allende?

Furthermore, the methods sometimes employed in a cold war are also morally repugnant. In its analysis of international Communism, a commission headed by former President Herbert Hoover advised in a secret report that:

> It is now clear that we are facing an implacable enemy whose avowed objective is world domination by whatever means and at whatever cost. There are no rules in such a game. Hitherto acceptable norms of human conduct do not apply. If the U.S. is to survive, longstanding American concepts of "fair play" must be reconsidered. We must develop effective espionage and counterespionage services and must learn to subvert, sabotage and destroy our enemies by more clever, more sophisticated, and more effective methods than those used against us. It may become necessary that the American people be made acquainted with, understand and support this fundamentally repugnant philosophy.[153]

But a democracy in a civilised state has a limited tolerance of reprehensible activities performed in its name. Eventually voters will turn against an Executive engaging in this behaviour irrespective of how much it protests that it's for their own good. Consequently it must shroud much of its activity in secrecy, not only against foreign spies but against its own citizens. Scandals like the CIA's *L'Armée Clandestine* become more comprehensible: a secret army in Laos composed of Thai mercenaries and Laotian ethnic mercenaries (like the Meo tribesmen), authorised by the Nixon administration despite the explicit laws of Congress concerning the hiring of mercenaries. Although under the Constitution only Congress shall declare war, Congress mightn't understand "the greater good" as well as the President knows he does, or act with the "necessary" ruthlessness, therefore Presidents have illegally waged secret wars in Guatamala (1954), against Communist China (during the 1950s), in Indonesia against Sukarno (1958), and in the early days in Vietnam. Congress and the general public were kept ignorant; most members of Congress were unaware of the covert war in Laos until 1969.[154]

This attitude of illegality for "the greater good" translated into activities within the United States: in testimony before the Church Committee ex-FBI agents admitted the FBI engaged in the kidnapping of suspected agents of foreign intelligence services in the early- to mid-1960s (although one of the captives might have actually been a legitimate US citizen rather than a sophisticated deep-cover spy). For mitigation of their offences they denied before the Committee that physical torture had been used, and protested that "none of [the] suspected espionage agents involved in these operations ever died as [a] direct result of kidnapping or interrogation or while attempting to escape".[155] Becoming worried by the mid-'60s that FBI Director J. Edgar Hoover wouldn't back them if something went wrong, agents refused to undertake more of this work without written authorisation, which Hoover was reluctant to give.[156]

After revelations in the *New York Times* over the existence and nature of the Schlesinger Report, CIA Director William Colby briefed President Ford over its contents. According to sources, part of these briefings included an oral addendum to the written report, on sensitive topics including several plans for the assassination of foreign persons. CBS News reported that "President Ford warned associates that if current investigations into [the] CIA went too far they could uncover 'several' assassinations of foreign officials in which the CIA was involved".[157] The White House Deputy Press Secretary subsequently refused to either confirm or deny the existence of these murders, and the President himself said it would be "inappropriate" to comment on them.[158] However, evidence indicates that a formal assassination capability was established within the CIA in 1961, and that the Agency worked in cooperation with senior Mafia figures in America and Havana in its attempts to kill Fidel Castro.[159] Allegations were also made that the CIA solicited the DEA (Drug Enforcement Administration, a federal body closely affiliated with the Agency) to purchase assassination equipment, prompting consternation in the Senate.[160]

Of course a real problem faced by an elected government engaged in dubious activities abroad is the threat of foreign *agents provocateur* inciting hostility within the domestic electorate, endangering the viability of these programmes

— and hence the national interest as perceived by the President. Testimony (including that of former CIA Director Richard Helms) indicates that in 1967 President Lyndon B. Johnson ordered the CIA to engage in illegal domestic surveillance of the anti-Vietnam War movement, to discover evidence of "foreign money and foreign influence".[161]

Perhaps President Johnson didn't know that the Agency had already been engaging in domestic espionage on a vast scale since the 1950s. Beginning as an exercise in counterintelligence, it rapidly evolved into a species of lawless behaviour justifying its own existence, not through counterintelligence dividends but through the political power the resultant knowledge yielded. In 1952 the Agency, with the active cooperation of the US Postal Service, began a massive mail-opening programme intercepting private correspondence between the US and the USSR, diversifying later to intercepting more general mail. Between 1953 and 1973 nearly a quarter of a million letters were opened and photographed, creating a computerized index of almost one and a half million names.[162] In 1974 Chief Postal Inspector William J. Cotter admitted to a House committee the complicity of the Postal Service, and said he believed every President since Dwight Eisenhower had been aware of it.[163] Even early CIA internal memos revealed an awareness of the illegality of this, one 1962 memo stating:

> since no good purpose can be served by an official admission
> of the violation, and existing federal statutes preclude the
> concoction of any legal excuse for the violation…it is impor-
> tant that all federal law enforcement and US intelligence
> agencies vigorously deny any association, direct or indirect,
> with any such activity as charged.[164]

In 1969 the CIA's director of security, Howard Osborn, confirmed "This thing is as illegal as hell".[165] And yet in the absence of any tangible evidence yielded by this interception — a 1961 inspector-general's memo reported "no tangible operation benefits had accrued…as a result of this project",[166] an assessment reiterated independently in the 1960s by both FBI domestic intelligence and CIA studies rejecting any significant link between American anti-war protests and the Soviet Union[167]— the counterintelligence operation continued and expanded into monitoring correspondence of Americans with no Soviet connection whatever, including that of one Richard M. Nixon. Similarly this behaviour diversified into warrantless wiretapping of telephones, and burglary.[168] William Colby admitted in testimony before the Church Committee that the CIA held files on 10,000 US citizens; the Rockefeller Commission report actually found 300,000 CIA files existed on individuals and organisations as a result of its "unlawful or uncontrolled domestic operations".[169]

All these past offences have had a rationale in the fact of the Cold War, but they serve also in drawing attention to the most obvious reason for executive illegality in a democracy: re-election. As Nixon aide John W. Dean III pointed out in his White House memo quoted earlier, the challenge for an unscrupulous Executive is to "maximize the fact of our incumbency in dealing with persons known to be active in their opposition to our Administration". During times of war, conventional or cold, the incumbent Executive holds an advantage through its power to define the national interest: "The power to define threats to the 'national security' is the power to draw limits of acceptable behaviour for leaders abroad and citizens at home".[170] Legitimate criticism of an elected government's policies can be re-cast as subversion, and the critics themselves, potential traitors.

In the United States the White House maintained a list of enemies to be attacked, some as security threats. Left-wing or social reformist groups were subjected to surveillance, burglary, infiltration and intimidation. But all this is merely a magnification of the faculty available to the Executive during the most tranquil periods of peace: the misuse of the legitimate instruments of government, including police and intelligence services intended to preserve the civil peace from internal or external violence, to smear, blackmail and intimidate political enemies deemed enemies of the "greater good". For example, Martin Luther King's reputation was smeared by a scandalous report on his private life, compiled by the FBI and disseminated with the apparent permission of President Lyndon Johnson.[171] Also revealed in 1975 was that President Johnson ordered the illegal bugging of King's hotel room (and those of other civil rights leaders) during the Democratic national convention in 1964; the FBI's response to this revelation was to assert it had been "collecting intelligence on [the] plans of subversive, criminal and hoodlum groups".[172]

Assisted by the Internal Revenue Service (IRS), the FBI under Director J. Edgar Hoover compiled dossiers on congressmen, senators, judges, federal officials and sundry other prominent figures from all walks of life in America, covering all aspects of their private lives, from their financial affairs and drinking habits to their sexual affairs[173] (including, as a handy cross-reference, possession of police records detailing the names of 300,000 people arrested for homosexual acts[174]). Hoover gave Presidents Johnson and Nixon regular personal briefings on the contents of these dossiers, for the purpose of helping them engage in useful blackmail. In the congressional inquiries following Watergate, Attorney-General E.H. Levi and Deputy Attorney-General Laurence H. Silberman confirmed the existence of these reports and their derogatory nature. Levi testified that Presidents of both parties misused the FBI for their own political and private purposes, and Silberman named three such offenders. Two were Richard M. Nixon and Lyndon B. Johnson. The third was John F. Kennedy.[175]

In his introduction to volume one of a collection of Watergate material William B. Dickinson, editor of Washington's *Congressional Quarterly*, wrote,

> A worry that cannot be easily dismissed centres on an unavoidable question: Does Watergate show some awful new flaw in the constitutional structure conceived by the founding fathers nearly 200 years ago?[176]

Although Dickinson didn't answer his own rhetorical question, it's tempting to reply "yes". In bittersweet irony the US Constitution, founded explicitly upon the principle that "only the people are sovereign, governed under the law, and that 'all offices of the government – from the highest to the lowest, are creatures of the law and are bound to obey it...' ",[177]in real life created a system of government in which the President is sovereign and his servants, by virtue of being his servants, are to a great extent above the law. Richard Nixon expressed the doctrine clearly when he said of the Presidency,

> it is quite obvious that there are inherently governmental actions which if undertaken *by the sovereign* in protection of the interest of the nation's security are lawful, but which if undertaken by private persons are not...[178]

He was neither the first nor the solitary adherent to this view. The practical immunity of servants of the Executive from prosecution was illustrated in July 1976, two years after Nixon's fall from power and exactly two hundred after the Declaration of Independence, when the Justice Department's lawyers

> recommended against prosecuting CIA officials involved in the mail-opening operation; they decided that presidential knowledge of the programme...was enough to authorize CIA officials to violate federal criminal statutes without fear of prosecution.[179]

Apparently these lawyers — and former Presidents — have believed the President holds some kind of suspending power over the laws of the land,[180] despite the fact that "there are no provisions in the Constitution, no statutes, and no court decisions that grant the [P]resident the authority to make illegal activity legal".[181] This apparent immunity to law has extended to perjury: when CIA Director Richard Helms "found it necessary to lie under oath"[182] about both domestic and international operations the Justice Department failed to indict him because "the general feeling within the Justice Department [was] that his duty was to lie".[183] Similarly the Department decided not to prosecute Helms for a burglary the Rockefeller Commission had cited as clearly illegal.[184] The Justice Department has also asserted a "presidential power to order warrantless wiretaps, bugs, and 'surreptitious entries' (break-ins) against American citizens for intelligence purposes".[185] One wonders whether this immunity to criminal statutes would also have extended to the FBI's confessed kidnappings, or the CIA's apparent assassination capability, if they had been conducted with presidential knowledge?

Unlawful orders appear to have enjoyed at least equal status with legitimate ones within the executive hierarchy. William Sullivan, the FBI's former Assistant Director for Intelligence, concluded that the legality of orders was never an issue "because we were just naturally pragmatists...As far as legality is concerned, morals or ethics, [it] was never raised by myself or anybody else".[186] I say "at least equal status" because former CIA Counter-Intelligence Staff Chief James Angleton has asserted a kind of legitimacy for executive lawlessness, stating "I find it inconceivable that a covert agency is expected to obey all the overt orders of the government"[187]. In his context, "overt orders" includes not only the laws and treaties of the United States but presidential directives inconveniently constrained by those laws.†

All this has a "bittersweet irony" because in contradistinction Her Majesty's realms throughout the world employ a modern interpretation of 17th Century principles, themselves based upon the ancient sovereignty of the monarch, to uphold the modern sovereignty of the people. First devised to constrain wayward monarchs, they now constrain wayward Prime Ministers, the modern wielders of executive authority. All executive authority flows from the Crown, the "King can do no wrong", therefore unlawful orders cannot have authority and so must be disobeyed by servants of the Crown. Since the Bill of Rights of 1689 the Crown has been deprived of any power to suspend or dispense with the laws of the land; from a strictly legal viewpoint Prime Ministers hold their authority purely as servants of the Crown, therefore Prime Ministers also cannot pretend to hold any power to suspend or ignore the laws of the land.‡ Thus the US Constitution, based explicitly upon the sovereignty of the people, has created instead a sovereign President, an elected autocrat, whereas constitutions defining Her Majesty's governments throughout the world rely upon the forms of a "sovereign" Crown to create the substance of a sovereign people. In America, an inheritor of English common law traditions, the clock's been ticking backwards: the Presidency regaining powers stripped from the Crown centuries ago.

Like an overdue reminder notice of an unpaid debt, the scandal exposed in 1986 revealed that US executive lawlessness remains, unresolved after Watergate. The events of the Iran-Contra Affair read more like the plot of a trashy airport novel rather than contemporary history, so to avoid accusations of sensationalism the following summary is drawn entirely from the account presented by the

---

† He was referring to an incident during the Nixon era, when the CIA secretly refused to destroy stocks of toxic substances in its possession. The US Senate had passed a treaty outlawing lethal poisons, signed by the President, and so Nixon issued a directive ordering the destruction of these substances, which was disobeyed by the Agency. Angleton was defending the general principle of this disobedience.(Halperin, Berman, Borosage and Marwick, *The Lawless State*, pp.224–225.)

‡ A modern perspective on the *Bill of Rights 1689* was provided by the New Zealand courts in the 1976 case *Fitzgerald v. Muldoon*. The New Zealand Prime Minister, Sir Robert Muldoon, had issued a public statement on the 15th December 1975 announcing the abolition of the superannuation scheme that had been established under the *New Zealand Superannuation Act 1974*. He warned that all contributions required under the Act should cease. In the light of this statement civil servants ceased to enforce superannuation contributions, despite the fact the Act had not as yet been repealed by Parliament. Fitzgerald, an employee of the Education Department, appealed to the Supreme Court for a declaration that the Prime Minister's statement was illegal, as it constituted the exercise of a pretended power of suspending laws outlawed by section 1 of the *Bill of Rights 1689*.The Chief Justice of New Zealand, Wild CJ, upheld Fitzgerald's contention, stating that Sir Robert's announcement had been made in his official capacity as Prime Minister and hence made "by regall authority"[sic-quotation of s. 1]. Remarking "The sovereignty of Parliament is such that it has the right to make and unmake laws and no person or body is recognised as having the right to override or set aside the legislation of Parliament", Wild CJ declared the Prime Minister's announcement illegal.([1976]2 NZLR 615 at 615.)

---

joint *Report of the Congressional Committees Investigating the Iran-Contra Affair*, itself published by the US Government the following year.[188] In November 1986 a bizarre story broke: through revelations published in a Beirut weekly, *Al-Shiraa*, and subsequent statements by the US Attorney-General, it emerged that the Reagan Administration had been secretly and illegally selling arms to Iran in the 1980s, in an attempt to secure the release of American hostages in Lebanon. Senior White House figures had been siphoning off profits from these sales — which had proved lucrative irrespective of hostages — to provide illegal military funding to the Contras in Nicaragua. The Select Committees convened by a horrified Congress unearthed much more, involving President Reagan himself, two of his National Security Advisers (Robert C. McFarlane and Vice-Admiral John M. Poindexter), an NSC staff member[†] (Lt. Col. Oliver North), and — allegedly — the Director of the CIA, William Casey, who died before his testimony could be heard. The Committees discovered that President Reagan had personally violated the law, setting in motion an international covert agenda without notifying Congress or providing written authorisation. His servants had gone much further, not only secretly selling missiles to Teheran, but pouring the profits into a private organisation (melodramatically christened "the Enterprise") under a retired US Air Force Major General, Richard V. Secord. Possessing its own aircraft, pilots, operatives, airfield, ship, secure communications technology and millions of dollars in Swiss bank accounts, the Enterprise was created by these officials to enable the White House to engage privately in world-wide covert operations using non-appropriated funds, in secret defiance of Congress and its laws. Abroad the Enterprise gave lethal support to the Contras; at home it engaged in pro-Contra "white propaganda" to defeat hostile Congressmen. The Congressional Committees drew up a list of the laws violated by the White House in this affair: among others, section 501 of the *National Security Act*, the *Arms Export Control Act*, the Boland Amendments (forbidding military interference in Nicaragua) and the Appropriations Clause of the US Constitution itself. Also violated by senior White House staff were 18 U.S.C. Section 1001 (the statute concerning the making of false and fraudulent statements to Congress, a criminal offence) and the *Presidential Records Act* (for their falsification and shredding of official records). The joint Report bleakly concluded that "beyond doubt…fundamental processes of governance were disregarded and the rule of law subverted".[189]

After Watergate commentators groped for a title to describe the elective but arbitrary autocracy the office of President had clearly become. They found it in a phrase coined by a Kennedy aide, Arthur Schlesinger, who referred to the position as the "imperial Presidency";[190] its occupant, the elected emperor. For

---

† As the Central Intelligence Agency explains it, "The National Security Council was established by the National Security Act of 1947 to advise the President with respect to the integration of domestic, foreign, and military policies relating to national security. The NSC is the highest Executive Branch entity providing review of, guidance for, and direction to the conduct of all national foreign intelligence and counterintelligence activities. The statutory members of the NSC are the President, the Vice President, the Secretary of State, and the Secretary of Defence. The Director of Central Intelligence and the Chairman of the Joint Chiefs of Staff participate as advisers". (**http://www.ic.gov/facttell/sections/eover.html**; as of update of 14th October 1994)

epitaph, the hazard this figure poses to the United States was expressed in 1976 at the beginning of the Carter administration, when the book *The Lawless State* was published. Written under the joint auspices of the American Civil Liberties Union and the Centre for National Security Studies, its authors (including two attorneys and an ex-Deputy Assistant Secretary of Defence and senior staff member of the National Security Council) rejected the proposition that the United States is under the rule of law. Pointing to post-Nixon offences (not to mention subsequent scandals like Iran-Contra) they criticised the attempted reforms after Watergate as empty and ridiculed President Ford's assertion that the American people would not elect an unreliable President (like Nixon), warning:

> With the executive branch alone standing between political freedom and a police state, we do not have a government of laws, but of men; and there is no inherent reason why the nation should expect to be luckier in its officials from now on.[191]

Since that protest was lodged the Cold War has ceased. The incumbent President is better known for his sexual follies than any unlawful agenda, and has suffered a harsher fate at the hands of Congress than Reagan ever did over Iran-Contra. But voices like that of John W. Dean remain, and with them, the shadow of the lawless State.

...I feel it my bounden duty to remind
you at once that you derive your
authority from His Majesty, through me,
and that I cannot possibly allow
the Crown to be placed in the position
of breaking the law of the land.

I must ask you, therefore, either
to furnish me with proof that the
instructions in the circular are within the
law, or, alternatively to withdraw the
circular at once.

I do not wish to press you unduly,
but the matter appears to me to be of
an urgency which admits no delay, and I
must ask for a definite reply by 11 a.m.,
tomorrow, 13th May.

Letter from Sir Philip Game, Governor of
New South Wales, to Premier Jack Lang,
1932.

Illegality and the Crown

The legality of orders may be a burning question for servants of the Crown, but what should — or could — Her Majesty's representative do personally when confronted with a delinquent government? Replying to that question necessarily involves answering another, namely, what do the Queen and her representatives actually *do* on a day-to-day basis? A popular misconception is that their role is purely ceremonial: making speeches, cutting ribbons, bestowing awards and opening fêtes. But, echoing Evatt, "It is a profound mistake to regard the royal functions as merely ceremonial or formal in character." Although rarely seen by the public, the main activity of the Crown is as the ultimate guarantor of constitutional government, an activity manifested most days by the tedious duty of the red boxes.

In the ordinary course of government, the Prime Minister and his Cabinet impose their will upon this country in an executive fashion, without the use of Parliament. They dictate orders relevant to their portfolios and these orders are obeyed directly by the Public Service, through the departmental

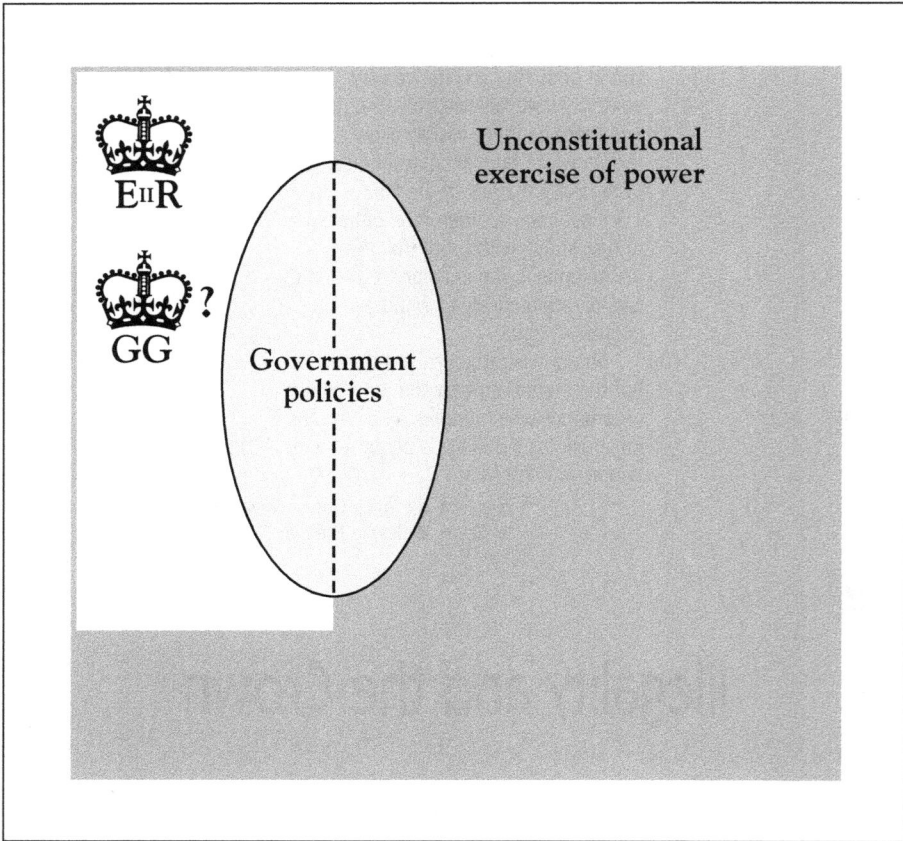

Under modern ministerial responsibility, the Crown is a potent witness of executive government. So what is the Crown to do when it witnesses flagrant executive illegality?

hierarchies, and imposed upon the public. Although these orders are devised and written by elected politicians, they are formally issued in the name of the Crown and take one of two forms: ordinary ministerial directives, and Orders in Council.

An Act of Parliament (say, a Motor Vehicle Registration Act) creates a law concerning some aspect of community life (in this example, commanding that all cars be registered before driven on public roads). It will often refer to the Minister responsible for administering it (here, the Transport Minister) and give him or her discretionary powers to make regulations to make the law work (to flesh out all the details and guidelines). The details of these regulations can be written, revised and revoked by Ministers on their own authority whenever they think it necessary; the personal instructions issued by Ministers to their own staff to do this are "ministerial directives".

The same Act may also confer much broader discretionary powers to Ministers over the administration of the law it creates (say, the power to command different scales of fees for different sorts of vehicles). Given the inter-departmental rivalry between Ministers (a Transport Minister may want to impose a hefty levy upon heavy trucks thundering along his roads, while the Agriculture Minister may protest that those same trucks are the lifeline for her farmers to get their produce to market, and shouldn't be disadvantaged), a safeguard over the way these broader powers are wielded is for the Act to require them to be exercised "by Order in Council".

An Order in Council is a formal document embodying a decision that a particular executive power is to be exercised in a specific way. Its content, decided by the relevant Minister, must also have the unanimous support of Cabinet (expressed in Queensland by their initials scribbled on its folder), a useful constraint. More relevant to our concerns, the Order also requires for its validity the final signature of the Governor or Governor-General. Orders in Council are commands issued by the Executive Council, i.e. the Cabinet plus the Queen's representative. Technically speaking, they are orders given by the Governor for the administration of his government; in reality this is an almost empty historical form, and has been for well over a century.

In fact the Cabinet is the issuer of the commands, Her Majesty's representative merely a witness. Yet as the Orders are given as a consequence of his signature, it's the Governor's responsibility to understand what is being done in his name by the true Executive. For the Governor to understand the implications of signing all of this documentation he has to read it, before attending the Executive Council meeting. Rather than by some glittering coronet, the emblem best embodying the Crown's work is the "red"† box that Cabinet papers are traditionally carried in.

My father tells the story of how, when he was a newly-elected backbencher in the 1970s, he was first confronted by "the boxes". At that time Queensland's Executive Council would meet virtually every week in the year, and at each meeting the Governor would sit at a table, attended by a quorum of Ministers (usually including the Premier). On this table would be a stack of Orders in Council awaiting signature, a stack usually eighteen inches or more in height per meeting, and for each Order there might also be a bundle of accompanying papers explaining it…amounting to a considerable pile of documents to be read. One day, my father was proudly showing a group of schoolchildren from his constituency around Old Parliament House. Barging into an anonymous-looking room with the children, he realised it was already occupied by a elderly man sitting at a desk, surrounded by paperwork. It was Governor Sir Colin Hannah, "doing his boxes" in private preparation. Much chastened, my father retreated before a baleful viceregal glare.

But for the Governor, the vital phrase earlier is "*almost* empty historical form": although the Queen's representative is reduced to being a witness, the role enables him to exercise the famous rights "to be consulted, to encourage and

---

† Although traditionally made of red leather stamped with a Crown, black synthetic now appears to be the fashionable choice for Cabinet boxes among some of Her Majesty's Governments.

to warn" as a non-politician observing politicians. How much notice ministers take of his advice depends on them; the transient nature of viceregal office implies he won't have the lifetime's experience of such briefings that lends weight to the Queen's advice, although the fact he's a distinguished Australian suggests life experiences that would make his opinions worth hearing. And when such a witness within the highest echelons of the Executive discovers unlawful behaviour being committed in his name, what is he to do about it?

In 19th Century Canada this problem was contemplated by Alpheus Todd, who wrote that if a Governor has "reason to believe that their [that is, the Cabinet Law Officers'] legal judgement has been unconsciously biased by political considerations, so that he cannot accept their interpretation of the law", he is not bound by these opinions and is "free to ask further assistance from elsewhere to aid him in his judgement".[192] Todd's view gained some weight in a despatch from the Colonial Secretary Sir M. Hicks-Beach on the 5th of June 1878, warning that a Governor couldn't shelter himself behind the responsibility of his Ministers in justifying the legality of any questionable proceeding. The dispatch stated that in all doubtful cases the Governor should require a written memorandum from the Colonial Law Officers certifying that no infraction of law is involved — a memorandum from them in their capacity as lawyers, not as political advisers. If no such memorandum was forthcoming, then the Governor's responsibility to his office might require him to delay the controversial action advised by his Ministers until he could decide, upon the circumstances, whether to accede to the advice or to refuse. This refusal might cost him the resignations of his Ministers.[193]

This view proved controversial, the chief danger being that, for a Governor to decide to act upon the illegality of ministerial advice, he would need impartial legal advice identifying its illegality. For a Governor not learned in law this implies external advice, from lawyers who might well have private political agendas colouring their opinions. Merivale, a British permanent Under-Secretary for the Colonies, had warned that for a Governor:

> His responsible Ministers may (and probably will) entertain views quite different from his own And the temptation to surround himself with a *camarilla* of special advisers, distinct from these Ministers, is one which a Governor must carefully resist.[194]

Merivale's warning has been embraced and magnified by a number of authorities, including Evatt, who pointed to some modern precedents adhering to it. One of these took place in South Africa in January 1914, when General Smuts deported ten Labour leaders from Natal.

> To intimidate the strikers [Smuts] decided to deport without legal authority ten leaders…The step taken was wholly illegal…It was found that General Smuts had admitted that he had had recourse to the illegal deportation because he

knew that Parliament would never give him authority in cold
blood to expel the men in question.[195]

Apparently when the South African government engaged in these expulsions
the consent or concurrence of the Governor-General, Lord Gladstone, "was
neither sought for nor obtained",[196] although he was informed of the event and
acquiesced. Consequently Evatt later wrote that,

> constitutional practice excludes from the consideration of the
> Governor in any Dominion the determination of all legal
> questions because direct responsibility for the action of the
> Governor in assenting to Bills or any proposed administrative
> act rests upon the Ministers holding office.[197]

Were any other principle adopted, he warned, it would cause difficulties:

> Unless the Governor is a specially trained lawyer…he will be
> unable to determine the disputed legal issue without seeking
> advice from outside the circle of his responsible Ministers.
> How can he be sure that the official advisers are wrong, and
> that the outside advisers are right? He is on perfectly safe
> ground if he allows all legal questions which are at all suscep-
> tible of argument to await determination at the hands of the
> judicial power.[198]

But Evatt's view is vulnerable to a number of strong criticisms, and precedents exist for supporting Todd. The most obvious was a crisis in Australia
during the Depression.

New South Wales in 1932 had as its Premier one John T. Lang, or "Jack" Lang,
a Labor Premier who had been re-elected in October 1930 with a large
majority in the NSW Lower House (the Legislative Assembly). Four months
later his government had run into trouble with its attempts to abolish the
NSW Upper House (the Legislative Council) without referendum, attempts
thwarted by the High Court of Australia who, in March 1931, had declared a
referendum would be necessary. Lang, having resolved to appeal to the Privy
Council in London against this decision, promptly found himself engaged in
political warfare by the NSW Upper House, in which his own supporters were
in a minority. It rejected his Bills.

The Lang Ministry retaliated by advising the NSW Governor, Air Vice-
Marshal Sir Philip Game, to appoint eighty additional Labor members to the
Legislative Council, thus swamping it. Angered at what he saw as grossly
improper advice, Sir Philip refused, reminding Lang of the existence of the
reserve powers. The latter responded publicly: the *Sydney Morning Herald*
reported the Crown Law Department had been ordered to draft documents to
be dispatched to London demanding the recall of the Governor. At the time
the risk of terminal confrontation was defused by Sir Philip, who wrote a letter

to Lang warning him that although advice to override the Legislative Council by stacking its membership wouldn't be acceptable, he saw no reason to demand Lang's resignation or to take any further action. The recall documents were not sent to London.

Observing at the end of June that the struggle between Lang and the Council persisted, he wrote another letter to Lang offering his assistance in mediation. In Britain a recent crisis among political parties had been resolved by King George V exploiting his position as apolitical Head of State: he had summoned a Conference in London, inviting all relevant political leaders to participate for the good of the country. Politicians who would never have responded to their opponents' overtures were able to accept the King's invitation without loss of face, and resolve some of their grievances around a table. Game offered to do the same in Sydney, providing a neutral venue for political differences to be resolved and pleading with the Premier to attempt it, but Lang rejected his offer of mediation, angrily describing it as "impertinance",[199] and refused to avert a confrontation over the Council. Finally in November 1931 Sir Philip acquiesced to Lang's demands and appointed twenty-five new Labor nominees to the Council, provoking public outrage. (The *Sydney Morning Herald*, for instance, telephoned Government House to inquire whether its occupants were all mad, and condemned the appointments in an editorial leader.) As events would show, even this measure would prove inadequate for some of the Premier's legislation to pass through the Council.

Trouble had already been brewing on another front. Crippled by the Depression, wool and wheat prices having collapsed, New South Wales found itself owing both the Commonwealth of Australia and overseas private investors considerable sums of money, of which it was unable to pay even the State's interest liabilities. The entire country was already deep in debt to overseas sources in London and New York. The Federal Government of Labor Prime Minister James Scullin had implemented earlier the Niemeyer Plan (named after Scullin's adviser, the Bank of England's Sir Otto Niemeyer) to manage the current financial crisis. Part of this had involved the Melbourne Agreement — an agreement among the Federal and all the State Governments to strive to balance budgets, avoid further overseas loans, seek no internal loans but for reproductive works, and to pay all interest on accounts falling due into a special account with the Commonwealth Bank. Commonwealth and State debts had been amalgamated, with the Federal Government assuming responsibility for the States' public debts. The NSW Labor Party had been in Opposition at the time of the Agreement, and many of its members — including Lang — hated both Niemeyer and his proposals, attacking both in incendiary terms. Lang subsequently called Scullin "only a small country grocer who found it difficult to think in terms of millions, instead of half-pennies",[200] and as Premier, refused to abide by the Agreement.

Becoming desperately short of money, the Lang Government failed — indeed, flatly refused — to pay its debts, embarrassing Canberra and isolating New

South Wales. Federal Labor disowned Lang,[†] renounced its NSW counterpart and threatened to expel its members. At the same time Government House was inundated with petitions demanding Lang's sacking. Newspapers throughout the State published editorials, articles and letters to this effect, sentiments echoed throughout the rest of the country. The *Canberra Times*, for example, demanded (30th April 1931) that under the circumstances "the need for a review by the electors of the vote given last October is now a matter of extreme urgency. Every possible step towards that object should be taken immediately, the most important being to urge the Governor to dismiss his present advisers".[201] Sir Philip, mindful of the previous mandate given to Lang — and aware of the cost of a general election to a near-bankrupt State — refused.

In February 1932, after the Scullin Government had been defeated at the general elections by the United Australia Party headed by the ex-Labor Joseph Lyons, the new Federal Government served a writ:

> To the State of New South Wales.
>
> We command you that within fourteen days after the service of this writ upon you, inclusive of the day of such service, you do cause an appearance to be entered for you in our High Court of Australia in an action for the full amount due to the overseas bondholders, a sum officially stated to be £958, 763 — including between £200, 000 and £300, 000 for exchange and remittance charges.[202]

In the interests of Australian credit the Lyons Government paid the overseas debts owed by the renegade State…and then moved to ensure its own sacrifice was repaid. On St Valentine's Day the Federal Parliament passed legislation to seize the revenues of New South Wales. All people owing taxes to that State were to pay the money to the Commonwealth instead, and *only* by paying the Commonwealth could they discharge their tax debts. The response of the Lang Government was both extraordinary and illegal. It, and Sir Philip's reaction, are best expressed by reproducing the actual correspondence, beginning with an unlawful Government directive to all public servants.

> **The Treasury, New South Wales,**
> **Sydney, 12th April, 1932**
>
> Subject: Collections and expenditure — Procedure
>   to be followed.
>
> Will you please instruct your departmental officers and officers of your sub-departments, and other collecting officers, including industrial undertakings to —
>
> (1) Refrain from meeting any Governmental expenditure by the drawing of cheques until further advised.
>
> (2) Hold all moneys collected coming under their control until forwarded as mentioned hereunder.
>
> (3) Under no circumstances to pay receipts into any bank.

---

† The New South Wales Federal Labor Executive sent a cable to the Dominions Secretary in London (who would have become involved if Lang had demanded the recall of Sir Philip Game), stating "The Hon. J.T. Lang has broken away from the Australian Labor Party and has now no mandate or authority from either the Australian Labor Party or the electors comprising such party". (B. Foott, *Dismissal of a Premier*, pp.116–117.)

(4) All collections to be made in cash or, if in any case it is necessary to take a cheque, such cheque must be cashed, if practicable, or, if the cheque or cheques cannot be cashed, such cheques must be "bearer" cheques made payable to "cash" or to a number, and crossed.

Cheques with specific crossings must not be accepted.

On no account must a cheque be officially marked either by stamp or otherwise.

(5) All cash and cheques collected to be delivered to the Treasury, either direct or to the departmental head office. Banks must not be used for this purpose, but safe and suitable arrangements should be made for forwarding cash and cheques to the Treasury. For this purpose, it is suggested that it may be possible to use the organisation of the railways.

For the information of the departments, it might be stated that value envelopes may be obtained from the railway stations, and, where the money is remitted through the railways, such envelopes containing the remittances should be addressed to the head office of the department or to the Treasury, full details of the collections to accompany the remittances. The Transport Commissioners have undertaken to facilitate arrangements through their organisation for the remittance of cash to the Treasury.

(6) Immediate action in this connexion is necessary.

C.R.CHAPMAN,

Under-Secretary.

CIRCULAR

Premier's Department, Sydney, 10th May 1932.

Subject: Collection and Expenditure — Procedure
              to be followed.

Reference: Treasury Circular letter of 12th April 1932.

I am to inform you that this matter was considered by Cabinet yesterday and that the following decision was approved, viz:-

That as forced labour without payment by the Authority who would use such forced labour or in other words, slavery, has been abolished in the British Empire for over 100 years, and as the first charge on revenue in every civilised community is the payment of those who collect the revenue for the Government, it is the decision of Cabinet, for the guidance of, and as instruction to, all servants of the State and of State Statutory Bodies, in order that the essential and social services of the State of New South Wales may be carried on, that the method of collecting revenue and paying same shall be as outlined in the Treasury Circular of 13th April, Subject: "Collections and Expenditure — Procedure to be followed"— and shall continue to be as directed by Treasury Circular under Government instruction from time to time.

C.H.HAY,

Under-Secretary

Government House, 12th May

Dear Mr. Lang,

I have received the copy of the circular for which I asked you. It appears to me that the terms of this circular direct public servants to commit a direct breach of the law as set out in proclamation No. 42 of 1932, published in the Commonwealth of Australia Gazette of 5th May, and the notice issued in accordance with the last paragraph of that proclamation and published in the Commonwealth of Australia Gazette of the 6th May. I feel it my bounden duty to remind you at once that you derive your authority from His Majesty, through me, and that I cannot possibly allow the Crown to be placed in the position of breaking the law of the land.

I must ask you, therefore, either to furnish me with proof that the instructions in the circular are within the law, or, alternatively to withdraw the circular at once.

I do not wish to press you unduly, but the matter appears to me to be of an urgency which admits no delay, and I must ask for a definite reply by 11 a.m., tomorrow, 13th May.

PHILIP GAME,

Governor

Premier's Department, 13th May 1932

Dear Sir Philip,

I received your letter of the 12th instant at 6 p.m., and must say that it is hard to understand how you do not wish to press unduly and yet insist on a definite reply by 11 a.m., on the 13th instant.

The circular of which you do not appear to approve represents the decision of the Cabinet, and no doubt was arrived at after consideration of the primary duties of maintaining the essential and social services of the State.

The only reply you can be given is that the circular cannot possibly be withdrawn.

JOHN T. LANG,

Premier.

Government House, 13th May

Dear Mr. Lang,

I have just received your letter of to-day's date. I gather from it that you do not dispute my view that the circular in question is a breach of the Federal law.

You will, I am sure, realise that I cannot allow the matter to rest where it is. Before considering what further action I may feel bound to take I should prefer to discuss the whole position with you. I shall be available at any time to-day convenient to you.

PHILIP GAME,

Governor.

Government House, 13th May

Dear Mr. Lang,

At our interview this afternoon you requested me to communicate my views by letter.

The position as I see it is that Ministers are committing a breach of the law. While you did not admit this, you did not deny it. Your case, as I understand it, is that Ministers are determined on their action in order to carry on the essential services of the State.

Into the aspect of justification it is not, as I conceive it, my province to inquire. My position is that if my Ministers are unable to carry on essential services without breaking the law my plain duty is to endeavour to obtain Ministers who feel able to do so.

As I have already pointed out to you in my letter of 12th instant, it is impossible for me to put the Crown in the position of being a party to illegal action.

If Ministers are not prepared to abide by the law then I must state without any hesitation that it is their bounden duty , under the law and practice of the Constitution, to tender their resignations.

I await an early reply, as I am sure you will agree that the present position cannot be allowed to extend over the week-end.

PHILIP GAME,

Governor

Premier's Department, Sydney, 13th May, 1932

Dear Sir Philip,

If your letter of to-day's date means that you are requesting the resignations of Ministers, you are hereby informed that your request is refused.

As to other matters mentioned in your letter, you are referred to my previous letter to you of to-day.

Yours faithfully,

JOHN T. LANG,

Premier

Government House, 13th May, 1932

Dear Mr. Lang,

Your letter informing me that Ministers are not prepared to tender their resignations has just reached me. In view of this and of your refusal to withdraw the circular, I feel it my bounden duty to inform you that I cannot retain my present Ministers in office, and that I am seeking other advisers. I must ask you to regard this as final.[203]

PHILIP GAME,

Governor

In reading Sir Philip's letters, a few more remarks must be made in parentheses to clarify the circumstances surrounding his final sacking of Lang. At the end of April the Full Court of the High Court began sitting in judgement upon the legality of the Federal legislation seizing the State revenue. While awaiting its decision seven King's Counsel sent a letter to Sir Philip, signed by them all, stating:

After discussion, the undersigned King's Counsel have come to the following conclusions and respectfully submit the same to His Excellency the Governor.

The Governor is entitled on action being taken by his Ministers in breach of the law of the land whether Federal or State (or where such action manifests the clear intent to frustrate such law, when such action interferes to a considerable degree with the carrying on of the King's Government) to take steps under the letters patent constituting his office to seek new advisers.

Any or all of the signatories hereto humbly express their readiness if it should seem good to His Excellency to discuss any matters bearing thereon.[204]

April 11th, 1932.

Chambers,

Signed,
A.B.Shand
R.Windeyer
G.E.Flannery
R.Clive Teece
H.E.Manning
F.A.A.Russell
A.V.Maxwell.

Sir Philip tersely declined the offer to consult with them. The High Court's decision confirmed the validity of the Federal legislation, and a second ruling, on the 22nd April, upheld the Lyons Government's seizure of the State's money deposited in bank accounts. By the 23rd April, when Sir Philip sent a telegram to the Secretary of State reporting on the events then unfolding, he had already been handed the NSW Auditor-General's opinion that the Audit Act of 1902 was being flouted, and had received the Chief Justice's opinion stating that in the absence of any other responsible advisor it was ultimately the Governor's task to decide upon the legality of the Circular of 12th April. Sir Philip had therefore met with Lang and demanded formal reassurance on the matter: as the telegram put it, he "told [Lang] that I wanted my doubts cleared up because if the Audit Act was disregarded I felt that if I remained inactive I would be in the position of condoning illegality. The Premier promised to send me the opinion of the Law Officers of the Crown…"[205] Meanwhile large sums of money were being hoarded and guarded in government offices in Sydney, with the New South Wales Railways being used to distribute the cash required for paying government servants.

The advice from the Law Officers never came. Lang eventually refused to provide any formal assurance that his Government was remaining within the law, despite the fact both Sir Philip and the Chief Justice felt his Government's instructions were violating federal law. On the 13th of May Lang was sacked and the Leader of the Opposition, Mr Stevens, was invited to Government House, where he was sworn in as Premier. Parliament was prorogued and then dissolved, and general elections held, which the Stevens caretaker government won, going on to form the Stevens-Bruxner coalition government.[206]

Although Evatt refused to condemn Sir Philip's conduct, it's clear from his assessment of both the Game-Lang affair and Todd's doctrine that he believed Sir Philip should have acquiesced to Lang and left the matter to the courts to decide.[207] But with the benefit of hindsight Evatt's general doctrine of royal or viceregal acquiescence, which relies instead on the courts to remedy illegality, has grave shortcomings.

The blanket statement that a Governor should allow "all legal questions which are at all susceptible of argument to await determination at the hands of the judicial power", if applied as a universal principle, creates a logical absurdity. Our system of law expects ordinary citizens witnessing a crime to take reasonable steps to aid prevention of the crime or eventually help apprehend the criminal. To this end all citizens possess the power of "citizen's arrest", whereby they can incarcerate a suspect if certain that police in the same predicament would do the same. Having a duty to help uphold the law, ordinary people — without taking any special oath or occupying any special office — are endowed with some powers to enable them to fulfil that duty. But Evatt's proposal suggests the Queen's representative, who has solemnly sworn a specific oath to defend the Constitution and the laws of the land, who represents a Queen who swore a similar oath at her Coronation and a Crown which since 1689 has held its power through a contract exchanging allegiance for this guardianship, who holds reserve powers over appointment and dismissal of Ministers, isn't to use them. We have a witness of illegality able to intervene but to be stripped of the duty to do so. Worse: Evatt's doctrine imposes a duty *not* to intervene. So ordinary citizens who haven't sworn an oath to defend the laws of the land are to exert themselves upholding those laws, but the one citizen who *has* promised to defend the laws is to be forbidden to do anything of the kind.

A valid way of appreciating the value of an institution is by observing what happens when that institution is lost or non-existent. The authors of *The Lawless State*, writing on behalf of the American Civil Liberties Union, weren't protesting about something rotten in the state of America for the sake of a good whinge but for the purpose of reform. A major obstacle to their endeavours in establishing a polity under the rule of law was (and still in 1999 remains) the Executive branch and its partisan self-interest: in the Intelligence community, for example,

> the only authority to whom a lower-echelon official with a troubled conscience can turn is the President's…Oversight Committee set up by…executive order. There are literally no provisions for taking information of wrongdoing outside the executive branch's system of self-interests. An official with knowledge of abuses is told to go through channels within the hierarchy that spawned those abuses, a process guaranteed to be ineffective.[208]

Within the highest council of *our* hierarchy is someone normally passive, whose interests are different from those of the elected politicians who wield the active power of government; someone to whom information of wrongdoing *can* be given by a "lower-echelon official with a troubled conscience", and who, in direst emergency, holds the reserve power to do something about it. Surely this is an inheritance we should be very reluctant to lose?

What legal argument is *not* "at all susceptible of argument"? For centuries questions of law have enjoyed a reputation for obscure complexity and the plausibility with which both thesis and antithesis can be argued. The courtrooms of the world are filled each day with reluctant lawyers advocating defences for people caught with a corpse, a smoking gun and the plea they Didn't Do It. It would be an inept lawyer who'd be incapable of putting any defence at all, so the obvious ploy for a guilty Executive is to "get closer to [its] attorney". If Tea Pot Dome, the scandals of the Truman era and Watergate offer any guide, it's that the Attorney-General of a government caught playing in the mud is likely to have got as dirty in the game as other members of the Cabinet. So what can we expect an Attorney-General to tell a Governor-General? Do we seriously expect the following conversation to take place:

G-G: Is this legal?

A-G: Ah…well no, actually. I was hoping you weren't going to ask that question. Damn…

Instead I regret to suggest that Attorneys-General may deal in pork pies, dine out on whoppers, exhibit ontological inexactitude, display a weakness for Little White Ones or a proclivity for Big Black Ones. In short, they may be untruthful.

"Unless the Governor is a specially trained lawyer" he may have difficulty ascertaining the illegality and implications of advice tendered him. But that doesn't imply he must be delivered entirely into the hands of his ministers. The very existence of reserve powers implies that, in times of dire crisis, Her Majesty's representative can consult informally beyond the circle of his responsible ministers.[†] Already there's a long list of Australian precedents for the Governor-General to consult with the Chief Justice, published[‡] in the years following 1975, although it would perhaps be better for distinguished lawyers to be consulted who are not members of the High Court. Merivale's objection, that these legal consultants may be politically biased against the ministers, could surely be better resolved by recruiting them from across the political spectrum rather than by abandoning them altogether. In the next chapter the idea of a judicial aristocracy shall be contemplated, a body of life-

---

† In Canada, Forsey argued this in the 1980s for Her Majesty's Realms throughout the Commonwealth (Forsey, "The Present Position of the Reserve Powers of the Crown", *Evatt and Forsey on the Reserve Powers*, pp.lxxvii-lxxx) and Sir Winston Churchill attested to it in the British House of Commons during World War II (see later). The necessity and history of the existing convention in Britain, the Queen's ability — through her Private Secretary — to obtain independent information from other political and legal figures beyond her Ministers has been argued in the context of commissioning minority governments by Professor Vernon Bogdanor (Bogdanor, *Multi-Party Politics and the Constitution*, pp.131–132) and Dr David Butler (Butler, *Governing Without a Majority*, pp.80–84).

‡ In this country alone, at least eight Governors-General and three Chief Justices have engaged in this practice, which has been approved by a number of other authorities. In reply to a challenge made by Senator Gareth Evans, D.J. Markwell (then of Trinity College, Oxford) cited three Chief Justices: Sir Samuel Griffith (1903–1919), Sir Owen Dixon (puisne judge 1929–1952, Chief Justice 1952–1964) and Sir Garfield Barwick (1964–1981). The seven Governors-General he cited were Lord Northcote (1904–1908), Lord Dudley (1908–1911), Lord Denman (1911–1914), Sir Ronald Munro Ferguson (1914–1920), Lord Casey (1965-1969), Sir Paul Hasluck (1969–1974) and Sir John Kerr (1974–1977). (D.J. Markwell, "On Advice from the Chief Justice", *Quadrant* July 1985, p.38, and *Quadrant*, October 1985, p.5.) Richard Lucy (Senior Lecturer in the school of Political Science, UNSW) subsequently added to this list the name of Governor-General De L'Isle, who "said he would have consulted the Chief Justice if no party had gained a majority in 1961" (*Quadrant*, September 1986, p.8). Other authorities who approved of this practice include Sir Edmund Barton (puisne judge 1903–1920), Sir Keith Aickin (1976–1982) and Sir Murray Tyrrell (Official Secretary to Yarralumla for twenty-seven years).

---

tenured judges whose expertise in the law is used as an excuse for granting them far-reaching legislative and executive authority, for which they have no particular competence or public accountability. A conspicuous irony of the republican debate is that the same people who favour the creation of such a body condemn the prospect of consultants to a Crown fenced about by responsible ministers, despite the fact that the latter offers far less scope for judges' personal political views to shine through their legal opinions.

Meanwhile, what's to become of servants of the Crown confronted with the unlawful orders derived from the Executive's unlawful agenda? Our system of government demands their disobedience, but surely we can only expect to impose this turmoil upon them provided we can promise them relief from the displeasure of their renegade superiors? Spare a thought for people like R.H. Beardsmore, an accountant in the Lands Department who, confronted with Lang's circular on the 11th May, refused to follow these orders which appeared clearly to conflict with the law and his duty to obey it. He was forced by Lang's Minister for Lands to go on leave immediately. (It's interesting to note that Sir Philip intervened the next day, demanding a copy of the offending circular, which prompted his subsequent letter of the 12th May.)[209] Given that public servants are put in this way of harm through being servants of the Crown, surely the Crown ultimately has the duty to protect them in their service to the rule of law? Then a Governor's refusal to intervene surely can only be justified provided the Crown's courts of law can provide adequate remedy against lawlessness. This is certainly where Evatt, as a Justice of the High Court, expected relief to come from, and when this relief is available he's right to have said that for a Governor to intervene over apparent illegality "may amount to an attempt to deprive the ordinary Courts of law of their exclusive responsibility for exercising the judicial power".[210] But in modern retrospect Evatt's faith in the courts' ability always to provide remedies appears excessive.

Despite his presence on the Bench — or perhaps because of it, in a country and era that never knew thorough executive lawlessness — Evatt's civilised mind seems to have failed to grasp the nature of the beast. One of the bizarre aspects of the Lang-Game crisis, for instance, was the covert civility with which it was conducted. In public Lang ranted against Sir Philip, claiming in 1931 that "[t]he Governor had torn the charter of democracy in two, and the people do not count",[211] and (in 1958) that Sir Philip had "loved power no less than Governor Bligh",[212] so that although he "made every effort to convince me that he was friendly, I was under no illusions. He hated my guts".[213] In private reality relations between the two men were generally cordial, to the extent that they exchanged gifts after the sacking and parted as friends: Game gave Lang a pipe and a book, who replied in a private note expressing appreciation of the gift and enjoyment of their past talks, and giving Sir Philip a book in return.[214] The crisis was not played by either protagonist with a hard ball: Sir Philip gave Lang ample warning of his misgivings, despite the risk the Premier might demand the Governor's recall by London; Lang never took this obvious step despite its tactical advantage. We as late-20th Century observers have an advantage over Evatt, in that we've witnessed in France the authority of the judiciary eroded by an Executive engaging in flagrant illegality and setting up kangaroo courts to sentence political rivals to death; in the United States, a lawless Executive whose servants have been able to engage in decades of outrageous behaviour, immune to the sanctions of law; in Italy, judges like Giovanni Falcone murdered by the same criminal organisation that permeates the government and the Parliament. By the modern standards of the Western world the Game-Lang affair appears mild-mannered and courteous.

In real life the courts may fail to cope with a government's sins in a number of ways. An offence may theoretically be dealt with by the courts and yet in reality never see the light of day for three reasons: knowledge, time and money. Civil servants executing an illicit plan devised by their political masters are often bound by — among other things — the *Official Secrets Act*, making exposure of scandals difficult. If this public exposure fails to occur within adequate time then the implications of an offence may have escalated beyond the hope of adequate redress. (One example is a hypothetical near-bankrupt State engaging in an illicit financial agenda with disastrous consequences. By the time knowledge of this agenda becomes public, allowing the matter to come before the courts, the economy may have collapsed entirely. Another is a government planning military overthrow of the Constitution. By the time the relevant unlawful activities from the prelude of the *coup* come before the courts, soldiers may be in the streets.) And once this exposure takes place, what private citizen or company has the resources — the money — to litigate against the Government? These obstacles are about getting a matter before the judiciary, but it's at this point that the real nastiness begins. The challenge to a government fearing exposure is to "use the available federal machinery to screw [its] political enemies" — use of "national security" concerns, for instance, to silence witnesses. Silence can be procured by other means. "You know that if the administration gets its back to the wall, it will have to take steps to defend itself". These measures can be applied, not only to witnesses, but to judges themselves: either Watergate-style blackmail or Falcone-style murder, achieved through misusing the instruments of State.

In contemplating the behaviour of individuals, we speak of their acts as being either lawful or unlawful. But in contemplating the unlawful acts of governments a new line must be drawn, between simple illegality and catastrophic illegality, the former being offences that may readily be remedied in a court of law and the latter, offences that threaten the continued functioning of the civilised State under the rule of law, that threaten the operation of the courts themselves and so cannot find secure remedy within those courts. We possess at the moment what other countries lack, and in its absence find danger: an apolitical figure — Her Majesty's viceregal representative — drawn from within our own community and seated at the top of the Executive hierarchy, under all normal circumstances quiescent, obeying the advice of elected politicians, but who in times of emergency has the capacity of stripping an apparently unlawful agenda of its catastrophic implications by stripping its architects of executive office. Why should we be in haste to throw this institution away?

In 1975 CIA Director William E. Colby was asked if he would refuse a presidential order to carry out an operation he regarded as improper. He replied by saying he had both the authority and the commitment to the US Senate to refuse.[215] This question and its answer provide a stark contrast to Her Majesty's Governments throughout the world, in which patently unlawful orders could never carry legitimate authority to the servants of the Crown, and so must be disobeyed — irrespective of seniority or a commitment to Parliament or to anything else. The Crown on the uniforms of its servants is a symbol of promise, warning and twofold sanctuary: the promise and warning over the nature of executive authority flowing through the hierarchy, a sanctuary to its servants confronted with unlawful orders...and through this, sanctuary to all citizens under the Government. The title "Her Majesty's Government" has changed greatly in its meaning since the 17th Century, but one of its implications, the most important, remains unaltered: the formal symbolic source of executive authority "cannot command ill or unlawful things. And whatever ill events succeed, the executioners of such designs must answer for them".

Niccolò's Ghost You seem to be rather obsessed with English-speaking countries, my boy. Although the United States is obviously defective, I've heard nothing yet about Europe. What about France, or Italy? And what of Ireland? Perhaps they furnish better role models for a republic...

3

▪ BEYOND OUR SHORES ▪

> Although the terrorism of the OAS and
> the FLN provided a reasonable and
> immediate excuse, his special courts
> bore an uncomfortable resemblance to
> the "People's" court of Nazi Germany
> and the infamous tribunals of the Vichy
> régime. To traditional Republicans it
> seems that only the existence of
> Parliament stood between the French
> people and absolute dictatorship.
>
> Aidan Crawley, *De Gaulle*. [On President
> De Gaulle's destruction of judicial
> independence in France in the 1960s]

―――――――――――▪■▪―――――――――――

Although Australia's recorded history is brief, yet within that brief span we have become one of the six oldest living democracies in the world. Only Britain, the United States of America, Canada, Switzerland and Sweden can look back upon longer periods of democratic government, uninterrupted by self-imposed dictatorship or foreign conquest and occupation. Of these six, three are under various forms of the Westminster system with Elizabeth II as their Queen, four are constitutional monarchies, and four are British in origin.

Perhaps more importantly, it cannot be assumed that a country with a republican *form* of government, an elected president instead of a monarch, is a country embodying what may be called the republican *ideal* of government, a polity which embodies government "...of the people, by the people, for the people". The French commentator Alexis de Tocqueville, writing in 1836, remarked:

> I am not about to compare Switzerland with the United
> States, but with Great Britain. When you examine the two
> countries, or even if you only pass through them, you
> perceive, in my judgement, the most astonishing differences
> between them. Take it all in all, England seems to be much
> more republican than the Helvetic [Swiss] Republic. The
> principal differences are found in the institutions of the two
> countries, and especially in their customs (*moeurs*). In almost
> all the Swiss Cantons liberty of the press is a very recent

thing. In almost all of them liberty is by no means completely guaranteed, and a man may be arrested administratively and detained in prison without much formality. The courts have not, generally speaking, a perfectly independent position. In all the Cantons trial by jury is unknown. In several Cantons the people were thirty-eight years ago entirely without political rights. Aargau, Thurgau, Vaud, and parts of the Cantons of Zurich and Berne were in this condition.[216]

He went on to describe how these observations, true of the institutions of the two countries, were even more noticeable in their customs.

In many of the Swiss Cantons the majority of citizens are quite without taste or desire for *self-government*, and have not acquired the habit of it. In any crisis they interest themselves about their affairs, but you never see in them the thirst for political rights and the craving to take part in public affairs which seem to torment Englishmen throughout their lives.[217]

Furthermore,

The Swiss seem still to look upon associations from much the same point of view as the French, that is to say, they consider them as a means of revolution, and not as a slow and sure method for obtaining redress of wrongs. The art of associating and making use of the right of association is but little understood in Switzerland.[218]

So a country wearing a republican *form* and a country possessing the republican *ideal* are two clear different things. Britain, with a constitutional monarchy, had succeeded in creating a society "much more republican than the Helvetic Republic", and one that more effectively upheld the civil liberties of its citizens.

This is less strange than it appears. In the continual struggle for power which is the hallmark of all human society, the constitution of a nation provides a yardstick whereby the legitimacy of an act may be measured. The burden of a nation's constitution is to protect the system of government its citizens deem most desirable, so that actions performed by politicians seeking to preserve their own political hides do not endanger the survival of that system. A democratic nation must prevent the government of the day from using its temporary mandate and authority, loaned to it by the people to govern during its term of office, to acquire or seize more permanent power and authority beyond the electorate's power to revoke. Parliament must be denied the ability to extend its own life without recourse to its electors; the Prime Minister and his friends must be subject to the same laws as any other citizen, without amnesties, exemptions or exceptions.

Accepting this, then the "system with most elected officials" need not be "the most democratic system". An elected president isn't *ipso facto* more democratic than an appointed governor-general or an anointed monarch. In a parliamentary democracy like our own, it is for the Head of Government, the Prime Minister, to be elected; the other figure's task is to ensure these axioms aren't violated. At the moment we're free citizens of a free and independent democracy; it works. What legitimate case has been brought for tampering with our safeguards? In the absence of any physical urgency advocates have claimed the presence of a "moral" imperative, a principle grossly misnamed. Precious little morality resides in their arguments for destroying communal emblems among countries. For "moral", read "nationalist".[†]

Opposing this "moral" imperative remain strong ethical considerations. As holders of the power to alter the Constitution, we may alter the balances of power and the delicate mechanisms of liberty in this country for ever, a heavy responsibility…and a heavy burden of proof upon republican shoulders. If by our actions we deliver future generations of Australians into a state of oppression, then we as individuals shall be more deserving of their lasting ridicule and contempt than will be the particular dictator who oppresses them. Despots, like rats, are opportunistic creatures, coming to flourish wherever and whenever the environment exists that allows them to prosper. As it lies within our power to create such an environment in this country, so is it our responsibility to prevent such circumstances from occurring. There is no imperative existent in this debate save the ethical one of responsibility for our actions or inaction; no treason, but treason against existing and future generations.

Despite their awe-inspiring contributions to human civilisation, all modern European countries have been at best ordinary, and at worst political failures, if success is to be measured by the preservation of stable parliamentary democracy.

Italy, for example, produced two thousand years ago one of the greatest experiments in large scale administration the world has ever seen. For all that, the modern republic of Italy has become legendary for its decades of political instability and corruption. When the Ciampi government was brought down by a no-confidence motion in January 1994, it was the fifty-second government to fall in the forty-nine years since the end of World War Two. By the end of the same year its successor had itself collapsed. A referendum was held in 1993 to dismantle the Italian system of parliamentary proportional representation, in a desperate attempt to inject stability into the republic.

The corruption attendant upon such instability is of epic proportions. By January 1994, one in every five deputies in the Italian parliament was under investigation for alleged corruption and Mafia links. The current so-called *dolce rivoluzione* (sweet revolution) in the Italian political system has been an attempt to establish order in a landscape of chaos, described by commentators as a "radical

---

† Here I follow the example of George Orwell, and distinguish between the concepts of "patriotism" and "nationalism"; see An "Australian Head of State".

process of political transition" that will "determine whether Italy will emerge as one of the strongest countries in the European Union, or be shunted aside by Brussels as a Latin American-style banana republic beset by Mafia crime." [219]

◙ ◈ ◙

The experiences of many of the republics of central Europe this century have been scarcely more edifying. Both Imperial Germany and the Austro-Hungarian Empire held elected parliaments, but these parliaments possessed little or no genuine power. To describe the monarchies of these countries as "constitutional" is impossible in our context. Parliamentary democracy was established in the ashes of World War I, following the abdication of Kaiser Wilhelm II of Germany and Emperor Charles I of Austria-Hungary and the dissolution of their empires into an assortment of independent sovereign states. The remnants of Germany and Austria were each declared republics, as were the newly-established countries of Poland and Czechoslovakia. By the late 1930s only Czechoslovakia remained a genuine democracy, all of the other republics having collapsed into self-imposed authoritarian government.

Germany had the Weimar Republic, established in August, 1919. On a super-ficial level the Weimar Constitution was an enlightened document. It attempted to guarantee civil liberties, many of which it explicitly encompassed in a declaration of rights: freedom of speech, travel, association and assembly being among them. It provided a republic in which both the *Reichstag* (the parliament) and the President were directly elected by universal suffrage. The President appointed and dismissed the Chancellor (the prime minister), who headed the government in the Reichstag. All government ministers were to be held responsible to the Reichstag. This Constitution, which would seem upon reading to protect and uphold parliamentary democracy, instead possessed within itself the instruments by which the liberty of German citizens would be crushed, and allow Adolf Hitler to plant the eagle-and-swastika standard of the Third Reich in Berlin.

In having a Chancellor and a President both directly elected, and hence polit-ically partisan, it provided ample reason for friction between the occupants of the two posts, and tacitly encouraged an atmosphere of political intrigue. Most dangerous was Article 48 of the Constitution, which placed enormous resources and power at the disposal of the President for the restoration of "public order and safety" in the advent of an emergency. There is nothing wrong in the existence of reserve powers; later chapters will argue their neces-sity in curbing the ambitions of a recalcitrant government. Yet in trying to define the extremity of scope of such powers, and in placing such powers in the lap of a politician, the authors of the Weimar Constitution had created a Holy Grail, an ultimate prize that could be seized in the quest for political supremacy in Germany.

The situation was exacerbated by the facts: that the elderly President von Hindenberg did indeed engage in partisan intrigues involving his Chancellors, that a number of unstable governments succeeded one another in Berlin, and that the German economy was disastrously crippled with the combination of war debt and the onset of the Great Depression. When the German coalition government broke up in March 1930, Hindenberg appointed Heinrich Brüning of the Catholic Centre party as Chancellor. Denied a parliamentary majority in the Reichstag following the 1930 general elections, Brüning governed by presidential decree under Article 48, under circumstances which came to resemble a presidential dictatorship. The parties in the Reichstag were too divided to override the decrees. Such parties included not only the Catholic Centre party and the Social Democrats, but also the Communist Party with seventy-seven seats and Hitler's National Socialists with one hundred and seven seats.

To a backdrop of increasingly strident nationalism, Brüning struggled to remain in control, but ultimately failed and was dismissed by Hindenberg. He was replaced by the right-wing Franz von Papen, a personal confident of the President's, who was sworn in as Chancellor in June 1932. This dismissal took place despite the fact that Brüning still enjoyed the confidence of the Reichstag, which was subsequently dissolved by Hindenberg, who claimed that it "no longer represented the will of the German people".[220]

Hindenberg himself had been re-elected as President two months previously, in April 1932. In the face of the parliamentary paralysis among the parties in the Reichstag, Hindenberg and his circle of advisors had become the effective government of Germany. Elections in July gave Papen's coalition government enough seats in the Reichstag to govern, provided they retained the tacit support of the largest single parliamentary party, the Nazi Party. Hitler demanded to be made Chancellor, but Hindenberg refused, preferring Papen.

November elections reduced the Nazi party's seats, and increased those of the Communists. Papen resigned in December, to be replaced by Kurt von Schleicher. Hindenberg's clique trusted Schleicher even less than they trusted Hitler, so Papen intrigued with Hindenberg to make Hitler a puppet Chancellor, with Papen holding the strings as vice-Chancellor. On the 30th of January 1933, Adolf Hitler became Chancellor of Germany. In this way the democratic republic found itself with a thoroughly evil man as Chancellor, who held an elected parliamentary government (although not a majority government) and had become Chancellor by constitutionally legal means.

On the 27th of February 1933, the Reichstag building in Berlin burnt down, and a mentally ill Dutch communist was blamed as the arsonist. Hitler claimed the existence of an immediate Communist threat against the government, issued an Emergency Decree under Article 48, and proceeded to have alleged Communists arrested. In early March another Reichstag general election was held, in an atmosphere of anti-Communist fear and Nazi propaganda. Although the Nazi party only acquired 43.9 percent of the votes, Hitler managed to persuade the new Reichstag to pass an Enabling Act on the 23rd of March 1933. This Act allowed Hitler to rule by decree, removing all effective political restraints for four years. The puppet had cut his strings, and remained standing. Hindenberg's death in August 1934 removed a symbolic inconvenience, and Hitler inherited his powers. The Third Reich had begun.[221]

The Weimar Constitution was never formally repealed or amended. Such alterations were unnecessary. That "enlightened document" was simply superseded by the February 1933 Emergency Decree and the March 1933 Enabling Act. To establish the foundations of dictatorship in a parliamentary democracy does not require the storming of Parliament, the shooting of the judiciary or acts of collective madness. All it requires is a crippled economy, a disillusioned populace willing to accept nationalism as an opiate, and a badly-written Constitution. All else can follow at leisure.

◙　◈　◙

Republicanism's bravest phrase is in the centuries-old cry of the revolutionaries, *liberté, égalité, fraternité*. Yet one doesn't need to return to the grim days of the Terror to find disillusionment in the history of France. Simply looking at the last days of the Fourth Republic, its collapse in 1958 and the reigns of Presidents de Gaulle and Pompidou in the current Fifth Republic are enough to give warning.

> For almost two centuries the French experiences with government have been relevant to students of the Westminster system, for during that period the example of Westminster has been strongly influential upon constitutional authors in Paris.
> [T]he two constitutional monarchies (1815–48), the third republic (1870–1940) and the fourth republic (1946–58) sought to import and adapt the British model as the French misunderstood it. The constitutional monarchies, in particular, did not learn the lesson of the failure of George III's attempt to govern personally and thought the British practice involved an active, politically implicated head of state; while the conspicuous absence of the religious, economic, social and political solidarity that allowed Britain to achieve the simplicity of a two-party system led to unstable republican government, the third republic having reduced the president to the role of master of constitutional ceremonies.[222]

The days to which we now look are the dying ones of the Fourth Republic, a republic which had

> curtailed the power of the second chamber and increased the importance of the prime minister and of the political parties, to come into line with the twentieth-century British model. However, the reversion to government by assembly and weak coalition that disintegrated when faced with each controversial problem left the régime vulnerable.[223]

In 1956 the Fourth Republic was wrestling with the question of Algerian independence. Algeria had been under French rule since 1830, longer than any other French North African possession. Algerian and French communities had become interwoven both in North Africa and Metropolitan France; of almost nine million inhabitants in Algeria more than one million were European, half of these French. They weren't just the wealthy planters and landowners but shopkeepers, artisans, civil servants and labourers, with generations of family ties in both North Africa and Europe. Similarly, hundreds of thousands of Algerian Arabs had settled in France, living and working there. In the view of many citizens Algeria, unlike Tunisia, Morocco or Indo-China, was part of France itself.

This opinion was particularly strong in the French armed forces, professional and conscript alike, fighting in Algeria against the separatist FLN (*Front de Libération Nationale*) independence movement. Almost the entire French army's fighting strength of four hundred thousand soldiers (half of them conscripts) was now deployed against the FLN, many of the professionals among them embittered by the French defeat at Dien Bien Phu in Vietnam and determined not to repeat the experience. The recently elected Socialist Prime Minister of France, Guy Mollet, found himself inextricably bogged down in the problem, with terrorist attacks and murders now taking place in Metropolitan France itself.

Disaffection and discontent permeated not only the armed forces but the police force, the civil service and cabinet ministers. The Minister of Defence and the Minister of the Interior intrigued against the Prime Minister, arresting a delegate of the FLN whom Mollet had invited to Paris for talks. Civil servants concealed information from ministers, while ministers intrigued and concealed the actions of subordinates from the scrutiny of Cabinet colleagues. Journalists and writers protesting against the torture of Algerian dissidents were themselves arrested without trial while the torturers went unpunished. Newspapers were confiscated under emergency powers, public meetings banned, and the now openly partisan police marched in Paris in protest against the very Assembly and government they were supposed to be obeying. Mollet's government fell in May 1957. So too did the next government, led by his former Defence Minister Bourès-Maunoury, which resigned in September. For five weeks France was without a government, and teetering on the brink of anarchy.[224]

During that winter groups right across the French political spectrum realised the republic was about to collapse, and wondered how to turn that event to their advantage, plotting outright revolution. Conservatives, Poujadists and leaders of Old Comrades Associations were all making their plans for such an event, while the Communists hoarded caches of weapons and ammunition, planning armed insurrection. Marshal Juin and General Koenig were "not unsympathetic" to establishing some form of military government in Paris, while the hardline right-wing settlers in Algeria, the *Ultras*, were envisaging the establishment of an autonomous white republic in the provinces of Oran and Algiers.

Two groups in particular were to play a significant role in the months to come. Senior army officers in Algeria and Metropolitan France planned a military *coup* in Paris, a military conspiracy codenamed "Operation Resurrection". On the 10th of May 1958 the French army entered the arena as an independent political force, led by its Commander-in-Chief in Algeria, General Salan. A telegram was sent to General Ely, Chief of the General Staff, to be passed on to the President of the Republic, René Coty, warning of the army's "reaction of despair" if Algeria were to be abandoned — a thinly-veiled ultimatum. It was signed by Generals Salan, Allard, Massu, and Jouhaud.

Operation Resurrection was already organised. To be led by General Miguel of the South-Western Command headquarters in Toulouse, and involving most of the Metropolitan army and air force, it had the open support of four of the nine Regional Commanders in France and secret support from most of the others, including Ely's own aide-de-camp General Beaufort, who was to lead the *coup* in Paris. The opening phase was activated on the morning of 13th May. General Petit of the Air Force sent air transport to Algiers for the embarkation of paratroopers under the command of General Massu. Petit's orders were confirmed by the Air Force Commander-in-Chief.[225]

At the same time members of another group based in Algeria were making their own preparations. The Committee of Vigilance, a group of collaborators including wealthy landowners, fascists, Poujadists, the students and schoolboy's unions, and the Ex-Serviceman's Associations, had as its objective the formation of a government in Paris committed to *Algérie Française*, or if that failed, outright independence of Algeria as a French colonial-style State. Organising an all-out revolt in Algiers and Paris, they declared a general strike in the first of the two cities, and mass demonstrations in the second. On the day of the general strike a touch of unintended humour tinged the tension. Several hundred schoolboys stormed the entrance of the Government-General Building in Algiers, there to be confronted by riot police and tear gas. Serious brawling broke out, aggravated by the arrival of senior students who waded in on the side of the schoolboys. The police cleared the forum by charging, then were ordered to withdraw at the arrival of paratroopers. Far from maintaining the peace, these soldiers offered to lend the students a truck to help them break down the building's gates. The police finally retreated and the building was sacked, its library burned, although the soldiers prevented access to the secret files stored in the building. In the looting one student absconded with the bust of Marianne, emblem of the Republic, at which a paratroop officer remarked "No casualties fortunately, except the Republic and that's not serious". Algiers was now in a revolt controlled by the Committee, a member of which now rewarded the schoolboys for their part in the riot. Summer examinations were cancelled that year.[226]

On the 17th of May four separate military missions flew from Algiers to France as the final phase of Operation Resurrection prior to the *coup* itself, planned to take place in Paris two days later. At this stage General Charles de Gaulle intervened. A cult figure among the Free French from World War II, he persuaded the ringleaders of Resurrection to suspend the final blow. Despite this a demonstration of the immediate danger was provided on the French

Mediterranean island of Corsica where, on the 25th May, the Corsican military garrison and police (including 120 riot police flown in from Nice) overthrew the civilian administration. When the civilian government in Paris ordered the recapture of the island, the French navy refused to obey. Under no illusions about the reality of impending overthrow and bloody civil war, President Coty requested de Gaulle form an emergency government in Paris. By now enjoying the support of General Salan — support engineered by Léon Delbecque of the Committee of Vigilance — de Gaulle dictated terms, which included not only emergency powers but a complete constitutional re-write. Coty had no choice but agree or see France lapse into war. The Fourth Republic had fallen.[227]

In the writing of the Constitution of the Fifth Republic which now took place, the Westminster system proved once again influential. In its drafting de Gaulle employed two men,

> Michel Debré, Keeper of the Seals and, therefore, chief draftsman, and Jacques Soustelle, Minister of Information, whose duty it was to sell the Constitution to the nation. Both were brilliant men whose sustained and contemptuous attacks had steadily undermined the authority of the Fourth Republic. Debré, an admirer of the British parliamentary system, genuinely desired to create a Republic in which a government could be strong while remaining democratic; Soustelle, caring less for the form, saw the Constitution as a means of building a multi-racial state and uniting fifty million Frenchmen.[228]

This constitution, although drawing heavily upon Westminster, had a few idiosyncratic twists. Before observing the differences, consider first the similarities.

The republic was to be a parliamentary democracy, with a Prime Minister and a President. The President was endowed with reserve powers analogous to those of the Crown, except that he didn't require some alternative ministry to take responsibility for his actions if he defied the incumbent Prime Minister.[229] These reserve powers included the appointment and dismissal of the Prime Minister; the right (under certain restrictions) to dissolve the legislative assembly, and the right when confronted by the imminent collapse of society itself (through, say, civil war or invasion) to assume emergency powers for the preservation of the State (Article 16; analogous to the ultimate reserve power of the Crown made famous in the 1983 Grenada crisis).

The President also was given traditional Westminster-style powers supposedly to be exercised under the advice of the incumbent Prime Minister, including:

❖ The appointment and dismissal of other ministers;

❖ The chairing of the council of ministers;

❖ The promulgating of statutes, and the signing of ordinances and decrees, including the right to refuse or delay signing provided ministers were willing to assume responsibility for this;

- ❖ Appointment of officials to senior judicial, military and administrative posts;
- ❖ The position of "protector of the independence of the judicial authority";
- ❖ The position of commander-in-chief of the armed forces.[230]

Some deviations from the modern Westminster model were also incorporated to try to correct perceived weaknesses of the Fourth Republic, the most obvious being that although the Prime Minister had to enjoy the confidence of the assembly, and all ministers were to be held responsible to the assembly "in accordance with British parliamentarianism",[231] no minister was permitted to belong to that assembly. The President was to retain policy control over foreign, defence and postcolonial affairs as part of being the ultimate guardian of France's integrity.[232] Yet France's constitution was written close enough to a "minimalist" Westminster republic for an observer to be startled at the abuses of power that now followed.

Transgressions in three fields of presidential power are of particular interest . One is the use of the reserve powers to protect the Constitution. These powers were abused in the Fifth Republic, in the partisan appointment and dismissal of ministers and dissolution of Parliament, leading further to gross abuses of the Constitution. Another is protection of the independence of the judiciary: in the Fifth Republic, so abused in the establishment of special courts under specially nominated judges to try political crimes against the State, that "constitutional" government became meaningless. The third is the position of commander-in-chief of the armed forces: although originally a formal post to be exercised under the advice of responsible ministers, it was transformed into an astoundingly powerful office, the occupant of which came to wield solitary prerogative right of launching France's strategic nuclear arsenal, without consultation.

Soon after Charles de Gaulle became President it became clear he intended to extend his presidential powers at the expense of Parliament. Where the written Constitution denied him power it was to be ignored — as he imperiously put it, events were more important than constitutional texts, of which France had possessed no fewer than seventeen in one hundred and fifty years.[233] When farmers, angered at farming prices, petitioned for a recall of Parliament and gathered enough signatures to satisfy the Constitution, he simply refused to sign the necessary decree. When Mali and Madagascar demanded full independence he realised their requests had to be satisfied swiftly for French influence to be retained. As, in his opinion, the constitutional procedure was unsatisfactory on this matter he proposed amendments, ignoring the protests of Legalists and Fourth Republicans that he was now violating his own constitution. Exploiting public disaffection with the war in Algeria he imposed an unconstitutional referendum on Algerian independence in April 1962, winning it and giving independence to that troubled Department of France (also illegally).

When his loyal Prime Minister Debré requested an immediate general election after this referendum, to ride on the back of its goodwill, de Gaulle decided such an election would be inconvenient to his agenda. He therefore sacked

Debré secretly, replacing him with Georges Pompidou, a man inexperienced in political office. When the change became publicly known,

> every parliamentarian at once recognised that, though Pompidou might bear the title of Prime Minister he, like Couve de Murville at the Foreign Office, would be little more than a disc recording his master's voice.[234]

On a later occasion, when for the first time Pompidou's government was defeated on the floor of the Assembly, his resignation was offered to de Gaulle, whose reply was to dissolve Parliament rather than accept it.[235]

An obvious question is to inquire why the people of France tolerated this behaviour. One answer lies in de Gaulle's control over information. At the beginning of his reign his Minister of Information, Jacques Soustelle, exercised control over radio and television broadcasts. Purging his civil service staff of all politically uncooperative members, Soustelle engaged in propaganda not only transmitted through the media, but through information distributed to the public by government departments, newsreels displayed in cinemas, posters (both government and approved "private" ones) pasted up in public places, and the propagation of material to "fringe" radio stations through the *Centre de Diffusion Française* (a body compared by a British historian with the British Council).[236] Another answer rested in the Algerian war. As Guy Mollet remarked, although eighty per cent of the population might be against de Gaulle on most things, eight-five percent were with him over Algeria.[237] A third answer also came as a consequence of Algeria: repeated assassination attempts against the President, including a bomb explosion in front of his car at Pont-sur-Seine. To replace de Gaulle one needed a rival candidate, and with both FLN and the ultra-right wing OAS (*Organisation Armée Secrète*) employing terrorism as a means of persuasion, few were willing to step forward.

Niccolò's ghost   But what of the judiciary? Where were they when de Gaulle was acting illegally?

Author   As you of all people should concede, the judiciary is vulnerable to the same brutal logic that led Josef Stalin to inquire of the Pope how many divisions of troops he had. It's quite irrelevant what judges call legal or illegal when you have the army on your side, and de Gaulle was entirely ruthless whenever he suspected it was not on his.

Already the independence of the judiciary had been destroyed when de Gaulle had set up special courts, under judges he selected, to try people for political crimes against the State.

Although the terrorism of the OAS and the FLN provided a reasonable and immediate excuse, his special courts bore an uncomfortable resemblance to the "People's" court of Nazi Germany and the infamous tribunals of the Vichy régime. To traditional Republicans it seems that only the existence of Parliament stood between the French people and absolute dictatorship.[238]

When in May 1962 one of his own special courts refused to condemn General Salan to death — a man who, like many of the other generals who had originally backed de Gaulle, now felt he had been betrayed by the President and so was vehemently opposed to him — de Gaulle dissolved the court and established instead a military tribunal, composed of six officers and six NCOs, for the purpose of sitting in judgement upon people accused of crimes against the State. The president of this tribunal was to be General de Larminat, one of de Gaulle's oldest supporters and, like him, a Free French hero. Confronted by this impossible predicament, de Larminat resorted to what he apparently regarded as the only honourable way of refusing the office. He committed suicide.[239]

Following de Larminat's death a less extreme form of tribunal was established which continued to operate until 1981, when it was abolished by François Mitterand.[240]

A second kind of judicial suicide was to follow. Presented with de Gaulle's proposed referendum amendments to the Constitution — amendments that even one of his own Cabinet ministers, Pierre Sudreau, found impossible to swallow, pleading instead with de Gaulle not to become a symbol of illegality — the Constitutional Council, a judicial body empowered under the Constitution to declare proposed legislation *ultra vires*, refused to confront the President. The Council of State (another body through whose hands the legislation had had to pass) had already declared these amendments unconstitutional, despite lacking the power to impose this verdict upon the government, yet the Constitutional Council evaded confrontation by claiming that although it had power to strike down parliamentary legislation, the Constitution was silent on laws passed by referendum. In the reproachful words of Gaston Mannerville, President of the Senate, the Council had committed suicide through its cowardice.[241]

A vivid symbol of the presidential seizure of power in France was the transformation of the formal post of Commander-in-Chief to something other. In 1964, when the first Mirage IV strategic nuclear bomber became operational, de Gaulle passed a decree, ostensibly based upon being Commander-in-Chief, giving himself solitary power over nuclear launch.[242]

After Charles de Gaulle resigned from the presidency following the 1968 Paris riots and the rejection of his 1969 referendum, he was succeeded by Georges Pompidou. As one foreign analyst was later to remark bitterly,

> Before Pompidou succeeded de Gaulle as president of the republic, anyone who had predicted that the new president would not merely maintain but accentuate the subordination of the prime minister to him would have been regarded as indulging in eccentric humour.[243]

Yet only six months after becoming President, Pompidou declared "I have conducted the affairs of France with the help of the prime minister and government I appointed. My first decision was to devalue".[244] Not words to be spoken in a parliamentary democracy, but uttered in the strange hybrid the Fifth Republic had become.

In 1969 *Le Figaro* published the results of a public poll on the role of Parliament. The good news was that Parliament as an institution had become more popular over the last eleven years. The disturbing news was the parliamentary role now deemed most important: not to "represent constituency interests in Paris" or "make government accountable", but to "protect liberty".[245]

A foreign political analyst awarded a scholarship by a Fourth Republic government re-assessed the French political landscape in 1973, when he dismissed its historically numerous written constitutions as "periodical literature", describing its current constitution as:

> merely a treaty provisionally settling the allocation of power to suit the victors in a political struggle. The constitution is only a partisan procedural device setting out the formal conditions according to which the government is entitled to rule. It is not endowed with the sacredness or permanence attributable to a constitution that symbolizes fundamental agreement about political values as well as about political procedures. In France, there is no clear separation between the prevailing institutional arrangements and the supporters of the government currently in power. Each régime is fragile because its legitimacy is always open to question and its duration depends on the hegemony of the political forces that established it.[246]

Do we really want to walk the path to the Elysée Palace?

◙ ◈ ◙

Another republic influential in this debate, both in Australia and the British Isles, is the Republic of Ireland. The Turnbull Committee commissioned a report on the Irish presidency through the Australian Embassy in Dublin in May 1993, to be delivered in July the same year to the Committee in Canberra. The consequent highly detailed report, written by an Irish scholar expert on the Irish office of President, proved less than flattering. He wrote:

The Presidency of Ireland has not been a highly successful office...As this study will show, de Valera created a poorly defined presidential office which for most of its existence has existed in a form of limbo, ignored by successive Irish governments and the media. Even past Presidents have admitted to finding the office as conceived difficult to manage and frustrating. Indeed one leading political scientist went so far as to describe the job as created "inherently unsatisfactory", a description which, with some reservations, I came to agree with when studying the office for a political science thesis in 1990.[247]

The report revealed serious shortcomings in the Constitution of the Irish republic (*Bunreacht na hÉireann*). Control over nomination of presidential candidates rests entirely in the hands of senior politicians:

Since 1938, seventeen candidates have been nominated for the presidency. All were nominated either by Oireachtas [the Parliament] members or, if incumbent Presidents, by themselves. It is hardly surprising that to date no one has ever been nominated through the local authorities, given the extent to which the national parties dominate local government in Ireland. On at least four occasions, independents have tried and failed to secure the required four local authority nominations.[248]

Furthermore,

[w]ithin the Oireachtas, the selection of candidates has been further centralised, with the strength of the party system and leadership loyalty within parties ensuring that it was the leaders, not the backbenchers, who chose the candidates. Only on one occasion have backbenchers forced a candidate on an unwilling party leadership.[249]

Not surprisingly, then, "Every candidate nominated since 1938 could be said to belong to the political elite, in so far as each had previously either sought election or been appointed to the Oireachtas."[250] Moreover,

presidential elections only take place when it is thought to be in the interest of the politicians to hold one. In 1938, 1952, 1974, 1976 and 1983, it was thought unnecessary, with the result that one candidate, often the incumbent President, was put in office without having a single vote cast in his favour in a public ballot.[251]

This presidency, described as merely "an appendage to the nationalist power-structure"[252] not only has failed as a constitutional check upon the actions of the government, but has failed even to serve as a potent unifying symbol, as the *elu* or spirit of the nation.[253] Consequently the report from Dublin suggested we retain our "Nominal Chief Executive" system (currently embodied by the Governor-General), and strongly urged that, should Australia decide to become a republic, it avoid Irish precedents.[254] If to be an Irish republican is to embrace the *Bunreacht na hÉireann*, then such republicanism in Australia and Northern Ireland is profoundly flawed.

Casting a summary eye over the republics of Western Europe, the very best of them have merely emulated our success with parliamentary democracy, while none have surpassed us. Nor, with the notable exception of Switzerland,† have any European democratic republics even approached the vintage of representative government in Australia: the current span of democratic government in Germany (counting West Germany and re-unified Germany as one) is less than half that of the Commonwealth of Australia, and only one-third as old as elective responsible government upon Australian soil (dating the latter from the 1855 enactment of the New South Wales and Victorian Constitution Statutes,[255] themselves inspired by existing Canadian legislation.[256]) If age is an indication of success, then we need not look to contemporary republican Europe for any tuition upon the art of government.

⬚ ◈ ⬚

Unlike Western Europe, in this region of the world democratic government even as an abstract concept is by no means universally admired. The number of functioning democratic constitutions that have survived even twenty years can be numbered on the fingers of one hand. The political systems of Japan, India and Malaysia have all been influenced in the past by the Westminster model; the decay of Malaysian democracy into Mahathir's autocracy appears to have followed the decay of the King's authority, while India's 1975 encounter with near-dictatorship under Indira Gandhi reveals the danger of entrusting reserve power to a politician as President. The constitutional monarchy of Japan, however, retains a stable parliamentary democracy.

But what of other Asian republics? The morning newspaper at my elbow tells its own story, a story anyone who's been reading newspapers over breakfast for the last ten years ought already know. In the republic of South Korea two of its former presidents, Chun Doo-Hwan and Roh Tae-Woo, have been imprisoned for treason and mutiny, based on their roles in a 1979 military *coup* and the subsequent Kwangju massacre of 1980. They also faced separate trials on bribery charges.[257] During his first months in office in 1993 the incumbent president, Kim Young-Sam, purged the armed forces of a dozen senior generals: " 'There is no possibility at all of a *coup*', he said, 'I have purged all the officers interested in politics. I have complete control over the army.' "[258]

---

† Given Switzerland's appalling record regarding female suffrage, one could argue that even they have had less experience with fully representative government.

At the moment I was writing these words in a manuscript draft, Taiwan was engaging in its brave new experiment in democracy, while the People's Republic of China performed war games nearby in the Taiwan Strait as intimidation for the upcoming Taiwanese presidential election, the island's first ever.[259] Mainland China's own views on democracy and civil liberties have been made patently clear by its atrocities in Tibet and the massacre of pro-democracy protesters in Tienanmen Square in 1989. The People's Republic leaves precious little freedom for its people.

Indonesia, a country in which the army is heavily politicised, remained effectively a one-Party state under Suharto's regime. Indeed, in 1993 he went so far as to exhort the younger generation in the armed forces to play a more active role in the domestic political life of the country — *as* members of the military.[260] Opponents of the government found themselves confronted by the guns of the soldiers, as the protesters in the cemetery at Dili realised. Whether the country under Habibie will ever approximate a democracy in its tolerance of divergent opinion remains to be seen.

In the Philippines no-one has forgotten the dictatorship of Ferdinand Marcos, while in Bangladesh a senior member of the Opposition recently warned the Government of the risk of civil war,[261] arousing bitter memories of the numerous attempted or actual *coups* which have plagued that country since its creation in 1971.[262] Far less dramatic but nonetheless disturbing, in Singapore the People's Action Party has been in power continuously since 1959, and has come under repeated criticism for its authoritarian government. Singaporean Opposition politicians have repeatedly complained of State persecution and oppression.[263]

Stalinist North Korea remains isolated, a relic of the Cold War, while Vietnam and Laos remain under Communist-era regimes. Burma, or Myanmar as its dictators sometimes like it to be called, suffers under the brutal oppression of a military *junta*. It has been enduring military dictatorship since 1962, despite UN denunciation of abuses including the arrest of political opponents, torture, slave labour, systematic gang rapes of women and girls by soldiers, mass murder, and forced relocation and internal displacement on a large scale.[264]

As Nobel-prize winning dissident Aung San Suu Kyi has remarked, totalitarian governments within Asia reject democracy and human rights by arguing they are Western concepts opposed to national culture.[265] Doubtless eating scrambled eggs on toast in the morning tends to distract one's attention away from the message on the printed page, but it returns again now in the form of a question: precisely *who* are we trying to impress here with our hypothetical republic?

The history of the 20th Century has been dominated by the struggle against dictatorships of the Left and Right, and for the majority of the century totalitarianism has been the triumphant protagonist, losing wars but winning the peaces. Now in the final closing years we are fortunate witnesses of the blooming of democracies in the fertile soil of former killing fields. Joy in their blossoming should neither distract us from the probability of their eventual extinction nor delude us that we are witnessing the dawn of some enlightened era, what some might actually name an Age of Aquarius, benign New World Order, or (God help us) the End of History, a millennial Era-of-Peace-and-Prosperity summoned into being by the mercantile interests of the global *bourgeoisie*. The world has seen such blooms before, in the postwar ashes of World War I, when the brave new democracies sprung up throughout central and eastern Europe. With the proud exception of Czechoslovakia, all of these withered from internal diseases, decayed into dictatorships, and the poisons of their rotting blackened the gardens of all Europe. The brave Cold War flowers of Budapest and the Prague Spring were trampled before their time, teaching a moral recently repeated in Tienanmen Square: that unarmed noble sentiments are no protection against bayonets and overwhelming violence. Unless the diseases which poison democracy are understood and inoculated against, we may read our future in the annals of the past.

The most striking thing about watching film of Soviet soldiers marching in goose-step before the Kremlin isn't a sense of anachronism between the grim mediaeval citadel and the modern soldiers, but quite the opposite, a sense that they are appropriate, that they go together. The totalitarian regimes of Left and Right that have defiled human history this century have possessed primitive natures — primitive because despotism itself is intrinsically primitive, being founded upon the right to rule through violent strength, no matter how the iron fist is disguised or excused by the ideological velvet glove. Hitler and Mussolini both were aware of the archaic air of their regimes. Hitler went so far as to exploit it by reviving Teutonic rituals and incorporating archaic elements into the panoply of Nazism, such as the eagle standards of the Reich and the sixteenth-century Swiss daggers worn by the SS and SA. The Fascists also seemed keen on resuscitating ancient emblems and rituals: after all, the word "fascist" itself comes from the ancient Roman *fasces*, the bundle of rods with the axe in the middle which was an ancient ensign of authority revived by these modern extremists. Both *Der Fuehrer* and *Il Duce* enjoyed the trappings of despotic monarchs, yet with all these archaisms adorning primitive-hearted and bestial ideologies can we seriously describe Nazism or Fascism as "horse and buggy obsolete"? With the recent resurgence of neo-Nazism throughout central Europe, and the re-emergence of Fascist politicians in Italy, this question is more than merely academic for Europeans confronted by their return. If we cannot describe even brutal and primitive regimes as obsolete, how can we be so free in using the term to ridicule successful democracies?

❂ ◈ ❂

Niccolò's ghost So you refuse to defer in this matter to any republic in the world. Indeed you mock the republicans for themselves "tugging the forelock" to countries whose constitutional successes are merely pale imitations of your country's own. But couldn't they in turn accuse you of being too deferential to the driftwood of history, relics of a bygone era that have survived to the modern world through accident rather than design? I seem to remember a famous writer has made that suggestion already…

[*Author looks up at him, scowls, and returns to writing.*]

4

■ BAGEHOT REVISITED ■

> To state the matter shortly, the sovereign
> has, under a constitutional monarchy such
> as ours, three rights – the right to be
> consulted, the right to encourage, the
> right to warn.[266]
>
> Walter Bagehot, *The English Constitution*

■■■

In October 1994 the British edition of the international journal *The Economist* carried a front cover photograph of the Crown, with the caption "An idea whose time has passed". Inside, the editorial asked,

> Is Prince Charles a suitable future monarch? That is the question on millions of lips, and not only those of republicans or the editors of salacious newspapers.
>
> Yet it is also the wrong question. The right questions, though few dare to pose them in serious company, are the ones Bagehot would have asked: whether a monarchy is any longer a suitable part of Britain's constitutional arrangements, and whether those arrangements remain collectively suitable for this modern democracy. The answers, in *The Economist's* view, are that the monarchy's time has passed; that the only powerful argument against abolition is that it is not worth the trouble; and that there is an even stronger case for reforming other parts of the constitution, which anyway cannot be done without addressing, and hence altering, the monarch's role.[267]

Who was Walter Bagehot? This same editorial described him as "the finest and most influential writer ever to have been editor of *The Economist*, when in 1865–67 he defined — some would even say created — the constitutional role of the modern British monarchy."[268]

The work so grandly alluded to is Bagehot's famous book, *The English Constitution*. It is, of course, utter humbug to suggest he or any other writer of the 1860s† "created" the constitutional role of the monarchy. It is even false to suggest that he "defined" it; the best that can be said about his study is that he "described" the Crown as he saw it, and many subsequent writers heeded his description.

But how well did he describe it? Ask questions about Westminster conventions of a lawyer in a hurry to get to lunch and he or she will tell you to "go read Bagehot". He is regarded as an authority — by some as *the* authority on the subject. If you follow the advice, and read his work in isolation, you may even believe it, depending upon how cynical you feel. Read other, more recent authorities, however, and those same propositions begin to come unstuck.

Some of his propositions are undoubtedly accurate. The extract quoted at the beginning of this article is regarded as a good description of three constitutional rights that are held to exist, and are desirable. At the time he was writing, the Crown's rights of consultation and private reply already existed‡, but his description of those rights is often used to encompass the interaction between the Crown and its ministers in their working relationship.[269] Yet in the words of Sir Ivor Jennings,

> Most writers have been led astray on the subject of the monarchy, for instance, by Bagehot's exposition. The material now available makes it evident that Bagehot's analysis was in many respects faulty.[270]

D.J. Markwell, a former Fellow and Tutor in Politics at Merton College, Oxford, notes of the extended passage from which that extract is taken:

> ...Bagehot was writing about what *ought* to be the case in his view, not what was or is the case. He was stating neither the law nor the practice of his day. Sir David Lindsay Keir has shown that 'a study of Queen Victoria's interpretation of the constitutional function of the monarchy suggests that Bagehot's analysis was at the time inaccurate'.[271]

In other respects Bagehot's analysis is more than faulty — it is profoundly flawed — and it is upon his misconceptions, explicitly stated, as in *The Economist*, or implicitly followed, as in the tabloid press, that present republican sentiment in Britain is standing.

The flaws that pervade his work are of two forms. The first is his misunderstanding and disregard of the existence and nature of the Crown's reserve powers. Neither did he know of any authorities whom he could consult to achieve understanding, remarking,

---

† Not even Alpheus Todd LL.D, Librarian of the Canadian House of Commons, whose analysis was far more rigorous than Bagehot's.

‡ "Lord Beaconsfield [Benjamin Disraeli] *was certainly describing an unbroken practice* when he told the Queen in 1881, when he was out of office and close to death, that she had 'a right, which it would be wise always to exercise, to express [privately] your Majesty's opinion on every point of the policy of your Minsters, and to require and receive explanations'." Le May, *The Victorian Constitution*, p. 23; comments and italics mine.

> Some good lawyer ought to write a careful book to say which
> of these powers are really useable, and which are obsolete.
> There is no authentic explicit information as to what the
> Queen can do, any more than of what she does.[272]

So Bagehot confesses his ignorance. He lectures about the Crown with the authority of a man who lectures about leopards, knowing little about their habits, or whether they eat meat or grass, but only that they possess spots; so he argues that the true essence of a leopard is its spottiness, to which all else is incidental.

And yet, even if he had read *On Parliamentary Government in England*, written by the Canadian scholar Alpheus Todd and published two years after *The English Constitution* came out in book form; even if he had lived to read the writings of subsequent scholars, like Anson, Dicey, Evatt and Forsey, he could not have drawn their conclusions. He could not have declared as Dicey[†] declared nearly fifty years later, that the guiding principle behind the Crown's use of the reserve powers had become that "the final decision of every grave political question now belongs, not to the House of Commons, but to the electors as the representatives of the nation."[273]

For Bagehot's second flaw was that he despised and feared most of his fellow citizens.

> We have in a great community like England crowds of people
> scarcely more civilized than the majority of two thousand
> years ago; we have others, even more numerous, such as the
> best people were a thousand years since. The lower orders, the
> middle orders, are still, when tried by what is the standard of
> the educated 'ten thousand', narrow-minded, unintelligent,
> incurious...Those who doubt should go out into their
> kitchens. Let an accomplished man try what seems to him
> most obvious, most certain, most palpable in intellectual
> matters, upon the housemaid and the footman, and he will
> find what he says seems unintelligible, confused and erro-
> neous — that his audience think him mad and wild when he
> is speaking what is in his own sphere of thought the dullest
> platitude of cautious soberness.[274]

Of the working class he said,

> It must be remembered that a political combination of the
> lower classes, as such and for their own objects, is an evil of the
> first magnitude; that a permanent combination of them would
> make them (now so many of them have the suffrage) supreme
> in the country; and that their supremacy, in the state they now
> are, means the supremacy of ignorance over instruction and of

---

† A.V. Dicey KC (1835–1922), Vinerian Professor of English Law and Fellow of All Souls, Oxford.

---

numbers over knowledge. So long as they are not taught to act together, there is a chance of this being averted.[275]

The heart of Dicey's proposition, that the general public should be allowed to decide crucial political questions directly, was condemned by Bagehot: "constituency government" as he called it, even when the constituency was composed entirely of male middle- and upper-class members, was a

> government of immoderate persons far from the scene of action, instead of the government of moderate persons close to the scene of action; it is the judgement of persons judging in the last resort and without a penalty, in lieu of persons judging in fear of a dissolution, and ever conscious that they are subject to an appeal.[276]

But an appeal to whom? The opinion of a representative public meeting

> could not be moderate; could not be subject to effectual discussion; could not be in close contact with pressing facts; could not be framed under a chastening sense of near responsibility; could not be formed as those form their opinions who have to act upon them.[277]

Granted, public meetings can degenerate into beer-hall rallies, but if the opinions of a public meeting could *never* be moderate, never subject to effectual discussion, never in close contact with pressing facts, then surely democracy itself would be fatally discredited. What is the verdict of a general election but the vote of a vast community, cast after weeks or months of exposure to political speeches, articles and advertisements. In a sense it is a "virtual" assembly, for the millions of citizens do not gather in a single huge hall, but the speeches and articles enter their homes in the form of pamphlets and newspapers (and in more recent times via radio and television broadcasts). Yet in essential respects the "virtual" assembly resembles a real one enough to wonder how Bagehot can denounce public meetings in the way he did without logically denouncing the democratic process itself. For parliamentarians to appeal to an electorate over an issue — and all elections involve at least one issue, that of who should govern — surely it must be a necessary condition that the opinion of the electorate is at least *sometimes* moderate, subject to effectual discussion and in close contact with pressing facts. Otherwise the democratic process would founder in chaos.

Even Bagehot's conception of "moderate persons" was suffused with prejudice. According to him, they were "men of business" who had

> got rich themselves by transactions of which they could not have stated the argumentative ground — and all they ask for is a distinct though moderate conclusion, that they can repeat when asked; something which they feel *not* to be abstract

argument, but abstract argument diluted and dissolved in real life…we like to have the rigidity taken out of an argument, and the substance left.[278]

Founded on his prejudices, Walter Bagehot's analysis of the Westminster system is based upon the division of political institutions into the "efficient" and the "dignified".

Niccolò's ghost	What's wrong with that? We can say that *all* people and all institutions possess on one hand an efficient aspect, and on the other, a dignified one, where we define "efficiency" as the ease with which we impose our wills upon our surroundings, and "dignity" as the amount of respect that those who inhabit our surroundings give us! I remember pointing out centuries ago what's obvious to commonsense — namely, that our efficiency is improved by possessing dignity, and hampered by lack of it. In a complex body of institutions, one part might improve its efficiency by employing the dignity of another to advantage; so what's your problem?
Author	But Bagehot's analysis was much cruder than yours. To him, government was composed of a multitude of parts, true; some parts "did" things, and other parts possessed public respect, or as he put it "excite and preserve the reverence of the population."[279] The bits that "did" things he put into one pile, and christened "efficient", and the others he put into a second pile, and labelled "dignified", although he conceded that the two piles were "not indeed separable with microscopic accuracy, for the genius of great affairs abhors nicety of division."[280]

According to this influential writer of the 19th Century, the purpose of the dignified was to deceive the "lower classes" into accepting the efficient parts of government. This was his rationale for the Crown: that it was a useful instrument of deception, for it

acts as a *disguise*. It enables our real rulers to change without heedless people knowing it. The masses of Englishmen are not fit for an elective government; if they knew how near they were to it, they would be surprised, and almost tremble.[281]

For men of affairs, however — clever chaps, like W. Bagehot, Esq. — Britain was already a "secret republic". They realised that a "Republic has insinuated itself beneath the folds of a Monarchy."[282]

How accurate is Bagehot's vision of the role of the Crown? His basic hypothesis is false, that the Crown merely sits on the top of the "dignified" pile, his error stemming from his belief that the Crown's most vital discretionary power, the royal power of dissolution[†], no longer existed. He erroneously claimed "The Queen can hardly now refuse a defeated Minister the chance of a dissolution, any more than she can dissolve in the time of an undefeated one, and without his consent."[283] (This error was echoed in *The Economist*'s editorial, which boldly declared "In the monarchy's current state, there are virtually no true checks and balances in the British constitution..."[284]) The powers of dissolution and refusal of dissolution — the power to decide, subject to the conventions of ministerial responsibility, whether or not to dissolve Parliament and hold fresh elections — must place the Crown firmly upon the "efficient" pile. Close upon its heels follow other powers: the right to dismiss a government that no longer holds the confidence of the House, the power to prorogue or not prorogue Parliament. All these refute the suggestion that the Crown is an empty ornament, a useful bauble with which the Prime Minister beguiles the childishly "heedless people".

Consequently, when we look at Bagehot's offerings on why the Crown is useful we find a platter of red herrings, cooked in a sauce of misconceived ingredients. To appreciate this, we must taste them one by one. His fish are as follows:

❖ The Crown acts as a disguise: that the monarchy remains the most intelligible part of the political system for the ordinary people, who still believe the Queen actually governs;

❖ That monarchy "commonly hidden like a mystery, and sometimes paraded like a pageant"[285] strengthens government with the force of religion, the idea of "mystic duty" and Divine Right;

❖ That the Queen as head of society spares us from the tyranny of social adventurers clambering for the top spot;

❖ That the Crown has come to be regarded as the head of our morality.

How was the Crown to act as a disguise? It can't have been a terribly convincing one if foreign observers like Alexis de Torqueville and Emile Boutmy, "even if [they] only pass through" Britain and Switzerland, could "perceive...the most astonishing differences between them" and declare that "England seems to be much more republican than the Helvetic [Swiss] Republic" or that "England is in reality a republic wearing the semblance and invested with the forms of a monarchy".[286] Are we expected to believe that when ministries collapsed, when Russell, Palmerston and Gladstone wielded power and lost it again, that no-one in the country noticed apart from the "upper ten thousand"? What were the disenfranchised public supposed to think of general elections? That they were nothing more than some kind of race meeting, to which they were not invited?

---

† The royal power of dissolution will be discussed in *The Reserve Powers*.

And what of women and their struggle to acquire the right to vote, briefly alluded to by Bagehot in his discussion of "ultra-democrats"?[287] If the Crown concealed so effectively the true position of power from these people who "care fifty times more for a marriage than a ministry",[288] then why were they campaigning so convincingly for the right to vote ministries in and out of office?†

The 19th Century was a period of considerable military activity, with British armies in the field maintaining and extending the far-flung reaches of Empire. In times of strife the ordinary soldier becomes politically aware (as does his family). He has, after all, a personal stake in the matter; his life lies in the balance of a political decision. Are we expected to believe that the "lower classes" entirely failed to notice the role of Pitt the Younger during the war against Revolutionary France, or the Duke of Wellington's prime ministership thirteen years after Waterloo, or the power that they wielded? The London mobs had been quick enough to make their opinions of individual ministers known during the American Revolution — they cheered or hissed them in the streets, depending on their policies. Why now were Londoners suddenly overwhelmed with ignorance or apathy? Maybe in peace few questions are asked, but surely the bloody mess of the Crimean War provoked a few.

Even two centuries earlier, the English common soldiers of the 17th Century disproved Bagehot's smug description of being "narrow-minded, unintelligent, incurious"; some of the most lucid declarations of democratic political principle to come from any century issued from their councils held following the English Civil War. In 1647 five mutinous regiments drew up a manifesto entitled *The Case of the Army Truly Stated*, calling for manhood suffrage (rather than the right to vote being restricted by the requirement of property ownership) and for the election of a Parliament of supreme authority, embodying popular sovereignty of the widest sort. In late October that year the Parliamentary Army held debates at Putney, in which ordinary soldiers participated and are identified by such titles as "Buff Coat" and "Bedfordshire Man". At these debates a set of proposals entitled *The Agreement of the People* was presented. These proposals called for a new Parliament of four hundred members to be established, to be elected every two years by an electorate which included all "housekeepers of twenty-one who had not aided the King or impeded the Army", although "persons on alms, wage-earners or servants" were to be excluded from the right to vote. This proposed Parliament would then "appoint a Council of State, erect and abolish law courts, and generally make laws to which everyone within the realm would be subject." [289]

Whether the right to vote should be qualified by the possession of property or not was hotly debated. Since the earliest days of Parliament under Edward I's reign in the late 13th Century‡, it had been believed that representation

---

† This right was granted to them in the colonies of New Zealand and South Australia in 1893–94, and in Great Britain in 1918 and 1928; an early example of how the Westminster system's development surged ahead in the "colonies".

‡ The genesis of the House of Commons (Commons from *Communitates*, communities of the realm) as an

should be linked with the possession of property or a position in society. Most of the soldiers at the Putney debates did not own land, and demanded the right to vote. Henry Ireton, Oliver Cromwell's son-in-law, was angered by what he saw as a veiled attack upon the rights of property-owners, and declared,

> This doth make me think that the meaning is, that every man that is an inhabitant is to be equally consider'd, and to have an equal voice in the election of the representers...and if that be the meaning then I have something to say against it...I think that no person hath a right to an interest or share in the disposing or determining of the Kingdom, and in choosing those that shall determine what laws we shall be ruled by here, no person hath a right to this, that hath not a permanent fixed interest in this Kingdom.

Colonel Rainsborough, infuriated,

> replied by insisting passionately on the people's rights: the foundation of all law lay in the people and 'I do not find anything in the law of God that a Lord shall choose twenty burgesses, and a Gentleman but two, or a poor man shall choose none.'[290]

Another radical dissident of the time, John Lilburne,

> moved to the idea of man as a citizen who had the right to give his own agreement to the government; man could rule over individuals 'no further than by free consent, or agreement, by giving up their power each to other, for their better being.'

At the time of the October debates Lilburne was incarcerated in the Tower of London. He had plenty of time to reflect, for he spent much of his time in prison, being a scathing critic of contemporary governments. Even Oliver Cromwell visited him in the Tower and begged him to "stop speaking in such bitter terms of Parliament".[291] Lilburne was a popular figure for discontent. Exiled abroad, he returned to England in 1653, during the republic, and was

---

organised representative assembly were established earlier by Simon de Montfort. In December 1264 he "laid the foundations of the House of Commons, by issuing writs directing the sheriffs to return not only two knights from each shire, but also two citizens from each city, and two burgesses from each borough. This famous Parliament met at London on 20th January, 1265, to deal not merely with the granting of supplies, but with the business of the nation generally". De Montfort himself was killed at the Battle of Evesham by the Royalist forces of Henry III, but his reforms survived as precedents. By 1347 Parliament had become clearly divided into the Houses of Lords and Commons, "the House of Lords being the aristocratic and official chamber, and the House of Commons the representative chamber, consisting, as it does to this day, of representatives of the shires and representatives of the boroughs...During the long reign of Edward III (1327-77) the power of the Commons was consolidated, and they succeeded in establishing the three great principles that taxation without the consent of Parliament is illegal, that the concurrence of both Houses is necessary for legislation, and that the Commons have a right to inquire into abuses of administration". (Quick and Garran, The *Annotated Constitution of the Australian Commonwealth*, pp.306–307)

BAGEHOT REVISITED

promptly imprisoned again. Popular petitions flooded in for his release, remembered in the rhyme:

> And what shall then honest *John Lilburne* die?
> Three score thousand will know the reason why[292]

These, then are voices of the "narrow-minded, unintelligent, incurious" lower and middle orders to whom the dullest platitudes on government are to sound "mad and wild", "unintelligible, confused and erroneous".

Based on this view of the people, and astride his "intelligible" theory, Bagehot makes his famous declaration,

> The best reason why Monarchy is a strong government is, that it is an intelligible government. The mass of mankind understand it, and they hardly anywhere in the world understand any other. It is often said that men are ruled by their imaginations; but it would be truer to say that they are governed by the weakness of their imaginations. The nature of a constitution, the action of an assembly, the play of parties, the unseen formation of a guiding opinion, are complex facts, difficult to know and easy to mistake. But the action of a single will, the fiat of a single mind, are easy ideas: anybody can make them out, and no one can ever forget them. When you put before the mass of mankind the question, 'Will you be governed by a king, or will you be governed by a constitution?' the inquiry comes out thus – 'Will you be governed in a way you understand, or will you be governed in a way you do not understand?' [293]

This is not only patronising but utterly false. First, it effectively suggests that the general public would prefer dictatorship over democracy because the former is more comprehensible. Second, it establishes a dichotomy of public perception between monarchy and constitutional government, a dichotomy which is reprehensible to a modern monarchist, who believes that the only tolerable government is constitutional government; that constitutional government, to be maintained, must be actively defended;[†] and that the justification of a constitutional monarch over a president lies in the motivation to defend. Finally, defending *constitutional* monarchy on the basis of ease of comprehension was always absurd. The bloodstained Renaissance pragmatism of the Tudor despotic monarchies was easy to understand, as was the arbitrary rule of the republican Rump of the Long Parliament.

---

† To say that the Crown actively defends constitutional government is not to suggest that the Queen, Governor-General or Governor is permanently poised to cause a crisis. Rather, it may be said that the Crown actively defends the constitution in the same sense that a watchdog in a garden actively defends the grounds, even when he sleeps in his kennel. Most prospective burglars, aware of the danger, will prefer to let sleeping dogs lie and refrain from an attempt at burglary. For his own part the dog would prefer to sleep. Only the trespasses of those intrepid few who still dare to violate the grounds will rouse him to the fury of his office.

Niccolò's ghost A child could understand the theory behind Oliver Cromwell's Protectorship. Military dictatorship is merely a more sophisticated version of the polity that bullies struggle to establish in every schoolyard.

But modern constitutional monarchism is more subtle, a combination of republican ideals and the acknowledgment of the human condition, leading to the precautions against human nature needed for these ideals to be implemented. The Westminster system is indeed a "secret republic" that has "insinuated itself beneath the folds of a Monarchy", but the presence of the monarchy is an active, integral part of the preservation of this "secret republic", not through deception or false display, but through ensuring that the power entrusted to a few to govern on behalf of the many can be revoked and transferred to a new choice of the many. This is neither a simple concept, nor obvious, but necessary.

Bagehot's second herring is his talk of a religious aspect to the Crown. He is not referring to the Queen's position in the Church of England, nor should he; Henry VIII became Head of the Church of England so that he could not be dictated to by bishops, not that he might be mistaken for one. Instead what Bagehot is referring to is the idea that citizens have a "mystic duty" to the Crown, a sense of awe inspired by an oath of allegiance invoking God which, through the Crown, "strengthens our Government with the strength of religion":[294]

> If you ask the immense majority of the Queen's subjects by
> what right she rules, they would never tell you that she rules
> by Parliamentary right, by virtue of 6 Anne, c.7. They will say
> she rules by 'God's grace': they believe that they have a
> mystic obligation to obey her.[295]

Bagehot never says that this belief in Divine Right is good, indeed he calls it a "mischievous sentiment" — but he holds it to be a useful one.

It is neither good nor useful, but degrading equally to the dignity of the Crown and that of the citizen. Members of the general public may not be able to declare that Elizabeth II reigns by virtue of 6 Anne, c.7 (presumably he was referring here to 6 Anne c.41, the *Succession to the Crown Act 1707*, which secures the succession laid out in the Act of Settlement), but the important matter is that they be able to declare the grounds upon which the *monarchy* reigns; no Divine Right but Revolution Settlement, a 17th Century pact between the Crown and the people of the realm, by which the Crown was given to William and Mary, their heirs and successors "in all times to come" by the representatives of "all the estates of the people of this realm" in return for the solemn oath to "preserve [the people] from the violation of their rights, which they have here asserted" and from all other attempts upon their rights, laws and liberties.[296] This pact killed Divine Right and the Act of Settlement buried it. Duty is owed, not through a mystic obligation to God's anointed, but through a desire to preserve the rule of law, to a guardian established by pact devised by the Convention Parliament. Although Bagehot once declared "We must not let in daylight upon magic",[297] the Westminster system isn't founded upon magic but on a love of liberty. Not only *can* it be illuminated by daylight, it *should* be illuminated by daylight.

In its characteristically terse, businesslike manner the Australian Constitution shines a spotlight upon the true political role of the Crown as a constitutional guardian, not a dignified disguise or deceit of the ruling cognoscenti:

> The legislative power of the Commonwealth shall be vested in a Federal Parliament, which shall consist of the Queen, a Senate, and a House of Representatives, and which is here-inafter called 'The Parliament' or 'The Parliament of the Commonwealth'...The executive power of the Commonwealth is vested in the Queen and is exercisable by the Governor-General as the Queen's representative, *and extends to the execution and maintenance of this Constitution, and of the laws of the Commonwealth.*[298]

Thus Bagehot's error is renounced by the Australian authors of our written Constitution, in what has already been identified as a Tory (as distinct from Whig) formulation of political authority. Indeed, while his manifesto was wooing the English mercantile classes, its principles were being steadfastly ignored by Imperial and colonial legislators alike, and have remained ignored by the written constitutions of Her Majesty's realms throughout the 20th Century.

Bagehot's third red herring: that the Queen as head of society spares us from the tyranny of social adventurers. He suggests,

> the House of Commons is thronged with people who get there merely for 'social purposes'.... that they and their families may go to parties else impossible...If the highest point in conspic-uous life were thrown open to public competition, this low sort of ambition and envy would be fearfully increased.[299]

It would have been more sensible to suggest that she spares us from the tyranny of *political* adventurers, for his contention's barely worth a reply if he's claiming that the Crown shelters us from the atrocities of those cocktail conquistadors who roam parties and ruthlessly dominate the social pages of *Vogue*. All the wit of mankind has failed to devise a shelter against them, unless it be to be so obnoxious that we're not invited to parties at all. Anyone stupid enough to enter political life for the sake of the parties deserves every minute he or she gets.

Bagehot's final herring is his suggestion that the Crown represents the head of our morality. Although George III and Victoria represented and upheld the moral ideals of the societies in which they lived, he notes with dismay that the marital arrangements of Georges I and II and William IV were not so impeccable, and George IV's lifestyle was positively dissolute. Sancti-moniously Bagehot pronounces a sentiment to warm the cockles of a tabloid editor's heart:

> It should be observed, too, in fairness to the unroyal species of
> Cabinet government, that it is exempt from one of the
> greatest and most characteristic defects of the royal species.
> Where there is no Court there can be no evil influence from
> a Court. What these influences are every one knows; though
> no one, hardly the best and closest observer, can say with
> confidence, and precision how great their effect is.[300]

What he is awkwardly discussing here is *sex*, and the damnable intrigues of royal mistresses.

Niccolò's ghost	The damnable intrigues of other royal lovers, too, but these don't seem to score a mention.
Author	For over a decade our evening news has been full of sex, politics, and the influence of private advisers. After Monica Lewinsky and Bill Clinton, tomahawk missiles and a semen-stained dress, Nancy Reagan and her astrologers, the collapse of the younger Windsors' marriages and the sordid gossip of their lovers, the debaucheries of President John F. Kennedy and of his brother Robert, there is little we *haven't* heard about the intertwining of sex and government. Time to turn this harsh light of reality upon Bagehot's claims.

After what we've seen at the end of this century, how are we supposed to believe that royalty is more susceptible to "illicit" sexual activity than a presidency? Why on earth would anyone expect unroyal Cabinet government to be "exempt"? It is not an idle and gilded youth which is the principle cause of marital breakdown in public life, royal or unroyal. Rather, as anyone born into a political family can attest, it's public life *per se* that places an immense strain upon family life, through stress, long hours and a life lived in a goldfish bowl. The parliaments of Australia and the United Kingdom are littered with the debris of broken marriages and the consequent gossip of lovers, and the dirty laundry aired during the Clinton impeachment has revealed the United States to be no exception.

There may be, of course, more chance of breakdown in matches constrained from the very beginning by political forces, rather than dictated entirely by love, and in this royalty is made more vulnerable. Apart from this, royal infidelity merely provides more colourful theatre than the mundane kind, and so attracts more idle viewers. Unroyal Heads of State obviously do engage in affairs of the heart and other organs. But royal or unroyal, what is the relevance of all this to the State?

The current loss of faith in the monarchy owes a great deal to the linking of sex and State, yet although a moral monarch is desirable, an immoral one unfortunate, and a conspicuously immoral one causes a few scandals, strict morality need play no necessary part of the job description of constitutional guardian.† If we *do* assume these people's private lives are relevant, why should we assume that their lovers are intrinsically harmful, or at least more harmful than their legitimate spouses? Nell Gwynn, for example, was a far less dangerous proposition than Lady Macbeth, despite the latter's respectably married state. For those who wish to avoid the theatrical (apart from some great dialogue by Marlowe), it was not Edward II's gay lover Gaveston but Edward's wife Isabella who conspired, with her lover Mortimer, to usurp the throne in 14th Century England. Mary, Queen of Scots had a thoroughly awful time after she married Lord Darnley, because he thought saying "I do" qualified him to run Scotland instead of keeping to his proper vocation of Queen's consort. Modern history does not protest that the actress Lillie Langtry ever conspired to straddle the British Empire, despite her intimacies with Edward VII. There's doubtful correlation between the sanctity of marriage and the propriety of a companion's political agenda.

The troublesome "influence" envisaged by Bagehot was the risk of royal favouritism when choosing a Prime Minister. Yet here is a danger that party discipline has largely rendered obsolete. Following a general election, if there's a dominant party possessing the confidence of the new House, then a Head of State with the power of choice must invite its parliamentary leader to form a government. Were another member of that party to be invited instead, he or she would simply decline in favour of the leader, otherwise his or her own position would rapidly become untenable within the party. If there's no clear dominant party in the Lower House, then the discretionary power to choose *among* parties a party or coalition capable of retaining the confidence of the House must nonetheless exist. President Scalfaro has been vexed with precisely this problem in the republic of Italy, to prevent government collapsing into anarchy. There is still the risk of favouritism here, yet the greater risk lies in republics. Bagehot himself conceded "It is absurd to choose by contested party election an impartial chooser of Ministers"[301].

Niccolò's ghost [*shifting uncomfortably in his chair*]: If Henry Kissinger was right when he said that power is the ultimate aphrodisiac, then we ought to be looking elsewhere. As you yourself have conceded, nowadays it's the Prime

---

† We will go on to argue that in a well designed system, the duties of guardian are entirely coincident with her own self interest. It is only in a poorly designed system that one requires a guardian to have strong moral qualities to be useful.

	Minister, not the Queen or her representatives, who wields the active power.
Author	Well, here again Bagehot's fallacy raises its ugly head. Even in 19th Century England the British statesman W.E. Gladstone was moved to comment "I have known ten Prime Ministers, and all but one of them were adulterers".[302] Clearly, elected politicians aren't immune to sin or influence. If presidents are similar creatures to prime ministers, where now is Bagehot's "exempt" unroyal government?

Not all cliques of closet advisers exercise sexual influence. Most possess their influence purely through their shrewd judgement, or reputation for political soundness, or old friendships. Simply looking abroad further discredits allegations of a particular association of a Crown with private advisers. During the reigns of presidents De Gaulle and Pompidou in the 1960s and '70s, the hidden influence of private presidential advisers hostile to Parliament and the government led to the bitter French proverb "France, like Britain, has a 'shadow cabinet' but in her case it is in office".[303]

Monarchs, presidents, governors-general and prime ministers will all have informal advisers, whose relationships with them may take many varied forms. It must be so, unless we are to have a polity composed entirely of celibate, solitary philosophers. Not only is it nonsense to suggest an unroyal form of government is exempt from this, but foreshadowed in the previous passage is a serious argument that presidents are more likely to be influenced by unscrupulous advice than their royal counterparts; an argument derived not from reverence or sycophancy, but from simple self-interest.

Bagehot's failure to grasp the common human condition infuses his work. Even his famous extract quoted at the beginning of this essay is promptly spoiled by his next sentences:

> And a king of great sense and sagacity would want no others. He would find that his having no others would enable him to use these with singular effect. He would say to his Ministers: 'The responsibility of these measures is upon you. Whatever you think best must be done. Whatever you think best shall have my full and effectual support. *But* you will observe that for this reason and that reason what you propose to do is bad; for this reason and that reason what you do not propose is better. I do not oppose it, it is my duty not to oppose; but observe that I *warn*.' Supposing the king to be right, and to have what kings often have, the gift of effectual expression, he could not help moving his Minister. He might not always turn his course, but he would always trouble his mind. [304]

Lord Balfour, former British Prime Minister and a member of the House of Commons for nearly fifty years before his elevation to the House of Lords, the statesman who presided over the Imperial Conference of 1926 which declared the equality of the Dominions, described this passage quoted above as reflecting "naiveté" and "a certain unintended humour".[305] The politicians of Mr. Bagehot's acquaintance must have been meek and timid souls, to lose sleep over the criticisms of someone who by established convention could not publicly criticise her ministers, and who by Bagehot's hypothesis should have no other power apart from that right privately to criticise them. The editor of the local newspaper would be more threatening to a Prime Minister than this hypothetical constitutional indoor nag. Would a Monarch of great sense and sagacity really want no other powers?

Niccolò's ghost   To possess no other power is to possess no power at all, not even to uphold this right to express a private opinion. To be told you occupy a position endowed with rights but devoid of power is to be told a pleasant lie. Without power there are no rights.

This question was answered by the collapse of conventions surrounding the presidency of the Republic of Ireland. At its inception these "rights" of consultation were possessed by the earliest President, Dr Douglas Hyde, and his successor, Sean T O Ceallaigh, both regularly briefed by Eamon de Valera, author of the Constitution and the first Taoiseach (Prime Minister). Both presidents were personal friends of de Valera, who had, moreover, bestowed these rights upon them in the written Constitution, which declared (Article 28.5.2) "The Taoiseach shall keep the President generally informed on matters of domestic and international policy."[306] As de Valera himself explained it during the Dáil debates in May 1937 on the draft Constitution,

> [The President] will be kept in touch with the position of affairs generally in the country by the Government or by the head of the Government from day to day or from week to week. The Government ought to be able to persuade him, giving him the inner knowledge that they have about the situation, while they may not be able to persuade a body like the Seanad.[307]

But as so often happens, the theory — even when supposedly enshrined in written law — differed from reality. The quality of the briefings declined under the second Taoiseach, John A Costello, a long time political opponent of President O Ceallaigh. By the 1970s this tradition of consultation was in tatters. Taoiseach Liam Cosgrave briefed President Childers (1973–74) so rarely that Childers "suggested to friends that he received more information on government policy from the newspapers than he received from Cosgrave".[308] President Ó Dálaigh (1974–76) went further, writing in his private papers an accusation against Cosgrave, of engaging in "an act of constitutional defiance" by not briefing him more fully.[309] Ó Dálaigh wrote "Brevity I admire, taciturnity I can respect, but silence, of almost two years, in the face of a constitutional obligation to keep the President informed...baffles me."[310] Particularly galling to him was the fact the government hadn't even warned him in advance of its 1976 decision declaring a national emergency.[311]

The Irish scholar who presented the report on the Irish presidency to Australia's Republic Advisory Committee contrasted this state of affairs with the weekly detailed briefings Elizabeth II receives from her British government and the similarly regular and detailed briefings Queen Margrethe II of Denmark receives from her government in Copenhagen. Also contrasted in his report were the sections of the Australian Constitution quoted earlier, vesting the executive power of the Commonwealth in the Crown, and the very different Irish provision (Article 28): "The executive power of the state shall, subject to the provisions of this Constitution, be exercised by or on the authority of the Government."[312] He warned,

> Few Irish political and legal experts have paid much attention
> to what appears such a simple, uncontroversial statement in
> the Irish Constitution, yet that very provision is largely
> unique to the Irish Constitution and has had a *fundamental*
> impact on the position of the President of Ireland in Irish
> constitutional structures. It means, for example, that the presidency is totally bypassed in executive matters.[313]

In this manifesto it will be argued that it lies in the mutual interest of both Crown and public for the Crown to possess other, albeit limited, powers than these of consultation: for example, it is vital for the Crown to be able to dismiss ministers acting illegally or who have lost Parliament's confidence, appealing to Parliament or the public to confirm this decision.[†] (Of course, even this limited power is ill-fitted to defend directly the right of private consultation, and doubtless nine times out of ten a Prime Minister or Premier can treat this private right contemptuously. Yet surely it would be foolhardy for a Prime Minister to treat the Crown with contempt three hundred and sixty-four days in the year when on the final day there may be a crisis in which the Crown is called upon to intervene). As outlined in later chapters, the Crown indeed has this power; that Bagehot failed to recognise this fact leads to the last of his major misconceptions.

Given his hypothesis that the Crown should have no other powers than those stated by him, he concentrates upon the idea of a monarch as an adviser, and concedes that years of experience during her reign may make her opinions valuable. For example, Elizabeth II's political memory stretches back to at least

---

† Here we are simply discussing the powers within the conventions of Westminster. Dismissals based on

the beginning of her reign, when her prime ministers in Britain and Australia were Sir Winston Churchill and Sir Robert Menzies. She has witnessed the evolution of both countries at the highest levels of power for half a century. But Bagehot becomes obsessed with this advisory aspect of kings; in arguments based upon the Hanoverian kings, he notes with dismay that "A constitutional sovereign must in the common course of government be a man of but common ability",[314] and hence his advice be of an indifferent quality.

But Bagehot's hypothesis of "no other powers" is wrong. The monarch's reserve power to dismiss her ministers transforms the emphasis of her duties: the more important role is not the Queen *as an adviser*, but *as one who is advised*; more precisely, the Queen, whose formal executive concurrence is required, as an observer of when she is being unconstitutionally or illegally advised.[†] Even if she *were* a person of only ordinary ability, it is a characteristic of many ordinary people that they are acute judges of when they are being conned. If she does this well, then she serves the country well.

Yet, finally, Bagehot's distortion of the role of the Crown was due to his misunderstanding of the people who wore it, a misunderstanding fed by his own arrogant prejudices and his belief that throughout their youth heirs to the throne led idle lives of self-indulgent luxury. Although this was doubtless an accurate description for George IV, it was not true even for his brother William IV, who had a naval upbringing, served under Nelson in the West Indies, and before his accession (in the words of Jennings) "led the life of a worthy burgess".[315] Nonetheless, Bagehot pronounces in patronising tones:

> A constitutional sovereign must in the common course of government be a man of but common ability. I am afraid, looking to the early acquired feebleness of hereditary dynasties, that we must expect him to be a man of inferior ability. Theory and experience both teach that the education of a prince can be but a poor education, and that a royal family will generally have less ability than other families.[316]

What novel theory of genetics and environment is it that asserts — as a general physical principle — that the holder of an hereditary office shall, *ipso*

---

powers in our written Constitution also involve an appeal, but not necessarily to confirm this decision. For example, section 57 of the Australian Constitution contemplates the predicament of parliamentary deadlock, with rival intransigent factions dominating the Representatives and Senate and important legislation being shuttled from one House to another without resolution. Under this section the Governor-General may dissolve both Houses in a forced election for both. The question placed before the electors is not "will you confirm my dissolution?" but "which faction should win and govern?"

† It is important to distinguish between merely very stupid advice, and advice which is illegal or unconstitutional. The Queen has no right to oppose in public even the most foolish ordinary advice of her elected Ministers, although she may employ her private rights to argue against their perceived stupidity with them in private, hoping to change their minds. But confronted with advice that attacks the democratic fabric of the Constitution or precipitates revolutionary change without mandate, she may invoke her reserve powers. In 1943 Forsey suggested criteria of attempted advice which would justify the Crown's use of reserve powers. These criteria are quoted in *The Reserve Powers*.

facto, possess and exhibit *less* than average ability? Where do the Tudors fit into his scheme of things? Are we to pretend that this highly educated and intellectually brilliant hereditary dynasty of the Renaissance are merely a conspiracy of historical novelists? In the intellectual firmament viewed from the 20th Century, Elizabeth I and Henry VIII still shine far brighter than Mr Bagehot himself.

When most people think of Henry VIII they summon the image immortalised by Holbein, of the bloated and tyrannical despot who went through wives the way other people went through pocket handkerchiefs. Yet here was a man who in his youth was regarded throughout western Europe as the archetype Renaissance prince: whose brilliance in arguing theology against Martin Luther's doctrines earned him the papal title "Defender of the Faith" before he embraced the Reformation; who resurrected the Royal Navy, and realised early the implications of deck-borne cannon for naval tactics; who managed to keep the small nation of England afloat and independent despite the deep religious dissensions at home and the turbulent rivalry of hostile Powers abroad.

What of his kinswoman Lady Jane Grey, who as a girl displayed considerable learning and intellectual talent, tragically cut short when she was dragged into politics, becoming Queen of England for nine days in 1553 before being arrested and beheaded by her rival, Mary Tudor? And what of Mary's other rival, her own younger half-sister Elizabeth, who ascended the throne in 1558 at the age of twenty-five to become Queen Elizabeth I?

Here was a woman whose formidable intellect and abilities became famous throughout all Europe. As well as possessing an acidic wit in English she spoke fluent Latin, French and Italian, and good Greek. Like her father Henry she was skilful in music. For pastime she delighted to engage in long theological arguments, even as in negotiations she excelled in political ones. All in all she was a strong-willed and subtle diplomat who even early in her reign proved capable of outwitting and exasperating foreign ambassadors present at her Court and their monarchs abroad. If the praise of her courtiers and allies is not to be believed on this, look to the testimony of her enemies.

Scotland at the time of her coronation was a kingdom under the rule of France, Mary Queen of Scots being both descended from and married into the French royal House of Guise. Mary's mother, Mary of Guise, was Regent of Scotland. In May 1559 a revolt led by Protestant lords broke out in Scotland against their foreign overlords. Elizabeth promptly formed a secret inner council composed of herself and two close advisers, Sir William Cecil and Sir Thomas Parry. All clerks were dispensed with, Cecil writing and encoding the secret dispatches himself. Elizabeth also communicated with Cecil in cipher written by her own hand. This council provided the rebels with secret funding — even, in December, an "unauthorized" naval blockade by English warships which raided and destroyed ships sent across the Channel to suppress the revolt. When events rendered it necessary, Elizabeth sent out her spies in Europe to rescue the Scottish Earl of Arran, a fugitive on the Continent on the run from the French. He was safely smuggled to England, and sent north to aid the uprising.

There was no doubt money and supplies were being smuggled into Scotland from south of the Border, yet try as hard as he might in personal audiences and covert inquiries the French ambassador to the English Court found it impossible to ascertain the extent (if at all) that the Queen was herself implicated in assisting the rebels. Baffled and frustrated, he wrote to the Regent in September, complaining "There is more dissimulation in her than honesty and goodwill; she is the best hand at the game living".[317]

As the leading Protestant prince of Europe, Elizabeth was regarded by Protestant and Catholic alike as the natural enemy of the Catholic Powers, yet when Pope Pius V issued a Papal Bull in February 1570 excommunicating her and attempting to incite her subjects to overthrow her, the reaction of these same Powers is noteworthy. Having negotiated with her on some occasion in the past, and hence possessing a keen appreciation of her ability, Philip II of Spain and the Duke of Alva, Spanish Governor of the Netherlands were annoyed at the Bull. So was the Emperor of the Holy Roman Empire, and France went so far as to refuse bluntly to publish it against her.[318]

Much later in her reign, when she had sat on her throne for almost thirty years, another Pope took a radically different view to that of his predecessor:

> 'She certainly is a great Queen' said the new Pope, Sixtus V,
> 'and were she only Catholic she would be our dearly beloved.
> Just look at how she governs! She is only a woman, only
> mistress of half an island, and yet she makes herself feared by
> Spain, by France, by the [Holy Roman] Empire, by all.'[319]

Where now is the early acquired feebleness of hereditary dynasties in this daughter and granddaughter of kings; the lesser ability, the poor education?

Nor is a good education unique to the Renaissance princes, for even in exile Charles II took lessons from the scholar Thomas Hobbes, and upon his Restoration was a powerful patron of mathematicians and other scientists, founding the Royal Society. Perhaps intellectual brilliance itself is a rare and elusive quantity, but a good education is not. It is instead a discipline that serves to make the best of whatever native qualities the student does possess, be he or she ever so "common" in ability. Here remains something a single-tiered monarchy can do that an elective presidency cannot: guarantee the education of the occupant.

Even if we do as Bagehot does, and confine ourselves entirely to the Hanoverians and the Saxe-Coberg-Gothas, his theory remains flawed. What of Victoria herself, patronised famously by him as that "retired widow" walking on the slopes of Windsor? In her youth this woman and her husband established a formidable foreign intelligence network throughout Europe, based on their blood relatives abroad, which provided information "nearly always different in emphasis, and sometimes more accurate, than that transmitted by British ambassadors and ministers abroad".[320] The first extended arguments Victoria had with her Foreign Minister, Lord Palmerston, were over Portuguese affairs, for "the Court's information came more quickly than that reaching the Foreign Office".[321] These arguments were, of course, in private. It was believed by some sections of the public that Victoria's personal allegiances abroad were defined in terms of her in-laws, but "those who assumed she was automatically on the side of those countries into whose ruling houses her children had married did not know her very well".[322] Even in old age she remained formidable:

> Bagehot, in his 'right to be consulted', never did justice to the Queen's pitilessness as a letter writer; she did not demand a right to be 'kept in the picture' but to argue and be argued with. Her talents were buttressed by a memory of astonishing exactness. (Sir Henry Campbell-Bannerman[†] told Ponsonby[‡] that once, when he was trying to persuade the Queen to withdraw an objection to some measure, she said: 'I remember Lord Melbourne using the same argument many years ago, but it was not true then and it is not true now.' Campbell-Bannerman said that he felt 'like a little boy talking to his grandmother'.)[323]

Her advice "was often shrewd, and she had excellent intuition of how the middle orders of her subjects were likely to react".[324] There is little here to substantiate Bagehot's claim of "early acquired feebleness" and "lesser ability".

A brief overview of British monarchs since the time of Bagehot erodes his case even further. What of Edward VII, that "unemployed youth" (again, Bagehot's words) whose personal diplomacy in Europe proved valuable during the *Belle Epoque*, particularly in Paris where he helped secure the approval of the French public to the Anglo-French *Entente Cordiale*, and who at home supported the large scale military reforms prior to World War I? And what of George V, that "competent and conscientious naval officer, of a conservative cast of mind, although not a party politician",[325] who

> was in constant communication with such people as Mr St Loe Strachey, Colonel Unsworth of the Salvation Army, Mr Hagberg Wright, the Bishop of Chelmsford or Canon Woodward, whose activities brought them in touch with different sections of the community.[326]

Here was a man who, throughout the difficult and dangerous Home Rule debates, it is "reasonably accurate to say…never made a mistake",[327] and who was,

---

† Sir Henry Campbell-Bannerman (1836-1908), Chief Secretary for Ireland 1884-85; Secretary of State for War 1886, 1892–95; Leader of the Liberal Party in the Commons 1898; British Prime Minister 1905-08.

‡ Sir Henry Ponsonby (1825–1895), Private Secretary to the Queen 1870–95.

BAGEHOT REVISITED

in many ways a typical grouse-shooting squire, interested in people, and therefore possessing an instinctive knowledge of ordinary people which neither the intellectuals nor the curious collection into which 'society' was developing could have acquired.[328]

Was the conscientious reign of George VI, eulogised by H.V.Evatt earlier in this book, such an anomaly? Or that of Elizabeth II herself? Bagehot's vision of an inferior idle king seems far from a general principle. Like his vision of the Crown itself, it seems more a product of his imaginings than an accurate description of his surroundings.

In summary, Walter Bagehot occasionally provides elegant and accurate descriptions, yet nowhere in his book do we hear the echo of the debates of 1689 or the earlier struggles of the Commonwealth of England; nowhere do we sense the spirit of revolution and reform of the 18th Century. Rarely do his postulates of monarchs and their relations with their ministers tally with reality. This is not 19th Century literature being used as a medium to reflect the English Constitution, but the English Constitution being used as a medium to reflect 19th Century prejudice. Perhaps the politicians of that age really believed that this was what their institutions had come to exist for: to provide an elaborate Punch and Judy show for the masses, while a clique of cognoscenti got on with the business of governing. Certainly it is a natural thing for an arrogant politician of any era to believe. In a more liberated age, wishing to understand the institutions which serve us on the threshold of the 21st Century, the narrow world view of one class-obsessed 19th century man will not do. The "masses" of our country have their own good reason for desiring the preservation of the Crown: precisely because they *are* "fit for an elective government", rather than the rule of a clique of clever chaps. The time is long overdue for Bagehot to be left neglected on the bookshelf.

In its October edition *The Economist* declared,

> On principle, this newspaper is against monarchy.
> Constitutional or not, it is the antithesis of much of what we
> stand for: democracy, liberty, reward for achievement rather
> than inheritance…It may be a symbol of unity but it is also a
> symbol of aristocracy, of feudal honours, of baseless deference.[329]

More rigorous authorities have declared that constitutional monarchy is *not* antithetical to democracy or liberty; rather, it is a weapon by which these most precious of our possessions are defended. The voices of some of these authorities have already spoken in these pages, and more will speak. Nowhere in their arguments will be heard baseless deference to symbols of aristocracy or inheritance, or covetousness for feudal honours, but an appreciation of the dangers which threaten democracy and liberty, and a knowledge of effective safeguards.

Any representative democracy left undefended can be swiftly destroyed by the conflicts on which it is based. Without a democratic structure, liberties do not long survive. Without personal liberty there can be no freedom of expression and hence no meritocracy, no true "reward for achievement" — indeed, in such regimes there are few rewards of any kind apart from the patronage of the ruling clique. Until such time as editors of *The Economist* are willing to look more deeply at the foundations of political institutions, they would better serve their readership by confining themselves to discussing economics.

Civil Politics and the Crown

There are plenty of instances of a constitution
which according to its law is not democratic,
but which owing to custom and training is
democratic in its workings; conversely, there are
in other places constitutions which according to
law incline towards democracy, but by reason of
their customs and training operate more like
oligarchies. This is especially apt to happen after
a change of constitution. The citizens do not at
once discard their old ways, but are *at first*
content to gain only moderate advantages from
their victory over the opposing side, whichever
that may be. *The result is that the existing laws
continue to be valid, but power is in the hands
of those who have brought about the change in
the constitution...*

Aristotle, *The Politics* (emphasis mine).

▪ THE NECESSITY FOR RESERVE POWERS ▪

> When freedom is imperilled in a territory of
> which Her Majesty is Queen, her representative,
> the Governor-General, has a reserve power to
> take such steps as are necessary to avoid the
> extinction of the territory as a civilised state and
> to preserve the society and its inhabitants.[1]
>
> Chief Justice of the High Court of Grenada, 1983

> [I]n abnormal times in the case of any attempt
> to disregard the Constitution or the laws of the
> Commonwealth or even the customary usages
> of Australian government, it would be the
> Governor-General who could present the crisis
> to Parliament and if necessary, to the nation
> for determination. It is not that the Governor-
> General (or the Crown) can overrule the
> representatives of the people, but in the ultimate
> he can check the elected representatives in any
> extreme attempt by them to disregard the rule
> of law or the customary usages of Australian
> government and he could do so by forcing
> a crisis.[2]
>
> Sir Paul Hasluck, former Governor-General of the
> Commonwealth of Australia.

Existence (and Need for Existence)

▪■▪

Few, if any, authorities would now question the existence of the reserve or "prerogative" powers of the Crown. A school of thought existed early this century which held that such powers had attenuated through the passage of time to such an extent as to be virtually non-existent: in the words of the late Canadian constitutional expert, Dr Eugene Forsey, the reserve powers were regarded by some to have become a "Cheshire Cat: nothing remained but the smile".[3]

Such a proposition could only retain its credibility in the absence of a public demonstration. Government ministers who have witnessed the exercise or the private threat of such powers could not deny their existence, and throughout the last three centuries a number of them have publicly acknowledged and discussed the nature of these powers. Although the author is unaware of any occasion in the last fifty years in Britain in which they have been publicly invoked, they have been energetically exercised during times of crisis in the younger Commonwealth realms. So far has the pendulum swung towards their use, or advocated use, that Forsey complained in recent years that at the expense of parliamentary privileges, "More and more people seem to feel that if anything is amiss in the body politic, the Governor-General is (to borrow a phrase from P.G. Wodehouse) 'the chap to kiss the place and make it well'."[4]

The reserve powers don't exist to usurp the privileges of Parliament but quite the opposite: namely, to provide a last line of defences against any assault upon parliamentary democracy, as powers normally exercised under the advice of incumbent ministers, but which can be invoked under the ancient form of ministerial responsibility should events require it. The absence of their use in Britain has led Lord Hailsham of St. Marylebone, a former Lord Chancellor of the United Kingdom, to remark in 1978,

> The parts of a machine work well almost in inverse propor-
> tion as they attract attention to themselves. The Queen
> attracts plenty of attention as a symbol. But her most impor-
> tant working function as part of the machinery of government
> never attracts attention precisely because it is working exactly
> as it was designed to do.[5]

Irrespective of Britain, in the face of disproof throughout the rest of the Commonwealth adherents to the notion of the "Cheshire Cat" have gone the way of its torso, and faded away.

The value of the reserve executive powers has been tacitly recognised by some members of the republican camp, in their call for a "minimalist" republic. Before discussing the impossibility of "minimalist" change, or attempting to enumerate and describe the reserve powers in any detail, it's necessary to wonder why they might be desirable in the first place.

It dwells in the nature of the human condition to desire power: to ensure our survival, to acquire wealth and prestige, to impose our will upon our surroundings, and to remake our environment in fulfilment of our desires. This consideration must lie at the heart of any discussion of politics, or of politicians.

In a parliamentary democracy such as our own, the political sovereign, the people, invest their collective power into an instrument of government, namely Parliament, an assembly of representatives. The dominant faction in Parliament's Lower House becomes the Government, and its leader, the Prime Minister. The power vested in Parliament to govern lies at the disposal of the

Prime Minister and other Government ministers to wield, subject to the confidence and scrutiny of Parliament, the rules and conventions of the Constitution, and the rule of law. But how are these rules and conventions to be enforced? How is one to prevent government ministers from using their vast but temporary powers to acquire more permanent power, beyond the control of Parliament and the electorate to revoke? Given that the government ministers possess their power for a finite duration of time in office, and that disgruntled constituents must represent the eventual death sentence for most minister's political careers, these questions are central to the survival of parliamentary democracy. There's a conflict of interest inherent in representative democracy between citizens wishing to preserve and exercise their democratic right to hire and fire their political representatives, and the politicians, struggling to achieve tenure despite the tides of public opinion.

One might hope that the personal moral code of politicians is such to prevent this scenario of constitutional subversion from taking place, but to make the moral integrity of politicians a basis for our constitutional creed is to render our liberties an article for common prayer. A well-written Constitution is a partial solution, but even the best-written one merely disperses the problem into smaller elements, rather than dissolving it. The legal profession gains much of its wealth from the fact that no written document is fully proof against a hostile intelligence probing for weaknesses and challenging definitions, and in this respect a written Constitution is a legal document like any other. Having the full bench of the High Court — an active judicial intelligence scrutinising government actions and legislation — is a useful and desirable safeguard. But it is not enough. Avenues of behaviour are open to the government that, although outrageous in their effects and pernicious of liberty, are perfectly legal. Our panel of judges are powerless to prevent this behaviour, although they might disapprove of it.

Consider a hypothetical scenario: an ultra-nationalist political party and its allies gain a majority of seats in both Federal Houses of Parliament. Its members have a secret agenda: they believe that immigration from overseas should be reduced to zero, that migrants should be discriminated against and, if possible, repatriated. They begin by repealing the 1976 Federal anti-discrimination legislation that provides a safeguard against discriminatory State legislation. This of course can be passed due to their parliamentary majority, and is perfectly legal. Their next success is in some of the States. In Queensland (which has a unicameral Parliament) they repeal the right to vote of all Queensland residents born overseas. Despite the obnoxious content of such an Act, it might well survive a legal challenge. A bench of judges can do nothing if the forms of law have been obeyed. All they can do is hope that the majority of the new electorate, now restricted to native-born Queenslanders, is sufficiently disgusted eventually to elect another government that will undo the damage.

This is an example of a *non-justiciable* issue: one which demands action, but cannot be redressed in a court of law, for no legal principle has been violated.

Judges can only protect the Constitution on *justiciable* issues. On other issues they are as powerless as any other private citizen.

Superficially this hypothetical may appear extreme and silly. It *is* extreme, which is why it was chosen to expose our problem at hand. It exposes some disturbing issues. Although its threat to democracy is conspicuous, it would be less dangerous in its implications than legislation already presented before the High Court of Australia.

Simply stripping groups in the community of the right to vote doesn't destroy expectations that a fully representative democracy will return in the foreseeable future. If the machinery of free election remains intact — freedom of speech and dissemination of information, freedom to associate and form political groups, the right of those still possessing a vote to exercise choice among the candidates freely, the certainty of knowing that if sufficient votes are raised against the incumbent government it will be removed and replaced by one reflecting the electorate's choice — then a representative democratic system may be restored. Even with a limited franchise, if these mechanisms are preserved then those disenfranchised sections of the community, by public campaigning, arguing their case to the members of the limited electorate, may fight to regain their lost right to vote in the same way that right was originally gained for universal male suffrage, women's suffrage, and most recently, full citizenship and voting rights for Aborigines.

The more dangerous, real, legislation was attempted by the Keating government in 1992, to censor political advertising. Despite having extreme implications, it was regarded by that Government as being within its powers and safe from legal challenge. In the 1992 landmark court case *Australian Capital Television Pty Ltd v. The Commonwealth of Australia*, the High Court of Australia struck down the attempted legislation on the grounds that it attacked the foundations of representative government; it would entrench existing politicians, silence all associations in the community not actually proposing candidates for election, and unjustly hinder attempts by new associations to have their candidates elected. The proposed laws would do this by distorting the exchange of information throughout the community; in the passionate words of the late Sir Maurice Byers QC, a former Commonwealth Solicitor-General now standing in court to oppose the Commonwealth Government, "In a democracy the right to freedom of speech is part of the fabric of society. There cannot be democracy if the voters are gagged and blindfolded".[6]

Niccolò's ghost You're straying from the topic, surely. Get back to your anti-immigrant supremacists! Couldn't their attempts be easily thwarted by establishing a Charter of Rights, rendering all assaults upon civil liberties justiciable, within the capacity of your High Court to oppose?

In 1988 the issue of an Australian charter of rights was a topic of heated debate.[7] Its inspiration came from the first ten amendments of the US Constitution, otherwise known as the US Bill of Rights, and the French Declaration of the Rights of Man written in 1789. The modern impetus for such a charter owes some of its strength to Canada, which has possessed a Charter of Rights and Freedoms since the "patriation" of her constitution in 1982. The central problems of this concept are of drafting (what words should be written), implementation (persuading the voters to agree to these words both in themselves and how they affect the federal structure), interpretation (who shall say what these words mean, and why) and potency (what power these words wield, and the power their interpreters wield), as well as the ethical issue of whether we possess the right to write one at all. The writing of a document which encompasses and enunciates the fundamental rights in our society, to be enshrined within our written Constitution, is no idle matter of coffee shop composition over a cappuccino and cigarette. The opponents to it raised the ghost of Thomas Paine, who in 1791 asserted in the *Rights of Man* that "Every age and generation must be as free to act for itself, *in all cases*, as the ages and generations which preceded it".[†] To enshrine an explicit and comprehensive statement of rights in a written constitution is to dictate terms, however benevolently intended, to future generations, and contradicts this principle.

The authors of our written Constitution decided against inflicting this. Apart from a few limited statements,[‡] they placed their faith in the processes adopted from Westminster for the protection of our liberties. As traditionally practiced in England, the law has two levels: the fundamental or lower level ("common law"), a combination of legal precedent — being centuries of history of judicial decisions upon a particular point of law — and the legal philosophy which underlies them, and an imposed or upper level ("statute law"), provided by legislation passed by Parliament.

Because the United Kingdom has no written constitution, the supreme lawgiving authority is the "Crown in Parliament", being the threesome of the House of Commons, the House of Lords and the Queen. The House of Commons, being an assembly of democratically elected citizens, proposes legislation in the form of a motion or "Bill". The House of Lords, being traditionally a body of hereditary and life peers, reviews it and may recommend amendments. Once the Bill passes through both Houses it is delivered to the Queen, who gives it her royal assent, turning the Bill into an Act of Parliament. Acts may override existing common law, where the two conflict. Similarly, a new statute eclipses existing statute law, as it is a more recent

---

† Quoted from P. Hanks, "The Democratic Case against Constitutional Rights", *Change the Constitution?*, pp. 60–66. Ironically, Paine himself was in favour of declarations of rights; he seems to have been unaware of the underlying contradiction in his book, being ignorant of the implications of such a declaration and believing as he did that rights were unalterable in nature.

‡ On trial by jury for offences against Commonwealth laws, the acquisition of property by the government on just terms, and a prohibition against the Commonwealth establishing a religion or prohibiting the "free exercise" of any religion.

expression of the will of the people's representatives. What one parliament does, a later parliament can undo, as the will of successive generations of society changes. In this way each generation may design the society within which it lives.†

But allowing the populace from year to year to design society involves a dilemma, because democracy itself has within its own body the capacity for tyranny, the so-called "tyranny of the majority". Government by popular consent can easily involve policies against unpopular or disenfranchised minorities within society, who are successfully oppressed by sheer weight of numbers. Even in times of peace and stability, a philosophy of government of "the greatest good for the greatest number" of citizens can be oppressive to those not included in that number. In times of crisis, when societies become paranoid, it's common for minorities to be used as scapegoats. History provides a palette of diverse examples within democracies, from Jewish conspiracy theories to "Papist plots", from the trials of the Salem witches to the trials of the alleged communists in 1950s America. Public paranoia or prejudice can be manifested in persecution and execution and yet be democratic. How does one construct a sieve that allows society to echo the voices of a crowd but not the voices of a mob?

These ingredients of oppression would lie even in a political system which worked like an inanimate mirror, reflecting perfectly the will of the electorate, with no other complicating factor. Yet in a representative democracy composed of living, breathing human beings there's another, different danger. Aristotle argued that society is composed of three elements: the democratic, the oligarchical and the monarchical. For at least the last three centuries the English-speaking world has given his words an interpretation along the lines of the traditional structure of the English Constitution, with the democratic element represented by the elected House of Commons, the oligarchical represented by the hereditary and appointed House of Lords, and the monarchical represented by the Crown. Even within this century when this traditional structure, interpreted literally, was obsolete, it has remained a useful metaphor for a society in which the effective "monarchical" element has been the Prime Minister, the "democratic" the representatives in Parliament of the masses of citizens whose usual political power resides solely in their votes, and the "oligarchic" those individuals whose positions outside the democratic frame-work — as media barons, say, or leaders of trade unions — have given them particular power over the society, and hence influence over the policies of government. However there is a different interpretation which may be cast on Aristotle's words, an interpretation which would remain valid in the centuries ahead even in a Utopian society which somehow imposed perfect equality of

† The exception to this is the *Bill of Rights(1689)* itself. Although strictly speaking it is simply a piece of legis-lation devised by the Convention Parliament and enacted by William and Mary, its central position in defining the contract between the Queen and her subjects means it is unlikely that attempts to violate it through future legislation would succeed. For this reason it has sometimes been described as the closest thing Britain has to a written Constitution (Adams, *Constitutional History of England*. pp. 358–359).

wealth, equality of opportunity, equality of ability among its citizens — and a representative democracy. Be everything else ever so equal, representative democracy itself creates what might be described as an elective oligarchy,† dividing society into two "classes",‡ between which exists friction.

It has been said that a commonwealth is a State in which the citizens have in effect made a pact with one another for each to surrender part of their autonomy, this surrendered authority from each citizen to be given to some central Power to be exercised for the mutual benefit and safety of all.§ This Power we name the government, and the power it wields over the citizens is the accumulation of the authority surrendered by all the citizens. Yet this itself creates a class structure. What might be described as an *elective oligarchy* is that class of people who have a personal vested interest in the wielding of this power, apart from the common interest in the common good. It consists not only of these parliamentarians who actually wield the power of government, but the parliamentarians in Opposition who may come to wield that power if the fortunes of political war shift, and the apparatchiks on both sides, those whose livelihoods and ambitions depend upon the continuing patronage of parliamentarians. From this oligarchy is drawn the "monarchical" element — the Prime Minister — whose single will guides and sometimes dictates the policies of government. And below…is the other class, the *constituency*, composed of all those citizens of the community not actively involved in the political process. (Some might say this view of representative democracy ignores the existence of conflicting parties, but this isn't so. Both elective oligarchy and constituency are divided into parties and followers of parties, dominated at present by the two warring alliances of factions and parties of Labor and the Coalition, and those other constituents who follow neither grouping but cry a plague upon both their Houses.)

The strength of a democracy in remaining intact is the inability of the elective oligarchy to shake free of the constraints of the constituency. For Opposition parliamentarians to gain government they must rely upon gaining the support of voters, by adopting (or appearing to adopt) the wishes of enough members

---

† Some readers might be offended at my use of the word "oligarchy" within a modern democratic context. After all, an oligarchy is a government by a handful of aristocrats, isn't it, and we live in an egalitarian representative democracy, don't we? The literal translation of the term "oligarchy" is "rule by the few" (from the ancient Greek, *oligoi* few + *arkhō* rule). Inasmuch as our government is conducted by a Cabinet of ministers theoretically responsible to Parliament, this term doesn't appear immediately inappropriate. Whether this rule by the few may be described as democratic (Gk *dēmos* the people + *kratos* power) surely depends upon how accountable these ministers can be held to the people. Objection may be made that "oligarchy" usually has an implication of life tenure. As we shall see, it's a point in my argument that government ministers desire precisely this.

‡ Once again some readers may object to my use of the word "class" in describing a division of the public into two groups, between which some conflict exists; a classification of society which however has nothing to do with economics or ownership of the means of production or membership of the proletariat. But if one is to "classify" then one must have "classes", and our classes, like those discussed by Marx, are identified by their roles in a transaction, although the transaction which interests us here has nothing to do with labour.

§ Hobbes'definition, from *Leviathan*. It is to be *hoped* that all modern countries that name themselves representative democracies can be described as commonwealths, in which the authority to govern rests on the consent of the governed, and is given in the expectation that it shall be employed for the public good.

---

of groups in the constituency into their agenda to win the next election. The government mustn't allow this to happen, and so adopts (or appears to adopt) enough of the wishes of rival groups in the constituency to retain the votes to remain in power. When the constituency is alert — instead of wishful, apathetic or fatally cynical — it's dangerous for members of the oligarchy to rely upon deceit to achieve votes, dangerous to rely continually upon pretending to incorporate popular policies without actually implementing them. So long as freedom of association and the integrity of the electoral process are preserved there is always a risk that angry and frustrated citizens shall form new parties and elect new representatives, displacing former parliamentarians from their positions and forcing them into reluctant exile among the constituency. One must therefore either implement election promises from time to time, or search for alternative solutions to the problem of the constituency; the problem posed by the very existence of the voting public.

The obvious alternative solution available to the oligarchy is to use its temporary power to shake free of the constraints of the constituency. The only members of the oligarchy able to do this are those with the power to do it: those parliamentarians sitting on the Government benches. Their enemies sitting on the Opposition benches may resist these attempts if they have the numbers to do so. No-one likes to see their enemies endowed with permanent power. Yet what if the Opposition lacks the numbers, the cohesion or the political will to provide effective resistance against these measures attempted by the Government? More cynically, what if these measures can be turned to mutual advantage on both sides of the House? Clearly what is needed then is a will external to Parliament, capable of intervention at these times.

Niccolò's ghost At last we're coming to it! I mean, the profound difference between the reserve powers of the Crown and a declaration of rights. But to reach this difference, you must answer the question: what actually *is* political power? Neglect your talk of commonwealths, and search for an answer to this question which holds true for all political systems throughout the centuries behind and ahead of us, be they enlightened or tyrannical, inspired by liberty or grounded upon slavery. Better yet, I'll tell you.

A clever Florentine gentleman provided one way of perceiving political power when he described it as the means by which we impose our will upon our surroundings.[†] The quantity of political power we possess can be measured by the extent to which we can alter our environment to our own advantage. If we are shrewd in our use of power, these alterations will be made to ensure future impositions of our will are easier to inflict and

---

† Deeper implications of Machiavelli's writings are frequently lost in translation. Subtle and precise in his use

more profound in effect; increasing our future political power. If we are a government, constitutions, written or "unwritten", exist to prevent the power associated with that will from becoming absolute.

In modern times both the reserve powers and a proposed declaration of citizen's rights in our system of government are a tacit recognition of the dangers of a parliamentary oligarchy, and both attempt to curb the power of the government, but in profoundly different ways. Understanding the difference is crucial. Crudely speaking, the reserve powers are a weapon against the manipulation of the *substance* and *nature* of political power by the government, whereas a declaration of rights protected and interpreted by a High Court is a weapon merely against *expressions* of political authority, laws imposed upon citizens by the government. This distinction between the two was clearly demonstrated in Germany by Adolf Hitler as Reich Chancellor during the last days of the Weimar Republic.

It's an interesting question whether he could have begun his later programme of detention, torture and extermination had the Constitution retained its strength. Declarations in the Republic's constitution that "The freedom of the person is inviolable. Curtailment or deprivation of personal freedom by a public authority is only permissible on a legal basis" (Article 114), or "All Germans have the right to assemble peacefully and unarmed without giving notice and without special permission" (Article 123), or "All citizens without distinction shall be eligible for public office in accordance with the laws and according to their capabilities and achievements" (Article 128) don't sit well with the society of the Third Reich. Although the operation of these declarations of rights could be suspended by the exercise of the President's reserve powers during times of national emergency, government by presidential decree could only be perpetrated "so long as his [the president's] measures were not rejected in parliament".[8]

From when he was appointed Chancellor by President Hindenberg on the 30th of January 1933 to when he arranged fresh elections held on the 5th of April after the Reichstag fire, Hitler did not possess a majority in parliament:

> His appointment was quite unnecessary. His coalition government, in which Hugenberg's Nationalists were the only other

---

of language, he was fond of employing puns and apparent paradoxes in his original Italian to force the reader to puzzle out the implications of his statements. In *The Prince* his term "*lo stato*" is usually translated as "the State", but when it clearly isn't referring to a particular regime controlling territory with formal geographical boundaries, translators have often written words like "dominion", "rule", "government", "reign" and "power" instead. But political historian and translator Leo Paul S. de Alvarez has argued persuasively that this destroys meaning, and Machiavelli was self-consistent in his use of *lo stato*: "The [S]tate is the realisation in act of the will of someone. It indicates the extent to which one's will is introduced or imposed...[it] is certainly not a territory, and it is more than rule, power, dominion or government. It is the ordering of inchoate nature into a human form. It is entirely an artificial construct, dependent upon man's capacity to invent and to manipulate things". (Niccolò Machiavelli, *The Prince* (transl. L. P. S. de Alvarez), pp. ix–x.) A logical consequence is that the distinction between "domestic" and "foreign" politics becomes almost a false dichotomy.

party represented, had no majority in the Reichstag. The Nazis could not have threatened the State if they had been denied power. Their movement was waning.[9]

Of Germany in 1932 it could still be said:

> It should be stressed that at this time there was no reason why Hitler should have been regarded as an invincible force in German politics. Indeed, the nation had, by its votes, shown that it rejected dictatorship from the left or the right. Had the President and the army leaders been determined to defeat Hitler they could easily have done so.[10]

Rather than attempting to impose his will upon Germany with the limited political power he then possessed — a move which, given his agenda, might have been effectively opposed by the judiciary, fatally discrediting himself and his party — Hitler shrewdly moved to increase the substance of his power. His Emergency Decree following the Reichstag fire, arresting or dispersing Communists accused of planning a Bolshevik *coup*, broke their opposition both within parliament and outside it in a way which was legal. His passage of the Enabling Act through parliament in March 1933 then exploited the complacency of the Centre Party, the electoral defeats of the moderate Right and the outnumbering of the Social Democrats. None of this could be opposed by the judiciary wielding declarations of citizens' rights, because — apart from the attack on the Communists, legally defensible under Article 48 empowering the Emergency Decree — nothing in these manoeuvres actually violated anybody's rights in any justiciable way. All the judges could do was sit on their benches, watching the thunderhead of Nazi power gain in strength on the horizon, and wait for the storm to break over Germany with enough accumulated force to wash away the rights of the citizens.

A declaration of rights doesn't fulfil the purpose of the reserve powers. Opposing direct oppression by the government upon the citizens, it is impotent in preventing the government from acquiring further power by other means behind the scenes, power amassed and hoarded until there is enough of it to make the Prime Minister irresistible in will — at which time the government may unleash that power to impose that will upon the citizens, too strongly for the judiciary to resist.

Conversely, the reserve powers don't fulfil the purpose of a declaration of rights. The powers of the Crown exist to prevent unconstitutional alterations in the substance and nature of power wielded by the government, and to perform the fundamental duties of the Crown imposed after the Revolution of 1688. Apart from that, the legitimate usual authority of Parliament may be employed in many ways which alter or destroy civil liberties, ways which a declaration of rights could oppose but the reserve powers may not. Of this usual power of Parliament Lord Hailsham has written,

> There is no right, however sacred, of the individual or of a
> majority which cannot be infringed or abolished by an Act of
> Parliament. The sole sanctions restricting this almost unique
> authority rest in the consciences of the members of each
> House, the influence of public opinion, the necessity for peri-
> odical general elections…and the power of Parliament to
> reverse or amend its own legislation.[11]

This authority to re-model the nature of rights within a society from parliament to parliament is essential for the social order to adapt to its changing
environment in a way that can be described as democratic. It's traditionally
regarded as having been inherited by the Australian Parliament, with our
written Constitution deliberately silent on declared rights. This is, however, a
dangerous ability to possess, and silhouetted against this background the
activism of the High Court of Australia in the early '90s may best be understood. If, as most of its members asserted in 1992, it's possible to read the existence of "implied" rights in a document which is deliberately silent in stating
them, then a profound shift in the power structures of our society may have
taken place, with the High Court marching to capture territory traditionally
held by Parliament.

A traditional tenet of faith is that the High Court's concern is with the *substance*
of authority wielded by the legislature, rather than how Parliament chooses to
wield it in policies. Yet this distinction between substance and the way it's
wielded is crude: for example, if Parliament chose to abolish blonde-haired
suffrage, by one interpretation it would be a legitimate (although reprehensible)
exercise of usual parliamentary authority.[†] From another perspective it would
represent a serious alteration in the fabric of the Constitution: if opinions and
voting patterns for the government are divided along lines of hair colour, then
abolishing the right of blondes to vote could change significantly the nature of
elections, as well as altering the modern view on the consent of the governed.
There's a grey margin in politics and law where Parliament, by wielding its usual
power to alter civil liberties, may be said to have acquired unusual power.

One parliament's ability to alter civil liberties is only tolerable if subsequent
parliaments possess the ability to change them back again. Physicists argue
Nature abhors a reversible process; political philosophers reply that in legislation, liberty abhors an irreversible one. The wanton behaviour of one parliament
must not be permitted to steer constitutional government down a blind alley,
salvageable only by revolution. If a line must be drawn, over which a parliament
may not step without challenge, that line must be where alteration to the fabric
of society, imposed by the will of Parliament, precipitates irreversible change.

But what form should this challenge take, and who should issue it? If the line
can be drawn in legal terms, then the High Court can adjudicate a complaint

---

† It would of course have to be done in the States before being done federally, in order to comply with s.41
of the Commonwealth Constitution.

issued by an aggrieved party. Not all such lines may be drawn with legal instruments without a declaration of rights, nor even with one will the lines all be placed where we need them; placed so the elective oligarchy cannot seize further power. But put aside for the moment these fears, and return to the arena of the Court, where the battle was fought in 1992 over an attempt by the Keating government to alter liberties and seize entrenched power through political censorship. Members of our community cling to the belief that our elected politicians would never attack the institution of democracy itself, never attempt to erect a sham façade behind which an effective one-party State could be created. In '92 came disillusionment.

It seems (at least to this author) that the case of the plaintiffs in *Australian Capital Television Pty Ltd v. The Commonwealth of Australia*, propounded by Sir Maurice Byers QC and K. Mason QC[†] (Solicitor-General of New South Wales) and upheld in the decision of the Court, rested on three points: the attempted ban on political advertising imposed by the Keating government was, first, an attack upon the political integrity of the States and Australia's federal structure: in the words of Mason QC, sections of the attempted legislation would

> impede the capacity of the States to function and the
> processes by which their legislative and executive powers are
> exercised, thereby threatening their structural integrity. They
> also contravene the protection of State constitutions guaran-
> teed by [sections] 106 and 107 of the Constitution…The ban
> on political advertisements by State Governments and
> government authorities goes far beyond the protection of any
> legitimate federal interest in relation to federal and Territorial
> elections…The capacity of State Governments and their
> authorities to protect themselves and to communicate infor-
> mation vital to their interests and proper functioning is
> severely impaired. Because of the definition of 'political
> matter', [sections of the legislation] would prohibit broadcasts
> on behalf of a State Government during a federal constitu-
> tional referendum in which there was a Commonwealth
> proposal to amend the Constitution by extending the
> Commonwealth Parliament's concurrent or exclusive powers,
> or to abolish the States or make applicable to the States a
> controversial bill of rights.[12]

Secondly, it was a calculated and disgraceful attempt by members of the elective oligarchy to pervert the democratic process, to entrench themselves in power. In the words of Byers QC:

> This regime [imposed by the legislation] discriminated against
> persons or parties not already represented in a Parliament or

---

† It is important to distinguish in this account between K. Mason QC, Solicitor-General of New South Wales, and Sir Anthony Mason, Chief Justice of the High Court of Australia.

legislature. The constitutional freedom [of movement and communication] is totally taken away…[a section of the legislation] substitutes for the right of freedom of political discussion a regime under which those parties represented by members in the Parliament obtain ninety percent of the total time allowed for broadcasting political material. Non-party Senators take the next five percent. No other person has a right to time. He must apply. The obligation [in the legislation] to provide free time is invalid because it compels the broadcasting of political information or, alternatively, because it compels the broadcasting of political information discriminating in favour of political parties already represented in a Parliament or legislature. The provisions cannot be justified as falling within the area of any permissible regulatory power. They are not proportionate to the attainment of any legitimate governmental objective.[13]

This concern was echoed by Mason QC, who insisted,

The Act is also unfair in its allocation of free time in favour of existing parties. It operates to entrench them and deter new entrants. It imposes burdens on innocent persons because of a perceived need to prevent the corruption of major political parties.[14]

a concern confirmed and upheld by Chief Justice Sir Anthony Mason, who later wrote in his judgement:

It is obvious that the provisions of [this legislation] regulating the allocation of free time given preferential treatment to political parties represented by the preceding Parliament or legislature which are contesting the relevant election with at least the prescribed number of candidates. Their entitlement amounts to ninety percent of the total free time. Others must of necessity rely on the exercise of discretion by the Tribunal. As among the political parties, the principle of allocation to be applied will tend to favour the party or parties in government because it gives weight to the first preference voting in the preceding election. Furthermore, a senator who seeks re-election is given preferential treatment over a candidate, not being a senator, who stands for election to the Senate. The former, but not the latter, is entitled to a grant of free time…The provisions of [the legislation] manifestly favour the status quo. More than that, the provisions regulating the allocation of free time allow no scope for participation in the election campaign by persons who are not candidates or by groups who are not putting forward candidates for election. Employers' organisations, trade unions, manufacturers' and farmers' organisations, social welfare groups and societies generally are excluded from participation otherwise than through the means protected by [a particular section of the legislation]. The consequence is that freedom of speech or expression or electronic media in relation to public affairs and the political process is severely restricted by a regulatory regime which evidently favours the established political parties and their candidates without securing compensating advantages or benefits for others who wish to participate in the electoral process or in the political debate which is an integral part of that process.[15]

Those who doubt that members of the elective oligarchy of this country are actively attempting to subvert the democratic process need look no further than to the Chief Justice to see that he, at least, was painfully aware of the implications of what lay before him. Later he acidly warned "The Court should be astute not to accept at face value claims by the legislature and the Executive that freedom of communication will, unless curtailed, bring about corruption and distortion of the political process."[16]

The third, closely related, point was the direct attack by the government on freedom of communication. Parliament's general right to alter and amend the rights and liberties of the community was claimed in full by the Government's defence counsel in court, Commonwealth Solicitor-General G Griffith QC:

> The Court should not strike down the legislation unless it is satisfied that it so impairs the democratic process that it can no longer be said that Parliament is being directly chosen in an informed way by the people…The Court must accept that Parliament had reasonable grounds for apprehending the problems to which the legislature is addressed, and cannot inquire whether the solution adopted was necessary or even desirable. For invalidity, it is not enough that the Court considers the law to be inexpedient or misguided…Once it is accepted that the right of freedom of expression is subject to some regulation in the public interest, it is for Parliament and not the courts to determine what the public interest requires.[17]

Sir Anthony Mason warned "[T]he overseas experience does not refute the proposition that [this legislation] impairs freedom of discussion of public and political affairs and freedom to criticise federal institutions in the respects previously mentioned",[18] namely "the freedoms previously enjoyed by citizens to discuss public and political affairs"[19]. Traditional freedom of speech was under attack, and government politicians being entrenched. What could be done about it?

> The framers of the Constitution accepted, in accordance with prevailing English thinking, that the citizens' rights were best left to the protection of the common law in association with the doctrine of parliamentary supremacy.[20]

THE NECESSITY FOR RESERVE POWERS

Consequently, unlike the United States we're able to say of our system that "The great underlying principle is, that the rights of individuals are sufficiently secured by ensuring, as far as possible, to each a share, and an equal share, in political power".[21] But where did this leave us in 1992?

This was the pivotal point of Sir Anthony's decision — without the freedom to disseminate information throughout the community it could not be said that members of the public were able to "build and assert political power, including the power to change the men who govern them".[22] Under these conditions it couldn't be said that citizens possessed "each a share, and an equal share, in political power". Democracy was being destroyed in this country. The federal system also came back into play:

> The concept of freedom to communicate with respect to public affairs and political discussion does not lend itself to subdivision. Public affairs and political discussion are indivisible and cannot be subdivided into compartments that correspond with, or relate to, the various tiers of government in Australia. Unlike the legislative powers of the Commonwealth Parliament, there are no limits to the range of matters that may be relevant to debate in the Commonwealth Parliament or to its workings... Notwithstanding that a particular matter at a given time might appear to have a primary or immediate connexion with the affairs of a State, a local authority or a Territory and little or no connexion with Commonwealth affairs.[23]

In his judgement the fact the authors of our written Constitution had deliberately rejected an enshrined declaration of freedom of speech was

> no answer to the case [argued by Byers QC and Mason QC] which the plaintiffs now present...that a guarantee of freedom of expression in relation to public and political affairs must necessarily be implied from the provision which the Constitution makes for a system of representative government...because such a freedom is an essential concomitant of representative government, it is necessarily implied in the prescription of that system.[24]

Through this elaborate process of reasoning, invoking in part the federal structure, Mason CJ ruled against the attempts of the government to bias political communication and entrench themselves in power.[25]

This decision wasn't unanimous. Justice Sir Daryl Dawson dissented with the entire judgement, not because he approved of anything the Keating government was attempting, but because in his view,

> in this country the guarantee of fundamental freedoms does not lie in any constitutional mandate but in the capacity of a

democratic society to preserve for itself its own shared values…The question is not whether the legislation ought to be regarded as desirable or undesirable in the interests of free speech or even of representative democracy…it is for Parliament, within the limits prescribed by the Constitution, to provide the form of representative democracy which we are to have and in so doing it may adopt measures about which there may be a considerable variation of opinion.[26]

Of these conflicting opinions, the interpretation traditionally regarded as the correct one is that expressed by Justice Dawson. It is the judicial opinion of Chief Justice Mason (and for that matter, Justices Deane and Toohey, who "reached 'a firm view' that the Constitution contained implications of freedom of communication extending to all political matters apt for an ordered and democratic society"[27]) which is radical.

The battle illustrated two aspects of the guardianship of the political order of society by a High Court.

1. The Court is not reliable in the consistency of attitude of its members, nor consequently in its stance against controversial legislation. This doctrine of implied rights, law today since 1992, was proposed in the 1970s in the High Court by the late Justice Lionel Murphy — and was roundly rejected by his fellow judges. This doesn't mean Murphy was a true prophet of future days: in another twenty years time it may be this doctrine will again be roundly rejected, and a more traditional interpretation restored — or a more radical one adopted. In saying this, no blame or stigma is intended to be laid upon the judiciary. Generations of judges come and go, and with their books and baggage are carried different judicial philosophies, and so different interpretations of the matters before them. When legislatures from time to time compose an Act to acquire wrongful power, the extent of opposition encountered from the Bench will depend not only on the judge's personal beliefs, but the prevalent legal doctrine of the day.

    Hence the Court, although a valuable and desirable check upon the executive and the legislature, is insufficient both in the scope of its power — only able to adjudicate justiciable issues — and in the consistency of its adjudication, to provide an acceptable final defence against abuses of powers.

    Inspired by our recent salvation by lemon juice rights discovered in the Constitution, which in the heat of crisis appear written on the paper, brownly, some have suggested that the first half of this problem — the scope of what's justiciable — could be dealt with by writing (in black indelible ink) an entrenched charter of rights *in conjunction with* a Constitution which addresses the substance of all power, so by addressing all aspects of society in law, the Court is empowered to resolve everything under the sun. Unless all the conventions of which our system of government is composed — including the reserve powers — are also codified into hard law, this belief is invalid. This is neither the time nor place to discuss the codification of the reserve powers. That task kept for later chapters. Sufficient to say here that the Westminster system of government is a political system composed almost entirely of historical conventions and principles, and these conventions are not themselves justiciable. Their violation is an issue of naked political power, and their remedy must (until they themselves find complete legal expression) also be political. This is the emergency that demands the existence of reserve powers.

It would be an act of madness to attempt a comprehensive legal codification of the conventions of Westminster. Not only is precise codification an impossible task, but even if by some Herculean effort it *were* possible, this would be largely undesirable. For example, even if the entire doctrine of ministerial responsibility could be neatly summarised in a legal formula, only a fool would want to incorporate it in the fabric of law in a way that could ever be erased. Statutes can be eclipsed or revoked. Constitutional law can be altered by referendum or (as we have just witnessed) by a change in judicial interpretation. Nothing short of a revolution should be permitted to tamper with ministerial responsibility, for by its alteration or suspension the rule of law could easily be destroyed.

Even implementing the easy part of the proposition — endowing the Bench with an entrenched declaration of rights to defend — yields ominous results, for the inconsistency of judicial decision-making is vastly amplified in its implications. As shall be argued in more detail later when we look at the United States experience, the variation in judicial opinions would not be reduced by even one punctuation mark, but the repercussions for the community would be manifoldly increased by the levers placed in the hands of these quarrelling scholars. This brings us to the second of the insights:

2. What we've been witnessing is the struggle of oligarchy against oligarchy, the parliamentary majority in the legislature being opposed by the Justices of the High Court who, through not having an interest in parliamentary power, may be expected to oppose it when appropriate. The decision of the High Court is final. There is no appeal from these lofty heights. One has consulted with the Delphic Oracle, whose words now hang over one's destiny with an awful finality.

The proposal mentioned earlier, of attempting to bring all political disputes within the aegis of the High Court — a proposal solemnly advocated by prominent republicans — would exalt its members even higher, to a positively godlike status.

Niccolò's ghost: The names of Zeus, Hades and Apollo would have been joined by those of Mason, Toohey and Brennan, Gaudron, Dawson, Deane and McHugh JJ. Not to mention their learned successors.

Is it really desirable that when confronted by an elective oligarchy out of control, our only solution is to oppose it by another oligarchy? That when politicians become more outrageous in their attempts to acquire power, our solitary reply is to invest yet more authority in the judiciary? Even if all political struggles *could* be reduced to a set of legal questions, is it really appropriate that all political struggle be sent to a secluded assembly of scholars to be resolved? Where now are the privileges of Parliament, the ability of parliamentarians hostile to the government to oppose and defeat its measures *as* parliamentarians (rather than as litigants), resolving the quarrel on the floors of the two Houses? Where would be the power of Parliament, in this country which boasts of being a democracy? Finally, where would the power of the people themselves have gone? When all the final decisions of weight are made by the wisdom of unelected judges, where now is the voice of the people? Apart from ordinary elections, there seems to be no place for it at all in this struggle of gods and titans. The more we elevate the positions of the Powers that brawl, the more remote they become from the actual source of sovereignty in this country. Surely in any genuine democracy the final resolution of many forms of political conflict should be, and must remain, trial by ballot box.

In these past few pages voices have spoken, saying our founders had placed their faith in the processes of the British Constitution for the security of future liberty. With no written constitution that country has no analogue with our High Court, no opportunity for British judges to oppose unscrupulous legislation in the manner of their Australian counterparts, no chance to "do a Mason". Yet the elective oligarchy in that country, although far stronger than its Australian equivalent and further strengthening its grip in the first three quarters of the 20th Century, has not successfully shaken free from the constituency. One must ask why.

It's not due to any sanctity on the part of British politicians, of an awareness imbued in the occupants of the offices of Westminster and Whitehall that usurping power, like wearing a waistcoat with a double-breasted jacket, just Isn't Done. What power the residents of 10 Downing Street *have* managed to acquire this century would indicate they have a common appetite with politicians throughout the rest of the world. That in the absence of obvious restraints they have yet been restrained, unable to indulge fully this appetite, is interesting. It suggests there is an alternative way to oppose the excesses of the elective oligarchy than erecting another oligarchy against and above it.

The political authority that dwells in London SW1 is divided between two elements, from which the whole is composed. One is active, the other passive. The "active" dwells in Whitehall, the elected politicians in government. These are the vocal, visible, active wielders of political power, the people who wield all the aspects of day-to-day authority which the executive can employ without real check by the legislature. Their wills devise foreign and domestic policy, altering the circumstances of daily life for ordinary Britons and the disposition of Britain's nuclear-armed submarines in the North Sea for NATO. When the voice of Britain formally speaks, these are the people who have written the script.

The "passive" element dwells in Buckingham Palace. Her Majesty cannot speak in public in Britain or any country *other* than her Commonwealth realms without the permission of her British Prime Minister, for the Prime Minister must take responsibility in the House for Her Majesty's words.[†] Under all usual circumstances she must follow the advice of her government ministers, and the servants of the British Crown obey the commands issued from Whitehall.

Yet the Crown isn't an empty cipher. Imagine a pair of old-fashioned scales, the balance of usual power. In one tray rests Whitehall, in the other, Buckingham Palace. Whitehall's share of power is overwhelmingly heavier than that possessed by the Palace, whose only counterweight is represented by the Queen's private rights "to be consulted, to encourage and to warn". In extraordinary circumstances however, the Queen can briefly tip the balance in the Palace's favour by throwing her sword into the scales. The "sword" she possesses is her power to force the government to endure the verdict of Parliament at Westminster (in effect, the verdict of the House of Commons) or submit to the test of the constituency's verdict at forced general elections.

This is an entirely different approach from resorting to the verdict of a judicial aristocracy. Unlike a High Court, Her Majesty does not and could not herself decide solutions to problems of policy, for she has no deliberative power to do so. What she does possess the authority to do, the purpose of all her existent reserve powers, is to prevent the elective oligarchy from escaping from the constituency, the true political sovereign.[‡]

Being an extremely dangerous course of action for her to take, this will only happen in rare circumstances. The reserve powers of the Crown represent a weapon of final solution, and like most other weapons of this kind, are ill-fitted for use in smaller scale conflicts. If the Crown wants to oppose the advice of the existing ministry pushing a disastrous or repugnant measure, and the incumbent Prime Minister refuses to back down or compromise, then alternative parliamentarians must be found, willing to take personal responsibility for sacking the incumbent. This necessity of finding people, most likely recruited from the front bench of the Opposition, willing to jeopardise their

---

[†] The nature of the impositions of the Queen and her representatives, imposed by the government of each realm, shall be discussed in detail in *Realm against Realm*. Meanwhile, remain mindful of the fact the British and Australian Crowns are distinct. The *Australian* — not British — Prime Minister takes responsibility for all words uttered by the Queen under the Australian Crown, irrespective of Britain.

[‡] In discussing "sovereignty" in the Westminster system, one must distinguish between the legal viewpoint and the political viewpoint. From the purely legal perspective the sovereign is the Crown in Parliament, possibly — as in Australia and most other Commonwealth realms — constrained by a limited written Constitution interpreted by a High Court. From the political viewpoint, it is the people. In a third, titular sense it is the Queen herself who is Sovereign; as we've already seen, even this is useful in terms of executive orders and the rule of law.

political careers for this controversial action of the Crown, imposes a check. The harsher constraint upon exercising this power except in grave emergency is the extreme personal danger its use represents. In the United Kingdom the Queen must be certain that the repugnance she feels for a particular measure is reflected strongly in the general community. If a general election is forced and the members of the former government are defeated, she may be vindicated, but if they're re-elected to dominate the House of Commons she might well be forced to abdicate.

Politicians in Britain have been able to take advantage of the absence of other constitutional defences to acquire enormous power, keeping a wary eye on the Palace while doing so. Consequently, British prime ministers this century have enjoyed a concentration of power fiercely criticized by a number of British political writers, most notably R.H.S. Crossman[28] and Lord Hailsham. Hailsham has gone so far as describe the present situation as being one of elective dictatorship: once a party acquires government at elections, there is virtually nothing now which forces it to be accountable to the constituency or Parliament except the Crown. The imbalance in that country is stark. Without the Crown's powers, it would be fatal. In Dr Forsey's words,

> The enormous increase in the power of the Cabinet, and
> especially of the Prime Minister, raises the question whether
> the reserve power of the Crown to force or refuse dissolution
> may not be one of the few safeguards against dictatorship by
> 'the leader of the junta wielding for the moment the power
> of office'[29].

We who advocate the necessity of retaining the reserve powers have been accused of having insufficient faith in our country. That accusation can be refuted, and the case for reserve powers advanced, using the words of James Madison. The chief author of the United States Constitution, he wrote a series of articles in 1787–88 defending aspects of his draft. In one article he wrote,

> It may be a reflection on human nature that…devices should
> be necessary to control the abuses of government. But what is
> government itself but the greatest of all reflections on human
> nature? If men were angels, no government would be neces-
> sary. If angels were to govern men, neither external nor
> internal controls on government would be necessary. In
> framing a government which is to be administered by men
> over men, the great difficulty lies in this: you must first enable
> the government to control the governed; and in the next
> place oblige it to control itself. *A dependence on the people is,*
> *no doubt, the primary control on the government; but experience*
> *has taught mankind the necessity of auxiliary precautions.*[30]

In Australia there are many such precautions: a written Constitution, a High Court, a powerful Senate and a federal structure. Yet, beneath everything, the essential transaction underlying representative democracy — the assignation of power from all citizens to their representatives in government — establishes a conflict of interest that is irreconcilable and permanently threatens to crack the foundations of democratic society. Abstractly we know this to be true. In recent history we've actually witnessed a reprehensible attempt by our government to demolish our democracy leaving only a façade, to deliver the electorate "bound and gagged" into the hands of the Prime Minister, an attempt opposed by the Chief Justice of the High Court. We can no longer pretend this struggle between the constituency and the elective oligarchy doesn't exist in the Lucky Country, or is played according to 'gentlemen's rules'.

This is a struggle in which politicians hold most of the cards to be played. An external force is required, to intervene when the game is played too unscrupulously. A choice exists, between two alternatives: invest the power of intervention entirely in another, independent oligarchy — the judiciary — by attempting to re-write the Constitution to be all-encompassing, or alternatively, impart at least some of this power of intervention to an executive figure, also not a member of the elective oligarchy, who has no power to dictate solutions but can force the issue to the verdict of Parliament or the constituency.

For practical reasons the judiciary provides an unsatisfactory final line of defence against usurpations. For ideological reasons also, judges are an intolerable replacement for the executive witness mentioned above. She or he, having no power to dictate solutions, may nonetheless force the issue to the judgement of the constituency, the people, who are the true sovereign of this country. If the people wish to remain the true sovereign, to be consulted in a crisis, then the reserve powers of the Crown must be retained. Discard this avenue of appeal, and you shall cease to be sovereign.

The newspapers supporting Ministers assert
that, under modern constitutional practice,
the Prime Minister for the time being 'always
has a dissolution in his pocket'...In my opinion,
similar 'intimations' are a very serious
interference with the regular processes of parliamentary government...

The Rt. Hon. Dr H.V. Evatt,
The Discretionary Authority of Dominion Governors.

*Debate in the British House of Commons,
29th March 1944:*

Mr Price (Forest of Dean): He is claiming for
the Executive now to dissolve Parliament and go
to the country...

[Sir Winston] Churchill: I never said anything
of the sort. I must make it absolutely clear that it
does not rest with any Prime Minister to dissolve
Parliament. The utmost he can do is tender
advice to the Crown...This is one of the exceptional circumstances when the Prerogative of the
Crown comes into play and where in doubtful
circumstances the Crown would refer to other
advisers. It has been done on several occasions.
I must make it absolutely clear that it does not
rest with the Government of the day. It would be
most improper on my part to use any language
which suggested that I have the power to make
such a decision.[31]

Granting or Denying
Dissolution or Prorogation

Legal texts on the reserve powers speak of three facets of the Crown's traditional power of dissolution of Parliament: namely, to grant dissolution, to
refuse dissolution, and to force its dissolution. But why all this talk of the
Crown's power? Under extraordinary circumstances it might be desirable for

the Crown to be able to appeal directly to the electorate, but surely under all but revolutionary conditions it should be the Prime Minister, as head of the elected government, who should have complete authority to decide whether or not to dissolve Parliament?

The answer to that question is a resounding NO, most obviously because neither the Prime Minister nor the entire Cabinet represents the democratic will of the nation assembled. That honour belongs to Parliament, in particular the entire Lower House of Parliament gathered together, being the assembly composed of all the elected representatives of all the constituencies of the nation, and it is an honour to be jealously guarded. The will of a complex society is by its nature divided, and for this reason the portion of it, the faction of it, that best commands the confidence of the assembly is granted the power to govern; yet the belief that the government of the day is the paramount democratic authority is a conceit to be condemned by any who admire parliamentary democracy.

Sometimes Prime Ministers give themselves presidential affectations, but ask yourself this question: who votes for our Prime Minister? In the parliamentary system the premiership or prime ministership isn't a directly elective position. The only people who vote for him directly are the members of his own constituency sympathetic with his party. Other Australians throughout the country who want to see him in power, vote for whatever — at the time of writing, Coalition — candidate is running in their electorate. Those who wished to see other parties, and their leaders, in power — be they Labor, Australian Democrats, Greens, Socialist Worker's Party or whoever — vote for their appropriate local candidate. At the end of the day, a party or grouping with enough seats to command the confidence of the House of Representatives gains the right to govern, but that is not to say that they gain the right to pretend to speak for all Australians, or to pretend to a direct mandate beyond that given via Parliament. What of the constituencies throughout Australia represented by parliamentarians of other parties? This is why the voices of Parliament are more important than the single voice of the Government, for it is the dialogue of the many which has the better claim to represent the mind of the nation. It is also why, traditionally, the Leader of Her Majesty's Loyal Australian Opposition is supposed to be accorded a similar level of respect to that of the Prime Minister. In this emphasis on the dialogue of the many rests one of the strongest reasons why parliamentary democracy is preferable to an American presidential system.

The fiery words of Edmund Burke, speaking in the House of Commons on the 14th of June 1784, outline the dangers of conceding to Cabinet the power to dissolve Parliament at will:

> If there must be another mode of conveying the collective
> sense of the people to the throne than that by the House of
> Commons, it ought to be fixed and defined, and its authority
> ought to be settled: it ought not to exist in so precarious and
> dependent a state as that ministers should have it in their
> power, at their own mere pleasure, to acknowledge it with

respect or to reject it with scorn. It is the undoubted prerogative of the crown to dissolve Parliament; but...it is, of all the
trusts vested in his Majesty, the most critical and delicate,
and that in which this House has the most reason to require,
not only the good faith, but the favour of the crown...We are
to inquire and to accuse; and the objects of our inquiry and
charge will be for the most part persons of wealth, power and
extensive connections...A House of Commons respected by
his ministers is essential to his Majesty's service: it is fit that
they should yield to Parliament, and not that Parliament
should be new-modelled until it is fitted to their purposes. If
our authority is to be held up when we coincide in opinion
with his Majesty's advisers, but is to be set at nought the
moment it differs from them, the House of Commons will
shrink into a mere appendage of administration, and will lose
that independent character which...enables us to afford a
real, effective and substantial support to his government.[32]

Burke argued that if a House of Commons could be dissolved by Cabinet
ministers as a punishment for its criticisms, then,

no other consequence can result...but, in future, the House of
Commons, consulting its safety at the expense of its duties,
and suffering the whole energy of the state to be relaxed, will
shrink from every service which, however necessary, is of a
great and arduous nature, — or...will exchange independence
or protection, and will court a subservient existence through
the favour of those ministers...who ought themselves to stand
in awe of the Commons of this realm.[33]

At the time Burke was speaking it was extremely rare for an incumbent government to be defeated at general elections, due to its influence through patronage.
Consequently the holding of elections was a potent threat against Opposition
parliamentarians. A similar threat holds true today whenever the Opposition is
weak and divided, or crucial seats for the balance of power are held by
Independents with limited resources and narrow margins in their constituencies.

More modern, but no less passionate words were spoken on the topic in 1926
in the Canadian House of Commons, during a constitutional crisis in which
the then Prime Minister, Mr Mackenzie King, erroneously believed he was
entitled to dissolve a Parliament while the Commons was debating a censure
motion against his government. The Governor-General, Lord Byng, refused
and Mackenzie King promptly resigned. Byng sent for Arthur Meighen, the
leader of the Conservatives, and asked him to form a government.[†] Speaking
in the House, Meighen said,

---

† There was no clear majority in the Commons: King's Liberals held 101 seats, Meighen's Conservatives
116, and the balance of power was held by Progressives, Labour and Independents with 28 seats.

THE NECESSITY OF RESERVE POWERS

Never in the history of parliamentary government as we have it today, has any Prime Minister ever demeaned himself to ask for a dissolution while a vote of censure was under debate. A dissolution very manifestly should not be granted when its effect is to avoid a vote of censure…The Prime Minister said to His Excellency: 'This jury must disappear; this Parliament must be dissolved'. The effect of that advice was simply this: 'If Parliament shows signs of going against me, even if that Parliament was elected on my own appeal, that Parliament must not live'. If such advice must always be accepted, then the supremacy of Parliament would be over, and the Prime Minister would be supreme himself…To demand such a right is not to plead for responsible government; it is to plead for irresponsible government; to demand such a right is not to uphold our parliamentary institutions; it is really to stifle those institutions; to demand such a right is not to plead the cause of parliament; it is in effect to choke and strangle and prevent parliament from expressing its will…

Of the duties of Governor-General, Meighen declared:

The sphere of discretion left to a Governor-General under our constitution and under our practice is a limited sphere indeed, but it is a sphere of dignity and great responsibility. Within the ambit of discretion residing still in the Crown in England, and residing in the Governor-General in the Dominions, there is a responsibility as great as falls to any estate of the realm or to any House of Parliament…Within the sphere of that discretion the plain duty of the Governor-General is not to weaken responsible government, not to undermine the rights of parliament,…it is to make sure that responsible government is maintained, that the rights of parliament are respected, that the still higher rights of the people are held sacred. It is his duty to make sure that parliament is not stifled by government, but that every government is held responsible to parliament, and that every parliament is held responsible to the people.[34]

Meighen was speaking at the beginning of what has become known as the Byng-King crisis of 1926. Meighen misjudged his own ability to form an alternative government to King, for a number of members of the Progressive Party "suddenly reversed their attitude towards the new Government after helping to defeat the want of confidence motion of June 30",[35] and so he was forced within three days of Parliament's sitting to advise Byng to dissolve Parliament after all. In the ensuing elections King was re-elected with enough supporters to become Prime Minister again, and Byng, severely embarrassed by the incident, subsequently returned to Britain. None of this diminishes the accuracy of Meighen's speech, nor the necessity of this discretion to remain beyond the reach of the Prime Minister. When the Parliament was finally dissolved it was not to gag a censure motion, but because it could not longer transact the business of government.[36]

In Australia, Dr H.V. Evatt once complained,

> Cases have occurred where, owing to the existence of three or four political parties in the popular House, or of a revolt within a Ministerial party, Ministers brought face to face with a critical vote of the House assert that they possess an unconditional right to dissolve…and in the event of an adverse vote, will assert such right…The newspapers supporting Ministers assert that, under modern constitutional practice, the Prime Minister for the time being 'always has a dissolution in his pocket'…In my opinion, similar 'intimations' are a very serious interference with the regular processes of parliamentary government…They are designed to put pressure upon members of parliament who are thus hindered in the free exercise of their duty to vote in accordance with the interests of the electors.[37]

What physical harm could come to society if the Prime Minister did always have "a dissolution in his pocket"? What could the damage be? Evatt again replies,

> Of course, in one sense, every appeal to the people, whatever circumstances exist when it takes place, represents an attempt to get a decision from the political sovereign. In this sense a series of repeated dissolutions of the Parliament may be said to represent the 'triumph' of the people as political sovereign. In actual fact, however, by means of defamation and intimidation and the deliberate inculcation of disillusion and disgust, a series of repeated dissolutions would probably be the very means of first delaying and ultimately defeating the true popular will, and so represent a triumph over, and not a triumph of, the electorate.[38]

So the power to grant or refuse dissolution of Parliament to a Prime Minister, vested in the Crown, exists to protect the privileges of Parliament from abuse by the government of the day, and to prevent exhaustion of the popular will. This power must then be retained beyond the Prime Minster's group…but why entrust it to the Crown?

To whom else could it be given? Certainly not to the legislature — the whole point of these powers is that they are entrusted by the legislature to someone outside the struggles of the two Houses, to keep them safe from the temporarily dominant faction. What of giving it to the judiciary? For judges to be able to decide a matter as judges, then the matter before them, if not expressed in legal formulae, must at least be expressible in terms of such formulae. The complex web of conventions that clings to dissolution is not expressed in legal terms at all, but is spun from historical precedents and political principles, and its precise dimensions are a topic of ongoing debate. The issues to be caught are slippery and elusive, and they are political in nature: can an alternative Ministry transact business in that particular House, or is able to negotiate so it can? Has a significant new issue of public policy arisen? Has a major change in the political landscape of the nation occurred, for which the Parliament is no longer representative? Are the issues of change of an urgent nature?

How are considerations such as these to be codified in law? How does one describe the flux of crisis or national mood in legal terms? Codification of the reserve powers is a controversial topic, but here there exists doubt as to whether accurate codification is actually possible. Even if they could be codified so that these questions were in at least one case accurately expressed in law, would judges be competent to know the answers? The answers don't rest in the law but in the political circumstances, and in circumstances of crisis there are rarely enough "facts" to hang a hat on. Instead there are merely interpretations of ongoing events, and opinions as to their outcome. At the end of the day it would be the political discretion of the judges, and not their legal knowledge, which would govern their actions. Although sitting on the bench in a court of law, the decisions emanating from these people would be executive in nature. For the well being of the community behaviour of this kind is best left to figures who are publicly and explicitly executive, rather than creating a second, secret executive from amongst the judiciary.

Furthermore, a purely practical problem: is the usual legal apparatus really appropriate to respond to fluid political issues? During times of instability would it not require judges to be perpetually hovering, anxiously watching and waiting for events to unfold? In the problem of dissolving Parliament there's a strong emphasis on the acquisition of information. The Queen in London and her Governor-General in Canberra individually possess their own private staff, the Queen's headed by her Private Secretary at Buckingham Palace and the Governor-General's headed by his Official Secretary at Yarralumla.† A duty of this staff is to collect and analyse information about contemporary events in order to provide private counsel‡ to the Crown, so that it has other sources of information than simply what it is told by the Prime Minister. In times of parliamentary unrest, with the possibility of an alternative minority government enabling refusal of a dissolution to the existing government, an important function of the Official Secretary would be to take discrete and diplomatic soundings from parliamentary leaders and Independents as to the viability of an alternative government.§ Our hypothetical judges are unlikely

---

† In reality there are differences in practices of the Private Secretary and the Official Secretary; Australian politicians have rarely been keen to see the staff at Yarralumla achieve the same status as that of Buckingham Palace, because then Australia's viceregal Head of State would find it easier to exercise his independent discretion- not a comfortable thought for the Prime Minister. Buckingham Palace represents the proper model for the privileges and duties of viceregal staff, and shall be regarded as such throughout this discussion.

‡ This is "counsel" as in advice with a small "a", as distinct from legal counsel from, say, the Chief Justice, or Advice from responsible ministers.

§ This role, performed by the Queen's Private Secretary in the British context, has been discussed by a

to have this kind of support staff keeping them informed. Presumably their long-suffering associates would have to start making clippings from the newspapers. Future constitutional crises in Canberra might be heralded by the sight of a graduate law student on a bicycle wobbling off to take soundings from the Opposition parliamentary leaders…

So neither the legislature nor the judiciary are suitable to be entrusted with this power. That only leaves the Executive, but the effective Executive is precisely that faction and its leader from whom these powers must be kept. There is only one executive figure without a personal stake involved in parliamentary censure or votes of no confidence, a figure who can afford to watch dispassionately as a government is defeated in a hostile House and torn from office. That figure is Her Majesty's representative.†

A number of republics throughout the world have also acknowledged this need to keep the power of dissolution beyond the Prime Minister. A translation of the 1958 Constitution of France's Fifth Republic states "The President of the Republic can, after consulting the Prime Minister and the Presidents of the Assemblies, pronounce the dissolution of the National Assembly", without requiring ministerial counter-signature.[39] This appears to give the French President far more draconian powers to govern dissolution than Westminster conventions concede to the Crown. "To consult" is a delightfully vague verb, encompassing everything from a summit meeting to a cup of tea.

How is any dissolution of Parliament attempted, and what *are* the guidelines for granting or refusing this request? A proper answer to that question lies beyond the scope of this book; Forsey dedicated his doctoral dissertation to this question, later published as *The Royal Power of Dissolution of Parliament in the British Commonwealth*…all two hundred and seventy-one pages of it. Sufficient to say here that it is the right of the Prime Minister, and a right possessed by the Prime Minister alone, to ask the Crown to dissolve Parliament. If his or her request is granted then Parliament is dissolved, fresh elections are held, and — if the Prime Minster is popular or has a good sense of timing — he or she is returned to power. If the Crown refuses then the Prime Minister must either accept this or resign. This is why during periods in which the House is dominated by a disciplined party this power of the Crown is never witnessed. If the government, the dominant party, desires a dissolution, circumstances prevent refusal, because refusal would require alternative ministers to take responsibility in the House, ministers who would have to come from the lesser party. Such a ministry couldn't hope to avoid defeat in the House, and the Crown would be obliged to dissolve Parliament after all. It

---

number of authorities: in Oxford, Professor Vernon Bogdanor (Bogdanor, *Multi-Party Politics and the Constitution*, pp. 131–132) and Dr David Butler (Butler, *Governing Without a Majority*, pp. 80–84).

† This importance of a viceregal discretion, to refuse dissolution to a Prime Minister, has been explicitly mentioned in the modern written constitutions of Her Majesty's realms of Belize, St Lucia, and St Vincent and the Grenadines, and recognised in official documents of the Canadian Government in 1969 and 1978. (Forsey, "The Present Position of the Reserve Powers of the Crown", *Evatt and Forsey on the Reserve Powers*, pp. xxxii–xxxv.)

would have failed in the objective of refusal, the preservation of that parliament, and failed in a publicly humiliating manner. There's no salvation here in public endorsement of its actions, for there is no formal way for the Crown to appeal to the general public over the granting or refusing of dissolution. In this, the final battleground is the floor of the Lower House. In times of a disciplined majority in the House, and only in these times, can it be said that a Prime Minister "has a dissolution in his pocket". This is why a significant third party or collection of Independents which holds the balance of power in the House is so important for the preservation of parliamentary privileges, for it is then the Crown can discharge the duty entrusted to it by Parliament, and the principle can be enforced, that:

> The House of Commons is *prima facie* the exponent of the national will; and if the Ministry does not possess the confidence of the House of Commons, it ought to resign...Far from having an inherent personal right to dissolve, a Minister must always show why he does not resign and why he dissolves...He must show that there are special reasons why immediate recourse should be had to an extraordinary and irregular manifestation of the national will...Either he must show that the national will has not been declared in the existing Parliament, because through the equality of parties, the shufflings and vacillations of members, or the varying views to which the House commits itself, there is no manifestation of the national will in the deliberations and decisions of the House; or else he must state that, on some great question, the national will is not really expressed by the existing Parliament, and to the best of his belief, a new Parliament would take a very different view, and represent the nation far more adequately.[40]

Of course, the Crown must be very wary about the exercise of this power. Even if the wielder of the Crown's powers had both eyes fixed only on the Constitution, he or she would have to remain mindful of Evatt's words, now pleading caution:

> The mere fact that some sort of alternative Ministry is possible does not, and should not, prevent the grant of a dissolution by the King's representative. Presumably the Governor would never lose sight of the popular 'mandate' possessed by the existing Assembly. Again, it might be disastrous to democratic feeling to permit the continuance of an Assembly if (say) the alternative Ministry would have little or no popular backing or if it proposed to act, or wait dependent upon the support of members who were proposing to act, in flagrant disregard of pledges to the electors.[41]

Yet this caution is still a far cry from opinions bandied about in a debate conducted in *The Times* in late April to early May 1950, when it was suggested that to avoid controversy the Crown should always oblige Prime Ministers in their requests for dissolutions. The right of reply must go to the then Private Secretary to King George VI, Sir Alan Lascelles, whose letter to *The Times*, written under the pseudonym "Senex", was published on the 2nd May 1950:

> It is surely indisputable (and common sense) that a Prime Minister may ask — not demand — that his Sovereign will grant him a dissolution of Parliament; and that the Sovereign, if he so chooses, may refuse to grant this request. The problem of such a choice is entirely personal to the Sovereign, though he is, of course, free to seek informal advice from anybody whom he thinks fit to consult.
>
> In so far as this matter can be publicly discussed, it can be properly assumed that no wise Sovereign — that is, one who has at heart the true interest of the country, the constitution and the Monarchy — would deny a dissolution to his Prime Minister unless he were satisfied that: (1) the existing Parliament was still vital, viable, and capable of doing its job; (2) a General Election would be detrimental to the national economy; (3) he could rely on finding another Prime Minister who could carry on his Government, for a reasonable period, with a working majority in the House of Commons. When Sir Patrick Duncan refused a dissolution to his Prime Minister in South Africa in 1939,[†] all these conditions were satisfied: when Lord Byng did the same in Canada in 1926, they appeared to be, but in the event the third proved illusory.[42]

So much for the Crown's discretionary power to grant or refuse dissolution of Parliament. What of proroguing Parliament? What, first of all, does "proroguing" mean? During the life of an elected Parliament it doesn't sit in session all the time, nor should it, for parliamentarians of all parties have homes to go to, constituencies to look after, and in the case of ministers and shadow ministers, departments to administer or scrutinise. Yet, understandably, opinions differ as to how many days a year Parliament *should* sit, depending on whether one is inside government or outside it. From the viewpoint of the government benches, Parliament need only sit long enough to pass the annual budget, or to sit when the government wants to change laws.

---

† Upon the outbreak of World War II in 1939 British South Africans favoured declaring war upon the Third Reich, whereas an element among the Boer Afrikaners actively supported Nazi Germany. The then-Prime Minister, General Herzog, favoured neutrality, as did a minority of his party and just less than half the Cabinet. The majority, whose spokesman in this matter was General Smuts, Minister of Justice, favoured declaring war, although not the despatch of troops overseas. In the Assembly the Prime Minister moved a resolution embodying his policy. General Smuts countered with a proposed amendment to it expressing his policy, which won the approval of the Assembly 80–67 on the 4th of September, and the amended motion was carried on the same division. Apparently General Herzog, now effectively defeated in the House and supported by only a minority of the Cabinet, then approached Governor-General Sir Patrick Duncan and requested a dissolution. Observing the circumstances, Sir Patrick refused, prompting General Herzog's resignation. Sir Patrick then sent for General Smuts, who agreed to form a Government in the existing Parliament. This he did without difficulty, and served as Prime Minister during the War with the confidence of South Africa's Parliament. (Forsey, *The Royal Power of Dissolution of Parliament* pp. 251–256.)

Any other time the Houses are sitting they're just a nuisance. Parliamentarians outside the government start asking damned awkward questions, and if the Speaker is impartial rather than a government hack, the ministers actually have to answer them. It is better that the whole nasty predicament goes away. Prorogue quickly, and run the country without interference.

Understandably the view from the Opposition benches is rather different. One feels one is supposed to be there to scrutinise government, and it is rather difficult to scrutinise events in Canberra from, say, Launceston, or Robe River, or Weipa. It is even more difficult to get ministers to answer curly questions from that distance. They tend to hang up on the telephone. One needs to be in Canberra, on the floor of the House, with that most wondrous of God's creatures, an impartial Speaker, to uphold the privileges of the House — like the right of members to have their questions answered. The longer the House sits, the greater the chance the Opposition can have an effect.

The conventions surrounding this power to silence Parliament are similar to those surrounding the power to dissolve it. The right to request that Parliament be prorogued belongs to the Prime Minister. The right to decide whether to grant that request belongs to the Crown. Under all normal conditions the Crown must follow the Prime Minister's advice, but under unusual circumstances — say, a motion of censure or of no confidence in the government being debated in the House, and a viable alternative ministry being present and willing to continue the debate — the Crown might decide to refuse. As for the power to refuse dissolution, much depends on the circumstances, particularly upon the existence of a viable alternative ministry. If no such alternative exists then the debate, however worthy, may still be silenced by the Prime Minister.

This was illustrated vividly in Canada, in 1873. On the 13th August of that year the Canadian Parliament, having adjourned some months earlier, met and was at once prorogued on the advice of the Prime Minister, Sir John Macdonald. This was done to silence the Liberal leader, Alexander Mackenzie, who was about to move a vote of censure. In November the next parliamentary session began, amid fierce criticisms by the Liberals that the prorogation had been an invasion of the rights of Parliament and the people. Macdonald's answer was that these rights were in no danger because the Crown's prerogative was wielded on the advice of responsible ministers. Edward Blake, regarded as one of Canada's greatest constitutional authorities, retorted angrily,

> It made no difference to a free people whether their rights
> were invaded by the Crown or by the Cabinet. What was
> material was to secure that their rights should not be invaded
> at all…It was very well to tell the people that they were all-
> powerful, but if they handed over to a Cabinet inordinate
> powers, not susceptible of being kept under control, they
> might be deprived of the free expression of the popular will
> which was necessary to popular government. The honourable
> gentleman [Macdonald] said that the prerogative could not be
> used against the people under the advice of responsible

Ministers. They [Blake and his colleagues] alleged that it *had* been used against the people under the advice of responsible Minister — *in order to prevent the action of the people's representatives, in order to withdraw from the cognizance of their representatives the great cause pending between Ministers and their accusers.* In this very case they found an instance of the evil which the honourable gentleman had ridiculed as a fancy of the imagination, and an instance of the necessity of preserving to the uttermost the forms and principles of the Constitution and the rights of a popular body which our ancestors had handed down to us. The most dangerous doctrine which a Parliament could listen to was that it was to part with some of its ancient liberties.[43]

Further insights into this matter were provided in the South Pacific in 1994, in the Solomon Islands. An independent Queen's Realm of the Commonwealth, the Solomons' Constitution attempts an at least partial codification of the reserve powers. Based, as a judge would later remark, upon the assumption that the national Parliament would meet on a regular basis, one oddity of the codification is that it apparently removes power over appointment and dismissal of the Prime Minister from the Governor-General and vests it instead explicitly in the Parliament, with curious results.

Towards the end of 1994 the Solomon Islands found itself immersed in crisis. Elected in June 1993, the government of Francis Billy Hilly held the narrowest of parliamentary majorities: in an assembly of forty-seven members he held twenty-four votes while his rival held twenty-three. By the beginning of October 1994 six members had defected from his party, including five ministers. Parliament, however, had not been called since January. It had remained prorogued, and in its silence Billy Hilly remained Prime Minister. Disturbed by these circumstances the Governor-General, Moses Puibangara Pitakaka, arranged to meet on the 2nd of October with the Prime Minister to discuss whether his administration was still capable of transacting the business of government in the House. At that meeting Billy Hilly promised to provide the Governor-General with a list of his supporters in the House, promising to resign if he lacked sufficient numbers. The list was to reach Pitakaka the next day. It failed to arrive.

Responding to further viceregal urging, Billy Hilly wrote to Pitakaka on the 5th of October admitting he no longer had the numbers but requesting a week to consider his position. This was granted, the Governor-General telling him his response was expected by noon Wednesday 12th October. On the previous day the High Court of the Solomon Islands had handed down its decision in *Abe v. Minister of Finance and Attorney-General*,[44] finding that the Billy Hilly government had violated the Constitution in borrowing over ten million dollars in excess of the sums approved by Parliament. Pitakaka awaited the outcome of the next week with some trepidation.

Contemplating the possibility that the Prime Minister would refuse to resign, he requested advice from the Attorney-General over the alternative way to re-assert the authority of the House: to revoke the existing prorogation and summon the House to assemble, in defiance, if necessary, of the incumbent Prime Minister's advice. It could then vote for a replacement Prime Minister, one who did enjoy its confidence and thus had rightful claim to govern. The Attorney-General advised Pitakaka that the Governor-General didn't have the authority to remove the Prime Minister, and refused to draft the order Pitakaka requested. Deprived of legal assistance, the Governor-General prepared the Order himself, and proclaimed it on Thursday the 13th October 1994.

In the name of Queen Elizabeth II, Queen of the Solomon Islands, he commanded the Speaker of the National Parliament to convene Parliament on the 31st of the month, declared the Billy Hilly government to be in the interim only a caretaker administration and removed Billy Hilly himself from office as Prime Minister, although inviting him to head the caretaker government. Pitakaka also directed the Commissioner of Police to execute this warrant, and warned that disobedience or civil disorder committed by the incumbent ministry or its followers might be seditious under the law. The Leader of the Opposition, Solomon Sunaone Mamaloni, was willing to tender advice to this effect although was unable to do so formally due to the way the Constitution's codification had been constructed.

Billy Hilly described this Order as "unconstitutional" and his Attorney-General called it "a worthless piece of document". Prior to the reconvened Parliament choosing a new Prime Minister the question of the constitutionality of the Governor-General's actions went before the High Court of the Solomon Islands, which referred it to its Court of Appeal, in session at the time, in the case *Francis Billy Hilly & Others v. Governor-General of the Solomon Islands*.[45] On the 22nd of October the Court of Appeal, consisting of Connolly P, Williams JA and Los JA unanimously upheld the Governor-General's forced summoning of Parliament against the advice of the incumbent Prime Minister.

Observing that constitutional practice in the Solomon Islands differs from that in Australia or the United Kingdom, in that the Constitution only provides for dismissal of a Prime Minister after a vote of no-confidence is passed in the House, the joint judgement of Connolly P and Los JA remarked,

> What at least is established in our judgement is that a Prime Minister who hangs onto office while conceding he has no majority is in no position to insist that the Governor-General's functions can only be expressed on his advice.[46]

Consequently, as the Constitution of the Solomon Islands vests in the Governor-General the function of appointing the place and time of the holding of sessions of Parliament, "in the circumstances there can be no doubt about the validity of [Pitakaka's] order"[47] commanding Parliament to assemble.

Under these conditions their Lordships concluded "We find it unnecessary to discuss the existence and extent of the reserve powers of the Governor-General".[48] In his separate judgement the third Justice of Appeal, Williams JA, concurred with his fellow Justices yet went further, declaring,

> In the circumstances in my view the Governor-General has the power under [relevant sections and Standing Orders of the Constitution] to direct that Parliament convene on a specified date. If that is not the correct interpretation of those provisions, I would be prepared to hold that he was entitled to do pursuant to a reserve power vested in the Governor-General. If a Prime Minister without majority support in Parliament sought to continue governing without convening Parliament I am of the view that the reserve prerogative powers would authorise the Governor-General to direct that Parliament be convened.[49]

Inasmuch as any invocation of the Crown's powers in defiance of the advice of the incumbent Prime Minister or Premier can be described as a resort to the reserve powers, all three members of the Court of Appeal could be regarded as approving the existence of a reserve power to revoke prorogation of Parliament, the viceregal exercise of which is entirely justified under some circumstances. But whereas Connolly P and Los JA thought it unnecessary to go beyond contemplation of explicit powers written in the Constitution, Williams JA apparently proved willing to look beyond the written Constitution, to a latent reserve power in the Crown. Moreover, what was approved by the Court wasn't merely the Crown refusing to prorogue a Parliament then in session, but the more extreme case of the Crown *defying* its incumbent ministers and summoning Parliament.

The echoes of these disputes in Canada and the Solomons hold an immediate relevance to a contemporary crisis which has afflicted New South Wales, and to rather odd doctrines that currently appear prevalent in that State. Upon the approaching retirement of Rear-Admiral Peter Sinclair as Governor of New South Wales in early 1996, the Carr Labor Government of that State announced his successor, Gordon Samuels QC. At the same time Mr Carr unveiled disturbing proposals affecting the office of Governor. It was to be reduced to a part-time position, its ceremony stripped, its occupant removed from Government House and expected to live at home in the suburbs. Mr Justice Samuels was, moreover, to be permitted to retain his former job as chairman of the NSW Law Reform Commission,[50] raising immediate doubts over conflict of interest. These concerns, and the broader issue of a preemptive move to a republic without popular mandate or adequate debate, angered members of both Parliament and community.

Angry members of the NSW Upper House (the Legislative Council) insisted that body be recalled to debate the matter. After being petitioned by a majority of members, its Liberal president duly ordered the Council to reconvene on the 13th of February. The Government retaliated by advising Admiral Sinclair at an emergency Executive Council meeting held on Saturday the 27th January to prorogue the Upper House until April, thus gagging it. This advice was formally given by the Treasurer, Mr Egan. The day before the meeting Mr Egan claimed the Governor had already assured him the prorogation would be granted, a claim Admiral Sinclair denied, retorting,

> Nothing has been put before me yet…what I will do is follow
> due constitutional process.
>   That is what governors are for…whatever is put before me
> I'll do the right thing by the people of NSW.[51]

Mr Egan, however, had asserted the prorogation would proceed, saying "there should never have been any doubt about that…[The Governor] gave the Government an assurance he would act with utmost constitutional propriety".[52] During his last formal speech as Governor, Sinclair did his best to articulate to the Carr ministry what constitutional propriety actually *means*, explaining,

> The Governor has a fundamental role to play in the
> Government of NSW and in helping on behalf of the
> community to safeguard the constitutional and lawful
> processes under which we are all governed.[53]

Egan's depiction of these events was as "a political conflict between a modernising government and the bunyip aristocracy of the Opposition and the Upper House", claiming "The facts are it is no longer appropriate for NSW affairs of State to be conducted over cucumber sandwiches in draughty old castles with batmen and footmen and butlers".[54]

Other community leaders entered the fight. In what has been described as "one of the strongest attacks by a religious leader upon a State premier" the Anglican Archbishop of Sydney, Dr Harry Goodhew, denounced Mr Carr for having "eroded the integrity of the governor's office and in doing so invited the distrust and cynicism of the people of this State".[55] He called for the Premier to "take this matter to the people", a call endorsed by the Council of Churches, representing ten of the nation's Protestant churches, which warned Carr not to interfere with the office of Governor without consulting the public.[56]

Professor Geoffrey Winterton of the UNSW Law School now chipped into the controversy. Expostulating that for Admiral Sinclair to block prorogation would be "outrageous", that he would be behaving "unconventionally and improperly", Winterton asserted that prorogation was "not considered" to be among the Governor's reserve powers, claiming,

> I cannot think of an example in modern times when advice
> to prorogue has not been followed. Perhaps in some obscure
> Canadian province somewhere — but for England, Australia

and Canada the convention is that the viceroy [sic] follows the advice of the executive.[57]

His claims were enthusiastically championed by a number of republican journalists, one of whom reiterated in an article entitled "Sinclair must do Government's bidding" that "[c]onstitutional experts could find no precedent yesterday for a viceregal representative acting any differently in a similar situation".[58] He went on to assert that the suggestions the Governor should intervene to allow a parliamentary debate over a decision to scale down the ceremonial aspects of the viceregal office were "absurd", because the actual legal powers of the Governor remained unaltered and hence were not affected "one iota" by the changes.[59]

Even Winterton conceded[60] more was at stake than mere ceremony, for the potential conflict of interest between the Governorship and Samuels' presiding as chairman of the Law Reform Commission — a post controlled by the government, thus interfering with the independence of its occupant — raised serious questions of propriety. Yet even if no other questions had been posed but of those ceremonial differences between a full-time Governor residing in Government House as New South Wales' acknowledged viceregal Head of State, and a reclusive part-time Governor living in the suburbs, rarely seen except by Ministers and then only reluctantly, leaving the Premier alone on the landscape to declare *l'Etat c'est moi*, then this in itself would have held serious political implications which even a journalist would be naive not to appreciate. What hope has this second species of Governor, shy and nocturnal, of invoking the reserve powers, however legitimately, in a public forum which he doesn't know and which doesn't know him? Such a figure is stripped of the dignity of office required in the public eye for a challenge to be made. De Valera must have appreciated as much when he, similarly, stripped the Governor-General of the Irish Free State of all ceremonial dignity in 1932, preparatory to declaring a republic. One can distort the balances in a Constitution without amending the text.

But what are we to think of Professor Winterton's professed opinions on this matter? Unless "modern" is to denote some more obscure timeframe — say, the time since Phar Lap won the Melbourne Cup — surely the relevant epoch for a scholar to be contemplating is that of Responsible Government, a period which in Canada includes Edward Blake and his arguments? The national Parliament of Canada is hardly the legislature of an "obscure province", and even in the absence of any more substantive event surely Blake's propositions would have enough merit to give pause to the thoughtful. Nor is it any great feat of logic to realise that Evatt's and Forsey's arguments (among others) upon the Crown's right to refuse dissolution might have some implications for prorogation. Finally, surely a more meticulous scholar would have kept abreast of events in Her Majesty's other independent realms in the Commonwealth, being as they are co-equal with Australia and Britain, lest one of them furnish

THE NECESSITY OF RESERVE POWERS

an example — such as a crisis that took place less than two years previously, in a country not 1600 km from the Queensland coast?

In reckoning up abuses committed by politicians employing even their partial control over prorogation, we needn't go very far. Newspaper columnist Frank Devine has remarked on the fact that former West Australian Premier Carmen Lawrence twice misused prorogation to silence unwelcome debate; her behaviour elicited a caustic response from the University of Western Australia's professor of politics, the late Patrick O'Brien, who observed that Charles I had only engaged in that behaviour once before being beheaded by an angry Parliament.[61] Nonetheless, there's no doubt that the Crown should under all but extraordinary circumstances obey the advice of incumbent ministers. If those ministers hold a disciplined majority in the House the Crown has in any case limited choice, because even if an alternative ministry were willing to assume responsibility for the Crown's refusal, this alternative government would be unable to hold the House's confidence, creating a dangerous situation for the Crown. Yet under the conditions whereby a debate of no-confidence was being conducted in the House with sufficient numbers for it to be passed, then the Crown would be faced with both a possible moral obligation to permit the debate continue and a possible practical way of realizing that obligation. Provided those members contemplating a vote against the Government are willing to take responsibility for the debate continuing, then the Crown can defy the incumbent Premier or Prime Minister who is demanding the House be silenced.

The real questions over the prorogation of the NSW Legislative Council were therefore never the actual possession of the Governor's power to refuse prorogation, nor his right — under rare circumstances — to exercise it. What should have been the central questions are, first, were the proposed executive measures of urgent importance to Parliament, being an attack upon its rights and privileges? Given that they were, would a debate in the Council have been able to generate any *effective* counter-measures unattainable by debate in the community at large (e.g. a resolution to block legislation related to the measures if some were needed)? Assuming the answer to both of the above is "yes" — and that assumption is debateable for the latter question — did an alternative ministry exist capable and willing to take responsibility in the Lower House for the Governor refusing to silence the Upper? Assuming the Crown appealed to its reserve powers and the resultant crisis triggered a general election, was the issue sufficiently critical both in fact and in public perception for this election's upheaval in the community to have been countenanced?

Admiral Sinclair finally chose to accept the Carr Government's advice to prorogue Parliament. When he left Government House for the last time on the 30th of January, to enter retirement, he was greeted by cheering monarchists waiting outside the gates in a rally intended as a final gesture of support. More than ten thousand people then marched through the streets of Sydney in protest against the Carr Government's alterations to the viceregal office.[62]

In this matter neither the presence nor absence of butlers or footmen is relevant. It's the presence or absence of debate in our parliaments on matters touching upon our communities and constitutions which is of critical concern to us, debate which some in our community appear keen to stifle. This sanctioned silence is one cause of our anger, which has brought the thousands of protesters out upon the streets of Sydney. A remedy — imperfect, perhaps, but better than any alternative yet put before us — rests in the Crown.

Forced Dissolution and Refusal of Assent

Understanding the use and nature of the reserve powers is easier during hours of crisis than in more mundane years. We will therefore contemplate two of the most ancient and extreme weapons, tarnished with antiquity and disuse. Both have been significant in 20th Century history, although neither of them have been actually exercised. The very fact of their existence — even hidden away at the back of the closet — exerted a sobering influence during the Great Depression and the Irish Home Rule Bill, and aroused considerable debate.

In the United Kingdom, co-operation by the Queen with any legislation that violated a modern interpretation of the Revolution Settlement would destroy her own authority, both in its actual constitutional source and its public image. Hailsham, describing a British scenario similar to the Nazis' seizure of power in 1930's Germany or Mussolini's in Italy, argued,

> The one way in which a revolutionary regime could install
> itself without abolishing the monarchy would be if it first
> captured a majority in Parliament at a general election, and
> then proceeded to pass laws to preserve its own existence or
> subjugate the majority under the authority of the Royal Assent.
> It might be able to achieve this for a time by deceiving the
> palace advisers of the Crown. But the very difficulty of doing so
> would be a very powerful deterrent, and, if it succeeded in
> doing so for any length of time it would certainly destroy the

monarchy or at least the occupant of the throne. It was the
failure of the Italian King to withdraw before it was too late
royal support from the tyranny of Mussolini which destroyed
the Italian monarchy. It is not altogether without significance,
especially in view of this fact, that it was the dismissal of
Mussolini by the King, too late though it was to save his
throne, which ultimately destroyed Mussolini.[64]

But how could Her Majesty, or her representative, oppose a Prime Minister
turned tyrant? Two ancient weapons that remain in the hands of the Crown to
oppose such a regime are the royal powers of forced dissolution of Parliament,
(obliging all members of the Lower House to seek re-election in a forced
general election) and of veto (the right to refuse assent to obnoxious legislation pressed upon the Crown by an unscrupulous ministry).

In Great Britain the royal veto was last used by Queen Anne in 1707. It hasn't
been exercised since, largely because the nature of parliamentary government
has changed considerably since the reign of Anne. The executive veto was an
important administrative tool at a time when the executive and legislature occupied distinct spheres and conflict between them was commonplace. For the last
two centuries the Westminster system has abandoned this separation of powers
between the effective executive and the legislature: all Cabinet ministers must
now be parliamentarians, and cannot govern without the confidence of the
House of Commons. Policy struggles that previously occurred between Crown
and Commons are now resolved on the floor of the House of Commons itself.

This absence of exercise of the veto led Walter Bagehot to believe it had atro-
phied with disuse. Smugly and inaccurately he stated that "the Queen has no
such veto. She must sign her own death-warrant if the two Houses unanimously
send it up to her".[65] The 19th Century political philosopher John Stuart Mill
more wisely described the veto power as an ancient instrument of political
warfare that "no one desires to see used, but no one likes to part with, lest [it]
should at any time be found to be still needed in an extraordinary emergency".[66]

Alpheus Todd[†] threw his own considerable weight into the argument. After
pointing out the changes in parliamentary government which had caused the
ancient form of veto to fall into disuse, he argued,

> But, if need be, the dormant power of the Crown to veto a bill
> presented by the two Houses of Parliament for the royal assent
> could be revived and exercised; — provided only that a
> ministry could be found to assume the responsibility of such an
> act — for 'her Majesty has no constitutional right to abdicate
> that part of her prerogative which entitles her to put a veto
> upon any measure she thinks fit'. And 'although no minister

---

[†] Alpheus Todd was librarian of the Canadian House of Commons in the late 19th Century. His study of
the British parliamentary system, written with the Canadian context in mind, remains significant a century
after it was written.

can introduce a measure into either House without the consent of the Crown, such consent is only given in the first instance in the executive capacity of the sovereign. It implies no absolute approbation of the measure...As a branch of the legislature whose decision is final, and therefore last solicited, the opinion of the sovereign remains unshackled and uncompromised until the assent of both Houses has been received. Nor is this veto of the English monarch an empty form. It is not difficult to conceive the occasion, when supported by the sympathies of a loyal people, its exercise might defeat an unconstitutional ministry, and a corrupt Parliament'.[67]

Adolf Hitler's government has since provided an obvious foreign blueprint for when a veto should be exercised to defeat an "unconstitutional ministry, and a corrupt Parliament". Had his March 1933 Enabling Act been struck down by an appropriate figure, modern history might have been very different.

Circumstances other than an obnoxious Bill also arouse thoughts about the dismissal of ministers and the forced dissolution of Parliament. In times of extreme crisis, be it economic, social, military or induced by natural disaster, it is sometimes necessary to bestow upon prime ministers and their governments extraordinary powers for temporary use, to tackle the problems at hand. Consider the Great Depression:

> Respect for authoritarianism, even in Britain and France, was strengthened in these years [the 1930s] by their own experience of the need to abandon normal parliamentary procedures in an effort to meet the Great Depression...it became common to entrust drastic emergency powers to "national governments", broad coalitions usually conservative in character. The considerable extension of presidential authority by President Roosevelt in his New Deal was the American counterpart, just as the use by President Hindenberg of his special powers under Article 48 was the German counterpart. In most democratic systems, indeed, some form of constitutional dictatorship had to be initiated. But much depended on how this was done, and there were important differences between British and French practice.[68]

Where were these drastic emergency powers to come from? In Britain,

> the prerogative powers of the Crown had always provided a reserve of emergency authority. These were enhanced by the Emergency Powers Act of 1920, which broke with precedent and permanently delegated to any government the right "to make exceptional provision for the protection of the community in times of emergency". The type of emergency visualized was a strike or series of strikes likely to deprive the nation of such essentials of life as food, water, fuel, light or transport.

But a limit of one month was fixed for the validity of any proclamation issued under the act, and parliament had to be immediately convened.[69]

However the economic crisis of 1931 forced the British government to different and arguably more drastic measures:

[T]he National Government of Ramsay MacDonald was given emergency powers by five separate Enabling Acts. They constituted so radical a break with normal procedure that general elections were held in which the government asked for a "doctor's mandate". When it gained 554 seats as against only 52 Labor seats and a total opposition of only 61, it could claim to have such a mandate. With so large a majority any legislation that the government wanted could be passed intact, and emergency powers were not again invoked until the outbreak of war in 1939. Then the Emergency Powers (Defence) Act, while preserving parliament's right to annul regulations, gave the government very wide powers to conduct the war with efficiency.[70]

In France a different path was attempted:

[T]he main device was the emergency delegation of law-making by parliament to the cabinet. The government was empowered, for a limited period and specific purposes, to issue decree-laws which became immediately operative but could later be annulled by parliament.[71]

This approach worked for a considerable length of time.

This [emergency power of decree-laws] was given to Poincaré in 1926 to enable him to stabilize the franc; to the Doumergue-Tardieu ministry of 1934, again to meet the economic crisis; to Pierre Laval's ministry of 1935 "to prevent speculation and to defend the franc"; and to the Chautemps government of 1937 for the same purpose.[72]

In all of these instances cited above, parliamentary control of government was retained. Unfortunately,

[t]he abuse of the power by Laval, who issued under its aegis 500 decree-laws, exposed the dangers of the device. It was Edouard Daladier's ministry, which held power from April, 1938, until March, 1940, which made fullest use of it. During these two years of acute crisis and war, four Enabling Acts were passed which in aggregate meant a surrender of all lawmaking power to the executive authority. They were couched in sweeping terms, and the chambers virtually

abdicated power to the government two years before their
more formal abdication to Marshall Pétain in July, 1940.[73]

Once "constitutional dictatorship" is established, how is it to be revoked? In
Britain, even as the Crown provided the source of extraordinary powers for the
government, so too the King's prerogatives provided a safeguard for the public
against abuse of these powers. Not only was it necessary to hold in reserve the
threat of ministerial dismissal, but — in the hypothetical scenario of Ramsay
MacDonald's government turning rogue to retain its extraordinary power —
nothing short of George VI's reserve power to force a dissolution of parliament
could have forced the government to relinquish its grip on power. With a
parliamentary majority of 493 seats, an appeal to the Commons would have
been pointless.

It's no accident the British and French experiences with emergency government during this period ended differently. In the latter country "ministers
entrusted with such powers were apt to abuse and discredit them".[74] In the
absence of an effective safeguard, the temptation for ministers to employ emergency powers to entrench themselves in office is obvious.

In 1913 the threat of civil war in Ireland made the royal power of veto a matter
of urgent debate. The Asquith Liberal government had been elected in
December 1910. Once in office, the government was determined to enact a
Home Rule Bill for Ireland, to pass into law in 1914. Controversy broke out
whether the government had a popular mandate for such an act. More
ominously, it was argued by Conservative leaders that passage of the Bill into
law in its current form would lead to the outbreak of civil war. In a constitutional debate conducted in autumn of 1913, in the form of letters to *The Times*,
Conservatives demanded that the government put the Home Rule Bill to the
test of a general election. It was suggested that, should the Asquith ministry
refuse to advise an election on the issue, that,

> a refusal of the Royal Assent to the Home Rule Bill after its
> third passing might no doubt be represented as a challenge to
> the democracy; but no such reproach could be levelled
> against a decision of the Sovereign to satisfy himself, before
> the House of Commons is finally committed to a decision
> which must change the History of his Kingdom, that House
> does indeed represent the democracy of to-day.[75]

On the 8th of September Balfour declared in *The Times* that Parliament should
be dissolved (hence forcing fresh elections) before any attempt was made to
advise the Sovereign to pass the Bill, so that it would be impossible to say that
"…Ulster is the victim of a revolution on which the people of this country
were never consulted".[76]

Two more constitutional authorities now weighed into the debate. The first was
Sir William Anson, who on the 10th of September outlined the circumstances

and manner in which he thought the prerogative powers of dissolution and veto could be exercised, remarking that measures of high importance (relating to Home Rule in Ireland) "have never been fairly submitted to the consideration of the electorate" and that against the danger of civil war "our only safeguard…is to be found in the exercise of the prerogatives of the Crown".[77] Five days later A.V. Dicey, the second authority, expressed in *The Times* his "complete agreement with Sir William Anson's masterly exposition of the principles regulating the exercise of the prerogative of dissolution". Although Dicey much preferred the option of dissolution of Parliament, preventing the escalation of controversy by immediately forcing fresh elections at which the issue could be decided without resorting to the veto, as "Every advantage by way of appeal to the electors, in consequence of the exercise of the so-called Royal veto, can be far better and more regularly obtained by a dissolution of Parliament",[78] he declared of the veto that, in the words of Edmund Burke,

> The King's negative to Bills is one of the most undisputed of
> the Royal prerogatives, and it extends to all cases whatsoever
> …it is not the propriety of the exercise which is in question.
> Its repose may be the preservation of its existence, and its
> existence may be the means of saving the Constitution itself
> on an occasion worthy of bringing it forth.[79]

One must be clear on the difference between a forced dissolution and a veto. The power of veto is a power triggered only (if at all) once a Bill, poised to become law, is actually placed before the Crown for its assent. It represents our executive witness' final chance to prevent the Bill passing into law. The power of forced dissolution, on the other hand, is the power of the Crown under extreme circumstances to force the government to hold general elections,† by dissolving Parliament. These two powers possess a common element. If certain dangerous activities of a government may be resisted by the Crown, then surely a Bill attempting to legitimise or entrench these activities may also be resisted by the Crown. Conversely, if (as was suggested about the Home Rule Bill) attempted legislation is so revolutionary as to justify resistance by the Crown, then surely the better response is to require fresh elections over the issue early in the peace, before passions are roused and tempers lost, while the act of saying "no" is still able to avoid crisis rather than merely precipitating it.

Phrases like "royal power of veto" and the idea of the Crown being able to say "no" conjure up an image of majestic or viceregal despotism, of an unelected figure pursuing a private agenda by vetoing the personally unpalatable legislation of an elected Parliament, rendering farcical the democratic process. This image is entirely mistaken, a misconception of what the veto in contemporary

---

† Whether that government goes to the elections *as the government* depends on whether the Prime Minister submits to the demand for elections under threat of a forced dissolution, or whether he or she is stubborn in refusal, forcing the Crown to actually invoke its reserve power. In the latter case the conventions of ministerial responsibility require that Prime Minster to resign or be dismissed, to be replaced by another temporary Prime Minister. It is widely accepted that whoever goes to the polls as the incumbent government holds a certain advantage which any sensible Prime Minister would be loath to surrender.

circumstances entails. Dicey stated that the modern guiding principle behind the veto, as behind all of the reserve powers of the Crown, is that "the final decision of every grave political question now belongs, not to the House of Commons, but to the electors as the representatives of the nation."[80] It's easy in theories of democratic government to overstate a principle of plebiscites, and it is often said of Dicey that he did so. As Burke once remarked, it must never be forgotten that elected parliamentarians are not merely their constituents' representatives but also their agents, elected not merely to enact specific policies but also to transact general business according to the philosophy of their party. On one hand, repeated appeals over the heads of these agents is subversive of representative government. Yet on the other, there is a risk whenever a client employs an agent in any kind of business that the latter shall be over-zealous, or negligent, or misguided. For the people's sovereignty to be preserved, in emergencies it must be possible for them to change their agents. Much water has flowed under the bridge since the days of Burke, and in the evolution of our political system over the last two centuries a mechanism for achieving this has emerged. Contrary to Dicey's belief, the Crown is not a weathercock of public opinion, forcing governments to the polls when the winds of public mood have shifted direction, but it *is* a potent witness of disastrous government.

But how do we tell the difference between a revolutionary Bill that demands consultation with the electorate, and a merely controversial one? Forsey asks,

> But what is a 'revolutionary measure'? Does it mean only a bill which would work a revolutionary change in the political Constitution? Would the term extend to economic change: socialization of the banks or of industry, abolition of the co-operative movement, prohibition of trade unionism? It would be easy to multiply examples, and it is clear that what one honest man might consider 'revolutionary' another would think merely part of the normal process of development... Obviously much would depend on whether the government had a 'mandate' for the measure in question, whether, that is, the electors at the previous general election, had it clearly put before them that in voting for Party X they would be voting for the abolition of the monarchy, or that a vote for Party Y meant a vote for the abolition of cooperative societies. But, as the discussions of 1913 showed, it may not be at all easy to find out whether the measure in question was 'the' issue, or even 'an' issue, at the previous election. It seems clearly undesirable that a party which has got into power on, say, the issue of a defensive alliance with the United States and the Soviet Union [Forsey was writing this during World War II], should be able, without consulting the electors afresh, to abolish trade unions, or socialize the banks, or deprive women of the franchise, or allow a Roman Catholic to succeed on the Throne, whatever the merits of any of these measures; on the other hand it is as clearly undesirable that a government elected on a platform which announced plainly an intention

to socialize the banks and big industry, disestablish the Church of England and abolish the House of Lords, should be compelled to undergo a series of general elections on each of these issues successively.[81]

In his conclusion upon forced dissolutions, he said,

It is probably safe to say that under modern conditions forced dissolutions will take place only if the Crown considers them necessary to protect the Constitution or to ensure that major changes in the economic structure of society shall take place only by the deliberate will of the people. In other words, the power to force dissolution is now likely to be used only negatively, preventatively; never as a means of bringing about some positive end desired by the King himself or his representative.

If the Government won an election by means of flagrant and notorious fraud, corruption, violence or terrorism, or some combination of these, the Crown could properly dismiss such a Government and call to office a new Government which would hold new elections under proper conditions.

Or if the Crown were asked to 'swamp' the Upper House (in jurisdictions where such a power exists), or to assent to some major change in the electoral system, a widening or narrowing of the franchise, abolition of the ballot, abolition of the Upper House or of the monarchy, prolongation of the life of Parliament otherwise than by general consent, a change from private to social ownership of the means of production (or vice versa), then it might well insist that any such change should first be submitted to the judgement of the electors.[82]

But is it enough that members of the former government urging the revolutionary Bill or engaging in other unconstitutional activity are defeated at the subsequent forced elections for the Crown to be vindicated? Would not the Crown be indelibly tarred with the brush of partisanship, the allegiance of the defeated party diminished or extinguished? It has been suggested by some participants in British discussions of the reserve powers that the Crown must always acquiesce to the advice of incumbent ministers, in order to remain (as one put it) *au dessus du combat*.[†]

If the Crown always followed this doctrine then it would be fit to be described in the words of Clemenceau in France: "There are two things in the world for which I have never seen any use: the prostate gland and the president of the republic."[83] More than this, permanent acquiescence by the Crown represents

---

[†] See letters to *The Times* of 26th April 1950 and 13th May 1969, reproduced in Appendix 4 of B.S. Markesinis, *The Theory and Practice of Dissolution of Parliament*, pp. 260-261, 267. It is interesting that a further argument put forward for acquiescence was that the Crown "should be bound by a clear and simple rule" to avoid claims of partisanship. It is surely foolish to speak of "clear and simple rules" in a complex and difficult environment.

an abdication of its responsibilities, expressed historically in the contract of 1688, legally in the written Constitution in Australia and ceremonially in the Coronation Oath, taken by the modern monarchs at Westminster Abbey and binding upon their representatives throughout the Commonwealth. A pragmatic Prime Minister is unlikely to respect the Constitution, so for the Crown *always* to submit to the advice of incumbent ministers is for it to surrender its guardianship of the Constitution, hence violating the basis upon which the office of monarch or Governor-General exists. Even with a written Constitution, a High Court and a powerful Senate it is necessary on occasion — fortunately very rare — for the Crown to walk a different path than that urged by its incumbent advisers.

Finally, acquiescence is potentially suicidal. In the words of Lord Hailsham, in a commentary on the British and the Australian Crowns published in 1988,

> But there are lessons here [in Whitlam's unconstitutional activities and his potentially illegal solutions to his predicament] too for the Crown [in Britain]. Though it be the business of British statesmen to avoid a situation which may bring reserve powers into action, the Crown cannot avoid its obligations if they fail to observe this rule...It is clear that sovereignty lies with the people. But the Queen is a trustee for her people. Trustees are not ciphers, and cannot safely act as rubber stamps...If the Crown makes a mistake, and is not endorsed by the electorate, there are only two possibilities, admission of error and reconciliation, or abdication in favour of a successor. That is the fate of trustees, and the sanction which must sober their use of power.[84]

Acting entirely as a rubber stamp is dangerous, for not only action invites responsibility, but also calculated inaction. Although it's said that for the Crown to oppose ministers violating constitutional conventions is for the Crown to appear partisan, yet for the Crown to abstain from opposing these ministers would also be to act in an apparently partisan fashion — as Victor Emmanuel of Italy discovered to his cost over Mussolini's Fascists. The Crown is a symbol of national unity, which is why it is the moral duty of statesmen not to immerse it in conflict, but it is of a different kind of symbolism to that of a flag. It isn't an insensate piece of coloured bunting but a living symbol of an active political institution, namely constitutional parliamentary democracy. If a great party of the nation treats parliamentary democracy with contempt, then for the Crown to oppose this party isn't to destroy its symbolism of unity, but merely illustrates the nation wasn't united in the first place in its attitudes to democracy.

Even with all its warnings and exceptions, this idea of the Crown's ultimate appeal to the electorate over matters of government is a profoundly democratic one — far more so, than the principles guiding the United States of America. In the legislative controversies among the Congressional Houses and the President there is no place, no voice for the ordinary American voter. Nowhere is his or her opinion sought on a particular, disastrous Bill or measure. It is regarded as sufficient that the members of Congress and the President were at some time in the past (maybe years previously) elected by the voters, and that at another time to come (maybe years in the future) shall be forced to confront the voters again at elections. These elections are never due to any specific issue confronting the country, but only the monotonous regularity, like a dripping tap, of a fixed-term Constitution.

It seems a curious irony of history that parliamentary government in a monarchy should produce conventions of government more democratic than those of a republic, but an irony neither accidental nor trivial. Argued later will be the contention that this "irony" is a logical consequence of establishing an executive guardian of a democratic Constitution who is given powers to defend that Constitution, is well motivated to defend it, is not a member of the government and could never pretend to an existing electoral mandate as the excuse for her actions.

King George V agonised over the decision which confronted him on the Irish question. He consulted constitutional authorities, but the opinions he received from them were coloured by their political views on Ireland. The Unionists on the Opposition benches were openly threatening civil war, encouraging armed resistance in Ulster and the British Army to mutiny, while threats emanated from the Liberal government benches of using the Royal Navy on Belfast. The debate was made more heated by the recent passage of the *Parliament Act (1911)*, which had destroyed the House of Lord's traditional right to block Supply and ensured that any other Bill, except one to extend the life of Parliament beyond its limit, should be:

> deemed to have passed the Lords after having been passed by
> the House of Commons in three successive sessions, provided
> that at least two years had elapsed between the second reading
> in the first session and the third reading in the third.[85]

Thus the Lords, which had a Unionist majority, could no longer force an election; the only power which could force the Commons to the people was direct prerogative action by the King. Bonar Law, leader of the Unionists in the Commons, warned the King after dinner in early 1912 that his only chance lay in the government resigning within two years: "If they don't you must either accept the Home Rule Bill or dismiss your Ministers and choose others who will support you in vetoing it — and in either case half your subjects will think that you have acted against them."[86]

By 1913, both the Unionists and the Liberals had come, despairing, to the conclusion that "a general election would settle nothing: Ulster would not accept the result if it went one way, and southern Ireland would not accept it if it went the other way."[87] In an audience with the King at Balmoral in August 1913, Asquith admitted that he had not expected such extreme reactions when the Home Rule Bill had been drafted, however, he told the King that there was now no solution in an election.

> What would be the use of it, since Sir Edward Carson says that Ulster would not accept its verdict if the Government was returned to power. If, on the other hand, the Opposition win, the South and West of Ireland will be in revolt, and the new Government will be 'up against Home Rule again'. [88]

Furthermore, Asquith opposed a referendum on the issue because he claimed it would undermine the basis of representative government, and would be misleading anyway, as it would be conducted along party lines. George V, haunted by Bonar Law's warning, reminded him that the Crown had been put in an impossible predicament by the government's actions.

> Asquith's standard reply was that the King acted only upon the advice of his Ministers and therefore could not be held personally responsible for the result. But the stubborn fact, as the King saw with agonised clarity, was that in this dilemma a disturbing number of his subjects had demonstrated that they *would* hold him personally responsible. He produced a list of formidably hard questions for his Prime Minister to answer: the reply amounted to a reiteration…that there were some questions to which the verdict of the electorate, refracted as it must be by party allegiance, prejudice and the impossibility of singling out a particular issue, would be no answer.[89]

The King was unimpressed with this reply. He wrote a long memorandum in his own hand, undated, but attributed to a date before May 1914, the earliest date under the Parliament Act that the Home Rule Bill could pass through Parliament. Warning that when the Bill was presented to him for his assent he would remember "how it was forced through the House of Commons, pages of it never even discussed, and yet rejected three times by the House of Lords", he said,

> Whichever course I follow, never again shall I be able to set foot in Ireland. Is it right, is it just, to place the Sovereign in such an intolerable predicament? Whether Home Rule should be given to Ireland or not is a matter on which I have no opinion. But there *is* an opinion yet unsought, the opinion of my people, and I maintain that, in an appeal to it, is to be found the only sound solution of this momentous question.[90]

The final decision regarding the King's stance was made by him after consulting Lord Loreburn, the retired Lord Chancellor, who was now chancellor of the Duchy of Cornwall. Loreburn's opinion was that the King "should give his assent to the Home Rule Bill, but only after he had received written advice from his Ministers that he should do so, given in a form that could be published"[91]. On the 31st of July 1914, George V wrote a letter to Asquith, stating that refusal of assent had been contemplated, but that,

> the King feels strongly that extreme course should not be
> adopted in this case unless there is convincing evidence that
> it would avert a national disaster, or at least have a tranquil-
> lising effect on the distracting conditions of the time. There
> is no such evidence.[92]

In that letter he requested that Ministers "should provide him with a full state-ment of the reasons why they advised him to grant his assent", to be presented "in a form which can be put on record for the use of his successors and referred to if any necessity should hereafter survive"[93]. The letter was never sent, for amid these events Britain, like the rest of Europe, toppled into the War to End All Wars.

The constitutional struggle within the British Isles, unresolved, was deferred to a later time. George V assented to the Government of Ireland Bill on the 18th of September 1914, shortly after the outbreak of World War I. The Act was suspended by a subsequent Act of Parliament.[94] Yet although the veto was never used, its shadow forced a reassessment of controversial measures. It placed an ethical burden on the King, and a practical one on his ministers, grilled and cross-examined, and ultimately compelled to a degree of account-ability they had doubtless hoped to avoid.

In 1955 the Crown's powers of veto and forced dissolution were once again discussed, in Pakistan, at that time an independent Queen's Realm of the Commonwealth (as Australia is now). During a constitutional crisis in that country in the early 1950s the Governor-General, Mr Ghulam Muhammad, had forced the dissolution of the Pakistani Constituent Assembly (which had been acting in an illegal manner) in order to avert impending disaster. Aspects of this crisis and the role of the Pakistani Crown came to the attention of the Supreme Court in *Federation of Pakistan v. Moulvi Tamizuddin Khan* (1955) and subsequent cases[†]. In his decision the Chief Justice of Pakistan, Munir CJ, gave a detailed discussion of the role of Governor-General in a Commonwealth country. Observing that "the free exercise of a discretion or prerogative power at a critical juncture is essential to the executive government of every civilised country",[95] he stated:

> There may be occasions, however remote their conception may
> be, where the Governor-General would be entitled to withold
> his assent from a [sic] particular legislation. In the United
> Kingdom, if the House of Commons passes a law which strikes
> at the very foundations of the constitution, as for instance
> where Parliament indefinitely prolongs its life or trifles with the
> right of the electors to vote, the Sovereign may, and perhaps
> would, whether the Ministry advises it or not, exercise his

---

† The Moulvi Tamizuddin Khan named here had been President of the dissolved Assembly.

reserve powers of witholding assent or dissolution. The same is the position of a Governor-General in the Dominions.[96]

Australia is among the Commonwealth realms where the Governor-General (*not* the Queen†) retains on paper the right of veto. Section 58 of the Australian Constitution explicitly states:

> When a proposed law passed by both Houses of the Parliament is presented to the Governor-General for the Queen's assent, he shall declare, according to his discretion, but subject to this Constitution, that he assents in the Queen's name, *or that he withholds assent*, or that he reserves the law for the Queen's pleasure.
>
> The Governor-General may return to the House in which it originated any proposed law so presented to him, and may transmit therewith any amendments which he may recommend, and the Houses may deal with the recommendation."[97]

Prominent republican journalist Donald Horne once asked the rhetorical question "The Constitution also describes how the Governor-General can veto a Bill or send it back to Parliament with viceregal suggestions. Would a majority of Australians want to keep that in?"[98] Given that the viceregal veto can be regarded now as an ultimate weapon, whereby revolutionary legislation can be placed before the community in a forced election to receive its verdict,‡ does he seriously believe the community should be *deprived* of this safeguard?

Contemplated here have been the most extreme reserve powers named to exist in Australia, or indeed, the UK; dusty and long-disused weapons, that "no-one desires to see used, but no-one likes to part with, lest they should at any time be found to be still needed in an extraordinary emergency". Yet a Bill so revolutionary as to awaken thoughts of the veto is one which may arouse society to flashpoint before assent is due. If appeal is to be made to the electorate while heads are still cool, while an election can still avert conflict rather than merely express it, then forcing dissolution before assent is due remains important to our society. Finally, if in times of emergency extraordinary powers are to be endowed upon the government, some watching figure must nonetheless remain capable of dismissing this ministry and forcing new elections if the government becomes corrupted by its power. The ability to force dissolution, not in reply to a particular Bill but in response to executive behaviour, remains a far from idle issue. These are contemporary matters, not mere relics of a bygone age, nor "a fiction of the past".

---

† In discussing the supposed powers of reservation and disallowance, the Constitutional Commission stated "Whatever might be comprised in 'the reserve powers of the Crown', it clearly does not include the power of the Queen to refuse assent to a Bill duly passed or to disallow a law against ministerial advice". See Final Report of the Constitutional Commission, vol.1 p. 83.

‡ Canada, for example, has retained the veto in its revised 1982 Constitution.

"Do you think," said Martin, "that hawks
have always eaten pigeons
when they could find them?"

"Of course I do," said Candide.

"Well," said Martin, "if hawks have
always had the same character, why
should you suppose that men have
changed theirs?"

Voltaire, *Candide.*

Of Hawks and Pigeons

In establishing a constitutional guardian to oppose tyranny in a Prime Minister, we must be careful to avoid creating the kind of official that will seize power for itself. Paradoxically the guardian must possess the extensive reserve powers required to solve crises, but not the inclination to wield them as a common event.

In an emotional appeal for the republican cause, author Tom Keneally once declared that "if we cannot discover loyalty, sanity, human decency and leadership among our own people then we are finished as a nation". This statement is passionate, accurate and…entirely beside the point. No-one is questioning the presence of these attributes among the Australian people. The point is that no political system of any nation in the annals of history has ever been able to guarantee qualities of honesty and selfless integrity in its political leaders. Political philosophers have wrestled with this problem since the days of Plato and his treatise *The Republic*, written nearly twenty-five centuries ago. It cannot be pretended that public elections ensure a moral meritocracy. To be sure, the assemblies of our parliaments throughout this country have often been composed of honest, honourable and courageous men and women whose presence has endowed honour both upon this nation and the institution of Parliament. Those same seats in Parliament have also from time to time been occupied by bullies, cheats, liars and snake-oil merchants of every description, who through their hypocrisies have boasted a democratic mandate. These latter specimens have displayed a distressing aptitude for acquiring and retaining power — which is hardly surprising, given that this is the whole point of lying, cheating and bullying in the first place. Popular elections are an essential part of government "of the people, by the people, for the people", and they may well reject the worst of these rogues, but an election is not some act of alchemy which infallibly separates the noble metals from the base, or from two bad candidates creates one good.

In order to preserve the democratic process that Mr Keneally values so highly we must study the motives and inclinations of political leaders, and use methods more rigorous than a maudlin appeal for everybody to be nice to one another. Our own moral considerations have no place in analysing others' desire to usurp the power of government. We are not discussing what people morally or ethically *should* do, but what they *may* do. In this context the only reliable instinct is not that of *noblesse oblige*, but of self interest, and here rests the essential difference between a constitutional monarch and a politician.

The niche of President is transient in its occupation, filled by any one person for a handful of years. No matter how well the occupant does the job, he knows he will be out again in the street after, say, six years. All he will have is a healthy pension, a life's subscription to garden parties and the memory of power. If he did his job exceptionally well he might even be popular at the garden parties.

From an amoral viewpoint there's no good reason for a president to uphold or defend the Constitution which will terminate his lease on power, and, given an appropriate chance, excellent reasons to subvert it. Why defend the instrument of your own obsolescence when by intrigue, decree or simple violence you can overthrow it and perpetuate your own power indefinitely? The only reasons for not embarking on such a course of action are external ones. If the country is peaceful and prosperous, the elected government popular, and the army is in favour of constitutional modes of government, then it would be foolish to be seen to undermine the Constitution. To do so would be to set in train a sequence of reprisals from the government and public that could be beyond the control of the president to overcome. One could be unseated from power, and probably imprisoned. On the other hand, if the government is sufficiently unpopular due to prevailing social and economic conditions, the populace disillusioned and the army disaffected, then presidential subversion of the Constitution becomes a feasible course of action. Under these circumstances, if an amoral president *can* subvert, according to his own lights he *should*, to his own advantage. Restraint would appear to him an act of naivety or sentimental weakness. The crucial question for him is not of what's ethically proper, but of what one can get away with before power slips from one's grasp.

A constitutional monarch, on the other hand, occupies for life a unique position within society, created by the ongoing processes of the Constitution.

Provided these processes aren't disrupted she will hold it until the end of her life, and after her death one of her children will inherit her position. For someone in this situation, political power of the form enjoyed and exercised by the Prime Minister represents a poisoned chalice, because an essential corollary of government is public resentment at perceived misgovernment. This perception must always exist; a cabinet minister may possess the wisdom of Solomon, yet the formulation and implementation of policy will always excite criticism and anger from those quarters of society disadvantaged by that policy. The more complex the society, the more this truth is evident, with the trade unions in conflict with upper echelons of business and industry, urban interests estranged from rural, the tensions inherent in ethnicity, hierarchy and political philosophy. Much of the symbolic power of the monarchy lies in her being above the struggle of warring factions. Although the Queen has the right to be consulted, the right to encourage and the right to warn the Prime Minister, in the end he takes full and final responsibility for policy and its popularity. His head is the ultimate political trophy for the actions of government; a trophy that must be thrown to the angry people when required.

An elderly Sir Winston Churchill expressed this truth at a banquet held in the Canadian capital of Ottawa:

> If a great battle is lost Parliament and the people can turn out the Government. If a great battle is won crowds cheer His Majesty. Thus, while the ordinary struggles, turmoils and inevitable errors of healthy democratic government proceed, there is established upon an unchallenged pedestal the title deeds and the achievements of all the Realms and every generation can make it contribution to the enduring treasure of our race and fame.[99]

To do otherwise would be for Her Majesty to be identified with a particular faction and its policies, to surrender her unique position above the arena to descend into it; from being a singular power above the struggle, she would merely become one power among many. Her head would be transformed into another political trophy, and the Crown upon it.[†]

This principle has ancient echoes. It was Machiavelli who, after observing the polity of Renaissance France, remarked,

> Among the kingdoms that are well ordered and governed in our time is France, and there we find numberless good institutions *on which depend the liberty and security of the king*; of these the chief is the parliament and its authority, because he who established that kingdom, knowing the ambition and insolence of the great nobles, deemed it necessary to have a bit in

---

† This of course assumes that the public understands how the Constitution works; otherwise the sort of distortions that cling to the Whitlam dismissal are believed, and the Crown will be reproached for doing its duty.

their mouths to check therein. And knowing on the other hand the hatred of the mass of people against the great, based on fear, and wishing to secure them, he did not wish to make this the special care of the king, to relieve him of the dissatisfaction that he might incur among the nobles by favouring the people, and among the people by favouring the nobles. He therefore established a third judge, that, without direct charge of the king, kept in check the great and favoured the lesser people. Nor could any better or more prudent measure have been adopted, nor better precaution for the safety of the king or kingdom. From which another notable rule can be drawn, that princes should let the carrying out of unpopular duties devolve on others, and bestow favours themselves.[100]

[The Ghost, who has dozed off in his chair, awakes.]

Niccolò's ghost   Eh? What? Oh yes…not a bad passage, even if I do say so myself. I even remember writing it. It was in the months between spring and autumn of 1513.

I was outcast and poverty-stricken, living in my father's house just outside Florence. Spent the time composing a little treatise advising the Medici on government. Suspicious bastards — wouldn't give me my job back. Of course, the king I was referring to was Louis XII. Spent considerable time at his Court, on diplomatic missions. Marvellous days. Louis' gratefully remembered in French history as *Pére du Peuple*[†]. Had the Sun King, Louis XIV, payed more attention to the methods of his predecessors rather than declaring his own belief in the Divine Right of Kings, perhaps the ill-fated Louis XVI might not have lost his head at the guillotine. People really ought to read my books more often…

Author   Irrespective of this speculation, the essential principle is as true now as it was when written in Florence in 1513; that in a society divided into parties and factions, a strong and representative parliamentary government is not only a noble institution from the citizens' viewpoint, but an expedient one from the perspective of a constitutional monarch. It provides a vessel in which the Crown may remain afloat above the currents and tides of popular opinion, in which all political ministers must swim, and in which they all inevitably drown.

† French, "Father of the People".

Given a Constitution that creates and destroys governments by the will of the people, the monarch is not only its guardian by public duty but also by private policy. Unlike a republic, two of the most basic motives of human nature — the instinct for self-preservation, and the desire to create and impart a familial legacy — are here employed to provide the foundation of political structures, upon the sturdiness of which our liberties depend. Powers which must exist, to be exercised for the public benefit, are given to and guarded by someone whose natural self-interest coincides with the public interest. *This* is the central principle of modern constitutional monarchism in Britain, Australia and the other realms throughout the Commonwealth: not that some people are superior to others by reason of birth, but that people whose lives intimately rely upon the preservation of the existing Constitution make the best guardians of that Constitution.

Contrasted with this, a powerful and assertive parliament is unlikely to appear expedient to a politicised president, a transient official already dependent upon a constituency within society and therefore already doomed to swim. He may be either nobly stoic about his fate, or else climb upon the shoulders of a clique of fellow swimmers, relying upon their strength for his survival. If he abandons stoicism for a more active bid for survival then any extra power he acquires is likely to be won at the expense of Parliament and its privileges.

It is reasonable to expect someone who attains her position by right of birth, not by political intrigue and patronage, who from childhood is inculcated with a strict ethical code particular to her future political duties, who is forbidden from childhood to engage in politically partisan activities, join a political party or vote at any elections, and is sensible to the peculiarity of her position in society, will abstain from political partisanship when she assumes the Crown. It isn't reasonable to expect one can have a republic in which the president is not politicised, holding partisan allegiances. As even Bagehot conceded,

> The most dignified post in the State must be an object of
> contest to the great sections into which every active political
> community is divided. These parties mix in everything and
> meddle in everything; and they neither would nor could permit
> the most honoured and conspicuous of all stations to be filled,
> except at their pleasure…The strongest party would select
> someone who would be on their side when he had to take a
> side, who would incline to them when he did incline, who
> should be a constant auxiliary to them and a constant impedi-
> ment to their adversaries. It is absurd to choose by contested
> party election an impartial chooser of ministers.[101]

More importantly, it's absurd to expect such a personage to be impartially vigilant in scrutinizing the actions of those ministers. It is not reasonable to expect politicians, whose meat and drink throughout their careers has been overt adherence to a political party and the belligerent advocacy of its policies, *"…doth suffer a sea-change// into something rich and strange"*,[102] namely an apolitical guardian of the Constitution, upon assuming the presidential mantle.

It is therefore not reasonable to expect presidents, in any but exceptional circumstances, to emulate a constitutional monarch or be worthy of the same degree of trust, when endowed with analogous powers to protect the Constitution. Instead, one of two leaps of faith is required. The first is that of Frances' Fifth Republic, in which significant power is invested in the President in the (dubious) hope that it shall be used benevolently. The second is that of the Irish republic, in which the President is little more than the puppet of the Prime Minister, the (equally dubious) hope being that the latter will always act for the public benefit. For my part I like neither leap, relying as they do upon the good intentions and charity of politicians. In an essay in which he contemplated enlightened behaviour within a system of government, John Stuart Mill warned:

> Governments must be made for human beings as they are, or as they are capable of speedily becoming…And it cannot be maintained that any form of government would be rational which required as a condition that these exalted principles of action should be the guiding and master motives in the conduct of average human beings.[103]

He established an appropriate way to judge a well-designed political post when he wrote,

> But political checks will no more act of themselves than a bridle will divert a horse without a rider. If the checking functionaries are as corrupt or as negligent as those whom they ought to check, and if the public, the mainspring of the whole checking machinery, are too ignorant, too passive, or too careless and inattentive, to do their part, little benefit will be derived from the best administrative apparatus…The ideally perfect constitution of a public office is that in which the interest of the functionary is entirely coincident with his duty. No mere system will make it so, but still less can it be made so without a system, aptly devised for the purpose.[104]

This is the litmus test. A constitutional monarchy fulfils this specification, and from this comes its success. A republican presidency fails it, and from this is born the multitude failure of republics.

Some may feel affronted at the suggestion that a modern political problem may be solved by the use of an ancient institution, but the problem of empowering a guardian is a problem of human nature, namely the desire to acquire and retain personal power. As such it is not a "modern" problem but one, like the human condition itself, as eternal as the hills. Shakespeare's tragedies retain their popularity and relevance, not through an insatiable public hunger for theatre in iambic pentameter, but because ambition, treachery and deceit are as comfortable in the trousers of a lounge suit as in an Elizabethan codpiece. There's no means of commissioning this guardian — be she or he elected, appointed, anointed, chosen by college of cardinals or suckled by a she-wolf, nominated by the army or nominated by a burning bush — that is in any way intrinsically good or bad, except inasmuch as it assists or impedes our shared purpose, the preservation of an accountable and stable parliamentary democracy. If incorporation of an hereditary element best assists this, why discard it?

Niccolò's ghost Nothing in this argument guarantees a monarch shall behave well, or a president, badly.

Author No political system in history has ever been able to guarantee the behaviour of the humans populating it. Yet what a system can do is transform what might under some circumstances be an act of amoral shrewdness into one of self-destructive stupidity — or the reverse. Quite possibly some presidents might be tempted to preserve democracy for its own sake, and some monarchs might be tempted to do like Alfonso XIII of Spain and establish some favourite minister as dictator.

Niccolò's ghost So you argue that, although no system can abolish the risk of usurpers, surely a system that transforms usurpation by a guardian from being the clever act of a knave to the self-destructive one of a fool is preferable to a system that actively tempts its guardian to do wrong, yet expects him to look the other way — and is shocked when he succumbs to the temptation, conspiring to seize such tools as he needs to overthrow legitimate government. [*pauses*] So much for the desire to usurp government. But an ideal guardian should also lack resources to usurp the instruments of government. If he possesses enough resources but lacks the active desire, errors of judgement or policy may still lead to the disruption of democratic government. What do you say of the resources?

Prospero: ...To credit his own lie, he did believe
He was indeed the Duke, out o'th'substitution
And executing th'outward face of royalty,
With all prerogative. Hence his ambition
growing – Dost thou hear?

Miranda: Your tale, sir, would cure deafness.

Prospero: To have no screen between the part he played
And him he played it for, he needs will be
Absolute Milan. Me, poor man, my library
Was dukedom enough.

The Tempest, Act I Scene 2

Appointment

To many people, the word "resources" summons images of police and soldiers. Yet when attempting any dubious enterprise, the most valuable resource of all is the semblance of legitimacy. In a Westminster-like system the "Head of State", elected, appointed or anointed, is not a member of the elected government. When striving to subvert democratic government, the most useful weapon is the outward appearance of a democratic mandate. This weapon is possessed in abundance by a directly elected president, in moderation by a president elected by Parliament, and not at all by a monarch anointed or governor-general appointed under the Constitution.

In the ten years between the downfall of the Fourth Republic and the Paris riots of 1968, perhaps the shrewdest manoeuvre of Charles de Gaulle was a 1962 constitutional amendment that rendered the presidency directly elected by the people. He had already violated the French Constitution over issues of domestic agriculture and the independence of Mali and Madagascar, and had violated the independence of the judiciary by setting up special courts to try political crimes against the State. He had displayed contempt for Parliament by ignoring it; frequently his ministers only knew of government policy by reading about it in the newspaper. An example was the trip de Gaulle and Pinay, his Minister of Finance, took to French Africa. The first Pinay knew of the granting of independence to the colony of Guinea was when he read about it in the local papers.

To entrench his existing controversial position and shroud future violations in the blanket of a popular mandate, it was useful for de Gaulle to change the method of election of the President, from being the choice of the College of Notables, as set down by the Constitution, to being by referendum. He argued that power must be derived from the people through universal suffrage, and that he intended to become completely and directly dependent on that suffrage, so what could be more democratic?

His actual motive was less exalted. Gaston Monnerville, the President of the Senate and next in line for the Presidency were de Gaulle to die or be assassinated, accused him of planning a "deliberate, calculated and outrageous attack on the Constitution in order to establish a system of personal power".[105] The Council of State pronounced de Gaulle's proposals as unconstitutional; the Constitutional Council remained silent, although a number of members, including the Gaullist President Léon Noël, were known to have been critical. When Prime Minister Pompidou's government was defeated by Parliament over the issue, de Gaulle dissolved Parliament and asked Pompidou and his cabinet to remain in office until 27th November 1962. He then decreed that a referendum on his reform be held on the 28th of October, to be followed by a general election three weeks later. Pompidou issued secret instructions to all Prefects in France, stating explicitly that,

> although government servants were to adopt an attitude of
> neutrality in the general election for the Assembly, they were
> to exert themselves with the 'utmost energy' to secure the
> vote for the President of the Republic in the Referendum.[106]

Despite the large number of opponents to de Gaulle, the internal dissent and disunity of the parties of the Left meant there was only limited coherent opposition. He won the referendum with sixty-two percent of the votes cast at the polls. Nearly a quarter of the electorate abstained.[107]

All this effort, all this intrigue on the part of de Gaulle, Pompidou and their supporters was not due to an over-zealous love of democracy. Once elected by popular vote, the President would have his term of years in office, employing his presidential powers to remake the Constitution and country in his own image, excusing trespasses against ministries and parliaments on the pretext of a democratic mandate. And so it was for President de Gaulle and his successor, President Pompidou.[108]

Many prominent republicans and monarchists in Australia are agreed that a directly elected president wielding significant reserve powers represents the worst of all possible worlds. Such a presidential office possesses all the vices of a republic in an acute form: the mortality of office, the adherence to a political party, and the semblance of legitimacy when trespassing against the government or Parliament. This president, this supreme constitutional symbol of our nation would hold an explicit constituency within our society. Admired by his supporters, he would be despised and resented by all the elements of society whose interests conflict with his policies, whose political leaders were defeated by him in the struggle for the supreme post. Support or subversion of the Constitution would become a recurrent dilemma in the policies of parties and associations. As the Constitution becomes associated with a partisan political will, so would subversion become a natural manifestation of opposition to that will in society. It isn't startling that the Fifth Republic was accused in 1973 of having:

> concentrated on giving the executive every facility to govern while denying to the 'oppositions' the constitutional means to oppose short of rendering the country ungovernable. This has stimulated the proliferation of extra-constitutional and illegal forms of opposition by groups motivated by sectional interest or ideology whose activities range from being a minor irritant to being a threat to the whole organization of French society.[109]

The concept of a president elected by Parliament carries the same weaknesses but to varying extends. This method of appointment is intended to prevent partisanship, although under general circumstances it would fail to do so, giving as it does the power of appointment to members of the elective oligarchy. It also fails to address motives engendered by the mortality of office, or whether it might not be dangerous to establish a President who could claim to be more representative of Parliament than the Prime Minister.

Underlying this scheme of appointment rests the argument that, if enough rival factions in Parliament can agree on a candidate, then this in itself will provide a fairly good guarantee the candidate will be apolitical. This argument is flawed in three essential ways.

* The first is the belief that members of Parliament, overtly partisan politicians elected purely for the duties of government, are appropriate people to be given the power of choice over future Heads of State. The Australian people are rightly suspicious of endowing parliamentarians with this privilege — "jobs for the boys" is a political principle as old as civilisation itself. If the purpose of reserve powers is to prevent the elective oligarchy from cutting its bonds of accountability to the constituency, then to give members of that oligarchy the right to choose the wielder of these reserve powers is to commit an act worse than stupid.

* Ignoring this, the second flaw lies in deciding what constitutes "enough" rival factions.

* The third flaw is the belief that a candidate who appears apolitical will remain apolitical. To this third problem there appears no ready solution apart from removing inducements to corrupt behaviour, and in this we return to the issue of mortality of power.

Putting aside all our other objections, how many are "enough" rival factions, and how can their vote be representative of the public will?

The path suggested has been to require a certain proportion of members of Parliament to vote for a particular candidate: some say fifty percent, others seventy-five, while some demand ninety or more. In nominating a figure we steer between two disastrous scenarios, one an outcome of requiring too few votes, the other, too many.

The first may be found in the idea suggested by Gough Whitlam, of requiring the support of only fifty percent of members to choose a president.[110] The folly of this scheme is that it transforms a general election, which should be a question of choice of government, into a lottery for absolute power. Whosoever wins fifty-one percent of seats takes all: government, president, Parliament and armed forces in an elective dictatorship. Far from freeing the presidency from the infection of partisan politics, it renders the president a creature of party.

A remedy suggested has been to "up the ante"; to require the president to be chosen by a two-thirds majority vote of either the House of Representatives or some arrangement of both Houses of Parliament, the argument being "No Government in the post World War II period has had a two thirds majority overall".[111] This is as scientific as arguing that it won't rain tomorrow because it didn't rain yesterday. In periods of two-party parliaments as in periods of drought, such reasoning appears valid in the absence of a demonstration of its fallacy. The composition of Parliament, like the nature of the weather, is changeable and impermanent, even more so than the society it represents. The hypothesis that no faction or coalition of like-minded factions will ever control two-thirds is born of the assumption that future parliaments will, as now, be dominated by two mutually conflicting groups of the Left and Right, whose respective constituencies will provide a balance in representation. It isn't difficult to conceive of circumstances in which parliaments dominated by two or three parties shatter into Houses filled by a multitude of factions, either due to the inability of existing parties to adjust to swift-changing circumstances of society, or by a simple change in the electoral system. Given that even the basic ideologies of "Left-wing" and "Right-wing" are now fading in our post-Industrial era, with new industrial technologies and global capital transforming political perceptions, our current political parties may conceivably cease to exist over the next century, replaced by new groupings and controversies.

This figure of two-thirds is not a magic number, not a result obtained by sophisticated computations, but is an arbitrary high water mark. It represents not a line carved in marble but one drawn in sand, retaining a semblance of permanence only until some higher political tide should come and wash it all away.

In striving to remain above the waterline of partisanship we encounter the second danger, that of requiring too many votes in consensus. An assembly of representatives of society is by its nature a House divided, reflecting conflict as a mirror of that society. Require a full consensus before a candidate is appointed and that candidate shall never be appointed. This dismal truth was realised by the Italian parliament when they sought to appoint a President of the Republic in 1992.†

---

† More recently, it has also been realised by the Eastern European republic of Slovakia. On the 2nd of March

The President of Italy wields powers comparable to those of the Governor-General of Australia. He has the power to dissolve Parliament, and in the absence of a clear parliamentary majority, chooses the Prime Minister. He himself is chosen by an assembly composed of the members of both Houses of Parliament augmented by 58 regional representatives from all over Italy — a total of 1,014 electors, who squeeze into the 630-seat Chamber of Deputies (Italy's Lower House) for a vote by secret ballot. The first ballot requires a two-thirds majority to elect the President. If that ballot fails, a second one is held, again requiring a two-thirds majority for election. If that fails, a third ballot is held which requires a simple majority — 50% of the vote plus one — to elect the President.

The general elections held on the 6th and 7th of April 1992 caused the proportion of seats held in the Chamber of Deputies by the dominant Christian Democrats to collapse to its lowest level in decades. The Socialists also lost seats throughout northern Italy, although they overtook the Democratic Party of the Left (PDS, Italy's renamed communist party) in the south, while a massive protest vote saw the Northern League win 20% of the vote in Lombardy. The overall result throughout Italy was to cause a parliamentary deadlock, with the majority held by the former governing coalition under Christian Democrat Giulio Andreotti being too slim to provide a viable new government. Under these circumstances it was up to Italian president Francesco Cossiga to choose Mr Andreotti's successor as a prime minister who could command the confidence of Parliament after it met on the 23rd of April.

Later described in an article on Mafia corruption as "a creature of the night from the first republic and an historic opponent of the independence of the judiciary",[112] Mr Cossiga had his own problems. Originally ascending to the presidency via the Christian Democrats, with whom he had subsequently quarrelled, his mandate was due to expire on the 3rd of July. Voting for his successor was due to begin on the 4th of June. Cossiga had had bitter public quarrels and reconciliations with both Giulio Andreotti and Achille Occhetto, the leader of the PDS. Bettino Craxi, leader of the Socialists, had withdrawn his own candidacy for the prime ministership due to investigations of corruption. Confronted with a tangled parliamentary problem, Cossiga's solution was simple. On the 26th of April, without having chosen a prime minister, he tearfully declared his resignation.

The result was chaos. Italy now had neither a prime minister or a president, and until Parliament elected the latter the former could not exist. Giovanni Spadolini, the recently re-elected President of the Senate, plugged Cossiga's gap as temporary President but had no constitutional authority to appoint a prime minister. (For obvious reasons — making a gift of presidential powers to

1998 outgoing President Michal Kovac's term expired. Five months later, at the end of July, the Slovak Parliament had to cancel its eleventh attempt to find a replacement president, because no candidates had been put forward. The Slovak Constitution requires a three-fifths majority in Parliament to elect a candidate, and the parties refused to agree on a candidate, leaving the country in limbo. (The *Age*, 29th July 1998.)

a partisan "stand in" would conceivably allow him to appoint a like-minded prime minister; they could then prorogue Parliament and rule as they please.)

This national chaos lasted for weeks, while the assembly gathered in the Chamber of Deputies in Rome remained ineffectual, divided and irresolute, unable to decide upon a president. The frustration of delegates led to brawls and fistfights breaking out between members of rival parties in the chamber.

The crisis was finally resolved by a murder. Judge Giovanni Falcone, a prominent campaigner against organised crime, was assassinated on the Palermo motorway in Sicily by a Mafia bomb. Party bosses attending the funeral were jeered by mourners chanting insults, protesting over the absence of a government. Badly shaken, they finally chose Oscar Luigi Scalfaro, the Christian Democratic Speaker of the Chamber of Deputies, to be President almost two months after the general elections. As *TIME* magazine put it, "Scalfaro must now tackle the same Mafia terror to which he owes his election."[113]

The chaos caused by the refusal of the House to resolve its collective mind in appointing a president is a priceless political weapon for the Opposition. If the Government requires the support of the Opposition to appoint a president, it can reply by threatening the Government with the spectre of a government unable to govern; an Executive Council without a Head to ratify treaties or issue proclamations; a Parliament unable to create laws, without anyone to assent to its legislation; a Parliament which cannot be prorogued or dissolved unless it expires from old age; a nation's armed forces deprived of a commander-in-chief. A rudderless ship of State cast adrift, unless the government of the day purchases the Opposition's support by acceding to its demands. Should we allow this instrument of political blackmail to come into existence? This thought has occurred to the Republican Advisory Committee, and its reply is feeble:

> If the objection is made that this allows an Opposition, if it were so minded, to refuse to cooperate (thus denying a two-thirds majority) unless certain political demands were met, the answer would be that government could continue to function, with an acting head of state (or possibly the outgoing head of state staying on), until the situation was resolved.[114]

This proffered solution is unserviceable in a number of ways. If the chaos of an unoccupied presidency is to be averted, there must be (by implication) an emergency process of appointing an acting Head which is faster than the two-thirds parliamentary method. If this is so, then why go to all the trouble of creating a slow and elaborate mechanism to select an impartial president if the deadlock of this mechanism allows the hasty appointment of a more partisan acting Head of State wielding the same powers? Certainly it would allow government to "continue to function" — but with all the vices and abuses that the original mechanism was intended to prevent. The strategy a government would adopt to exploit this loophole is obvious: offer an official candidate who is known to be unacceptable to Parliament, and when the appointment mechanism grinds to a halt, invoke the emergency clauses to appoint a loyal puppet as acting President.

The straw clutched by the Committee, of relying on the outgoing Head of State to fill the breach until a replacement can be found, is a forlorn hope. What if the former President has been impeached, or resigned in disgrace, like Richard Nixon in the United States? On a more mundane level, what if he's died? Non-hereditary Heads of State are often elderly, and the prospect of death in office is an immediate one. Human mortality, a likely cause for a new president to be required, sinks the hopes of the Committee.

Selecting a president by choice of Parliament is like trying to find a place to stand on the sand between a rock and the tide, between the obdurate irresolution of a House divided and the high water mark of political patronage. Even if the selection is performed and a president is sworn in, does this president represent a desirable circumstance, able as he is to claim to be more representative of Parliament then the Prime Minister?

Our Westminster system defines the relationship between the Crown and Prime Minister by a set of conventions which gain their strength not so much from their own existence as from the environment in which they exist. Their power is derived from the fact that the monarch or her representative could never pretend to possess a popular mandate as the source of their power, whereas the Prime Minister relies on one, owing his or her authority to the confidence of an elected House. Thus, struggle between the two figures is manifested in terms of the Crown appealing to Parliament or the electorate, to revoke the Prime Minister's democratic authority rather than endowing any extra to the Crown. Far from being a source of embarrassment, an obviously unelected "Head of State" is an asset in that it provides a clear demarcation line: the privileges of Parliament are partly protected from abuse of the reserve powers by the fact that such abuses require a breach of convention which cannot be concealed by a pretended mandate. The two branches of subversion described earlier, the desire to subvert and the resources to do so, are here seen to be tangled. The knowledge that she cannot camouflage her abuses is a strong disincentive for a monarch or her representative to attempt them. Self-interest protects Parliament from a pragmatic monarch; the absence of the camouflage of being "a voice of the people" helps protect it from an idealistic one.

To see what happens when this environment is destroyed we need look no further than the Fifth Republic, where the President can claim a direct mandate and government involves an ongoing power struggle between President and Prime Minister, with the advantage sometimes resting with one and sometimes the other. A former prime minister of France, Jacques Chaban-Delmas, stated the situation somewhat ruefully in January 1970, during a period of presidential ascendancy, when he said,

> Our constitution has an Achilles heel. This weakness can be
> summarized as the requirement of close, almost intimate rela-
> tions between the president of the republic and the prime

minister, between whom mutual trust must be complete…[The latter's] subordination should not be rigorous or rigid…They must work together, it being understood that the final decision lies with the head of state…[115]

The conventions of our system of government have succeeded where the laws of many republics have failed, in entrenching the position of the Prime Minister so that struggle between the Heads of Government and State does not destroy or diminish the power associated with the post of Prime Minister. Who is a Prime Minister but a parliamentarian possessing the confidence of the Lower House — fifty percent of its members plus one — and commissioned by the Head of State to govern? If the President can boast of being more representative of Parliament than is the Prime Minister, having been elected by half or two-thirds of the Lower House or of both Houses, then why should he feel obliged to consult with either the Prime Minister or Parliament over the exercise of the reserve powers, able as he is to claim already to be the single most representative figure on the political landscape?

The modern republican movement is founded upon the belief our Head of State should hold a popular mandate from the people through the way he or she is appointed to the post. In devising some means of appointing a Head of State with a popular mandate grave difficulties are encountered: on one hand the infection of party politics, on the other the stubborn refusal of rival parties to countenance a candidate. On a deeper level republican logic is based upon a false premise, for the wielder of Westminster-like reserve powers must *never* be able to claim to represent the popular will before the eruption of a constitutional crisis. The Queen and her representatives are accorded a trust as guardians, but no existing claim to the popular will. Thus, when they invoke reserve powers to uphold this trust they must appeal to Parliament or the electorate, to clothe their actions with popular legitimacy; a legitimacy to which they could otherwise never pretend. Not a shred or rag of an existing mandate should be permitted to conceal the nakedness of these powers. For fear of embarrassment let their wielder crave to borrow clothes.

Your first letter to me was most improper and your second letter to me is not only improper, it should not have been written at all.

When I took my oath as Chief Justice 13 years ago I promised to uphold the Constitution and the Law of Papua New Guinea. You did the same when I swore you in as Governor-General of Papua New Guinea. Your letter on the third instant is an attempt to induce me to breach my oath of office. It is not my intention to violate my oath of office.

Letter by Chief Justice Sir Buri Kidu
to Governor-General Sir Serei Eri, 1991.

Dismissal

If the election of presidents should be condemned for its susceptibility to infection by political patronage and partisanship, then what of the current mode of appointment of Governors and Governors-General in Australia, by advice of the Premier or Prime Minister? Assuming the current method of appointment lends itself to establishing a politicised Governor or Governor-General — a fair assumption for a critic to make — then how is a partisan viceregal Head of State any better than or preferable to a partisan president? If we regard politicisation of the Head of State as a disease of the body politic, then a bipartite monarchy possesses a remedy impossible in any republic: swift and drastic surgery.

A single-tiered monarchy deals with the danger by preventative means, by removing inducements to partisanship. In a two-tiered monarchy, where the effective, viceregal Head of State is appointed to the position on the advice of politicians and holds it only for a finite term of office, there cannot be so effective a defence against politicisation. However, if the Governor-General reveals himself later to be corrupt or partisan, the Prime Minister can appeal to the Queen to dismiss him swiftly. A dramatic case of this took place in Papua New Guinea, in 1991, in what has become notorious as the Diro Affair.

Edward "Ted" Diro, first Commander of the PNG Defence Forces, entered the national politics of that country in 1982. Ethnically Papuan, by the next elections in 1987 he had created the People's Action Party, a Papuan-based political party which acquired a formidable presence in Parliament. In the same year Diro's encounters with the law began, when he was cleared of six counts of perjury by a technicality, and so avoided fourteen years imprisonment. The 1987 Barnett Commission of Inquiry, investigating mismanagement and corruption in the PNG timber industry, recommended in early 1988 that criminal charges be laid against him, and against a number of businessmen and public servants. Diro, now a cabinet minister in the Wingti government, was not going to be put away so easily.

On the 9th of March 1988, shortly before the Barnett Inquiry was to table its final report, Diro supporters confronted the then Prime Minister Paias Wingti, and attempted to dictate terms to him: that "Ted Diro's case be done away with", to be done "within seven days, no later". To his lasting credit, Wingti's response was to state,

> No Prime Minister should interfere with the course of justice;
> he should not interfere with police matters, he should not
> interfere with the public prosecutor's office and he should not
> interfere with the proceedings of a commission of inquiry.[116]

Eleven days later Diro wrote a letter to an Opposition member, and asked that it be passed on to Opposition leader Sir Michael Somare. The contents were straightforward, an offer to transfer allegiance of Diro's People's Action Party to the Opposition, away from Wingti's People's Democratic Movement, which would then fall from government. In return for this he had two demands: a promise that the Barnett Inquiry be buried, and the post of Deputy Prime Minister in the new government to be given to the PAP.

Thus Paias Wingti's integrity lost him government; he lost a vote of no confidence in July 1988 when PAP voted with the Opposition, and Rabbie Namaliu became the new Prime Minister. As agreed, Diro was rewarded with the deputy prime ministership — but the Inquiry remained active, and its final report was referred by Namaliu to the fraud squad.

By now Diro had positioned himself to be third in line to become Prime Minister in June 1992, after Namaliu and Wingti. In 1989 the new Police Commissioner, Ila Geno, announced that there was "no case" in pursuing the Inquiry's findings. It seemed Ted would escape again.

Confronted by this prospect the Ombudsmen Commission fought to have him brought to trial. In 1991 it submitted to the Public Prosecutor, Kina Bona, that he be charged with 73 counts of bribery, corruption and misuse of office. Some of these charges derived from the Barnett findings, while others were independent offences. After considering this list, Bona advised the Chief Justice to appoint a leadership tribunal to try Diro on a total of 86 charges. Ted Diro did everything in his power to evade trial. First he claimed the Ombudsmen Commission didn't have lawful jurisdiction, then he forced a change of chairmen, and finally, unsuccessfully, attempted to block the evidence from the Barnett Inquiry. When all legal avenues were exhausted he moved to more irregular methods.

The Governor-General of Papua New Guinea at the time was one Sir Serei Eri, a former president of the Peoples' Action Party who had been conveniently appointed Governor-General in January 1990, on Diro's recommendation. Now was time for Ted to call for his old friend and ally to repay political debts. Sir Serei twice wrote letters to Chief Justice Sir Buri Kidu, first hinting and then bluntly requesting that charges against Diro be dropped.

Sir Buri wrote back:

> Your first letter to me was most improper and your second letter to me is not only improper, it should not have been written at all.
>
> When I took my oath as Chief Justice 13 years ago I promised to uphold the Constitution and the Law of Papua New Guinea. You did the same when I swore you in as Governor-General of Papua New Guinea. Your letter on the third instant is an attempt to induce me to breach my oath of office. It is not my intention to violate my oath of office.[117]

The Leadership Tribunal under Justice Graham Ellis proceeded, and within three weeks pronounced Diro guilty on 81 charges of bribery, corruption and misuse of office, and recommended his dismissal from office for each of 71 counts. These included attempts to prevent the course of justice, violating the leadership code and the Constitution by secretly holding directorships in several companies, and — perhaps most disturbing for national security — accepting K140,000 in secret political donations from General Murdani, the Commander-in-Chief of the Indonesian armed forces at the time.

In a final desperate attempt to derail the system, Sir Serei refused to sign the dismissal papers, "thanked" Ellis for "a job well done", flatly rejected the Tribunal findings and fully reinstated Diro as Deputy Prime Minister, only fining him K3,000. Papua New Guinea now found itself in a full-scale crisis, with both the man responsible for discharging the duties of Head of State and the Deputy Prime Minister out of control, ignoring the judiciary, subverting the Constitution and the rule of law.

Fortunately the Constitution of PNG has an efficient way of dealing with a recalcitrant viceregal Head of State. Prime Minister Namaliu contacted Queen Elizabeth II as Queen of Papua New Guinea, briefed her on the recent unpleasant turn of events, and advised her to dismiss Sir Serei. Realising he was outmanoeuvred by Namaliu and the Queen, Eri resigned, and the Queen appointed an acting Governor-General on Namaliu's advice who promptly dismissed Diro and restored the proper processes of law. Thus constitutional government was restored: swiftly, legally, without ambiguity or bloodshed.[118]

Consider the same crisis in a "minimalist" republic. The judiciary and the exercise of law they represent are being flouted by "President" Eri, who is

Commander-in-Chief of the armed forces and the police. Existing judicial decisions are being ignored and the Chief Justice bullied. The next logical step is for the President and like-minded ministers to issue directives to the police through the usual chain of command, to ignore certain judicial directives.

Such a presidential directive destroys "the rule of law" — which is to say, the regulation of a society through a framework of laws that apply universally to citizens, and which can be altered only through an established mechanism consistent with the existing framework — and replaces it with "the rule of the prince" — in other words, arbitrary discretionary government. Civil liberties may be found in a society under the rule of law, but in a society under an arbitrary government guaranteed civil rights cannot exist, only a despotic largesse. This leaves the police and other instruments of State with an unpleasant decision to make, either to acquiesce in the new despotism or to resist. It is to be expected that political and personal loyalties and conscience will induce some officers to choose one path and some the other, a split into factions which in the absence of a swift political resolution would decide the issue through use of force. This is the path of civil war.

So we should examine the political devices used by republics to deal with a recalcitrant Head of State, while remaining mindful of three necessities: the removal procedure must not be too easy, nor too slow. It should not be driven by partisan political vendettas but by the desire to give impartial justice, to chastise only to preserve democratic constitutional government,.

It is obvious why removal mustn't be too easy. The first task of ministers attempting to subvert the Constitution would be to eliminate or emasculate its guardians. Even conscientious guardians cannot be expected to be effective if at the first hint of trouble they can be replaced by more pliable officials, puppets of the Prime Minister.

The process mustn't be too slow. Events can escalate into a dangerous national crisis very rapidly. A maverick who wields reserve powers, and is the ultimate head of the disciplinary instruments of State — the police and armed forces — can wreak immense damage unless stopped swiftly and decisively. Consider the timescale of the Diro Affair: Sir Serei first began exhibiting odd behaviour on the 3rd of September, when he wrote private letters to the Chief Justice pressuring him to drop charges. Within *twenty-four days* PNG was plunged into total crisis, with Sir Serei ignoring the judiciary on the 27th and reinstating a corrupt senior cabinet minister with a strong parliamentary backing. The Prime Minister and Queen of Papua New Guinea then forced him into checkmate in three days. He tendered a letter of resignation on the 30th of September.

Finally, the process should be decided by someone impartially motivated to preserve the democratic Constitution for its own sake, rather than use crisis as a party-political tool. For example, if the process involves Parliament sitting in trial upon a popular president belonging to a party hostile to those dominating Parliament, it doesn't take Richelieu to realise that circumstances permitting, an innocent shall still be sentenced to be as guilty as Judas, and, stained with "guilt", removed in the name of political expediency.

This problem of devising an acceptable republican trial for dismissal doesn't seem to have been taken seriously by the Republican Advisory Committee. After making the patently silly remark that "Australians would have a right to expect that [a provision allowing for the removal of the Head of State] would never need to be used",[119] the Committee proceeded to recite the impeachment mechanisms of the constitutions of the republics of Singapore, Malta, Israel, Ireland, India, the Philippines, the United States, Trinidad and Tobago, Germany, Sri Lanka, Austria, Iceland and Finland — without bothering to ascertain whether any of these tools were actually useful to our circumstance, or worthless artefacts to be discarded. For reasons that will now be argued, the devices of our current Constitution can be used to provide a superior removal process to that of any of these republics. Furthermore, that as the mechanisms of these countries appear to be representative of the entire family of sensible procedures in a republican context, the proposition of an Australian republic remains totally unacceptable until a viable and superior trial and dismissal procedure is devised.

Niccolò's ghost [*reaches for a book*] The Concise Oxford Dictionary defines the verb "to impeach" as meaning to:

> Call in question, disparage, (character etc.); accuse (persons) of, charge (with); find fault with (thing); accuse of treason or other high crime before competent tribunal,[120]

and it's in this last sense, of accusation before a competent tribunal, that the word is applied to the trial of a president or other political figure. This immediately inspires the question of what, in a republic, is a "competent tribunal"? Is it a panel of judges, one or both Houses of Parliament assembled, or the entire citizenry of the country? Do any of these assemblies, when used as a tribunal — an authority that sits in judgement upon a person, to decide innocence or guilt — satisfy the three necessary conditions you have stated?

The most obvious people to use in a tribunal are judges — say, the full bench of the High Court. But before judges can be used to decide a matter, the law must encompass the matter to be judged. If the law exists as a sieve to sift through the actions and transactions of a community, separating those acts which are consistent with the well-ordered functioning of a society from those which are not, then for the courts to judge an act requires consideration of the context of that act. To see the value of context, ask the following question: is it tolerable behaviour for a boy to throw stones? If he is alone in an empty paddock then yes, it probably is; his actions do not represent any kind of threat to the well being of the rest of the community. However, if the same boy throwing the same stones smashes the windows of a house, his actions obviously cease to be tolerable. Is it acceptable for private citizens to be deprived of their liberties and be locked up in a small room? If this deprivation of liberty were arbitrary then no, it would be utterly abhorrent to us, and yet when police constables imprison criminals we are relieved and grateful. It is the particular relationship between the community, "police constables" and "criminals" which empowers police to perform actions unacceptable in ordinary citizens. Clearly the particular context of an act is important in deciding whether that act inspires admiration or imprisonment. Therefore, before we can use judges to decide whether a president is guilty of "wrongdoing", we must decide in legal terms what executive wrongdoing actually *is*.

There are two ways of doing this.

❖ One, is to attempt to codify precisely what behaviour is tantamount to wrongdoing. This attracts two criticisms, the first being that surely an attempt to define with precision what the president should *not* do may in part delineate in legal code what he *should* do, which immediately and irrevocably destroys the relevant previous Westminster conventions, wherever they conflict.[†] A second criticism is the question of what if the president engages in behaviour clearly detrimental to the survival of constitutional government, but sufficiently novel as not to have been included in our legal formulation of wrongdoing. Will that make his behaviour legitimate, and render him safe from dismissal while he vandalises executive government? Can we seriously expect to have addressed *all* manner of emergencies with precision in our formula of words?

❖ The alternative is to be content with avoiding exact specification of wrongdoing, instead using a provision like the republic of Israel's, which states that the President may be removed for "conduct unbecoming his status as President". What does this mean, precisely? It means nothing precisely. Certainly this nebulous formula encompasses criminal and civil offences against the existing laws of our society, but the President could be

---

† This was illustrated before the Privy Council by *Adegbenro v. Akintola(1962)*, arising from the 1962 Nigerian constitutional crisis. At the time, Nigeria was one of Her Majesty's independent realms, with a written federal Constitution and partly-codified reserve powers. At the time of the crisis, the Governor of the Western Province was Sir Adesoji Aderemi, Oni [paramount chief] of Ife. His sacking of his Premier, Alhaji D.S. Adegbenro, although in accordance with the written text of the Constitution, was in apparent violation of Westminster convention. Mr Adegbenro's supporters took the matter to the Nigerian Federal Supreme Court, which overturned the dismissal as unconstitutional because it violated Westminster principles. Mr Adegbenro's enemies — including the new Premier, Chief S.L. Akintola — appealed to the Privy Council in London, in *Adegbenro v. Akintola(1962)*, which, while acknowledging the violation, upheld the Premier's dismissal and overturned the Supreme Court ruling. The ruling of the Judicial Committee of the Privy Council stated "it is...the wording of the Constitution itself that is to be interpreted and applied, and this wording can never be overridden by the extraneous principles of other Constitutions which are not explicitly incorporated in the formulae that have been chosen as the frame of this Constitution". (Quoted by Forsey, "The Present Position of the Reserve Powers of the Crown", *Evatt and Forsey on the Reserve Powers*, p. lxxxiv; see also [1963] A.C. 614.)

tried for such offences anyway, as a private citizen appearing before the courts within their usual sphere of competence. This vague phrase "conduct unbecoming" encompasses far more than actual violations of the law, and it is this *terra incognita* of executive misconduct, this twilight land stretching between stark illegality and benignly "proper" behaviour which we now expect intrepid judges to roam, mapping the territory as they track the spoor of a straying president.

We should not stomach this second approach to the trial of a Head of State. To begin with, it's a cop-out by constitutional drafters. Given a difficult problem, the trial of a Head of State, they borrow judicial robes and finery to imbue with legal dignity a process which should have nothing to do with the courts: namely, the question of whether or not to strip office from someone who has not actually violated the laws to be found on the statute books or in the common law, and so who stands before them to be judged on grounds alien to their expertise.

Under parliamentary sovereignty, the servants of justice in an ordinary court of law — the judge, the jury and the counsel prosecuting and defending the accused — aren't personally responsible for the sanctions imposed by the court, provided the trial is properly conducted. They are sheltered from personal culpability by statute books and the Common Law, by Parliament, precedent and established procedures. The purpose of counsel for the prosecution and defence is to submit cases arguing the guilt or innocence of the accused, of alleged crimes and offences that stand defined and treated in existing law, through thesis and antithesis argued by barristers and moderated by the judge. The jury decides whether the accused has been proved guilty of the alleged offences, and upon that verdict the judge either acquits or pronounces sentence upon the prisoner in the dock. Such decisions are made in the light of existing laws, not illuminated by fanciful laws devised by the servants of the court. This rule protects not only the liberty of the citizen standing accused in the dock, but also the judge and jury themselves; for not being the authors of laws that punish, and being obliged to enforce them, these people are not culpable for the impositions they mete out. Appeals to higher courts exist to correct errors of judgement, but when the laws themselves are foolish it is ultimately for Parliament, not the courts, to remedy them. It is Parliament, not the courts, that is ultimately responsible for bad or inadequate laws, as either the architect that created them or the authority that should have replaced them. Provided this principle is understood, public rage at bad law will pass over the courts to its proper prey, parliamentarians, who will be removed and replaced at general elections by people who would change the law.[†]

On the other hand, in political trials the accused are being judged on offences not found on the statute books; their conduct is measured by conventions and

---

† The exceptions to this are matters relating to a written Constitution, the entire purpose of which is to place certain laws beyond the control of Parliament. A Parliament cannot be held responsible for a constitutional law deliberately set outside its reach.

THE WIELDER OF THE RESERVE POWERS

perceptions of conduct not rigidly defined. This has the virtues of flexibility, so that each case may be judged according to its own peculiar merits; vital virtues when judging exercise of the reserve powers, where circumstance is all-important. Actions like those of Sir Paul Scoon in Grenada, which in that particular time and place were essential to save democratic rule, would as a general rule destroy democracy. The reserve powers are *emergency* powers, and cannot be rigidly codified, for emergencies are by nature unpredictable. When a storm destroys the roof of a house we use ropes and tarpaulins to provide temporary shelter over the damaged structure: flexible materials, that can be adjusted to fit the particular problem. So too, the conventions of the reserve powers are intended to be flexible, their exercise discretionary, to give shelter when crisis devastates our political structures.

But what of when these ultimate powers are abused? Emergency power resides in the Crown as does water in an old-fashioned well: a vast reservoir exists, but conventions of ministerial responsibility confine the way it can be brought into the light of day; conventions reinforced by the peculiar positions of the Governor-General and Queen, their reluctance to see their authority abused. Republican constitutions inspired by Westminster have acknowledged the importance of granting the Head of State a broad discretion in direst emergency: France's current Constitution, for example, states (Article 16):

> When the institutions of the Republic, the independence of
> the Nation, the integrity of its territory, or the execution of
> its internal commitments are endangered in a grave and
> immediate manner and the regular functioning of the consti-
> tutional organs of government is interrupted, the President of
> the Republic shall take all measures required by these circum-
> stances after consulting the Prime Minister, the President of
> the Assemblies and the Constitutional Council.

Yet even when partly codified for a President, ultimate power provides a Holy Grail for politicians to seize as part of their quest to subvert proper government. President de Gaulle used the power of Article 16 for his personal convenience during the April 1961 "general's insurrection". The insurrection collapsed within a week; de Gaulle refused to release France from the iron grip of his emergency powers for over five months.[121] President Hindenberg's abuse of his emergency powers under Article 48 of the Weimar Constitution enabled his Chancellor, Adolf Hitler, to destroy German democracy and erect the Third Reich.

If we're to try renegades who have siezed the Grail and been defeated, we must give the appointed tribunal the latitude of being able to define the nature of the political sins the president is accused of having committed. This latitude is bought at a high cost, that of personal responsibility. Members of a political court, who sit as judge, jury and executioner upon the accused, cannot hide behind the law for their denunciations, and hence find no refuge behind Parliament. They are the entire authors of punishments they inflict, and so bear a heavy burden of responsibility.

By giving judges a loose discretion we are in serious danger of creating a judicial aristocracy, a council tenured for life, endowed with power beyond that based on their authority in law and able to wield unaccountable political power in an executive manner. This council and its actions would not be hedged about with the safeguards we have placed about our executive government, the responsibility of cabinet ministers to Parliament, nor in their usual capacity would it be appropriate to surround judges with such constraints. The liberties of the citizen in daily life relies upon a judiciary independent from political pressure exerted by the dominant faction in Parliament. This same independence from the executive and legislature, so necessary for an effective judiciary acting in its ordinary capacity, render judges totally unacceptable for an extraordinary capacity, to sit in judgement upon a president charged with no proper crime or misdemeanour but of "conduct unbecoming". How can the people be regarded as sovereign in any country in which the Head of State may be removed by a completely unaccountable council? At present, advice to the Queen to dismiss her Governor-General rests with responsible ministers in the country of that Governor-General. Yet this judicial council would be responsible to no-one.

Or are the ministers to accept responsibility for the judges' dismissal of the President? Executive prerogative decisions based on ministerial responsibility are not analogous to decisions based on legal reasoning; we *cannot* have a hybrid system in which judges, ostensibly acting on the basis of their knowledge of the law, are influenced in prerogative action and shielded from responsibility by responsible ministers. It's impossible to have a workable system in which "the judges can do no wrong". The way the ancient form of ministerial responsibility worked — preserved in the rare instances the modern reserve powers are exercised — was to offer the King complete freedom within the boundaries of the law to devise his actions. His plans would then be constrained in reality by what his ministers would be willing to accept personal responsibility for in Parliament; thus royal policy was indirectly shaped by the opinions of Parliament. If ministers refused to accept responsibility for a course of action the King had to cast around to try something else. Yet modern judges are supposed to have their judicial actions dictated — or at least circumscribed — by legal reasoning. If ministers refuse to take responsibility for a judicial dismissal, what are judges supposed to do? Renounce all reasoning in the name of political expediency? Sit in deadlock? Either the integrity of legal reasoning or ministerial responsibility ends up being discarded. Or are you going to give the judiciary the power to sack ministers who refuse to accept responsibility for decisions beyond their control?

Even if we attempt, as the Israeli drafters did, to evade the problem of defining executive wrongdoing and waive the implications of judicial aristocracy, we are still confronted with the trial process itself. Surely if a president is to be tried before a court of law then he is entitled to the same rights of trial as any other citizen: in this country, the presumption of innocence, the rules of evidence, the requirement of proof of charges beyond reasonable doubt. And if our tribunal of judges is not a court of law, then what do the judges do there?

The due process of law is notorious for the time it takes, and here the idea of a judicial tribunal fails one of our three necessary conditions, the requirement that the trial not take too long. Executive emergencies can evolve in days, yet the trial to stem the emergency may take a month or more before reaching a verdict. Which demands the question: while the President is standing in the dock, who is wielding his powers in his absence?

It would be foolhardy in the extreme to allow the President to retain his executive powers while on trial for his liberty, yet if they are confiscated from his grasp then *someone* must be given them. Who will this surrogate president be? A politician? Appointed by whom? Accountable to whom? Will this surrogate possess full presidential power until a verdict is decided? Alternatively, what if the surrogate is only given caretaker powers and an emergency arises requiring a proper president? These are dangerous questions and they demand more serious analysis than the glib assertions of the Committee, that this provision "would never need to be used".

In summary, judges are no good for our "competent tribunal" because the matter to be decided — whether to sack a president — is not really justiciable. If the President's role is defined by conventions, breaches of these informal rules cannot be dealt with by the courts. Attempts to replace conventions by legal code not only destroy flexibility but incur two risks: if the code is written too specifically it creates a danger of loopholes, and if it is written too loosely we will have created a judicial aristocracy imposing its will over us. In any case the trial process of a court of law would take too long to be serviceable. We must therefore leave the judges in peace, to preside happily over their usual courts, and look elsewhere.

The obvious place to turn is to Parliament, the traditional source of tribunals for judging executive offences. Two forms of trial present themselves to us: one descends from the traditional English method formally titled "impeachment", which uses both Houses of Parliament, each in a distinct manner we've encountered earlier, whereas the other uses members of one or both Houses gathered in a single assembly to sit in judgement upon the accused.

The ancient method of impeachment as originally practised in England employed the House of Commons to decide whether a particular minister or other public figure should be put on trial. Once a vote had been passed favouring this, the House of Lords, being competent to act as a court of law, provided the actual court in which the accused was tried and either found guilty or acquitted. When the Constitution of the fledgling United States was being written its authors adopted and adapted this process for their own ends. The House of Representatives adopted the role of the Commons and the US Senate that of the Lords, except that, being wholly elected, it had no judicial competence and so could only judge the accused in a purely political sense, the "guilty" verdict being reached by two-thirds of the senators present voting in favour of it.

The problems with this adaptation are obvious. Even without the blinkered rigidity of modern Australian-style party politics, contemporary impeachment is (in the words of Washington's *Congressional Quarterly* at the time of Watergate) an "infrequent and often political move" historically often associated with "sensationalism and partisan politics".[122] That journal noted that "[d]espite revelations, accusations and denials surrounding the Watergate scandal and alleged coverup attempts" the leaders of both congressional parties had at the time "been reluctant to discuss the subject of presidential impeachment".[123]

In the Clinton impeachment, the world recently got a ringside view of this procedure in action. Its most interesting feature is that once the momentum of events forces trial proceedings to commence, the presidential incumbent's innocence or guilt becomes superfluous. His presence before fellow-politicians sitting on the tribunal — his vulnerability to their verdict — poses a much more important question to them: is it more advantageous to me for him to retain power, or for him to be stripped of office?

Putting it in language made infamous by the Vietnam War, the question isn't whether he's a sonofabitch, but whether he's *our* sonofabitch (or perhaps can be forced to be ours in future). Alternatively, the question may be: is he so unpopular with the public — through, say, having sex with pretty young White House interns and then lying about it afterwards — that his inconvenient presence can be removed from the Oval Office? The necessary ingredient isn't justice but a reasonable excuse, so that tribunal members can appear to have acted from honest and honourable motives in reaching their verdict. Prosecution and defence in a political trial judged by politicians are cynical exercises, less a matter of persuasion of guilt or innocence than of purveying excuses for the tribunal members to justify the verdict they already want to give. What strains the voices of advocates inside the chamber and of journalists outside the chamber is the effort required to persuade enough members that a particular excuse to acquit or condemn will or won't be publicly palatable.

Having contemplated all of this, the final factor which determines the condemnation or acquittal is arithmetic. For congressional impeachment to begin the US House of Representatives must approve, so at least half of the congressmen present have to vote against the President. Having passed that hurdle, for the President to be found guilty at least two-thirds of senators present at the trial must vote accordingly. So all the President needs is a third plus one of the senators present to remain loyal for impeachment to fail, or control over one half plus one of congressmen present in the House for it never to get off the ground. Is it really so surprising then that no US President has *ever* been successfully impeached and found guilty?

During the trial of President Clinton, the international media repeatedly claimed that this was only the third time this move had been attempted in US history. That claim was false. It is true that only one previous President has ever undergone trial in American history: Andrew Johnson survived eleven articles of impeachment in 1868 when in three successive votes the Senate fell one vote short of a conviction, then adjourned *sine die*, never to resume the trial. But apart from Johnson at least five other Presidents have had motions of impeachment, or investigation for the possibility of impeachment, introduced against them in the House prior to Watergate: Nixon again (1972), Harry S. Truman (1952), Herbert Hoover (1932 and 1933), Grover Cleveland (1896) and John Tyler (1843). All these motions failed.[124] Even Nixon was never actually impeached, resigning when it finally appeared inevitable that impeachment would proceed.

Were less stringent measures required for a guilty verdict to be returned — say, only a simple majority in the Senate — or the whole bicameral nature of impeachment dispensed with, the tribunal becoming instead one or both Houses gathered in a single assembly to pass sentence — this change in arithmetic would cause a swing to the other extreme in passing judgement: instead of party discipline shielding the accused, it could now be used to secure a "guilty" verdict against even the innocent. Thus trial by parliamentary tribunal fails at least one of our three criteria: that a trial should be motivated to preserve constitutional government, not be a weapon of partisan vendetta or a shield against true accountability.

Both trial by single assembly and impeachment also fail a second criterion of the three: impeachment drags on like a judicial trial, for weeks or months, while a single assembly gains its admirable swiftness by the ease with which it destroys, becoming a blunt instrument of rough justice.

If a judicial tribunal is unsuitable and a parliamentary one undesirable, are we really expected to admire republics which rely upon these measures (either singly or combined) for their preservation: Bangladesh, Germany, Greece, India, Ireland, Israel, Italy, Malta, Mauritius, Portugal, Singapore, Trinidad and Tobago, the United States or Vanuatu?[125] A handful of countries (e.g. Austria and Iceland) have the general public act as the tribunal through referendum, but this merely poses the question, who decides that a referendum should be held? For what remains a political trial, the answer given by these two countries remains the elective oligarchy,[†] and the criticisms of this group as a tribunal still remain.

The proposed Republic laid before you answers the problem by not answering it at all, in a breathtaking display of cowardice and irresponsibility. The Exposure Draft of the *Constitution Alteration (Establishment of Republic) Bill 1999* declares that the President may be sacked by the Prime Minister, although the Prime Minister "must *seek* the approval of the House of Representatives for the removal within 30 days", while a "President who has been removed is eligible for re-appointment, through the mechanism for choosing a President set out in the Constitution".[126] After witnessing all the troubles overseas, outlined briefly in the last nine pages, this proposal deserves nothing but our contempt; a poorly-drafted recipe for disaster.

---

† Austria requires the application of two-thirds majority of Parliament for referendum, confirmed by a simple majority of both Houses sitting jointly, while Iceland requires a three-quarters majority of members of both Houses of Parliament acting jointly for a referendum to be called. (Turnbull Report vol. II p.4.)

Niccolò's ghost [*distracted by a fountain pen*] It's easy to be negative, but look to your own precious constitution. Does it obey your three "necessary conditions"? Certainly dismissal of a Governor-General can be done swiftly, but surely it's too easy for a corrupt Prime Minister to arrange the dismissal of an honest Governor-General by tendering this advice to the Queen? For this dismissal procedure to be "driven by the desire to give impartial advice" surely the Queen would have to hold the power to refuse such unscrupulous advice? You've argued that her unique position is enough to motivate her to be impartial, but the *desire* to act impartially is surely insufficient. She needs the *power* to be impartial— which requires the power to refuse to sack a good Governor-General. [*Looks up.*] Does she possess this power?

THE WIELDER OF THE RESERVE POWERS

Of Dogs and Wolves

Professor Geoffrey Winterton has published his formula for a minimalist republic:[127]

> Until the Parliament otherwise provides, the President shall
> exercise and perform his powers and functions in accordance
> with the constitutional conventions which related to the
> exercise and performance of the powers and functions of the
> Governor-General, but nothing in this section shall have
> the effect of converting constitutional conventions into
> rules of law.[128]

Perhaps this "minimalism" appears adequate to an academic lawyer. In a republic contrived from a single-tiered monarchy, Winterton's proposal would be utterly unacceptable. Endowed with the same privileges and powers, the difference between their former wielder and a President would be the difference between an Alsatian and a wolf, the one domesticated through centuries of experience to provide protection against the other. But what of Australia, a bipartite monarchy already sometimes described as a "crowned republic"?

Under two differing interpretations of that phrase our polity warrants the description. Under the first, all countries employing forms of Westminster system under the Crown are "crowned republics" because their systems of government employ hereditary monarchy to uphold the republican ideal; an elected government rules the country, and the monarchy and its representatives help (to differing extents, depending upon the individual constitution) to uphold constitutional government. Under the second interpretation Australia and all other *bipartite* monarchies are "crowned republics" because the powers of the Crown are wielded by the Governor-General, effectively a *de facto* president appointed by the Queen on the advice of the government of the day. But if these

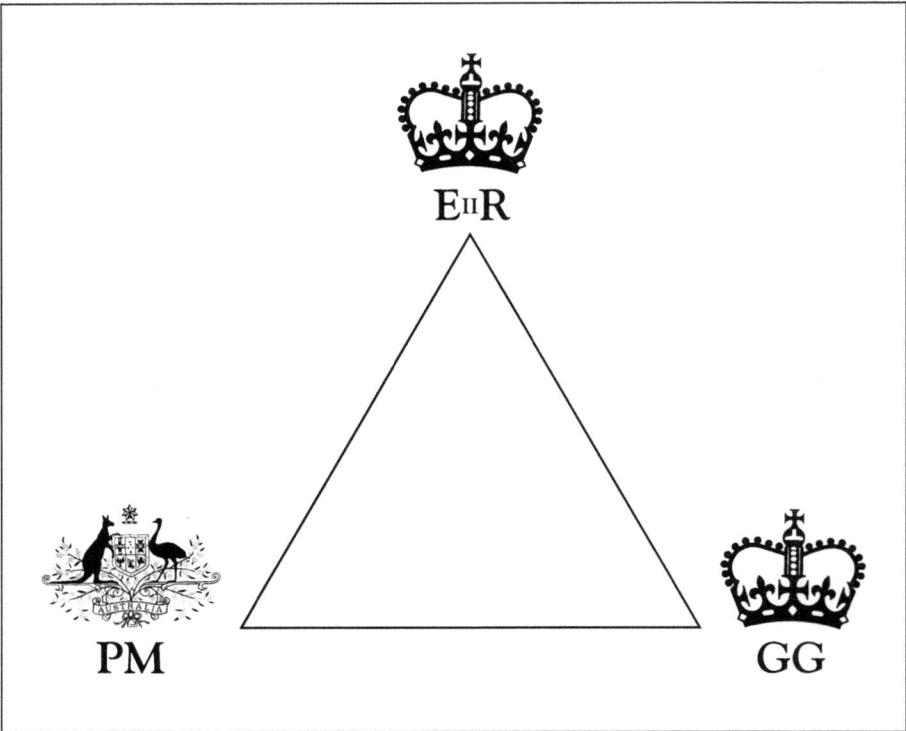

Our two-tiered ("bipartite") Crown generates an elegant power triangle, with the Prime Minister (PM) wielding the active power, the Governor-General (GG) holding the reserve powers, and the Queen as arbiter between the two in a crisis.

countries possess *de facto* presidents, how is it they've not suffered from the same ailments and collapsed the same way explicit republics do?

An answer is the provision for swift and drastic surgery, the Queen and her Prime Minister possessing the instruments to excise a malignant Governor-General, but this remedy, although vital, is of limited utility. Even as surgery for a human patient is only a remedy for certain ailments and not for others, so is this swift dismissal of the viceregal Head of State. Our body politic is exposed to more insidious dangers; for example, viceregal figures in this country are appointed by the Queen on the nomination of the relevant Prime Minister or Premier, and can be dismissed the same way. What happens if the Governor-General and the Prime Minister belong to the same political party? What if, in a re-run of the 1991 Papua New Guinea crisis, Ted Diro had been Prime Minister instead of merely his Deputy, so that while Sir Serei Eri was watching his mate's back, Diro was repaying the favour? Deprived of appropriate ministerial advice, the Queen would possibly have been helpless, sidelined like the Chief Justice proved to be.

This predicament was envisaged here by Sir Robert Menzies, who wrote,

> Close observers have not failed to notice that, as the Governor-General holds office *at the Queen's pleasure*, a pleasure to be exercised on political advice, an enforced appointment of a political Governor-General, 'enforced' because the Queen had no choice, could be followed, on a change of Government, by an enforced termination. Carried to its grimmest logical conclusion, this could mean that Governors-General would go in or out with Governments, all pretence of neutrality being abandoned.[129]

To date, Australian viceregal representatives have been admirable in maintaining the integrity and neutrality of their position, yet this can't be expected to continue indefinitely. Elements of our community condemn impartial behaviour by their holders of public office, a conclusion gained by observing the aftermath of two controversies.

Following the 1975 dismissal of the Whitlam government by Sir John Kerr, himself originally appointed on the advice of Whitlam, protests against the sacking turned into personal vilification of the Governor-General, vilification led by Whitlam himself exhorting his followers to "maintain the rage". On a subsequent occasion a brick smashed through the Governor-General's car window during a protest, injuring an aide in the face. In Melbourne yellow paint was thrown at the car, projectiles hurled and marbles were thrown under the hooves of escorting police horses. In Sydney, the church in which a service attended by Sir John was to be held was desecrated, a slogan painted on its wall.[130]

Most interesting about these protests was the repeated belief that Kerr was a "traitor to Whitlam". The slogan "Judas" was repeatedly used; as Sir John replied in some bewilderment; "Where is the Messiah whose disciple I am supposed to have been? To whom or to what cause can it be claimed I was a traitor? Can anyone seriously claim that I was or should have been Mr Whitlam's disciple?"[131] Gough Whitlam himself apparently thought so;

> [He] certainly gave every appearance of assuming that he had the Governor-General in his pocket — that the Governor-General would act only on his advice. Mr Whitlam's former Deputy, Dr Jim Cairns, has recalled that "he always said something like 'he's my man' when speaking of the Governor-General". As Edward St John has put it, "Whitlam suffered from the strange illusion that Kerr was his creature, to do what he willed, and Kerr, if he wished to retain the potential for action which the Constitution required of him, had perforce to allow him to continue in that illusion."[132]

The Prime Minister laboured under the delusion that advising the appointment of someone as Governor-General placed that official under some sort of burden of loyalty. Kerr's refusal to behave in this manner made him a "Judas" to Whitlam's enraged followers.

The other controversy comes from an earlier year, 1951. Governor-General Sir William McKell had been appointed to that office in 1947 on the advice of the Chifley Labor government. A former Labor Premier of New South Wales, McKell's appointment was attacked by Opposition Leader Mr (Sir) Robert Menzies as a cynical handout to a partisan politician. Attacked also was McKell's behaviour in continuing to engage in the internal affairs of his political party after the appointment had been announced. However, McKell's partisan activities had ceased by the time he took viceregal office, as had Menzies' attacks on him.[133]

By 1951 Menzies had become Prime Minister, and in that year was confronted by what appeared to be a parliamentary deadlock, with the Senate having failed to pass a Bill once, then, on being presented with the same Bill after more than five months had elapsed, having referred it to a committee. He advised Sir William to grant him a double dissolution of Parliament under section 57 of the Constitution, but left it clear that this was a decision upon which the Governor-General was entitled to exercise his own discretion. McKell was furnished with opinions from the Attorney-General, Senator John Spicer, and the Solicitor-General, Professor Sir Kenneth Bailey. He decided he was satisfied with the opinions of these two law officers, and granted Menzies his dissolution of both Houses. At the time this issue was actively discussed in the Press, it being suggested that Labor members believed McKell would refuse Menzies his request.[134] When the announcement was made that the request had been granted, Labor supporters denounced McKell as a traitor. "In the view of the former doyen of the Federal Parliamentary Press Gallery, the late Allen Reid, the abuse which the Labor Party heaped on Sir William McKell was as bad as anything done to Sir John Kerr."[135]

Corruption in this country is not merely a creature of venality but more, a distortion of the noble idea of mateship into something grotesque and detestable. Some members of our community are willing to see the impartiality of our officials prostituted to favour those who advised their appointment, the excuse of "mateship" applied like lipstick to make the act more attractive. Worse, those who've refused to be complicit in this behaviour have been publicly reviled for failing to "do the right thing by their mates". Honourable behaviour has been greeted with contempt, revealing that the current method of appointing viceregal representatives must be reformed. A corrupt representative appointed by a corrupt Premier or Prime Minister, willing to smile benignly while the latter engages in unscrupulous acts, is rightly damned. An honest representative willing to oppose the unscrupulous acts of the Premier or Prime Minister who advised his appointment, or one who refuses to oppose the proper advice of the enemies of that former Premier or Prime Minister, is also damned — for putting his duty above the interests of his "patron" and party. This is an unendurable state of affairs, imposed by partisan "discipline".

Earlier when we examined the mechanisms of dismissal, the assumption was made that it was the Governor-General who was the renegade; that in contacting the Queen, the Prime Minister was acting from motives of

THE WIELDER OF THE RESERVE POWERS

propriety. But what if the Governor-General's the one who is acting properly and the Prime Minister's the scoundrel? Under these conditions is the Queen bound to accept the advice of the Prime Minister? Constitutional authorities are divided into two camps on this question, one asserting that she's bound, the other that she can refuse. Consider first the apparent implications if she's bound to accept.

A. Berriedale Keith believed the consequence of this doctrine was that "in truth the representative of the Crown may be said to have no possibility of exercising authority outside the social sphere".[136] He was clearly wrong, as subsequent events throughout the Commonwealth have shown, although his justification for his belief was sound: that at the first hint of viceregal opposition a Prime Minister embarking upon an unscrupulous scheme would, if cunning as well as determined, telephone Buckingham Palace, advise dismissal, and advise a more compliant replacement.[137] Thus Lord Hailsham has written,

> The Governor-General may be the representative of the
> Sovereign. But he is not the Sovereign. He can be dismissed
> at pleasure, and in modern practice this means at the pleasure
> of the Commonwealth Prime Minister for the time being.
> This means he is in danger of becoming a puppet on a string,
> and should he deem it his duty to use the reserve powers of
> the Monarchy against a would-be Mussolini, or a Prime
> Minister who wishes to govern unconstitutionally, he must
> make his preparations in secret or not at all. He must exercise
> the powers of the Crown before the Prime Minister advises
> the Queen to take them away from him.[138]

Sir John Kerr subscribed to this doctrine, which explains the swiftness of his actions on the day of the eleventh of November 1975. Certainly Whitlam's response that day, "I must get in touch with the Palace at once", uttered after Kerr had warned him at Yarralumla that he felt obliged, under the circumstances, to withdraw his commission as Prime Minister, but before Kerr had actually done so (and hence when there still existed an opportunity for Whitlam to alter his advice and go to general elections for both Houses as Prime Minister) appears to justify Kerr's precaution.[139] Whitlam had already made his own views clear on the subject. A formal dinner had been held at Yarralumla on the 16th October 1975 in honour of the Malaysian Prime Minister, the late Tun Abdul Razak. Before the dinner began Whitlam, Kerr and Tun Abdul Razak were talking in the Governor-General's study, when Whitlam turned to the visiting dignitary and told him that the constitutional crisis then unfolding might finally be decided by whether Whitlam sacked Kerr or Kerr sacked Whitlam first. Later it was reported that this was intended to be humorous, but we have an impartial assessment on the "joke": Tun Abdul Razak's own reports on the incident, given later to his staff and diplomatic associates.

> The reports gave Tun Abdul Razak as observing that though
> Whitlam's contribution to the conversation might on the
> surface be intended as humour there was an undertone of real

threat and that Tun Abdul Razak would not be surprised if in certain circumstances the humour vanished and was replaced with seriousness.[140]

Belief in the doctrine of inevitable dismissal, and exposure to Whitlam's veiled threats, prompted Sir John Kerr to make his preparations for Whitlam's dismissal on the eleventh of November in secret.

Because of this need for stealth the notion of inevitable dismissal has been condemned internationally. The late D.P. O'Connell QC, an expatriate Australian and Chichele Professor of Public International Law at All Souls College, Oxford, wrote that in context of the events of 1975,

> If there is such a convention [of inevitable dismissal by the Queen] it is wrong and the events showed that. For it prevented the Governor-General of Australia from giving proper warning to the Prime Minister. It led to unseemly appearance, and it certainly aggravated the situation politically. For that reason the Palace should think again about this supposed convention.[141]

Otherwise,

> the constitution is destabilized at its heart. Any Governor-General is liable to intimidation by a Prime Minister, and the two offices of Head of State and Head of Government are apt, in practical terms, to coalesce. That is likely eventually, in one Commonwealth monarchy or another, to lead to a grave constitutional crisis.[142]

The importance of Her Majesty's independent discretion over the dismissal of her representatives, to prevent their intimidation and manipulation (and hence the intimidation and manipulation of the guardians of the Constitution) has been expressly stated in Canada. On the 9th of August 1978 the Premiers of the Canadian provinces were meeting in Regina. Confronted by plans by Prime Minister Pierre Trudeau to replace the old Canadian Constitution, they objected vociferously to a number of aspects of its successor. Of these aspects, the one that stirred them most was that of the monarchy.

Since 1947, when the Canadian Letters Patent were revised, the Governor-General of Canada has effectively been Viceroy under the Canadian Crown. "The difference between a Viceroy and a Governor-General has been pointed out in the Courts. A Viceroy is one with complete delegation of the royal prerogative."[143] The effect of this in Canada has been that instead of State Governors and a federal Governor-General acting independently of one another (as in Australia) there are Lieutenant-Governors and a Governor-General; "the Crown is centralized because the Lieutenant-Governors [of the

Provinces] depend upon the Governor-General"[144] for their appointment and dismissal. Australian State Governors depend directly upon the Queen.[†]

So the question was posed: if the Queen of Canada is advised by her Canadian Prime Minister to dismiss her Governor-General, would she automatically be obliged to do so? Given this Governor-General possesses "full delegation of the royal prerogative, so that even [under the pre-1982 Constitution],[‡] when the Queen is not in Canada, he acts in fact, if not in name, as Head of State",[145] the suggestion that this figure could automatically be dismissed on the advice of a hostile Prime Minister, to be replaced by a more compliant appointment, aroused the anger of the Premiers. Every Premier (including that of Quebec) insisted that Queen Elizabeth II retain discretionary powers over the appointment and dismissal of her Canadian Governors-General:

> They argued that Canada needed an arbiter standing above the political scene, outside Canada, not involved in the cultural issue of English-French relations and that the Queen plays that role. Their unanimous view was that Canada's parliamentary system requires an ultimate authority not appointed by or subject to dismissal by the Prime Minister.[146]

On this protestation, O'Connell wrote from All Souls "The Canadian Premiers now have it in their hands to rejuvenate the monarchy if they can successfully tackle this issue."[147]

In the same article he lucidly expressed the essential problem confronting us over dismissal.

> [I]t is evident that the monarchy cannot function as it is intended to function unless the Governor-General is made secure for the tenure of his office and liable to dismissal by the Queen only for misuse of that office. The old colonial practice of recalling a Governor who made mistakes has, apparently, turned into a convention that he must enjoy the confidence of his Ministers. That is the real colonial hangover that is open to criticism, not the representational character of the office.[148]

The arguments asserting the Queen has no discretion are readily refuted. The most obvious assertion is that, under the conventions of modern responsible government, Her Majesty is *always* obliged to follow the advice of her incumbent ministers. As we've seen, this is only true over the policies of government. For the handful of aspects of parliamentary democracy entrusted to the

---

† In the republican debate in Australia, those who rely upon the report of the Turnbull Committee for information are readily recognised, for they adopt its ridiculous misuse of terminology in describing all our viceregal representatives as "viceroys".

‡ The 1982 Constitution Act has entrenched both the monarchy and the office of Governor-General; see E.A. Forsey, "The Role and Position of the Monarch in Canada", *The Parliamentarian* LXIV No.1, pp. 6–11.

Crown beyond the total control of the Prime Minister, for which a royal or viceregal discretion exists, the ancient form of ministerial responsibility remains available to be invoked under extraordinary circumstances. So the question becomes: does the dismissal of a viceregal representative belong in the enormous basket labelled "policy", or in that small one marked "discretionary matters"? The documents of appointment appear to yield an answer.

Three instruments define the powers and functions assigned to the Governor-General: the Letters Patent, Instructions under the Royal Sign Manual and the Signet, and the Governor-General's Commission.[149] All three are exercised subject to the written Constitution (in countries where it exists) which will itself stipulate certain specifications of the office. In Australia section 2 of the Constitution states that the Governor-General has and exercises his powers *during the Queen's pleasure*; the revised 1984 Letters Patent for the Commonwealth of Australia echoes this, declaring "the appointment of a person to the office of Governor-General shall be during Our pleasure by Commission under Our Sign Manual and the Great Seal of Australia",[150] warning "We reserve full power from time to time to revoke, alter or amend these Letter Patent as we think fit".[151] Although both "the Queen's pleasure" and any alteration to these Letters Patent would be under the advice of Australian ministers, the wording of these documents appears to emphasise the existence of a royal discretionary power, and hence the availability of the ancient form of ministerial responsibility.

In this country another argument favouring the existence of a royal discretion can be devised from first principles. Employing as it does the ancient Tory formula of the Crown as the source of all sovereignty, the written Constitution vests[152] the executive power of the Commonwealth of Australia in the Queen, a power which extends to the execution and maintenance of the Constitution and the laws of the federal Commonwealth. Even as the Governor-General, empowered under the same section to exercise that authority on her behalf, is entitled to invoke discretionary reserve powers when the Constitution is threatened, surely the Queen in like manner also has a discretion when the Constitution is endangered by threats levelled against the Governor-General? Otherwise the particular choice of words in that section would be empty of meaning.

Canada's 1982 Constitution also preserves the same Tory axiom, established by the *British North America Act (1867)* which stated in part that "the executive government and authority of and over Canada is hereby declared to continue and be vested in the Queen",[153] so one could argue an analogous discretion exists for Canada on the same grounds.

One could also argue the Coronation Oath, binding the Queen to reign over her various realms "according to their respective laws and customs" has the same effect. Certainly in Oxford Dr Geoffrey Marshall has argued the conclusion of the question of the Queen's discretion must be,

> that the removal of a Governor-General is a personal prerogative to be exercised on the Queen's responsibility as Queen of

THE WIELDER OF THE RESERVE POWERS

the Commonwealth country concerned, and in principle it would seem that she would not in every case be bound to accept advice to dismiss. As with ministerial advice on dissolution, it would be a matter of assessing the issue and the political consequences of a refusal to act.[154]

The other, more sophisticated argument against the Queen's discretion points at the way the ancient form of ministerial responsibility works. Under this system, given one set of ministers are attempting to force reprehensible advice upon the Crown, if the Crown chooses to exercise its discretion against them it must force them to back down, or tender their resignations, or else sack them and appoint an alternative ministry willing to accept responsibility for the Crown's decision. But in any realm having a viceregal representative, that representative wields this reserve power to fire and hire whenever the Queen is overseas. So if the Queen is contacted at Buckingham Palace and advised by the relevant Prime Minister on the other side of the world to dismiss the Governor-General of, say, Belize or Tuvalu, and she disagrees strongly with that advice, she can't dismiss that Prime Minister in order to obtain new advisers consonant with her discretion. How, then, can she exercise a choice when she can't commission the ministers required for that choice?

Two solutions present themselves. We are worrying about a constitutional crisis in which the Prime Minister and the Governor-General are trying to sack each other, a duel between the Governor-General revoking the Prime Minister's commission and the Prime Minister formally advising the Palace to dismiss him before this happens. For the Prime Minister to be sacked, the Governor-General must already have lined up replacement ministers willing to take responsibility for this action. If they're willing to take responsibility for the Crown (Governor-General) engaging in this action, then surely they may be held to have taken responsibility for whatever other actions of the Crown (Queen) may be reasonably and logically deemed necessary for this event to take place — including the Queen saying "no" to the old Prime Minister long enough for her representative to perform the dismissal, dispensing with the necessity for the Queen to appoint the new ministry?

Alternatively, confronted by unwelcome ministerial advice urging dismissal during a crisis, the Queen's other option is to stall for time. As Marshall has remarked, this discretionary power is unlike any other exercised by the Crown, in that "a tactical delay to consider the advice would permit the Governor-General to exercise the power of dismissal, and remove the Ministers before their advice could be acted on."[155]

In criticising aspects of the 1975 Dismissal, the late Sir William McKell made the same point. In an interview with John O'Hara, Sir William said,

> "I couldn't go along with dismissing a duly elected Prime
> Minister without giving warning. But something had to be
> done. With the Senate blocking Supply and the Government

in danger of running out of money to pay public servants, I would have called both Mr Whitlam and Mr Fraser to Yarralumla and warned them I would have to intervene unless the crisis was resolved by a specified date. I would have made it clear I would not tolerate any breach of the Constitution, or any attempt to embroil the monarchy...I would not have been influenced by any threat that Mr Whitlam might call on the Queen to dismiss me beforehand." With a sly smile, he added: "I would have made sure the threat wasn't carried out". How? "Well, you know, the Queen can be hard to contact. She's a busy woman."[156]

Without needing any overt gesture from the Palace, the Queen's discretionary power over dismissing her representatives remains. Sir William could only have "made sure" the threat wasn't carried out by privately persuading the Queen of the justice of his actions. Were she to be persuaded by him she could have delayed a response to advice from the Prime Minster; unconvinced, and she could have responded immediately by revoking the viceregal commission. The beauty of this is that simple delay in responding isn't an overt public action, and hence doesn't require any minister to take responsibility.

Niccolò's ghost	But how much delay makes the difference between a sacked Governor-General and a sacked Prime Minister? Surely the Governor-General could forestall any royal discretion by sacking the Prime Minister as soon as word gets out that a Queen's Messenger has left for London?
Author	The communication channels between the Queen and her Prime Minister and the Queen and her representative are distinct and independent. The Governor-General needn't know the Prime Minister has been talking to the Queen or dispatched a courier to her. The fact that both of these officials have private lines of communication to the Queen, and neither official is privy to the conversations of the other, is an effective disincentive against embroiling the Palace in local feuds, and an external threat against allowing such feuds from becoming too heated.

A problem remains. This gesture of silence is an excellent institution — in a fight. But this entire argument is based on the assumption of an existing crisis; that if the Prime Minister's the villain, the Queen can keep the heat off her representative long enough for him to sack the PM and appeal to Parliament or the people. Yet the reserve powers are constructed assuming that reprehensible circumstances exist at the time of their summoning, so Parliament or the people are aware of these circumstances and accept the basis for the appeal. The problem is, shrewdly unscrupulous Prime Ministers might get rid of any potentially troublesome Governor-General *before* embarking on a dangerous ploy, and replace him with their creature. In times of apparent peace the public aren't going to countenance any use of reserve powers, and so the Queen's discretion, so important during conflict, is rendered useless in periods of quiet; effective against high crimes, but impotent against petty misdemeanours.

This was illustrated in the Irish Free State in July 1932. Prime Minister de Valera desired an obedient puppet as Governor-General, and so sought a petty excuse for the removal of the incumbent, Mr MacNeill. The opportunity was provided one evening by a reception at the French legation. When Mr MacNeill appeared there as a representative of the Crown, de Valera's ministers walked out. Afterwards he remonstrated with them for their studied discourtesy to him, but de Valera's only response was to contact George V and demand MacNeill's dismissal, which, in the absence of a crisis, the King felt obliged to grant.

> The result was…the continuous debasement of the office of Governor-General [in the Irish Free State]. The new appoint-ment [Domhnall Ua Buachalla] refused to cross over to London…retired to a villa in the suburbs, and agreed to pay back £8000 of his salary and to perform no function other than that of signing Bills when so instructed.[157]

He became an empty cipher, declining even to appear in public. De Valera dismantled a fundamental constitutional safeguard simply so he could thumb his nose at the British and achieve his own agenda of a republic.[158]

Niccolò's ghost But how could you defend against this dismissal over trivia?

A popular response among those few writers who have addressed the problem is to make the dismissal procedure more complicated. Lord Hailsham, for example, has suggested that our Governor-General be made answerable to an Australian Council of State.[159] Some more recent constitutions of Her Majesty's realms have other dismissal procedures than a simple message to the Queen by the Prime Minister: the Solomon Islands requires an address to the Queen from its Parliament, supported by the votes of at least two-thirds of the members thereof, before dismissal can take place.[160]

This kind of precaution, although admirable in motivation, is flawed in substance, representing a return to dangers outlined for the dismissal of presi-dents. The swiftness of emergency dismissal is lost in guarding against abuses over petty matters, the twin threats of political partisanship and irresolution return, as do doubts over the effect this has on the Queen's discretion. To refuse the advice of incumbent ministers, appealing to a simple majority of the Lower House and then if necessary to the public, is difficult enough, but to refuse the advice of two-thirds of Parliament? An honest Prime Minister faced with a bad Governor-General and a tough Opposition can't scrape up a two-thirds vote, hence the Queen can do nothing. And a dishonest Prime Minister backed by a corrupt two-thirds[†] can advise the removal of an honest viceregal Head of State. To refuse this advice the Queen must defy in a single stroke both the incumbent government and most likely the members of the alternative government as well. Not a pleasant prospect.

An entirely different means of securing the same end, the protection of Governors and Governors-General from the petty dismissals by their chief ministers, can be devised by putting a twist on T.S. Eliot's words "In my beginning is my end".[161] There's no point arranging the sacking of an honest guardian when you're planning mischief, unless you can replace him or her with a more reliably dishonest one. On a less disreputable note, there's no use replacing one damned awkward scrutinizer and questioner of government with another equally difficult individual. Control over the replacement is of paramount importance. If the Prime Minister were deprived of the power of nominating the successor, the incentive for his arbitrary dismissal of the Governor-General would be effectively removed.

The scope for conspiracy between Prime Minister and Governor-General is reduced, as the Prime Minister can neither ensure the appointment of a particular candidate nor be confident of his dismissal, therefore is hindered in either jobbery or coercion. The existing method of removal remains, but is only likely to be invoked in a real emergency, under which conditions the Queen's discretion can be exercised. On quieter days the adage "Better the Devil you know" would keep the peace, to the mutual advantage of all honest players. The Prime Minister retains a mechanism for swift dismissal of the Governor-General, who in turn is given more room to warn the Prime Minister over impending constitutional crisis without fearing retaliatory immediate dismissal. The Queen is kept out of domestic brawls unless absolutely necessary, with no mad scramble for telephones to the Palace until a crisis actually forces the hand of one of the other two members of this power triangle. The responsibility therefore remains with whoever *does* nominate particular candidates to ensure they're as impartial as possible.

Niccolò's ghost All this is assuming the power of nomination can be removed from the Prime Minister, but what evidence have you of this?

---

† Recall that in Italy in 1994 one-fifth of the entire parliament was under police investigation for corruption and Mafia links, across the entire political spectrum. For a Parliament to be corrupt when party discipline is tight, it's unnecessary for everyone to be corrupt, merely for their leaders to be so.

Author   The relevant passage can be found in the resolutions of the 1930 Imperial Conference. On the topic of appointing Governors-General, the resolution was made that

1. The parties interested in the appointment of a Governor-General of a Dominion are His Majesty the King, whose representative he is, and the Dominion concerned.

2. The constitutional practice that His Majesty acts on the advice of responsible ministers applies also in this instance.

3. The ministers who tender and are responsible for such advice are His Majesty's ministers in the Dominion concerned.

4. The ministers concerned tender their formal advice after informal consultations with His Majesty.

5. The channel of communication between His Majesty and the Government of any Dominion is a matter solely concerning His Majesty and such Government...

8. The manner in which the instrument containing the Governor-General's appointment should reflect the principles set forth above is a matter in regard to which His Majesty is advised by his minsters in the Dominion concerned.[162]

So section eight allows us to alter how the Queen's representative is chosen, provided it's obedient to sections one to five.

Papua New Guinea has already taken advantage of this passage by establishing that its Governor-General is nominated by a simple majority vote of Parliament, conducted by secret ballot. The National Executive Council is then obliged to advise the Queen to appoint whoever is chosen by this vote, with the consequence that the Prime Minister is obliged to take responsibility for this advice.[163] Thus the viceregal Head of State of Papua New Guinea isn't only a *de facto* president through delegation of the Crown's powers, but is an elected *de facto* president.

Were Australians to be immovably determined to possess an elected effective Head of State, in all ways chosen by the Australian people, this could be accommodated without changing to a republic. We would merely need to make a PNG-style amendment to the Constitution to have the Governor-General elected (by the public or by Parliament) under the Crown of Australia, differing from a republic in that he would be removable by the Queen acting on the advice of her Australian ministers. But would this be wise? Although the PNG measure is the wisest of all elective means of nomination proposed so far, it's not the wisest of all possible schemes. It *does* remove power from the Prime Minister's hands, merely to put it in those of his or her fellow-travellers, other members of the elective oligarchy.

If we allow ourselves to be unconstrained by the republican superstition that the Head of State of a parliamentary democracy must be elected to be worthy, then we can devise a way of nominating a viceregal representativethat doesn't allow him to appear more representative than the PM; a nomination outside both the elective oligarchy's immediate grasp (unlike election by Parliament) or its attainable grasp (unlike direct election by the public). A solution could be to employ alternative hierarchies in the community, beyond the control of politicians, to provide the deliberative body to nominate the candidates for Governor-General. This body non-politic could be drawn, for example, from leaders of non-government welfare groups, like the Salvation Army and St Vincent de Paul; leaders of the principal religious denominations in our society: bishops and archbishops of the Anglican, Roman Catholic and Orthodox Churches, moderators of the Uniting Church and the free Presbyterians, chief rabbis of the Jewish faith and imams of the Moslem. Chancellors and Vice-Chancellors of our universities, Justices of our courts; retired officers of the General Staff of our armed forces, former Governors and Governors-General, Companions of the Order of Australia. Were these people to form the convocation or council charged with the duty of nominating a list of candidates for the Governor-Generalship, engaging in informal consultations with the Queen over the list,[†] they could reasonably be expected to suggest a Governor-General representative in spirit of the Australian people without any claim to being politically representative of the same. The formal advice for the candidate's appointment would then be tendered to the Queen by the Prime Minister.

Committees that approve nominees to high office tend to harden into inquisitions. Nominees to the US Supreme Court, for instance, have their private lives and opinions raked over in humiliating detail by US senators, to the senators' own political advantage. This can be avoided in our convocation, by virtue of the fact its members, unlike politicians, gain no political or party advantage by preferring one candidate over another. They gain no advantage by humiliating anyone.

Niccolò's ghost	What if the Prime Minister doesn't like the choice of candidate?
Author:	Should we care? Provided a professional working relationship is viable, why should prime ministerial personal

---

† Such consultations are largely a courtesy, instead of presenting Her Majesty with a single name as a *fait accompli* for her representative. Because these consultations are expressly "informal" there's no reason why they need be conducted via government ministers. Furthermore, by presenting the Queen of Australia with a shortlist of possible candidates, rather than a single name, the inquisitorial aspect can be further diminished.

likes and dislikes be relevant? And if such a relationship were to prove impossible, this in itself would justify advising dismissal of the Governor-General.

A Governor-General so appointed would have no claim to a electoral mandate and no liability to the elected oligarchy. Through rejecting the notion of a vote-based mandate, we have also dispensed with the constraint of making a contemporaneous choice. A president given a "mandate" to reign one election has no claim to reign later, as popularity shifts; a fact that forces republics to make a contemporary choice at the time of death or dismissal, with disastrous results, else have some surrogate stand in with no real right to be there except that he was "the last man standing". But viceregal appointment by a convocation deliberately avoids endowing any competitive mandate. Hence it discards any requirement for viceregal names to be chosen at any particular moment. At the time of the convocation's choosing a new candidate for Governor-General, its members could also draw up a secret list of successors should the incumbent be removed from office before his appointed time, providing the viceregal equivalent of the ancient monarchical principle that the Throne is never vacant: "The King is dead, long live the King". This list could be updated at the beginning of each Governor-General's term in office. This approach would provide a strong source of stability, while avoiding the quagmire of presidential election discussed earlier.

Niccolò's ghost A novel solution, certainly…But you began this essay by posing Juvenal's question "Who is to guard the guards themselves?" What did you mean by it?

Author The two-tier monarchy creates an ingenious triangular power structure, whereby prime ministers are endowed with all the active power they need for the business of government, the Governor-General's entrusted with the dormant reserve powers, armed with which he guards the Constitution from the Prime Minister, and the Queen is armed simply with a discretion over assenting to advice to dismiss her Governor-General — so she guards the guard himself.

At present in this country this structure is hindered from working properly because of the way the Governor-General is appointed on the advice of the Prime Minister. Scope for improper collaboration between these two figures exists, and when the Governor-General refuses to participate in this collaboration he is damned by sections of our community for betraying his "mate". This weakness also endangers the Queen's discretion, allowing an unscrupulous Prime Minister to force the dismissal of a Governor-General in a time of calm, in preparation for victory in an impending crisis. The same weakness inspires Governors-General to make their preparations in stealth, dismissing a Prime Minister swiftly in a crisis without giving much prior warning, thus provoking unnecessary hostilities with the elected government of the day when reconciliations might have been possible. So the occupant of each vertex of our triangle currently has his or her position weakened by our current mode of appointing our viceregal Head of State.

Each occupant's office would be strengthened by removing this power of appointment from prime ministerial hands and entrusting it to the members of a convocation or council drawn from community hierarchies, beyond the control of the politicians. The superiority of our existing system of government over the republics of the world rests not simply in the availability of surgery upon the body politic, but also the present scope for improving its resistance against the diseases of corruption that threaten all governments. The advantage of the Crown in the Westminster system rests not merely with what it is, but with what it may readily become.

THE WIELDER OF THE RESERVE POWERS

MILITARY CONSIDERATIONS, OR UNCIVIL
▪ POLITICS AND THE CROWN ▪

> *Antonio*:   …Here lies your brother,
> No better than the earth he lies upon,
> If he were that which now he's like, that's dead;
> Whom I, with this obedient steel, three inches of
> it, Can lay to bed for ever…
>
> *Sebastian*:   Thy case, dear friend,
> shall be my precedent; as thou got'st Milan,
> I'll come by Naples. Draw thy sword: one stroke
> Shall free thee from the tribute which thou
> payest; And I the King shall love thee.
>
> *The Tempest*, Act II Scene 1.

Niccolò's ghost   At last! I was wondering when you were going to get to the soldiery.

Author   [*worried*] Actually I'm not sure I should cover this aspect at all. Readers might think me alarmist, or extremist, or melodramatic.

Niccolò's ghost   [*sharply*] Were you to omit it I'd think your study inadequate. Attempting to comprehend *lo stato* while neglecting the issue of armed force is an exercise to be left to fools. *Der Krieg ist nicht anderes als die Fortsetzung der Politik mit anderen Mitteln.*

Author   Eh?

Niccolò's ghost   I'm quoting von Clausewitz. *Vom Krieg*. "War is nothing other than the continuation of politics by other means". But you delay. Get on with it.

[*Author writes.*]

◙ ◈ ◙

Ultimate power comes out of the barrel
of a gun.
Mao Tse-Tung

The Issue of Military Command

Irrespective of democracy, a common role of many Heads of State is as supreme commander of the armed forces, for a reason succinctly put by Chairman Mao. Apart from the purpose of waging war upon others, countries arm and maintain standing armies to protect themselves in times of domestic crisis, such as foreign invasion or acts of terrorism, civil riot or revolution, and natural emergencies or disaster: earthquake, cyclone, floods or bushfires. However the same weapons that were purchased to defend a society can be turned against its citizens; the same army that serves to defend our society's freedom from foreign aggression can be used as an instrument of domestic oppression. The rule of law and the preservation of liberty rely on a disciplined army, held in check by an authority that soldiers and society both acknowledge. Consequently the Head of State in many political systems provides that acknowledged authority, and holds the armed forces in leash, so that the rule of law and civilian society can function in peace and security. Our Westminster system treats such power as being too dangerous to be bestowed entirely upon a politician, who might be tempted to manipulate it to political ends. That such manipulation does occur can be readily seen in the Commonwealth republics of Africa and countries throughout Asia, the republics of the former Soviet Union, Central and South America.

Our system places ultimate command (at least in a symbolic sense) of the armed forces in the hands of the Crown, as no mere relic of history but an active and contemporary political principle, foreshadowed in the earlier history of ministerial responsibility. A blunt reminder of it can be found in the letters of Queen Victoria to her Prime Minister, Lord Derby in 1859. Apparently confronted by the prospect of the British administration in India raising an army not under the Crown, she wrote,

> the Queen thinks it incumbent upon her not to leave Lord
> Derby in ignorance of her firm determination not to sanction,
> in any form, the creation of a British Army, distinct from that

known at present as the Army of the Crown…Such an Army would be freed from the proper control of the constitutional monarchy. It would be removed from the direct command of the Crown, and entirely independent of Parliament. It would throw an unconstitutional amount of power and patronage into the hands of the [British] Indian Council and Government; it would be raised and maintained in antagonism to the Regular Army of the Crown; and professional jealousy, and personal and private interests, would needs drive it into a position of permanent hostility to that Army.[164]

The modern, extremely limited purpose of the symbolic command of the Crown is to prevent the armed forces from becoming independent of Parliament and the law — either from being manipulated by the government in a struggle against Parliament, or being manipulated by ambitious officers to be independent of them both. Crown command of the armed forces does not represent a distinct reserve power in addition to its civil powers, nor is it exercised in any way except upon the advice of incumbent responsible ministers. It isn't driven by any policies except those of an elected government, yet neither is it a role of empty ceremony, of white gloves and marching bands. Instead it is the iron fist in the velvet glove of constitutional government — the ultimate force, if force is needed, by which the democratic Constitution is defended.

The most usual form this defence takes is the upholding of legitimate elected government against foreign aggression, an act of terrorism or in a domestic emergency, whereby soldiers of the Crown are controlled by the Defence Minister. Another form it can take is against a renegade government trying to govern without Parliament, whereby the Crown can invoke its civil reserve powers to defend Parliament by dismissing its former ministers and, acting on the advice of new ministers responsible to Parliament, places its soldiers under the control of those new ministers.

During the Solomon Islands crisis of 1994, when Prime Minister Francis Billy Hilly's minority government attempted to govern despite Parliament's clear lack of confidence in it, Governor-General Moses Pitakaka's position as commander-in-chief of the Solomon Islands armed forces was regarded as significant in the enforcement of parliamentary government, as the final threat of force in the struggle between legitimate Parliament and illegitimate Prime Minister.[165] The third, rarest form was exemplified by Grenada, with ministers dead, the country invaded and the polity disintegrating, when the Governor-General's position became essential in re-asserting order and the rule of law.

The Australian Crown's responsibility for the Australian armed forces resides in our commander-in-chief, the Governor General.[†] In the military context the sole duty the Queen has is to watch him anxiously, to appoint and dismiss him upon the advice of her Australian ministers. If the Prime Minister wishes

---

† Section 68 of the Australian Constitution states "The command in chief of the naval and military forces of

to call out the armed forces for any purpose, he or she must advise the Governor-General to that effect.[†] In legal parlance, the Prime Minister seeks *military aid to the Civil Power* from the Crown. If the Prime Minister's advice is legitimate the Governor-General is obliged to give his assent under the Westminster conventions; a proclamation is issued, formally calling out the troops. But what if the internal deployment of troops is unwarranted — say, preparatory to some sort of government *coup*? When contemplating executive lawlessness, an additional distinction was drawn between "ordinary" illegal behaviour and catastrophic behaviour, a distinction that must be remembered now when considering armed force. Were the advice to deploy be in some sense unconstitutional the Governor-General might be justified in exercising his civil reserve powers, to dismiss that government.

(To use an analogy, it's as if the Constitution gives the Governor-General a car but no driver's licence, and gives the Defence Minister and Prime Minister driver's licences but no car. Having no licence, Governor-General cannot take his car out onto the roads himself. Should the ministers decide they want to take it for a drive, they must ask him for permission and the keys. Under normal circumstances he is required to oblige them. Once they've got the car out of the garage they are free to take it wherever they like, with the proviso that the Governor-General is sitting anxiously in the back seat ready to protest if the car is misused, and other members of Parliament are bystanders watching the journey from the roadside.

If the Governor-General is convinced the ministers are drunk at the outset he can refuse to give them the keys, or if they become intoxicated during the journey he can confiscate the keys and give them to other members of Parliament to drive him home. If he does this he must appeal to either Parliament or the electorate to confirm his decision. If they concur then disaster is averted; if they hold the original ministers to be sober then the Governor-General may be forced to resign and the Constitution will then give the car to his successor, who shall re-join the original ministers on their adventure.)

Here again the Oath of Allegiance arises as an issue. Under the old form of Oath Australian soldiers swore allegiance to Queen Elizabeth II as Queen of Australia. As well as underlining the fact that soldiers are servants of the Crown (with all the implications that holds for culpability for obeying orders) this traditional Oath holds practical implications in times of crisis. Under a crisis inflicted upon the country governed under normal circumstances, it

---

the Commonwealth is vested in the Governor-General as the Queen's representative". In his Opinion appended to the Hope Report Sir Victor Windeyer commented upon this section, noting that unlike some other sections of the Constitution it doesn't refer to the Governor-General in Council, and hence remarked for a Commonwealth-initiated call-out "It follows that orders by the Governor-General to the Defence Force, including calling it out, are given by virtue of the authority of command in chief. That does not mean that His Excellancy may act without ministerial advice. He must act on the advice of a responsible minister; but not necessarily by an Order-in-Council after a meeting of the Executive Council". (Appendix 9 to the Hope Report, pp. 280–281; quoted also by Mr Justice Hope on p. 146.)

† Sir Victor notes that under some circumstances the Commonwealth government can call out troops without viceregal permission: see *Military Aid to the Civil Power.*

translates as members of the armed forces and police obeying directives from the incumbent elected government [exemplified in Australia in 1978, and in Canada in 1970]. During a government crisis in which ministers are behaving outrageously, forcing the Governor-General to dismiss them [similar to Solomon Islands, 1994], it would translate as obliging the armed services to obey the new set of ministers (who are to be held responsible to Parliament and the constituency for this use of the reserve powers). During an emergency when it's the Governor-General who's turned rogue [Papua New Guinea, 1991], it would translate as obliging the armed forces to obey whatever new Governor-General is appointed upon ministerial advice to the Queen, ignoring further orders emanating from the disgraced former commander-in-chief.[†] During the most extreme emergency of chaos, with all government ministers killed by an act of terrorism and the forms of government collapsing, it casts a spotlight on the Governor-General himself, as the figure to reassert legitimate constitutional government [analogous to Grenada, 1983].

If for some bizarre reason the monarch herself turned rogue the effect would be minimal for us, because the military aspects of the Australian Crown are exercised by her Australian representative under Australian ministerial advice. In all it's an elegant arrangement for resolving civil emergencies without risking escalation into civil war. Replacing this Oath with one to "the Commonwealth of Australia" or "Australia and its people" is both foolish and dangerous in its ambiguity: in a crisis, *who* is Australia? *Which* signature on a decree ordering deployment of soldiers in the streets or ordering them back to barracks is the valid one? *Which* voice over the radio, ordering them to open fire upon a crowd or to lay down their arms, is the proper one? This is the danger engendered by fashionable ambiguity, inviting personal political allegiances to be expressed with a gun.

There has been discussion in our newspapers suggesting that the role of commander-in-chief should be removed from any hypothetical future president's powers. Assuming that the proponents of this suggestion are not suffering from a touch too much sun or actively planning a dictatorship, such a notion displays a staggering naiveté on their part. The only other member of the executive who could take supreme military command is the Prime Minister. We are arguing that a politicised army is a threat to our liberty, and they are suggesting that the army be placed under the direct control of the person most likely to abuse that power.

Suggesting the ultimate commander of our military forces be a third figure in the executive is pointless. In the power struggle between the government and the Head of State any such person would end up in one of the two factions, under the effective influence of either the President or the Prime Minister. A republic removes all politically neutral points of reference to which such a third figure could otherwise adhere.

---

† All orders formally issued by this new figure would of course be written by government ministers.

Given that a standing army is necessary for the defence of the nation, how does a society prevent the acquisition of a domestic politically partisan agenda by the supreme commander of the armed forces, and given that the commander-in-chief has acquired a partisan agenda, how does a society prevent the implementation of such an agenda, involving as it does the use of military force?

A single-tiered hereditary monarchy resolves the problem of political partisanship by removing any inducements for such behaviour, for drinking from "the poisoned chalice" earlier described. For the United Kingdom the symbolic supreme commander is the monarch herself, born into the position and trained for it throughout her youth, forbidden from birth from engaging in any overtly partisan political activity. Because of this neutrality soldiers may owe her their military allegiance without conflict with their personal political sympathies. This is true even if they are personally of republican opinion — although they might then criticise her accession to her post, her administration of it could provoke no reasonable criticism.

In bipartite monarchies as exemplified by Australia, New Zealand or Canada, we see more complicated versions of the same idea. In Canada the Queen is commander-in-chief of the armed forces, although the Governor-General discharges her duties on her behalf, including the declaration of war upon the advice of his Canadian ministers.[166] In Australia the Governor-General is commander-in-chief, as the Queen's representative. His post is a combination of the political neutrality of the Crown with an attempt to impose a meritocracy, rather than relying upon the vagaries of birth. Yet he may have held previous political affiliations. Although the challenge for our country is to ensure the impartiality of this State figure, if we fail the political neutrality of the Crown imparts its own stability on what would otherwise be a dangerous situation. As was witnessed in the Diro Affair, a bipartite monarchy can deal efficiently with the situation of a maverick commander-in-chief acquiring a political agenda: the Prime Minister can contact Buckingham Palace and advise dismissal to the Queen, replacing the incumbent with a more law-abiding appointment within twenty-four hours and ordering any deployed soldiers back to barracks.[†]

In a republic, the commissioning a Head of State is an inherently political act. We can constrain partisanship through a neutral monarch, plus appointment through the use of an Australian Convocation of State. However, no such neutral restraints exist in a republic, where all commissions are the consequence of party political manoeuvring in parliamentary or popular elections. A republic therefore not only has difficulty resisting the acquisition of a partisan agenda by the commander-in-chief, but its structure inherently encourages political partisanship at all levels. Having failed to prevent the acquisition by the armed forces of a political agenda, a democratic republic is

---

† This point has been made in the Australian context by our then Governor-General, the Hon. Bill Hayden, in an interview with former Prime Minister Bob Hawke, in which he advocated the retention of our current system.

left with the problem of preventing its implementation at gunpoint. Such an agenda may be manifested in one of three forms:

❖ Within the context of military aid to the Civil Power;

❖ The army, under the President, suppressing democratic freedoms within the nation, or

❖ The army revolting against the President.

Niccolò's ghost   You're fond of quoting Shakespeare. What would he have said now? "Cry, 'Havoc!' and let slip the dogs of war"…Not from *The Tempest*, unfortunately.

> When dissent turns to violence,
> it invites tragedy.
> President Richard M. Nixon, Kent State
> massacre 1970.

Military Aid to the Civil Power

Although the phrase "military aid to the Civil Power" may be unfamiliar, the concept underlying it exists in all civilian governments throughout the world. Many emergencies can confront a country that exceed the capacities of a civil administration to resolve.[†] Consider a large-scale natural disaster — bushfires, a cyclone, floods or an earthquake — followed by disruption in communications and the supply of food and medicines. A subsequent collapse in the rule of law manifests itself in looting and other violent criminal activities, beyond the capacity of available police resources to handle. Under such circumstances, the civil administration (the "Civil Power") may request military aid from the armed forces, to help re-assert the rule of law. Alternatively, a society may be confronted by terrorist attack, in which case it is essential for the government to be able to provide a swift military response. In political systems such as our own where it's felt to be unwise to make a gift of unfettered military force to the incumbent politicians, they must request such a weapon from the Governor-General.

This is not an unused and dubious power in this country. On the 13th of February 1978 a bomb concealed in a rubbish bin outside the Sydney Hilton exploded, killing two people and injuries seven more in an event often described as Australia's first terrorist attack. Its intended victim is believed to have been the Indian Prime Minister, Mr Desai, who was present in Sydney at the time for the Commonwealth Heads of Government Regional Meeting. Neither Mr Desai nor the other visiting Heads of Government were injured in the blast, but further assassination attempts were feared. In order to safeguard Australian national and international interests and fulfil Australia's obligation

---

[†] Note we're not going to be contemplating more routine assistance like coastal surveillance, or unarmed technical or logistical support, or bomb disposal of non-terrorist ordnance (like old explosives). What interests us here is the problem of armed military deployment in a civil emergency, where there's scope for concern about civil liberties (one of the major concerns of the Hope Report).

to protect internationally protected persons, Prime Minister Malcolm Fraser advised Governor-General Sir Zelman Cowan that military assistance was required. As a result Australian military units were called out to prevent or resist further terrorist action.

> The call out of the Defence Force in February, 1978 was reported to have involved over one thousand Army personnel deployed in the field, as well as Air Force personnel who provided helicopter support. Major units involved were reported to include 2 Cavalry Regiment R.A.A.C., 1 Field Regiment R.A.A. and 5/7 Battalion R.A.R., with supporting signals, engineers, transport, supply and other units. Rules of engagement, which embodied the doctrine of "minimum force", were issued by the Chief of Defence Force Staff, though…no call for their application actually arose.[167]

The Army remained deployed in New South Wales for seven days until the 20th of February, when, following further advice from Malcolm Fraser, Sir Zelman ordered them back to barracks[168].

In Canada soldiers were used to assist Provincial governments in controlling riots until the 1930s. In 1970 about 20,000 members of the armed forces were called out after the Canadian government invoked the *War Measures Act*, in response to the kidnapping by the Quebec Liberation Front of the Quebec Minister for Labour and Immigration, Pierre Laporte, and British trade commissioner James Cross. The Canadian armed forces were again used in the security arrangements for the 1976 Montreal Olympic Games.[169] But the most immediate examples in the Commonwealth are in the United Kingdom, where British military units are deployed in Northern Ireland to assist the RUC, and from time to time in Great Britain to counteract terrorist threats from the IRA and other organisations.

When military aid is given to the Civil Power it should be granted both in a politically impartial way and be *seen* to be granted in an impartial way, otherwise the distinction between quelling a riot and suppressing valid political dissent becomes blurred. When casualties are involved the distinction becomes downright murky. Because it's in the nature of a republic to politicise the post of supreme commander, the political partisanship of this figure may taint his decisions; it will certainly be perceived as doing so in the opinion of the protestors.† Consider the Kent State Massacre of 1970.

---

† A source of complaint against my argument is to remark that to Irish nationalists the soldiers and police of the Crown shall always appear politically hostile. Axiomatic to this argument has been the assumption that the polity is a commonwealth, based upon the consent of the governed, the problem then being how to prevent the armed servants of the polity from becoming pawns of the great parties within the society. The answer is then as argued, a neutral Crown represented by a figure belonging to neither party and with interests other than theirs. But to those inhabitants who are opposed to the entire polity, its armed servants are always going to appear oppressive.

Kent State University is to be found in the State of Ohio, and was placed on the map of modern American history by the events of the night of Saturday 2nd May, 1970, as what TIME magazine described as "...a bloodstained symbol of the rising student rebellion against the Nixon Administration and the war in Southeast Asia".[170] On that night a student rally was held on the ten-acre Commons of the campus of Kent State University. Intended to represent a combined protest for an increase of numbers of black students admitted to the university and against the Vietnam war, permission to hold the rally had been granted by the university authorities. Militant anti-war protesters took control of the 800-strong rally and played upon student resentment of recent police heavy-handedness. The protest turned ugly. The crowd "attacked the one-storey Army ROTC building facing the Commons. They smashed windows and threw lighted railroad flares inside. The building caught fire."[171] The protesters then obstructed the efforts of firemen to extinguish the blaze.

What happened next is the crucial. In 1970 the President of the United States was a Republican — Richard Nixon — and this rally had been organised to protest against his policies. Sitting in the chair as Governor of Ohio was another Republican, James Rhodes, who was thus confronted with a riot based on a hostile political protest. His response was to call out Ohio's National Guard and set them on the rioters, with deadly consequence. The National Guardsmen "fired indiscriminately into a crowd of unarmed civilians, killing four students."[172] In the ensuing international scandal, Nixon refused to criticise either Rhodes' actions or those of the National Guard, saying merely that "when dissent turns to violence, it invites tragedy."[173] Over twenty years after the event, Rhodes' motives remain controversial; whether he called out the National Guard because he was confronted with a riot, the political origins of which were purely incidental, or whether the political nature of the protest was the principal incentive, and the subsequent riot a convenient excuse for overwhelming force. What cannot be disputed is that it is difficult to retain respect for a nation's institutions when there is clear scope for their manipulation in the name of political expediency.

Contrast this system with ours, where the soldiers may be deployed but their chain of command passes through a witness of the highest echelons of executive government; a witness with a reserve power to intervene, who can afford to be dispassionate through being appointed, not elected. His mandate comes from the Constitution rather than the electoral winds of change. Only the tendering of legitimate advice, not the Prime Minister's political embarrassment, can impel this passive observer to obey the Prime Minister's will. Thus an appointed Governor-General can act as a sieve to separate the act of maintaining civil order from the suppression of legitimate political dissent. This sieve is imperfect: clearly there are circumstances under which he would feel obliged to obey the directions of the Prime Minister, but protesters could still claim that force has been directed against them for partisan purposes. What at least can be said is that the soldiers are acting as servants of the Australian Crown; perhaps misused by Cabinet, perhaps misused badly, but not the henchmen of the Cabinet. Although this sieve may be imperfect, its presence is better than its absence.

The differences between the two political systems in the use of armed force to maintain civil order go deeper. Assume that a large-scale political protest against the government is taking place, and that this protest has degenerated into a politicised riot, with widespread looting and acts of arson. This level of violence is beyond the scope of the police to control, and so the Prime Minister has advised the Governor-General that the police require the support of military units. The Governor-General has complied to this request, and issued a proclamation accordingly. Infantry units have been deployed in the streets under the command of senior officers to provide armed support to the police, if needed.

Part of the operational deployment of soldiers involves the issuing of "rules of engagement". These rules embody the level of aggression of a response deemed appropriate in a particular situation; the way an infantryman reacts to a looter in a riot should not have the same level of violence as his response to an enemy soldier during a war. Rules of engagement are issued before deployment by the senior commanding officer, and are updated during the crisis as it develops.

The political loyalties of this senior commanding officer now become significant. At the moment Australian military officers are "soldiers of the Queen", which is to say their allegiance rests with the Crown through the Governor-General of Australia, the chain of command passing through the senior ranks up to the Governor-General acting on the advice of the Minister of Defence. As servants of the Crown, officers obey the directives of the elected government, but it is to the Crown and its courts of law that they are accountable for their actions; echoing Brigadier-General Sir Victor Windeyer, it is the duty of all servants of the Crown to disobey patently unlawful orders. Here the Crown's interests are distinct from those of the Prime Minister. Troops have been deployed to assist police in maintaining civil order, irrespective of the political nature of the riot. The rules of engagement issued under the Crown should therefore incorporate the doctrine of minimal force, which is to say, the implementation of only that degree of force required to achieve the objective of maintaining order. Unlike the government of the day, the Crown has no interest in quelling the hostile political dissent that was the source of the protest, but merely with restoring the peace.

That doesn't deny events in history when soldiers serving under one of the Crowns have committed outrages, for instance, the April 1919 massacre of civilians in the Indian city of Amritsar, a massacre committed by riflemen under the command of (British) General R.E.H. Dyer. A mob had run amok three days earlier, burning and looting shops and banks; three British men had been killed and two women assaulted. The District Commissioner of the area, unable to keep control, handed over his powers to General Dyer, the commanding officer of the local garrison. Three days later, Dyer and a large column of British and Indian soldiers marched through Amritsar for two hours with drummers and the town crier, "who, at nineteen places in the city, read a proclamation in Urdu and Punjabi", concluding with a warning: "Any... processions or gatherings of four men will be...treated as an unlawful assembly and dispersed by force of arms if necessary".[174] Later that afternoon at Jallianwala Bagh, a principal meeting place in Amritsar, a crowd assembled peacefully. Later estimated anywhere between fifteen thousand and fifty thousand strong, it had gathered for a variety of reasons: political protest, the horse and cattle fairs, the Sikh festival of Baisakhi. Upon entering the Bagh, Dyer and his fifty riflemen simply saw a defiant crowd...and opened fire, killing 379. In the aftermath an official committee of inquiry was held; disgraced, Dyer was forced to resign his command by the Viceroy's Council, and was shipped back to England. His proclamation on the morning of the massacre had provided him with a legal pretext for his atrocity, and probably spared him from being hanged as a murderer. Despite this, and British nationalist support at the time, he was forced to retire for betraying the trust invested in him.[†]

But contemplate a situation where the command structure itself has become politically partisan, and the senior commanding officers owe their allegiance to the Prime Minister, or to a President politically allied to the Prime Minister. In such a circumstance the soldiers are dealing with protesters who are not merely disturbing civil order, but are also political enemies. One may expect more belligerent rules of engagement. As the authorities to whom the soldiers are accountable for their actions are politically sympathetic, one may also expect diminished discipline upon their excesses; the "trust" invested in army officers by politicians is of a different kind to the interests of the people. Incidents such as that of Kent State can be seen to be nothing more than the natural consequence of a politicised command structure, itself the natural result of a partisan commander-in-chief.

Niccolò's ghost So much for "military aid". Time, I think, to go a step beyond; to armed might for its own sake.

---

† Personally I think he deserved to be hanged. During the Queen's 1997 visit to India protestors demanded a formal apology from her for the Amritsar massacre. The request was erroneous in its logic: asking the Queen to apologise for atrocities committed by a renegade officer is like asking the rightful owner of a stolen car to apologize to the victims of hit-and-run crimes committed by the thief.

The Army and the President

The spectacle of the armed forces of nations being used by governments to execute their political will upon their own citizens is a distressingly common one, having occurred in recent years in a multitude of nations scattered throughout the world. It is so common that many Australians, on reading of such oppression in the newspapers over breakfast, think little more of it. The prevalent attitude is that such things happen — elsewhere, of course — and it generally takes an atrocity in central Europe, or events of the magnitude of the Dili or Tienanmen Square massacres to occur, before we pause in astonishment over pouring another cup of tea.

Regrettably, as the recollection of the events of Europe in the Thirties fades from public awareness, of the atrocities of General Franco's dictatorship of Spain and the oppression of Fascist Italy, Salazar's Portugal and pre-war Nazi Germany, and as it becomes increasingly unfashionable to mention more modern events, like the military *junta* that ruled Greece in the 1970s or the crimes of the former Stalinist governments of Eastern Europe, it is easy for us to develop a very West European ethnocentric attitude, whereby the use of armed force to put down democracy is regarded as an exotic phenomenon — it happens elsewhere, of course, but it couldn't happen here. If any positive benefit has emerged from the geopolitical tragedy that was once Yugoslavia, it's that this dressing-gown whimsy of the breakfast table has been shaken. The notion that any ethnic group or country is exempt from the spectre of domestic military oppression is completely untenable.

It's easy to devise comforting rationalisations for the Tienanmen and Dili massacres. Assertions are heard that such events occurred because the soldiers were Communist or Muslim, or displayed some sort of ethnic proclivity for acts of violence. Such assertions are not only insulting but self-deluding. The essential, unpalatable truth is that incidents like these have occurred because mass murder and the use of soldiers to quell the public have been politically expedient. The soldiers were brutal because they could afford to be brutal and it was useful to be so; atrocities and military oppression will remain tools of political expediency whenever and wherever domestic political safeguards and international pressure fail to combine to render them otherwise.

We must address ourselves to the prospect of a member of the political executive attempting to use military force as an instrument of domestic political oppression, a topic seeming unduly alarmist or melodramatic until the debates of the authors of the constitution of the United States of America are read. For four months in 1787, a convention was held in Philadelphia for the purpose of framing a constitution for the Union of independent States, these States being the thirteen former British colonies in North America which had fought against the Crown in the American Revolution and declared themselves independent in July of 1776.[176] Participating were some of the finest political philosophers and legal intellects of the North American colonies, including Benjamin Franklin, James Madison and Alexander Hamilton. George Washington chaired the debates.[177] Such men were not given to empty constitutional posturing, nor were their sensibilities so delicate that they recoiled from unpleasant considerations, such considerations having been shown by the history of nations to be essential to the continued liberty of private citizens. "One of the many problems confronting the delegates to the convention in Philadelphia was how to reconcile the fear of a standing army, which was inimical to personal freedom and liberty, with the need to defend the fledgling nation."[178]

There were clear historical grounds for the fear of a politicised standing army. In the period of the English Civil Wars and Interregnum, in particular in the period of years between 1647 and 1660, the republican Parliamentary army set itself up as a political power in its own right, directed by a "General Council of the Army". It repeatedly interfered in the political settlement of the nation, declaring with some justification that "All wise men may see" that,

> Parliament privileges as well as royal prerogative may be
> perverted or abused to the destruction of those greater ends
> for whose protection and preservation they were intended, to
> wit, the rights and privileges of the people and the safety of
> the whole.[179]

However democratic the army's objectives were, it backed them up by the threat of armed violence. When it felt its petitions to Parliament were being ignored, it resorted to an act now notorious as "Pride's Purge". In November 1648 the military General Council presented a *Remonstrance* to the House of Commons — and then ordered the army to march on London. By seven o'clock in the morning of the 6th of December the army was camped in Hyde Park, and soldiers had been stationed around the House. At the entrance of the House stood Colonel Pride and Lord Grey of Groby. Pride had a list of parliamentarians who were proscribed by the army. These men were identified by him or Lord Grey, and were turned away. All who resisted were arrested. It is estimated that some one hundred and forty members were purged from Parliament by the army, leaving only eighty in the House (the "Rump" of the Long Parliament). When Colonel Pride was questioned by a bystander during the purge as to the source of his authority, he replied by indicating his sword.[180]

Five years later, on the 20th of April 1653, Oliver Cromwell used military force to exert his political influence when he marched five or six files of his own musketeers into the House of Commons of the English republic, the Commonwealth of England. He expelled the remnants of the Long Parliament and eventually established a military dictatorship, with himself as Lord Protector of England, Scotland and Ireland. After his death, the English republic under his son Richard was witness to a continual power struggle between the army and Parliament, which was only resolved in 1660 by the integrity of General Monck and the Restoration of constitutional monarchy in the person of King Charles II.[181]

After the death of Charles II in February 1685, his younger brother James, Duke of York, became King James II. After successfully defeating the insurrections of the dukes Argyle and Monmouth, James refused to disband his army, despite the protestations of the English Parliament, which was suspicious of a standing army. In a society already taut with religious and political tensions he established a despotic regime which subverted the rule of law, and hence the private liberty of the individual. When his English parliament refused to provide funds for his army, he prorogued Parliament and finally dissolved it completely. His army was the instrument of his regime; James encamped sixteen thousand soldiers outside London to intimidate the citizenry of that city.[†]

Finally his own army abandoned him, and in the Revolution of 1688 he was forced to flee for France. The Bill of Rights of 1689 states "That the raising or keeping a standing army within the kingdom in time of peace unless it be with consent of parliament is against law".[182]

Most recently, the American colonies had been oppressed by the military units of George III, for which reason the Declaration of Independence lists as a grievance "He has kept among us, in times of peace, Standing Armies without the consent of the legislatures. He has affected to render the Military independent of and superior to the civil power."[183] To have kept standing armies in times of peace without the consent of Parliament was clearly contrary to the Bill of Rights of 1689 and would have been illegal if attempted in England. However,

---

† G.B. Adams, *Constitutional History of England*, pp. 352–353. In his *History of England*, first published in 1756, David Hume states that after Monmouth's rebellion James would encamp his army on Hounslow Heath each summer, both to improve its discipline and "...by so unusual a spectacle overawe the mutinous people". See D. Hume, T. Smollett and W. Jones, *History of England*, (this edition published late 19th Century, precise date unknown), Vol. II, p. 2244.

the constitutional safeguards effective in England were inappropriate mechanisms to a colonial context, forcing the colonists to more extreme measures.

It was pointless for the delegates in Philadelphia to debate the acquisition of a political agenda by their commander-in-chief. It is inherent in the nature of all republics to render partisan the supreme military commander. Even if a modern — as distinct from 18th Century — constitutional monarchy could have been contrived at the time, this alternative solution had become impossible under the circumstances. As one delegate put it, after arguing the relative merits of a British-style constitutional monarchy over a republic in another debate, "A limited Monarchy however was out of the question. The spirit of the times — the state of our affairs, forbade the experiment, if it were desireable."[184] Having decided the future United States of America was to be a republic, it would possess a supreme commander with politically partisan policies. The challenge confronting the constitutionalists was to devise a way of preventing the President from using the armed forces to implement his policies when confronted by the opposition of the citizenry.

The only purely political process whereby a republic's Parliament can dismiss a renegade President being some form of impeachment, dismissal is either partisan or time-consuming, unwieldy and unpredictable, requiring a focus of political intent, an accord across conflicting factions and a consistent resolution of purpose difficult to maintain in an assembly. The entire mechanism of impeachment is a profoundly optimistic one, based upon the hope that the army will remain quietly in barracks while its supreme commander is on trial in the dock, under threat of dismissal. The attempts of the Russian Parliament to impeach Boris Yeltsin provided an example of the difficulties of this process, abruptly concluded when its chamber in Moscow was shelled by pro-Yeltsin tanks.

Given that the citizens of a republic may be confronted in the future by a President acting unlawfully, and impeachment alone isn't an effective safeguard, the delegates needed to contemplate a military option to oppose a politicised standing army.[185] Their solution — one of apparently only two effective republican solutions — was the Second Amendment to the Constitution, otherwise referred to as Article Two of the U.S. Bill of Rights, the so-called "right to bear arms". They concluded that there *was* no effective way of halting a politicised army except by arming the collective community, so that the domestic effectiveness of the army turning its weapons upon American citizens would be minimised until the President could be deposed.

Article Two of the U.S. Bill of Rights, ratified on the 15th of December 1791, states "A well-regulated Militia, being necessary to the security of a free State, the right of the people to keep and bear Arms, shall not be infringed."[186] This "right" exists specifically to render effective Article I, section 8 of the U.S. Constitution,[187] under which provisions "the military was precluded from accruing too much power by recognition that Congress had the authority to raise a standing army; the militia could be called forth 'to execute the laws of the Union, suppress insurrections, and repel Invasions' ".[188] In short, given that constraints are required upon a professional standing army, and that a republic both exacerbates that requirement and fails to provide an effective political solution to military partisanship, a military countermeasure is imperative to restrain a partisan army. The action taken in the U.S. Constitution is to arm the people, to constitute militias, and to oppose tyranny by posing the threat of civil war. Thus the American solution for the preservation of liberty is the permanent, institutionalized threat of civil war, and the penalty for this liberty is the fact that American society is immersed in armed violence.

In grief and revulsion after the tragedies in Port Arthur and Dunblane, the legislatures across our entire continent moved to abolish (with few exceptions) the civilian possession of automatic or semi-automatic weapons, so that never again by mass murder will our community be stained with blood. Our civil peace is more than the absence of war, but the absence of armed violence or its threat. Ours is a highly civilised society which has no need of such weapons in its households. To this end, to maintain and consolidate the peace which we have come to regard as our birthright, our elected representatives have at last spoken with a single coherent voice, the voice of our community gathered in mourning, to eradicate senseless guns.

Yet for every freedom a price must be paid. The price for eradicating weapons from our society is the exacerbation of the imbalance between the civilian populace and the servants of the Executive, whereby only the police and armed forces are now to possess rapid-fire weapons. This leaves our community more vulnerable to domestic oppression, although it's a vulnerability we can almost certainly tolerate under our present political conditions.

In a letter written two months after the end of the Philadelphia convention Thomas Jefferson wrote "The tree of liberty must be refreshed from time to time with the blood of patriots and tyrants. It is its natural manure." One of the signal glories of the Westminster system is that three of the six oldest continuous democracies in the world — Great Britain, Canada and Australia — have demonstrated that the so-called "tree of liberty" can be sustained by nothing more bloody than the processes of Parliament and the Crown, raked over by the peaceful succession of governments. We have been able to maintain a professional standing army for our defence in conjunction with a peaceful and (even hitherto) largely unarmed society, devoid of military concerns. In lieu of patriots manning barricades against the soldiers of an ambitious politician, a courier sent from The Lodge to Buckingham Palace can swiftly de-commission a partisan commander-in-chief. We have never needed to contemplate arming the general populace in peacetime. The very notion is alien and reprehensible to most Australians.

Our sensibilities are the natural consequence of our society, protected by a political system designed to guard against the brutal realities of life, our familiar juxtaposition of an unarmed society and a small elite standing army only safe with sufficient precautions. Our subtle balances now employed cannot exist in a republic, where impeachment of a powerful President is slow and unpredictable, and the alternative — a concentration of political and military authority in the Prime Minister — highly undesirable. In such a predicament, our aversion to an armed populace, admirable in our present social and political system, becomes a self-indulgent and self-destructive luxury. Republicans among us will need to give the Second Amendment a long, hard look.

The alternative to the Second Amendment is to emulate the European republics and abandon altogether the maintenance of a voluntary standing army in favour of the doctrine of the army as "the nation in arms", advocated by the Prussian military officer and theoretician Karl von Clausewitz and his disciples, such as Colmar von der Goltz. In short, an army based upon conscription.

Arguments for conscription are usually couched in terms of the desirability of deploying vast numbers of soldiers against a foreign aggressor. Their validity is debateable, a contrary school of thought countering that a highly trained and motivated army of professional soldiers provides a more daunting prospect to an adversary than a multitude of conscripts pressed into half-hearted soldiery. Following that proposition, the principal virtue of an army based upon conscription is not its effectiveness abroad but its obstructiveness at home, its resistance to oppressive deployment within the borders of the home nation. In the republic of Switzerland, every able-bodied male citizen is obliged by law to serve as a reservist soldier in the Swiss armed forces until he reaches the age of retirement. For the commander-in-chief to use the army against the Swiss citizenry would be difficult, for the simple reason that the army consists of members of almost every household in the land. Similar measures are taken in the republics of Singapore and Israel, while less extreme illustrations of "the nation in arms" have been provided by the European republics of France, Germany and Greece, until recently enforcers of conscripted "national service" for young male citizens for a specified number of years. These conscripts have constituted a large proportion of the armed forces of these European republics, augmented by career soldiers. Their presence has rendered the internal application of military force for political oppression more difficult, although it must be stressed that it still remained possible (as France discovered in 1958). The effectiveness of this arrangement in obstructing the misuse of military force relies on both the cross-section of the community conscripted into the armed forces and the homogeneity of distribution of these conscripts throughout the military units. The Swiss model, where all soldiers are conscripts at all levels of expertise, will be a more effective obstruction than the "national service" model, where the conscripts are young and inexperienced, allowing a segregation between conscripted and elite units and a consequent politicisation of those elite units.

Either military measure — arming the citizenry coupled with a provision for raising militias, or enforcing conscription within the doctrine of "the nation in arms" — provides a de facto constitutional safeguard in lieu of the genuine article attainable with a neutral supreme commander with a personal stake in preserving the Constitution. The effectiveness of these de facto safeguards for a republic depends not upon the constitution but upon the rigour with which these measures are pursued. Errors of judgement in military policy may have grave constitutional implications for the preservation of liberty.

Creating a republic places the military policies of this country squarely between Scylla and Charybdis, between two unpalatable and undesirable options, between which we must choose. The first option is that of the Second Amendment. It is repellent, in both the innate concept of arming the households of this country, and in the effects this will have upon the civil peace of our society. The second option, that of "the nation in arms" requires the surrendering of Australia's military traditions of a volunteer professional army, to be replaced by an army composed of conscripts, and is deeply distasteful. The only other path is that of wishful ignorance, whereby we cling to the discredited doctrine of "minimalist" republican change. To walk that path is to invite the same fate as almost every republic to have walked it before us, which is to say, eventual dictatorship.

Niccolò's ghost	You quoted me before as saying (in your English translation, alas, a waste of superb Italian prose) "and it is not reasonable that he who is armed willingly obeys him who is unarmed, nor that the unarmed be secure among armed servants". Obviously you regarded the sovereign people as being "the unarmed...among armed servants", but I would have thought a slightly different interpretation would have been more obvious.
Author	Ignoring popular sovereignty completely, the unarmed person surrounded by armed servants is the President himself. [*Thinks.*] Yes. Consider now the rebellion of these servants.

One of the worst nightmares for a civil society is the spectre of the army acquiring its own political agenda, a nightmare experienced during the English republic. Although no polity apparently can be completely immune to this danger (save one without a standing army, and that invites a neighbouring army to provide a somewhat different nightmare), it takes no leap of genius to realise that a supreme commander without the taint of party-political affiliation is more likely to hold the loyalty of the armed forces than one with a particular partisan following within the community. In times of unrest, should military officers acquire an appetite for more active power, the strength of this loyalty between the supreme commander and the ordinary soldiers may become critical in asserting the authority of the civil state over the usurpers. It's therefore in the interests of the law-abiding members of the civil state to attempt to preserve a State figure beyond active politics, for their own security.

The attempted Fascist *coup d'etat* in Spain in February 1981 demonstrated this. Following the death of the dictator General Franco in 1975, King Juan Carlos had been restored to the Spanish throne. This Restoration of a constitutional monarchy had been a central component of the establishment of parliamentary democracy in 1978. It proved its worth three years later, when armed Fascist paramilitary civil guards under Lt. Colonel Tejero stormed Parliament and took hostage Spain's three hundred and fifty MPs. General Jaime Milans del Bosch, a senior Fascist general, promptly declared martial law, "suspended political parties, issued a nine point program 'to fill a power vacuum', sent troops to all major city intersections, and warned citizens to stay home".[189] However, the revolt collapsed when King Juan Carlos, dressed in his uniform as the Commander-in-Chief of the armed forces, made a speech broadcast on national television, in which he "ordered civilian and military leaders to 'take the necessary measures to maintain constitutional order' and asked the people to have faith in the nation's five-year-old democracy".[190]In his speech he said "The Crown, the symbol of the permanence and unity of Spain, cannot tolerate any actions by people attempting to disrupt with force the democratic process which Spaniards approved in a referendum."[191] He thus provided the soldiers in the armed forces with a clear choice; to persist in the coup, which would be clearly unlawful, as would be any further orders given by their superior officers to that effect; or to acquiesce to the lawful command structure. General Bosch realised this, and chose the latter. Minutes after the monarch spoke, the General capitulated, swore support for the King and annulled his own declaration. King Juan Carlos retained the loyalty of the commanders of the seven other military districts, and that of other civil guard and police units, leaving isolated the Fascist civil guards holding Parliament. Outgunned, outmanned and stripped of any semblance of legitimate military authority, Colonel Tejero and his men surrendered. Parliamentary democracy in Spain had been rescued, after seventeen hours of crisis, by monarchical intervention.

A more intrigueing variation on the same theme has been traditionally provided by the Kingdom of Thailand, where the army is very much part of the partisan political landscape and *coups* happen frequently. However the King of Thailand is once again above the partisan struggles, a fact that lends him considerable authority to intervene when necessary, without himself resorting to armed force. This he did early this decade, terminating a savage power struggle in Bangkok following a massacre of demonstrators by politicised troops.

By virtue of past political associations — including those necessary to gain the top job — a President will necessarily be tainted in the eyes of the people whose submission to his authority is vital for the civil state to survive. Assuming that in a two-party system both parties are well represented somewhere in the ranks, the Presidency cannot avoid this contempt. Military frustration at government policies will not be restricted to the elected government, but directed at the State itself, as France's Fourth Republic discovered to its cost. Regardless of whether Australia is a monarchy or a republic there must exist a member of the political executive whose authority can bring soldiers onto the streets of our cities. The existence of an army necessitates the existence of a supreme commander, to translate the will of the government into legitimate military directives for the armed forces to obey. In the military context, the monarchist grievance against a republic is this : a republic can neither prevent the acquisition of a partisan political agenda by the commander-in-chief, nor provide an effective mechanism to prevent the implementation of this agenda, or prevent the politicised backlash of resentment within the ranks.

Yet once again the Crown carries answers, in the tradition of "Her Majesty's Loyal Opposition". Not only are both royal and viceregal offices non-partisan, but they traditionally emphasise that one can be loyal to the country and its human face while being disdainful and critical of the government of the day. Ruling politicians are fond of declaring themselves to be the nation's embodiment, in a fantasy that peaked in popularity here a few years ago, when even a Prime Minister's spouse was described by the Press as the "First Lady" and their family, "the First Family". That American notion is deeply distasteful: if politicians can claim for themselves to embody the State, and elevate their own domestic arrangements to some grand social emblem† — if they can, in short, pretend to some sort of mystical national legitimacy deeper than the temporary confidence of the House — then they can claim the partisan policies they advocate are somehow married to the spirit of the country in a wedlock denied their critics. To disagree with them becomes "un-Australian", a McCarthyist phrase already disturbingly popular. To disagree with them is to be a traitor.

This insult to freedom of thought and choice must be averted. In providing a non-partisan viceregal figure embodying Australia, the Crown provides an alternative face to represent the nation, and traditions that uphold the right of Opposition members to criticise without having their own patriotism impugned. As servants of the Crown, soldiers are themselves forbidden to express publicly partisan opinions while in uniform; but by the same token, they may hold such opinions in private without being regarded traitors, and hear civilian advocates of their opinions freely speak in the forums of the nation, their resentments peacefully aired…and channelled from damaging the polity itself.

A final word remains to be said. Wielders of active power love to dress in the spectacle of armed splendour: marching soldiers, ponderous tanks, the martial array of obedient uniforms. As dramatic effects go, a big military parade invests a grandeur that Press Secretaries and campaign directors find hard to beat. Presidents love them. In providing an emblem of passive authority under which all wielders of lawful coercive force are made servants; an emblem held by a distinguished member of our own community, a person who could be nominated by our community hierarchies rather than by the elective oligarchy, the Crown can deny politicians the ability to appropriate military splendour entirely to themselves. Our troops move, make war and make peace by the will of elected politicians, but those soldiers themselves are on loan, not owned; lent by the trustees of common liberty, whose emblem the soldiers wear.

---

† If one *must* obsess about someone else's family — and I for one have never understood the necessity of it — then at least sentimental obsession with the Royal Family is less harmful than creating personality cults around a Prime Minister's family. For democracy to survive, individual politicans must remain expendable — and so too their sisters and their cousins and their aunts.

These dilemmas of a standing army in times of peace are hardly new; Jonathan Swift thought them so obvious he even made passing reference to the matter in *Gulliver's Travels*, and expected his audience to understand the allusion. And yet these military issues associated with a change to a republic have not been addressed by the republican advocates — the implications probably haven't even occurred to them. Now these issues have been raised, it will be interesting to see whether the ARM will have the integrity to address them.

The Flies of a Summer

But one of the first and most leading principles
on which the commonwealth and the laws are
consecrated, is lest the temporary possessors
and life-renters in it, unmindful of what they
have received from their ancestors, or of what
is due to their posterity, should act as if they
were the entire masters; that they should not
think it amongst their rights to cut off the
entail, or commit waste on the inheritance, by
destroying at their pleasure the whole original
fabric of their society; hazarding to leave to
those who come after them, a ruin instead of a
habitation – and teaching these successors as
little to respect their contrivances, as they had
themselves respected the institutions of their
forefathers. By this unprincipled facility of
changing the state as often, and as much, and
in as many ways as there are floating fancies
or fashions, the whole chain and continuity of
the commonwealth would be broken. No one
generation could link with the other. Men would
become little better than the flies of a summer.

Edmund Burke, *Reflections on the Revolution
in France*.

If the Queen or some other member of
her family opens the [Sydney Olympic]
Games, we will be inviting the rest of
the world to conclude that we are
something less of a nation.[1]

Malcolm Turnbull, Australian Republican
Movement Chairman.

Historical Inevitability?

Stephano: I prithee now, lead the way
without any more talking. – Trinculo,
the King and all our company else
being drowned, we will inherit here.
Here, bear my bottle.

The Tempest, Act II Scene 2.

■■■

The most lucid defence of the monarchy I've ever heard argued on British soil
was delivered in Edinburgh on a freezing winter day in 1993. In a university
debate touching upon Scottish nationalism, a young barrister rose after the
formal speeches and spoke from the floor of the House, pleading that whatever
Scotland chose to do regarding the United Kingdom, it not become a republic.
Two things about him I will never forget. The first, that he was from one of the
London Inns of Court, the second, that he was black. His parents and family had
fled one of the African Commonwealth countries after it had become a republic,
for it had collapsed into dictatorship. He stood now for an unfashionable truth:
that the question of a republic's success or failure ultimately isn't one of ethnicity
or economics, but the simple temptation of power upon the human condition.

He spoke with an eloquence and a passion lacking in his other English
colleagues, inspired by physical experiences foreign to them. His speech was

regrettably short, confined to the few minutes dictated by the debate, but it left an indelible impression on my mind. His argument was remarkably similar to the one formulated by me in Queensland some months previously, and the resemblance set me thinking. Listening to his speech, I remember wondering how many of his fellow British barristers or students were likely to sympathise. Looking around at their Celtic or Anglo-Saxon faces, fed upon a diet of Bagehot and postcolonial insularity, led to a gloomy conclusion. He and I were isolated by bland scepticism.

Supporters of the Crown are diverse in nature, but for clarity's sake a distinction must be drawn among them, dividing into two schools of allegiance. One has its loyalty founded upon sentiment: "*I did but see her passing by// And yet I love her 'til I die...*" But the allegiance of the second is drawn from a different source, of political principle and philosophy. Members of the first I name royalists, and the second, constitutional monarchists. My African-British *confrère* and I belong to the latter fellowship. Royalists have no need of a manifesto, as their ties of emotion are enough to justify their continued loyalty. But for those of us whose determined allegiance is more calculated, an exposition is required.

The fabric of much republican argument is woven from one single fundamental thread of error, namely the proposition that the monarchy is simply symbolic. From this thread an entire suit of clothes has been woven, which we are expected to wear without question. The garments handed to us are as follows:

❖ That the monarchy's desirability depends on the proportion of the population of British descent.

❖ That the degree of its active support is a measure of the political conservatism of the supporter.

❖ That the Crown's purpose, being purely symbolic, may be readily replaced by a republican construct.

Were the monarchy purely a cultural icon then its relevance would largely be for citizens to whom the British culture is relevant. Given that our society is now culturally diverse, support for the Crown might then also be regarded as a symptom of a general political conservatism. Its relevance (being only symbolic) might then wane to the extent its replacement becomes desirable... although never imperative.

This single error — a kind of inverted royalism — has been recently championed by a clique of academics whose politically fashionable, albeit shallow, views on history have ensured them a place in the limelight. Their presentation of the monarchy as a purely cultural construct rather than one of intrinsic political value, and their attempts to deduce its obsolescence from the emergence of an independent Australia, does them no credit, intellectually or otherwise. For the layman whose only knowledge of the monarchy might be gained from magazines and television it's understandable to believe that the Crown is a symbolic cipher. After all, the media only ever display royal weddings and garden parties, never meetings of Executive Council. However, for academics to encourage this fiction serves either to promulgate a politically useful misconception, or to reveal that they have nothing to declare except their ignorance. Either action brings disgrace.

Claiming that an Australian republic is "inevitable" implies that our future is no more than a juggernaut grinding down the steep slope of the decades, which we're powerless to resist, and so must acquiesce else be crushed in empty resistance. Its basis is solid ignorance of the role of the Crown, of political philosophy emerging throughout the Commonwealth, and of the profound space between the postcolonial obsessions of the 1970s and the needs of modern countries of the 21st Century. The case laid before you now has argued that these needs must draw from a deeper well, from the human condition itself, in comparison to which all else is ephemeral.

The republican case attempts to build upon these ephemera, to hide behind them and exploit them as an apologia for its deficiencies. But we are renovating for the future, for the centuries ahead; no map less than the entire globe is adequate for our study. In the words of John Donne, "No man is an island... Any man's death diminishes me, because I am involved in Mankind; And therefore never send to know for whom the bell tolls; it tolls for thee."

When we point to common collapse of polities throughout the world, we are rebuked for arguing "by quantity, not quality". We are expected to take permanent refuge in our current social, cultural and economic landscape — despite the fact this is transitory, even as the landscapes of the 1950s or 1900 have vanished. And indeed, who even at this moment beyond our shores represents "quality"? The United States? France? Both countries have suffered worse degeneracies of government in the last forty years than have many "Third World" Commonwealth realms.

Our system has grown out of centuries of history and bears the fruits of struggle, an elaborate system of safeguards to preserve parliamentary democracy derived from the experience of the Stuart autocracies, from Cromwell's military dictatorship, the corruption of the Long and 18th Century Parliaments and the strife of civil war and revolution. Its precautions are stringent and assume that politicians may be mendacious, grasping and amoral; that soldiers may be ambitious, parliamentary factions willing to denounce the criticisms of their opponents as treason, the prime minister corrupt, the monarch, prone to every human weakness. They are precautions that recognise power may bring out the worst in human nature, and place countermeasures accordingly.

In particular the Crown's modern purpose is to oppose the infection of salient institutions by political partisanship, and to impose non-partisan limits upon the government of the day, so politicians cannot use their immense but temporary power to acquire illegitimate authority, extend their reach beyond constitutional limits or place themselves beyond the accountability due to Parliament and the people. As the traditional adage puts it, the chief virtue of the Crown rests not in the power that it wields, but in the power it denies others.

If this is true, we might expect the other two dubious garments, reliant on this principal error for their existence, to unravel also — which indeed they do. My African colleague demonstrated the lie restricting the Crown to Anglo-Saxon/Celtic blood. The majority of citizens in most of Her Majesty's sixteen realms throughout the world are his colour;† their independent, democratically elected governments are black majority governments. Countries such as Papua New Guinea, the Solomon Islands and Grenada are not noted for their Anglo-Saxon populations, although their constitutional monarchies under Queen Elizabeth II have done good service, and continue to do so, in preserving their parliamentary democracies. In the case of Papua New Guinea this has taken the form of forcing the dismissal of an allegedly corrupt deputy Prime Minister and the resignation of a Governor-General who was acting unconstitutionally;[2] in the case of Grenada, it was the Governor-General who invoked the Crown's reserve powers in a situation of social and political chaos to restore order,[3] and in the Solomon Islands, a Governor-General who prevented a recalcitrant Prime Minister from escaping the verdict of Parliament.[4]

The Papua New Guineans seem to understand something many of our own leaders have failed to grasp; namely, that the desirability of a political system can exist independently of the ethnicity of its Head. Symbolic objections raised by a Melanesian nationalist are circumvented by the appointment of an indigenous Governor-General to exercise the Queen of Papua New Guinea's powers, the residue of his objections disdained as inspired by an ethnic prejudice unworthy of any mature country intent upon an internationalist stance. It's often argued that a multicultural Australia has no place for the Queen, yet the essential difference between third-generation citizens and many immigrants to our shores isn't language or ethnicity, but that to discuss a politicised army under a despotic government with third-generation Australians is to ask them to exert their imaginations, whereas to discuss the same scenario with many immigrants is to ask them to recollect their memories. The citizens of this country who have most in common with the architects of Westminster are not those of Anglo-Saxon ancestry, but those who understand most clearly the dangers here discussed, and the need for precautions. Rather than being the death-knell to the monarchy, a multicultural society may yet prove its salvation.‡

The prevalent image of monarchists lies in the mould of Sir Robert Menzies, of political conservatism and that of old age. Obviously at the core of political conservatism lies an awareness of, and an emphasis upon, the burden of proof in any form of political change. But on the converse side of the coin, the

---

† The sixteen are: Antigua and Barbuda, Australia, the Bahamas, Barbados, Belize, Canada, Grenada, Jamaica, New Zealand, Papua New Guinea, St Lucia, St Christopher and Nevis, St Vincent and The Grenadines, the Solomon Islands, Tuvalu and the United Kingdom.

‡ This was vividly brought home to me before the 1992 debate held in the Council Chamber of Queensland's Old Parliament House. In the fifteen minutes before the speeches began, prominent members of Brisbane's Greek and Serbian communities, seated in the audience, came up to me to offer their support and best wishes. They made it very clear to me that they understood what was at stake, even if the UK-born republicans debating against me did not.

OF NATIONS

popular belief that equates monarchism with conservatism is mistaken, and the belief the Crown's eradication represents reform, simplistic.

Repeatedly throughout this book, the words of the Canadian constitutional historian Dr Eugene Forsey have been quoted. Perhaps the reader assumed he was a political conservative. In reality he was a staunch socialist. Born in Newfoundland, later a Rhodes Scholar for Quebec, Forsey became active in the Canadian labour and socialist movements in the 1930's, visited the Soviet Union in 1932, and was an influential member of the Canadian Congress of Labour. A social radical, he was a keen advocate of reform and was appointed to the Canadian Senate by Pierre Trudeau in 1970. In 1943 his doctoral thesis *The Royal Power of Dissolution of Parliament in the British Commonwealth* was published for the first time. It has been subsequently re-published in 1968 and 1990, and remains a classic study of aspects of the Reserve Powers of the Crown. Forsey remained a staunch monarchist throughout his life (he died in 1991) and wrote a vigorous defence of the actions of Sir John Kerr in 1975, providing a rude shock to those who regard the Whitlam dismissal in the context of some right-wing conspiracy. A civil libertarian, he regarded his commitment to the political processes of constitutional monarchy as logical and consistent with his dedication to social reform.[5]

The other classic text on the Reserve Powers was written by an Australian socialist, namely the Labor statesman Dr H.V. Evatt. A complex figure of a man, it is difficult to fathom his precise personal beliefs, but it does seem unlikely that the author of *The King and His Dominion Governors* and the personal mentor of John Kerr was a republican, as has been recently claimed. Evatt attended Elizabeth II's Coronation in Westminster Abbey, and was a member of her Privy Council. In his arguments a civil libertarian and defender of the Constitution, he described Menzies' attempts to legislate to outlaw the Communist Party of Australia as being "to write into this great document [the Australian Constitution] provisions which were utterly non-British and the very antithesis of the glorious traditions of our race."[6]

These aren't the sentiments of a Keating republican, nor indeed of any species of republican. After the royal opening of Federal Parliament in 1954 he said of the Queen,

> Her direct participation in the constitutional processes of this National Parliament must recall, as indeed the Speech does, the close association of the Royal Family with Australia. That personal link is greatly valued by all the people of this country, especially by those who served in the great wars…it is true to say that the memory of the Queen's father, King George VI, is revered by the people of Australia. His name will go down in history as that of a Sovereign who, during the most critical period of the history of the British nation and perhaps of the world, inspired the British and allied peoples by his long sustained fortitude and courage and by his wise and effective contribution to leadership. As yet, too little is

known of his calm and helpful counsel during some of the great emergencies that confronted the leaders of Great Britain and Australia during the last world war.

May I also pay tribute to the great national service rendered to Australia by the Queen's mother. The value of what she did, even more, what she was, both during the King's reign and since, will never be forgotten…With these illustrious examples before her, Queen Elizabeth's self-dedication in her Coronation broadcast expressed in felicitous terms the new conception of the democratic British monarchy, and of the special link that binds the Sovereign to her people.

He continued,

…therefore, we do right to join together to pay tribute to our Sovereign. She has more than fulfilled the most ardent expectations of her people…Every member of this Parliament is privileged to acclaim Her Majesty's presence here today. It is something we shall never forget. It is quite wrong, as the Prime Minister has properly stressed, to regard the visit to the Parliament of Her Majesty as being only ceremonial or formal.

And he concluded by quoting a stanza of the then-National Anthem:

Thy choicest gifts in store,
On her be pleased to pour,
Long may she reign.
May she defend our laws,
And ever give us cause
To sing with heart and voice,
God save the Queen.[7]

This man, one of the Australian Labor Party's most eminent intellectuals, was in fact a staunch supporter of the Crown and vehemently opposed to views such as those espoused by Paul Keating and his ilk.[8] For that matter Ben Chifley, possibly Labor's finest Prime Minister in our history, expressed the monarchist creed well in a speech to the House of Representatives:

We members of the British Commonwealth of Nations are free nations bound together with the King as the constitutional link. To us, the throne in no way usurps the rights of the people. It is a symbol of the liberty of the people. With us, the prerogatives of the Crown have become the privileges of the people.[9]

Removed from the confines of class and prejudice that still permeate modern Britain, it isn't difficult to distinguish between the political institution of constitutional monarchy and the general problems of social inequity of class.

The issue of a monarch's wealth is distinct from the question of her existence; she is by definition merely someone born into a hereditary position that is a constitutional solution to a political problem, and who enters into a political contract with society upon accession to the throne. Proudly egalitarian societies such as those of Australia, New Zealand and Canada can and do enjoy the political benefits of a Crown, as does Norway beyond the Commonwealth.[10] Conversely, a Los Angeles car journey from South-Central to Beverley Hills provides a swift reminder that gross inequities of wealth, education and quality of life can and do exist in democratic republics.

Where does this leave us? As the rest of this chapter will argue, ceremonial and diplomatic functions corresponding with a distinctively Australian Head of State can already be performed by our Australian Governor-General. The protocol for this has existed for over half a century, although neglected in this country in earlier decades. The belief that trading rivalries — or for that matter, even military tensions — between realms provide a sound basis for becoming a republic is ill-founded. We are neither oppressed by a despotic monarch, nor could our monarch directly oppress us even if she wanted to be despotic. We aren't required to defend her other realms and territories. We aren't even expected to contribute to her upkeep, except when she is visiting this country. The American Declaration of Independence puts the matter succinctly when it warns that governments are instituted among men to secure rights for the governed, signal among these being life, liberty and the pursuit of happiness; and whenever any form of government becomes obstructive of these ends, it is the right of the people to alter or abolish it, instituting a new form most likely to "effect their Safety and Happiness". Neither effigies on coins nor toasts at diplomatic banquets are a proper excuse for tampering with that safety.

Machiavelli's warning, in the first pages of this book, now comes back to haunt us. Already we have seen evidence that "the same troubles [that] generally recur in all republics" may take root in our soil. Even in this young country which is one of the world's oldest living democracies, a dispassionate appraisal of history denies a comfortable complacency about our future, for it reveals the vices and weaknesses of the human condition reside in our political leaders as well as across the sea. In 1932 Jack Lang as Premier of New South Wales attempted to violate the Audit Act and evade payment of government debts. When he refused to provide an undertaking that his government was not engaging in illegal activities he was finally dismissed by Sir Philip Game, the Governor of New South Wales, who then called fresh elections, which members of the Lang government lost.

In 1974–75 the Whitlam Government engaged in secret negotiations through Tirath Khemlani, to borrow up to US$4,000 million from Middle Eastern sources for a period of twenty years. This was done through irregular channels, without the knowledge of the full cabinet or the approval of the Loans Council which the Constitution required. When confronted by a hostile Senate refusing to pass the budget until Whitlam agreed to call a new election, he attempted to govern without Parliament rather than seek a fresh mandate from the electorate. As a consequence he was sacked by the Governor-General, leading to fresh elections in 1975, which members of Whitlam's former government lost.

Australia's Federal Parliament has an appalling record for being prorogued and dispersed, pathetic by the standards of major English-speaking democracies throughout the world. Remembering that our government is meant to be subordinate and accountable to Parliament, one would expect that the Lower House be given the opportunity to sit frequently, so it can ask meaningful questions and extract meaningful answers from the government of the day. Since 1950 Australia's House of Representatives has averaged a woeful 63.4 sitting days per year, compared with the British House of Commons (164 days), the Canadian House of Commons (146 days), and the New Zealand House of Representatives (89 days). Even results from the United States House of Representatives — in a country where the Executive *isn't* subordinate — although limited to the years 1985 to 1991, reveal a superior average of 146 days a year. In 1993 the British House of Commons sat for 164 days over 35 weeks, with Prime Minister John Major being subjected to 70 Question Times. The same year our House of Representatives sat for only 47 days, in 14 weeks, with our Prime Minister absenting himself for some of these days, leaving an ineffectual Speaker and an impotent Opposition with questions rendered futile, unanswered.[11]

The Crown and the right of parliamentary scrutiny are not the only aspects of the Australian Parliament for which Paul Keating displayed disdain, his most notorious phrase being his denunciation of our Upper House of Parliament as "unrepresentative swill". His opponents accused him of purging or politicizing senior public service positions[12] and silencing dissent from all those who desire government work; political commentator Padraic P. McGuinness described it thus:

> What the government has now signalled…is that no one who works for the government is safe in expressing views which are politically unacceptable to it.
> That is no public servant, no consultant, no appointee to a public body or to an administrative role is permitted to freely express his or her opinions without threat of penalty. This is not democracy.[13]

On Tuesday the 20th of December 1994 the *Australian Financial Review* published two disturbing articles. The first began on the front page, captioned "Revealed: how Keating bullies business". In an interview by correspondent Pamela Williams with Mr Dick Warburton, chairman of Du Pont and a prominent member of the Business Council of Australia, he revealed that the Keating government had been engaging in a "Cold War" with its alleged corporate critics since the last election. He said,

> We have been getting in much closer to the politics of hate…
> In other words: 'If you don't agree with me, I'll not only hate you, but destroy you'.

So one of the problems business has is that while an individual is prepared to stand up and say what he means, you have to run a business. And you can't afford to have your business destroyed. So you have got to be very circumspect.[14]

Pamela Williams went on to report "Mr Warburton said the tactics had stifled debate because of the concerns of corporate leaders that their own businesses could be targeted for retaliation by the Government."[15]

Dick Warburton's criticisms were not those of a "class enemy". As Ms Williams commented,

> Mr Warburton's comments will come as a shock to the Government, because he is widely regarded as a moderate and supportive business leader and has been appointed to a string of government boards and advisory bodies. He is a director of the Reserve Bank of Australia, chairman of Wool International, chairman of the National Occupational Health and Safety commission, chairman of AusIndustry, and chairman of the Australian Best Practice Demonstration Program.[16]

The second article, on page eight, was written by Malcolm McGregor, a long time member of the NSW Right of the Labor Party. It carried the title "How fragile is our right to speak out and express dissent". Mr McGregor had acted as a campaign consultant to the Housing Industry Association, an organisation which campaigned against the Keating government in the 1993 elections because it was deeply worried about legislation which it feared would "radically alter the way the housing industry operated."[17] It spent several million dollars on a grassroots campaign and a High Court challenge, despite being warned research revealed that the Keating government would win the election, and inflict heavy reprisals upon perceived opponents. Sure enough the Government won and ostracised the HIA for daring to speak against it, dumping it from government advisory bodies and informing bureaucrats in the Department of Housing that "the HIA was absolutely banned from consultation with the Government in all forms."[18] McGregor was himself subjected to an attempt at personal intimidation by a senior minister: "For my part, Laurie Brereton took the trouble, on March 25, 1993, at Sydney Airport, to push his ruggedly handsome profile up to mine and warn: 'I really hope we manage to get you'." [19]

In the words of P.P. McGuinness, discussing elsewhere the dismissal of a government adviser,

> The disturbing thing…is that [the dismissal] is not unique, but is part of a pattern of behaviour by the present Government. From the Australia Card through the political advertising ban and on, it has attempted to infringe civil liberties. It has threatened retaliation against those who campaigned against it in the last election campaign, and acted upon those threats, even ejecting the Housing Industry

Association from consultative panels. There have been suggestions that companies which have been seen to have the wrong political associations or which have taken political stances critical of the Government might have trouble getting contracts, or information, regardless of considerations of cost or efficiency.[20]

The same tactics can be attempted by future governments determined to dismantle all checks and balances between themselves and ultimate power, suppressing dissent along the way. I therefore suggest there exists a *prima facie* cause for concern for the integrity of our present and future liberty.

Our two-tiered monarchy is capable of responding to a broad spectrum of illegitimate actions by the Prime Minister, Governor-General, or by the Queen herself, and able to survive traumas that would cause the collapse of democracy in a republican structure. Conversely, in crises which have destroyed bipartite monarchies such as the Fiji *coups* of 1987, a republic would fare no better. The dismantling of checks and balances required to render Australia a republic endangers the preservation of parliamentary democracy, because it must result in a concentration of power in the hands of either (or both) the Prime Minister and the President, an event which is inherently politically regressive. At best it leads to the kind of disastrous bipolar power struggle witnessed in the Republic of Pakistan over the last ten years; at worst, it leads to a monopoly of power and dictatorship. Either way it represents a return to power struggles of a form rendered obsolete by the Westminster system over a century ago.

Underlying the assumption of an "inevitable" republic is a broader cultural myth, that we are confronted by a mutually exclusive choice of political heritages: that retaining Westminster implies rejecting Asia, and we must embrace Asia, "therefore" must renounce Westminster. This tacit contention, that interaction with one set of cultures implied renunciation of others, would be laughable if it were not so serious. Cultural assimilation would become a kind of bulimia: gorging then purging, gorging then purging. Is our brave new society to spend half its time staring glassy-eyed down the toilet bowl of history, expelling that which should have given it strength? At the moment our polity appears to be in the middle of a long dry retch. It's an irony that one of the institutions which appears to be first down the bowl when the revolution comes, is a delicacy derived from Imperial China…via the British.

Contrary to modern conventional wisdom the successful administration of a far-flung and logistically over-extended Empire in previous centuries demanded some degree of cultural sensitivity, for the most pragmatic of reasons. Failure to appreciate the cultural, administrative or military sophistication of other societies on the landscape carried with it the risk of disaster: witness the massacre of British regular forces by Zulu *impis* at Isandhlwana, or the 19th Century cold war between Britain and Russia in northern India, or the tensions underlying the Indian Mutiny. Local Imperial administrators required an accurate appreciation of the complex and potentially threatening societies that occupied their environment, a sensitive diplomatic task to be attempted by envoys and agents. Among at least the members of this small caste of Imperial officials the cultural richness of the observed societies left its imprint.

During the 19th Century envoys of the British Raj in India observed the functioning of the Imperial Chinese Court in Peking. One of the aspects of the Court which impressed them deeply was the Mandarinate, what we would now described as an *élite* civil service, members of which were required to pass formidable examinations and were inculcated with an *esprit de corps* that rendered them difficult to corrupt. The institution was regarded as so admirable by the envoys that it was imitated in British India in what became famous as the Indian Civil Service, the 1,200 members of which were recruited from privileged backgrounds (predominantly British, although from 1869 Indians were also included). They were required to sit rigorous exams and expected to be conversant in whatever local Indian languages were appropriate to their posting, as well as having a good grasp of classical Greek and Latin, in which they frequently corresponded with one another. They were again inculcated with a powerful collective ethos to create a class of people frequently compared by historians with Plato's Guardians, an ancient Greek paradigm also influential upon British thinking at the time.

A prosaic reason existed for creating such an *élite* body in India long before any counterpart existed at home. Early British administrators had accepted gifts and bribes from maharajas, some of whom were fabulously wealthy. The scope for corruption — and if push came to shove in the other direction, extortion and looting — was immense. In the long view, for Imperial administration of India to remain viable the administrators had to be incorruptible, and in the absence of any effective external enforcement of this the discipline had to be self-imposed. What was required was a caste apart, the members of which would not only abstain from financial profiteering but would also despise it. The Indian Civil Service provided the solution to this problem, proving remarkably successful at corruption-free government irrespective of what one thinks of other aspects of the Raj.[21]

Along with a taste for Chinese tea and Chinese silk, this institution was conveyed to the British Isles by expatriates returning home, where it replaced the former inefficient and corrupt system of patronage indigenous to the English political system. The British Civil Service dates from the reign of Queen Victoria, an aloof body bound by its own subculture which has traditionally refused to deign to engage in party-political intrigue, preferring instead to remain neutral in its relationship with the government of the day. Although neither its Chinese origins nor its adopted form in India had anything to do with democracy, transplanted in British soil it came to provide an essential support to parliamentary democratic government, and from there it came to Australia.[22]

Through this neutrality, ministers newly in office following a change in government can rely on the permanent civil service staff of their department to continue to provide them with the expertise required for transacting the business of governing, expertise the politicians lack, acquired from years of experience under previous governments. Without this experience every new administration would be crippled, but for such expertise to remain accessible the minister must remain confident of the bureaucrat's professional neutrality. If bureaucrats can't be trusted to remain non-partisan then they must be purged, for they come to know enough confidential information to embarrass their minister seriously — even dangerously, given a politician's reliance upon public opinion. But if they're purged then their experience is lost, and hence the capacity of the nation's government to function effectively is diminished. Thus, in our parliamentary democracy, civil servants who violate their neutrality to pursue partisan political agendas betray not only the traditions of the civil service, but also the trust of their fellow-citizens. We cannot make free choice of the government which is to be given power over us, unless we can remain confident that our choice will be served fully and impartially by the national bureaucracy. By breaking this neutrality public servants partisan to the old government distort our freedom of choice and cripple the new-chosen government, an abuse and betrayal of the electoral process.

The Chinese origins of the Westminster system's non-partisan civil service haven't been entirely forgotten. Members of the Indian Civil Service — perhaps tongue in cheek — used to be commonly referred to as "the heaven-born", while senior British and Australian civil servants were at least until recent years nick-named "mandarins". As has been remarked earlier, one of the most alarming developments in recent Australian history has been the politicisation of senior public servants. It would seem the wheel is slowly turning back to pre-Raj days, to an inefficient and corrupt mendicant bureaucracy, its members pandering to their own political patrons for preferment. Our polity is losing the fragrance of Peking duck, coming instead to smell of the lame variety.

This very idea of historical inevitability is flawed: its vision of history, as a ponderous wheel grinding inexorably towards a predefined series of outcomes, has a dubious basis in reality, and is an affront to the human condition. Marx and Engels were fond of the belief in "inevitable history", the Hegelian Dialectic of Thesis and Antithesis and All That Jazz. Casting a jaundiced eye over recent history, one could uncharitably suggest they were mistaken.

If, then, it's true that a republic is inevitable for us, then this is a bitter pill to swallow. It not only reveals the future in a bleak light, but raises doubts in the present tense: either our free will as a people is illusory, or else our judgement is lacking. It damns our society, as being incapable of assimilating and preserving cultural legacies that would help preserve it. The flaws in the "inevitable" republic are best exposed by Evatt's words, "It is a profound mistake to regard the royal functions as merely ceremonial or formal in char-acter."[23] The doctrine of an inevitable republic is founded upon this delusion of empty ceremony, and the Oz Republic has its genesis in this "profound mistake", buttressed by misconceptions about our society, historical and current. The day the Australian populace realises what the Oz Republic puts at jeopardy, is the day the republic will cease to be inevitable.

Niccolò's ghost   So far you've only considered the doings of your own little community within itself, like some Tuscan peasant careless of the fact his village belongs to a larger world. Kindly desist in this parochial examination, and lift up your eyes. Where does the rest of the world stand in your philosophy?

Author   [*frowns, and pauses.*] You mean, how does the rest of the world see us on a day-to-day basis? And how can we retain a shared monarchy as an independent sovereign country? And doesn't it impede our independence? All fair questions. Back to work, I suppose. [*Resumes writing.*]

The Queen is actually,
and not merely nominally,
Queen of Australia: in that capacity
separate and distinct from the Crown
of the United Kingdom.

Sir Garfield Barwick, former Chief Justice
of the High Court of Australia.[24]

An Australian Crown

A debate in the green chamber of the House of Representatives. A jeering Prime Minister Keating, taunting the monarchists on the Opposition front benches, accuses them of being "lickspittles", "tugging the forelock" to a British Queen. Behind these childish and unpleasant jibes lies a serious allegation: that the basis of monarchist beliefs is servility to a foreign power, and that deference to the Queen is part of an irrational deference to Britain. If our defence of the monarchy were founded upon preserving some sort of British political hegemony over Australia, then such an allegation could be justified. But if no such hegemony exists, and the Australian Crown is independent, and our defence is expressed in terms of our own national interests, where is the forelock-tugging?

Our national interests in the matter, political stability and democratic accountability, have already been established. And considering whether to become a republic isn't a question of whether Australia should sever her ties with the *British* monarchy but whether Australia should dismantle her *own* form of monarchy, the head of which is resident in London. Dismantling this monarchy will not render us more independent. To understand this, consider its genesis.

At the beginning of this century the Australian Governor-General held a dual position, being both the King's representative for the Commonwealth of Australia (appointing Prime Ministers and dissolving Parliament) and the agent of the British Government in Australia, reporting back to the Colonial Secretary in London as the formal channel of communication between the British and Australian Governments.[25] So too were the Governors-General in the Empire's other self-governing communities, then known as "Dominions".†

---

† The title "Dominion" is of Canadian coinage. At Confederation in 1867 the founders of modern Canada

This second role was clearly incompatible with Dominion independence, and was scrapped in 1926, when an Imperial Conference in London adopted the "Balfour Formula".[26] Intended (in the words of Leopold Amery, then the Dominions Secretary) to "get rid of every last vestige, not only of substance, but also of mere historical form which might be thought to limit the complete independence and equality of the dominion governments",[27] this was a declaration that defined the status of the Dominions and their relationships with Great Britain to be of:

> autonomous Communities within the British Empire, equal in status, in no way subordinate one to another in any aspect of their domestic or external affairs, though united by a common allegiance to the Crown and freely associated as members of the British Commonwealth of Nations.[28]

The Dominions were to be "subject to no compulsion whatever" from Britain. As an essential consequence of this equality of status, the declaration stated that,

> the Governor-General of a Dominion is the representative of the Crown, holding in all essential respects the same position in relation to the administration of public affairs in the Dominion as is held by His Majesty the King in Great Britain, and that he is not the representative or agent of His Majesty's Government or of any Department of that Government.[29]

From that time on, the official channel of communication between the Australian and British Governments would be direct. Stripped of his Imperial role, our Governor-General would now act only on behalf of the King within Australia, and the job of representing British interests in each Dominion was handed over to the British High Commissioners.[30]

Four years later another Imperial Conference went further, enunciating certain principles flowing "naturally from the new position of the Governor-General as representative of His Majesty only", in particular the question of who was the appropriate authority to advise the King upon the appointment of Dominion Governors-General. It stated that the King would make his appointment on the advice of the ministers of the Dominion concerned (as distinct from British ministers) and "the ministers concerned [would] tender their formal advice after informal consultations with His Majesty."[31]

---

desired to include in the formal title of their new country "a tribute to the monarchical principle, which they earnestly desire to uphold". Consequently they wanted to christen their country "Kingdom of Canada". Afraid of offending the Americans, the British Government objected and insisted they choose a different form of words. The Canadian response was to make an oblique reference to Psalm 72: "He shall have dominion also from sea to sea, and from the river unto the ends of the earth". (E.A. Forsey, *How Canadians Govern Themselves*, Government of Canada, 1980.) The term became a shorthand description for the kind of autonomous community within the Empire that Canada exemplified, and remains to this day in the formal title of two countries: The Dominion of Canada, and the Dominion of New Zealand. It refers to the existence of a monarchy, and has no implication of British hegemony.

Through these two Imperial Conferences the relationship between the King and his Australian ministers became a direct one, quite independent of Britain or British interests. This situation was reinforced in law by the Statute of Westminster, passed in the British Parliament in 1931 and adopted by the Australian Parliament in 1942. It was acknowledged in the coronation of King George VI in 1937, when his Coronation Oath explicitly named the independent countries in the Commonwealth — including Australia — over which he would be King. In the words of the Canadian Prime Minister of the time, W.L. MacKenzie King, "...for the first time, in this great ceremony, it was recognised that the relationship between the King and [the] people of [the Dominions] is direct and immediate".[†]

When in 1953 Elizabeth II was crowned Queen of her realms, her Coronation Oath obliged her to reign over them, not in accordance with English law, but "according to their respective laws and customs",[32] prompting Sir Robert Garran, a founding father of the Australian Constitution and former Solicitor-General, to remark

> Our Queen comes to us, not as Queen of a far-off country,
> representing authority exercised over us from the other side of
> the world, but as one of ourselves: as our own Queen of
> Australia, who reigns here, not in accord with her despotic
> will, but by and with the advice of her Australian Ministers.[‡]

Historical precedents exist for a single monarch ruling over independent realms with different constitutions and laws. The independent nations of England and Scotland shared Kings from 1603 to 1707,[§] as did Britain and Hanover between 1714 and 1837.[ʃ] As Sir David Smith, until recently Official Secretary to the Governor-General, put it, "With over two centuries of shared Monarchs as precedent, our position today is neither novel nor unique."[33]

---

† Quoted from Markwell, *The Crown and Australia*, p.12. Consequently, whenever ministers of any of Her Majesty's Governments throughout the Commonwealth wish to communicate with her they do so directly, without either the involvement or knowledge of any other government. Specifically the British Government is neither involved in nor privy to communiqués between the Palace and Her Majesty's other governments. Such communications are handled by the Queen's Private Secretary, over whom she has complete discretion of appointment and dismissal, without any ministerial involvement. For obvious reasons the Private Secretary is not a member of the Civil Service, and needn't necessarily be British: for instance in the late 1980s he was an Australian, Sir William Heseltine.

‡ Quoted from Markwell, *op. cit.* p. 12. The doctrine of "the Crown, separate and divisible", as it is known, has in recent years even been used as the basis for judicial decisions. In 1982 the English Court of Appeal referred to it when passing judgement in the case of *Regina v Secretary of State for Foreign and Commonwealth Affairs; ex parte Indian Association of Alberta & Others (1982)*, whereby it was declared that the monarchies of Canada and Great Britain were separate and distinct, although both were exercised contemporaneously by Queen Elizabeth II (Barwick, *The Monarchy in an Independent Australia*, pp. 10–11).

§ From the accession of James VI of Scotland to the throne of England, to the Act of Union in the reign of Queen Anne.

ʃ From the accession of George, Elector of Hanover as King George I, to the accession of Queen Victoria to the British throne (counting the Electorship as a monarchy).

In 1983 a stark illustration of the mutual independence of Elizabeth II's Crowns was provided by the Caribbean island nation of Grenada. Independent since 1976, Grenada has remained a two-tiered monarchy under the Queen. From the early 1950s until the late 1970s political affairs on the island had been dominated by one Eric Gairy, a controversial politician who, despite a turbulent and dubious career, survived to become the country's first Prime Minister and win the first election after independence.

> Despite strong popular support, his government became known for mismanagement and encouraging violence against its political enemies…Demonstrations against him and the prospects of independence under his government in 1973 and 1974 ended in violence with the opposition cowed, having failed to change his policies or delay independence. At the first post-independence elections in 1976 a united opposition challenged him strongly but lost, alleging that electoral irregularities had denied them victory. By early 1979 the Gairy years had left Grenada with a ruined economy, growing discontent and strong pressure for change.[34]

On the 13th March 1979, while Gairy was abroad on a foreign visit, he was overthrown by the Marxist-Leninist New Jewel Movement (NJM), the most radical of his opponents, in an "almost bloodless and immensely popular"[35] *coup d'etat*. They promptly proclaimed a People's Revolutionary Government (PRG), promulgating People's Laws. In some of these laws they reenacted sections of the independent Constitution of 1973, including (People's Law Number 3, 25th March 1979):

> The Head of State shall remain Her Majesty the Queen and her representative in this country shall continue to be the Governor-General who shall perform such functions as the People's Revolutionary Government may from time to time advise.[36]

The Governor-General at the time was Sir Paul Scoon, a former Grenadian Cabinet Secretary. "When Gairy was overthrown, Scoon, like a majority of Grenadians, probably felt relieved."[37] Why did Marxist-Leninists preserve the Crown? It's been suggested the "PRG did have something to gain from the relationship, and apparently felt that [the Governor-General's] retention conferred some measure of constitutional legitimacy upon them".[38] Having acquired both legislative and executive powers at the time of the *coup*, perhaps the PRG assumed the Crown was now an empty figurehead of ceremony. Perhaps they assumed Scoon would remain, mouselike, quiescent in Government House regardless of subsequent events. This was a tactical blunder.

Why did Scoon tolerate the New Jewel Movement? He seems to have had little choice. Gairy and his governments had proved disastrous, and the integrity of the electoral system in providing an alternative was questionable. The NJM were — at least initially — popular, and they invited non-Party members into the PRG. Despite the more unsavoury aspects of their ideology, the NJM successfully proceeded to undo much of Gairy's legacy of mismanagement, reduced unemployment from fifty percent to between fifteen and twenty percent, and improved public welfare and education. Unfortunately they proved haunted by paranoia (not entirely unfounded, in the light of contemporary events), and "[a]s Marxist-Leninists they did not believe that even with fair elections the parliamentary system was appropriate for Grenada".[39]

Slowly the regime began to disintegrate. The leader of the NJM, Maurice Bishop, claimed in April 1979 to "know that the dictator Gairy is organising mercenaries…to restore him to his throne."[40] Meanwhile, in the Caribbean "[m]anoeuvres by US armed forces…generated fears of invasion. Internal security thus became a major priority, and the armed forces came to be increased with the help of agreements with Cuba, the USSR and other allies."[41] The PRG became oppressive, silencing dissent and losing its popularity. An internal power struggle between Bishop and a rival, Bernard Coard, led to Coard and his followers going into hiding by 8th October 1983, fearing assassination. Imprisoned by the Party, Bishop was freed by a mob who then seized control of the military headquarters at Fort Rupert. PRG soldiers, apparently ordered in by members of the Central Committee of the Party, stormed the headquarters. Bishop (who until the previous week had headed the government) and his followers were murdered. The army seized control in a short-lived Revolutionary Military Council. In what appears to be a handwritten record of the last Central Committee meeting, on the 24th October, there is only a single item, emphasised in the original document: "*Bogo* [Major Leon Cornwall of the Revolutionary Military Council] *to brief G.G. tomorrow.*"[42] It is unknown what was to be said; perhaps an offer to invite civilians into the government. The briefing never took place, for the next day US and Caribbean Commonwealth troops invaded.

The official story is that the Governor-General secretly requested the Organisation of Eastern Caribbean States to intervene, using a "confidential channel to transmit an appeal to the OECS and other regional states to restore order on the island".[43] The late Prime Minister of Barbados, Tom Adams, revealed that this confidential channel was "a friendly government, albeit non-participating".[44] Certainly on the 24th October Scoon, apparently seeking help, communicated with Brigadier Lewis, commander of the military forces of Barbados, but doubt exists whether he desired a full-blown foreign invasion spearheaded by US troops. The Governor-General's letter formally requesting intervention because "there is a vacuum of authority in Grenada following the killing of the Prime Minister and the subsequent serious violations of human rights and bloodshed"[45] was signed a few days *after* the invasion. It's entirely possible the US invasion had no lawful basis, in which case the "request" was a mutually useful excuse: it reasserted Grenadian sovereignty over events beyond Grenada's control, and it veiled US actions with a veneer of legitimacy. As the British House of Commons' Foreign Affairs Committee later remarked,

Both the timing and the nature of this request, which is said by the United States Government to have been a critical factor in providing a legal justification for their decision to act, remain shrouded in some mystery, and it is evidently the intention of the parties involved that the mystery should not be dispelled.[46]

Irrespective of the request, in the days of crisis that followed the mouse roared. Accurately described by a US official as "the sole remaining source of Governmental legitimacy",[47] and placed under the protection of the invaders on the 26th October, Sir Paul Scoon invoked the ultimate reserve power possessed throughout the world by all viceregal representatives of Queen Elizabeth II — a power later upheld by the High Court of Grenada[48] — to reestablish a government from chaos by summoning a Crown advisory council. This council provided an alternative government to that of the US military forces and diplomats, who "indubitably did regard themselves as saviours and were reluctant to return to more mundane activities".[49] Once certain the crisis had been resolved and there existed political groups within Grenadian society willing and able to uphold the 1973 democratic constitution, Scoon held elections in December 1984, which an anti-Gairy and anti-NJM coalition won. Parliamentary democracy had been restored to Grenada under the Crown.

What role did Britain play in this drama? Absolutely none. Replying to a parliamentary question in the British House of Commons, Prime Minister Margaret Thatcher made clear that "no request from Sir Paul Scoon for military assistance had been passed through United Kingdom channels, and no such request was reported to the United Kingdom".[50] In replying to a question put by a journalist, Sir Paul Scoon expressed the doctrine of the Crown, separate and divisible, very clearly:

Journalist: Was there some problem about the fact that you did not contact Her Majesty's Government [of the United Kingdom]? Being the Queen's representative in Grenada, do you regard your action in going to the Organisation of Eastern Caribbean States and the possibilities that arose from that to be in any way in conflict with your appointment?

Scoon: They don't conflict at all. Her Majesty has many governments...The Queen is the Head of Grenada and the British Government can't dictate to the Government of Grenada what to do, nor can the British Government give any orders to the Governor-General of Grenada...I don't understand all this about the British Government. I had not thought at all of contacting the British Government.[51]

A more curious example was provided by an incident in Fiji while a draft of this manuscript was being written. Despite having become a republic after the 1987 military *coups*, Fiji is perhaps the most reluctant republic in the world. Among my papers as I write these words are three shiny Fijian coins. The oldest was minted (by the Canadian Mint) in 1990; the other two are more recent. All three bear the profile, not of some Fijian politician, but of Her Majesty Queen Elizabeth II. Government departments in the Pacific republic are still officially departments of HM the Queen of Fiji, and proudly display the emblem of the Crown. A decade after the *coups*, speculation began to grow of a Restoration of the monarchy…which is where our tale begins. According to newspaper reports, during a private audience with the President of Fiji in mid-1997 the British ambassador was foolish enough to suggest that the Government of Fiji would have to apologise formally to the Queen for the events of 1987 before the monarchy could return. The President curtly reminded him that the Crowns of Fiji and Britain were distinct; that Elizabeth II had been Queen of Fiji independently of Britain, and that any negotiations concerning her Restoration were strictly a matter between the republic of Fiji and Buckingham Palace. The British ambassador was then shown the door for his impertinence.[†]

Prime Minister Rabuka made it clear that he wanted to hold a referendum on restoring the monarchy, given Fiji's recent restoration to the Commonwealth. Restoration of Elizabeth II as Queen of Fiji is expected to be popular among the Fijian people…and would deliver a signal throughout the Pacific that they are more politically astute than our own republican leaders. With each Crown existing for the benefit of the people of that country, 1970s-style postcolonialism is dead. In Australia, however, we are being urged to wear the ideological equivalent of flared brown hipsters and gold chest-medallions.

An Australian judicial perspective was provided by the controversial former Chief Justice of the High Court of Australia, Sir Garfield Barwick, when he delivered a lecture in 1982 entitled "The Monarchy in an Independent Australia":

> The Queen is actually, and not merely nominally, Queen of
> Australia : in that capacity separate and distinct from the
> Crown of the United Kingdom. She as Queen of Australia, not
> as Queen of the United Kingdom, is one of the components of
> the Parliament. The monarchy in Great Britain relates and is
> limited to a different territory; is held under a different consti-
> tutional regime to the monarchy in Australia. Each is isolated
> from the other. None of the powers vested in the sovereign in
> or in relation to the United Kingdom can be exercised so as to
> control, affect or influence Australian affairs : and this is so
> notwithstanding the fact that the succession is determined by
> the laws of Great Britain…The monarchy in Australia can

---

† Despite humiliating diplomats who haven't done their homework, this doctrine of distinct Crowns is of mutual benefit to the UK and Her Majesty's other, independent realms.

OF NATIONS

properly be regarded as an Australian institution separate and distinct from the monarchy in Great Britain, albeit that the one person exercises a monarchy separately attaching to each territory and that the succession to the throne is not directly determined by Australian law.

Thus, the stimulus to republicanism which the involvement of the British monarchy in Australian affairs formerly and understandably provided should no longer exist: its basis has long since gone.[52]

In 1985 the Hawke/Keating government established a Constitutional Commission, to report revisions to our Constitution required to "adequately reflect Australia's status as an independent nation".[53] The final report from the Commission was presented in 1988, and in it was set out our nation's historical progress to full constitutional and legislative independence, concluding,

> It is clear from these events, and recognition by the world community, that at some time between 1926 and the end of World War II Australia had achieved full independence as a sovereign state of the world. The British Government ceased to have any responsibility in relation to matters coming within the area of responsibility of the Federal Government and Parliament.[54]

The final conclusion of the Commission was that "[T]he development of Australian nationhood did not require any change to the Australian Constitution."[55]

> We recommend no change to Australia's status as a constitutional monarchy or to the position of the Queen of Australia as head of State. The only changes we recommend affecting the powers of the Queen under the Constitution are in relation to assignment of powers to the Governor-General pursuant to section 2 of the Constitution, reservation of Bills passed by the Houses of the Federal Parliament for the Queen's personal assent, the power to disallow Federal Acts, and the power to authorise the Governor-General to appoint deputies.[56]

It also testified to the existence of distinct monarchies corresponding with the various realms over which Elizabeth II is Queen.

> The disappearance of the British Empire has therefore meant that the Queen is now Sovereign of a number of separate countries such as the United Kingdom, Canada, Australia, New Zealand and Papua New Guinea, amongst others. As Queen of Australia she holds an entirely distinct and different position from that which she holds as Queen of the United Kingdom or Canada. The separation of these 'Crowns' is underlined by the

comment of Gibbs CJ in *Pochi v. Macphee* that 'The allegiance which Australians owe to Her Majesty is owed not as British subjects but as subjects of the Queen of Australia'.[57]

In the light of this report, Keating's bombast about an Australian republic being necessary for our nationhood is clearly empty rhetoric. He must surely be aware of the existence of this document — didn't he read his own government's reports?

But what would happen to us if the United Kingdom became a republic? If it became a republic at midnight tonight, Her Majesty would remain Queen of Australia until such time as we arranged otherwise. In the absence of such an arrangement Australia would remain a bipartite monarchy, irrespective of any British political changes, with no additional effort on our part. It would be "business as usual", provided the Queen retained some support staff, a fax machine and a telephone. The only impediment rests in the current reliance of Her Majesty's other realms upon the British laws of succession. Given the above hypothetical scenario, it is entirely conceivable (indeed, arguably necessary) that her remaining realms would devise a mutually acceptable Act of Succession, passed in their respective parliaments. In such an eventuality the realms could then function normally, completely ignoring the British republic. From a purely legal perspective it matters nothing that the United Kingdom is a member of the EU and has surrendered sovereignty to Brussels; nothing, within the span of a single reign, if the United Kingdom declares itself a republic, and little, beyond that span.

A precedent already exists for this, set in 1952–53. After the death of King George VI the Prime Ministers of the United Kingdom, Canada, Australia, New Zealand, the Union of South Africa, Pakistan and Ceylon met in London, in December of 1952. Their purpose was to modify the royal titles of the monarch before the coronation of Queen Elizabeth II, to bring them in line with the changed political circumstances within the Commonwealth. In particular it was desired that the Queen's titles emphasise the fact that she was Queen separately and individually of these realms, independently of the United Kingdom. The outcome of that meeting was the *Royal Style and Titles Act*, passed in the parliaments of all seven countries in 1953. By this act Elizabeth the Second became explicitly Queen of Australia at her coronation in 1953, her Australian title being "Elizabeth the Second, by the Grace of God of the United Kingdom, Australia and Her other Realms and Territories Queen, Head of the Commonwealth, Defender of the Faith." To emphasise the constitutional irrelevance of Britain to our monarchy the Whitlam government modified this Act in 1973, so that her Australian title became "Elizabeth the Second, by the Grace of God Queen of Australia and Her other Realms and Territories, Head of the Commonwealth."[†]

---

† It seems, however, that the Whitlam government was not motivated by patriotism, although this was the ostensible reason given for the change; see **The Ending of States.**

OF NATIONS

To write a revised Act of Succession, the relevant mechanism is to be found in the Statute of Westminster, which states in part,

> [I]t would be in accord with the established constitutional
> position of all the members of the Commonwealth [of
> Nations] in relation to one another that any alteration in the
> law touching the Succession to the Throne or the Royal Style
> and Titles shall hereafter require the assent as well of the
> Parliaments of all the Dominions as of the Parliament of the
> United Kingdom.[58]

So the laws of royal succession can be changed, and the Parliament of the Commonwealth of Australia has a crucial share in their change. In his call for a republic, ex-Federal Attorney-General Michael Lavarch has based his demands on the fact that the existing laws of succession discriminate on the grounds of gender and religion, claiming that for this reason the Crown has become unacceptable to the Australian people. He's implied there is no middle ground: either we must retain the status quo or abolish the monarchy altogether. But this well-established mechanism shreds his argument's credibility to tatters. As he *should* already know, it's entirely possible to retain the monarchy despite updating the laws of succession so that they are no longer sexist or offensive on religious grounds. How we do so is a matter for the people of this country to consider carefully; but in Lord Archer's Bill the British Parliament has already signalled its willingness to contemplate change.

The Crowns of the Australian States evolved more slowly and along a somewhat different path from their federal counterpart. Explicitly exempt from the *Statute of Westminster*, the States remained technically self-governing communities under the British Crown long after the distinct Australian Crown had emerged federally. Until the *Australia Acts 1986* (*Commonwealth* and *UK*) passed at Westminster, Canberra and the Parliaments of each of the States severed these States from the British Crown, their dealings were conducted under the Crown of the United Kingdom, and so a Premier's advice was transmitted to the Queen by a British minister. But by convention, British ministers acted as messengers and did not attempt to interfere with the Premier's advice.[†] It's interesting to note that even into the 1980s many State Premiers — including at least one who has subsequently claimed he was always a republican — fiercely resisted any amending of these traditional arrangements, for while Premiers remained nominally under the British Crown the reality was they each enjoyed a constitutional relationship with the Queen independent from federal Australian interference, and from which British ministers abstained from interfering.

---

† A rare exception to this rule occurred in 1976, when "the British government declined to advise the Queen to re-appoint Sir Colin Hannah [the Governor of Queensland] because in 1975 he had made partisan public remarks".(D.J. Markwell, "The Conventions of Ministerial Resignations: The Queensland Coalition Crisis of 1983", *Constitutional Heads and Political Crises: Commonwealth Episodes 1945–85* (ed. D.A. Low), p. 163.)

In 1986 the relationship between the Queen and her State Premiers became direct. Some people even go so far as to describe Australia as an "heptarchy" composed of seven monarchies. Although an unpopular view in some southern capitals, governments in Western Australia and Queensland have fiercely asserted their possession of independent monarchies, entrenching the Queen as "Queen of Western Australia" and "Queen of Queensland". Whether or not these State Crowns are entirely distinct from the Federal one, it's certain they belong to this continent.

In all of her Crowns upon Australian soil Her Majesty's role is limited. For the federal Commonwealth, for example, the duties of monarch when out of the country are virtually restricted to appointing and dismissing the Governor-General upon the advice of Australian ministers; all other powers and duties of the Crown are wielded by the Governor-General. Within each State the Governor discharges the Queen's duties as Queen of that State in an analogous manner.

All other powers and duties? What about disallowance? Republican journalists have harped upon the section of the Constitution that claims for the Governor-General the right to reserve the Royal Assent to a Bill, and for the Queen the right to disallow an Act of Parliament for up to one year after the Governor-General has given Assent. The historical ignorance of these journalists is behind their repeated complaints; they are drowning in a mirage. Reservation and disallowance were never royal powers at all but Imperial ones, to aid the administration of a far-flung empire. In the earlier years of the Empire disallowance enabled British ministers to overturn in the King's name ill-conceived laws enacted by inept colonial Governors in distant parts of the world. In the later Empire, when responsible government had been established throughout its autonomous communities, reservation and disallowance acquired a new use: to coordinate legislation concerning the administrative integrity of the colony, to prevent violation of treaty obligations held by the Imperial Government, and to harmonise laws governing trade and shipping among the various British dependencies throughout the world.[59]

This power was exercised in 19th Century Canada and the Australasian colonies, but has never been invoked for the Commonwealth of Australia. By 1929, when the Conference on the Operation of Dominion Legislation and Merchant Shipping Legislation was held, it had long since fallen into dormancy and disrepute. The Conference resolved that "the power of disallowance can no longer be exercised in relation to Dominion legislation";[60] that reservation, if exercised at all, could only be done by the Governor-General in accordance with local constitutional practice; and that in such conditions the British Government could not interfere by advising the King to act against the views of the Dominion government concerned, as "it is the right of the Government of each Dominion to advise the Crown in all matters relating to its own affairs".[61]

Imperial reservation and disallowance were thus terminated. Her Majesty's power of disallowance expressed in section 59 of the Constitution sleeps as if dead, by international convention. And yet a threat remains, neither from the Queen nor from London, but from an Australian Prime Minister under whose advice it might be reawakened from Canberra. An unscrupulous politician freshly in office, confronted with legislation recently passed through Parliament by his predecessor but not yet enacted, and unable to pass another Bill through both Houses revoking the first, might conceivably advise the Governor-General to reserve the offending Bill with a view to advising the Queen of Australia to disallow it, thus effectively flouting Parliament. Unlike reservation, disallowance should therefore be buried; not because of bogeymen abroad, but because under the Australian Crown the threats to our constitutional integrity are home-grown ones.

Our Australian monarchy has existed independently of Britain or British interests for over fifty years. It has been independent as a matter of political convention since the Imperial Conferences of 1926 and 1930, as a matter of Australian and British law since the Australian adoption of the *Statute of Westminster* in 1942, and has been emphasised as a matter of international protocol and public ceremony since the *Royal Style and Titles Act* of 1953. For the Australian States the *Australia Act* of 1986 merely provided a formal expression of a situation which had really existed for decades, in which the British Crown had previously served simply as a convenient cover to protect them from Canberra. Those nationalists who would now like Australia to become a republic to be "finally independent" of Britain are over half a century too late. We have become fully independent without them.

[*Throughout the Author's reading aloud of his manuscript, the Ghost has been leaning back in his chair, with his eyes closed and his fingers cradled, listening in the attitude of an elderly schoolmaster. Secretly hoping he might have fallen asleep, the Author pauses, puts down his pen and stretches. At this the old man's eyes flutter open, and he stares accusingly across the table.*]

Niccolò's ghost   And...?

Author   [nonplussed.] And what?

Niccolò's ghost   Well that's all very good, but I hope you're not going to leave it there! All right, so your monarch is independently Queen of your country, and almost all of her duties are exercised here on her behalf by your — what d'you call him — Governor-General. But practical government is about more than getting your fingers inky signing decrees. What of receiving foreign ambassadors and dignitaries? Who presides over your masques and banquets, your most solemn festivities?

How can your Queen, when she spends most of her time abroad?

Author [*Resigned, reaches again for his pen.*]: I was just getting to that. [*Begins to write again.*]

Trinculo: A strange fish!…Legged like a
man! And his fins like arms! Warm, o'my
troth! I do now let loose my opinion,
hold it no longer. This is no fish, but an
islander…

The Tempest, Act II Scene 2.

An "Australian Head of State"

A great deal of agonising has gone on in this debate about having or not having an "Australian Head of State", without much pause to ask what is *meant* by such a phrase, by what actions is the incumbent of that office recognised…or indeed whether the term holds meaning within our shores. The title is a cardboard tag pinned to sundry people throughout the world: the President of the United States and that of Israel, although two very different creatures, wielding dissimilar powers and serving unlike roles, are penned together in this loose enclosure of convenience. The term is alien, both to Australia and the older traditions of Westminster, but now introduced we must address it. What do we *mean* when we speak of a "Head of State"?

Two different aspects spring to mind, the first a dusty legal form, the second of formal pomp and circumstance, and when the two coincide the figure created is the one we recognise as the occupant of this vague office. On one hand the ultimate source of all executive authority, the signature on Bills that turns them into law, the supreme commander of the armed forces; on the other, the international ceremonial figure, the cutter and bestower of ribbons, the titular personage delivering speeches and waving at crowds, a human face of the country. When all these images are conjoined like tiles in a mosaic, a recognisable pattern emerges, the "Head of State". But what of when these tiles *don't* all come together? They often don't.

Sweden, for example, has a King. His face adorns Swedish stamps and coins, he occupies a formal position in Swedish society, and to many of us foreigners he is the ceremonial embodiment of his country. And yet he is not a source of executive authority; he has failed to fill that legal job description we associate with a "Head of State" since 1974, when the ruling Social Democrats stripped the monarchy of all its powers and handed many of them to the Speaker of

Parliament. (This was a misguided attempt at reform, and has subsequently come under international criticism.) Technically speaking, Sweden is under an "Orphan Model" of government.

Every time Irish republicans in Australia have held up the Irish President as a distinctively national "Head of State" and urged we follow suit, they've unwittingly shored up the defences of our Governor-General's job description; for the Irish Republic, like the Kingdom of Sweden, is under an Orphan Model, and if the Irish Presidency has had any diplomatic success overseas, it has demonstrated that one needn't be the constitutional source of all authority at home to be regarded as the country's distinctive face abroad. An immediate consequence of a two-tier monarchy is the designation of not one but two figures of State, one royal, the other viceregal; the Queen of Australia at Buckingham Palace and the Governor-General of Australia at Yarralumla. Because Elizabeth II is Queen of sixteen independent countries, and when not within one of her realms represents the United Kingdom by default, we have the question of whom should represent each of the other fifteen countries as distinctive "Heads of State" in diplomacy abroad. Since 1926 the answer has rested in their Governors-General, with a protocol established decades ago and encouraged by Buckingham Palace: our Governor-General should engage in foreign diplomatic visits with all due ceremony and courtesy as Australia's distinctive State figure. In the words of Sir David Smith, the former Official Secretary to the Governor-General at Yarralumla,

> Buckingham Palace has long had a much better appreciation
> and understanding of the diplomatic role which a Governor-
> General is capable of discharging on behalf of his country
> than has any Australian Prime Minister, even to stipulating
> that Governors-General should be received by foreign host
> governments as the head of their country, and with all the
> proper marks of respect due to a visiting head of state.[62]

This is a logical consequence of the Imperial Conference of 1926, and was swiftly recognised as such by Canada, which started sending its Governors-General on official visits abroad in 1927. The fact our own Governors-General weren't sent overseas on such diplomatic initiatives until 1971 is due to the slowness of successive Australian governments in recognising the potential of such visits in terms of international self-assertion.

The subsequent success of State visits overseas has made it clear that our Asian and Pacific neighbours regard our Governor-General as a State figure in his own right, and not simply as the Queen's nominal representative in this country:

> All of the host countries visited by Governor-General Sir
> Paul Hasluck, Sir John Kerr, Sir Zelman Cowen, Sir Ninian
> Stephen and Mr Bill Hayden have indeed acted in this way
> during 27 State and official visits made to 20 countries, and
> all but one of them in Asia or the Asia-Pacific region.
> Australian Governors-General have even been accorded

special courtesies by foreign Heads of State and their governments when travelling abroad privately and unofficially while
on leave, so it is just humbug to speak of this country needing
to become a republic in order to be properly recognised and
accepted by other countries.[63]

An unambiguous confirmation of this occurred at the 1989 coronation of
Emperor Akihito of Japan. Following his coronation, the new Emperor of
Japan granted audiences to all visiting Heads of State or their representatives,
with one clear distinction: that Akihito would grant a private audience to all
actual Heads of State present, whereas he would grant only a collective audience to all the *representatives* of Heads of State. The Governors-General of
Australia and Canada were each granted a private audience, a clear signal from
the Chrysanthemum Throne that they were regarded, not simply as "stand-
ins" for the Queen, but as "Heads of State" in their own right.[64]

Republicans have countered that the Queen, not the Governor-General, is
the source of all executive authority under the Australian Constitution, and
so therefore she, not he, must be "the" Head of State, while some monarchists
have riposted with the other extreme, that he *is* "the" true Head of State and
the Queen's merely a symbol. This rather childish squabble hasn't been helped
by otherwise distinguished figures jumping into the fight with fists flailing…
particularly as both sides are wrong. The crude concept of a single, monolithic
Head of State — the mosaic described earlier — is applicable to the US
President, or Elizabeth II as Queen of the United Kingdom. At the time our
Constitution came into force in 1901 it was also applicable to Queen Victoria
in the Australian context, and so she could unambiguously be described as our
single Head of State through wearing the British Crown. But our
Constitution's reliance upon convention made it a flexible document, its
interpretation open to evolution. Imperial Conferences, the emergence of "the
Crown, separate and divisible", the *Statute of Westminster*, the *Royal Style and
Titles Acts*, all have lead to the mosaic's dissociation across the decades and the
formation of newer and more subtle patterns.

Irrespective of where our polity puts the font of executive power, our
Governor-General can discharge his duty as our Australian-born figure representing us as a diplomatic "Head of State", even as Sweden's and Ireland's
figures do. Indeed, he stands closer to the font than they, wielding as he does
the Crown's reserve powers. Buckingham Palace has proved more determined
to assert his moral and legal authority, as an Australian figure resolving
Australian problems, than our politicians have done. The day after the 1975
Dismissal of the Whitlam government, G.G.D. Scholes as Labor's Speaker of
the House of Representatives petitioned the Palace, requesting that Her
Majesty restore Whitlam to office as Prime Minister, reversing Sir John Kerr's
decision to sack him. The Queen's Private Secretary replied from London:

> I am commanded by The Queen to acknowledge your letter
> of 12th November about the recent political events in

Australia...As we understand the situation here, the Australian Constitution firmly places the prerogative powers of the Crown in the hands of the Governor-General as the representative of The Queen of Australia. The only person competent to commission an Australian Prime Minister is the Governor-General, and The Queen has no part in the decisions which the Governor-General must take in accordance with the Constitution. Her Majesty, as Queen of Australia, is watching events in Canberra with close interest and attention, but it would not be proper for her to intervene in person in matters which are so clearly placed within the jurisdiction of the Governor-General by the Constitution Act.[65]

Historical neglect of a distinctively Australian State figure isn't a sin of the Palace but of the Lodge, for while ambiguity has remained over the viceregal role, prime ministers have been able to exploit this to their own advantage. At Yizhak Rabin's 1995 State funeral in Israel, where the world's leaders gathered to grieve his assassination, one would have thought Australia's appropriate figure should have been present to represent our country in a non-partisan manner. In fact he was not. Nor was the Leader of the Opposition invited. Only Prime Minister Paul Keating went, claiming the right to go representing all Australians — a ridiculous pretension in a parliamentary democracy, in effect claiming *l'Etat c'est moi*.[†] The solution to both prime ministerial pretension and ambiguity over our State figures rests not in denouncing our Queen but in exalting our Governor-General, requiring only a change in political attitude.

Naturally this solution doesn't commend itself to Malcolm Turnbull or the other leaders of the republican movement, nor should we expect them to concede it: were they to acknowledge the existence of this historical solution their own hardline position would be badly compromised. But one must inquire, if Yarralumla says that for diplomatic purposes abroad "Head of State" means our Governor-General, and Buckingham Palace has agreed for decades, and the Australian people can persuade the Lodge to surrender its previous tenacious ambiguity over the issue, then...who is left standing in the way? Only the republican leadership itself, living in a state of denial. They refuse, not an abstract proposition, but an important diplomatic protocol which has long since been in use by other Commonwealth realms. By their denial they deprive our country of the independent symbolic figure they claim to desire. If they're sincere, desiring only a distinctive Australian State figure — rather than perhaps other, more personal ambitions — why don't they embrace this opportunity to create such a figure within our current Constitution?

This denial is only one of many distortions that contort this country's "debate" on the Crown. It's almost impossible to determine whether the distortions

---

† For a contrast, consider the British delegation, which included Prime Minister John Major, Leader of the Opposition Tony Blair, and Prince Charles representing the Queen in her British capacity. Thus *both* sides of the House were represented, as well as the apolitical Head of State.

OF NATIONS

solemnly pronounced by our "experts" have been the result of unfeigned ignorance, or whether the effort of providing a proper analysis has simply been too inconvenient. Assertions that to acquire an elected State figure requires a shift to a republic, and that choice of the Governor-General's identity "must" be in the hands of the Prime Minister, are patently false, despite being claimed by republican lawyers and believed by the public. Were an elected figure required for Australia to represent itself properly, this could be easily achieved by reforming the post of Governor-General; the neglected provisions for this have been sitting on bookshelves since 1930, and are employed by countries like Papua New Guinea. Did the "experts" quoted in the Press not know, or did they merely think that we didn't need to know?

It would be best if we could discard entirely the cardboard cut-out title "Head of State", a crude and foreign term, when discussing the subtleties of our modern system and its posts of State. No single modern figure in our polity conforms with its crude expectations; the demarcation of responsibility between Queen and Governor-General is too sophisticated to be encompassed by the title. The ARM's complaint that currently "no Australian can be Australia's Head of State" is as ridiculous as complaining no Australian can be our God-King or Doge. But subtlety is sadly lacking in this debate, where few phrases that aren't slogans survive. Perhaps the least violence to the truth is done if we say we have two Heads of State, one royal and the other viceregal. When the two are put together, the Crown — rather than either of the individuals wielding it — satisfies all the criteria of our mosaic.

We're told it's undesirable to possess as Queen someone who is Queen of another country. The obvious reply is to inquire "why?" As our viceregal post already provides a niche for an eminent Australian to fulfil the republican President's job description, why is the prospect of a Queen shared with other realms a cause of unmitigable rage? Elizabeth II being Queen of her various realms in a distinct and independent fashion, her constitutional powers regarding Australia in no way jeopardising our nationhood or independence, there's no high political motive behind the rage at a Queen of many realms. The actual motive is base, unpleasant and ugly, although in our current social climate it's judged otherwise. In a word, nationalism.

The aridity of our political landscape, starkly littered by some of our current and recently departed leaders, is such that in the present atmosphere nationalism is applauded by those who would formulate opinion — politicians and the media — instead of being denounced. Unlike patriotism, nationalism is no virtue but a vice, a contemptible trait. George Orwell, better known for his portrayal of totalitarian societies in *Animal Farm* and *1984*, distinguished between the two when he wrote,

> Nationalism is not to be confused with patriotism. Both
> words are normally used in so vague a way that any definition
> is liable to be challenged, but one must draw a distinction
> between them, since two different and even opposing ideas

are involved. By 'patriotism' I mean devotion to a particular place and a particular way of life, which one believes to be the best in the world but has no wish to force upon other people. Patriotism is of its nature defensive, both militarily and culturally. Nationalism, on the other hand, is inseparable from the desire for power. The abiding purpose of every nationalist is to secure more power and prestige, *not* for himself but for the nation or other unit in which he has chosen to sink his own individuality. A nationalist is one who thinks solely, or mainly, in terms of competitive prestige.

Orwell concludes the distinction by stating,

Nationalism is power hunger tempered by self-deception. Every nationalist is capable of the most flagrant dishonesty, but he is also — since he is conscious of serving something bigger than himself — unshakeably certain of being in the right.[66]

Enlarging on this distinction, a patriot is one who loves his or her country without feeling any need to disdain other countries or their symbols to do so. Nationalism, on the other hand, is the mentality of the stadium applied to the world at large.

When we support a team at a football match we engage in a scenario of strict competition between teams, our own and a rival. Collaboration between teams is unthinkable, as is the wearing of the rival's colours. Any team not our own is a rival, and therefore an opponent, formidable if superior in ranking, vanquished or vanquishable if inferior, as are its supporters, the wearers of its colours and emblems. Such is the nature of football, and there is no offence in this. The offence lies in applying this attitude beyond the stadium, and most particularly at our national borders.

There are those who would argue that it's no sin to apply the mentality of the stadium to the world at large, for they hold that the world itself lies within a stadium, as the playing field upon which nations struggle. Truly between nations there exists competition and struggle — even wars — over trade, the distribution of wealth or debt or territory, over ethnicity and religion and historical prejudice. What liberates the community of nations from the confines of the stadium is the opportunity to share goals, to cooperate for the common good in a kinship of thought, in a shared commitment to aspirations beyond national differences. In this context the Crown of the Commonwealth realms is a remarkable symbol, an emblem of kinship and shared aims that transcends national borders. Within any given realm the Westminster system under the Crown strives to preserve the institutions of parliamentary democracy. Beyond our shores, this emblem of the Crown that surmounts the parliamentary systems of Australia, New Zealand, Canada, the United Kingdom and the other twelve realms of Queen Elizabeth II also displays a shared commitment to parliamentary government, declares a common heritage and denotes

OF NATIONS

a kinship between countries, more so than among Commonwealth republics or by mere membership of the UN.

These sixteen realms, as independent countries defending their own interests, contend against one another in the daily melee of international politics on such issues as trade, but as the dust of the fight settles the shared emblem of the Crown serves as a reminder that those things that our countries possess in common transcend that which divides us. *Even if* the Crown were no more than an empty cipher (which it is not), in providing this emblem of common focus in sixteen parliaments of the world it would remain a valuable instrument, beyond the haggling of the marketplace or the disquiet of personal political egotism on the world stage.

Upon the issue of symbols patriots and nationalists must diverge, especially on historical symbols. The heartbeat of history is the intercourse of nations, and no great nation ever emerged from obscurity a virgin. The fundamental symbols of a society are for the most part inherited, heirlooms bearing the hallmarks of history, not devised overnight to comply with our latter-day sensibilities. For this reason, close inspection of a country's emblems will often reveal traces of another nation, and it is this which offends a nationalist's sense of ethnic cleanliness. Patriots, however, in loving their country may love its symbols, irrespective of their foreign "taint", for that they are emblems of their country's history, foreignness and all. Regiments of the Australian army are no less Australian for that their traditional insignia consist of a blend of indigenous and British symbols, just as British regiments have been no less British for that some of their insignia incorporated German symbols from the Hanoverian period. The desire to expunge historical symbols of kinship between countries because those symbols *are* common to both countries is pure nationalism, a sublimation of hatred, and like most manifestations of hatred, essentially irrational. A case in point was the lunatic suggestion of a government committee that Australian soldiers should no longer march to the skirl of bagpipes, for bagpipes are a Scottish instrument, "therefore" not Australian, "therefore" unacceptable. This proposition not only rejects the strong historical influence of the Scots and Scotland upon our armed forces and their traditions, but is also ridiculous in its logical consequences — presumably our soldiers shall in future march only to didgeridoos, clap-sticks and the martial sound of wobble-boards.

Our history, for all its blemishes — and only a child expects history to be devoid of stains or shame, beginning as a fairytale ends, "happily ever after" — is one to be proud of. It's a history of courage and tenacity, and of a lasting struggle against adversity. Yet for all this, it doesn't lend itself well to nationalistic jingoism. To this end it must be re-written, cast into a more malleable and convenient form; history as it "should" have been, written either by master novelists like the late Manning Clark, or by his less adroit disciples. Old tensions and grievances must be aroused and magnified; old friendships, kinships, shared allegiances and alliances for the common good derided and belittled. To this end also must our heritage be demolished or deleted, its old emblems effaced from common view — for these emblems, being tokens of our true history, expose the lie of our pseudo-history. Old friendships are easier forgotten if the photographs and letters are destroyed, and old wounds are easy to remember if we rub scars until they ache.

Nationalism is the last resort of those in power incapable of leadership. Unable to rally their disillusioned fellow citizens to united purpose by positive endeavours, they strive to do so by creating external tensions, manufacturing jealousies and magnifying petty hatreds. To this end they find it necessary to re-write history, discarding those emblems we possess in common heritage with other countries as being inconvenient to their purpose. It isn't undesirable for our country to possess as Queen someone who is Queen of other realms — merely inconvenient for past and future leaders that we do so.

Perhaps equally importantly, this desire to re-write history, deliberately erasing the influences of past cultures, surely represents a betrayal of the values of multiculturalism. Orwell described such an irony in his dictator's maxims: War is Peace; Freedom is Slavery; Ignorance is Strength. Republicans could be said to have added a fourth: Elimination of Heritage is Multiculturalism. Twisting the maxim even further (and still unconscious of the irony) they claim that a British-born Queen is incompatible with and unacceptable to a modern multicultural Australia.

Insisting upon an Antipodean Queen as well as a Governor-General sounds as petulant as demanding an Antipodean Pope. That a Queen of sixteen realms must be foreign-born to fifteen of them is a phenomenon owing more to the mechanics of childbirth than those of colonialism. It must be remarked, however, that we may have come very close to having an Australian-raised heir to the throne — Prince Charles' second son — potentially to reign over Britain, Australia and the other realms.

In the early 1980's it was public knowledge that the Fraser government wanted to recommend Prince Charles as Governor-General of Australia, an exception to the general practice of restricting this post to eminent Australians. There were (and remain) strong cases to be made both for and against such an act. The case against the appointment is obvious in the light of the previous arguments established. A self-assertive sovereign nation needs duties performed by the occupant of this post which could and should be performed by a visibly Australian figure; the viceregal tier of the Crown should be one of national symbolism and focus here and abroad, just as the royal tier is one of international symbolism here and overseas. On the other hand, the case in favour of the Prince as Governor-General ought not to have been lightly dismissed, as it held some persuasive virtues, in the general argument as well as in the particular individual concerned.

The most conspicuous point of the general argument was the fact that the Prince of Wales is the heir to the throne. The future King of this country would have served first as our Governor-General, and thus have seen the view of the world from the windows of Yarralumla as well as from those of

Buckingham Palace. This might not only have been to our advantage in how the monarch sees the world but in how the world see the monarch, as it would have emphasised the affiliations of the monarchy with realms other than Britain; in particular, Australia. Prince Charles' personal history and abilities weighed in favour of this. In his youth he was educated for a time in this country, as a schoolboy at Geelong Grammar. Commissioning him as Governor-General would therefore have been an extension of his existing association with Australia, in addition to serving as a link of goodwill between our country and Great Britain. The high esteem in which he was held by many Australians at the time — particularly rural Australians — would have ensured that the commission would have been a popular one.

The choice of the 1983 Adelaide Constitutional Convention, held by the newly-elected Hawke government following Fraser's defeat at the polls, was to decide against such an appointment. This was done in a motion debated on the afternoon of Wednesday the 27th of April 1983.[67] Intended to serve as a convention for future governments, it stated in part: "Appointments to the office of Governor-General are made from Australian citizens with back-grounds relevant to the constitutional responsibilities of the office."[68] Although not legally binding in any way, it was intended to entrench existing practice with regards to the viceregal position by stating such a practice formally, rendering future violation unlikely. Delegates from Queensland, who were in favour of the appointment of Prince Charles, objected to this and other "Practices" in the motion.[69] Senator Gareth Evans defended the motion, arguing that the resolution excluded the possibility of appointing the Prince of Wales or future members of the Royal Family for a number of reasons.

> It is not a matter of anyone having any lack of respect or affection for the Prince of Wales or a belief as to his capacity to perform the job. It is not a matter necessarily of any lack of enthusiasm for the Monarchy or for the continued existence of the Crown as the Crown of Australia. Least of all, is it any question of disloyalty that lies under this proposed confining of the positions of future Governors-General to Australian citizens. Rather, it is simply an affirmation of Australian citizenship and Australian nationhood that is involved in this particular proposal.[70]

Its adoption by the Convention ruled out the future appointment of Prince Charles or other members of the Royal Family to the viceregal post.

It doesn't require a Richelieu to realise that, had the Prince of Wales become our viceregal Head of State — or even had he simply been resident within our country — it's quite possible that at least one heir to the throne, namely the young Prince Henry, could have been either born or at least raised upon Australian soil. The recent royal marriage two years previous must still have been fresh in the memories of the delegates in Adelaide. It's difficult to believe that the issue of the heir escaped the scope of their deliberations. History has revealed circumstances whereby a King is succeeded by his brother: James II succeeded Charles II in 1685, due to the absence of legitimate children to the older brother, and George VI became King in 1936 following the abdication of his older brother Edward VIII (later Duke of Windsor). It is entirely conceivable that King William V may be succeeded by his brother as King Henry IX, in which case within two generations a British-born Queen might have been succeeded by an Australian-raised King to sit upon the thrones of the United Kingdom, Australia and His Majesty's other realms and territories. That this cannot now occur is due to a deliberate forfeiture by our elected leaders, yet many of those who now complain of a foreign Queen applauded the measures taken which prevented the possibility of an Australian King. It would seem that some people are never satisfied.

Already there is reason enough to reject the assertion of the "incompatibility" of a "foreign" monarch with a multicultural Australia. Our form of the Westminster system contains mechanisms that render it attractive to any country committed to the preservation of parliamentary democracy, irrespective of ethnicity. When such a political system already exists as part of our heritage, a flourishing cultural diversity provides no genuine incentive to change. The enriched political experience provided by multiculturalism may indeed serve to strengthen the support for our current Constitution, a support I have witnessed first-hand, having had the honour to campaign alongside Greek- and Italian-Australian monarchists. Yet even if we entertain this assertion of "incompatibility", we see that it demands a number of questions.

Is it that a multicultural Australia has room for the foreign-born in every capacity except as our Queen, or is it that the architects of the Oz Republic will allow every culture except the British cultures that provided the genesis of non-aboriginal Australia? One must question the sincerity with which the self-ordained bishops of the Republic incorporate multiculturalism into their creed, when the phrase "foreign-born" is employed to be derogatory of the Queen. It gives cause to wonder whether the true motivating passion is indeed love of foreign-born cultural diversity, or merely dislike of Britain, for which the existence of other ethnic groups in this country is being exploited. For those of us who enjoy cultural diversity and wish this country to take an internationalist — as distinct from and opposite to a nationalist — stance, the Crown is a desirable international symbol of commonwealth, able to reflect in a single elegant symbol both British and multicultural Australia, through a British-born Queen being represented by an Australian Governor-General of non-British ancestry. Clearly not only is the Crown compatible with a culturally and ethically diverse Australia, it could be employed to reflect both our past and present more elegantly than any president could.

Niccolò's ghost   [*Stirs restlessly in his chair.*] **So you're asserting** [*ticking off on his fingers*] **one**: the Queen is Queen of Australia, and you're arguing over the future of the Australian

Crown, not the British. *Two*, the Governor-General can fulfil the entire presidential job description demanded by the republicans (and more besides), and *three*, more sense can be found on a Swedish postage stamp than in the ARM's speeches on a "Head of State". But so far in all your ponderings on national symbolism, you've been arguing by refuting negative claims of incompatibility, rather than proposing any comprehensive reason why your country (or any other) would actively want to retain the monarchy or its symbols. Does one exist? One that embraces the rest of the world, rather than just nodding to it? For instance, can you justify the continued existence of this commonwealth of countries in the 21st Century, rather than disbanding it in favour of more recent associations?

> The Commonwealth is not against anyone; it is a source of common sense in the world where that quality is sadly lacking. It cannot negotiate on behalf of the world, but it can caution the world and help it to negotiate. The more the Commonwealth preserves its coherence across the oceans and continents, the better for all — including my own country.[71]
>
> Dr Richard von Weizsacker, President of the Federal Republic of Germany, 1987.

Realm Against Realm

History is littered with the debris of faded treaties and extinct alliances, outworn oaths once solemnly sworn now remembered only by the elderly in their cups. Tacit in the republican debate is the assumption that the [British] Commonwealth of Nations is destined soon for the same fate as the Hanseatic League or the Holy Roman Empire, confined to the pages of a history book. But is this belief valid? Seeking the answer requires understanding what the Commonwealth is, does and may become.

Constructed from out of the former British Empire, the Commonwealth is a free association of independent sovereign countries which, unlike its Imperial predecessor, exists neither to perpetuate some sort of British hegemony nor is founded upon the interests of trade. Spanning countries from the First to the Third World, it's founded on a mutual heritage of language, experience and institutions. Member countries engage in an exchange of scholars and civil servants and offer one another assistance in matters from education to agriculture, including — if needs be — police and military assistance. But the relationship runs somewhat deeper.

Australia has neither an embassy nor an ambassador in London, nor has the United Kingdom these appendages in Canberra. Neither has either country either formality in New Delhi, Ottawa, Karachi, Wellington or any other capital of approximately fifty countries. All countries of the world send ambassadors to foreign counterparts and build embassies to house them in, but as an explicit rejection of this notion of being mutually foreign, Commonwealth countries employ neither in their relationships with one another, preferring instead to send High Commissioners housed in their host's capital in High Commissions. Traditionally High Commissioners enjoy privileges denied ambassadors: instead of communicating through the host's Foreign Minister they have a traditional right of access directly to its Prime Minister. This rejection of foreignness has nothing to do with ethnic statistics; Valetta wasn't accorded an Australian High Commissioner through any stipulation of the percentage of Maltese in the Australian community, but through fellow membership of this international community. Consequently this mutual courtesy between Australia and Malta (and Canada and Greek Cyprus and so on) based upon a shared heritage needn't be endangered by multiculturalism. It may indeed be strengthened by an ethnically diverse society now drawn in part from these countries.

Within the Commonwealth a division exists between those countries and peoples who identify strongly with this community and those who don't. In previous decades some have attempted to define it using race, by referring to the "white" and the "black" Commonwealths, assuming that people whose ancestries were drawn from the history producing the common heritage would feel more closely bound by that trait than those who had this heritage imposed upon them. Not only has this attempt an unpleasantly racist flavour, in the personal experience of the author it is also simply wrong. A better way of drawing the line would be to observe how a country and its citizens treat the institutions and emblems of that common heritage, to define an "inner" and "outer" Commonwealth based upon the extent to which nationalism or allegiance to some other external association has triumphed over this sense of community. The most obvious litmus test, most obvious institution and symbol is the monarchy and its occupant: Queen Elizabeth II, Head of the Commonwealth and independently Queen of sixteen realms.

The strongest argument for demolition of these monarchies is the assertion that they somehow hinder the operation of the sixteen realms as independent sovereign countries; that the Crown makes awkward the expression of tensions and rivalries created by modern trade alliances. Run first with the republican assumption that these modern alliances find no expression in partnerships among the sixteen realms; that they're made with foreign countries unlikely to be patient with our historical ties. Contemplate then the situation where modern interests bring us into conflict with another of Her Majesty's realms.

Consider tensions between two such realms with bipartite Crowns, provoked over trade or territory. Imagine a scenario inspired by recent tensions nearby, whereby territory belonging to the fictitious realm of Melsapap, including a valuable copper mine, is in a state of armed insurrection. The insurgents have an affinity with neighbouring Polynea and allegedly flee across the waters separating the two countries when pursued by Melsapapean soldiers or police; once in Polynean waters they're safely beyond the jurisdiction of their pursuers. Undermanned and under-equipped, the Royal Polynean Police Force is unable to monitor the entire coastline and consequently cannot prevent small-scale incursions. Frustrated by perceived inaction on the part of the Polynean authorities, Melsapapean forces cross over into the other country's sovereign territory in pursuit of wanted insurgents, provoking a sharp diplomatic rebuke. Replying from his capital city, the Melsapapean Prime Minister states that his forces shall continue to take whatever measures necessary to protect his own country's sovereignty. Aggrieved, the Polynean Prime Minister responds by establishing refugee camps to provide a haven for people fleeing the crisis; anti-Melsapap insurgents use these camps, providing as they do food, shelter and medical aid to all comers, as bases from which to launch further strikes against Melsapap's forces. Tensions escalate.

Niccolò's ghost How does any of this differ from an international crisis between any other countries?

Author Overtly, it doesn't — that's just the point.

Although both countries have Elizabeth II as their Queen, each holds in its Governor-General a distinctively national viceregal Head of State who, acting upon ministerial advice, may express the national interest to the world. Thus (in our hypothetical scenario) the viceregal representative of Queen Elizabeth II of Polynea may, upon the advice of his Prime Minister, denounce the aggression of Melsapap, whose Queen's representative may retaliate on the advice of his Prime Minister by deploring the complicity of the other country in recent insurgent attacks upon his country.

But advantages for both countries being Her Majesty's realms in the Commonwealth are there beneath the surface. Commonwealth membership for both doesn't preclude friction (even outright war, as witness India and Pakistan) but it means that the traditional right of access of High Commissioners to the Prime Ministers can be employed to full effect, for each protagonist communicating its views directly to the head of the opposite government and for other member States to express their disquiet. The advantages of both being Her Majesty's realms, rather than republics, are more tangible in their private and public aspects. The Queen possesses formal rights of consultation with her other governments throughout the world analogous to those in a British context, "to be consulted, to encourage and to warn". In reality the fact her powers are exercised on her behalf in these realms by her Governors-General renders royal consultations virtually pointless under normal circumstances. However if two of her realms appear on a collision course to war she has both a right and a duty to intercede privately with both Prime Ministers, urging a more peaceful resolution of the problem. Similarly she may communicate privately with her representatives to express her doubts. But if the Prime Minister and the Governor-General on each side are in accord over their nation's interests, she can do nothing more. The Prime

Minister of a realm may advise the Governor-General to declare war in the name of Queen Elizabeth II, Queen of the realm, and he shall do so despite Her Majesty's private and vehement protests, even to declaring war upon one of her other realms.

Niccolò's ghost	Couldn't she command her representatives not to declare war?
Author	Certainly not. Although Governors and Governors-General are Her Majesty's representatives they are not her agents. They're distinguished citizens of the particular realm, acting on the advice of the realm's government.

Without the advice and support of that government's ministers she cannot compel, merely attempt privately to persuade. But she's in a unique position to attempt persuasion, occupying a unique symbolic office within each country and endowed with a supra-national authority as royal Head of State of many countries. Able to act privately as a mediator whose authority and good will to both parties is acknowledged, the limitations set upon her office prevent her from endangering their national sovereignty or thwarting their determined wills.

Niccolò's ghost	But wouldn't the British government interfere with this mediation, perhaps preferring one country to go to war with another if it suits its own national interests? Wouldn't it therefore insist upon her following its own scripted agenda?
Author	In this scenario Elizabeth II would be acting in her capacity as Queen of Melsapap and Queen of Polynea; British ministers have no more authority to compel her actions in her other realms than they have to compel those of Margrethe II as Queen of Denmark.

Because this mediation is behind closed doors, not involving any public act, it's neither embarrassing to the British government nor would require ministerial responsibility, any more than her private conversations with her British Prime Minister require anyone to take formal responsibility. And finally, whatever agenda the British government chooses to follow it can pursue using its own diplomats and servants. If it desires Her Majesty to make a public statement on its behalf as Queen of the United Kingdom she would of course do so; if this involves conflict with her private views expressed in mediation overseas, she can easily emphasise that this public statement is (like most other speeches she makes) of the views of her British government. Obviously she has a particular duty to the United Kingdom as its solitary Head of State to express in her public words and actions British interests, but for one skilled in diplomacy there's little difficulty in reconciling this public role with that of private mediator in rare crises among her other realms.

When in one of her other realms, her speeches and actions are performed there under the advice of her local ministers.[†] It's conceivable that they would take advantage of her presence to send a strong international signal: for example, when in New Zealand her relevant ministers may ask her to deliver a speech expressing their abhorrence of French nuclear testing in the Pacific, in stark contrast to the views of her British ministers. But she lives in Britain and must return there; an embarrassing contrast in the stances of the two countries might perhaps be better handled by the Governor-General of New Zealand, representing her, delivering the speech in Her Majesty's presence and that of the international Press. Either way, notice that the strength of the message is due in part to the fact it isn't delivered in a nationalist manner. Instead it's one parliamentary democracy using symbols it shares with another to say "We have much in common in our heritage and our faith in parliamentary institutions, and *because* of our fellowship this issue that divides us must be given urgent consideration". It's a much more civilised way of expressing dissent between nations than by burning flags or effigies in the streets.

Beyond the human occupying the throne other related symbols and ceremonies held in common among these realms serve a purpose, in rendering absurd the idea of (say) Her Majesty's Melsapapean forces going to war against Her Majesty's Polynean forces, without physically impeding this process. An institution that can make war among parliamentary democracies ridiculous without hindering any country's actual capacity to defend itself is rare and valuable to human society; this very aspect detested by nationalists among us holds the admiration of more enlightened observers like von Weizsacker. Given the geographical groupings of Her Majesty's realms throughout the world (Australia, for instance, has as immediate neighbours New Zealand, Papua New Guinea and the Solomon Islands, with Tuvalu, the Cook Islands and Niue not far away), this is an asset to our peace it would be stupid to destroy.[‡]

A vivid illustration of the strength of this international symbolism was provided in 1995 over the so-called "Turbot War" between Canadian coastguard vessels and Spanish fishing trawlers off Newfoundland waters, whereby

---

† Obviously they can't advise her in terms of her other Crowns, only in terms of their own realm's. So New Zealand ministers can't advise her to do anything, say, under the British Crown, but only under the New Zealand Crown.

‡ This potential of the modern Crown as an inhibitor of conflict was recognised in the dying days of the British Raj in India, in a somewhat different form. Confronted with the emergence of two independent countries bitterly estranged on religious and ethnic grounds, and given that the two new countries of India and Pakistan (remember the latter then consisted of what's now modern Pakistan and modern Bangladesh) would initially be, like Australia or New Zealand, independent parliamentary democracies with bipartite Crowns, Jawarharlal Nehru suggested that the Governor-Generalships of India and of Pakistan should be held by the same person. This official, representing the Head of State of either country, would then have

Canadian sailors boarded the Spanish vessels and cut their nets in anger at apparent violations of accepted international fishing practices; violations that would destroy fish stocks. Spain responded by sending warships to patrol off Canadian waters, leading to a tense naval standoff. At the same time the two countries were eyeballing each other in the North Atlantic, pro-European figures in London denounced this so-called "act of piracy". In reply, the Cornish fishing fleet declared its own allegiance graphically, with vessels putting to sea flying the Canadian ensign; a pro-Commonwealth demonstration[†] that echoed British public sentiment, obliging members of the British Parliament eventually to side tacitly with Ottawa against Madrid and European hostility. As reported in one British newspaper,

> Fishermen in Newlyn, Cornwall,…are flying Canadian Maple
> Leaf flags — flown over after a media appeal — from their
> boats…Each time British MPs have signalled their support
> there has been a sigh of satisfaction. [Canadian newspapers]
> reprint editorials and Hansard reports to show that Canada's
> forefathers have not forgotten them.[72]

London's veto scuttled proposed EU sanctions against Canada, leading to a Canadian victory over the dispute. Listening to the BBC World Service from Germany I heard a British official in Gibraltar grumbling at the initial chill in relations between Spain and the Crown Colony following the incident; Spanish officials were warily waiting to see how many of Her Majesty's other governments throughout the world would declare for Canada.[73]

And yet these ties of sentiment leave unbound our deliberate acts of will. We could, if we chose, declare unstinting hostilities upon another realm of Elizabeth II and show in favour of its enemies, boycotting its exports, banning its citizens and denouncing its government in the forums of the world. We could be belligerent enough in every particular of foreign policy to dispel all doubt in the hearts of foreign onlookers and bring a smile to the lips of the dourest nationalist. Our ambassadors throughout the world are paid already to state our distinctive stances and clarify our policies to other eyes, and if we wish to remove all traces of ambiguity we could send our Governor-General overseas as well.

---

constitutional access to both governments and be titular commander-in-chief of both sets of armed forces, thus able to act as a mediator in times of conflict and rendering warfare between the two at least symbolically absurd. Under this plan the first person to have held the dual seat was to have been Lord Louis Mountbatten, who as the final Viceroy had already held the formal allegiance of the army from which the two armies were to be drawn, would be neutral in Hindu-Muslim feuds, and was himself widely respected on both sides. The plan failed when vetoed by one of Pakistan's independence leaders, Mohammed Ali Jinnah, who insisted on being his country's first Governor-General (it later transpired he was dying of tuberculosis and, understandably, wanted to be Pakistan's viceregal Head of State before he died). Mountbatten went on to be independent India's first Governor-General. India became a republic soon after. (See Lapping, *End of Empire*, pp. 87–90.)

† The demonstration cut deeper than the issue at hand: had it been Spanish sailors cutting Canadian nets over violations it's most unlikely the Cornish vessels would have put to sea flying the Spanish ensign.

All this has been based upon the assumption that ties no stronger than heritage and symbolism would bind the sixteen realms, that in every other respect their regional and trading interests would be disparate and conflicting. But in the 1990s that assumption, so apparently prophetic in the '70s, looks decidedly shaky. We've been told we live in a time in which Australia shall and should look entirely to Asia, and Britain, entirely to Europe. Entering a century in which ease of global transport is unparalleled in human history, suddenly we are taught to think ourselves constrained by geography in a way never experienced by our ancestors in their wooden ships.

When travelling across Germany in 1995 there was nowhere I couldn't buy New Zealand apples. Every greengrocer from Munich to Hanover seemed to stock them proudly, and it wasn't only this homesick Antipodean who enjoyed the seductive fruit of the Land of the Long White Cloud. But every time I bit into one I felt like a modern Adam: guilty and enlightened. Where were their Tasmanian counterparts? Why did I never see the fruit of Australian orchards being bought by German housewives with their eco-friendly shopping bags and their eager Deutschemarks? The wineshops of Germany are filled with the weary juice of downtrodden grapes, row upon row of overpriced and mediocre bottles not only from within the European Union but imported from beyond its borders. No German I spoke to was even aware Australia produces wine, let alone had tasted the genius of our vineyards. It seems hardly sensible to neglect this marketplace of millions.

Conversely, until the recent worldwide collapse in emerging markets Britain was looking to Asia for investment and trade, and to a renewed relationship with Australia to facilitate this. In 1989, as part of the first full-scale visit to Australia by a British Prime Minister since Macmillan's 1957 visit, Margaret Thatcher advocated a trading, investment, political and diplomatic renaissance between Australia and Britain, declaring "We want to step up our contacts at every level with Australia, including more regular ministerial visits…let us increase our contacts as two strong, proud, independent successful nations each with its own specific contribution to make."[74] Thatcher's Minister of State for the Foreign and Commonwealth Office, Lord Brabazon of Tara, argued that mutual advantage lay in this renaissance for both countries:

> [F]or Britain, the advantage of a close partnership with a
> stable, friendly, like-minded country situated near the fast
> developing Asian Pacific Rim; for Australia, the advantage of
> having a leading member of the Western alliance and the
> European Community as interlocuteur.[75]

He argued that this reversal of the post-war trend of each country ignoring the other in favour of concentrating upon its regional ties was a renunciation of the former quasi-colonial relationship between them; that the proposed re-invigorated relationship was a recognition of the contemporary imperatives of the 1990's for both Britain and Australia to maintain global interests, rather than being hedged in by provincial interests. Enthusiastically supported by then-Prime Minister Bob Hawke, the co-equal nature of this new relationship was illustrated by the 1988 ministerial talks in London between senior Cabinet ministers of the two countries, talks that, in Brabazon's words, "resembled the summits which the UK now holds with its major European partners".[76] At the same time as these talks, an Australia-Britain Trade and Investment Conference was held in London, addressed by the two Prime Ministers and attended by about 150 business leaders from each country.[77]

Although Mr Hawke's successor appeared to do nothing positive for it, investment figures during his term pointed to an existing, albeit invisible, axis between the two countries. In 1994 the *Financial Times* noted that Australian investment in Britain had soared to almost A$16 billion (£7.4 billion), making Britain "the biggest single offshore home for Australian investment", Australia being "the fourth largest overseas investor in the UK".[78] A report by the Allen Consulting Group revealed that this investment, representing about 35% of our country's offshore direct investment, was "eight times more than could be expected from the size of the UK economy".[79] In turn "Britain is the second largest investor in Australia, although only 7 per cent of its offshore direct investment goes in this direction".[80]

An even stronger case than Brabazon's for pursuit of this political and trading axis was provided by Professor Katharine West at the Institute of Commonwealth Studies, University of London. Despite the fact her proposal has been put on ice for now by the 1998 global slump in emerging markets and Asian currencies, both her particular suggestion and its underlying reasoning are worth considering for the future. In 1994 she remarked,

> Whatever the British Government's political preoccupation with the EU, the balance of British trade is tilting heavily away from Europe. Indeed, the Oxford Economic Forecasting Group claims Britain's trade with China and the Pacific Rim economies will double well before the end of the century, outstripping the US as a market for British goods. According to the British financial journalist Bill Jamieson, many leading British companies — such as GEC, P&O, Courtalds, Johnson Matthey, Trafalgar, and BOC Group — expect that, by the end of the century, the China and Pacific Rim economies will account for between 20 per cent and 30 per cent of their company turnover.[81]

As further evidence for British engagement beyond Europe, she noted that over the last ten years more than three-quarters of its direct investment and (in 1993) an even greater proportion of its portfolio investment were invested outside the European Community (EC); similarly, in 1992 although 56% of Britain's visible exports went to EC countries, only 45% of total British exports went there, as 65% of her "invisible" exports again were sent to destinations beyond Europe. In 1993 the EC's share of total British trade was even lower, leading Professor West to state "While Britain's political face remains turned to Europe, its economic feet are striding elsewhere, notably to the Asia-Pacific region".[82]

She argued that British companies would employ traditional Commonwealth links — in particular, Australia — to pursue this agenda, because of a shared "Commonwealth business culture", based on shared English language, legal, administrative, accountancy and financial practices, following Professor Samuel Huntingdon's adage that "close economic cooperation normally requires a common cultural base".[83] Or as Professor Dennis Austin put it in 1988,

> The value of the Commonwealth connection arises when there
> is a coincidence of interests, and when friendly assumptions,
> based on language and practice, help to facilitate relationships...
> Most businessmen will admit to a preference for markets where
> English is spoken and the legal system is familiar.[84]

Although tarnished by the recent economic crisis, the long-term prospects of the Asia-Pacific region remain good, and Australia's own political and economic stability in the face of that collapse has illustrated our value as a safe regional headquarters. More importantly, this new vision of diversified trade across the globe's regions, taking advantage of shared cultural links to create trade axes and exploit market opportunities, remains sound. No region is immune from some form of economic crisis from time to time; if the abstract political arguments proposed in this book are applied to the EU's flawed political structure, even Europe's future can be seen to be somewhat troubled.[†] So what? Even as private investors are always warned never to put all their eggs in one basket, so too should countries diversify their interests, and the Commonwealth provides a worldwide means of doing so, ready-made. In an earlier century the world was divided by Papal decree into two spheres, one to be dominated by imperial Spain and the other, by imperial Portugal. The myth of this domination was exploded by the audacity of smaller maritime powers determined that no chart less than a globe should define their mercantile interests. Confronted by "Europe", "Asia" and "North America" the time has come again for audacity, this time by traders and investors moving through a community of countries that spans the globe. Currency crises come and go, but the world remains, and so does our need to trade across its seas.

Some would regard a mercantile renaissance of British-Australian relations as prostitution on our part. Isn't Britain the country that betrayed us thirty years ago: destroyed our traditional markets, revoked our British passports, stripped

---

† More precisely, it's easy to see federal Europe is likely to collapse within the span of the 21st Century, in a backlash of virulent neo-nationalism. The Eurocracy — the supra-national hierarchies of bureaucrats in Brussels, Strasbourg and elsewhere, administering the EU and its directives — is far too powerful, too unaccountable and too rigid for its own survival. Its malaise is exacerbated every time a fresh country is incorporated into the Union, increasing the complexity of the society to be governed, and hence shortening the polity's lifespan further. The recent anti-EU fishing protests and farmers' pickets, truckdrivers' blockades and rallies of the unemployed, are not transient phenomena. A Lord Chief Justice of England outlined the essential danger in the 1920s; see *Epilogue*.

us of our right to work there even as it precipitately withdrew its troops from East of Suez, leaving our defences looking naked but for the intervention of the United States? Hasn't Britain already displayed enough treachery to its formerly kindred countries throughout the world, selling them down the river for the sake of Europe? Like most other Australians and New Zealanders, I cannot enter or leave the United Kingdom without feeling systematically insulted by the British Government. Historically our countries proved fiercely loyal to Britain, our citizens volunteering to fight to defend her interests in wars throughout the world. In 1939 we were proud to stand alongside her, declaring war on the Third Reich and its Axis partners. In 1941, when the rest of the world had fallen into darkness or still hid in neutrality and the British Commonwealth stood alone against the Axis powers we held the line, preferring extinction at the hands of Hitler's forces rather than deserting to make a separate peace.[†] Yet within fifty years of what Sir Winston Churchill described collectively as our "finest hour" at the Battle of Britain, holders of Australian or New Zealand passports arriving in Britain are classified as "Other" in the Immigration queues, and treated as undesirables. Young Commonwealth citizens are granted (once only) the dubious honour of working in desultory and menial jobs for up to a year in a holiday visa; no longer is permitted, for fear we may occupy jobs — any jobs — "better" granted to continental Europeans. Heathrow and Gatwick teach an apparent lesson, that Britain betrays her most loyal allies within two generations. We didn't abandon them at Dunkirk, but they abandoned us at Brussels. And the British probably don't even realise they impose this conclusion upon everyone who sets foot on their soil.

Little wonder that even relatively moderate voices, mistakenly equating our Crown with Britain, have denounced Australian monarchism as a betrayal of our national interests, a Fifth Column topped with a Crown. But their indignation is flawed. The *Australian* Crown is not merely a bilateral emblem linking our country with Britain, but a multilateral one linking us with an international community, with New Zealand and Canada and the rest. Repudiation of it isn't merely a rejection of links with Britain, but of our mutual ties with all these countries. Irrespective of Britain, both New Zealand and Canada have remained our close and loyal friends. On the floor of the UN General Assembly we informally belong together in the so-called "CANZ Bloc" — Canada-Australia-New-Zealand — standing up as middle-ranking powers, multicultural parliamentary democracies with a shared heritage. Why be ashamed of an emblem we share with these two?

Even denouncing British treachery is a little premature. For a start, blaming the Queen for the actions of her British ministers is a weird inversion of constitutional reality. She's hardly to blame if, say, Sir Edward Heath acted disgracefully. And if we want to underline our independence from England, it's hardly clever to destroy our own independent arrangements with the Queen

† The option was there: the Irish Free State was neutral throughout World War II, and the Union of South Africa contemplated neutrality.

in the name of thumbing our noses at English politicians; the opposite signal would be sent, that actions in London can excite us to respond regardless of our own self-interest. But more importantly, has Whitehall's behaviour constituted "treachery"? And even if Whitehall's corridors of power are populated with nasty people, does their misconduct translate as "British" treachery, the sort to inspire us to strike off all insignia in common?

When, on a drizzling March day in 1995, the author suggested to diplomats in Whitehall that Britain's behaviour had engendered a sense of betrayal, they were incredulous and somewhat offended. It is an obvious truism that any Australian politician who dared suggest that in the event of a war we could expect British military support or aid would be ridiculed off the podium; but this remark, so mundane here, was viewed as bizarre there. Had the interview taken place a few days earlier it probably would have been dismissed outright. Fortunately a copy of a New Zealand defence newspaper had found its way into the building a few days beforehand; one of its columnists had remarked casually that the UK could no longer be trusted as a reliable ally, eliciting the kind of shocked disbelief of a dowager confronted by a condom. The fact that throughout the Cold War — particularly after its troops precipitately pulled out of their Asian bases — London failed to provide any formal commitment to uphold Australian or New Zealand territorial integrity, despite Washington's signing of the ANZUS treaty, close attention from the White House and the perceived Communist threat, was seen as immaterial.

They were unaware that London's actions had led even the conservative Holt Cabinet to write off the British as an ally, confirmed in the 1967 Cabinet papers. They were innocent of the perception of Britain widely held after the "winds of change" and before the Falklands War: of a diminished country that lacked even the backbone or integrity to defend its own territories and citizens elsewhere in the world, of a country obsessed with Europe and its relationship with the United States. (How else did they think Argentina believed it could get away with invading the Falklands?) The diplomats' reply was that formal treaties are necessary only among nations where formal expression of commitment is demanded, a natural understanding being absent; and that such kindred countries as Britain, Australia and New Zealand had no need of such artifices, being so closely tied by history, blood, language and outlook that the UK's loyalty and commitment to us were "obvious".

Obvious? After our traditional markets have been destroyed, our trading rivals favoured over us, our citizens banned from working? After Britain sided with France over nuclear testing in the South Pacific; after the citizens of the country that bombed the *Rainbow Warrior* are free to enter and dwell in the UK while New Zealanders and Australians are treated as foreigners? The diplomats and I stared at one another in mutual bafflement: they, that I could dare suggest a widespread sense that we'd been sold down the river; I, that professional diplomats could think they understood our world view while failing to grasp something so obvious. At this height of Keating's anti-British rhetoric, one of the two men sitting opposite me said he thought Anglo-

Australian relations were as good as ever; as evidence, he said, consider the British dance troupe invited to tour Down Under. I sourly contemplated this new-look diplomacy. Presumably if bilateral relations had deteriorated further they would have sent in an entire *corps-de-ballet*.

Sitting in that dimly-lit office while the rain fell in the street outside, an image of Foreign Office policy took shape in my mind's eye; of an over-ambitious juggler convinced of his ability to keep many balls aloft simultaneously. Performing before an audience, he tosses ball after brightly-coloured ball into the air, his hands moving rapidly. But so rapt is he at his own virtuosity, he barely notices he's dropped a ball; it sits ignobly on the ground, apparent to all but its handler. Another falls…and another. And when he finishes and takes his bows, instead of the applause he expected, the audience is unimpressed. Some even jeer. And the bewildered juggler has no idea why. Insular post-colonial self-delusion, rather than deliberate treachery, underlies London's botching of its relations with its former Commonwealth allies: a belief that neglected alliances don't wither, that kinships can be ignored without giving offence, and that the silence of our expatriates indicates no problem exists, when it really means the insult's so obvious we think it tasteless to mention in polite conversation.

Yet the Cornish fishermen have succeeded where Whitehall has failed, in providing a tangible gesture of solidarity. The Newlyn fishing trawlers flying the Canadian flag are eloquent reminders of the distinction between official policy and the opinions of the ordinary British people. Their influence over government policy as the "Turbot War" unfolded and Downing Street realised ordinary voters sympathised with Canada rather than Europe cannot be ignored. Our countries have been wronged by individual British politicians, not by the British people, and the British Crown symbolises the latter. Attacking this emblem misses the proper object of our anger. Indeed, by maintaining our links to the Queen we are able to lobby someone with the constitutional right to express our concerns to the British Prime Minister in private audience. He may ignore her comments — his fault, not hers — but surely her position in London makes her one of our greatest assets, not a liability, particularly considering our future interests throughout the world. Our problem with London is one of communication. If our diplomats are being ignored by Whitehall, our premiers and prime ministers, governors and governors-general should be expressing our grievances in their private *communiqués* to the Palace. We need to use the Palace *more*, not less. In cutting our private hotline to the Queen, we defeat ourselves.

In a surreal touch of bread and circuses, the ARM have repeatedly insisted we must strike off the monarchy in time for the Sydney Olympic Games; more specifically, in time for its opening ceremony. They've elevated an obscure bye-law in the IOC rules outlining the procedure for the Opening Ceremony to the status of holy writ: subsection 1.1 of an unnumbered bye-law to Rule 69 states "The Olympic Games shall be proclaimed open by the Head of State of the host country", *therefore* (according to republican sources) the Queen or a member of her family has to open the Games…and this will be terribly shameful and reveal us to be "something less of a nation" to the rest of the world. Changing your polity for the sake of the Games is perhaps taking sport a little *too* seriously (although while we're at it, why not go all the way and declare ourselves a nation of team players: have the Games opened by a *junta*?). It's too easy a shot to point out in reply that the Montreal Olympics were opened by the Queen of Canada, while the Calgary Olympics were opened by the Canadian Governor-General. Better to raise our eyes slightly to Rule 69 itself, to rebut Mr Turnbull's odious assertion at its source. Rule 69, on which the controversial passage above was tacked as an afterthought, declares (s.1) "The opening and closing ceremonies…should reflect and portray the humanistic principles of Olympism and contribute to their spread".[85] What humanistic principles? Why, the ones that inspired Pierre de Coubertin to found the modern Olympics in 1894, its goal being "to place everywhere sport at the service of the harmonious development of man, with a view to encouraging the establishment of a peaceful society concerned with the preservation of human dignity. To this effect, the Olympic Movement engages…in actions to promote peace", to "contribute to building a peaceful and better world by educating youth through sport practiced without discrimination of any kind and in the Olympic spirit, which requires mutual understanding with a spirit of friendship, solidarity and fair play".[86] As von Weiszacker and others have noted, the Commonwealth already represents a kindred spirit in the world: "the more [it] preserves its coherence across the oceans and continents, the better for all — including my own country [Germany]". And within the Commonwealth its principle glory, its supra-national emblem of community, kinship and parliamentary democracy, is the Crown.

The greatest test of strength the Olympic Games offers to individuals and countries alike is neither weightlifting nor discus but the moral strength to reject nationalism. Many countries participating in the Games fail this test in their daily transactions with the outside world. In our country individuals like Turnbull have already failed. The challenge is whether Australia itself will pass the test, as a country truly worthy to be inheritor of the Olympic spirit. Rejoicing in Her Majesty's position as Queen of many realms is a sign of our success, a more profound embracing of a "spirit of friendship, solidarity and fair play" than most countries can show; rejecting her as Queen of another country shall be itself ignominious failure of the Games' most important trial. Having the Queen open our Games may, in the eyes of nationalists, make us "something less of a nation"; but in the eyes of the more enlightened, it makes us a great deal more as a country.

> Then Snowball (for it was Snowball who was
> best at writing) took a brush between the two
> knuckles of his trotter, painted out MANOR
> FARM from the top bar of the gate and in its
> place painted ANIMAL FARM. This was to be
> the name of the farm from now onwards. After
> this they went back to the farm buildings, where
> Snowball and Napoleon sent for a ladder which
> they caused to be set against the end wall of the
> big barn. They explained that by their studies of
> the past three months the pigs had succeeded
> in reducing the principles of Animalism to seven
> commandments. These seven commandments
> would now be inscribed on the wall; they would
> form an unalterable law by which all the animals
> on Animal Farm must live forever after. With
> some difficulty (for it is not easy for a pig to
> balance himself on a ladder) Snowball climbed
> up and set to work, with Squealer a few rungs
> below him holding the paint-pot.
>
> George Orwell, *Animal Farm.*

■■■

At first glance the topic of a declaration of rights and that of the existence and powers of the Crown appear entirely disparate. As argued earlier, crudely speaking, the reserve powers of the Crown are a safeguard against abuses in the substance and distribution of power, whereas a declaration of rights is intended to be a safeguard against abusive *expressions* of power manifested against citizens. Yet three important links connect these two concerns.

The first rests in an observation made earlier, that the distinction between these two forms of abuse is an imprecise one with no clear line of demarcation. Some abuses can be dealt with by invoking the reserve powers but not by appeal to a declaration of rights upheld by the judiciary. Others may be remedied by the latter institution but not the former. But what of those abuses which may be opposed by resort to the reserve powers *or* by appeal to a judiciary interpreting an enshrined declaration? An overlap certainly exists, obliging us to pause and consider how we view such a document.

The second link is one of political principle. Enshrined declarations of particular rights are (at least in the public mind) intended to uphold these rights of the citizens against attack by their government. As we shall see, it's dubious whether such declarations actually achieve this noble objective, yet it's certain they severely compromise the sovereignty of the people — and perhaps destroy it. Elected government becomes supplanted by a judicial aristocracy.

If we could accept permanent, active government by an unaccountable and effectively irremovable handful of figures, on the grounds that they represent an enlightened rule, better understanding our needs and interests than we could possibly understand them ourselves — the usual excuse for entrusting a supreme collection of judges with executive and legislative power beyond the reach of "the tyranny of the majority" or its elected representatives to negate — then that surely opens the door for other oligarchies also to use their supposed enlightenment as a pretext for claiming permanent authority over us, a claim which this entire manifesto rejects and opposes.

The third link is an historical one. During the early stages of the French Revolution Radical dissident groups sprang up throughout Britain, taking their inspiration from contemporary events across the Channel and the recent revolution in the American colonies. A debate broke out over the future of the British monarchy and the Constitution. In a famous book, *Reflections on the Revolution in France*, Edmund Burke defended both monarchy and Constitution. In angry reply the English radical *émigré* Thomas Paine produced the manifesto *Rights of Man*. The debate was followed keenly by the British public: Burke's *Reflections*, released on the 1st November 1790, sold nineteen thousand copies within six months and had gone through eleven editions by September 1791.[87] The *Rights of Man*, part I of which was published on the 16th of March 1791 and part II eleven months later, has been estimated to have sold possibly two hundred and fifty thousand copies within two years.[88] As is the way of most debates, both cases had flaws: Burke was too deferential to the *status quo* and inaccurate in his account of contemporary French events,[89] whereas Paine was almost totally ignorant of history and uncomprehending of the implications of his own doctrines. Yet valuable political principles emerged from both sides of the debate, ideas which remain important today.

Ironically Paine's denunciation of monarchy, the principle theme of his *Rights of Man*, is invalid when applied to modern constitutional monarchy[†] but incomparably eloquent as a denunciation of enshrined declarations of rights. In his work he accuses Burke of describing the Revolution of 1688 and the resulting pact as events in which the people of England bound themselves and their successors for ever to the monarchy, renouncing for eternity any future

---

† His central denunciation of monarchy is its implication of hereditary government. Inasmuch as hereditary government is an absurd notion this argument held validity for his own era, when the King was supposed to be the head of the government and its policies. In the 20th Century Westminster system a constitutional monarch is simply a potent impartial witness to democratic government, not the head of it herself.

A DECLARATION OF "POSITIVE" RIGHTS

right for themselves or their descendants to reject the monarchy and assert a republic.[90] (If Burke did assert such a statement then he was clearly wrong, as the modern experiences of Commonwealth realms in becoming republics illustrates. Provided a constitutionally proper path is walked, a realm can become a republic, and the compact between that Crown and its subjects terminated.) Yet Paine argued further. Assuming Burke's statement to be accurate, he replied,

> The English Parliament of 1688 did a certain thing, which, for themselves and their constituents, they had a right to do, and which it appeared right should be done: But, in addition to this right, which they possessed by delegation, *they set up another right by assumption*, that of binding and controlling posterity until the end of time. The case, therefore, divides itself into two parts; the right which they possessed by delegation, and the right which they set up by assumption. The first is admitted; but, with respect to the second, I reply —
>
> …— Every age and generation must be as free to act for itself, *in all cases*, as the ages and generations which preceded it. The vanity and presumption of governing beyond the grave, is the most ridiculous and insolent of all tyrannies. Man has no property in man; neither has any generation a property in the generations which are to follow. The parliament or the people of 1688, or of any other period, has no more right to dispose of the people of the present day, or to bind or control them in any shape whatever, than the parliament or people of the present day have to dispose of, bind or control those who are to live a hundred or a thousand years hence. Every generation is, and must be, competent to all the purposes to which its occasions require. It is the living, and not the dead, that are to be accomodated. When man ceases to be, his power and his wants cease with him; and having no longer any participation in the concerns of this world, he has no longer any authority in directing who shall be its governors, or how its government shall be organised, or how administered.[91]

This passage fails to refute the essential world view of Burke's *Reflections*, of society as a contract between citizens,

> a partnership in all science; a partnership in all art; a partnership in every virtue…As the ends of such a partnership cannot be obtained in many generations, it becomes a partnership not only between those who are living, but between those who are living, those who are dead, and those who are to be born.[92]

Traditions are a valid expression of that partnership, and are hence intrinsically valuable to a community. Moreover, former generations have a legitimate interest in the welfare of those who come after, even as grandparents possess a legitimate interest in the wellbeing of their grandchildren. Yet when the latter come of age that family interest can no longer be expressed in terms of coercion or compulsion, merely persuasion, which adults are free to choose to ignore. Similarly, earlier generations surely have a right to attempt to persuade a future generation "how its government shall be organised, or how administered", but arguably not to "dispose of, bind or control" it.

How does this fit into a discussion of enshrined rights? Paine himself believed the "rights of men in society, are neither devisable, nor transferable, nor annihilable, but descendable only; and it is not in the power of any generation to intercept finally, and cut off the descent".[93] This is clearly false, for by this argument we would still be caught in the 18th Century: women could never have acquired the *right* to vote, nor could the *right* of a man to dispense with his wife's property have been rescinded, nor the principle which tied the *right* to vote with possession of property have been amended. He says that if "the present generation, or any other, are disposed to be slaves, it does not lessen the right of the successive generation to be free: wrongs cannot have a legal descent."[94] And yet one generation's meat is another generation's poison; as perceptions of wrongs change, so too must the perception of rights change. If it is the right of every generation to be free, so too it must be the right of every generation to be free in defining what freedom *is*, so that perceived wrongs and injustices do not have a legal descent.

Do we dare boast we have at last attained the true Age of Enlightenment, that our moral and ethical philosophies at this instant deserve carving in stone to last a thousand years? Yet if, instead of stone, our rights are to be made on clay, to be re-moulded and shaped by successive generations, then what guarantee have we that members of a particular generation won't ruin entirely the legacy handed down to them, so that their children are delivered into an immutable tyranny without any rights at all? Is it better to have bad "rights" but set in permanent stone, or enlightened ones vulnerable to extinction?

Paine's words awaken considerable doubt whether any particular generation of citizens holds either the right or the moral authority to impose its views upon all future citizens, by codifying a "positive" charter of rights to be enshrined. Yet ignore these concerns, and push on with the task of writing. Immediately we are confronted with a new problem, that of drafting the document itself, composing the sentences for (an admiring) posterity.

What will we say? These are words that shall cast a silhouette over all the actions of future parliaments and future households of our country for centuries to come. Every Act passed by Parliament shall be held up to them for its legality to be decided, every controversial action in the community shall be examined in their shadow. The same attribute which provides the strength of a well-written Constitution renders a badly-written one so dangerous: its permanence. The purpose of including any section, clause or phrase in a written Constitution is to make the law described by those words difficult to alter, by making the words themselves very difficult to alter. Once a sentence is written in, it requires a national referendum with a majority of voters in a majority of states, and a majority of Australians overall, to amend it in any way or blot it out again. Understandably then the original authors of our Constitution were very cautious with what they said in it, restraining themselves to writing terse statements that provide the essential backbone and ribcage of the Federal Commonwealth, leaving the softer organs for the Parliaments, conventions and the common law to define: Cabinet government, ministerial accountability, the respective positions of legislation and common law; the complex myriad of precedents and political forms from which parliamentary democracy is constructed. They were following the British tradition whereby a written Constitution is not seen as a necessary part of a parliamentary democracy, and so where the Constitution, in speaking, might interfere unduly with the traditional role of Parliament, it kept silent. It makes no codified declaration of rights.

For this the Australian Constitution is accused of being "Benthamite"[95]; Jeremy Bentham (1748–1832) was an English lawyer and political philosopher, a contemporary of Paine's who described the passionate 18th Century rhetoric of natural rights as "nonsense upon stilts". As far as Bentham could see, rights exist in a society because they are created and protected by the laws of that society, not because they sprout by some natural process like mushrooms in a paddock.

Unpalatable and deeply unfashionable as it may be to admit it, Bentham was right. Go tell the families of the Chinese dissidents executed in recent years — in the absence of anything worthy of being described as "due process of law", perhaps "murdered" would be a more accurate description — that the People's Republic of China was violating their natural rights when it killed them. Go tell the Burmese dissident Aung San Suu Kyi, in prison or under house arrest for the previous six years until 1995 that during that time she was entitled to the natural rights of freedom of speech and association, or indeed the right to walk out under the open sky. Go tell the Tibetans that the natural right is theirs for self-determination and enjoying their cultural inheritance. It won't stop the Chinese People's Liberation Army from murdering them, forcing abortions on Tibetan women and bulldozing temples, but it's a marvellous way of venting impotent indignation.

We like to say these people possess natural human rights which are being violated because it's much less frightening than admitting that rights of any kind exist only so far as does the political system which enables them to exist. Nature offers no rights apart from that to struggle for survival in a life of "continual fear, and the danger of violent death; and the life of man, solitary, poor, nasty, brutish and short."[†]

---

† In *Leviathan* Hobbes himself stated a belief that in a state of nature every man has a right to everything which may be useful in preserving his own life. It would have been more accurate to say in a state of nature every creature has the right to *attempt* anything useful in reserving his or her own life. If this alternative premise is accepted, Hobbes' thesis on the existence of inalienable natural rights collapses, for his argument was as follows: in a state of nature all humans have a right to everything which may be useful in

Declarations of "inalienable natural human rights" beyond the right to struggle are nothing more than a polite mockery of human experience. They belong to the same profound philosophy as speculation on the existence of Santa Claus: yes, Virginia, so long as there are people who believe in Christmas there will always be a Santa Claus, because then there will be people with the will and the resources to step in to fill in the gap of the Old Fellow's absence and fill up the stockings of their nearest and dearest, so his failure to manifest himself this Christmas will go without serious question in happy tousled heads.

An alternative explanation to quoting Bentham may be given for the absence of any declaration of rights in our written Constitution. In his course of lectures on English law given at Oxford in the early years of the 20th Century, A.V. Dicey remarked that there is "in the English constitution an absence of those declaration or definitions so dear to foreign constitutionalists"[96], for the idea of rights being bestowed from above by a written Constitution was utterly alien to traditional English legal thought, and hence to colonial legislators educated in its schools.

In Dicey's English view, rights exist at a grassroots level. They exist as part of the fabric of the common law, centuries of "mere generalisations drawn either from the decisions or dicta of judges, or from statutes which, being passed to meet special grievances, bear a close relationship to judicial decisions".[97] Consequently,

> the relation of the rights of individuals to the principles of the constitution is not quite the same in countries like Belgium, where the constitution is the result of a legislative act, as it is in England, where the constitution itself is based upon legal decisions. In Belgium...you may say with truth that the rights of individuals to personal liberty flow *from* or are secured *by* the constitution. In England the right to individual liberty *is part of the* [unwritten] *constitution*, because it is secured by the decisions of the courts, extended or confirmed as they are by Habeas Corpus Acts.[98]

The difference in perspective is this:

> The declaration of the Belgian constitution, that individual liberty is 'guaranteed', betrays a way of looking at the rights of individuals very different from the way in which such rights are

---

preserving their own lives; some individual rights are surrendered upon the formation of a society, but those individual rights pertinant to the survival of the individual could never be reasonably regarded as having been surrendered in forming any society, thus these rights are "inalienable". For example, no society can expect its citizens to commit suicide on its behalf, or destroy their own lives. Yet, employing Machiavelli's attitude of *lo stato*, in nature there is no State for any human, no region of imposed control, hence it's as meaningless to say "all humans have a right to everything which may be useful in preserving their own lives" as it is to say "all humans have the right to command the sun to be stationary at noon". Where there is no power to achieve an objective (be it preservation of one's own life, or whatever), it's meaningless to speak of a right to that objective; and if there's no right to begin with, then it's a futile exercise to wonder whether that right was ever subsequently surrendered.

A DECLARATION OF "POSITIVE" RIGHTS

regarded by English lawyers. We can hardly say that one right is more guaranteed than another. Freedom from arbitrary arrest, the right to express one's opinion on all matters subject to the liability to pay compensation for libellous or to suffer punishment for seditious or blasphemous statements, and the right to enjoy one's own property, seem to Englishmen all to rest upon the same basis, namely, on the law of the land.[99]

So in the years before 1901 there were three distinct practical grounds not to write a declaration of rights: the empty nature of "natural rights", the alien notion of fishing some rights from the common law and enshrining them on a constitutional mantelpiece as externally "guaranteed", and the folly of writing metaphysical speculations in indelible ink. But what *harm* can come from these? What actual harm can come, say, from writing indelible metaphysical speculations?

Consider the word "God". In particular, the word "God" in the Australian preamble: "Whereas the people of New South Wales, Victoria, South Australia, Queensland and Tasmania, humbly relying on the blessing of Almighty God, have agreed to unite in one indissoluble Federal Commonwealth under the Crown". At Federation the idea of including some formal recognition of God in the Constitution was a popular one. In their 1901 commentary, Quick and Garran said this "appeal to the Deity was inserted in the Constitution at the suggestion of most of the Colonial Legislative Chambers, and in response to numerous and largely signed petitions received from the people of every colony represented in the Federal Convention."[100] Yet there were a few petitions in opposition, and their arguments are worth hearing. In the Melbourne convention debates views were put by a Mr H.B. Higgins, who was opposed to constitutional reference to God, although not due to any atheism on his part. Instead, in his own words "I say frankly that I should have no objection to the insertion of words of this kind in the preamble, if I felt that in the Constitution we had a sufficient safeguard against the passing of religious laws by the Commonwealth."[101]

He cited the case *Church of the Holy Trinity v. United States*, which appeared before the U.S. Supreme Court in 1892, over the question whether the Church could employ a foreign rector (one E. Walpole Warren, a resident of England) in apparent contravention of federal statute forbidding the importation of foreigners to the US for the purpose of performing pre-contracted labour. The Supreme Court's decision was that, although technically the Church was in violation of the statute, it "was a familiar rule, that a thing might be within the letter of a statute, and yet not be within the statute, because not within the spirit, nor within the intention of its makers".[102] The purpose of the federal Act was to prevent the importation of cheap unskilled labour, not Christian ministers, so the Church's contract remained valid. But the Court went much further than this. Through the voice of Mr Justice Brewer, it declared that "beyond all these matters, no purpose of action against religion can be imputed to any legislation, state or national; because, this is a religious people"[103]; more specifically, a Christian people. To justify this rather curious assertion for a court of law to be making, the Supreme Court cited three documents. One was the Commission to Christopher Columbus from "Ferdinand and Isabella, by the Grace of God, King and Queen of Castile", which recites "that it is hoped that by God's assistance some of the continents and islands in the ocean will be discovered". The second was the first colonial grant of American soil, made to Sir Walter Raleigh in 1584 by "Elizabeth by the Grace of God, of England, France and Ireland, Queen, Defender of the Faith" etc., authorizing him to enact statutes for the government of the future colony provide that they "be not against the true Christian faith now professed in the Church of England". The third quoted was the Declaration of Independence itself:

> We hold these truths to be self-evident, that all men are created equal, that they are endowed by their Creator with certain inalienable Rights, that among these are Life, Liberty and the pursuit of Happiness…We therefore, the Representatives of the United States of America in general Congress assembled, appealing to the Supreme Judge of the World for the rectitude of our intentions, do, in the Name and by the authority of the Good People of these colonies solemnly publish and declare [etc]…and for the support of the Declaration, with a firm reliance on the Protection of Divine Providence, we mutually pledge to each other our lives, our Fortunes, and our sacred Honour.[104]

These references to God in documents, the most recent of which was well over a century old by this time, were used to declare formally that "no purpose of action against [Christian] religion can be imputed to any legislation, state or national".

Niccolò's Ghost Mentioning God in the Constitution is comparatively harmless. Illustrious a body as the High Court of Australia doubtless is, it is most unlikely that the Almighty will appear before it in the guise of a litigant. Other speculations are not so benign.

Imagine this passage from the Declaration of Independence was part of an Australian Charter of Rights. Its statement that all citizens possess an inalienable right to life is far more perilous than it seems. Consider: if future generations of Australians, adults and children alike, possess the constitutional right to life, when did they individually begin to possess this right? At the latest it must surely have been at their births. Was it when, red-faced and crumpled, they first drew breath and wailed at the world? Or was it when their umbilical cord was severed, cutting off all hope of return? Or…perhaps it was earlier, when they were still enwombed in their mothers' bellies. But if the foetuses in the wombs of women possess a right to life, *when* do they come into possession of it? At conception, or at three months? At the end of the second trimester, at six months? This is of more than academic interest to the mother, for as soon as the foetus comes into possession of rights, her own are compromised. Contemplate the predicament of a woman who discovers she is pregnant, and is subsequently told she suffers from any one of a number of medical conditions whereby her life is endangered by bringing the foetus to term. If that foetus does not possess a *constitutional* right to life, *and if the existing legislation allows it*,[†] she might have an abortion to preserve her own life. If, however, the foetus does have a constitutionally enshrined right to life, then she cannot (legally) attempt to preserve her own life this way, no matter how sympathetic a legislature might be to her plight.

Turning from one dilemma, we promptly stumble over another: euthanasia. If we possess a right to life, do we — could we legally — possess the right to abdicate life, say, when suffering from a fatal medical condition involving excruciating pain? Assuming the answer is "yes", our problems have just begun. If we choose death of our own free will, relinquishing our own lives, that's one thing. But consider circumstances under which we have lost our free will. Say, we have had a bad car accident, suffering from severe brain damage as a consequence. All our higher mental functions have been irreversibly destroyed, but our basic nervous system remains intact: so we can still feel pain. Pain we feel, for we have been physically badly hurt, being only kept alive by a life-support machine. Under these conditions many people would advocate euthanasia as an act of compassion, but whose finger will turn off the machine? We are no longer capable of voluntarily surrendering our lives, and if to live is our "inalienable right", who shall have the right to take it from us?

These are questions forced upon judges by vague speculative words being written into a Constitution. The answers lie entirely outside the expertise of judges to give. Commenting in 1990 on *Roe v. Wade*, the landmark 1973 United States trial in which the US Supreme Court gave women the right to seek abortions on demand, Mr Justice Scalia (himself a member of the Supreme Court) said in frustration,

> The point at which life becomes 'worthless' and the point at which the means necessary to preserve it become 'extraordinary' or 'inappropriate', are neither set forth in the Constitution nor known to the nine Justices of this Court any better than they are known to nine people picked at random from the Kansas City telephone directory.[105]

If this is true, then why not leave decisions regarding these issues to the assembly composed of all the representatives of all the names in the telephone directories — Parliament — to decide? Why not leave the rights of the foetus

---

† Note that this book doesn't take an active position on the question of abortion but simply argues that the public, through its representatives in Parliament, is the appropriate body to decide the resolution of that question, rather than a handful of unelected and unaccountable judges.

and the rights of the mother, the rights of the dying and the rights of their relatives, to Parliament to determine through legislation in accordance with the prevailing opinions of the community at large? *This* is the harm done by writing vague phrases on rights in indelible constitutional ink. Questions affecting the entire community are brought before a handful of people whose legal expertise is of no avail, whose speculative opinions are unlikely to be any better than anyone else's, whose views are unlikely to be particularly representative of the public's views, yet whose words are final.

Declarations of rights frequently go further than realms of conjecture, and enter the realm of mythology. What the unicorn is to heraldry, "freedom of religion" is to enshrined rights: a beloved motif, but one never witnessed by mortal eye.

Niccolò's Ghost Confronted by the riddle why this is true, you must ask yourself another question. From where do we acquire our views on rights and liberties?

For most of us, our opinions are not extracted from principles of pure logic. They are not part of some elaborate calculus differentiating right from wrong, not derived with the dispassion of a mathematical proof, nor can they be displayed with the self-consistent order of an ice crystal. We devise them coloured with passion, inspired by external moral and ethical influences, and for most people the most powerful moral influences are those of religion; either explicitly in their own beliefs, or implicitly in the beliefs of the community and culture in which they were raised. Our laws, our customs, our beliefs on the value of human life and human dignity, all bear a strong Judaeo-Christian imprint.

To say, therefore, that there can exist true freedom of religion within a single legal system is to indulge in an illusion. Whatever dominant group in society controls the writing of laws will write them in accordance with its own secular beliefs, influenced (although not always obviously) by its own religious beliefs. Smaller, weaker groups that find their inspiration in alternative beliefs shall find their religious differences with the dominant set given physical expression in secular laws which they find emotionally intolerable, but which the dominant element in the community regards as not negotiable. An example would be a religious minority in multicultural Australia that practiced ritual female circumcision. Mainstream society would react with shocked revulsion, and — in my own Anglo-Saxon/Celtic Judaeo-Christian inspired opinion — rightly so, preferring to describe it as "female genital mutilation" rather than "circumcision". Our displeasure would take the form (if necessary) of parliamentary legislation outlawing these practices — in effect outlawing this religious ritual of this minority group. Where now is their freedom of religion?

A legal formula has been devised by judges to resolve this conflict, which distinguishes between freedom of religious *belief* and freedom of religious *ritual*.

A DECLARATION OF "POSITIVE" RIGHTS

When a charter of rights promises "freedom of religion" what it actually offers (according to this formula) is freedom of belief, not of ritual. You can believe what you like, but if you start sacrificing virgins at the full moon, expect trouble from the police.

But if religious ritual is open to attack from Parliament, can we seriously describe what is left as freedom of religion? It's fair enough to protect the rights of virgins from rites, but where do we draw the line? If Parliament decides the Muslim festival of Ramadan, the Jewish celebration of Bar Mitzvahs or the Christian ritual of Holy Communion ("the body and the blood") offends its delicate sensibilities and so bars or heavily modifies them, can any of these faiths be said to possess freedom of religion? What of those rituals that affect day-to-day living? If Parliament declares the ritual slaughtering of cattle required for *kosher* meat, the slitting of the throat of the animal while it is still alive, is cruel and unnatural treatment and so bans the importation or production of *kosher* meat, where does that leave our Jewish community? Hungry or vegetarian. Similarly for Muslims and *halal*. If the lifestyle of the followers of a faith is made untenable, how can they be free to follow that faith?

No easy solutions are at hand for the problem of preserving religious harmony within a diverse society. The only apparent answer is to nurture a spirit of tolerance throughout the community, and that's beyond the capacity of any constitution, written or unwritten, to guarantee. In our quest to preserve harmony, we are left only with the knowledge that any document that claims to guarantee genuine religious freedom is offering us a unicorn it cannot provide.

Our steps finally lead to the last category of enshrined rights. Stumbling from the metaphysical and mythological, we now trip over the merely contentious, a declaration promising us all freedom from discrimination based on gender, colour, creed or sexual orientation. That sounds admirable if we cast "discrimination" in its negative sense, as something along the lines of "selection or exclusion based upon criteria other than those logically associated with the matter at hand; in particular based upon personal prejudices of the selector or excluder".

We aim at establishing a society in which all employment, all promotion, all affiliations are based upon fair criteria (whatever "fair" might mean). Writing this declaration into the Constitution would be done so that judges are set up as the guardians of this admirable state of affairs. The sticky question is: are we there yet? This shall come to vex us with the irritating consistency of a bored five-year-old on a road trip, for if fair selection is the normal way of the world then the judges' task is simple. Prejudice becomes a deviation from the norm; its failings, a failure to conform to this model, hence readily correctable. In our society, then, is fair selection the usual way of things?

If not, then life under this declaration becomes very messy very quickly, for these judges are not now guardians of the status quo. They could instead be described as constitutionally-appointed midwives assisting at the birth of a new society from out of this one; except that they will never be able to prove that the child has been born. The new society, in which fair selection is embodied as the way of life, exists as yet nowhere except in the minds of those overseeing its creation. The new society exists when they say it exists. This is a problem.

Voltaire once remarked acidly that if it is true God created Man in his own image, Man has certainly returned the compliment. The same could well be said of our hypothetical panel of judges and society. Imbued with ideas about the society which created them, they may well strive to model it anew to be enlightened as they conceive Enlightenment to be. This is a pity if those of us who are to live in that new society come to disagree with them and their conception. What they perceive as a fair society we may well call an unfair one. What use to us *then* is the Declaration?

Need these judges be given such a far-reaching discretion when interpreting words on discrimination? Although the High Court isn't bound by its own decisions, couldn't we expect its members to follow the principle expressed by Gibbs J., that:

> No Justice is entitled to ignore the decisions and reasoning of his predecessors, and arrive at his own judgement as though the pages of the law reports were blank, or as though the authority of a decision did not survive beyond the rising of the Court. A Justice, unlike a legislature, cannot introduce a programme of reform which sets at nought decisions formerly made and principles formerly established. It is only after the most careful and respectful consideration of the earlier decision, and after giving due weight to all the circumstances, that a Justice may give effect to his own opinion in preference to an earlier decision of the Court.[106]

Although Gibbs' principle is admirable, one we might pray is etched in the minds of all judges in the long years to come, it's surely unreasonable to expect our hypothetical judiciary to be so conservative in judgement when the words to be interpreted are so changeable in meaning. "Prejudice" is a culturally specific word, particular in meaning not only to the culture of a country but that of a generation and a decade, the *Zeitgeist*, the spirit of the age. For legal interpretation to keep pace with popular interpretation, surely it's necessary to grant this judiciary an unusual freedom of movement, that it may give the Declaration a culturally appropriate flavour?

What we've lost on the roundabouts we are attempting to make up for on the swings. What each generation has irretrievably lost in the way of power of an elected Parliament to define rights and liberties, through being eclipsed by a Declaration enforced by a judiciary, we are attempting to regain by endowing this judiciary with unusual freedom in the exercise of interpretation — in the hope this freedom is used in a culturally appropriate way.

In the meantime what's to be the fate of measures like "positive" discrimination? Confronted, for example, by sexism in the workplace, many people advocate policies of affirmative action: minimum quotas to be imposed upon the number of women occupying certain positions, and so on. If our declaration forbids *all* forms of discrimination based on gender, colour, creed or sexuality, then a literal interpretation of it would render all affirmative action illegal. Should our declaration, then, only forbid such discrimination as does not possess the sanction of Parliament?

Niccolò's Ghost [*frowning*] At best that would operate like ordinary legislation, and at worst it would lead to quarrels between Parliament and the High Court, with the former struggling to express its opinions while the latter dictates them back. Try a *bit* harder…

Or should we instead allow our judges to permit affirmative action by upholding that the end justifies the means: that preference despite individual merit is by us a formally acknowledged evil, but that we live in a world in which such evil abounds, and so to diminish this evil at large we must engage in it ourselves? If this is true of offences of discrimination, for what other offences supposedly prohibited by law could we make it true, pleading good intentions? Nothing in this argument is intended as criticism of affirmative action programmes, but merely illustrates the danger of careless declarations.

Niccolò's Ghost Enough. Ignore now your worries about wording, even as we abandoned your fears about your right to fetter future generations by writing a Charter in the first place. Throughout this entire discussion we have been edging around the issue of judicial interpretation like a shivering bather around a cold bath: occasionally dipping in a toe to test the temperature, glowering balefully at the frigid water and grimacing. Be a man and take the plunge properly.

In August 1993 the Electoral and Administrative Review Commission confidently stated that "[t]he declaration in a Bill of Rights of the rights and freedoms of people in Queensland will serve the purpose of clarifying what those rights are. It will demystify appeals to the common law or the heritage of English law and make it possible for everyone to know their rights."[107] These words are such stuff as flower-beds are made on. Phrases of a declaration of rights mean *nothing*, promise *nothing* of themselves. They only acquire meaning when a constitutional court says what they mean. This is the oddest part of a constitutional declaration of rights: the writing of it fetters future generations, but not in the way intended by its authors. They have control over what words they write, but none over how those words shall be interpreted by future courts in generations to come. The future judges have control over the power of interpretation, but none over the actual words handed down to them. Thus a creature evolves which is neither fish or fowl, neither precisely what the authors envisaged nor what the judges desire. The essential idea behind an enshrined declaration — that rights can be made immutable by declaring them in words made immutable — can now be seen to be a false hope, for even if the words are immortal, the judges ain't. As the judges change so will their interpretations, and hence the effective meaning, of the words.

Illustrating this principle is Magna Carta, the most ancient declaration of rights in modern Europe, simply by virtue of its antiquity. When one speaks of Magna Carta, two things must be remembered. The first and lesser consideration is that the version of Magna Carta which is still partially in operation today in the United Kingdom isn't the original one signed by England's King John at Runnymede in 1215 but a slightly altered document enacted in 1297, during the reign of Edward I. The second and far more important point is that in understanding the modern relevance of Magna Carta, what matters is not what was intended in the text when it was first written in the 13th Century, but how the text came to be interpreted in later centuries.[†] Consider the passage quoted earlier, talking about "the lawful judgement of [a free man's] peers". This passage planted the roots of modern trial by jury throughout the entire English-speaking world, yet when it was first written it was not intended to guarantee such a process. (Indeed, there exists a possible argument that it was, on the contrary, an attempt by the barons to resist the reforms of Henry II and establishment of trial by jury, in favour of preserving the pre-jury law of the land: trial by ordeal, battle and wager of law. What precisely was intended by the barons is still a matter of debate; it depends on how you interpret the phrase *Per legale iudicium parium suorum vel per legem terrae*, and what was meant by the barons when they wrote it.) However, trial by ordeal ceased after 1215, and mediaeval trial by jury, which had begun to be used in legal processes about the time of Henry II (reigned 1154–1189), was well established by the time of Edward I (reigned 1272–1307)[108].

Over the subsequent centuries interpretation of the Charter changed radically. At the time in which it was written,

> a liberty was then a special privilege or immunity. Liberties
> were the established rights by feudal law of particular people
> or places to be exempt from the arbitrary power of an over-

---

† Perhaps more important than any single section in Magna Carta was the sentiment underlying the entire document, a sentiment apparent from that first day at Runnymede in 1215. What we would now call the political executive, the feudal king, and all his actions, were not to be above the law. Instead they could be constrained by the law. Most importantly, the relationship between the king and his subjects could be defined in the law, and by its due process freemen could seek redress of grievances against the offences of the government and its servants. That mediaeval England possessed such a document at the heart of its legal system goes far in explaining the enormous difference in political evolution between England and the countries of continental Europe in subsequent centuries.

A DECLARATION OF "POSITIVE" RIGHTS

lord. The Charter promised to the freeman his liberties.
Probably the 'freeman' was the freeholder of feudal law.
Certainly in 1215 villeins were not comprehended in the
term *liberi homines*. But within two hundred years this had
been forgotten, and all Englishmen had come to be considered entitled to the benefits of the Charter. Liberties ceased
to be feudal privileges and became the right of all Englishmen
to be ruled by the law of the land — a law which both
government and people should obey.[109]

Within England Magna Carta again became a rallying-cry in the 17th
Century, when the Stuart kings claimed the existence of Divine Right and
attempted to enforce the principle "Rex is Lex": the King is the Law, an
obvious challenge to the principles of constitutional government represented
by the Charter. During the subsequent Civil War and Commonwealth, Magna
Carta was used by both Roundheads and Cavaliers as the ancient emblem of
constitutional government, a status it still enjoys today.[†] Its meaning has
shifted through the centuries, not because subsequent judges necessarily spoke
bad Latin, but because their interpretation of those words, appropriate to their
own time, necessarily became foreign to the circumstances of the authors. By
1500AD what Magna Carta meant by "liberties" and to whom it promised
them had altered substantially from 1215 AD. Those same words were again
dramatically reinterpreted in the 17th Century.

> In the days of the Stuarts, when once again despotism was
> challenged, Coke and his followers found in the Charter an
> assurance that the law of England gave to all men equal
> justice and liberty as a birthright. The Charter then became
> an assertion of individual freedom, a recognition of
> Parliamentary sovereignty, a guarantee of the continuance of
> the common law of England. All this was based on a misin-
> terpretation of the clauses of the Charter. To medievalists it
> is therefore an error. But in the history of England and of the
> British people it has been the truth; and we may hope it will
> remain the truth. In the letter of the law, it is an error. But
> this error has become accepted as, in truth, the law.[110]

Magna Carta was never drafted as a general declaration of abstract rights, but
was a catalogue of specific complaints and actions which could not be inflicted
upon "free men". The same curious process of evolution we have witnessed in
it exists also in all constitutional declarations of "positive" rights. Indeed we

---

† In a speech delivered in 1992 to the assembled Houses of the Australian Parliament in Canberra, US
President George Bush described it in these words:"This Parliament building displays an original copy of the
Magna Carta, I am told — one of only four such manuscripts to have survived to this day. The US National
Archives is home to another of those original manuscripts, and I can think of no more powerful symbol of our
shared commitments to the rights of the individual, to the rule of law and to the government of consent — by
consent of the people." (Address by President George Bush to the joint assembly on the 2nd of January 1992,
reported in *Parliamentary Debates* (House of Representatives) No 1 1992; this quote is from p. 2.)

can expect this evolution to be much greater for "positive" rights, due to their vagueness and culturally specific nature. This has important consequences, rarely so benign as for Magna Carta.

It is frequently suggested that a Charter of positive rights will protect the rights of minority groups from the tyranny of the majority. This faith is misguided, for by virtue of this process of change it is impossible to predict precisely what the same formula of words shall or shall not protect in future years. In the case of the US Bill of Rights I am indebted to an article written by Gabriel Moens, Professor of Law at the University of Queensland, for examples:

> In 1896, the equal protection of the laws provision of the Fourteenth Amendment to the United States Constitution was interpreted as permitting the segregation of black and whites. It was not until 1954 that racial segregation was declared unconstitutional in *Brown v. Board of Education*. Prohibition of slavery was interpreted as deprivation of 'property' without due process of law. During the height of preparation for war, the Supreme Court ruled that the Jehovah's Witnesses could not refuse to salute the flag despite their strong claim of religious convictions...The Supreme Court also upheld banishment and internment of Americans of Japanese ancestry during the Second World War. Eugenic sterilisation of retarded people was similarly upheld. In this context, the eminent judge, Oliver Wendell Holmes J commented that 'three generations of imbeciles are enough'.[111]

So unsympathetic judges may not necessarily uphold the "rights" of minorities appealing against maltreatment or oppression by the social majority. It's true that some of the negative rulings cited above have been subsequently reversed, but that neither protected the minorities at the time nor provides any guarantee that in future times similar rulings — say, on banishment and internment, or eugenic sterilisation — may not once again occur. To the other extreme, judges may uphold the "rights" of a minority against what might be described as reasonable legislation. For example, in 1990 a US Court held the opinion that nude dancing in public bars was a protected form of free speech and hence could not be banned. A dissenting judge, Justice Manion, said in exasperation,

> It takes little foresight to realize that three-fourths of state legislatures would not ratify a Twenty-Seventh Amendment that stated 'the right of citizens of the United States to entertain by dancing nude in public shall not be denied or abridged by the United States or by any State' It is a much simpler process for a handful of judges to protect nude dancing as entertainment by calling it speech.[112]

Even as future interpretations of a declaration of rights cannot be reliably established from present conditions, neither can a present interpretation be guaranteed from judgements of times past. The High Court of Australia raised legal eyebrows all across the nation when it recently discovered the existence of an implied right to free political discourse in our terse written Constitution, where no such right is actually declared. The chap who wrote about stout Cortez's men staring at each other with a wild surmise would have appreciated the reaction of legal counsel throughout Australia when the judgement was made known. To say, therefore, that a general declaration "of the rights and freedoms of people in Queensland will…demystify appeals to the common law…and make it possible for everyone to know their rights" is to make an assertion fit for fertiliser. It does, however, raise another interesting question. What of the peoples' own interpretation of the rights due to them from the declaration?

It doesn't matter a brass cent what the people think is owed to them. Public opinion plays no formal role in judicial decision-making, and neither it should. The Law cannot be defined by plebescites, nor are elected assemblies which draft legislation generally competent to define precisely how their handiwork will function in the context of existing law. Yet owners of land, buyers and sellers of goods, the participants in any transaction need to know from one day to the next whether their actions are legal or illegal. What is legal on Monday afternoon cannot be permitted to have drifted into illegality by Tuesday morning simply because public opinion seems to have drifted overnight. A more structured and formal process is demanded. For the sake of citizens constrained within whatever is the Law, the voice which, in speaking, interprets and defines law must be coherent and dispassionate; it must be learned in statutory interpretation, knowledgable in precedent, logical in reasoning and comprehending of the implications new legislation holds for existing law. It's therefore sensible to delegate this task of definition and interpretation to the courts of law, in the name of a coherent legal system, even as it makes sense to place Parliament above these courts in the English system of common law, in the name of democracy.

In this way the voices of public opinion, expressed through elected parliamentarians, can still be given a dominant position in defining rights and liberties without interfering unduly in the coherence of existing law. Parliament passes legislation and then hands it over to the courts, so that existing complicated structures of laws may be amended to incorporate the new Act. If parliamentarians are happy with the outcome, well and good. If not, then Parliament can invoke its superior position to pass another Act, responding to apparent shortcomings of the previous one revealed by judicial scrutiny. Provided judges remain dispassionately logical and subordinate to Parliament, the rules of cause and effect will enable the people's representatives to compel particular changes to the social fabric through successive Acts. What was legal Monday still might become illegal by Friday lunchtime, but it has to go through a formal public process to get there, and there's a similar process to restore it back to legality later, if enough angry people are elected to some future Parliament.

With a written Constitution all this threatens to come unstuck. The point of such a document being to set certain matters above the ordinary reach of

Parliament, judicial decisions about this document are also out of the reach of parliamentarians. This isn't so alarming when the document is as sparse as Australia's written Constitution, but it's downright dangerous when that piece of paper has vague and speculative words written on it. High Court judges can't be expected to acquiesce to ephemeral contemporary swells and troughs of public opinion when defining concepts in a declaration of rights. Not only haven't they any clear way of gauging public opinion directly (unlike judges confronted with an Act of Parliament, in which the votes of the House are a gauge of public opinion, and if it's an inaccurate gauge then that's a matter to be fought out between voters and politicians at the next election) but even if they *could* assess precisely the contemporary public mood on a particular topic, then if this determined the definitions to be used in judgements, the decisions handed down from the Bench would become as changeable as public mood. The legality of abortion might mean one thing in April and another in August, altered not by a formal process of debate but by the passions of demagogues. If transient shifts in the public mood may alter definitions and interpretations of the declaration, this alters the decisions handed down — which overrule all other forms of law issuing from Parliament or inferior courts. This would be an arbitrary and absolute tyranny of the majority.

The alternative is for our panel of judges to be allowed to devise their own interpretations of the words in an enshrined declaration, but what of when this judicial interpretation conflicts with a popular interpretation? Members of the community shall feel themselves to be deprived of what is "properly" theirs, deprived by an unaccountable panel of legal scholars perceived to be misruling either through ignorance or deliberate spite. Estrangement, anger and conflict with the Court are the most likely consequences, if the declaration says anything worth saying. In Hailsham's words,

> the only freedom which counts is the freedom to do what some
> other people think to be wrong. There is no point in demanding
> freedom to do that which all will applaud. All the so-called
> liberties or rights are things which have to be asserted against
> others who claim that if such things are to be allowed their own
> rights are infringed or their own liberties threatened.[113]

One of the most elegant attributes of representative democracy in a diverse society is that it feeds on estrangement and resentment, channelling these emotions into a form of non-violent conflict: party rivalry.† Frustration and anger at a government's policies, which in a more rigid political system would find expression in violence, can be expressed instead in campaigning to vote that administration out of office. Yet if it's a great strength of representative

---

† To what extent this channelling is effective would seem to be a function of how easy it is for disaffected and frustrated voters to form new associations and parties, which can acquire meaningful power at the expense of established parties. Westminster parliamentary democracy appears to be much better at this than US-style presidential government. In the latter the real battlefield is the presidential elections, requiring Ross Perot-style nationwide expenditure of millions of dollars. In the Westminster system a new party merely has to aspire to winning enough constituencies to hold the balance of power on the floor of the House.

democracy that public rage at bad policy or legislation can be expressed by pulling parliamentarians from out of their seats, then what of public rage at a High Court's rulings upon citizen's rights? By the same logic, if from a height beyond the reach of our votes these judges impose laws upon us affecting our rights and liberties — indeed, striking down all legislation offered by Parliament which offends their interpretations of our rights — then surely we should have the power to drag them also from their benches even as we can drag elected legislators from their seats? And yet, if judges may readily be dragged from their benches for unpopular decisions, the entire purpose of a written constitution is made void. We cannot establish a sturdy legal framework that withstands the transient passions of a society or the imperious dictates of a government if its interpreters and upholders are to be stripped of office for declaring an unpopular truth.

The US Constitution attempts an alternative solution, centred on appointment rather than dismissal. Justices of the US Supreme Court are appointed for life by the President (subject to good behaviour), but these appointments are subject to the approval of the Senate, which has the power to confirm or deny them, making its decision based upon cross-examination of the candidates over their attitudes on various topics. This attempted solution is a failure on two grounds.

The first is that it's based upon flawed thinking, reminiscent of some bizarre scheme of interviewing bulls before the Spanish *La Fiesta de San Fermin*. Each year in the Spanish walled city of Pamplona this festival is held, in which the famous "running of the bulls" takes place. For no readily apparent reason some of the wickedest bulls ever to dissolve the bowels of frightened tourists are penned up, then released into the cobbled streets where a number of young men nervously wait to display their machismo and inadequate survival instinct to the curious onlookers. The theory is simple. The bulls emerge. You run away, hoping your gym subscription gives you an edge over the other participants (also running away). As a sport, the best position to play this from is a nice high balcony (Ra ra runners! Ra ra bulls!). Now imagine someone came up with the bright idea of eliminating the potential tourist mortality rate by interviewing the candidate bulls before the festival began. ("So, Ferdinand, what are your feelings regarding humans…?") Perhaps this might reduce the subsequent casualty rate by weeding out the truly homicidal, but danger would still remain. The important question isn't how bulls feel about the abstract concept of a running man when they're standing quietly in their stalls, but how they feel when they actually see one shrieking down an alleyway, fleeing from their wicked horns. If there's a change of emotion now, it's too late. The bulls are loose on the streets.[†]

The other ground on which the American scheme fails is the obvious politicisation of the Supreme Court entailed. The President and senators, politicians all, will obviously want a Supreme Court Justice to be a person sympathetic to their own ideology and agendas, so that their own party's legislation is likely to

---

† Running from the bulls is thus the second most dangerous pastime for a traveller on the Iberian peninsula, surpassed only by being a pedestrian in Lisbon.

be upheld, and their opponents', struck down. This issue of ideology is already relevant for Australia's sparsely-written Constitution, but the ideologies being questioned are those relevant to the document. For instance, in a federal document such as our own one debate is between "centralist" judges (those who wish to concentrate power in Canberra) and "States' rights" judges (who desire the retention of considerable power and autonomy in the State governments). This dispute, influential on judgements, nonetheless doesn't find much expression in the left-wing versus right-wing polarisation of our politics, and so goes largely ignored by the public. But in a Constitution with a declaration of rights, which may touch upon all aspects of a citizen's life and hence encompass all manner of legislation brought before the Court, conventional party-political dogma becomes supremely important. A left-wing administration will attempt to appoint left-wing judges, and a right-wing administration will attempt the same for right-wing judges. The Bench will lose whatever vestiges of non-partisanship it now possesses and become a creature of party, the colour of its politics diluted only by the number of biased opposition members previous hostile administrations have been able to appoint.

So what are we left with? In a Court endowed with the independence from external pressure judges need to perform their duties properly, and given a declaration of rights to interpret which can strike down legislation from Parliament, we have nothing other than a judicial aristocracy, creating and destroying our rights and liberties without recourse to our votes or our representatives.

This stripping of power from voters was a deliberate aspect of the US Bill of Rights at its establishment. After the Declaration of Independence in 1776 a confederation was created between the thirteen former British colonies, now States loosely bound together in 1777 by a written constitution known as the Articles of Confederation. Dominated by reactionary sentiment against centralised authority, inspired by the struggle against the British government, the brief Articles period of American history was dedicated to the liberty of citizens and the supremacy of legislatures over the Executive and judiciary. All effective power was kept in the individual States, there being no central executive government or judiciary, only a legislative body consisting of a single House, the Continental Congress, in which each State held a single vote. This Congress had virtually no power apart from devising common foreign policy for the Confederacy. In their own freshly-devised republican constitutions, a number of these States gave full rein to English radical theories on democracy. The executive post of Governor was abolished in Pennsylvania and New Hampshire, and severely curtailed in authority elsewhere. In many States the judiciary was also rendered not only subordinate but subservient to the legislature, which would not only appoint judges and control their salaries and fees but also overturn their decisions and even take direct control of deciding cases on probate, debt, marriage and divorce. Most radical of all, Pennsylvania established a form of community-based anarchism, with its unicameral legislature representing an "upper" House, the "lower" being the entire citizenry of that State. Bills proposed in the House couldn't become law until they had been promulgated throughout the State, discussed and approved by local conventions in the towns,

A DECLARATION OF "POSITIVE" RIGHTS

and then voted upon in the next session of the House. Farmers in western Massachusetts attempted to push the idea even further, claiming each town had the right to reverse and annul any action taken by the State legislature.[114]

The result was chaos, arbitrary and irresponsible government. The pendulum of public opinion, having swung to a more extreme belief in the participation of the voter in government and the supremacy of the elected legislature over the Executive and judiciary than in any other period of history, then or since, of the English-speaking world, began to swing back against those same beliefs and the "politics of liberty". Sentiments began to be muttered, "When a man who is only fit to patch a shoe attempts to patch the state, fancies himself a Solon or Lycurgus…he cannot fail to meet with contempt".[115]

More extreme sentiments in the same vein were expressed by American revolutionary leaders. James Otis warned in 1776 that "when the pot boils the scum will rise", while ten years later Benjamin Rush, in a letter written to Price, remarked hopefully, "The scum which was thrown upon the surface by the fermentation of the war is daily sinking".[116] Belief in the inability of the lower classes to govern was expressed by John Adams, one of the leading figures in the Revolution,[†] who recounted in his autobiography an encounter with a man in 1775 whom he had in the past defended in court over issues of debt. This was in the colony of Massachusetts; in reply to Boston's rebellious behaviour Britain had closed, among other things, all the courts. This man was delighted, thanking Adams and the other rebel leaders, because "there are no courts of justice now in this province and I hope there never will be another".[117] Appalled, Adams later wrote in his diary,

> Is this the object for which I have been contending? said I to myself. For I rode along without any answer to this wretch. Are these the sentiments of such people and how many of them are there in the country? Half the nation for what I know; for half the nation are debtors, if not more, and these have been, in all countries, the sentiments of debtors. If the power of the country should get into their hands, and there is great danger that it will, to what purpose have we sacrificed our time, health and everything else? Surely we must guard against this spirit and these principles, or we shall repent of all our conduct.[118]

A similar moral was drawn by Governeur Morris, in a letter written in the 1770s. A Pennsylvanian delegate to Philadelphia, he was the Convention's most active debater, edited and revised the final draft of the US Constitution and was the author of its preamble.[119] Describing in his letter a public gathering, he warned,

---

† John Adams (1735–1826): helped draft and sign the Declaration of Independence, nominated George Washington to lead the American forces, was a member of the Continental Congress (where he argued for total independence from Britain, persuading his more reluctant colleagues to this action), served as a diplomatic emissary to France, the Netherlands and Britain, and finally served in turn as both Vice-President and President of the United States. (*The Book of the Founding Fathers* (ed. V. Wilson), pp. 8–9.

I stood on the balcony and on my right were ranged all the people of property, with some poor dependents, and on the other the tradesmen, etc., who thought it worth their while to leave daily labour for the good of the country…The mob began to think and reason. Poor reptiles! It is with them a vernal morning; they are struggling to cast off their winter's slough. They bask in the sunshine, and ere noon they will bite, depend on it.[120]

In short, one of Cornell University's professors of Government recently summed up the mood of those times by stating,

Part of the Federalist[†] response to the Articles period and of their sense of the excesses of radical democracy was a feeling that too much had been abandoned of the British inheritance in the years after 1776. This led, even before the [1787 Philadelphia] Constitutional Convention, to a desire in some circles to restore a more balanced and mixed government against the legislative supremacy characteristic of the Articles years.[121]

In the 1787 Constitution of the United States drafted in Philadelphia, the "classical" British separation of powers was utilised as a pattern — with some amendments. A triumph of centralised organised power over the levelling Articles view of diffused participatory democracy, the new Constitution represented a deliberate attempt to strip voters of much of their previous power. Included in that were the first ten constitutional amendments, drafted by Madison and collectively famous as the "Bill of Rights". Their purpose was to protect citizen's rights from the legislature's actions, not because the latter was occupied by an elective oligarchy hostile to the constituency, but because the legislature might be the voice of the Great Unwashed, ignorant of responsible legislation.

Far from being egalitarian, in many respects the US Constitution is intended to exploit the class system in American society. It is, as both its advocates and opponents were swift to point out during the ratification debates before its adoption, an instrument which is pro-aristocracy: not the titled European-style aristocracy, which was explicitly forbidden, but favouring a "natural aristocracy" of enlightened worthies drawn from the educated classes. This aspect has been submerged by subsequent American mythologising about the heroic lawgivers who drafted their system of government, but it was one freely admitted at the time of drafting, until popular revulsion whipped up by anti-Federalists forced Federalists "to minimize, even to disguise, the elitist elements in the Constitution"[122] during subsequent debates. James Madison envisaged rule by "representatives of enlightened views and virtuous sentiments", rather

---

† This was the name given to advocates of the new Constitution, eventually ratified by the individual States to become the United States of America. Opponents to that Constitution during the ratification debates became known as "anti-Federalists".

than the "men without reading, experience or principle" who filled the State legislatures.[123] Attacking the new Constitution, John Quincy Adams denounced it as being calculated "to increase the influence, power and wealth of those who have it already".[124] Another contemporary critic zeroed in upon the Supreme Court as having the makings of a "consolidating aristocracy".[125]

The traditional conception of a judicially enforced Charter of Rights is underpinned by a tacit belief in an enlightened minority, who better understand the public's best interests than the public does itself. What are these judges who interpret vague declarations on life and liberty but an assembly of "enlightened elders", "venerable sages" of our society? Whether, as in 18th Century America, this enlightenment is to come from their belonging to an educated and cosmopolitan upper class, or whether it is an individual thing, derived from years of sitting upon a Bench, listening to a monotonous recitation of cases and precedent that induces a Zen-like trance conducive to metaphysical transformation, is a question our modern advocates have yet failed to answer.

Niccolò's ghost If you can suspend your righteous indignation for a moment, you've got to admire the cleverness of the US Bill of Rights as an instrument of hegemony. Not only does it strip the masses of much of their power in a manner they're willing to countenance — but they actually think it's doing them a *favour* in the process! [*Wryly*] It's really most amusing.

The final proposition lingering for our attention is that an enshrined declaration of rights would be useful, in displaying to the world our committment for our society to retain certain attributes it now possesses. This provokes a number of replies.

That a written Constitution, a legal document that exists to serve a practical purpose, is the appropriate venue for expounding vague philosophies is a dubious proposition. Why do we feel an urge to drape tinsel over a prosaic instrument? If we want an "inspired and inspirational document", perhaps someone ought to write instead an Australian equivalent to the *Federalist Papers*. More importantly, an awfully high price is to be paid for the sake of sharing our views with the world. We would fetter future generations to a device that cuts the hamstrings of Parliament and diminishes the sovereignty of the people, preventing their representatives in assembly from defining the rights and liberties of their society according to their own morality, their perception of good and evil; a perception necessarily different from our own, made distant by advances in technology and alterations in society posing ethical dilemmas alien to our late-20th Century world view; a device which subordinates these generations and their democratic processes to the dictates of a Bench of elders, an oligarchy whose knowledge of the law is the excuse for their much broader authority over the community. All this, just so we can carve in a monument what we think. Is this statesmanship? Do we expect future generations to admire us for it? Surely this act, committed to immortalise our views, becomes an act of vandalism scrawled across the years; the declaration itself, however noble in sentiment, worse than any graffiti.

No declarations of positive rights actually promise anything when read in isolation, for they derive meaning only from interpretations by the relevant Court. The words written on paper are merely a shadow of what we desire. Only these judges can see the solid rights promised, because these objects exist only in their doctrines and imaginations. What we citizens possess are not solid rights but judicial promises, which acquire substance by being underwritten by the Crown and its servants (most notably, the police).

To pretend we can possess more than this is to engage in a comfortable delusion, and frequently citizens in countries endowed with a charter of rights possess less. Our metaphor of a shadow and a solid object breaks down here, because a shadow exists only when some object casts it, whereas a declaration of rights frequently exists where no rights can be found.

Take the People's Republic of China. Article 41 of its Constitution promises:

> Citizens of the People's Republic have the right to criticise or make suggestions to any state organ or functionary. Citizens have the right to make to relevant state organs complaints and charges against, or exposures of, violation of the law or dereliction of duty by any state functionary or organ; but fabrication or distortion of facts with the intention of libel or frame-up is prohibited.
>
> In the case of complaints, charges or exposures made by citizens, the state organ concerned must deal with them in a reasonable manner after ascertaining the facts. No one may suppress such complaints, charges and exposures, or retaliate against citizens making them.
>
> Citizens who have suffered losses through infringement of their civic rights by any state organ or functionary have the right to compensation in accordance with the law.[126]

One wonders whether dealing with criticism "in a reasonable manner" includes marching heavily-armed detachments of People's Liberation Army soldiers into Tienanmen Square at 2am on the 4th of June 1989, escorted by armoured personnel carriers and tanks; whether it includes opening fire upon the thousands of unarmed men, women and children they found there, or the bayonetting of the wounded, or the crushing of tents by armoured vehicles to kill the occupants; whether it includes the committing of similar atrocities in other regional capitals, or the imprisonment of surviving dissidents. One might even describe this sort of thing as "suppression" of "complaints, charges and exposures", although doubtless Deng Xiaoping would have disagreed. Words can fall from grandiloquent posturing into bitter mockery.

A DECLARATION OF "POSITIVE" RIGHTS

The most conspicuous case was remarked upon by Sir James Killen over a coffee with the author, when he commented that the Soviet Union's declaration of rights didn't save Solzhenitsyn from the Siberian prison camps. That same point was made obliquely by George Orwell in *Animal Farm*, his "fairy tale" of Soviet history transposed to an English farmyard. The animals had rebelled against oppression from humans, and established their own collectivist government based upon principles of liberty. Their system of government was gradually usurped by the pigs, eventually collapsing into dictatorship under a boar named Napoleon.

Orwell's fable can be used as an encapsulation of issues surrounding a charter of rights, one especially pertinent to Australia in the 1990s. The pigs ignored whether they had the right to codify Animalism into commandments and impose these upon Animal Farm. They did it anyway. The pigs (especially one named Squealer) appointed themselves interpreters of these commandments apparently promising rights, but the meanings of which proved more changeable as the regime became more corrupt, eventually condoning exploitation and murder. As this occurred, the principles and liberties which had originally underlain Animalism were eroded, and finally destroyed. Finally the pigs' regime, by now entirely arbitrary and absolute in power, did away with these commandments altogether, replacing them with a single article which summarises the ethos of the US Bill of Rights as an instrument of class hegemony: All Animals are Equal, but Some Animals are More Equal than Others.

Times and countries in human history come to pass when an enshrined declaration of rights is needed as a lesser of two evils. In communities divided by sectarian or ethnic violence and prejudice reflected in their legislatures, and in which there exists a smaller population, unafflicted by these prejudices, from which a Bench of judges may be drawn, then a future confined by that device is better than no future at all. Yet our country isn't in this lamentable condition, and is blessed with rights and liberties without recourse to that contrivance. If we must write more words of praise in our Constitution, we could do worse than take as inspiration the tombstone of Sir Christopher Wren in St Paul's Cathedral, London. In that magnificent edifice of stone and gold, echoing air and symmetry rests its creator, interred in the crypt in 1723. Whereas three centuries of other famous people's graves scattered throughout the cathedral have themselves proclaimed in pompous marble, his quiet tomb is marked by a plain block of dark grey stone, inscribed in Latin LECTOR, SI MONUMENTUM REQUIRIS, CIRCUMSPICE. Translated: Reader, if you seek a monument, look around you.

[*The Ghost picks up Lewis Carroll's* Through the Looking-Glass, *lying among the Author's papers, and begins to read it.*]

"The time has come", the Walrus said,
"To talk of many things;
Of shoes – and ships – and sealing wax –
Of cabbages – and kings –
And why the sea is boiling hot –
And whether pigs have wings."

Lewis Carroll, *Through the Looking-Glass*

A Walk along the North Shore

▪■▪

The ARM's rhetoric concerning Australia is evocative of a poem, about two demagogues on the beach —

Niccolò's ghost [*reading aloud*]:

The Walrus and the Carpenter
Were walking close at hand;
They wept like anything to see
Such quantities of sand:
'If this were only cleared away',
They said, 'it would be grand!'

'If seven maids with seven mops
Swept it for half a year,
Do you suppose' the Walrus said,
'That they could get it clear?'
'I doubt it', said the Carpenter
And shed a bitter tear.

Professing to love a country while despising its history and traditions is like professing to love a beach while despising the sand of which it is composed.

What is loved then is neither the actual country nor the actual beach, but an ideal which exists nowhere but in the mind of the dreamer.

The attempted republic represents an agenda containing far more radical changes than simply the face upon our coins. Within it are to be found the abolition of the Senate and the States, the renunciation of the Australian flag and the forcing of fixed terms upon Parliament.

Previous referenda have revealed Australian society to be by its nature conservative, reluctant to countenance change to an established order unless a good reason is shown. To oppose this, members of the republican camp have attempted to inspire general discontent with the status quo through calculated iconoclasm, ridiculing traditional emblems within our society or portraying them as outdated, pushing a belief that their demolition is an inevitable as the coming of the year 2001. To this end the general public's lack of knowledge about the origin of many institutions (a lack shared by many "authorities" in the media) has proved useful, by making us more malleable.

This discontent has already been cultivated through the media. Proposals for change will now fall upon ears more willing to listen and acquiesce — the more so when the proposed remedy to this awful (induced) illness is presented using soothing words like "minimalist". It is always easier to persuade patients to endure an injection when they're frequently told they're ill, when the side-effects of the serum are understated, and when they're told it won't hurt a bit.

Niccolò's ghost   'Oysters, come and walk with us!'
                    The Walrus did beseech.
                    'A pleasant walk, a pleasant talk,
                    Along the briny beach;
                    We cannot do with more than four,
                    To give a hand to each.'

Persuading all members of the community that institutions which have served them well for almost a century are diseased and should be destroyed is a difficult task. Many older citizens in particular are alienated by attempts to ridicule and remove symbols dear to their hearts. To this end rather odd suggestions have emerged from the republican camp, that older citizens should be disenfranchised, excluded from any vote concerning the future of the Australian monarchy.

Niccolò's ghost   The eldest Oyster looked at him,
                    But never a word he said:
                    The eldest Oyster winked his eye,
                    And shook his heavy head —

Meaning to say he did not choose
To leave the oyster-bed.

Instead there's been concentration upon the younger generations, not because they'll be the inhabitants of the brave new society, but cynically, because the republican movement hopes to exploit the (perceived) willingness of youth[†] to drag a republican monument within our Constitution, while dismantling whatever safeguards stand in the way.

Niccolò's ghost But four young Oysters hurried up
All eager for the treat:
Their coats were brushed, their faces washed,
Their shoes were clean and neat —
And this was odd, because, you know
They hadn't any feet.

Four other oysters followed them,
And yet another four;
And thick and fast they came at last
And more, and more, and more —
All hopping through the frothy waves,
And scrambling to the shore.

---

† As a member of the so-called "Generation X", the author is always startled when republican Baby-Boomers start laying down the law about what his generation does or does not believe.

A Change of Standard

Contemplate what Burke described as the "unprincipled facility of changing the state as often, and as much, and as many ways as there are floating fancies and fashions". Even as floating fancies and fashions are frequently expressed in clothing, ornaments and symbols, look to our national emblems. Other than the Crown, the emblem most likely to be mothballed by the republican movement is our flag.

Although Paul Keating strongly linked the two issues, some republicans have denied that scrapping the flag is part of their agenda, and certainly there's only a tenuous link apparent between preservation of the Crown and preservation of a flag composed in part of a British emblem. The British Union Flag ("Union Jack" to those fond of nautical terminology) has been removed from the flags of many Queen's Realms such as the Solomon Islands and Papua New Guinea, the Caribbean realms and Canada.[†] Conversely in the South Pacific there are republics that proudly retain the Union Jack: Fiji (which was once a British colony) and the US island state of Hawaii (which never was). Also in this region are two fully independent Queen's Realms retaining the emblem, Australia and New Zealand, as did a third, Tuvalu, until October 1995. The Prime Minister of Tuvalu responsible for the change, Mr Kamuta Latasi, later lost office on a vote of no confidence and his successor, Prime Minister Bikenibeu Paeniu, restored the traditional flag incorporating the Union Jack. The flags of Australia's six original states also cannot be forgotten, nor those of New Zealand's Associated States[‡] of Niue and the Cook Islands. This makes a total of twelve governments

---

[†] Although note the provinces of British Columbia, Ontario and Manitoba have retained it, and a number of Canadians, particularly in rural regions, still fly the old Canadian flag which incorporates it. Furthermore the province of Nova Scotia retains a reversed Cross of St Andrew and the royal lion of Scotland, and Newfoundland's flag appears to be a dissected Union Jack.

[‡] An Associated State isn't an internal province but a fully self-governing entity, for whose external affairs and defence a member country of the Commonwealth takes responsibility.

in the region, none of them colonies, which fly the Union Flag as part of their own flag because it has some particular validity for their own history. The presence of the Union Jack upon another state's flag doesn't necessarily imply a colonial status — or indeed any contemporary link — nor does its absence necessarily imply the absence of strong links with Britain.

Having said that, our flag will be a logical casualty if Australia becomes a republic, due to the nature of the transition. When Fiji became a republic this wasn't a gesture of symbolism, but because Colonel Rabuka's regime was more feasible in a republic without all the inconveniences of a bipartite monarchy. Its flag, dating from a more peaceful era as a Queen's Realm, remained. Hawaii was never a British colony, and has been a republic since its indigenous monarchy was overthrown in a *coup* backed by US sugar interests in 1893. It was annexed by the United States five years later. The Union Jack, adopted in the 19th Century by pro-British Hawaian kings in the face of American, French and German colonialism in the South Pacific, remains as a quiet reminder of a time when the Polynesians were free to negotiate their own alliances abroad. In both Fiji and Hawaii, the change to a republic wasn't effected to show post-colonial independence, but imposed by force.

If we adopt a republic of our own free will it will mean we're willing to discard an institution (the Crown) because of its symbolism held in common with the United Kingdom, irrespective of practical advantages. Countries like Jamaica, Barbados and the Bahamas have proved willing to change their flags but not their Crowns because the former are simply a matter of geographical heraldry, whereas the latter are a device which helps uphold parliamentary government. Like theirs, our Crown also justifies its existance for reasons other than heraldry. Yet if our national prejudice is such that we despise a political entity, however useful in function, because of its supra-national symbolism, how is our flag, purely a symbol, to survive? If we're so consumed by irrational passion that we must expunge all objects with symbols in common with the United Kingdom and New Zealand irrespective of the damage we inflict upon ourselves in the process, then that passion certainly won't limit itself to respect our traditional ensign. If that is the sort of people we've become then the joy departs any flag, however pretty. Flags in the hands of nationalists become tools of strife and division, not emblems of community.

So in the context of the current debate, a republic in Australia implies a new flag. Although it's possible to be a monarchist and desire a changed flag, in the existing political climate our flag provides an eloquent standard against the republican cause. It's an elegant illustration that historical emblems inherited from abroad and symbols indigenous to this continent can be combined to form a device distinctively Australian.

Turn now from the flag to the Senate and senators, those "unrepresentative swill" we're told should be denied the power to block Supply — indeed, perhaps should not exist at all.

Niccolò's ghost 'A loaf of bread' the Walrus said,
'Is what we chiefly need:
Pepper and vinegar besides
Are very good indeed —
Now if you're ready, Oysters dear,
We can begin to feed.'

ON THE BEACH

Supply

The obvious place to start is with the journalistic assertion that the problem of existence of and powers for the Senate and the analogous problem for the Crown are completely separate.

That assertion is rather naive, once one contemplates the issues already outlined in this book. We've established the Crown is the ultimate guardian and guarantor of the Constitution, against attacks by politicians already in office. In opposing its incumbent ministers the Crown is devoid of a elective mandate: appointed Governor, appointed Governor-General, hereditary monarch. This lack of mandate has been shown in earlier chapters to be a positive asset to the public and Parliament, as it leaves the Crown naked of any semblance of legitimacy in abusing its reserve powers. When those powers are invoked against existing ministers the Crown must appeal to Parliament or the people to clothe it in legitimacy by supporting its actions, else it's left embarrassed and vulnerable.

Yet this safeguard against Crown delinquency is bought at a price, that of limiting the Crown's own effectiveness against delinquent ministers. Confronted by outrageous government behaviour, the Crown relies upon an atmosphere of general outrage at this behaviour and its implications to make an appeal. Hence for an appeal to be contemplated, the Crown requires a) a crisis, b) media representation of this crisis, c) public appreciation of the gravity of the situation, and d) an electoral system in which the public's judgement can be accurately reflected in the composition of the Lower House. Neither the Queen nor her representatives can wage a public campaign against the incumbent ministers while the latter remain in office, for no words can be publicly uttered by the Crown except those for which a minister takes responsibility. Nor can the Queen or her representatives engage in protracted political warfare. Confronted by delinquency, they can only fight at most two pitched battles, namely an appeal to the Lower House or, if that fails, direct appeal to the electorate. Were this gambit to fail for the Queen in a UK crisis, she *might* survive on the throne without being forced to abdicate, but if a viceregal representative loses the appeals, he loses for ever.

Thus to guard the Constitution the Crown needs an earlier line of defence against transgressions, a defence which must be provided by someone else. What's needed is an institution which is vocal, and can engage in repeated public challenges to the government over its behaviour. An entity with enough power of its own to make those challenges meaningful, and which can afford to suffer earlier losses to win a later victory, without having to risk its entire future in a single fight.

Part of this role is fulfilled by the Opposition in the Lower House, but its scope is limited. If the government holds a simple majority in the House the Opposition can't prevent passage of legislation, however iniquitous. It can merely attempt to alert the public of whatever dangers are posed by a Bill which may be about to become law. An Upper House, however, if endowed with adequate powers can provide some of the forward defences needed. The extent of its powers and the freedom with which it can wield them of course depends on whether it's elected or appointed. If elected, the extent to which it opposes the government in the Lower House obviously depends on how different the electoral systems between the two Houses are, reflected in a different composition of parties in each House.

No Upper House could ever replace the role of the Crown. One reason is that such an assembly is only competent as a check upon the legislative branch of government, and so is of limited capacity as a protection against executive abuses. Another reason is that the members of an elected House would themselves be members of the elective oligarchy, and hence not necessarily hostile to all unscrupulous actions of the government.[†] Yet provided the Upper House is of sufficiently different political composition to the Lower, it will be reluctant to allow members of the Lower to entrench themselves via electoral redistribution.

The distribution of electorates throughout the community is fundamental to the operation of the Constitution, particularly the operation of the Crown's reserve powers. If the electoral system is rigged in favour of the incumbent government, how can the Governor or Governor-General hope to challenge it? What point is there in dismissing a renegade government and appealing to the public to confirm the decision, when those sections of the community critical of the government have already been muffled? When those electors uncritically sympathetic to the government, despite being inferior in number, have been given votes which drown out the voices of dissent? Even if the opponents of the renegade government formed a majority in the community and supported a principled stand by the Crown, under these conditions both

---

† For example, the legislation underlying *Australian Capital Television Pty Ltd v. The Commonwealth of Australia* attempted not only to entrench existing members in the House of Representatives, but also those in the Senate, both party and non-party.

they and the Crown's representative would be overthrown. The reserve powers defend the sovereignty of the people by appealing directly to the people; but how can this work properly in a gerrymander?

Niccolò's ghost	Assuming the electoral distribution was fair at some stage, then even if there were no Upper House and the majority of the Lower was pushing to rig the electoral system, surely at this point the Crown could act to protect both the Constitution and its own future ability to intervene?
Author	If the voters don't perceive the existence of a crisis, what can the Governor or Governor-General do? If the economy is booming and employment is good, who would support a Governor who dismisses the government over an electoral redistribution Bill? No: a better solution may be found by observing that parties generally recruit their grassroots supporters from particular socio-economic groups in society. Corrupt electoral reorganisations are performed to favour these loyal groups based on where or how they live.[†] As conflicting socio-economic groups produce rival parties, the logical solution is to create another chamber, a forum possibly occupied by members of these rival groups to scrutinise this and other legislation.

To Queenslanders this issue is particularly bitter. In 1922 Queensland's Upper House, its Legislative Council, was abolished in the name of constitutional 'reform' by Labor Premier E.G.Theodore. A subsequent gerrymander was established, aimed at magnifying the effects of the right-wing Labor votes of shearers and other rural labourers. Following the internal splitting within the ALP over Communism in the 1950's, Premier Vincent Gair was expelled from the ALP in 1957 and founded the Queensland Labor Party (which later became part of the DLP). The Country-Liberal Party Coalition defeated him later that same year in general elections, and the gerrymander then served to protect the Coalition in government for decades. Later governments took full advantage of their power to give the phrase 'civil liberties' an ironic sound in our ears. We at least have learned that to be Australian offers no defence against oppression, a lesson perhaps citizens of other states had better learn before this constitutional debate proceeds any further.

[†] As to how a lifestyle is relevant to rigging an electoral system, look to British history. For example, if one allows citizens the right to vote in every constituency where they hold land, then if there's a class of wealthy landowners in society, its opinions and interests shall be magnified in Parliament at the expense of poorer classes, the members of which don't own land.

If an Upper House is to provide an early line of defence against the government of the day, then it must have sufficient power to provide an effective challenge to that government over alleged abuses. The most significant power to be granted to this House, and certainly the most controversial, is of blocking Supply.

The concept of Supply and the blocking of Supply originates in mediaeval English *realpolitik*, dating from a time when the King was the government and the early Parliament was wrestling with the task of restraining him. Restraint within the law wasn't enough; what was needed was some means whereby Parliament could steer the King's general policies regarding the realm. This could be achieved through a simple observation: governing without money is impossible. In the 14th Century Parliament aquired control of all taxation in England through use of a document of 1297 called the Confirmation of the Charters (*Confirmatio Cartarum*), approved during the reign of Edward I, which required prior consent for any tax beyond customary feudal payments. This was the genesis of parliamentary appropriations: the right of Parliament to demand that money granted for a specific purpose be used for that purpose.[127]

The most important aspect of this right, and one which remains valid to this day, is that it forces the government to be in some sense accountable to Parliament. Secret schemes become difficult for the Executive to maintain because it's illegal for money to be spent on them without being granted under an appropriations Bill granted by Parliament — and Opposition politicians are hardly going to smile upon a funding item listed as "secret scheme". It's not impossible for a government to get around this through the strategic use of vague wording, but provided Parliament is vigilant and suitably structured with adequate powers, life can be made unpleasant for the unscrupulous — which is, after all, the point of accountability.

Historically, this control over the flow of money for government gave Parliament a potent weapon over the King in subsequent centuries, one dramatically employed during the 17th Century. If the King's policies were offensive to Parliament it could refuse to grant the money he required to govern until it achieved 'redress of grievances'. Expressing this in modern terms, Parliament would block Supply until specific complaints were remedied — a powerful, if rather crude way of stopping injustices, or forcing changes in executive policy. Charles I refused to submit to it. Confronted by one hostile parliament in 1625 and another in 1626, both insisting that Supply be deferred until his favourite minister the Duke of Buckingham was impeached, he replied by dissolving each parliament in turn. With no taxation authorised and with war raging against Spain and France, he proceeded to raise money without parliamentary consent by imposing forced loans, collecting illegal taxes and contracting heavy debts. His actions led to the outbreak of civil war, culminating in his defeat and execution at the hands of the Parliamentary forces.

By retaining the "classical" separation of powers into the 20th Century and beyond, the modern United States has needed to retain the weapon of Supply in its ancient context: a Legislature denying money to a separate Executive in order to achieve redress of grievances. While a draft of this essay was being written, the Republican-dominated Congress used this power to strangle the Clinton administration, depriving it of funds in an attempt to force it to capitulate over policy — although the President, unlike an Australian Prime Minister, couldn't reply by advising a dissolution of Congress and declaring fresh elections to obtain a verdict from the constituency. Instead the US Government was frozen, with wages and pensions unpaid and administration shut down while Clinton haggled with Newt Gingrich and Senator Bob Dole over a compromise that might enable the United States to have a functioning government again.

In Britain, with the evolution of Cabinet government and modern ministerial responsibility in the last years of the 18th and throughout the 19th Century, the leading members of the party commanding the confidence of the House of Commons became the effective Executive, now subordinated to the Legislature. The House of Commons could make effective government impossible by refusing to transact business until the composition of the ministry had been changed. An elegant way of signalling this refusal was the passing of a vote of no confidence in the government, without all the drama and fuss of depriving it of money. The more primitive and extreme weapon of blocking Supply remained for both Commons and Lords, but fell into disuse by the Commons.

With this evolution in government came an alteration in the monarch's role. Her essential duty to uphold constitutional government and ensure it continued to function remained the same, but in the modern world this duty translated into different actions than those previously required of her. In older days she had had to ensure her own policies weren't so offensive as to provoke Commons or Lords to block Supply. Now the policies were imposed by her ministers. If these were so reprehensible that Parliament (i.e. the Lords) refused Supply she had to ensure constitutional government continued. Three possible avenues were available for this: invoke her private rights "to be consulted, to encourage and to warn" to persuade her Prime Minister to amend the offending policy so the Lords would pass Supply; agree to grant a dissolution requested by her Prime Minister, to prove through re-election he has a popular mandate for his policy, after which (if necessary) she would appoint as many new peers on his advice as would be necessary for passage of Supply; or (the most extreme course of action) if he refuses to amend his policy, dismiss him and find an alternative Prime Minister who could obtain Supply. In the modern world her role had been transformed from being active to being reactive: in older days refusal of Supply had forced her to ask herself "How do I amend my policies so that Parliament will grant me the money I need?" In the modern era refusal of Supply forced her to warn her Prime Minster "Devise some constitutional means of obtaining Supply — it's your choice whether you do it by modifying your policies, striking some bargain with them or advising a dissolution to me — or I'll have to find someone else who can".

For the House of Lords, which had no equivalent to a vote of no confidence, control of Supply remained significant as one of the few coercive weapons they had against an outrageous government. Unfortunately for them times had changed. It was one thing for hereditary or appointed lords to coerce policies devised by an hereditary monarch, quite another to coerce those devised by ministers supported by the elected Commons, thus holding a clear claim to be being more representative of the people than disgruntled peers did. The Parliament Act of 1911 effectively destroyed the power of the British Parliament to withhold Supply from any majority government of the day. In its preamble it declares it is merely as a temporary measure, until the Lords is substituted by "a second chamber constituted on a popular instead of hereditary basis", but sadly remarks "such substitution cannot be immediately brought into operation".[128] Almost ninety years later reform has only just begun, and still no parliamentary power (other than that of the Commons) to block Supply. Describing this legislation as a matter of throwing the baby out with the bath water would be inaccurate. Rather, the Palace of Westminster has a filled bathtub and a missing baby.

Strict party discipline, imposed within Cabinet government, threatens to pervert parliamentary democracy throughout the world. This appears an outlandish exaggeration until we remember our government is supposed to be subordinate to Parliament,[†] and responsible to it. Yet except for when particular conditions induce a minority government, the government of the day will command a majority in the Lower House. Which demands the question: what happens when ministers lie to the House or treat it with contempt? Before the days of rigid party discipline there was always the risk backbenchers of all parties and even fellow ministers might be disgusted by such displays and turn against the guilty member, but now provided prime ministers are willing to throw their weight behind an offending subordinate, party whips shall coerce backbenchers to support their disgraced minister — or lose preselection for their own seats at the next election. Within the House votes which should be based on censure of contemptible behaviour are reduced to simple arithmetic of Government and Opposition seats. Outside the House Prime Ministers can and have responded to public allegations or the formal findings of a Royal Commission against ministers, not by dismissing the ministers but by heaping ridicule and abuse upon those who dare make the allegations. The public, supposedly the final decider against these abuses, has long since surrendered to numb disgust by chronic exposure to them. The Lower House, be it called the House of Representatives (Australia and New Zealand) or the Legislative Assembly (the Australian States) or the House of Commons (Britain and Canada) is no longer capable of defending its privileges against the delinquency of majority governments. Provided the Prime Minister is game to back them, ministers can lie and cheat and engage in all manner of calculated deceit, and those who cry outrage to this, within the House and without, find

---

† That word is *Parliament*, not 'the Lower House'. That House is an organ of Parliament. Historically it's the dominant of the two Houses. But it couldn't be synonymous with 'Parliament' unless there were no Upper House at all. Even if the Commonwealth of Australia abolished the Senate the House of Representatives wouldn't equate to Parliament, because the latter is composed of three organs: the Representatives, the Senate...and the Queen, represented by the Governor-General.

ON THE BEACH

themselves the hapless targets of executive enmity. Is it any wonder that in Britain Lord Hailsham has written despairingly of modern government as an elective dictatorship; that in Oxford Dr Eugene Forsey warned "The danger of royal absolutism is past; but the danger of Cabinet absolutism, even of Prime Ministerial absolutism, is present and growing"; that in pre-republic South Africa Leif Egeland MP described the office of Prime Minister as "the leader of the junta wielding for the moment the power of office"? The privileges of Parliament, being privileges of the people, can no longer be protected by the Lower House against the man or woman most likely to violate them — precisely because he or she already controls the Lower House.

Niccolò's ghost   'But not on us!' the Oysters cried,
    Turning a little blue,
    'After such kindness, that would be
    A dismal thing to do!'
    'The night is fine', the Walrus said,
    'Do you admire the view?'

Constitutional design in Australia has drawn upon pre-20th Century history in Britain and North America to provide some alternative protection for parliamentary integrity. The Federal Parliament has two Houses, the Representatives and the Senate, both of which are elected. The Representatives is as the name suggests, a conventional Lower House, a chamber composed of members representing regional constituencies from all Australia, whereas the Senate is a federal 'States' House' composed along the lines of the US Senate, with a certain equal number of senators for each State (irrespective of relative population).[†] These States are:

> so represented for the purpose of enabling them to maintain and
> protect their constitutional rights against attempted invasions
> [by the federal government], and to give them every facility for
> the advocacy of their peculiar and special interests, as well as for
> the ventilation and consideration of their grievances.[129]

An incentive for this system was that if a federal government committed offences against the States, appeal to the federal High Court would be inadequate for justice, a danger felt more acutely in the less populous regions.

> In addition to the legal remedy it was deemed advisable that
> Original States at least should be endowed with a parity of
> representation in one chamber of the Parliament for the

---

† The reason for this equality of representation is that the Original States (the former British self-governing colonies) held an equal degree of sovereignty prior to federation, and in the Commonwealth of Australia are co-equal partners irrespective of relative population. Therefore in the States' House they each have an equal voice.

purpose of enabling them effectively to resist, in the legislative stage, proposals threatening to invade and violate the domain of rights reserved to the States.[130]

A formidable weapon of resistance was therefore placed in the hands of the senators against the government of the day. Section 57 of the Constitution states,

> If the House of Representatives passes any proposed law, and the Senate rejects or fails to pass it, or passes it with amendments to which the House of Representatives will not agree, and if after an interval of three months the House of Representatives, in the same or the next session, again passes the proposed law with or without any amendments which have been made, suggested, or agreed to by the Senate, and the Senate rejects or fails to pass it, or passes it with amendments to which the House of Representatives will not agree, the Governor-General may dissolve the Senate and the House of Representatives simultaneously. But such dissolution shall not take place within six months before the date of the expiry of the House of Representatives by effluxion of time.
>
> If after such dissolution the House of Representatives again passes the proposed law, with or without any amendments which have been made, suggested, or agreed to by the Senate, and the Senate rejects or fails to pass it, or passes it with amendments to which the House of Representatives will not agree, the Governor-General may convene a joint sitting of the members of the Senate and of the House of Representatives.
>
> The members present at the joint sitting may deliberate and shall vote together upon the proposed law as last proposed by the House of Representatives, and upon amendments, if any, which have been made therein by one House and not agreed to by the other, and any such amendments which are affirmed by an absolute majority of the total number of the members of the Senate and House of Representatives shall be taken to have been carried, and if the proposed law, with the amendments, if any, so carried is affirmed by an absolute majority of the total number of the members of the Senate and House of Representatives, it shall be taken to have been duly passed by both Houses of the Parliament, and shall be presented to the Governor-General for the Queen's assent.[131]

Proposed laws that can be rejected or simply not passed include Money Bills. In this way the Australian Parliament retains an intensely practical (if ancient) weapon against a delinquent government, to be wielded by senators in times of crisis.

Like so many other institutions throughout history, the Senate has altered in behaviour from that originally intended for it. Although its original prime directive was to uphold the rights of the States against incursions by the federal government, this role appears to have been submerged through the efficiency of nationwide party organisation and discipline among the elected senators. Until recently the two parties that dominate the Representatives have also dominated the Senate, and senators have voted as members of a party rather than representatives of a State. Yet due to the difference between the electoral systems employed for each House, the party which controls the Representatives doesn't necessarily control the Senate, hence Keating's inaccurate reviling of senators as "unrepresentative swill". Consequently the weapons endowed upon the Senate are now employed to curb abuses by the government against federal Parliament rather than abuses against the States.

It was senatorial control of Supply which forced the dismissal of the Whitlam government by Governor- General Sir John Kerr on Remembrance Day, 1975. The Senate deferred Supply, claiming the existence of reprehensible circumstances: namely, unlawful and secretive attempts by members of Whitlam's ministry to borrow from Middle Eastern sources a sum of up to four thousand million dollars US for a period of twenty years, the notorious Khemlani affair (named after the government's private financial agent, Pakistani businessman Tireth Khemlani). What this vast sum of money was needed for remains a matter for heated debate. Whitlam's explanation was that it was needed "for temporary purposes" to "deal with exigencies arising out of the current world situation and the international energy crisis, to strengthen Australia's external financial position, to provide immediate protection for Australia in regard to supplies of minerals and energy" and to deal with "current and immediately foreseeable unemployment".[132] His description of a secret loan of US$4000 million (plus interest) over twenty years as "temporary" didn't inspire confidence among Opposition senators, although it provided him with an excuse to attempt avoiding the Loan Council. The Opposition senators saw a more sinister possibility for the money: that Whitlam had seen the writing on the wall for his government, that sooner or later events would provoke Senate to block Supply and so he was hoarding money to govern without Parliament; that once again he was following his personal rule of "crash through or crash", but this time to commit a gross violation against parliamentary democracy itself. They therefore passed a motion in the Senate on the 16th of October declaring that the two Appropriation Bills:

> be not further proceeded with until the Government agrees to
> submit itself to the judgement of the people, the Senate being
> of the opinion that the Prime Minister and his Government
> no longer have the trust and confidence of the Australia
> people because of —
>
> (a) the continuing incompetence, evasion, deceit and
>   duplicity of the Prime Minister and his Ministers as exem-
>   plified in the overseas loan scandal which was an attempt
>   by the Government to subvert the Constitution, to by-
>   pass Parliament and to evade its responsibilities to the
>   States and the Loan Council;

(b) the Prime Minister's failure to maintain proper control over the activities of his Ministers and Government to the detriment of the Australian nation and people, and;

(c) the continuing mismanagement of the Australian economy by the Prime Minister and this Government with policies which have caused a lack of confidence in this nation's potential and created inflation and unemployment not experienced for 40 years.[133]

This denial of money proved swiftly corrosive to administration. In the House Whitlam's Defence Minister, Mr Morrison, warned on the 21st of October that defence preparedness of Australia would collapse; that after 30th November all weekly wages and allowances for all defence personnel would be unpayable, the Army immobilised, the Air Force grounded, coastline surveillance ceased and naval forces confined to port.[134] The day after that speech Whitlam's Treasurer, Mr Bill Hayden, warned of a budgetary shortfall of between $700 million and $800 million per month once the existing Supply expired, causing government contracts to dry up, and subsequent retrenchments of school-teachers and university staff.[135] During this crisis Senator John Wheeldon, Whitlam's Minister for Social Security, moved

> a resolution in [Labor] Caucus, seconded by Senator Wriedt and supported by about a quarter or a third of the Parliamentary Labor Party, calling on the government to put an end to the obstruction in the Senate by asking for a double dissolution.[136]

This Whitlam refused to do. On the 11th of November Sir John Kerr finally lost patience and sacked him, replacing his ministry with a Coalition caretaker administration under Malcolm Fraser, and declared a double dissolution.[137] In the consequent general election Fraser won a landslide victory, enabling him thereafter to form a substantive government in his own right.

In the twenty years since Whitlam's government fell, the events surrounding the Dismissal have been distorted in the reflections of a partisan Press. At the twentieth anniversary of the sacking the loose assertion was frequently made that the power of the Senate to refuse or delay Supply is inconsistent and incompatible with responsible government, i.e. a government contained within the framework of ministerial responsibilty.

In weighing up this assertion, there's a vital difference between a *caretaker* government and what might be described as a *substantive* government. The former, as the name suggests, is simply a ministry which exists "to hold the fort" until a specific event takes place, usually a general election. Until that event the caretaker administration takes care of the day-to-day running of government, ensuring that someone is at the other end of the ministerial telephone when needed. It has no authority to initiate new policy or make new appointments, and is only summoned into existence when some unusual power vacuum occurs.[†] On the other side, a substantive government is the sort we are all familiar with, a ministry entitled to devise and implement fresh policies, make new appointments and generally govern as it thinks best. Understanding aspects of the Dismissal requires clarity on that distinction.

Those who've made the claim of incompatibility labour under the belief that responsible government is entirely described by saying "the identity of the administration in power is dictated by whichever parliamentary faction is holding the confidence of the elected Lower House". Certainly in all versions of the Westminster system throughout the world this confidence of the elected Lower House is a *necessary* condition for a substantive government to remain in power. But is it a *sufficient* condition, i.e. is this confidence *enough* for power?‡ The answer to that question depends upon the individual constitution. In Australia it's deliberately insufficient, so senators can in extreme crises render government impossible until a general election is promised. In other countries like unicameral New Zealand, unless the Crown invokes its reserve powers, this confidence provides a sufficient condition also.[138] Is this desirable? If the confidence of existing representatives is the only criterion, surely this reduces democratic government to elective dictatorship? Surely it converts ministers into temporary autocrats?

Imagine voters as people standing on a hillside strewn with large rocks, people required to play a game. Administrations once placed in power acquire a certain momentum that helps them to retain that power, even as a boulder set in motion down a hillside acquires a momentum that helps it remain in motion, by breaking obstacles standing in the way. Draw an analogy between voters given a choice between candidate governments and our people on a hillside given a choice of boulders to set rolling. One boulder must be pushed even as one candidate must be chosen. Any great rock set in motion must eventually come to rest at the bottom of the hill, even as any elected government forced to submit to regular elections must eventually reach the end of its term in office. Being inanimate, rocks aren't susceptible to malice or ambition, even as they're not motivated by altruism or compassion. Yet, obliged to see a vast rock set rolling down a slope, confronted with the possible damage it may cause to life or property further down the hill, most sane people would insist there be safeguards imposed upon the exercise: that in the event of an emergency, the wrong rock crashing down the wrong path, some method should exist to stop it before it goes too far, before it reaches the end of its path. If we feel this caution about the restraint of

---

† In Australia a convention also exists whereby once an ordinary government has successfully advised a general election, it behaves in a self-imposed caretaker role until the composition of the new post-election House makes clear whether that government can continue to enjoy the confidence of the House.

‡ In formal logic, the distinction between a necessary condition and a sufficient one can be explained as follows: if the fact that Proposition A is true always implies that Proposition B is also true, **then** A is a *sufficient condition* for B (written mathematically $A \rightarrow B$). For example: Given that all wombats are ill-tempered, then if Cecil is a wombat then Cecil is ill-tempered. "Cecil is a wombat" is a sufficient condition for Cecil to be ill-tempered. On the other hand, if the fact that Proposition A is false always implies that Proposition B is false, then Proposition A is a *necessary condition* for Proposition B (written mathematically $\neg A \rightarrow \neg B$). (This is equivalent to saying that B can never be true if A is false). For example: For a parrot to be alive its heart must be beating. Eugene is a parrot. Question: Is Eugene alive? Answer: If Eugene's heart is not beating, then he can't be alive.

an inanimate object devoid of ambition or malice, how should we feel about the restraint of a human government set in motion?

The power of an Upper House to block Supply, like the Lords' former power to do so, can't be described as *incompatible* with responsible government, for it's simply a more ancient way of enforcing a form of ministerial responsibility to Parliament. However an immovable Upper House repeatedly inflicting this punishment upon an administration possessing the confidence of the elected Lower clearly castrates democratic government. If the purpose of this punishment is simply to force the government to seek again the public will, then surely renewed public confidence in the former government should carry with it a penalty against the members of the Upper House who invoked this extreme measure of disruption. Otherwise a hostile Upper House could time and again render government impossible despite the confidence of the elected Lower, without fear of backlash, destroying the very privileges of Parliament we argue control over Supply should uphold.

In Britain a crude form of punishment was conceived whereby the Prime Minister of a returned administration would advise the monarch to create as many lords as was required for a pro-government majority in the Lords — altering the balance of power in that House for years after. This action was threatened during the reign of William IV, whom Prime Minister Earl Grey forced to provide a written undertaking that as many Whig peers would be created as would prove necessary for the passage of the 1832 Reform Bill.[139] When the 1911 Parliament Bill passed into law it reduced the Lords into little more than an eloquent eunuch, who no longer needed to be warned against misbehaviour it was incapable of performing.

In Australia a more sophisticated reprisal against misuse of the power over Supply was devised, based upon punishment through public accountability rather than by stacking the post-election membership. Because the Senate is elected, section 57 quoted above allows the Governor-General to dissolve both Houses (a so-called 'double dissolution') under certain circumstances, forcing simultaneous general elections for both. The electorate can decide whether or not the previous government should be returned to power or not, *and* at the same time whether the senators were justified in their extreme behaviour (therefore deserving re-election) or not.

Thus the responsibility of ministers to Parliament can be enforced, through the threat of a forced consultation with the ultimate sovereign, the electorate. If the conditions of section 57 are fulfilled[†] the Prime Minister can acquiesce and advise the Governor-General for a double dissolution, in which case both the government and its opponents are brought before the ballot box for the public verdict upon who should govern. If the Prime Minister refuses to acquiesce and

---

† The Appropriation Bill required for supply of money to the government needn't itself be one of the Bills being blocked under section 57. In the '75 crisis the *Appropriation Bill Nos 1&2 (1975–76)* had been deferred only since the 16th October, but some twenty-one other Bills blocked by the Senate satisfied

ON THE BEACH

attempts to defy Parliament (as Whitlam did in 1975, boasting he would "tough it out" and "crush" or "smash" this "vicious" and "tainted" Senate[140]) then, provided an alternative ministry exists in Parliament willing to take responsibilty for these actions, the Governor-General can dismiss the recalcitrant Prime Minister and old ministry, replacing it with the new *as a caretaker government* and declaring the House dissolved.[†] Whether the entire Senate is also sent to the polls depends on the presence of a section 57 trigger Bill.

As it turned out, in the 1975 elections members of Fraser's caretaker administration were re-elected to serve as a substantive government with an overwhelming majority: in a House of Representatives composed of only 127 seats Fraser's Liberal-National Country Party coalition won by a margin of 55 seats over the Labor Opposition led by Whitlam, a post-war record and a resounding endorsement of their role in the Dismissal (however unfashionable it may be to admit it twenty-five years on).[‡] Similarly, the Coalition won a landslide victory in the Senate, an endorsement of its senator's actions.

Political journalists like Laurie Oakes remarked sourly at the time that the House of Lords had been stripped of its power to block Supply in 1911, and had the Australian Constitution been drafted after that event "the powers of the Senate would probably have been similarly circumscribed".[141] But is this opinion accurate? It ignores a central point made by Chief Justice Sir Garfield Barwick in his written opinion to Kerr prior to the Dismissal. The powers of the Senate weren't modelled on the Lords but on the Commons: the Constitution states,

> The powers, privileges, and immunities of the Senate and of
> the House of Representatives, and of the members and the
> committees of each House, shall be such as are declared by
> the Parliament, and until declared *shall be those of the
> Commons House of Parliament* of the United Kingdom, and of
> its members and committees, at the establishment of the
> Commonwealth.[142]

This provision compelled Barwick to write,

> There is no analogy in respect of a Prime Minister's duty
> between the situation of the Parliament under the federal

---

section 57. The special powers imparted to the Governor-General by this section were thus activated by non-essential Bills, but it was denial of Supply which forced his hand into invoking those powers.

† Alternatively, if the old ministry was a minority government then, provided the new ministry won the confidence of the Lower House, it could be permitted to operate as a substantive government without a dissolution. If, as in the 1975 example, the new ministry cannot win this confidence then it has no right to anything more than a caretaker role, pending an election.

‡ Indirectly it might also be construed as an endorsement of Kerr's own actions. The Fraser caretaker ministry had taken public responsibility for Kerr's actions, as constitutional usage required. If voters in the greater public had disapproved of Kerr's actions, they might be expected to have vented their anger upon his responsible ministers. They did not. Instead they rewarded those ministers with a resounding majority in both Houses.

Constitution of Australia and the relationship between the
House of Commons, a popularly elected body, and the House
of Lords, a non-elected body, in the unitary form of govern-
ment functioning in the United Kingdom. Under that system,
a Government having the confidence of the House of
Commons can secure supply, despite a recalcitrant House of
Lords. But it is otherwise under our federal Constitution. A
Government having the confidence of the House of
Representatives but not that of the Senate, both elected
Houses, cannot secure supply to the Crown.

But there is an analogy between the situation of a Prime
Minister who has lost the confidence of the House of
Commons and a Prime Minister who does not have the confidence of Parliament, i.e. of the House of Representatives and
of the Senate. The duty and responsibility of the Prime
Minister to the Crown in each case is the same: if unable to
secure supply to the Crown, to resign or advise an election.[143]

So although the experiences and debates of the Lords are *illustrative* of the
necessity and pitfalls of a second House possessing the power to block or defer
Supply, the Senate's *actual* power to do so is that of the Commons — a power
unaffected and unchallenged by the events of 1911.

If Barwick's letter were read without its historical context the reader might
draw the inaccurate inference that this power of the Senate's could and should
be invoked as readily as the Lower House's power to pass a vote of no confidence. Denial of Supply is a weapon of threatened catastrophe, to force a
recalcitrant administration to its knees by starving it of funds required for the
maintenance of all the instruments of government: among other things the
public service, the judiciary, police and the armed forces. It endangers everything from the six-figure financial affairs of all the country's banks through to
the dole cheques of the unemployed; everything, in short, in a financial relationship with the federal government. It therefore should be used only after
much soul-searching, for it has the capacity to inflict great pain not only upon
the government but upon all citizens until the crisis is resolved. How much
pain it actually does inflict depends heavily upon the willingness of the Prime
Minister to acknowledge the authority of the Upper House and the integrity
to advise an election or resign to prevent harm to the electorate, rather than
clinging desperately to power.

Four years after the Dismissal Whitlam published a justification for his intran-
sigence, declaring "I was determined to uphold the ancient and fundamental
principle that it is the lower House which must control the supply of money
to the elected government".[144] But this justification is invalid, being based (as
we have seen) upon a false analogy between the Senate and the Lords. More
intriguingly, Whitlam himself did not always accept this principle. In D.J.
Markwell's words,

This was not a principle he had believed in when, in 1958 and 1959, he put his name to the *Report from the Joint Committee on Constitutional Review*, which quite clearly acknowledged the right of the Senate to block Supply. It was not a principle he had believed existed when in 1970 his Party, under his leadership, sought to bring down the Gorton government by opposing Supply in the Senate. Nor had Mr Whitlam done anything in April 1974 to assert that 'principle' when he immediately called a double dissolution election in response to the Opposition-controlled Senate's threat not to pass the Appropriation Bills. Indeed, Mr Whitlam told the House of Representatives that, while it was inappropriate for the Senate "to cut off supply for the House of Representatives", he did "not have the same objection to the Senate or an upper house refusing Supply *if it also faces the people at the same time*...I am very happy for both Houses of this Parliament to face the consequences of any refusal of supply". In 1975 (as in 1974), it was open to Mr Whitlam to make the Senate "face the people at the same time" as the House of Representatives (which is what finally happened); but, as Clem Lloyd and Andrew Clark record, Mr "Whitlam's attitude to the rejection of Supply had *hardened immeasurably* since the narrow return of his government in May 1974".[145]

We've already ascertained (courtesy of H.V. Evatt) that the forcing of repeated elections within a short space of time can be an abuse of the democratic process, "the very means of first delaying and ultimately defeating the true popular will, and so represent a triumph over, and not a triumph of, the electorate". Whitlam allegedly feared that denial of Supply would become as habitual a practice in the Upper House as attempted votes of no confidence in the Lower. On the day of his dismissal he delivered a speech in the House, warning,

I am not sure whether [the people of Australia], or indeed all members of this House, yet fully realise the inordinate and unprecedented pretensions now being put forward by the Leader of the Opposition on behalf of the Senate...The new preposterous claim is that the Senate — not even an elected majority but a mere accidental half of the Senate — can dictate to the House of Representatives our own dissolution... The Senate cannot be dissolved except at the times and in the terms strictly laid down by the Constitution. This House has no power to dissolve the Senate. Yet the Senate now purports to have such power over this House. The Senate is saying that every six months it has the power to require an election for this House, while its own term must remain inviolate under the Constitution.[146]

Yet was he justified in asserting that this measure, if employed once, would become a commonplace threat holding the House to ransom? Previous

Australian experiences indicate the contrary. Victoria's Upper House (the Legislative Council) used its power to refuse Supply to the Cain Labor government in 1947, demanding a state election over the federal issue of bank nationalisation. As might be expected, Premier John Cain resisted at first the Council's ultimatum. Seeing the Council was obstinant in its demands he finally advised the Governor of Victoria, Sir Winston Dugan, to this effect and was granted a dissolution of Parliament so that elections could be held.[147]

On the 8th of July 1948 Tasmania's Legislative Council, confronted with a financial Bill to draw money from Consolidated Revenue for various purposes, passed a resolution returning the Bill to the Assembly. This was coupled with a request that the Assembly amend the Bill, reducing the Supply to be granted to an amount for two month's use "on the understanding that the Government seek an immediate dissolution of the House of Assembly for the purpose of a General Election".[148]Infuriated, the House protested that the Council was denying Supply to force an election over the government's support of a recent federal referendum for the transfer of powers over prices and rents to the Commonwealth. The Council rejected this assertion, instead defending itself rather oddly by saying its attitude was based upon the general loss of confidence in the government by the electors — precisely the attitude Whitlam later warned against. The House gave the usual retort that the Council, by established useage, had no right to refuse Supply. Now on firmer ground, the Council formally replied by pointing to a 1926 Tasmanian Act largely copied from the Constitution of the Commonwealth, which endowed the Council with powers analogous to those of the Senate. As part of this formal reply the Council stated,

> If the Federal Senate should reject a Supply Bill, it could not
> be suggested it had acted unconstitutionally. The action
> might of course be criticised on political grounds, but its
> constitutional power would be undoubted...The Legislative
> Council does not, by this statement, suggest there are no
> practical limitations upon these powers...[b]ut such limita-
> tions are of a political and not a constitutional character.[149]

Later, in a formal statement in the House the Premier made it clear he regarded the actions of the Council as improper, but that if it persisted in this way then "the Government in the interests of the people will recommend His Excellency the Governor to dissolve the House of Assembly forthwith".[150] This he did, and a general election was held.

The third and most complicated example took place again in Victoria in 1952. In office was the Country Party minority government of Mr John McDonald (with 13 seats), supported in the Assembly by Labor (with 25 seats, including an independent) and opposed by the Liberal Party (with 26 seats). A dispute over electoral reform for the Assembly had set the Country and Liberal parties in conflict with each other, the Liberal advocates for reform through redistribution being led by T.T. Hollway, a former premier. In July Labor withdrew its support for McDonald's ministry in the House but the Liberals offered theirs instead, propping up the government for a while longer. In September Hollway did a deal with Labor whereby he would perform a redistribution favouring the towns, provided Labor gave him its support. This was agreed, and with the support of six other Liberals he moved a motion of no confidence in the government, in an attempt to topple it which was defeated 32–31. The Supply Bill then passed up to the Council, where Labor decided to refuse Supply to any government except one led by Hollway. As members of the Council saw it, this would lead either to a Hollway government dedicated to convenient redistribution or a general election fought over the issue. In this action Labor members were supported by two Liberal and Country Party members who also wanted to see an election fought on the topic, and so Supply was refused 17–16. Existing Supply was due to expire on the 31st October, leaving the government rather poor. McDonald therefore requested a dissolution from the Governor, Sir Dallas Brooks, but the crisis had by now accelerated to such an extent that it appeared there was insufficient money for any government to continue to function. The Governor consulted with Hollway and, receiving his assurance he could obtain Supply, refused to call an election just yet. (In this the Governor and Hollway had very different motives. Hollway doubtless wanted office, whereas Brooks was confronted with an emergency in which his overwhelming public duty was to ensure the fabric of government did not collapse.) McDonald therefore resigned and the Governor called upon Hollway to form a government and ensure Supply. The Legislative Council, true to its word, passed Supply on the 21st October and the money came through. The new Premier wasn't so lucky with the Assembly: its members voted against him in a motion of no confidence (32–31), so he also asked for an election. The Governor noted there was now enough money for an election, that throughout this entire episode McDonald had enjoyed the confidence of the House (which Hollway never had) and that not only had both Premiers requested an election but one would normally take place in March or April 1953 anyway. He refused Hollway's request, required the Premier's resignation, and reinstated McDonald as Premier for his proposed dissolution now granted.† The general elections were held.[151]

The fourth and final example might be described as a Supply crisis that never was, being more notable for what was attempted than what was achieved, and still more memorable for the players in this drama and what they said. Five years later at least some of them and their fans would pretend it hadn't happened, like

---

† Sir Dallas Brooks' actions provide an illustration of the Crown's role as referee, separating justifiable motives from unscrupulous ones in an emergency. The majority of members in the Upper House wanted to force an election, well and good. More money was needed before this election could possibly be held, and such money would only be granted to a government led by Hollway. Brooks therefore commissioned Hollway so that the money came through, and gave Parliament the chance to attempt to transact business under its alternative leader. This attempt failed, and to allow Hollway now to go to the voters as Premier would have been undesirable. In the coming election it would have given him an unjustified advantage; unjustified because his presence as Premier was no longer necessary, his predecessor McDonald had proved himself clearly willing to take ministerial responsibility for advising an election, and held the confidence of the House. Under these conditions McDonald was clearly the better candidate to take responsibility, and hence was recommissioned Premier for the election.

a B-grade movie successful actors later pretend they never appeared in. But the script deserves to be resuscitated, and the actors' performances reviewed.

In June 1970 the government of Liberal prime minister John Gorton attempted to pass a taxation Bill through the Senate. With the uninspiring title of *States Receipts Duties (Administration) Bill 1970*, it was to provoke a fascinating exposition from Labor Senator Lionel Murphy, then Leader of the Opposition in the Senate, and later to serve as a Justice of the High Court.

After criticising the Bill, Senator Murphy promised the Labor Opposition would oppose it, saying,

> In doing this the [Labor] Opposition is pursuing a tradition
> which is well established, but in view of some doubt recently
> cast on it in this chamber, perhaps I should restate the position.
> *The Senate is entitled and expected to exercise resolutely but with
> discretion its power to refuse its concurrence to any financial
> measure, including a tax Bill. There are no limitations on the Senate
> in the use of its constitutional powers, except the limitations imposed
> by discretion and reason.* The Australian Labor Party has acted
> consistently in accordance with the tradition that we will
> oppose in the Senate any tax or money Bill or other financial
> measure whenever necessary to carry out our principles or poli-
> cies. The Opposition has done this over the years, and in order
> to illustrate the tradition which has been established, with the
> concurrence of honourable senators I shall incorporate in
> Hansard at the end of my speech a list of the measures of an
> economic or financial nature, including taxation and appropri-
> ation Bills, which have been opposed by this Opposition in
> whole or in part by a vote in the Senate since 1950.[152]

This list was indeed appended as he requested, entitled *Measures of an Economic or Financial Nature including Taxation and Appropriation Bills which have been Opposed by the Australian Labor Party in Whole or in Part by Vote in the Senate since 1950*. It ran to one hundred and sixty-nine examples.[153]

On the 25th of August that same year the Gorton government attempted to pass the second reading of its *Appropriation Bill (No.1) 1970–71*. In this debate the Leader of the Opposition, Mr Edward Gough Whitlam, rose to his feet and proposed a motion condemning the Bill. He went further, saying,

> Let me make it clear at the outset that our opposition to this
> Budget is no mere formality. We intend to press our opposition
> by all available means on all related measures in both Houses.
> If the motion is defeated, we will vote against the Bills here
> and in the Senate. Our purpose is to destroy this Budget and to
> destroy the Government which has sponsored it[154].

There is no ambiguity here, either in Whitlam's and Murphy's belief in the power and right of the Senate to refuse Supply, or that by destroying a Budget one can destroy the government which sponsored it. The difference was, in 1970 it wasn't Whitlam's own government being threatened.[†]

These, then, are modern Australian precedents for the blocking of Supply to force the removal of governments prior to 1975, and they provoke a number of comments. First, while they are enough so that a Supply crisis was by no means *terra incognita* in 1975, they're surprisingly few in number if control of Supply really does upset the balance of power to the extent Whitlam later claimed. One would expect members of Upper Houses to have made more energetic use of this lever if such power was theirs to be had for free. Second; these precedents display that, far from playing chicken with the Upper House over the Constitution, or turning the entire emergency into a matter of personal ego, the proper course of action for the head of a government confronted with such a crisis is to search for alternative legitimate solutions through compromise or mediation, and, finding none, to advise dissolution or resign. Provided the Upper House is also elective it should be possible for the electorate to express its displeasure at the manner of this forced election, if the voters really disapprove of it. Third; the second crisis in Victoria appears to have been inspired by the first. Not only was the '47 crisis cited at the time as a precedent for that of '52, but the Melbourne *Age* commented during the latter that it might represent historic retribution for the former in the reversal of party relationships.[155]

So why has Supply been so rarely rejected this century at any level of government where it's been possible? Why hasn't it been invoked "every six months"? It's not through senatorial ignorance of their ability to do so: this power had been openly discussed in both Houses in 1901 when the first Supply Bills were hotly contested.[156] It's not because the Senate's always been controlled by the party in government — it hasn't. Is it through permanent fear of public opinion? If opinion were always a prohibiting factor, then surely the more often the Upper House threatened to engage in this act, the hotter public indignation would become against it, reflected in the election of anti-blockage senators and therefore refuting Whitlam's fears of escalating high-handedness. Escalations would be quelled.

This alone is not persuasive across almost a century of history. Public indignation doesn't last forever. Even if the majority of a particular generation are agreed that refusing Supply is a Bad Thing, that's no guarantee their children will share their opinion. One must delve deeper, to find a more calculated reason for senatorial restraint.

---

† The threat failed to materialize that year. Gorton's government wasn't brought down until March 1971, when he refused to use his casting vote at a Liberal Party meeting tied over the issue of confidence in his prime ministership, thus effectively voting himself out of office. Whitlam went on to win the 1972 election, with Murphy the Leader of the Government in the Senate.

In politics, reluctance to engage in high-handedness isn't always due to high-mindedness, senators wringing their hands in woe because the lion shows no sign of lying down with the lamb. Retaining this ecclesiastical turn of phrase, the more likely reason for caution is that he who lives by the sword dies by the sword. In the most highly strung rhetoric of the period the events of '75 were christened a *coup d'etat* or *putsch*. The accuracy of this description is somewhat dubious. If the revoking of Whitlam's commission by Sir John Kerr was a *coup d'etat* then it was the wierdest *coup* in human history: discharged within a constitutional framework, aimed at compelling constitutional government, and firing the bullet…of a general election for both Houses. A *coup* that menaced the government by forcing it to stare down the slit of a ballot box?

Yet this exotic flight of mid-'70s fancy isn't entirely without merit. Some of the differences between the Dismissal and a *coup d'etat* are instructive — particularly with reference to Whitlam's fears of an upstart Senate.

Consultation with a dictionary revealed its definition of the word

> **coup**(kōō), n. Notable or successful stroke or move;
> (Billiards) direct holing of ball; ~*d'état*(dĕtah'), violent or
> illegal change in government; ~*de grâce*(de grahs), finishing
> stroke; ~*de main*(see Ap.), sudden vigorous attack;…
> ~*de théâtre*(tāh'tr), dramatically sudden or sensational act. [F,
> f.med.L *col(a)pus* f.L f.Gk *kolaphos* blow][157]

Sir John Kerr's revocation of Whitlam's commission as Prime Minister certainly wasn't illegal, and the only violence associated with it, then or afterwards, was committed against Sir John Kerr. And although events on the actual day of the eleventh of November took place with swiftness, prompting inaccurate journalistic captions like "Kerr's king hit", the logic of circumstances had been grinding slowly towards this conclusion since at least the 16th of October. This was a logic of which no-one with a good understanding of the Constitution could be ignorant. Consider: it's a fundamental rule in parliamentary democracy for the government only to be permitted to spend money appropriated with the approval of Parliament.[158] So government can't spend unapproved money; if Parliament refuses to pass the Appropriations Bills the government gets no new money; government without money is impossible. The Crown is the ultimate guarantor of the Constitution and the laws of the Commonwealth;[159] the Constitution requires the existence of a functioning government; it also stipulates certain payments which must be made by that government.[160] Hence if a ministry finds itself deprived of Supply and unable to obtain it, that ministry eventually ceases to be competent as a constitutional government — obliging the Crown, if all else fails, to dismiss it. Conclusion? Provided the incumbent government can be starved of money long enough, the Governor-General shall be forced to dismiss it. If the crisis can be made sufficiently extreme circumstances shall reduce him to little more than a senior piece on the political chessboard, moving and capturing with a logic understood by both players.

Whitlam must have comprehended all this. Hadn't he attempted the same manoeuvre as Leader of the Opposition in 1970? No astute political leader — certainly not one with his legal background — would have embarked on such a course of brinkmanship without thinking through the implications. (It's not a vast intellectual feat to have stopped and pondered: if Gorton's government is starved until untenable and he advises a double dissolution to Hasluck, well and good. But if it becomes untenable and he refuses to tender this advice…?) Whitlam knew what stakes Fraser and his Opposition senators were playing for because they were the same he and his Labor senators had once played for. The difference was the earlier attempt had failed to make the stratagem reach fruition, whereas the later effort left an administration ripe for picking; if not to be picked, then to fall regardless.

Yet between the passive place of usual viceregal duties, where despite personal doubts on their wisdom the Governor-General must follow the advice of his incumbent ministers, and the rare site of crisis where his active duty is (if necessary) to oppose and possibly sack them, there's an obscure territory to be crossed. How crisis is to be averted, or if not averted resolved, depends on personal qualities of judgement, tact and experience (or lack thereof) of both Head of Government and Head of State. To warn or not, to mediate or not, are decisions the Governor-General alone must make regarding the incumbent government; decisions sobered by his own clear lack of a democratic mandate. Perhaps Sir John Kerr could have acted otherwise than he did to resolve the emergency at hand, although conciliation was not the thing uppermost in the minds of belligerent politicians on either side. Perhaps a better path existed. This is a question for political analysts to debate for years to come. But to blame him for the fall of Whitlam's government is to misunderstand 1975. The writings prompted by international disgust at the vilification and misrepresentation of Kerr within Australia put the matter succinctly; two conspicuous examples will suffice. In Canada Eugene Forsey wrote:

> For the life of me, I could not see, and still cannot see, what else he could have done in the circumstances. The constitutional right of the Senate to refuse, or defer, supply, seems to me incontestable. Perhaps it should never have been given that right. But it was; and the result of its exercise of that right, and of Mr Whitlam's response to that exercise, was that, but for Sir John's action, the Government of Australia would have been left for some months with no funds to meet some 40 per cent of its expenses, except by the use of measures of very doubtful legal validity and even more doubtful effectiveness…
>
> Mr Whitlam's refusal either to resign, or to advise a dissolution (single or double), was a flagrant breach of the principles of responsible government. It would, on his own and his Ministers' showing, have led to 'utter financial chaos', 'a major economic collapse', and severe hardship for 'the suppliers of goods and services to the Government and the suppliers of goods and services to people who serve the needs of govern-

ment, community agencies, States and overseas governments',
no pay for the armed services. The only way to prevent this was
a dissolution, preferably a double dissolution. Only the people
could settle the question. Mr Whitlam was refusing to let them
do so. It then became the plain, indeed the inescapable, duty of
the Governor-General to give them the opportunity which Mr
Whitlam would have denied them.[161]

Remember Forsey was never part of any supposed right-wing conspiracy,
national or international. This was the voice of a fellow socialist deploring
Whitlam's actions. In Britain Lord Hailsham wrote,

Sir John Kerr was an honest man placed in an intolerable
position which was not of his creation. I personally believe
with Dr Forsey...that he had in fact no option. Be that as it
may, he acted honestly, and he should have been spared
insult and persecution...Where Mr Whitlam erred was not in
precipitating the crisis (though I myself think this an error)
but in not accepting the verdict of the sovereign people, and
in pursuing Sir John Kerr instead of Mr Fraser and his Party
on party political lines...a general rule for politicians who
suffer electoral defeat is to pick themselves up and dust their
trousers, and live to fight another day. There is no future in
whining about injustice, still less in assaulting the referee.[162]

So Kerr was not the perpetrator of the so-called 'coup' in '75; the hand which
moved the chesspieces opposing Whitlam's was the collective one of
Opposition senators. Accepting this, look closer still at the difference between
their actions and the essence of a genuine coup d'etat.

The most obvious aspect of a genuine coup d'etat for comment is that it's an act
contemptuous of constitutionality, being instead a direct appeal to the ultimate force in any human polity: violence. It's entirely an exercise in living by
the sword whilst attempting to avoid dying by the same. Crudely speaking, any
well-run coup therefore needs to satisfy three objectives. First, whatever inconvenient people are currently in positions of power must be removed. Second,
all positions of power must be acquired and controlled by oneself or one's own
reliable allies. Third, this power once achieved must be retained; rivals and
enemies cannot be permitted to acquire power themselves in the future, for
revenge is a most unpleasant phenomenon.

Now compare this with the senatorial act of refusing Supply. Far from being
contemptuous of constitutionality it's a manoeuvre that relies upon all political
moves being constrained by a constitution. Otherwise once the Constitution
were trampled this weapon of controlling appropriations would become meaningless; the government would simply borrow money illegally, without penalty
as it holds momentary control over the disciplinary instruments of State

(police and armed forces) and the senators would find themselves deprived of any weapon at all.

Furthermore, refusing Supply only achieves one of the three objectives required for a successful *coup*. Certainly it effectively forces the incumbent substantive government to resign (thus surrendering office) or to advise an election (thus throwing its power into jeopardy) or to be dismissed (when a ministry sullenly refuses to do either), but it's a tactic that fails to ensure the Opposition party acquires this power itself (which requires the confidence of the existing Lower House, or else the winning of enough seats in the future Lower House at the election).

Niccolò's ghost	Are you sure about this? What's to stop a Senate dominated by a particular party from holding the other House to ransom: "Our party governs, or else no party governs"?
Author	An answer once again rests in the flow of money.

The drafters of our Constitution introduced an elegant asymmetry into the relationship between the House and the Senate, analogous to that which enabled Sir Robert Walpole to become the first prime minister of Britain in the 18th Century.[†] Although the privileges of both Houses of Parliament are based upon those of the Commons, our Constitution states:

> Proposed laws appropriating revenue or moneys, or imposing
> taxation, shall not originate in the Senate…The Senate may
> not amend proposed laws imposing taxation, or proposed laws
> appropriating revenue or moneys for the ordinary annual
> services of the Government.[‡]

This is a deliberate gesture by the drafters to uphold the Westminster convention that the Prime Minister is the leader of the faction which commands the confidence of the Lower House. Rather than resorting to the crude methods championed in the 1990s by some modern republicans — to codify in law the status of the Prime Minister — they chose to reproduce the 17th and 18th Century conditions that *led* to the creation of this convention. This produces the same result, while keeping the judiciary from interfering in a conflict that should retain a purely political resolution: who within the Lower House should

---

[†] The circumstances surrounding Walpole's era have been outlined in the chapter *The Legacy of Revolutions*.

[‡] Extract quoted from section 53. The difference between 'revenue' and 'taxation' is that when a government appropriates revenue it's taking money from an existing Crown fund administered by the Treasury (like ordinary citizens withdrawing cash from their bank account). On the other hand, when the government imposes taxation it's raising fresh money from the taxpayers. The third term 'moneys' covers money borrowed by the government in loans. (Quick and Garran, *Annotated Constitution of the Australian Commonwealth*, pp. 665–666.)

actually become Prime Minister.† As Quick and Garran's commentary says of this provision in the Constitution,

> [It]…necessarily confers the monopoly of financial origination on the House of Representatives. This part of the section crystallizes into a statutory form what has been the practice under the British Constitution for over two hundred and twenty years…This exclusive power of initiating money Bills is one of the most valued privileges of the House of Commons, and one of its vital sources of constitutional strength and supremacy.[163]

Implementing government policies requires money. No Senate-imposed substantive government could function for a long period of time without the confidence of the House, because without this confidence none of the money Bills desired by the usurping government for its policies could be proposed to Parliament in the form required. This is because the only money Bills which could be put before Parliament would be those approved by the House (i.e. written by whatever wronged faction actually *did* command the House's confidence), and the Senate cannot amend these money Bills, only accept, defer or reject them. So in reply to the Senate saying "Our party governs, or else no party governs — we'll block Supply" the House can retort "You can refuse money Bills, but you can't write them. We're the only people who can do that, and the only political agenda we'll fund is that of the party which has our confidence and should govern". Bluff called.

Niccolò's ghost   An ingenious solution, but surely only a partial one. It hamstrings the usurping ministers, but it doesn't actually eject them from office.

Author   True…but they're left out on a limb, looking ridiculous, unable to pass any kind of legislation through the House or to fund their schemes. A caretaker administration might be quite happy to operate under these conditions during its short existence, but more ambitious and unscrupulous ministers would find them a serious impediment.

---

† Most of the drafters rejected the idea of judicial interference in what they thought should remain a purely political struggle. Consequently section 53 refers to 'proposed laws' rather than 'laws', in deliberate contrast to the equivalent sections of the US Constitution and the then Canadian Constitution. By referring to 'proposed laws' section 53 outlined what the constitutional practice should be, but leaves it to the President of the Senate, the Speaker of the House, and — if need be — the Crown to uphold according to their political judgement. If the section referred to 'laws', then any irregularities in the inception of an Appropriations Act might cause it to be struck down by the courts after passing into law — an event causing financial disaster (Quick and Garran, *Annotated Constitution of the Australian Commonwealth* pp. 663–665). A similar rejection of judicial interference can be seen in the recreation of the financial conditions which lead to the post of Prime Minister, rather than enshrining in law the office itself.

ON THE BEACH

Remember also that all members of Parliament must eventually face the voters at elections. Here the third objective of a well-run *coup* becomes relevant. Far from disarming potential enemies, denial of Supply will anger the party forced out of government, a party which may in future elections come to command a majority in the Senate…and retaliate in kind. It's an act which raises the heat of political warfare for years to come.

History reveals that warring opponents, each unable to achieve total victory, often devise protocols of behaviour for their mutual protection. Compare the threat of refusing Supply with two more ancient political weapons in the Westminster heritage: impeachment, and the Bill of Attainder. The process of impeachment achieved the removal (and in earlier centuries, the execution) of unpopular ministers. Attainder was a more brutally efficient method of achieving the same objective. Impeachment required a judicial trial in the House of Lords, with the consequent risk that the accused might be found not guilty, and aquitted. A Bill of Attainder was simply a piece of legislation declaring a particular government minister guilty of a particular crime which it described, and prescribed a punishment for him. For example: "Sir John Doe is hereby declared a traitor and implacable enemy to His Majesty the King. He is therefore to be hanged, drawn and quartered, and his head to be impaled upon a spike as public warning to his fellow conspirators". If this Bill was passed by a simple majority in both Commons and Lords, and received the royal assent, it promptly became statute law, and poor Sir John promptly found himself by definition a traitor forced to submit to this ghastly punishment.

Attainder was thus a handy way for politicians to get rid of rivals. Provided the King was compelled by current events, parliamentary or popular opinion to submit to signing the document, the dominant parliamentary faction of the day could have a wonderful time settling old scores. Problem was, what was sauce for the goose was sauce for the gander. Although it was doubtless most gratifying to see one's opponents strung up, cut down and disembowelled, no-one liked to have it happen to themselves. Fortunes of politics being change-able, the applauding spectator of today stood a chance of providing the entertainment himself next week.

Both attainder and impeachment shared the attributes we've discussed for refusing Supply. Although they were means of removing rivals from office, they didn't ensure one's own friends and allies subsequently got *into* office; their use failed to prevent enemies from acquiring control of the same weapons at a later date; and their employment provided a positive inducement for retal-iation and revenge.

As a consequence, both of these ancient threats fell into disuse by mutual consent. Despite the fact impeachment remained possible in Britain for many years after the more modern method of removing governments by votes of no confidence was introduced, it ceased to be invoked. Why? If you're doomed to remain susceptible to conquest by your enemies (and democracy, as long as it survives, necessarily involves keeping politicians vulnerable this way) it's wise to be gentle with them; to do unto them what you would have them do unto you.

Of course a violation of this protocol by one party would invite retaliation by the other. An obvious parallel emerges in the blocking of Supply in Victoria in '47 and '52, with the latter being "historic retribution" for the former. It's also interesting to speculate to what extent the '75 denial of Supply was inspired by the attempt in 1970.† Certainly in 1975 at least one of Whitlam's ministers warned of further retaliation: in Mr Hayden's speech to the House (22nd October),

> In all seriousness I urge the Opposition to weigh the situation carefully. In politics, sooner or later, the wheel always turns the full circle. Sooner or later, the roles are reversed. Even if the Opposition were to be ultimately successful in its present short-term exercise of a grab for power, it would then live to rue the day that it succeeded.[164]

This talk of a protocol is obviously based on the assumption that the same parties fighting over dominance of the Senate are fighting over dominance of the House. They don't want to engage in actions in the Senate which will queer their future chances of leading a successful government in the House. In recent years the balance of power in the Senate has been held by Democrats and Greens, small parties which have no significant presence in the House, and hence no need to subscribe to this 'gentleman's agreement'. Yet a number of factors logically constrain them also.

First, they have insufficient numbers to threaten Supply in their own right, and so to do so rely upon persuading the support of a larger party which does have interests in the House. Second, they have limited campaigning resources and membership in the Senate, and hence must be wary of the threat of a double dissolution which could jeopardise their own presence altogether. Is the gamble worth the risk of being silenced? Third, even if they held entrenched senatorial positions through their popularity in their States, and held the numbers to refuse Supply, and had no direct representatives in the House, would they become cavalier about refusing Supply? Surely they would rather use this threat to compel the incumbent federal government in the House to implement their policies, rather than carrying out their threat and forcing an election. Given that there would be rival parties competing for supremacy in the Senate, then even if these parties were all State-based with no federal interests in the House, alliances would emerge between Senate-based parties and House-based parties. The enemy of my enemy would become my friend. The Senate parties would

---

† There can be no doubt the 1970 precedent was influential. The speech made in the House by Mr Ian Sinclair (National Party) on the 22nd October 1975, quoting the speeches made in 1970 by Whitlam and Senator Murphy supporting the right to refuse Supply, reveals this. (See *Parliamentary Debates*, H. of R. 97, pp. 2523–2524.)

ON THE BEACH

acquire vested interests in the House parties...and a new, looser equilibrium, a fresh 'gentleman's agreement' would emerge.

Yet the presence of smaller parties in the Senate is a good omen for the privileges of Parliament. Representing by their presence voter disaffection with the larger parties, and hence having a vested interest in appearing to "keep the bastards honest", their conscientious custodianship of the power to block Supply is both pragmatically useful to them, and of high moral value to all of us. The most responsible approach is that held recently by the Green senators: a reluctance to threaten Supply, but a refusal to promise to refrain.

In summary it's surely inaccurate to write, as some have written,[165] that there was a "convention" in Australia before 1975 that the Senate wouldn't refuse Supply to a government holding the confidence of the House of Representatives. This power exists to be used: in Sir Robert Menzies' words, "It would be absurd to suppose that the draftsmen of the Constitution conferred these powers on the Senate with a mental reservation that they should never be exercised".[166] More importantly, this power needs to be used from time to time now party discipline has rendered government accountability to the Lower House little more than a cipher, allowing arrogant ministers to gag the House and cheat it of its privileges; the privileges of a parliamentary democracy.

For the most pragmatic of reasons a tacit protocol has nonetheless existed not to block Supply, and we can reasonably expect it to continue to exist, to be discarded only under extreme conditions. It was discarded in 1975, and this action — not Sir John Kerr — was the real reason the Whitlam government fell. Whether this breach of the protocol was justified under the circumstances, and to what degree it was provoked by an earlier attempted breach, is a matter for debate in the years to come.

A combination of this 'gentleman's agreement' and explicit measures in the Constitution prevent the Senate's financial power from overthrowing the Westminster convention that the government is the dominant faction in the Lower House. The power to block Supply therefore can and should be retained as a support to responsible government in the Westminster system.

Niccolò's ghost   And what of the Crown? If blocking Supply eventually forces the Governor-General to move and capture with a well-understood logic, why not write this logic into legislation, so that refusal of Supply triggers off a sequence of events enforced by law without any viceregal intervention? Surely this would remove the Crown from the controversy, and prevent a repetition of Whitlam's shooting the messenger?

Author   This solution was suggested by Sir Charles Court, the former Premier of Western Australia.

Court's proposed reform was for federal legislation to be passed, whereby a double dissolution becomes obligatory once the Senate has blocked or denied Supply for a period of thirty days. His idea has merits, compelling the entire Senate to face the electorate as a consequence of its actions, irrespective of whether section 57 has been fulfilled or not. It clarifies responsibility for this event, placing it squarely at the feet of the senators. Yet there are drawbacks to the proposal also. It's difficult to establish at what point deprivation of money causes the fabric of government to collapse, and hence the point at which intervention becomes necessary. The system wouldn't collapse all at once but would fail part by part as existing money drains out. What if some mechanisms of government grind to a halt before the thirty days are up? The failure of *which* mechanisms should be used as the signal for intercession on behalf of the electorate? What if — as in Victoria, 1952 — there's insufficient money left to hold elections? What of more intangible considerations, like business confidence? What if both senators and incumbent ministers are willing to fight out the crisis to the brink of financial ruin, confident in pinning blame for the resulting disaster upon the enemy in the eyes of the public?

Assignation of a maximum timeframe before intervention is a valuable idea, but it doesn't replace a conscious non-partisan figure capable of forcing an earlier double dissolution, or of avoiding one altogether if a compromise emerges. The decision to force such a dissolution is essentially one of political judgement and timing and hence executive, not judicial. Judges could not properly be employed for this office, acting within their legitimate capacity. Given the tool of Supply, to be wielded by parliamentarians to uphold the accountability of government ministers to Parliament and the people, an impartial umpire will always be needed to avert financial disaster. This is a current duty of the Crown. Replace an impartial Governor or Governor-General with a partisan President and the scope for catastrophe will be magnified. Abolish both Crown and power over Supply, and you have an elective dictatorship with every majority government.

ON THE BEACH

The Ending of States

Niccolò's ghost 'It was so nice of you to come!
And you are very nice!'
The Carpenter said nothing but
'Cut us another slice:
I wish you were not quite so deaf —
I've had to ask you twice!'

Voices have been raised calling for the abolition of the States, their complaints worded in terms of the overgoverned public, whereby we are burdened with too many tiers of government at the expense of the taxpayer. They claim we would be much better off removing the State governments, leaving only the Federal government and local shire councils. Their belief reflects a very urban viewpoint on life. To a dweller in a major city it is possible to believe that a city council possesses the resources to address local issues, and if not, then any serious problem would affect a sufficient concentration of voters to capture the attention of Canberra. Rural Australians are unlikely to share this viewpoint, living in regions ignored by Canberra, in communities stripped of even basic services and impoverished by drought, rural recession and floods.

Even in the driest, most rational terms, the fact the United States and Canada also employ three tiers of government suggests it might be the most appropriate number of governments for a geographically enormous country with disparate concentrations of inhabitants scattered across its surface. Effective government requires an understanding of local issues, the political will to address problems and the organisational efficiency to construct solutions. Even after abolition, much of the money currently paid in tax at State level would still need to be paid to Federal or local authorities to administer former State government concerns. If the combination of Canberra and local councils cannot administer this nation as effectively as the present system, then taxpayers will find themselves saddled with poorer value for money after abolition than before.

Yet beyond administration, many people obviously identify strongly with the individual states in which they live, their interstate rivalries manifested in everything from flying State flags on buildings, to State of Origin football matches, to the frictions between the State governments. From the conduct of this debate it has become clear that even our cultural attitudes and views on national identity are not homogeneous. These are cracks in the national consciousness that cannot be readily plastered over or ignored.

A third and most important reason remains for retaining our system of Australian States, these states which evolved in apparently haphazard fashion last century, and which were federated in 1901; a reason exacerbated by the prospect of a republic. The presence of State Premiers in a federal system means that no single head of government may dominate the political land-scape unchallenged. Unlike a Federal Opposition leader, State Premiers are themselves heads of government and so possess resources which allow them to challenge the Prime Minister in a politically significant fashion, forcing not only debate but even confrontation on controversial issues. A Kennett may challenge a Keating and a Keating may challenge a Kennett.

A republic makes this issue more poignant, a fact recognised in some circles for over two centuries. In 1789 it was raised at the Philadelphia Convention by John Dickenson, the so-called "Penman of the Revolution". A lawyer, political writer and revolutionary, he argued that,

> such an Executive as some seemed to have in contemplation
> was not consistent with a republic: that a firm Executive
> could only exist in a limited monarchy. In the British Gov.
> itself the weight of the Executive arises from the attachments
> which the Crown draws to itself and not merely from the
> force of its prerogatives. In place of these attachments we
> must look out for something else. One source of stability is
> the double branch of the Legislature. The division of the
> Country into distinct States formed the other principal source
> of stability. This division ought therefore be maintained, and
> considerable powers to be left with the States. This was the
> ground of his consolation for the future fate of his Country.
> Without this, and in the case of a consolidation of the States
> into one great Republic, we might read its fate in the history
> of smaller ones. A limited Monarchy he considered as one of
> the best Governments in the world. It was not certain that
> the same blessings were derivable from any other form. It was
> certain that equal blessings had never yet been derived from
> any of the republican form. A limited Monarchy however was
> out of the question. The spirit of the times — the state of our
> affairs, forbade the experiment, if it were desireable.[167]

ON THE BEACH

He went on to argue that the collapse of ancient republics proved that they were badly constituted, and that the delegates present ought to seek for every remedy for the weaknesses of such republics. "One of these remedies he conceived to be the accidental lucky division of this Country into distinct States; a division which some seemed desirous to abolish altogether."[168]

Now the orthodox view upon federations is that they're only transitory structures, eventually either collapsing into a unitary centralised government or disintegrating into a patchwork of autonomous countries where federal provinces used to be. An interesting thing about this orthodoxy is that it's based upon an old-fashioned mathematical method of analysing dynamic systems. In mathematics a *dynamic system* is an entity in motion — the swinging of a pendulum, the flight of birds, the passage of a summer thunderstorm through the atmosphere — this motion being described by what are known as *ordinary differential equations*. A traditional way of describing the salient behaviour of a particular system is to draw diagrams describing the system's motion, and then look for equilibrium points — configurations for which the system is at rest, motionless. The number and position of these points, and the system's behaviour in their immediate neighbourhoods, yields valuable information about the system as a whole.

But the really interesting aspect of these equilibria is the fact that although they exist, the system might never reach them. A rigid pendulum, for example, has an equilibrium when poised perfectly vertical *above* its axis, although this configuration is extremely difficult to attain in real life. Proper understanding of a system possessing isolated equilibrium points requires understanding its behaviour away from equilibrium conditions, and here the belief in the short lifespans of federations fails. A federation is an intrigueing kind of dynamic system, generating conflict between State and federal levels. Far from being an accidental or undesirable trait, this conflict is an essential attribute of a federation, whereby the power balances between the two levels of government shift from year to year, depending upon the exigencies of the time (in what a games theorist might describe in terms of a non-zero-sum differential game). The prediction of a short life span is based upon a very crude analysis; the equilibria are correctly identified as corresponding with the two situations for which the internal conflict ceases to exist (as one of the two levels of government has been extinguished) but a federation's behaviour when approaching these points isn't well understood, nor is its behaviour when far from them. Surely the kind of conflict which exists when a level of government is facing extinction is different from that when both levels feel secure, and surely in these times of security the extinction of the other needn't be on the agenda? Simply because a federation can die in two ways doesn't mean it *must* die, let alone die soon.

If extinction isn't imminent, Dickenson's hypothesis sits well in the framework of our existing arguments. In previous chapters we've argued that the natural tendency of an incumbent government is to entrench itself in power. Given that any set of policies imposed upon a complex society shall excite dissatisfaction and resentment among those factions disadvantaged by it, such dissatisfaction accumulating over time, it becomes clear that no elective government can hope to remain in power indefinitely by relying upon the popularity of its policies. Eventually politicians determined to retain power must attempt to tamper with the electoral mechanism itself: by distorting the flow of information to the public, sowing discord among, bribing or suppressing the Opposition, establishing a gerrymandered electorate, or achieving some grosser violation of the Constitution. We know already that in federations the demarcation line between federal and State interests isn't static but dynamic, so that even when both levels of government are dominated by the same political party each strives to acquire power at the other's expense: federal politicians attempt to look clean and sympathetic in controversies that have left mud all over their State counterparts, and vice versa.

Niccolò's Ghost **When the two levels are dominated by idealogically conflicting parties, this struggle over *lo stato* throughout the country becomes intense. Alarming accumulations of power by a government may be challenged by its rivals, in the political arena or courts of law, in a continual stirring that helps defer stagnation.**

To this day the United States has remained a federation of distinct States retaining for themselves considerable political power. Dickenson's warning remains as pertinent to Australia as it was to the United States, with a single salient difference, that in Australia a 'limited Monarchy' isn't out of the question but is incorporated in a far more sophisticated form into our existing form of government. Are we so sure that equal blessings can be derived without it?

The more imperative issue is that it's likely that Australia's States shall destroy the initial federal republic before the republic can destroy the States. The act of turning Australia into a republic is in clear violation of the original pact between the States at Federation, in becoming the Commonwealth of Australia. A *pact* is an agreement among people or states that each shall make a mutually agreed sacrifice in return for a mutual benefit. The preamble of our Constitution states that it was because the people of the various colonies had "agreed to unite in one indissoluble Federal Commonwealth under the Crown of the United Kingdom of Great Britain and Ireland, and under the Constitution hereby established" that the Constitution uniting Australia was enacted in the first place. There are no idle words in this preamble. Republicanism had been debated within the colonies...and rejected. The Federal Commonwealth was to be indissoluble under the Crown and under the Constitution hereby established.

It was upon the terms of this pact among mutually independent states, or their logical and consistent extension, that the States would surrender their autonomy upon the Australian continent to form a single nation and remain within an "indissoluble Federal Commonwealth". It may be difficult but is vital to remember that the only right the federal government has to exist or to be obeyed stems from the authority of this pact. Without the pact there's no legitimate federal government.

Within this Constitution, the States retain their own individual and independent constitutional arrangements, both in their relationships to the Crown and in the formulation of their respective parliaments. The later evolution of an independent Australian monarchy through the Imperial conferences and the enactment of the Statute of Westminster, although holding implications for "the Crown of the United Kingdom of Great Britain and Ireland" in the federal sphere, did not impose upon or affect those States which wished to retain ties with the Crown in a British context. When the Australia Act was passed in 1986, for the most part formalising existing political conventions, it was done with the explicit and individual assent of all the States and required each State Parliament to pass legislation resolving its own constitutional affairs in accordance with the Act. This could not have been achieved by any means other than the free will of the Parliament of each State concerned.

The State governments have good cause to be jealous of their constitutional integrity. When the Whitlam government amended the Royal Style and Titles Act in 1973 to remove all reference to the Crown of the United Kingdom, some States argued this was motivated, not by patriotism, but by a desire to acquire greater power, for which patriotism provided a convenient excuse. In 1973 the State Premiers all still formally dealt with the Crown of the United Kingdom for the appointment of their State Governors; only the Federal Parliament, its organs and instruments operated under the insignia of the Australian Crown. As soon as the amendment was passed it was "immediately exploited by Mr Whitlam to argue that the Queen of Australia could be advised in state matters only by him because he alone had access to her. That involved an attempt to seize the royal prerogative in state matters."[169] The Premiers envisaged that what Whitlam was attempting to do was to destroy the power of the States by transforming the Governor-General into a Viceroy, who would effectively replace the Queen in all capacities of the Crown within Australia. In other words Premiers and Governors would no longer be able to communicate with Elizabeth II, only with the Governor-General who would (hopefully) be Whitlam's "man in Yarralumla". In the words of the late D.P. O'Connell QC, Chichele Professor of Public International Law at All Souls, Oxford, and an expatriate Australian,

> What the Australian states feared was that, if the Governor-General were given a full delegation of the royal prerogative on the Canadian model, state Governors would in practice become Lieutenant-Governors. They would be appointed by the Governor-General, they would receive their instructions from him, and these could give the federal Government power over state legislation. It was believed that Mr Whitlam's design was to unravel the constitution and reduce

the states to administrative regions, through manipulation of the Crown. Whether or not that was the intention it has now been made an impossibility as the result of defences which have been erected.[170]

The separation of Crowns, the Crown of the Commonwealth of Australia and the Crowns of the States, is the "keystone of the federal system in Australia",[171] the "principal line of defence"[172] of the rights of the States against incursions by the Federal Government. Could the States expect their integrity to long survive the declaration of a republic?

Our Constitution allows amendment, provided such proposed amendments are put to the Australian people in a nationwide referendum and passed by both a majority of voters in a majority of States and an overall majority of Australians. Given a successful outcome to such a poll, that minority of States opposed to the amendment are expected to acquiesce to the wishes of the majority. Such compromises are in the nature of federation, for without it no association of states could last for long.

Yet never until now has a referendum been brought before the Australian people possessing inherent to it the proposition that the voters in a number of States can dictate to the citizens and residents of another how their State Parliament — indeed, the very concept of sovereignty in their own representative democracy — is to be constituted, against their collective and demonstrated will. (According to law, other States cannot even dictate to an unconsenting one any alteration to its federal boundaries, or diminish its proportionate representation in either House of the federal Parliament.[173]) Circumstances in which a federal referendum could justifiably force changes upon the constitution of a recalcitrant State can be readily conceived; after all, Quick and Garran were themselves swift to point out that any amendment extending the powers and functions of the federal government must almost necessarily imply a contraction of those of the States.[174] Yet although the referendum process allows enormous changes,[175] Quick and Garran made it clear that the scope of such changes by no means readily extends to the federation pact itself, warning,

> it is certain that, if amendments were passed which were
> inconsistant with such words as 'indissoluble', 'Federal
> Commonwealth', or 'under the Crown', strong arguments
> would be raised against their constitutionality.[176]

The wording of the federal pact was chosen carefully. Describing Australia as an "Indissoluble Federal Commonwealth" was a deliberate reference to the US Civil War of 1862–1864 and its political doctrines: that, because the US Constitution had held no declarations of the permanence and indissolubility of the Union, the Union was therefore a dissoluble compact among the American States which, if violated by the Federal Congress acting in excess of its powers, could be held to be nullified, permitting the States to resist further impositions by the federal government through the use of armed force or, if necessary, by revolution.[†] But this phrase is bound to another, "under the Crown". Quick and Garran stated that this was inserted "out of an abundance of caution "[177] rather than provoked out of doubt or necessity, but that it revealed, not only an imperial loyalty to the Queen (Victoria) as the central figure in the British Empire, but as an intrinsic attribute of the Commonwealth of Australia. Having been established by concurrence of the Queen, who was herself an essential part of the Federal Parliament, head of the Federal Executive and represented in the Commonwealth by the Governor-General, the words "under the Crown",

> standing as they do in the preamble to the Imperial Act, may hereafter be of service in answering arguments in favour of amending the Constitution by repealing the provisions above referred to [relating to the Queen's position in the Commonwealth of Australia; in order to create a republic]. Strictly speaking, such amendments might be proposed, however, strong arguments against their constitutionality, and even their legality, would be available in the words of the preamble. It might be contended with great force that such amendments would be repugnant to the preamble; that they would at least involve a breach of one of the cardinal understandings or the conventions of the Constitution, and, indeed, the argument might go as far as to assert that they would be *ultra vires* of the Constitution, as being destructive of the scheme of Union under the Crown contemplated in the preamble.[178]

A possible legal counter-argument exists that claims the amending power, although limited under section 128, isn't limited by the preamble despite the fact the two may conflict, and therefore in such case the enacting words (creating the power to amend) should triumph over the preamble and its attempt to enshrine the Crown. A republic would then be possible.[‡] Our High Court will eventually be forced to rule on the matter, and in so doing answer an interesting question: after a sculptor finishes crafting a statue, can the statue pick up hammer and chisel

---

[†] This doctrine had caused tensions between South Carolina and the Federal Congress in 1832, when the former had declared a federal law passed by Congress null and void, and refused to obey it. When President Jackson called out federal troops to enforce it, South Carolina's Governor Hayne replied by mustering and drilling twenty thousand volunteer militiamen. Both sides stepped back from conflict by resolving a compromise. Twenty-eight years later, on the 20th December 1860, the State of South Carolina in Convention assembled formally declared itself to have seceded from the United States, an example followed by six other States (Mississippi, Florida, Alabama, Georgia, Louisiana and Texas) which joined it in a Confederacy. The next year war broke out over Fort Sumter, a United States fortification now situated within a Confederate State, after which four more States crossed over to join the Confederacy (Virginia, North Carolina, Tennessee and Arkansas). The Civil War continued until 1866, when it was won by the Union. Seven of the defeated States were coerced into explicitly renouncing secession in their constitutions. No formal amendment was made declaring the US Constitution indissoluble, because it was felt by the Unionists that such an amendment following the War would represent an admission that previous doubt had existed over the issue (Quick and Garran, *Annotated Constitution of the Australian Commonwealth* pp.292–294).

[‡] To this case Quick and Garran replied in 1901 by drawing attention to the *Colonial Laws Validity Act 1865* and the fact that the Federal Constitution is an Act of the Imperial Parliament. In their time a legislative attempt by the Federal Parliament to remove the Crown would, by being repugnant to the preamble of the

to "improve" the sculptor? That is, after all, what it means for a Constitution, crafted on cardinal understandings, to pick up an instrument contained within itself, to chip away those cardinal features that created it. The republican referendum has forced this entire country to the border of surreal territory.

Speculation over how the High Court shall deal with this Dali-esque task of navigation must remain. As part of this speculation, views have been aired claiming that the Court, if presented with a referendum split but won among the majority of States for a republic, will and should acquiesce to this expression of popular opinion, instead of listening to legal objections querying its validity.

One wonders whether the minds of these opinion-voicers accept responsibility for the actions of their mouths. Their words evoke in reply a scene from Robert Bolt's play *A Man for All Seasons*. Based upon the life of Sir Thomas More, one of Henry VIII's chief advisors later executed for refusing to submit to the annulment of the King's marriage to Catherine of Aragon, it contains a scene discussing the nature of law. On stage an unreliable man by the surname of Rich has turned informer, and has just left More's house to betray him to the King. More's wife Alice, and a friend of the family's, Roper, reproach him for not stopping the informer:

> ALICE: (*exasperated, pointing after* RICH) While you talk, he's gone!
>
> MORE: And go he should if he was the Devil himself until he broke the law!
>
> ROPER: So now you'd give the Devil benefit of law!
>
> MORE: Yes. What would you do? Cut a great road through the law to get after the Devil?
>
> ROPER: I'd cut down every law in England to do that!
>
> MORE: (*roused and excited*) Oh? (*Advances on* ROPER) And when the last law was down, and the Devil turned round on you — where would you hide, Roper, the laws all being flat? (*Leaves him*) This country's planted thick with laws from coast to coast — Man's laws, not God's — and if you cut them down — and you're just the man to do it — d'you really think you could stand upright in the winds that would blow then? (*Quietly*) Yes, I'd give the Devil benefit of law, for my own safety's sake.

The purpose in having a written Constitution is to prevent a fool with an axe — or an assembly of fools with axes — from being able to chop down certain cardinal laws. These same laws can only be felled through an elaborate proce-

---

Constitution, have been repugnant to an Imperial Act intended for Australia, and as such been void and inoperable. (Quick and Garran, *Annotated Constitution of the Australian Commonwealth* pp. 295–296.) Of course this external safeguard has long since withered away. Yet the fact s.128 was never written to be competent to create a republic surely gives pause?

ON THE BEACH

dure involving the entire populace, the wisdom of a certain proportion of which is regarded as adequate for that particular task. And if certain fundamental understandings were put beyond the axes of even this proportion, might it not have been due to the belief that the wisdom of this proportion is not enough; that before these understandings could themselves be cut down, exposing the populace to "the winds that would blow then", the entire citizenry should express a more comprehensive consent of the governed? Were these elaborate precautions to be ignored by our High Court, cowed into obeying the republican agenda despite legal protests, we could be forgiven for remembering the ancient protest: "For if power without laws may make laws, may alter the fundamental laws of the Kingdom, I do not know what subject he is...that can be sure of his life, or anything he calls his own".[179]

If a referendum for a republic were passed *nem. con.* by all States (i.e. by a majority in each State, for every State) then one could argue that although such an act violates the original terms upon which Federation was based, the mutual and unanimous consent of all States would render a Federal Republic under a duly amended Constitution a logical and reasonable successor to the present Commonwealth of Australia, although hardly a desirable one. Under these conditions, even if every citizen of the Commonwealth of Australia voted in favour of a republic the resulting alteration could nonetheless be described as "revolutionary", even as the Glorious Revolution in 1688 in the British Isles was revolutionary: not through barricades in the streets or riots against the government, but because the new system of government is based on grounds distinct from those of the old Constitution, and which cannot be reached using the mechanisms of the old. There is no constitutional bridge between the two. A leap must be made, the transition made possible peacefully through the consent of the governed.† But it's already obvious this referendum will *not* be passed in all States, and controversy smoulders whether it will be passed in enough to allow a republic to succeed.

Let us consider the scenario where a referendum has been won for an Australian republic to be established, with four States having voted in favour of the question and the others against. What, then, should be the fate of those States whose citizens have demonstrated that they prefer the status quo and are loyal to Australia as it is rather than as it is fancied to become? Can a combination of republics and monarchies co-exist in a single united country?

---

† Professor O'Connell made a similar point in 1979, when discussing Canadian and Australian suggestions favouring alterations to their respective constitutions more drastic then anything the drafters had envisaged or made provision for in their amendment procedures. The belief in vogue in the 1970s that amendments to the former Canadian constitution could be made by mutual agreement, ignoring the legal basis whereby the British North American Act obtained its authority, would be "tantamount to constitutional revolution. In effect, by unilateral action Canada would have set up a constitutional convention to adopt a new constitution. It has happened before, of course, in 1689, and the Whig tradition has applauded that revolution. If Canada effects a revolution by this means the portents for Australia could not be ignored. The amending power in Section 128 of the Australian constitution goes only so far. **It does not affect the basic rules of the constitution in the broader sense, which include the constitutions of the states and the Crown as the keystone of the whole system.**"(O'Connell, "Canada, Australia, Constitutional Reform and the Crown" p. 6.) Canada did not choose to go down this path. Will we?

A federated conglomerate of republics and constitutional monarchies raises a serious difficulty, of reconciling the fundamental issue of sovereignty and its manifestations in military, political and social contexts between the two political systems. Even if reconciliation of these problems is possible, such a conglomerate conspicuously fails to achieve any of the objectives the republican movement claims as its goals. It would have not severed Australia's ties with the Crown; although the republican States would have cut their links, such links with the Crown would be reinforced in the loyalist States, particularly with the immigration of monarchist Australians from the republican States. Far from remaining a single nation, Australia would effectively have become a loose coalition of several nations, cobbled together into a Federal Republic chaired by a compromise President. Far from creating a symbol of unity, a new symbol of division and controversy shall have been introduced into our political consciousness and society. Compared with our current circumstance with the Commonwealth of Australia, nothing will be gained and much will be lost — not only the hundreds of millions of dollars required to fund this futile and extravagant exercise, but also our sense of national unity.

In the wake of this referendum outcome, if the prospect of a federal conglomerate is discarded as an impasse achieving nothing, one must ask how such a circumstance may be resolved. Two avenues lead from this state of affairs to resolution: abdication and dissolution.

The hopes of the republicans rest squarely upon the abdication of Elizabeth II as Queen of the loyalist States; upon this plank are balanced all their future plans. Former ALP President Barry Jones admitted as much in a televised debate when he drew the tenuous analogy between suspension of the Imperial honours in Australia for the sake of consistency among States, and the abdication of the Queen on a similar basis.[180] Trinkets of enamel and gold designed to adorn the breast of a jacket are a very different matter from that of the continued existence of a figure performing constitutional duties within a particular form of parliamentary democracy. It is unfortunate that Mr Jones appears unable to discern the vast differences in principle between the two issues, but it speaks volumes for the shallowness of the analysis that he is unable to do so.

Imperial honours were suspended in Australia by the Queen due to inconsistencies in practice between the various States and the Federal Government, due to the conflicting attitudes adopted to imperial honours by the various parties. This was not a victory for the republican camp, although it was wrongly hailed as such. It was instead a recognition of the pre-eminence of the Order of Australia of which the Queen is Head,[†] and which uses a recommendation procedure independent of the various governments. Australians also remain eligible for other honours from the Crown, such as the Order of Merit, which do not depend upon the vagaries of political affiliation. Nothing behind the suspension of Imperial medals can be extrapolated to suggest a willingness to future abdication.

---

† It is worth noting that a Knight of the Order of Australia — AK — outranks most British Orders of Knighthood.

Indeed abdication *per se* violates the Queen's Coronation Oath, which constitutes part of the contract between the Sovereign and her subjects. As such it can only be acceptable by the monarch in one of two predicaments. The first was seen by the world in the abdication of Edward VIII prior to his Coronation in 1936, whereby he was determined to marry a divorcee against the will of the British Parliament. He was determined to pursue actions that would have eventually violated the contract between Crown and people, and so chose to abdicate before the swearing of the Coronation Oath, thus forfeiting the Crown. Although strictly speaking his quarrel was only with the British Crown, the Dominions followed the British lead in accepting George VI as King.

The other predicament is when the monarch receives legitimate advice from a Prime Minister, that she should abdicate in conjunction with an appropriate constitutional amendment. This has been the basis of the Queen's peaceful abdication from former realms that subsequently became Commonwealth republics, the realm's Parliament having negotiated a termination of the contract on behalf of the Crown's subjects.

The final twenty years of Rhodesia revealed that neither controversy, nor force of intimidation, nor even the illegal declaration of a republic provides adequate grounds for abdication. In his illegal 1965 Unilateral Declaration of Independence, Ian Smith effectively declared Rhodesia to be a republic, circumventing the Rhodesian Governor, Sir Humphrey Gibbs, by appointing an "Officer Administering the Government" to be a kind of de facto president.[181] In 1969 he went a step further, holding a referendum in the predominantly white minority electorate that established a new republican constitution.[182] For the duration of its existence the Rhodesian republic was an illegal regime which managed to defy the Crown and the outside world.

At no stage did the Queen abdicate her claim to sovereignty over Rhodesia. Her refusal to do so was central to the eventual restoration of legitimate government in 1980 and the establishment of a black majority government, which led to the creation of Zimbabwe. After the dust had settled in 1965, defiance of the republic by the Crown proved largely symbolic, but still important. Gibbs didn't lead a political resistance movement to UDI but defiantly refused to leave Government House, remaining a formal symbol of opposition to Smith's regime.

> He thus challenged them [Smith's men] to order him to be man-handled, which they decided not to do. The Chief Justice of Rhodesia, Sir Hugh Beadle, moved in to join him, so that together they could symbolize true law and order. When Smith's regime cut off the Governor's salary, car and telephone, Rhodesians loyal to the Crown, many of whom came to sign the Government House visitor's book, raised funds to help keep Sir Humphrey going. He maintained the imperial style, with formal black-tie dinners and the toast to the Queen now invested with unaccustomed meaning.[183]

Back in London the Queen challenged the authority of Clifford Dupont, the Officer Administering the Government, particularly his right to authorise the execution of prisoners. She attempted to intercede in Rhodesia by commuting a number of death sentences to life imprisonment.[184]

The pragmatic political reality was that once Smith's regime was established, such protests carried little direct weight. Executions in the Rhodesian republic proceeded regardless of the Crown's objections. However, the defiance of the Crown served as a continual reminder of the illegality of the republic. The eventual restoration of the Crown's political sovereignty with the appointment of Lord Soames as Governor of Rhodesia was a central aspect to the establishment of a black majority government in 1980 and the birth of Zimbabwe. Robert Mugabe, the newly-elected Prime Minister of Zimbabwe, then went through legitimate channels in gaining the Queen's assent to establishing Zimbabwe as a republic. (That the republic of Zimbabwe under President Mugabe subsequently acquired the flavour of a Maoist one-party State is hardly Her Majesty's fault.)

The distillation of this is that if the majority of voters in, say, South Australia, Western Australia or Queensland support the monarchy at a referendum in defiance of a majority of republican States, then the Queen would not and should not abdicate from those loyalist States. Abdication would be a violation of the monarch's contract within the Westminster system, a betrayal of both Coronation Oath and the democratic process, with implications for the future of the Crown going far beyond our coastline. For her to violate deliberately her Oath to uphold our "laws and customs" would be for her to abdicate her moral right to reign…anywhere in the world.

The beauty of the legislation explicitly declaring Elizabeth II Queen of Western Australia and Queensland is that it also enables the citizens of these two States to signal their views publicly to the Palace, without ambiguity or the need to rely upon the integrity of Premiers. Not only must they be asked whether they renounce the Queen of Australia, but also whether they renounce her as Queen of their particular State. Given an explicit "no" vote, the relevant Premiers could hardly advise Her Majesty to abdicate, and if they did then the Queen and her representative would be justified in refusing, forcing (if necessary) a dissolution for the public to enforce their referendum verdict.

The rejection of a republic by loyalist States cannot simply be interpreted as a sentimental gesture favouring the Queen, but also a rejection of the prospect of arbitrary and oppressive government associated with republics throughout the world. Consequently citizens of these States are hardly going to tolerate the erection over their heads of a federal republic, the laws of which may override the legislation of their own parliamentary democracies. More importantly, they will not tolerate the systematic destruction, beneath their feet, of their own constitutional systems of government: the font of executive power, the due processes of the legislative, the source of authority of the judicial. Attempts by Canberra or republican States to coerce the polity of a loyalist

State would, if they succeeded, destroy forever the consent of the governed there. *Any* form of replacement government, no matter how enlightened, would be a puppet regime imposed externally, not chosen by the community. Canberra would be guilty of an outrageous act of imperialism, and would have also destroyed itself. After having forced a profound — indeed, absolute — constitutional transmutation upon member states by duress, a Federal Republic could no longer claim to be a legitimate and reasonable successor to the Commonwealth of Australia. With the original agreement underlying Federation violated, and confronted by a Federal Republic devoid of right or legitimacy, the future prospects of our federated nation would be bleak.

Under these conditions, the Premier of a loyalist State would be under no moral or ethical obligation to concede to the wishes of a republican federation, nor would there exist any patriotic duty to an as yet fictitious new nation in the process of invention. Deep-rooted allegiance to Australia and its institutions as we know them offers neither guidance nor support following the collapse of the *ancien régime*. In such a circumstance the overwhelming duty of the Premier as a head of government of a parliamentary democracy would to obey the collective will of that State's citizens. If the citizens'express will is to retain their constitution in disobedience of Canberra, then such disobedience becomes for the Premier not only a right, but a duty. To do otherwise, to collaborate with Canberra, would become a kind of Quislingism, leading citizens into servitude of a once-familiar entity turned foreign.

The Turnbull Committee has calmly sketched ways of coercing loyalist States into becoming republics. Yet in all their talk of what legally could or could not be done, republicans, particularly those in the southern mainland cities, appear to have no grasp of the stronger repercussions of their agenda, repercussions beyond their control. Imagine if the High Court rules that, although Australia is an indissoluble federal Union, the Crown at all levels can be expunged despite the protests of unconsenting States, who are to be forced. Easier, pretend as part of this hypothetical scenario that our federal Constitution's preamble had *never* made explicit mention of the Crown, so that the Court had no such impediment. Even then, were the High Court to declare a republic and attempt the coercion of States, a strong case would exist for loyalist rebellion and secession.

In all their perusal of republican texts, Mr Turnbull and his Committee seem to have overlooked the one most pertinent to what would be our distressed condition:

> We hold these truths to be self-evident, that all Men are
> created equal, that they are endowed by their Creator with
> certain unalienable Rights, that among these are Life, Liberty
> and the Pursuit of Happiness — That to secure these Rights,
> Governments are instituted among Men, deriving their just
> Powers from the Consent of the Governed, that whenever
> any Form of Government becomes destructive of these Ends,
> it is the Right of the People to alter or abolish it, and to

institute new Government, laying its Foundation on such
Principles, and organising its Powers in such Form, as to them
shall seem most likely to effect their Safety and Happiness.[185]

This passage teaches that we cannot literally possess an indissoluble federal
Commonwealth, for indissolubility is a kind of immortality beyond the power
of any assembly of any generation to confer; in the words of Tom Paine,

Immortal power is not a human right,[186] and therefore cannot
be a right of parliament. The parliament…might as well have
passed an act to have authorized themselves to live for ever,
as to make their authority live for ever.[187]

Yet describing the Commonwealth as indissoluble serves the Constitution
well, for although writing the adjective cannot abolish revolution, any more
than any text can ever prevent its own death in revolution, it serves to remind
that any action dissolving the federal Commonwealth will be nothing *less* than
revolutionary. We are to that extent spared the doctrines of South Carolina,
and cannot simply walk away from the federation.

However, despite horrifying some in Sydney or Canberra, secession is by no
means an unheard-of word among northern or western Australians. Already
the people of Western Australia have voted overwhelmingly in favour of anti-
Australian secession, in a 1933 referendum, although they failed in petitioning
the British Houses of Parliament (as the then-Imperial Parliament) to amend
the Constitution Act accordingly.[188] Secessionist murmurings have been heard
in Queensland during the 1980s, and from time to time in Tasmania.

As proud Australians, and believers in constitutional government, few monarchists would condone such sentiments except under the most extreme circumstances. Yet we would be entirely justified in seceding from a federal republic,
being supported by both history and logic in regarding this metamorphosis to
a republic as a transformation of the federation and its government into an
entity destructive of our traditional liberties, and hence an entity no longer to
have power over us. And having failed to persuade, if this entity attempted to
compel us it would indeed be our right to attempt to alter or abolish, by whatever means necessary, whatever claims it pretended to assert over ourselves or
our children, our land, law or communities.

Canberra would be stripped of all legitimacy in the eyes of citizens of loyalist
States, whose consent to be governed has been destroyed. Why would they pay
the taxes, obey the laws or acknowledge the authority of a regime in Canberra
imposed without constitutionality or consent; a regime that can never hold
their allegiance, being at best a flawed and foolish artifice and at worst a
threat? At the dissolution of the pact all instruments of the federation would
lose their legitimate authority, becoming instead merely the appendages of a
Power without law, the federal police and republican armed forces becoming
indistinguishable from any other vigilantes who don a beret and call them-

ON THE BEACH

selves Law. Were such appendages to impose themselves upon us, they would be met with the same revulsion and force that a free and unconsenting people have ever displayed against an arbitrary regime. If monarchists fail to prevail against the glib ignorance of the republican movement in the southern capitals, be under no illusion about the lasting hostility against the artefacts and monuments of this stupidity.

The arrogance of the republican leaders may yet lead to civil conflict in this country which has barely known it. This would be the second-worst possible outcome for Australia and her people, the worst being tyranny planted on this our own soil through the ignorance of those same leaders.

Niccolò's ghost	'O Oysters', said the Carpenter, 'You've had a pleasant run! Shall we be trotting home again?' But answer came there none — And this was scarcely odd, because They'd eaten every one.
	[*The Author stops writing, and stares across the table at the Ghost, who, at first oblivious to the effect of his words, keeps reading. Silence, until the Ghost looks up, and hastily puts away the book.*]
Niccolò's ghost	Having come so far in so short a time, covering so much territory, I think it time for pause, a recapitulation. My head aches. [*Puts his head in his hands and peers reproachfully at the Author.*] What is it you've argued?

Iustem et tenacem propositi virum
Non civium ardor prava iubentium
Non vultus instantis tyranni
Mene quatit solida.

The man who is tenacious of purpose
in a rightful cause is not shaken from
his firm resolve by the frenzy of his fellow
citizens clamouring for what is wrong, or
by the tyrant's threatening face

Horace, *Odes*

Epilogue

Abandoned, bread turns mouldy. Neglected milk goes first sour, then rancid. Untilled fields grow rank with weeds, and unturned ministries, corrupt. Political corruption is a natural state, even as mouldy bread, and our nationality is of limited protection. We are human foremost, before we are citizens, and the human condition fails to respect national borders.

While the old adage "All power corrupts…"[188a] holds true, it fails to pierce to the core of the matter. In 1929 Lord Hewart, Lord Chief Justice of England, recounted one evening's conversation between a distinguished Treasury official and the Chancellor of the Exchequer, after a rough time in the House of Commons in which the Department hadn't gained its desired measures. Frustrated, the civil servant expostulated over all this parliamentary palaver:

> After all, what was the good of the House of Commons? And
> how perfectly useless was the House of Lords! Why should the
> work of the expert be always at the mercy of the ignorant
> amateur? Why should people be allowed to govern themselves

when it was manifestly so much better for them to be governed by those who knew how to govern? "Seriously," he asked, "could not this country be governed by the Civil Service?" "Undoubtedly it could," replied the Chancellor of the Exchequer, "undoubtedly it could. And I am quite sure that you and your colleagues would govern the country remarkably well. But let me tell you this, my young friend: at the end of six months of it, there would not be enough lamp-posts in Whitehall to go round".[189]

The Chancellor of the Exchequer was wryly referring to a popular method of executing bureaucrats during the French Revolution, by hanging them from convenient posts. As an emblem of political principle the lamp-post should probably be resurrected today, as a reminder that the greatest problem in politics has never been how to get the right people into power, but how to get the wrong people out of it.

All societies, if they are sufficiently complex, lead to corruption in the governments over them. Any wielding of active authority over this complex mass of people, *any* imposition of government policy, excites resentments in disadvantaged quarters. These resentments slowly accumulate, and the consent of the governed begins to wane. Ruling a diverse society is like running a complicated engine: discontent is generated within its bowels as a byproduct, like heat, and slowly accumulates the longer the government operates, eventually leaking throughout the system. This will destroy the society, unless some means of shedding resentments can be found. Many limited ways are at hand; by carefully balancing the discomfort or by inspiring the collective imagination, by resorting to populist policies or indulging in "bread and circuses", by finding scapegoats for the discontent at home, or by manufacturing them abroad through nationalism. But the people will eventually get fed up, and want to change their rulers, whether these have been enlightened or rogues. Enlightened policies merely defer the execution, not commute it. Finally, more extreme measures will be required to retain power, or the grace to go quietly.

Representative democracy both inflames the problem and lances it. Free and fair elections are a form of catharsis, a kind of bloodless revolution, a fresh start; a way of dumping heat. Parliamentary sovereignty allows this frustration and discontent expression, dragging members of the House — the ultimate authors of all executive and legislative acts — from their seats by ticking a box next to some other candidate's name. This basic principle of discontent that inflames the conflict of interest between constituents and their members seems to have been forgotten by a disturbingly large number of people, but it's central to achieving the republican ideal of government "of the people, by the people, for the people".

Towards the end of the 19th Century Karl Marx claimed "The history of all hitherto existing society is the history of class struggles".[190] His statement still has a bit of life in it, particularly if we remove the word "hitherto". Stripped bare of the ideological clutter of economic class and traditional "class struggle", the transactions of representative democracy itself can be seen to create two "classes" in perpetual conflict, the constituency and the elective oligarchy. A great challenge democracy poses to (sufficiently amoral) politicians is to devise some way in which the vast and temporary power, lent by the electorate, can be converted into a more permanent form before the original mandate is revoked. The greater challenge presented to the constituency is to devise some scheme to prevent its representatives from doing precisely this — from abusing their mandate by employing it against its lenders. Although this conflict of interest cannot be permanently laid to rest, electors must at least ensure that during it they retain the upper hand over their representatives, or else see their own sovereignty and rights destroyed.

A number of partial solutions lie at hand. One is having a written Constitution guarded by a strong judiciary, but two dangers exist, being that judges are confined on abstract grounds only to address justiciable issues, and on practical grounds need the Executive to be actually containable within the rule of law. So if the armed forces and police are politicised, serving their political masters rather than the law of the land, or the Executive's grosser lawlessness is secret, or lawfully exempted from judicial scrutiny, or defended through further appeal to executive power wrongfully used, then these judges cannot fulfil their duties as guardians.

If the text is written too sparsely, these guardians' capacity to intervene is impaired; the net of justiciability woven too coarsely to catch enough game. But if the text is written too densely, then a judicial aristocracy will have been created. This is a third danger. Members of the constituency, in embracing the judiciary as their saviours against politician's abuses, may be protecting their sovereignty from one oligarchy by sacrificing it to another — rather like the fairytale story of the Sultan who, on finding his palace infested with rats, invited in large numbers of cats, who killed the rodents but ended up infesting the palace themselves.

This arrangement would also end in destroying the members of the judicial aristocracy. If an unaccountable and supreme judiciary commited legislative or executive actions that outrage us, dragging politicians from their seats would become inadequate. To re-assert our sovereignty we would have to drag the judges from their benches, an act destroying the rule of law. And yet a Constitution that failed to enable frustration and dissent against political acts from being vented through constitutional means would merely invite unconstitutional action: if the consent of the governed is withdrawn from those in power, but cannot be reasserted through peaceful force, it invites the use of violent force. Lacking consent, a time comes when that force would be justified.

An alternative, partial solution to sacrificing popular sovereignty to the judiciary rests in the few residual powers now remaining with the Crown, for which the ancient form of ministerial responsibility remains available in an emergency. The Crown is a valuable modern instrument for the constituency, as a usually passive device that in rare crisis can become active to counteract abuses committed by politicians; a device that cannot itself dispense solutions but only reflect the crisis to the floor of the House or to the constituency itself to resolve, reaffirming the ultimate sovereignty of the people. Chifley enunciated the matter clearly when he said "To us, the throne in no way usurps the rights of the people. It is a symbol of the liberty of the people. With us, the prerogatives of the Crown have become the privileges of the people".

As well as its reserve powers, the Crown holds also hierarchical implications that uphold the rule of law, helping to preserve practical justiciability of grievances and rights of the individual. Servants of the executive, being servants of the Crown, have their hierarchies constrained in a remarkable way, whereby patently unlawful acts must be disobeyed, else the individual servants must answer personally for their actions. This potent device was traditionally employed in "Her Majesty's" prisons to uphold *habeas corpus*, and in "Her Majesty's" post offices to preserve the integrity of private communication. It remains in use in "Her Majesty's" police, armed forces and courts of law, while the disastrous effects of its absence can be seen in contemporary US history.

A modern reading of Machiavellian doctrines, applied to a monarch in a parliamentary democracy, reveals that her own best interests are served by aiding the constituency over the elective oligarchy. By delivering up the wielders of active political power to the anger of the citizens, she can preserve her own personal stake in the Constitution's survival, a stake created and perpetuated by the hereditary principle. A constitutional monarchy therefore satisfies John Stuart Mill's criterion for a well-constituted office, while an elective presidency fails it. For the Queen's viceregal representatives a more complex arrangement is used, a power triangle, suspended from the permanent thread of her own discretion whether or not to sack her representative; a discretion bound up by her own self-interest in survival, and exercisable under the ancient form of responsibility, using Australian ministers and advisers. Her representative can be drawn from beyond the elective oligarchy, using whatever means of nomination we, the community, choose to establish.

As an ultimate guarantor of parliamentary government in sixteen independent realms throughout the world, she represents a human emblem above the disquiet of nations. The Queen is uniquely positioned to act as intermediary among her governments, behind closed doors, with rights of access unparalleled by any other official in the world by virtue of her constitutional place. What our prime ministers and premiers, governors-general and governors choose to communicate to her is up to them; but our just grievances with Britain demand communication, to be remedied. Discard the Australian Throne, and never again will we have this opportunity to speak and be heard. The *greater* the grievances with Britain, as one independent country with another, the more important our links with the Palace become. Our choice is truly one of maturity: whether to sulk over past injustices, or ensure our complaints are heard in

Whitehall through being understood in the Palace. Diplomats come and go, but the monarch remains.

Beyond the secluded corridors of power and parliaments assembled, the symbolism of the Crown can be employed in a more civilised manner than any nationalist emblem that would replace it. Governors and Governors-General serve as figures embodying our polity beyond party, around whom all sections of our community can rally, despite their partisan grievances. As distinguished personages, they can bestow the much-deserved formal dignity and recognition to charities and individuals that work with the poor, the hungry and the desperate, without demeaning these bodies with the "kissing babies" cynicism of re-election. And having no vested interest in elected office, they can embody the supremacy of the community over its politicians; serving as witnesses of the highest echelon of executive power who, in times of constitutional crisis, can force an issue to the people to decide.

All this is to be expunged in the name of an Australian "Head of State", despite the fact our Governor-General can easily fulfil that job description, and has already been accorded honours as such abroad. Only minor alterations need be performed before this figure is exalted properly, as a distinguished and distinctive Australian State figure, beyond the schisms of party and creed. Yet this is, in truth, inconvenient for our elected leaders; it abrades the gloss from their own temporary mandate. Hence we had a Prime Minister, on one hand extolling the virtues of a distinctive Australian "Head of State"... then on the other, going to Yizhak Rabin's State funeral alone, leaving the Governor-General at home. The Prime Minister giveth and the Prime Minister taketh away.

In this era the Australian people are filled with a justified disillusionment with our politicians, a righteous disenchantment with the elective oligarchy. Yet at the same time we have in our hands a way of exalting our community over its elected assemblies, of emphasising that our politicians are supposed to be our servants, not our masters. And in tragic irony, it's precisely this avenue of reform we are now being asked to lock off and destroy by becoming a republic.

What is the alternative? A genuine programme of reform.

❖ Our communities' links with Government House are direct, not reliant on a politician's favour to communicate. Few Australians are aware of their right to petition the Governor or Governor-General, or of this viceregal official's right to take up community concerns privately, urging them upon the ruling politicians behind closed doors. **These links should be strengthened, not attenuated.** The Carr Government's attempt to close the New South Wales Government House was an attempt to destroy the ability of the community to have its voice heard directly by an apolitical figure willing and able to question the Premier privately. This is intolerable.

- The **existing protocol should be promulgated**, formally recognising our Governor-General as being an appropriate figure to be accorded full dignity abroad as "Head of State", with an explanation of the distinct roles of Queen of Australia and Governor-General of Australia. Buckingham Palace has already recognised this role, and a formal declaration will protect the Governor-General from the real threat… an arrogant Prime Minister. If a formal declaration is made in conjunction with other Commonwealth realms, like Canada and New Zealand, any doubts that may linger among other countries over our arrangements can be easily dispelled.

- **Remove the power of viceregal nomination from the Prime Minister** and bestow it upon a Convocation of State, an assembly of distinguished Australians holding high office through apolitical community hierarchies, within the 1930 guidelines. This assembly would draw up a list of candidates representative in spirit of the Australian people, while having no claim to an existing electoral "mandate". This would stabilise the mutual relationship between Prime Minister and Governor-General, remove the impetus for either figure to "ambush" the other, prevent unnecessary involvement of the Palace in local controversies, and give the Australian community — not politicians — the choice of who should be our viceregal Head of State.

- **Enhance** the ceremonial profile of our Governor-General within Australia, in line with Canadian precedents. Our Governor-General already has a distinctive Crown and Wattle emblem, although few Australians have ever seen it.

- **Designate the body of legal advisors** with whom the Governor-General can privately consult. Although there is a long list of precedents of viceregal consultation with the Chief Justice, this clearly may cause problems if the matter under discussion subsequently comes before the High Court. Using a council of, say, retired Chief Justices, will also dilute the influence of the political opinions of any one judge on their advice.

- **Amend the Laws of Succession of the monarchy**, to remove the sexist and religious impositions upon the Australian Throne. The recent popularity of Lord Archer's Bill in the British Parliament, and the enthusiasm of the Blair Government for constitutional refurbishment, has made it clear that London is amenable to suggestions of reform, and presumably Ottowa, Wellington, etc. will be as enthusiastic as we are on the matter. Under the *Statute of Westminster (1931)* the accord and concurrence of all of Her Majesty's national Parliaments is required for this reform, on a co-equal basis.

- As a fully independent sovereign country, we should be **improving our communications and presence in the Palace**, not severing them. The Palace has enormous potential as a diplomatic sorting-house of information, among the sixteen realms and the other Commonwealth countries — over fifty countries in total. The Queen's Private Secretary in the late 1980s was an Australian, Sir William Heseltine. Her Majesty's Press Secretary is currently an Australian, Mr Geoffrey Crawford. (Even the

Queen's Goldsmith is Australian — Stuart Devlin.) In 1988 Australian troops guarded the royal Palaces, to mark the Bicentenary. We should not be turning our back on this remarkable resource.

❖ Incorporate **Aboriginal reconciliation**. The precise nature of this reconciliation is far beyond the scope of this book, but it must be noted that the Canadian and New Zealand Crowns have a doctrine of a particular relationship with the indigenous peoples, whereby a special burden of the Crown is to act as guarantor of Government treaties with indigenous races. This burden has limited public expression apart from the Crown's Courts of Law, but privately, if indigenous peoples have a direct right of petition to Yarralumla or the State Government Houses, their grievances can again be taken up by its occupant and urged upon an unwilling Prime Minister or Premier. The words of Jagera Elder and Australia's first Aboriginal Senator, the late Neville Bonner, might then ring out with a fresh resonance:

> I do not claim to speak on behalf of the entire Aboriginal community, but certainly I speak on behalf of my own vast clan [the Jagera], of those Aborigines with whom I have been in touch, and of those who have contacted me. And I warn those who advocate a republic: do not be mistaken in thinking that those of us who feel there is nothing to celebrate on the current Australia Day (26 January) would thus stand firm against constitutional monarchy for Australia. For, by a strange quirk, the "causes" are not necessarily joined... So in this, my own land, my absolute native land, I say: Here I stand, metaphorically, with woomera and spear in hand, in defence of Australian constitutional monarchy.[191]

Rather than becoming a republic for the Olympics in a triumph of nationalism, the Centenary of Federation and the new Millenium should be celebrated by exalting community within our country and internationally. It would represent a victory for true democratic accountability at home, an acceptance of the synthesis of our heritage, our present multicultural complexity, and our future.

Even the venue of this celebration will exist at the right time and place, more dignified than the bread and circuses of the Olympics. The Commonwealth Heads of Government Meeting (CHOGM) will assemble in Canberra for its 2001 meeting. Present will be over fifty of the world's prime ministers and presidents, including all the prime ministers required to begin the reforms to the monarchy's laws of succession, and Her Majesty the Queen. It would be a fitting time to declare formally to the world our reforms to the Australian Crown.

The undischarged burden of proof upon republicans has been to devise a way of dismantling the Crown that preserves and enhances these safeguards over the sovereignty of the people. But at this late stage of the debate it's inadequate merely to remark upon their failure to do so. At the end of the 20th Century a more serious accusation must be levelled: that imposing a republican *form* of government upon the Westminster system doesn't merely fail to enhance government "of the people, by the people, for the people" but is an actual betrayal of the democratic ideal."The danger of royal absolutism is past; but the danger of Cabinet absolutism, even of Prime Ministerial absolutism, is present and growing." *This* is the real threat posed to popular sovereignty next century, and a failure to comprehend it is a failure to understand much of the 20th Century, the bitter cycle of atrophy: fresh-faced idealism fades, as elected leaders grow corrupted by the conflicts of interest underpinning their power; democracy stagnates as politicians employ their transient authority to acquire permanent power. Discontent seeps up through the populace and cannot be dispersed, the wielders of active power having entrenched themselves. The government grows more repressive in reply to protests; halfhearted democracy is replaced by authoritarian rule, and a new dynamic equilibrium emerges, of mutual antagonism between the ruling cliques and the alienated majority. Eventually the equilibrium breaks down — usually violently — and the old cliques are overthrown unconstitutionally, to be replaced by a new order. Depending on who's done the overthrowing, the new rulers are either military — khaki oppression replacing the civilian variety — or else popular, in which case we're back to the fresh-faced idealism and the merry-go-round starts around again.

Up until now we've never had to go for a ride on this merry-go-round, although it's a distressingly familiar pastime to citizens of most of the rest of the world. Yet in Australia this threat has been seen in recent years. The Keating Government engaged in legislative attempts struck down by the High Court, to entrench the status quo of established parties, to favour the incumbent government and silence community groups not represented within the system.To echo the words of Byers QC "There cannot be democracy if the voters are gagged and blindfolded". In the words of other protesting voices the Keating Government has engaged in "the politics of hate… In other words: 'If you don't agree with me, I'll not only hate you, but destroy you'." "From the Australia Card through the political advertising ban and on, it has attempted to infringe civil liberties. It has threatened retaliation against those who campaigned against it in the last election campaign, and acted upon those threats."

We are now confronted by a Bill for a republic that can be only described as grotesque, its safeguards pathetic or non-existent, its structure a botched camel of an idea. But its hasty imposition upon us, and the demands of our compliance at the risk of ridicule, cut to deeper concerns.

In June 1993 the magazine *Independent Monthly* suggested a new coat of arms for the Australian Republic, supported not by the traditional kangaroo and emu but by a shark and a fat cat, with the Latin motto CUI BONO (translated, "For whose benefit?") written beneath. The republican campaign has been notable largely for the elbowing and pushing by people with vested interests in constitutional change: a former Prime Minister inciting nationalism, exploiting it to give flesh to his own antipathies, to write himself into the history books and dismantle the final safeguards between himself and more permanent power. A number of legal "authorities" given free rein in the Press, fashionable figures determined to create a judicial aristocracy, to acquire for themselves lasting executive and legislative power over the nation which their otherwise unremarkable careers would deny them. A queue of faces drawn from the Sydney cocktail circuit, determined to be dining at the top table when the spoils of patronage are divvied out after the declaration of the Republic. These are hardly the emblems of a polity dedicated to the public good.

Rather, they are warnings of what is to come if we continue to walk this ideological road laid before us. Our society, like that of other Western societies, seems to be descending into a kind of 21st Century feudalism, ruled by oligarchs. The flow of conventional information is dominated by a handful of media barons. Economic rationalism has been imposed by our governments, privatising even essential services like prisons and telecommunications, despite the profound implications for personal liberty. Wielders of vast amounts of capital moving globally, making and crippling governments, have emerged. All these are developments potentially poisonous to the liberty of the citizen. It is no coincidence that many are also anathema to the traditions of Westminster, which holds that governments only deserve the allegiance and obedience of the people provided certain traditional rights and liberties are upheld. It is impossible in this context to ignore the phenomenal wealth of the ARM's leading figures or the ways this wealth might be misused in the service of active power in a republic. It would appear the ARM is emerging as the party for the 21st Century barons.

The most disastrous myth of the 20th Century has been the belief that politics is merely a form of economics with the numbers removed for easier reading; that governments can be dismantled and constructed with cold and icy logic. But humans are more than units of consumption and supply; we do not associate and dissociate our societies and alliances like beads upon an abacus. Humans will not deny their own desires when endowed with the power of office, or swallow their discontent when in the streets. A failure to understand this, and a desire to dismantle our polity's safeguards in the name of greater "efficiency", threatens our future with arbitrary government by an entrenched oligarchy, leading to eventual tyranny. In this environment, the 21st Century barons leading the ARM may well flourish.

Yet it is the monarchists who have been mocked and ostracised as, at best, "lickspittles" and "forelock-tuggers" to a foreign Queen and a quaintly outdated world view, at worst despised as little better than a traitor-class to our own country, our allegiance supposedly prostituted to foreign interests. Labelled "rednecks" by scribblers whose own intellectual qualifications consist of a black turtleneck skivvy and a half-read copy of Derrida, we've been obliged to endure the lofty ridicule of conformity.

Niccolò's ghost [*laughs*] You should have read a letter I wrote in exile — in exile, although within my beloved Florence, following the restoration of the Medici. [*Quoting from his own letter to Francesco Vittori, 10th December 1513.*]

> When evening comes, I go back home, and go to my study. On the threshold I take off my work clothes, covered in mud and filth, and put on the clothes an ambassador would wear. Decently dressed, I enter the ancient courts of rulers who have long since died. There I am warmly welcolmed, and I feed on the only food I find nourishing, and was born to savour. I am not ashamed to talk to them, and to ask them to explain their actions. And they, out of kindness, answer me. Four hours go by without my feeling any anxiety. I forget every worry — I am no longer afraid of poverty, or frightened of death. I live entirely through them.[192]

The disdain of the brave new world is endurable, because it's neither brave nor new. Egotism and ignorance have been distinguishing traits of the modern republican movement in this country, traits also attendant upon the darkest periods of human history across thousands of years. The intellectual cowardice of the debate has been a refusal to address the implications of this history— the thought it may hold unflattering lessons about our own natures, which may demand precautions more stringent than glib assurances or maudlin appeals. Many diseases exist in the body politic, and shall continue to exist in the centuries to come, being derived not from peculiar circumstances but through the fact of our own mortality. In Westminster's constitutional monarchy and viceregal representations throughout the world an inoculation exists to some of these distempers. Derived from centuries of history, an inoculation drawn from the human condition that causes the disease, the Crown's neither a perfect remedy nor protects against all disorders…and yet so successful has it been that it remains the emblem of half the world's six oldest surviving democracies, and of others older than democratic government in many Western European countries. And at this time at the turning point of millennia, it also provides a partial defence against another plague afflicting the entire world, including my own country: nationalism. It is a sad indictment, that a foreign observer like President von Weiszacker can appreciate our Crown's quality in providing some protection against that most despicable and virulent of modern diseases, while our own scribbling and chattering classes cannot.

This debate has revealed a stagnant hypocrisy within our society; a "republican" hypocrisy of the arrogant, of little men boasting their willingness to do whatever it takes to seize and retain elected power; of conclaves of the wealthy, exploiting their privileges to ensure a spotlight shines upon their "egalitarian" poses, while tickets to their political soireés cost more than a week's rent. Of newspapers and publishing houses upholding every republic bar the republic of letters, every opinion bar the inconvenient. A suffocating orthodoxy has descended over the country, like a pall of bushfire smoke.

The ARM is guilty of a profound blunder, in what it fondly imagines to be a viable republic; a blunder it now tries to persuade Australia to adopt. Their Republic shall and must be a betrayal of the sovereignty of the people. Because of this betrayal, to swear allegiance to the Republic shall be to betray Australia; to believe in government "of the people, by the people, for the people" is to be at war with the proposed oligarchies of politicians and judges erected for and by the Republic, hence to be at war with its Constitution…and so, to be at war with the Republic itself. The proudest title it shall have to bestow upon any citizen has already been resolved: to be its enemy. The only long-term peace the Republic can know will be the sullen silence of a defeated people, a judicial aristocracy or the politicians' oligarchy triumphant.

We are the free possessors of a free society, remarkable in the eyes of the world, beautiful and rare. But it is also fragile, as all free systems of human society are fragile, and an ancient archive of human experience has gone into constructing the greenhouse that preserves it.

Edmund Burke defined society as a partnership in every virtue which, as its end can't be obtained except over many generations, becomes "a partnership not only between those who are living, but between those who are living, those who are dead, and those who are to be born." The decision now before the people is *not* whether they want "an Australian as Australia's Head of State". The wording of that question is dishonest and misleading; everything republicans want in the way of a distinctively Australian figure of State can be achieved already. Nor is the question merely one of whose face should adorn our coins. The true question before us is which political system best serves the trust placed in us, as the living tenants of the partnership among all genera-tions of Australians, living, dead or yet to be born. Our audience is a multitude across the centuries, regardless of how few they may be in our own time. And our choice shall cast light or shadow across their lives.

[*Author puts down his pen and sits, silently staring at the Ghost sitting opposite.*]

———————————————— ■■■ ————————————————

Endnotes

AUTHORS' INTRODUCTION

1   Thomas Hobbes, *Leviathan*, p. 82.

2   *Ibid.*, p. 112. Hobbes' italics.

3   *Ibid.*, Hobbes' italics and emphasis, my notes.

4   J. Quick and R.R. Garran, *The Annotated Constitution of the Australian Constitution.*

5   As implied from its preamble, the Constitution of the Commonwealth of Australia "is founded on the will of the people whom it is designed to unite and govern. Although it proceeds from the people, it is clothed with the form of law by an Act of the Imperial Parliament". (*Ibid.*, p. 285).

6   Report of the Republican Advisory Committee, vol.1 pp. 24–25.

7   Tardif and Atkinson, *The Penguin Macquarie Dictionary of Australian Politics*, pp. 352–353.

8   *Ibid.*, p. 353.

BOOK ONE

1   Niccolò Machiavelli "The Discourses" Chapter XXXIX; taken from Machiavelli, *The Prince and The Discourses*, p. 216.

2   Keir, *The Constitutional History of Modern Britain since 1485*, p. 230.

3   Quoted from Hume, *History of England*. vol. II p. 209.

4   *Ibid.*, vol. II pp. 186–219; Adams, *Constitutional History of England.* pp. 340–355.

5   Marginal note, Wood, *Athenae Oxonienses*. cols.649–650.

6   Text *Ibid.*, col.650.

7   *Ibid.*, col.649.

8   *Ibid.*

9   *Ibid.*, col.650.

10   *Ibid.*

11   Marginal notes, *Ibid.*, cols.649–650.

12   *Ibid.*, marginal notes.

13   *Ibid.*, marginal notes cols.649–652.

14   *Ibid.*, marginal notes cols.795–798.

15   See marginal notes, *Ibid.* cols. 797–806, cols.811–812; this extract quoted from pages of cols. 803–806.

16   Quoted from speech by Henry Polexfen, member of the House of Commons, marginal notes *Ibid.* cols.793–794.

17   See chapter XVIII of *Leviathan*, entitled "Of the Rights of Sovereigns by Institution".

18   Marginal notes in *Athenae Oxonienses*, cols.651–652.

19   The Bill of Rights, *1 William & Mary, sess. 2, c.2.*

20   *Ibid.*

21   *Ibid.*

22   Quoted from the speech of Sir Robert Howard in the debates of the Convention Parliament of 1689: Evans and Jack, *Sources of English Legal and Constitutional History*, pp. 348–352.

23   Todd , *On Parliamentary Government in England*, vol. II pp. 103–107; Hume *op. cit.* vol. II pp. 438–441.

24   This new foundation of the monarchy was explicitly acknowledged by the princes of the House of Hanover, who publicly declared that their "...only title to reign is the consent of the nation" (Adams *op. cit.* p. 374).

25   Adams, *op. cit.* p. 384, p. 390; Keir, *op. cit.* p. 298, pp. 318–319.

26   Adams, *op. cit.* p. 387–388.

27   Hill, *Sir Robert Walpole*, p. 74.

28   Hume, *op. cit.* vol.II pp. 400–402.

29   Hill, *op. cit.* p. 67.

30   *Ibid.*, p. 79.

31   *Ibid.*, p. 81.

32   *Ibid.*

33   *Ibid.*, p. 126.

34   *Ibid.*, p. 128.

35   *Ibid.*, pp. 128–131.

36   *Ibid.*, p. 128.

37   *Ibid.*, p. 144.

38   Todd, *op. cit.* vol. II p. 120.

39   Hill, *op. cit.* p. 206.

40   *Ibid.*

41   *Ibid.*, pp. 206–207.

42   Keir *op. cit.* pp. 319–320, pp. 332–333.

43   Adams, *op. cit.* p. 385.

44   Adams, *op. cit.* pp. 396–397; Keir, *op. cit.* pp. 323–324; Fiske, *op. cit.* vol.I p. 41.

45   Keir, *op. cit.* p. 324.

46   Adams, *op. cit.* p. 397.

47   Keir, *op. cit.*, p. 292.

48   *Ibid.*

49   *Ibid.*, pp. 298–299.

50   *Ibid.*, pp. 340–343.

51   *Ibid.*, p. 336.

52   *Ibid.*, p. 340; see also Adams, *op. cit.* p. 394 and p. 401.

53   Keir, *op. cit.* p. 335.

54   *Ibid.*, p. 297.

55   Adams, *op. cit.*, p. 404.

56   *Ibid.*, p. 395.

57   *Ibid.*, p. 399.

58   *Ibid.*, pp. 399–400.

59   *Ibid.*, pp. 400–401.

60   Keir, *op. cit.* p. 339.

61   *Ibid.*

62   Lord Elton, *Imperial Commonwealth*, pp. 182–184.

63   O'Brien, *The Great Melody*, p. 92.

64   *Ibid.*

65   J. Fiske, *The American Revolution*, vol. I p. 55.

66   *Ibid.*

67   Elton, *op. cit.* p. 203.

68   *Ibid.*

69   For a discussion of the history and nature of the North American colonies, see Keir, *op. cit.* pp. 349–357.

70   Fiske, *op. cit.* vol. I, p. 4.

71   Elton, *op. cit.* p. 207.

72   *Ibid.*, pp. 207–208.

73   Adams, *op. cit.* p. 402.

74   Elton, *op. cit.* p. 185.

75   *Ibid.*

76   Fiske, *op. cit.* vol. I pp. 11–16.

77   *Ibid.*, p. 15.

78   *Ibid.*

79   Elton, *op. cit.* p. 185.

80   *Ibid.*, pp. 185–187.

81   *Ibid.*, p. 185; Elton's italics.

82   Fiske, *op. cit.* vol. I p. 20.

83   *Ibid.*

84   Elton, *op. cit.* p. 186.

85   *Ibid.*, pp. 184–188.

86   *Ibid.*, p. 179.

87   Fiske, *op. cit.* vol. I p. 26.

88   *Ibid.*

89   *Ibid.*, pp. 26–28; Elton, *op. cit.* pp. 192–193.

90   Fiske, *op. cit.* vol. II pp. 11–13.

91   *Ibid.*, vol. I pp. 14–15, p. 28.

92   *Ibid.*

93   *Ibid.*, pp. 29–32; Elton, *op. cit.* pp. 192–194.

94   Fiske, *op. cit.* vol. I p. 29.

95   C.M. Kenyon, "The Declaration of Independence", *Fundamental Testaments of the American Revolution*, pp. 33–34.

96   *Ibid.*

97   Elton, *op. cit.* p. 203.

98   Fiske, *op. cit.* vol. II p. 6.

99   Adams, *op. cit.* pp. 405–406.

100 Fiske, *op. cit.* vol. I pp. 34–35.

101 Elton, *op. cit.* p. 204.

102 Hutson, *A Decent Respect to the Opinions of Mankind*, p. 5.

103 *Ibid.*, p. 6.

104 *Ibid.*

105 Elton, *op. cit.* p. 201.

106 Fiske, *op. cit.* vol. I p. 100.

107 *Ibid.*, pp. 112–113; Elton *op. cit.* p. 206.

108 Elton *op. cit.* p. 203.

109 *Ibid.*, p. 202.

110 *Ibid.*, p. 208.

111 Adams, *op. cit.* p. 406.

112 Fiske, *op. cit.* vol. II p. 285.

113 Elton, *op. cit.* pp. 210–211.

114 Fiske, *op. cit.* vol. II pp. 288–290; Elton, *op. cit.* pp. 211–212; Adams, *op. cit.* p. 408.

115 Adams, *op. cit.* pp. 413–414, p. 563.

116 *Ibid.*, p. 428.

117 *Ibid.*, p. 411.

118 *Ibid.*

119 Fiske, *op. cit.* vol. I pp. 34–36.

120 Oakes, *Crash Through or Crash*, pp. 13–14.

121 Jennings, *Cabinet Government*, pp. 337–338.

122 Windeyer, *Lectures on Legal History*, p. 234.

123 *Ibid.*; Adams, *op. cit.* p. 289.

124 Windeyer, *op. cit.* p. 234; Adams, *op. cit.* p. 289.

125 Adams, *op. cit.* pp. 289–290. A former Justice of the High Court of Australia also points to these speeches of Digges and Eliot as the early formulation of the modern doctrine of ministerial responsibility (Windeyer, *op. cit.* p. 234).

126 *Ibid.*, p. 348.

127 Emden, *Selected Speeches on the Constitution*, vol. I p. 17; Peel's speech is reported pp. 16–19.

128 Although this is a rather strong statement to make it shall prove justified in later chapters, despite recent assertions to the contrary by some republican academics.

129 Butler, *Governing Without a Majority*, p. 80.

130 Windeyer, *op. cit.* p. 234.

131 Jennings, *op. cit.* p. 178. He cites Bainbridge v. Postmaster-General, [1906] 1 K.B. 178.

132 *Ibid.*, p. 199.

133 Quoted from Appendix 20 of the Hope Report on Terrorism, p. 352.

134 *Ibid.*, pp. 349–357.

135 Hewart, *op. cit.* pp. 27–29; Dicey, *op. cit.* pp. 193–194, 208–225.

136 Hewart, *op. cit.* p. 37.

137 *Ibid.*, p. 38.

138 *Ibid.*, p. 37.

139 *Ibid.*, pp. 40–42.

140 Dickinson, *Watergate: Chronology of a Crisis*, vol. I p. 153.

141 *Ibid.*, p. 64.

142 *Ibid.*, pp. 3–4.

143 *Ibid.*, p. 44.

144 *Ibid.*, pp. 44–45.

145 *Ibid.*, p. 1.

146 *Ibid.*, p. 6.

147 *Ibid.*, p. 63.

148 The *New York Times*, 22nd December 1974; Boswell, "Welcome to the New CIA", *The Australian Magazine* 25–26 April 1992, p. 32; *The New York Times Index 1974*, vol.II p. 2567; *The New York Times Index 1975*, vol.II p. 2600; McGehee, *Deadly Deceits*, p. 179.

149 For the chronology of CIA Directors and Deputy Directors, see the CIA home page: <http://www.ic.gov/facttell/sections/tenures.html.>

150 *The New York Times Index 1974*, vol.II pp. 2554–2568; *The New York Times Index 1975*, vol.II pp. 2583–2602; Halperin, Berman, Borosage, Marwick *The Lawless State*, pp. 1–236.

151 Halperin, Berman, Borosage and Marwick, *op. cit.* p. 222; quoted there from the Final Report of the Select Committee to Study Governmental Operations with Respect to Intelligence Activities, US Senate, Book II p. 2. [This report hereafter referred to as "Senate Final Report", with relevant volume.]

152 Halperin, Berman, Borosage and Marwick *op. cit.* pp. 4–5.

153 *Ibid.*, p. 34; quoted there from Senate Final Report, Book I p. 50.

154 Halperin, Berman, Borosage and Marwick *op. cit.* pp. 41–46.

155 *The New York Times Index 1975*, vol. II p. 2601.

156 *Ibid.*

157 *Ibid.*, p. 2600; see also p. 2583 (Press photograph of Senators Church and Tower displaying CIA poison dart gun).

158 *Ibid.*, p. 2600.

159 *Ibid.*; Halperin, Berman, Borosage and Marwick, *op. cit.* pp. 44–46, drawn from An Interim Report of the Select Committee to Study Governmental Operations with Respect to Intelligence Activities, US Senate, "Alleged Assassination Plots Involving Foreign Leaders, November 1975".

160 *The New York Times Index 1975*, vol. II p. 2597.

161 *Ibid.*, p. 2596; Halperin, Berman, Borosage and Marwick, *op. cit.* pp. 135–136, p. 148.

162 Halperin, Berman, Borosage and Marwick, *op. cit.* p. 3.

163 *The New York Times Index 1975*, vol. II pp. 2601–2602.

164 Halperin, Berman, Borosage and Marwick, *op. cit.* p. 141, quoting from Final Report of the Select Committee to Study Governmental Operations with Respect to Intelligence Activities, US Senate, Supplementary Detailed Staff Reports on Intelligence Activities and the Rights of Americans, Book III (US Government Printing Office, Washington DC 1976) [hereafter cited as "Senate Book III", with report title],

"Domestic CIA and FBI Mail Opening", p. 609; see also *The New York Times Index 1975*, vol. II p. 2595, for other CIA officials acknowledging illegality.

165 Halperin, Berman, Borosage and Marwick, *op. cit.* p. 141, quoting from Senate Book III, "Domestic CIA and FBI Mail Opening", p. 605.

166 Halperin, Berman, Borosage and Marwick, *op. cit.* p. 142, quoted there from Senate Book III, "Domestic CIA and FBI Mail Opening", p. 577.

167 The *New York Times*, 22nd December 1974. This newspaper edition is famous as the first of the leaks regarding the Schlesinger Report.

168 *Ibid.*; Halperin, Berman, Borosage and Marwick, *op. cit.* pp. 141–143; *The New York Times Index 1975*, vol. II pp. 2584–2597.

169 *The New York Times Index 1975*, vol. II p. 2584, 2596.

170 Halperin, Berman, Borosage and Marwick, *op. cit.* p. 5.

171 *Ibid.*, pp. 63–89 and p. 231, from Senate Book III, "Dr Martin Luther King, Jr., Case Study"; *The New York Times Index 1975*, vol. II pp. 2597–2598, 2601.

172 *The New York Times Index 1975*, vol. II p. 2598.

173 *Ibid.*, pp. 2597–2602; *The Imperial Presidency:The Invisible Government of America*[sound recording], ABC Sydney 1978; Halperin, Berman, Borosage and Marwick, *op. cit.* pp. 234–235. The White House also had and abused its direct access to IRS files: see *The New York Times Index 1974*, vol. II pp. 2557–2560, 2566.

174 Halperin, Berman, Borosage and Marwick, *op. cit.* p. 148, from the Commission on CIA Activities within the United States, *Report to the President* (US Government Printing Office, Washington DC 1975), p. 249. [This is the report of the Rockefeller Commission.]

175 *The New York Times Index 1975*, vol. II pp. 2599–2600.

176 Dickinson, *op. cit.* p. 1.

177 Halperin, Berman, Borosage and Marwick, *op. cit.* p. 224, quoting *United States v. Lee (1882)*, 106 US 196 at 220.

178 Halperin, Berman, Borosage and Marwick, *op. cit.* p. 224, (emphasis added), quoted there from Senate Final Report, Book IV p. 157.

179 Halperin, Berman, Borosage and Marwick, *op. cit.* pp. 243–244. A similar belief had been expressed by senior Postal Service officials, including the Postmaster-General during the Kennedy and Nixon administrations (see *Ibid.*, p. 245; *The New York Times Index 1975*, vol. II p. 2601). In 1975 a CIA spokesman said that CIA Director William E. Colby "has told CIA employees he believes that none of them will face prosecution for any illegal activities" (*The New York Times Index 1975*, vol. II p. 2600).

180 Halperin, Berman, Borosage and Marwick, *op. cit.* p. 258.

181 *Ibid.*, p. 244.

182 *Ibid.*, p. 9.

183 *Ibid.*, p. 10.

184 *Ibid.*, p. 250.

185 *Ibid.*, p. 221.

186 *Ibid.*, p. 226, quoting Senate Final Report, Book II p. 141.

187 Halperin, Berman, Borosage and Marwick, *op. cit.* p. 225, from *Washington Post*, 23rd October 1975.

188 *Report of the Congressional Committees Investigating the Iran-Contra Affair (1987)*: the US Senate Select Committee on Secret Military Assistance to Iran and the Nicaraguan Opposition, and the US House of Representatives Select Committee to Investigate Covert Arms Transactions with Iran.

189 *Ibid.*, p. 11.

190 *The Imperial Presidency, op. cit.*

191 Halperin, Berman, Borosage and Marwick, *op. cit.* p. 246.

192 H.V. Evatt, "The King and His Dominion Governors", Evatt and Forsey *Evatt and Forsey on the Reserve Power*, p. 189; quoted there from Todd, *Parliamentary Government in the British Colonies* (2nd ed.), pp. 58–59.

193 H.V. Evatt, "The King and His Dominion Governors", Evatt and Forsey *op. cit.* pp. 189–190, citing Todd, *op. cit.* p. 727.

194 H.V. Evatt, "The King and His Dominion Governors", Evatt and Forsey *op. cit.* p. 191, quoting Todd, *op. cit.* p. 807.

195 H.V. Evatt, "The King and His Dominion Governors", Evatt and Forsey *op. cit.* p. 175, quoting A.B. Keith, *Responsible Government in the Dominions* (1927), vol.I pp. 199–202.

196 H.V. Evatt, "The King and His Dominion Governors", Evatt and Forsey *op. cit.* p. 175.

ENDNOTES

197 H.V. Evatt, "The King and His Dominion Governors", Evatt and Forsey *op. cit.* p. 188.

198 *Ibid.*, pp. 188–189.

199 For the letter and Lang's response, see Foott, *Dismissal of a Premier*, pp. 105–108.

200 *Ibid.*, p. 16.

201 *Ibid.*, p. 84.

202 *Ibid.*, p. 178.

203 Quoted from Morrison, "Dominions Office Correspondence on the New South Wales Constitutional Crisis 1930–1932", *J. Royal Australian Historical Society*, vol. 61 pt.5 March 1976, pp. 323–345; these letters quoted from pp. 341–343.

204 Foott *op. cit.* pp. 197–198. Sir Philip pencilled in the margin of the letter "Agree generally, but words I have put in brackets are too indefinite to be of any particular value. P.G."

205 Morrison, *op. cit.* p. 336.

206 H.V. Evatt, "The King and His Dominion Governors", Evatt and Forsey *op. cit.* pp. 157–174; Foott, *op. cit.*, Morrison *op. cit.* pp. 336–338. Foott's entire book is addressed to the Game-Lang affair. Her account of events is much more detailed than that of Evatt, and provides a somewhat different picture.

207 H.V. Evatt, "The King and His Dominion Governors", Evatt and Forsey *op. cit.* pp. 172–191.

208 Halperin, Berman, Borosage and Marwick, *op. cit.* pp. 249–250.

209 Foott, *op. cit.* pp. 207–208.

210 H.V. Evatt, "The King and His Dominion Governors", Evatt and Forsey *op. cit.* p. 185.

211 Foott, *op. cit.* p. 115.

212 *Ibid.*, p. 103, quoting from an article in *Truth*, 20th July 1958.

213 *Ibid.*, p. 102.

214 *Ibid.*, p. 12, pp. 222–223.

215 *The New York Times Index 1975*, vol. II p. 2600.

216 Dicey, *An Introduction to the Study of the Law of the Constitution*, pp. 184–185. De Tocqueville's numbering of remarks has been suppressed.

217 *Ibid.*, p. 185, his italics.

218 *Ibid.*, pp. 185–186.

219 The *Weekend Australian*, 15–16th January 1994.

220 Quoted from Kraus, *The Crisis of German Democracy*, pp. 174–175. This book also contains an English translation of the Weimar Constitution.

221 See Thomson, *Europe Since Napoleon*, pp. 688–691; Nicholls, *Weimar and the Rise of Hitler*, pp. 130–140.

222 Hayward, *The One and Indivisible French Republic*, p. 2.

223 *Ibid.*

224 Crawley, *De Gaulle*, pp. 324–328.

225 *Ibid.*, pp. 334–335.

226 *Ibid.*, pp. 333–338.

227 *Ibid.*, pp. 339–360; Schoenbrun, *The Three Lives of Charles de Gaulle*, pp. 216–232.

228 Crawley, *op. cit.*, p. 360.

229 The way the reserve powers of the Crown operate is discussed in later chapters.

230 Hayward, *op. cit.*, pp. 85–89.

231 *Ibid.*, p. 93.

232 *Ibid.*, p. 81.

233 Crawley, *op. cit.*, p. 388.

234 *Ibid.*, p. 390.

235 *Ibid.*, pp. 387–397.

236 *Ibid.*, p. 362.

237 *Ibid.*, p. 387.

238 *Ibid.*, p. 392.

239 *Ibid.*, p. 391; Ledwidge, *De Gaulle*, p. 311.

240 Ledwidge, *op. cit.*, p. 311.

241 Crawley, *op. cit.*, pp. 392–396.

242 *Ibid.*, pp. 430–431; Hayward, *op. cit.*, p. 86.

243 Hayward, *op. cit.*, p. 80.

244 *Ibid.*, p. 82.

245 *Ibid.*, pp. 78–79.

246 *Ibid.*, p. 1.

247 Turnbull et al., Report of the Republic Advisory Committee, vol.2, p. 117.

248 Turnbull, *op. cit.* vol. 2, pp. 144–145.

249 *Ibid.*, vol.2 p. 145.

250 *Ibid.*

251 *Ibid.*, p. 147.

252 *Ibid.*, p. 177.

253 *Ibid.*, pp. 177–178.

254 The report on the Irish republic is presented as Appendix 4 of *Ibid.*, pp. 109–185.

255 18 & 19 Vic. c.54.

256 Quick and Garran, *op. cit.*, pp. 41–47.

257 The *Australian*, 19th March 1996.

258 The *Australian*, 3rd September 1993.

259 The *Australian*, 19th March 1996.

260 The *Australian*, 6th October 1993.

261 The *Australian*, 19th March 1996.

262 The *Australian*, 20th March 1996.

263 The *Australian*, 19th March 1996.

264 The *Australian*, 23rd November 1994; 28th January 1994; 1st April 1993.

265 The *Australian*, 23rd November 1994.

266 Bagehot, *The English Constitution*, p. 111.

267 "An idea whose time has passed", *The Economist* (UK), 22nd October 1994, p. 15.

268 *Ibid.*

269 See, for example, Markwell, "The Dismissal", *Quadrant*, March 1984, pp. 11–21.

270 Jennings, *Cabinet Government*, p. 10.

271 Markwell, *op. cit.* p. 18.

272 *Ibid.*, p. 101.

273 Quoted from *The Times*, 15th September 1913.

274 Bagehot, *op. cit.* p. 65.

275 *Ibid.*, p. 277.

276 *Ibid.*, p. 163.

277 *Ibid.*

278 *Ibid.*, pp. 161–162. Note the change of pronoun.

279 *Ibid.*, p. 63.

280 *Ibid.*

281 *Ibid.*, p. 99.

282 *Ibid.*, p. 95.

283 *Ibid.*, p. 232.

284 "An idea whose time has passed", *The Economist* (UK), 22nd October 1994, p. 15.

285 Bagehot, *op. cit.* p. 92.

286 Le May, *The Victorian Constitution*, p. 17.

287 Bagehot, *op. cit.* p. 163.

288 *Ibid.*, p. 87

289 Quoted from Fraser, *Cromwell, Our Chief of Men*, p. 214.

290 *Ibid.*, p. 218.

291 *Ibid.*, p. 210.

292 *Ibid.*, p. 440. A good account of the Putney debates is given on pp. 210–219.

293 Bagehot, *op. cit.* p. 84.

294 *Ibid.*, p. 88.

295 *Ibid.*, p. 91. Of course the Queen does not rule at all, but reigns; a distinction he makes elsewhere, and is used in his overly-simple dichotomy of "dignified" and "efficient" parts.

296 The Bill of Rights, 1 William & Mary, sess.2 c.2.

297 Bagehot, *op. cit.* p. 102.

298 Sections 1 and 61, Australian Constitution; 63 & 64 Victoria, c.12; my italics.

299 Bagehot, *op. cit.* p. 93.

300 *Ibid.*, pp. 110–111.

301 *Ibid.*, p. 112.

302 Le May, *op. cit.* p. 69.

303 Hayward, *op. cit.* p. 88.

304 Bagehot, *op. cit.* p. 113.

305 Markwell, *op. cit.* p. 18.

306 Turnbull, *op. cit.* vol. 2 p. 157.

307 *Ibid.*, vol. 2 p. 158.

308 *Ibid.*, vol. 2 p. 159.

309 *Ibid.*

310 *Ibid.*

311 *Ibid.*

312 *Ibid.*, vol. 2 p. 155.

313 *Ibid.*

314 Bagehot, *op. cit.* p. 110.

315 Jennings, *op. cit.* p. 329.

316 Bagehot, *op. cit.* pp. 107–108.

317 Neale, *Queen Elizabeth I*, p. 94.

318 *Ibid.*, p. 94.

319 *Ibid.*, p. 288. Sixtus V seems to have been a remarkable man. An outspoken admirer, not only of Elizabeth but also of Sir Francis Drake, he voiced misgivings over the chances of the Spanish Armada even before the sea battle (*Ibid.*, p. 298). When the initial, false news came of the Armada's success over the English ships he was sceptical, and eulogised both Elizabeth and Drake (*Ibid.*, p. 304); his view was subsequently vindicated once genuine reports came in, telling of the disaster which befell the Armada.

320 Le May, *op. cit.* p. 66.

321 *Ibid.*

322 *Ibid.*, p. 73.

323 *Ibid.*, p. 66.

324 *Ibid.*, p. 92.

325 Jennings, *op. cit.*, p. 349.

326 *Ibid.*

327 *Ibid.*, p. 346.

328 *Ibid.*, p. 349.

329 "An idea whose time has passed", *The Economist* (UK), 22nd October 1994.

BOOK TWO

1 Quoted from E.A. Forsey, "The Present Position of the Reserve Powers of the Crown", Evatt and Forsey, *op. cit.* pp. xciv–xcv.

2 Quoted from Cowen, "The Australian Head of State", *Quadrant* April 1992, p. 69.

3 *Ibid.*, p. xlviii.

4 *Ibid.*, pp. xlviii–xlix.

5 Lord Hailsham, *The Dilemma of Democracy*, p. 142.

6 (1992) 177 CLR, p. 123.

7 See e.g. Crawford and Odjers, *Change the Constitution?* pp. 51–66.

8 Nicholls, *op. cit.* p. 30.

9 *Ibid.*, pp. 138–139.

10 *Ibid.*, p. 132.

11 Hailsham, *op. cit.* p. 126. When a written Constitution exists, as in Australia, this power may be limited if the proposed legislation apparently interferes with the functioning of that instrument.

12 177 CLR., pp. 113–114.

13 *Ibid.*, pp. 111–112.

14 *Ibid.*, p. 115.

15 *Ibid.*, p. 132.

16 *Ibid.*, p. 145.

17 *Ibid.*, pp. 118–120.

18 *Ibid.*, p. 131.

19 *Ibid.*, p. 129.

20 *Ibid.*, p. 136.

21 *Ibid.*

22 Mason here is quoting Archibald Cox; *Ibid.*, p. 139.

23 *Ibid.*, p. 142.

24 *Ibid.*, p. 136.

25 The judgement is also reported in (1992) 66 ALJR, from p. 695.

26 *Ibid.*, pp. 722–724.

27 *Ibid.*, pp. 775–777. This quote p. 776.

28 See Crossman's introduction to Bagehot's *The English Constitution*; Bagehot *op. cit.*

29 E.A. Forsey, "The Royal Power of Dissolution of Parliament in the British Commonwealth", Evatt and Forsey *op. cit.* p. 7. Forsey's own quote is taken from Leif Egeland MP, a South African parliamentarian writing in 1940, before South Africa became a republic.

30 Quoted from No. LI of Madison, Hamilton, Jay *The Federalist Papers*, pp. 319–320. Emphasis mine.

31 *Parliamentary Debates (Hansard)*, 5th Series, vol. 398, col. 1516; quoted in Appendix E of Forsey, *op. cit.* p. 302.

32 Forsey, *op. cit.* p. 9.

33 *Ibid.*

34 *Ibid.*, pp. 162–163.

35 *Ibid.* p. 159.

36 Forsey provides a detailed analysis of the Byng-King crisis, and criticizes the views of Keith and Evatt over it; see *ibid.* pp. 131–249.

37 *Ibid.*, p. 10, quoted there from "The Discretionary Authority of Dominion Governors", *18 Canadian Bar Review*, no. 1 pp. 8–9.

38 H.V. Evatt, "The King and His Dominion Governors", Evatt and Forsey *op. cit.* p. 109.

39 Articles 12 and 19, Constitution of the Fifth Republic of France.

40 This excellent description of Westminster convention actually originated from a Queensland colonial newspaper, the *Saturday Review*, 1868. It is quoted by Forsey, *op. cit.* p. 25.

41 Evatt, *The Discretionary Authority of Dominion Governors*, quoted by Forsey, *ibid.* p. 10.

42 Appendix 4 of Markesinis, *The Theory and Practice of Dissolution of Parliament*, has the debate reproduced; this letter is on p. 263.

43 Forsey, *op.cit.* p. 184. Italics and comments mine. Forsey also emphasises the italicized passage.

44 *Abe v. Minister of Finance and Attorney-General*, High Court of the Solomon Islands, No. 197 of 1994.

45 *Francis Billy Hilly & Others v. Governor-General of the Solomon Islands*, High Court of the Solomon Islands, No. 299 of 1994.

46 Quoted from joint judgement of Connolly P and Los JA, *Francis Billy Hilly & Others v. Governor-General of the Solomon Islands* (1994), p. 6.

47 *Ibid.*

48 *Ibid.*, p. 8.

49 Judgement of Williams JA, *ibid.* For further details of this constitutional crisis, see also the commentary of Palmer J (also of the High Court of the Solomon Islands) upon this case and the judge-

ments handed down, and the transcript of the Governor-General's speech to the nation, Monday 17th October 1994.

50 The *Australian*, 17th January 1996.

51 The *Weekend Australian*, 27–28 January 1996.

52 *Ibid.*

53 *Ibid.*

54 *Ibid.*

55 The *Australian*, 26th January 1996.

56 *Ibid.*

57 The *Weekend Australian*, 27–28 January 1996. Comment mine.

58 *Ibid.*

59 *Ibid.*

60 *Ibid.*; The *Australian*, 19th January 1996.

61 The *Australian*, 29th January 1996.

62 The *Australian*, 31st January 1996.

63 Le May, *op. cit.* p. 218.

64 Hailsham, *op. cit.* p. 143.

65 Quoted from Bagehot, *op. cit.* pp. 131–132.

66 Quoted from "Representative Government", J.S. Mill, *Utilitarianism, Liberty, and Representative Government*, p. 239.

67 Quoted from Todd, *On Parliamentary Government in England*, vol. II pp. 318–319. Todd's own second quotation is taken from Disraeli.

68 Thomson, *Europe Since Napoleon*, p. 663.

69 *Ibid.*

70 *Ibid.*, p. 664.

71 *Ibid.*

72 *Ibid.*, p. 663.

73 *Ibid.*

74 *Ibid.*, p. 664.

75 Evatt quotes this letter of The *Times*, 4th September 1913, in "The King and His Dominion Governors", Evatt and Forsey *op. cit.* p. 91.

76 *Ibid.* p. 92.

77 *Ibid.*

78 Quoted from The *Times*, 15th September 1913.

79 *Ibid.*

80 *Ibid.*

81 Forsey, *op. cit.* pp. 123–124.

82 *Ibid.*, pp. 270–271.

83 Hayward, *op. cit.* p. 80.

84 See Hailsham's forward to Sir John Kerr's *Matters for Judgment*, pp. xv–xvi.

85 Le May, *op. cit.* p. 213.

86 *Ibid.*, p. 216.

87 *Ibid.*, p. 217.

88 *Ibid.*

89 *Ibid.*, pp. 217–218.

90 *Ibid.*, p. 218.

91 *Ibid.*, p. 219.

92 *Ibid.*

93 *Ibid.*

94 For an account of these events, see *ibid.*, pp. 212–219; Evatt, *op. cit.* pp. 90–102.

95 Quoted from Sir Zelman Cowen's "Introduction to the *King and His Dominion Governors*", Evatt and Forsey *op. cit.* p. xxii.

96 *Ibid.*, p. xxi; for more details on the constitutional crisis, see pp. xix–xxii.

97 63 & 64 Victoria, chapter 12, section 58. Italics are my own.

98 Quotation from The *Courier-Mail*, 5th May 1993.

99 Quoted from Sir Winston Churchill's speech "Britain and Canada", given 14th January 1952. See James, *Winston S. Churchill, His Complete Speeches 1897–1963*, vol VIII p. 8322.

100 Quoted from Machiavelli, *The Prince*, pp. 69–70; italics are my own.

101 Bagehot, *op. cit.* pp. 111–112.

102 *The Tempest*, Act I Scene 2.

103 Quoted from John Stuart Mill's essay "Representative Government"; see J.S. Mill, *Utilitarianism, Liberty, and Representative Government*, p. 253.

104 *Ibid.*, pp. 194–195.

105 Quoted from Crawley, *op. cit.* p. 393.

106 *Ibid.*, p. 395.

107 *Ibid.*, pp. 393–396.

108 See Hayward *op. cit.* pp. 80–89, Crawley *op. cit.* pp. 386–397.

109 Quoted from Hayward, *op. cit.* p. 3.

110 The *Australian*, 1st April 1993. It was not, alas, an April Fool's joke.

111 Quoted from Turnbull, *op.cit.* vol. 1, p. 67.

112 Robb, "Lives of the Matyrs", *The Independent Monthly*, Australia December 1995–January 1996, p. 74.

113 Quoted from "Fresh Faces, Fresh Starts?", *TIME* (Australia), 8th June 1992, p. 12. See also the *Economist* (UK) "Italy's Earthquake", 11th April 1992, pp. 43–44, "Cossiga Fan Tutte", 2nd May 1992, pp. 62–65; "The Unique Art of Italian

Politics", *TIME* (Australia), 25th May 1992, p. 11.

114 Turnbull, *op.cit.* vol. 1, p. 67.

115 Quoted from Hayward, *op. cit.* p. 82.

116 Quoted from Kolma, "Triumph of Justice", *Pacific Islands Monthly*, November 1991, p. 9.

117 *Ibid.*

118 Kolma, *op. cit.* pp. 8–9; Grubel, "Sir Eri's Swansong", *Pacific Islands Monthly*, November 1991, p. 10.

119 Quoted from Turnbull, *op.cit.* vol. 1 p. 74.

120 Quoted from Fowler and Fowler, *The Concise Oxford Dictionary of Current English*, p. 606.

121 Hayward, *op. cit.* p. 86.

122 Dickinson, *Watergate: Chronology of a Crisis*, vol. 1 p. 55.

123 *Ibid.*

124 *Ibid.*

125 Appendix Two, Turnbull, *op. cit.* vol. 2 pp. 2–5.

126 Explanatory Statement to the Exposure Draft of the Constitution Alteration (Establishment of Republic) Bill 1999, p. 7.

127 Turnbull, *op.cit.* vol. I p. 94.

128 Winterton, "A Constitution for an Australian Republic", *Independent Monthly*, June 1993, section 60A.

129 Menzies, *Afternoon Light*, p. 254.

130 Kerr, *op. cit.*, pp. 376–396.

131 *Ibid.*, p. 388.

132 Markwell, "The Dismissal", *Quadrant* March 1984, p. 19.

133 Joske, *Sir Robert Menzies 1894–1978 — a new, informal memoir*, pp. 152–153.

134 Cowen, "Introduction to *The King and His Dominion Governors*", Evatt and Forsey, *op. cit.* pp. xxiii–xxvi; Kerr, *op. cit.*, pp. 135–141.

135 Smith, *Australian Constitutional Monarchy*, ACM Occasional Paper No 1, October 1992, p. 6.

136 Keith, *The King and the Imperial Crown: The Powers and Duties of His Majesty*, p. i.

137 *Ibid.*, p. 180.

138 Kerr, *op. cit.*, p. xi.

139 *Ibid.*, pp. 358–359.

140 Reid, *The Whitlam Venture*, pp. 369–370.

141 D.P. O'Connell, "Canada, Australia, Constitutional Reform and the Crown", *The Parliamentarian* LX No.1, January 1979, p. 9.

142 *Ibid.*

143 *Ibid.*, p. 11.

144 *Ibid.*, p. 12.

145 *Ibid..*, p. 9.

146 *Ibid.*, p. 9.

147 *Ibid.*, p. 10.

148 *Ibid.*

149 Nicholas, *The Australian Constitution*, p. 47.

150 Letters Patent Relating to the Office of the Governor-General of the Commonwealth of Australia, section IIa.

151 *Ibid.*, section VIII.

152 Section 61.

153 Section 9; see E.A. Forsey, "The Role and Position of the Monarch in Canada", *The Parliamentarian*, LXIV No.1, January 1983, pp. 6–7.

154 Marshall, *Constitutional Conventions: The Rules and Forms of Political Accountability*, p. 174.

155 *Ibid.*

156 Draft manuscript, D.J. Markwell, *1975: The Crown and the Constitution*; quoted there from The Sun Herald, 13th January 1985.

157 Keith, *op. cit.*, p. 430.

158 *Ibid.*, p. 180; *idem, The Constitutional Law of the British Dominions*, p. 18; Marshall, *op. cit.* pp. 173–174; Turnbull, *op.cit.* vol. 2 p. 115.

159 Kerr, *op. cit.*, p. xi.

160 The Solomon Islands Independence Order 1978, section 27(3b).

161 T.S. Eliot, *Four Quartets*, 'East Coker'

162 Keith, *Speeches and Documents on the British Dominions 1918–1931*, p. 222.

163 Constitution of the Independent State of Papua New Guinea, section 88.

164 Letter dated 5th February 1859; *The Letters of Queen Victoria*, vol. III p. 316.

165 *The Australian*, 14th October 1994.

166 E.A. Forsey, "The Role and Position of the Monarch in Canada", *The Parliamentarian* LXIV No. 1 January 1983, pp. 6–11.

167 Hiller, *Public Order and the Law*, p. 220.

168 *Ibid.*, pp. 217–221; the *Australian*, 14th and 15th February 1978; Appendix 15 and annexes of the Hope Report, *op. cit.* pp. 320–325

169 Hope Report, *op. cit.* pp. 154–155.

170 TIME (Australia), 18th May 1970, p. 18

171 *Ibid.*

172 *Ibid.*

173 *Ibid.*

174 Lapping, *End of Empire*, p. 38.

175 Quoted from *The Prince*, Chapter XIV; see Machiavelli (de Alvarez edition) *op. cit.* p. 88.

176 Madison, *Debates in the Federal Convention of 1787.*

177 Wilson, *The Book of the Founding Fathers.*

178 Quoted from Freedman, *The Privilege to Keep and Bear Arms*, p 45.

179 Army Remonstrance of 23rd June 1647, quoted from Firth, *Cromwell's Army*, p. 351.

180 The events are described in Fraser, *Cromwell Our Chief of Men*, pp. 266–270, and also Firth *op. cit.* pp. 359–360.

181 For an analysis of the political nature of the Parliamentary standing army, see Firth *op. cit.* pp. 346–381.

182 I Will & Mary, sess. 2, c.2.

183 Bakel, *The Right to Bear Arms*, pp. 300–302.

184 Quoted from Dickenson's speech of 2nd June 1787, Madison, *op. cit.*, p. 48.

185 See e.g. Colonel Mason's motion of 14th September 1787, Madison, *op. cit.*, p. 565, and the debate of 23rd August, *ibid.* pp. 454–455.

186 *Ibid.*, p. 690.

187 Bakel, *op. cit.*, p. 296.

188 Freedman, *op. cit.*, p. 45.

189 Quoted from *The Australian*, 26th February 1981.

190 *Ibid.*

191 *Ibid.*

BOOK THREE

1 *The Australian*, 22nd July 1996.

2 For a synopsis of the Diro Affair, see Kolma, "Triumph of Justice", *Pacific Islands Monthly*, November 1991, pp. 8–10.

3 E.A. Forsey, "The Present Position of the Reserve Powers of the Crown", Evatt and Forsey, *op.cit.*, pp. xciv–xcv; Fraser, "A Revolutionary Governor-General? The Grenada Crisis of 1983", *Constitutional Heads and Political Crises: Commonwealth Episodes 1945–1985*, pp.142–162.

4 *The Australian*, 14th October 1994; *Francis Billy Hilly & Others v. Governor-General of the Solomon Islands*, High Court of the Solomon Islands, No. 299 of 1994.

5 See Markwell, "Canada's Best", a review of *A Life on the Fringe: The Memoirs of Eugene Forsey* by Eugene Forsey, *The Round Table*, October 1991, pp. 502–505. Sir John Kerr also discusses Forsey as an example of a socialist monarchist; see Kerr, *op.cit.*, pp. 209–212.

6 Dalziel, *Evatt the Enigma*, p 3.

7 Speech made by the Rt. Hon. H.V. Evatt to the House of Representatives, 15th February 1954; reported in *Parliamentary Debates (Hansard)*, 3 Eliz. II, Vol. H of R.3, pp. 7–9.

8 For a discussion of Evatt's ability to reconcile his social democratic philosophy with his acknowledgment of the reserve powers of the Crown, see Kerr, *op. cit.*, pp. 52–68.

9 Quoted from speech made by the Rt. Hon. J.B. Chifley to the House of Representatives, 29th August 1945, reported in *Parliamentary Debates*, 9 Geo. VI, vol 184, p. 4953.

10 See Grainger "Monarchy: Mystery and Practicality", pp. 111–118.

11 These figures and the chart were reported in the *Australian*, 9th February 1994.

12 See, for example, Waterford, "Keating's Quiet Power Shift", *Independent Monthly*, June 1993, p.12.

13 The *Australian*, 28th July 1993.

14 Quoted from the *Australian Financial Review*, 20th December 1994.

15 *Ibid.*

16 *Ibid.*

17 *Ibid.*

18 *Ibid.*

19 *Ibid.*

20 The *Australian*, 28th July 1993.

21 For a discussion of the Indian Civil Service see Lapping, *End of Empire*, pp. 31–33.

22 Hailsham, *The Dilemma of Democracy*, pp.158–161.

23 Speech made by the Rt. Hon. H.V. Evatt to the House, 7th February 1952; reported in *Parliamentary Debates*, 1 Eliz. II, Vol. 216, p. 32.

24 Barwick, *The Monarchy in an Independent Australia*, p. 4.

25 Markwell, *The Crown and Australia*, pp. 9–10.

26 The formula was named after Lord Balfour, who presided over the conference.

27 Cowen, "The Australian Head of State", *Quadrant* April 1992, p. 68.

28 Keith, *Speeches and Documents on the British Dominions 1918–1931*, p. 161.

29 *Ibid.*, pp. 164–165.

30 Markwell *op. cit.*, p. 10.

31 Keith *op. cit.* p. 222, discussed in Markwell *op. cit.* pp. 10–11.

32 *A Queen is Crowned*, film footage of the Coronation of Queen Elizabeth the Second, J. Arthur Rank Organisation, 1953.

33 Smith, *Some Thoughts on the Monarchy/Republic Debate*, p. 8. However, the fact that all the realms share common laws of succession and must all legislate when certain amendments to the Queen's position is made *is* novel and unique; as shall be argued later, it's also desirable.

34 Fraser, "A Revolutionary Governor-General? The Grenada Crisis of 1983", *Constitutional Heads and Political Crises: Commonwealth Episodes 1945–85*, p. 142.

35 *Ibid.*, p. 143.

36 *Ibid.*, p. 154.

37 *Ibid.*

38 *Ibid.*

39 *Ibid.*, p. 143.

40 *Ibid.*, p. 144.

41 *Ibid.*

42 *Ibid.*, p. 155.

43 *Ibid.*, p. 156.

44 *Ibid.*

45 *Ibid.*

46 *Ibid.*

47 *Ibid.*

48 E.A.Forsey, "The Present Position of the Reserve Powers of the Crown", Evatt and Forsey *op. cit.* p p. xciv–xcv.

49 Fraser, *op. cit.* pp. 158–159.

50 Cowen, *op. cit.* p. 67.

51 *Ibid.*

52 Barwick, *op. cit.* pp. 4–5.

53 Final Report of the Constitutional Commission, vol. III (summary), p. vii.

54 *Ibid.*, vol. 1 p. 75.

55 *Ibid.*, vol. 1 p. 75.

56 *Ibid.*, vol. 3 p. 17.

57 *Ibid.*, vol. 1 p. 76.

58 22 Geo. V, c.4, quoted from Keith *op. cit.* p. 303.

59 Quick and Garran, *op. cit.* pp. 688–698; Keith, *Speeches and Documents on the British Dominions 1918–1931*, pp.174–176.

60 Keith, *op. cit.* p. 476.

61 See the report of the Conference on the Operation of Dominion Legislation and Merchant Shipping Legislation, 1929: *Ibid.*, pp. 173–205; this quote p. 180.

62 Smith, *op. cit.* p. 10–11

63 *Ibid.*

64 Personal communication with Sir David Smith.

65 Kerr, *op. cit.* pp. 374–375.

66 Orwell, "Notes on Nationalism", *The Penguin Essays of George Orwell*, pp. 306–307.

67 Proceedings of the Australian Constitutional Convention, Adelaide 26–29 April, 1983, Vol. I, pp. 66–81.

68 *Ibid.*, p. 67.

69 For their objections to Practice 5, see *Ibid.*, pp. 76–78.

70 *Ibid*, p. 79.

71 Quoted from Sir Shridath Ramphal, "Canada and the Commonwealth", *The Round Table* (1987), 304 p. 429.

72 The *Guardian*, 29 March 1995.

73 *The Times*, 18 April 1995; see also its articles on 17th, 14th, 12th and 7th April, 16th and 14th March; the *Guardian*, 29 March 1995; the *Daily Telegraph*, 13th and 15th March 1995; the *Observer*, 12th March 1995; the *Sunday Telegraph*, 12th March 1995.

74 Lord Brabazon of Tara, "1988–89: A Watershed in Britain/Australia Relations", *The Round Table* (1990), 313 pp. 34–38; this quote p. 35.

75 *Ibid.*, p. 36.

76 *Ibid.*

77 *Ibid.*

78 The *Financial Times*, 24th January 1994.

79 *Ibid.*

80 *Ibid.*

81 *Ibid.*, p. 410.

82 *Ibid.*, pp. 408–409.

83 *Ibid.*, p. 412.

84 *Ibid.*, p. 413.

85 See <www.olympic.org/charter/echch5d.html#69>.

86 www.olympic.org/charter/

87 See the introduction to Burke, *op. cit.* p. vii.

88 See introduction to T. Paine, *Rights of Man*, pp. 15–18.

89 Burke, *op. cit.* pp. vii–ix.

90 Paine, *op. cit.* pp. 40–41.

91 *Ibid.*, pp. 41–42.

92 Burke, *op. cit.* p. 96.

93 Paine, *op. cit.*, p. 124.

94 *Ibid.*

95 See e.g. Bottomley, Gunningham, Parker, *Law in Context*, p. 26.

96 Dicey, *An Introduction to the Study of the Law of the Constitution*, p. 197.

97 *Ibid.*

98 *Ibid.* Italics are my own.

99 *Ibid.*, p. 201.

100 Quick and Garran, *op. cit.* p. 287.

101 *Ibid.*, p. 288.

102 *Ibid.*, p. 289.

103 *Ibid.*

104 *Ibid.*, pp. 289–290.

105 Moens, "The Wrongs of a Constitutionally Entrenched Bill of Rights", *Australia: Republic or Monarchy?*, pp. 233–256; quote is taken from p. 235.

106 *Ibid.*, p. 238.

107 Quoted from endnotes of *Ibid.*, pp. 254–255.

108 For a discussion on trial by jury and Magna Carta, see Windeyer, *Lectures on Legal History*, pp. 66–69 and 87–91.

109 *Ibid.*, p. 88.

110 *Ibid.*

111 Moens, *op. cit.* p. 246.

112 *Ibid.*, p. 244.

113 Hailsham, *op. cit.* pp. 94–95.

114 See Isaac Kramnick's Introduction to *The Federalist Papers*, Madison, Hamilton and Jay *op. cit.* pp. 16–23.

115 *Ibid.*, p. 24 (quote originally taken from W. Goddard, *The Prowess of the Whig Club*, Baltimore 1787).

116 *Ibid.*, p. 24.

117 Introduction; Madison, Hamilton and Jay *op. cit.* p. 24.

118 *Ibid.*, quoted there from "Autobiography", *The Works of John Adams* (ed. C.F.Adams), Boston 1856, vol.II pp. 420–421.

119 Wilson, *op. cit.* pp. 56–57.

120 Introduction; Madison, Hamilton and Jay *op. cit.* pp. 23–24. Morris' warning casts an interesting light upon later events in his life. Of aristocratic sympathies — he had wanted the US Senate to be more heavily modelled upon the House of Lords, as a body representing the wealthy and propertied to counterbalance the more democratic Representatives — he was US Minister to France during the revolution in that country. Respected by his French revolutionary counterparts for his role in the American Revolution, he was found conspiring to smuggle out aristocrats and the King, to rescue them from the guillotine. He was required to return to the United States. See Wilson, *The Book of the Founding Fathers*, pp. 56–57.

121 Isaac Kramnick, Professor of Government, Cornell University; editors' introduction, *The Federalist Papers*, Madison, Hamilton, Jay *op. cit.* pp. 48–49.

122 *Ibid.*, p. 64.

123 *Ibid.*, p. 63.

124 *Ibid.*

125 *Ibid.* For a discussion of the class aspects of the US Constitution, see pp. 61–65 of Kramnick's introduction to the *Federalist Papers*. His article has been recently described by a former Chief Justice of the US Supreme Court as "an outstanding piece of work…I am strongly recommending its reading".

126 Translation quoted of Article as adopted on the 4th December 1982 by the Fifth Session of the Fifth National People's Congress of the People's Republic of China, and published in *Beijing Review*, No.52, 27th December 1982.

127 Adams, *op. cit.* pp. 188–207.

128 Evans and Jack, *op. cit.* pp. 377–378.

129 Quick and Garran, *op. cit.* p. 414.

130 *Ibid.*

131 *Ibid.*, pp. 683–684.

132 Whitlam's memorandum to the Governor-General is reproduced in Kerr, *op. cit.* p. 233.

133 *Ibid.*, p. 260.

134 *Parliamentary Debates*, H. of R.97, pp. 2331–2333.

135 *Ibid.*, pp. 2392–2399.

136 Wheeldon's words; quoted from Markwell, "The Dismissal", *Quadrant*, March 1984, pp. 12–13. See also Reid, *The Whitlam Venture*, pp. 378–379.

137 Kerr, *op. cit.* pp. 363–369. Despite protestations to the contrary, as Governor-General Kerr possessed this right to dismiss ministers both implicitly — as a traditional reserve power of the

Crown in the Westminster system —
and as a direct consequence of his
explicit power of appointing ministers
under section 64 of the Constitution. In
their joint legal opinions upon the
validity of the Dismissal, J.S. Lockhart
QC and R.P. Meagher QC also identified
a third source: "such a reserve power is
not only recognised by s.64 but is also
expressly referred to in Clause IV of the
Letters Patent of 1900 constituting the
office of the Governor-General."
(Lockhart and Meagher, *The Australian
Constitutional Crisis of 1975: Facts &
Law*, p. 15.)

138 New Zealand has no Upper House.

139 Adams, *op. cit.* pp. 438–440.

140 Kerr, *op. cit.* p. 333

141 Oakes, *Crash Through or Crash*, p. 140.

142 Section 49; italics mine.

143 Sir Garfield Barwick's letter is reproduced in a number of sources: e.g. Kerr,
op. cit. pp. 343–344.

144 Quoted fom Markwell, *op. cit.* p. 12.

145 *Ibid.*, Markwell's emphasis.

146 Oakes, *op. cit.* p. 7.

147 Kerr, *op. cit.*pp. 126–127.

148 *Ibid.*, p. 128

149 *Ibid.*, pp. 128–129.

150 *Ibid.*, p. 129.

151 *Ibid.*, pp. 130–131; Forsey, "The Present
Position of the Reserve Powers of the
Crown", Evatt and Forsey, *op. cit.* pp.
xvi–xvii.

152 *Parliamentary Debates* (Senate), 19 Eliz.II
vol. S.44, p. 2647. Emphasis mine.

153 *Ibid.*, pp. 2651–2654.

154 *Parliamentary Debates*, H. of R. 69, p. 463.

155 Kerr, *op. cit.* pp. 130–131.

156 An unpublished manuscript, part II of
D.J.Markwell's *1975:The Senate and
Supply* (part I has been published) sets
out in considerable detail the role of the
Senate regarding Supply, argued on both
legal and historical grounds, in systematic refutation of Senator Gareth Evan's
assertions regarding the Dismissal.

157 Fowler and Fowler, *op. cit.* p. 281.

158 This finds expression in the written
Constitution through sections 81 to 83.

159 The foundation stone of the
Westminster system, this is enshrined in
section 61.

160 e.g. the salary of the Governor-General
(section 3), of senators and members of
the House of Representatives (section
48), of Ministers of State (section 66)
and of High Court judges (section 72).

161 Eugene Forsey's opinion is expressed in
an epilogue he wrote to Kerr's book
Matters for Judgement; Kerr, *op. cit.* pp.
440–444 (this quote pp. 440–442).

162 *Ibid.*, pp. xi–xvi.

163 *Ibid.*, p. 667.

164 *Ibid.*, p. 2394.

165 Tardif and Atkinson, *Penguin Macquarie
Dictionary of Australian Politics*, p. 328.

166 Menzies' words were quoted on a number
of occasions during the '75 crisis; e.g. by
Mr Sinclair, *Parliamentary Debates*, H. of
R. 97, p. 2524.

167 Madison, *op. cit.* pp. 47–48; Madison's
italics removed.

168 Madison, *op. cit.* p. 48. It is worth noting
that Germany is a federation of states
and Switzerland is a confederation of
self-governing cantons, which would
appear to reinforce his point.

169 Quoted from D.P. O'Connell QC,
"Canada, Australia, Constitutional Reform
and the Crown", The *Parliamentarian* LX
No. 1, January 1979, p. 12.

170 *Ibid.*, p. 12.

171 *Ibid.*

172 *Ibid.*, p. 13.

173 Quick and Garran, *op. cit.* p. 991.

174 *Ibid.*, p. 990.

175 *Ibid.*, pp. 991–994.

176 *Ibid.*, p. 994.

177 *Ibid.*, p. 294.

178 *Ibid.*, p. 295.

179 Protest of King Charles I, at his unlawful
trial at the hands of the High Court of
Justice.

180 "The Republic and the President", *4
Corners* (ABC 1993).

181 Lapping, *End of Empire*, pp. 494–496.

182 *Ibid.*, p. 504.

183 *Ibid.*, p. 495.

184 *Ibid.*, p. 503.

185 Quoted from the US Declaration of
Independence, 1776. Although the question remains contentious whether life,
liberty and the pursuit of happiness are
actually inalienable rights, it surely won't
be denied in this society that their
preservation and security are the fundamental reasons why human governments
are instituted, from which reasoning the
rest of the passage may be accepted.

186 Or indeed possession, Tom!

187 Paine, *op. cit.* pp. 44–45.

188 After gaining the approval of the West Australian Parliament, the West Australian secessionist case was presented to the Imperial Parliament by the State Government in 1934, formally requesting restoration to self-governing colonial status: *THE CASE OF THE PEOPLE OF WESTERN AUSTRALIA in support of their desire to withdraw from the Commmonwealth of Australia Constitution Act (Imperial), and that Western Australia be restored to its former status as a separate self-governing colony in the British Empire*, Western Australian government printers, 1934. The book runs to 489 pages.

188a "All power corrupts, and absolute power corrupts absolutely"; popular version of Lord Acton's 1887 quote, "Power tends to corrupt and absolute power corrupts absolutely".

189 Hewart, *op. cit.* pp. 15–16.

190 Quoted from Chapter I of Karl Marx and Friedrich Engels, *The Communist Manifesto*, p. 79.

191 Neville T. Bonner, "Why an Australian Constitutional Monarchy?", *The Australian Constitutional Monarchy*, pp. 18–19.

192 Machiavelli, *Selected Political Writings*, p. 3.

Bibliography

[author unknown], "An idea whose time has passed", *The Economist* (UK), 22nd October 1994.

[author unknown], "Fresh Faces, Fresh Starts?", *TIME* (Australia), 8th June 1992.

[author unknown], "The Unique Art of Italian Politics", *TIME* (Australia), 25th May 1992.

[author unknown], the *Economist* (UK) "Italy's Earthquake", 11th April 1992.

A Queen is Crowned, film footage of the Coronation of Queen Elizabeth the Second, J. Arthur Rank Organisation, 1953.

ADAMS, George Burton and STEPHENS, H. Morse (ed.), *Select Documents of English Constitutional History*, Macmillan, New York 1918.

ADAMS, George Burton, *Constitutional History of England*, revised edition, Jonathon Cape, London 1935.

ALLEY, Roderic, "The Military Coup in Fiji", *The Round Table* 1987, vol. 304 pp. 489–496.

ARISTOTLE, *The Politics* (transl. T.A. Sinclair), Penguin, 1981.

ARNOLD, John, SPEARITT, Peter and WALKER, David (ed.), *Out of Empire*, Reed Books, Melbourne 1993.

ATKINSON, Alan, *The Muddle-Headed Republic*, Oxford University Press, Melbourne 1993.

Australian, 26th February 1981; 1st April 1993; 28th July 1993; 3rd September 1993; 6th October 1993; 28th January 1994; 9th February 1994; 14th October 1994; 23rd November 1994; 19th March 1996; 20th March 1996; 22nd July 1996.

AUSTRALIAN BUREAU OF STATISTICS, *The Social Characteristics of Immigrants in Australia*, Australian Government Publishing Service, Canberra 1994.

Australian Financial Review, 20th December 1994.

BAGEHOT, Walter, *The English Constitution* (introduction by R.H.S. Crossman), Fontana, London 1993.

BAKAL, Carl, *The Right to Bear Arms*, McGraw-Hill 1966.

BARWICK, Sir Garfield, *The Monarchy in an Independent Australia*, 1982 Sir Robert Menzies Lecture, Sir Robert Menzies Lecture Trust 1982.

BLACKBURN, Robert (ed.), *Constitutional Studies*, Mansell [London? Date?]

BOGDANOR, Vernon, *Multi-Party Politics and the Constitution*, Cambridge University Press, 1983.

BOLT, Robert, *A Man for All Seasons* [citation?].

BOSWELL, Bryan, "Welcome to the New CIA", *The Australian Magazine*, 25–26 April 1992, pp. 30–33.

BOTTOMLEY, S., GUNNINGHAM, N. and PARKER, S., *Law in Context*, Federation Press, Sydney 1994.

BURKE, Edmund, *Reflections on the Revolution in France* (ed. Leslie Mitchell), Oxford University Press, Oxford 1993.

BRABAZON of Tara, "1988–89: A Watershed in Britain/Australia Relations", *The Round Table* 1990, vol. 313 pp. 34–38.

BUTLER, David, *Governing Without a Majority*, Collins, London 1983.

BUTLER, David, *The Republican Question in Australia*, Robert Menzies Memorial Lecture, 16 November 1993.

BUTLER, David and LOW, D.A. (ed.), *Sovereigns and Surrogates*, Macmillan, London 1991.

CARROLL, Lewis, *Alice's Adventures in Wonderland and Through the Looking-Glass*, Illustrated Editions, New York.

CLANCY, G.B., *A Dictionary of Indonesian History Since 1900*, Sunda Publications, Sydney 1992.

COWEN, Sir Zelman, "The Australian Head of State", *Quadrant*, April 1992, pp. 63–69.

COWEN, Sir Zelman, *Australian Constitutional Monarchy and the Australian People*, Australians for Constitutional Monarchy keynote address, Sydney, 4 February 1994.

CRAWFORD, James and ODGERS, Stephen (ed.), *Change the Constitution?*, University of Sydney Faculty of Law, Sydney 1988.

CRAWLEY, Aidan, *De Gaulle*, Collins, London 1969.

CROSS, M. (ed.), *Watergate: Chronology of a Crisis*, Congressional Quarterly, Washington, [date?] vol. II.

Daily Telegraph, 13th and 15th March 1995.

DALZIEL, Allan, *Evatt the Enigma*, Lansdowne Press, Melbourne 1967.

DICEY, A.V., *An Introduction to the Study of the Law of the Constitution*, tenth edition, Macmillan, London 1959.

DICKINSON, W.B. (ed.), *Watergate: Chronology of a Crisis*, Congressional Quarterly, Washington 1974, vol. I.

DUVERGER, M., *The French Political System*, University of Chicago Press, Chicago 1958.

ELTON, *Imperial Commonwealth*, Collins, London 1945.

EMDEN, Cecil S. (ed.), *Selected Speeches on the Constitution*, vol. I, Oxford University Press, London 1939.

EVANS, Michael and JACK, R. Ian, *Sources of English Legal and Constitutional History*, Butterworths Australia, 1984 (No.56 of Limited Edition of 150 copies).

EVATT, Herbert Vere, *Australian Labour Leader, The Story of W.A. Holman and the Labour Movement*, Angus & Robertson, Australia 1940.

EVATT, Herbert Vere, and FORSEY, Eugene A., *Evatt and Forsey on the Reserve Powers*, Legal Books, Sydney 1990; being a reprint of H.V.Evatt's *The King and His Dominion Governors* (second edition, Frank Cass, London 1967) and E.A.Forsey's *The Royal Power of Dissolution of Parliament in the British Parliament* (revised reprint, Oxford University Press, Toronto 1968).

Exposure Draft of the *Constitution Alteration (Establishment of Republic) Bill 1999*, Commonwealth of Australia, 1999.

Final Report of the Constitutional Commission, Australian Government Publishing Service, Canberra 1988 [three volumes].

Financial Times, 24th January 1994.

FIRTH, C.H., *Cromwell's Army*, third edition, University Paperbacks, London 1962.

FISKE, John, *The American Revolution*, vols. I & II, Houghton Mifflin, Boston 1919.

FOOTT, B., *Dismissal of a Premier*, Morgan, Sydney 1968.

FORSEY, Eugene, "The Role and Position of the Monarch in Canada", *The Parliamentarian* LXIV No.1, January 1983.

FOWLER, H.W. and FOWLER, F.G., (ed.), *The Concise Oxford Dictionary of Current English*, Oxford University Press, 1964.

FRASER, Antonia, *Cromwell Our Chief of Men*, Weidenfeld & Nicolson, London 1973.

FRASER, Antonia, *Charles II, His Life and Times*, Weidenfeld & Nicolson, London 1993.

FRASER, P., "A Revolutionary Governor-General? The Grenada Crisis of 1983", *Constitutional Heads and Political Crises: Commonwealth Episodes 1945–1985* (ed. D.A. Low), Macmillan, London 1988, pp.142–162.

FREEDMAN, Warren, *The Privilege to Keep and Bear Arms*, Quorum Books, 1989.

GIBBS, Sir Harry, *The Australian Constitution and Australia's Constitutional Monarchy*, address to Australians for Constitutional Monarchy, Sydney, 4 June 1993.

GRAINGER, Gareth, "Monarchy: Mystery and Practicality", *Australia: Republic or Monarchy?* (ed. M. Stephenson, C. Turner), University of Queensland Press, Brisbane 1994, pp. 111–118.

GRAINGER, Gareth and JONES, Kerry (ed.), *The Australian Constitutional Monarchy*, ACM Publishing, Sydney 1994.

GRUBEL, Frank "Sir Eri's Swansong", *Pacific Islands Monthly*, November 1991, p. 10.

Guardian, 29 March 1995.

HAILSHAM, *The Dilemma of Democracy*, Collins, London 1978.

HALPERIN, Morton H., BERMAN, Jerry J., BOROSAGE, Robert L. and MARWICK, Christine M., *The Lawless State*, Penguin, New York 1976.

HARDIE BOYS, Sir Michael, "The Role of the Governor-General under MMP", address to the Institute of International Affairs (New Zealand), Wellington, 24 May 1996.

HASLIP, Joan, *Lucrezia Borgia — a Study*, Heron, Geneva 1968.

HAYWARD, J., *The One and Indivisible French Republic*, Weidenfeld & Nicolson, London 1973.

HILL, B.W., *Sir Robert Walpole*, Hamish Hamilton, London 1989.

HILL, Robin, "The Rocky Road to a Republic", *The Bulletin*, vol. 115 no.5866, April 20 1993.

HILLER, Andrew, *Public Order and the Law*, The Law Book Company Limited, Australia 1993.

HOBBES, Thomas, *Leviathan*, Blackwell, Oxford [date unknown].

HODSON, H.V., "Crown and Commonwealth", *The Round Table* 1995, vol. 333 pp. 89–95.

HUME, D., SMOLLETT, T. and JONES, W., *History of England* (three volumes; this edition published late 19th Century, precise date unknown).

HUTSON, James H. (ed.), *A Decent Respect to the Opinions of Mankind — Congressional State Papers 1774–1776*, Library of Congress, Washington 1975.

JAMES, R.R., *Winston S. Churchill, His Complete Speeches 1897–1963*, Chelsea House, New York 1974, vol. VIII.

JENNINGS, Sir W. Ivor, *Cabinet Government*, Cambridge University Press, 1936.

JENNINGS, Sir W. Ivor, *The Law and the Constitution*, third edition, University of London Press, London 1943.

JOSKE, Sir Percy, *Sir Robert Menzies 1894–1978 — a new, informal memoir*, Angus & Robertson, Australia 1978.

KEGAN, Elizabeth Hamer, *Fundamental Testaments of the American Revolution*, Library of Congress, Washington 1973. (Published from Symposia on the American Revolution.)

KEIR, Sir David Lindsay, *The Constitutional History of Modern Britain since 1485*, ninth edition, A&C Black, London 1969.

KEITH, A. Berriedale, *The Constitutional Law of the British Dominions*, Macmillan, London 1933.

KEITH, A. Berriedale, *The King and the Imperial Crown: The Powers and Duties of His Majesty*, Longmans Green, London 1936.

KEITH, A. Berriedale, *Speeches and Documents on the British Dominions 1918–1931*, (second edition?), Oxford University Press, London 1948.

KELLY, Paul, *The Unmaking of Gough*, Angus & Robertson, Australia 1976.

KENYON, C.M., "The Declaration of Independence", *Fundamental Testaments of the American Revolution*, Library of Congress, Washington 1973, pp. 25–46.

KERR, Sir John, *Matters for Judgement*, Sun Books, Melbourne 1988.

KIRBY, Mr. Justice Michael, "Topics", *The Australian Law Journal*, vol. 66 no.12, December 1992.

KOLMA, Frank "Triumph of Justice", *Pacific Islands Monthly*, November 1991, pp. 8–9.

KRAUS, H., *The Crisis of German Democracy*, Princeton University Press, Princeton 1932.

LAPPING, Brian, *End of Empire*, Granada, London 1985.

LE MAY, G.H.L., *The Victorian Constitution*, Duckworth, London 1979.

LEDWIDGE, B., *De Gaulle*, Weidenfeld & Nicolson, London 1982.

LOCKHART, J.S. and MEAGHER, R.P., *The Australian Constitutional Crisis of 1975: Facts & Law*, Institute of Public Affairs (NSW), Sydney 1976.

LOW, D. Anthony, "Buckingham Palace and the Westminster Model", *The Round Table* 1987, vol. 304 pp. 445–456.

LOW, D.A. (ed.), *Constitutional Heads and Political Crises: Commonwealth Episodes 1945–1985*, Macmillan, London 1988.

LUMB, R.D., *Australian Constitutionalism*, Butterworths, Australia 1983.

LUMB, R.D. and RYAN, K.W. *The Constitution of the Commonwealth of Australia, Annotated*, third edition, Butterworths Australia, 1981.

MACAULAY, *Reviews, Essays, and Poems*, vol. I, Ward Lock, London [date?].

MACHIAVELLI, Niccolò, *The Prince and The Discourses*, Random House, New York 1950.

MACHIAVELLI, Niccolò, *The Prince* (transl. Leo Paul S. de Alvarez), revised edition, University of Dallas Press, Irving, Texas 1984.

MACHIAVELLI, Niccolò, *Selected Political Writings* (ed. and transl. David Wootton), Hackett, Indianapolis 1994.

MADISON, James (ed.), *The Debates in the Federal Convention of 1787 Which Framed the Constitution of the United States of America*, Oxford University Press 1920.

MADISON, James, HAMILTON, Alexander and JAY, John, *The Federalist Papers* (ed. Isaac Kramnick), Penguin, London 1987.

MAJOR, Rt. Hon. John, *Speech by the Prime Minister to the Britain/Australia Society*, 21 January 1993.

MARKESINIS, B.S., *The Theory and Practice of Dissolution of Parliament*, Cambridge University Press, 1972.

MARKWELL, D.J., *1975: The Crown and the Constitution* [draft manuscript].

MARKWELL, D.J., "The Dismissal", *Quadrant*, March 1984, pp. 11–21.

MARKWELL, D.J., "On Advice from the Chief Justice", *Quadrant*, July 1985, pp. 38–42.

MARKWELL, D.J., *The Crown and Australia*, Trevor Reese Memorial Lecture, University of London, 1987.

MARKWELL, D.J., "Canada's Best", a review of *A Life on the Fringe: The Memoirs of Eugene Forsey* by Eugene Forsey, *The Round Table*, October 1991, pp. 502–505.

MARSHALL, Geoffrey, *Constitutional Theory*, Oxford University Press, London 1971.

MARSHALL, Geoffrey, *Constitutional Conventions: The Rules and Forms of Political Accountability*, Clarendon Press, Oxford 1984.

MARSHALL, G. and MOODIE, G.C., *Some Problems with the Constitution*, fourth edition, Hutchinson, London 1967.

MARX, Karl and ENGELS, Friedrich, *The Communist Manifesto* (ed. A.J.P. Taylor), Penguin 1967.

McGEHEE, Ralph W., *Deadly Deceits*, Sheridan Square, New York 1973.

McGEHEE, R.W., *Deadly Deceits*, Sheridan Square, New York 1983.

MENZIES, Sir Robert, *Afternoon Light*, Cassell, London 1967.

MILL, John Stuart, *Utilitarianism, Liberty, and Representative Government*, Dent, London 1948.

MOENS, Gabriel, "The Wrongs of a Constitutionally Entrenched Bill of Rights", *Australia: Republic or Monarchy?*, University of Queensland Press, Brisbane 1994, pp. 233–256.

MORRISON, A.S., "Dominions Office Correspondence on the New South Wales Constitutional Crisis 1930-1932", *J. Royal Australian Historical Society*, vol. 61 pt.5 March 1976, pp. 323–345.

NEALE, Sir John, *Queen Elizabeth I*, Penguin, London 1960.

New York Times, 22nd December 1974.

NICHOLAS, H.S., *The Australian Constitution*, Law Book Co. 1948.

NICHOLLS, A.J., *Weimar and the Rise of Hitler*, Macmillan, London 1991.

OAKES, Laurie, *Crash Through or Crash*, Drummond, Australia 1976.

O'BRIEN, Conor Cruise, *The Great Melody*, Minerva, London 1993.

Observer, 12th March 1995.

ORWELL, George, *The Penguin Essays of George Orwell*, Penguin, 1984.

ORWELL, George, *Animal Farm*, Penguin 1989.

O'CONNELL, D.P., "Canada, Australia, Constitutional Reform and the Crown", *The Parliamentarian*, vol. LX no.1, January 1979.

PAINE, Thomas, *Rights of Man* (ed. Eric Foner), Penguin, 1984.

PLATO, *The Republic* (transl. H.D.P. Lee), Penguin, 1955.

PREMDAS, Ralph R., and STEEVES, Jeffrey S., "Political and Constitutional Crisis in Vanuatu", *The Round Table* 1990, vol. 313 pp. 43–64.

Proceedings of the Australian Constitutional Convention, Adelaide 26–29 April, 1983, Vol. I.

QUICK, Sir John and GARRAN, Sir Robert, *The Annotated Constitution of the Australian Commonwealth*, reprint of 1901 edition, Legal Books, Sydney 1976.

RAMPHAL, Sir Shridath, "Canada and the Commonwealth", *The Round Table* (1987), 304 p. 429.

REID, A., *The Whitlam Venture*, Hill of Content, Melbourne 1976.

Report of the Congressional Committees Investigating the Iran-Contra Affair (1987): the US Senate Select Committee on Secret Military Assistance to Iran and the Nicaraguan Opposition, and the US House of Representatives Select Committee to Investigate Covert Arms Transactions with Iran; US Government Printing Office, Washington 1987.

ROBB, P., "Lives of the Matyrs", *The Independent Monthly*, Australia December 1995–January 1996.

SCHOENBRUN, D., *The Three Lives of Charles de Gaulle*, Hamish Hamilton, London 1966.

SHAKESPEARE, William, *The Tempest* (ed. Anne Barton), Penguin 1968.

SMITH, Harrison, *Lord Strickland: Servant of the Crown*, Scholars Edition, Amsterdam 1983.

SMITH, Sir David, *Australian Constitutional Monarchy*, Australians for Constitutional Monarchy, Occasional Paper No.1, Sydney, October 1992.

SMITH, Sir David, *Some Thoughts on the Monarchy/Republic Debate*, 1992 Ernest James Goddard Oration, address to the Australian Dental Association (Qld), Brisbane, 3 September 1992.

Sunday Telegraph, 12th March 1995.

TARDIF, R. and ATKINSON, A.(ed.), *The Penguin Macquarie Dictionary of Australian Politics*, Penguin, Australia 1988

THE CASE OF THE PEOPLE OF WESTERN AUSTRALIA in support of their desire to withdraw from the Commmonwealth of Australia Constitution Act (Imperial), and that Western Australia be restored to its former status as a separate self-governing colony in the British Empire, Western Australian government printers, 1934.

The Imperial Presidency — The Invisible Government of America [audio recording], ABC Sydney 1978.

The New York Times Index 1973, New York Times, New York 1974, vol. II.

The New York Times Index 1975, New York Times, New York 1976, vol. II.

The New York Times Index 1974, New York Times, New York 1975, vol. II.

The Republic and the President, 4 Corners (ABC television, 1993).

The Times, 15th September 1913; 14th March 1995; 16th March 1995; 7th April 1995; 12th April 1995; 14th April 1995; 17th April 1995; 18th April 1995.

THOMSON, David, *Europe Since Napoleon*, Penguin, London 1966.

TODD, Alpheus, *Parliamentary Government in England*, vol. II, Longman Green, London 1869.

Translation of Article 41 as adopted on the 4th December 1982 by the Fifth Session of the Fifth National People's Congress of the People's Republic of China, and published in *Beijing Review*, No.52, 27th December 1982.

TURNBULL, Malcolm *et al.*, Report of the Republic Advisory Committee, vols. I&II, Commonwealth Government Printer, Australia 1993.

VATIKIOTIS, M.R.J., *Indonesian Politics under Suharto*, Routledge, London 1993.

VICTORIA, Queen, *Letters of Queen Victoria* (ed. A.C.Benson and Viscount Esher), John Murray, London 1908, First Series 1837–1861, vol. III.

VOLTAIRE, *Candide* (transl. John Butt), Penguin, 1947.

WADE, E.C.S. and BRADLEY, A.W., *Constitutional and Administrative Law*, tenth edition, Longman, London 1985.

WATERFORD, J., "Keating's Quiet Power Shift", *Independent Monthly*, June 1993.

Weekend Australian, 15–16th January 1994.

WILSON, Vincent, *The Book of the Presidents*, sixth edition, American History Research Associates, Brookeville Maryland 1974.

WILSON, Vincent, *The Book of the Founding Fathers*, American History Research Associates, Brookeville Maryland 1974.

WINDEYER, Sir W.J. Victor, *Lectures on Legal History*, second edition, Law Book Company of Australasia, Australia 1949.

WINTERTON, George, "A Constitution for an Australian Republic", *Independent Monthly*, June 1993.

WISEMAN, John A., and VIDLER, Elizabeth, "The July 1994 Coup d'Etat in the Gambia: The End of an Era?", *The Round Table* 1995, vol. 333, pp. 53–65.

WOOD, Sir Anthony, *Athenae Oxonienses*, Tho. Bennet, London 1692, vol. II.

Index

I

Iceland, 204, 211

Impeachment, 16, 19, 44, 49, 51–52, 55, 120, 204, 209–211, 244–245, 359

Imperial China, influence on British institutions, 262

Imperial Conferences, 1926 & 1930, 123, 225, 267, 280

Independent information, right of Crown to seek beyond ministers, 87

Independent Monthly, the, 386

India, 105, 204, 211, 230, 240, 262–263, 292, 294–295

Indian Civil Service (ICS), 263–264

Indian Mutiny, the, 262

Inquisitorial nature of committees, 226–227

Internal Revenue Service (IRS), executive misuse of, 64, 70

Interregnum, English, 242

Iran-Contra, scandal of, 72–74

Ireland, 11–14, 90, 103–105, 123–124, 128, 171, 175–176, 180–182, 204, 211, 237, 243, 281, 310, 366–367

Ireton, Henry, 116

Irish Free State, the, 168, 223, 299

Irish Home Rule Bill, 171

Irish Republican Army (IRA), 237

Isabella, Queen, 121, 310

Isandhlwana, Battle of, 262

Israel, provision for Presidential dismissal, 205

Italy, 55–56, 89, 93–94, 107, 121, 171, 179, 196–197, 211, 224, 241

J

Jacobite, 11, 13, 15–17, 20

Jamaica, 256, 333

James I/VI, King, 10, 12, 14, 51

James II/VII, King, 6, 10–12, 25, 243, 288

Jefferson, Thomas, 27–28, 40, 245

Jennings, Sir Ivor, 58–59, 110, 125

John, King, 316

Johnson, Dr Samuel, 23, 28

Johnson, President Andrew, 210

Johnson, President Lyndon B., 69–70

Jones, Barry, 243, 372

Jouhaud, General, and "reaction of despair", 98

Juan Carlos, King of Spain, 247–248

"Judas", and expectation of partisan behaviour in viceregal appointees, 203–204, 215

Judicial aristocracy, 87, 151, 208–209, 304, 322, 381, 387, 389

Juin, Marshal, 97

Junta, military, 106, 152, 241, 302, 341

Juvenal, 213, 227

K

Keating, Paul, 59, 136, 144, 147, 257–258, 260–261, 266, 273–274, 282, 300, 332, 343, 364

Keir, Sir David Lindsay, 30, 110

Keith, Professor A. Berriedale, 87, 217

Keneally, Thomas, 185–186

Kennedy, President John F., 70, 73, 120

Kennedy, Robert, 120

Kennett, Jeff, 364

Kent State massacre, 236–238, 240

Kerr, Sir John, 87, 215–218, 257, 280–281, 343–344, 347, 354–356, 361

Khemlani, Tireth, and Whitlam loans scandal, 259, 343

Kidnapping, confessed FBI, 66, 68, 237

Kidu, Sir Buri, Chief Justice of Papua New Guinea, 200, 202

Killen, Sir James, 327

Kim Young-Sam, President, and purging of South Korean generals, 105

King, Martin Luther, 70

Kissinger, Henry, 121

Koenig, General, 97

Kovac, President Michel, 196

Kwangju massacre, 105

L

La Fiesta de San Fermín (see Pamplona, running of the bulls in), 321

Lamp-posts, as symbol of political principle, 380

Lang, John T. "Jack", NSW Premier, 75, 79–85, 88, 259

Langtry, Lillie, 121

Laos, 68, 106

Laporte, Pierre, kidnapped Quebec Minister for Labour and Immigration, 237

L'Armée Clandestine, CIA-backed, 68

Larson, Jeff, 65

Lascelles, Sir Alan, (letter to *The Times* as "Senex"), 162

Latasi, Kamuta, Prime Minister of Tuvalu, 332

Laud, Dr, Archbishop of Canterbury, 8